T0300877

Sustainability in the Political and Socio-Economic Spheres of Development in Zimbabwe

Edited by
Innocent Chirisa and
Charity Manyeruke

Langaa Research & Publishing CIG
Mankon, Bamenda

Publisher
Langaa RPCIG
Langaa Research & Publishing Common Initiative Group
P.O. Box 902 Mankon
Bamenda
North West Region
Cameroon
Langaagrp@gmail.com
www.langaa-rpcig.net

Distributed in and outside N. America by African Books Collective
orders@africanbookscollective.com
www.africanbookscollective.com

ISBN-10: 9956-551-51-1

ISBN-13: 978-9956-551-51-4

Notes on Contributors

Abraham Rajab Matamanda holds a BSc Degree in Rural and Urban Planning and MSc in Social Ecology from the University of Zimbabwe. Currently, he is a PhD candidate in the Department of Urban and Regional Planning at the University of the Free State, South Africa. His study focuses on Applied Systems Analysis in planning with reference to urban dilemmas and emerging human settlements forms nexus. Abraham has published more than 10 articles and book chapters in national and international peer-reviewed journals that include Springer and two book chapters in Urbanisation and Its Impact on Socio-Economic Growth in Developing Regions. His research areas are urban sustainability, environmental planning and management, rural development and the planning of cities and towns.

Alfred Zvoushe holds the following MSc Population Studies (University of Zimbabwe), BSc Honours in Psychology, University of Zimbabwe and a Certificate in Research Methods (University of Zimbabwe).

Ashton Murwira is a lecturer in the Department of Political and Administrative Studies, University of Zimbabwe. He has just completed his PhD studies in Peacebuilding with Durban University of Technology. Other qualifications include MSc International Relations and BSc Hons Political Science with University of Zimbabwe. His research areas include international relations, conflict and peace.

Benjamine Hanyani-Mlambo is a senior lecturer in the Department of Agricultural Economics and Extension, University of Zimbabwe. He holds a PhD in Agricultural Extension from the University of KwaZulu Natal (South Africa), an MSc in Agricultural Extension from Wageningen Agricultural University (The Netherlands) and a BSc in Agricultural Economics from the University of Zimbabwe. Benjamine has also conducted consultancies for international donors and NGOs in Nigeria, Ethiopia, Rwanda, Kenya, Tanzania, Malawi, Zambia, Mozambique, Botswana, Lesotho, South Africa and Zimbabwe.

Charity Manyeruke is an Associate Professor and former Dean of Faculty of Social Studies, University of Zimbabwe. She holds a DPhil (International Relations and Political Science), MSc (International Relations), BSc (Political and Administrative Studies), University of Zimbabwe, IPMZ (Human

Resources), LCCI Diploma (Public Relations) and Law and Management courses (UNISA). Her research interests are politics and natural resources management, international relations and the politics of gender. Currently, she is serving as Zimbabwean Ambassador to Rwanda

Dudzirai Chimeri is the Principal of Zimbabwe Theological Seminary in Gweru, which is an Associate college of Great Zimbabwe University in Masvingo. Currently he is a part-time lecturer in the Department of Religious Studies and Philosophy at Great Zimbabwe University. He holds a DPhil in Postcolonial Studies, MPhil in Postmodern Studies from the University of Stellenbosch in Cape Town, South Africa and a BTh in Biblical interpretation from the Baptist Theological Seminary of Zimbabwe in Gweru. His area of research interests are postcolonial and postmodern studies.

Elmond Bandauko is a Consultant and Research Associate with the Development Governance Institute (DEGI), a Harare based consulting and development research firm. He holds a Master of Public Administration (MPA) with specialization in Local government from the University of Western Ontario (Canada) where he studied as an African Leaders of Tomorrow (ALT) Scholar. He did his BSc. (Hons) in Rural and Urban Planning from the University of Zimbabwe. His interests are urban policy and governance, urban resilience, participatory policy making, policy innovation and policy diffusion, public management, program and policy evaluation, collaborative governance and the politics of urban development in cities of the global south.

Emelia Chimhowa-Chikoko (The late) was a D.Phil in Social Work Candidate from the University of Johannesburg. She was a holder of a Master of Science in Population Studies, Post Graduate Diploma in Project Planning and Management, Bachelor of Science (honours) Degree in Social Work all from the University of Zimbabwe. Her interested were childhood studies, demography etc.

Francis Machingura is an associate professor at the University of Zimbabwe, Curriculum and Arts Education Department. Currently is the Chairperson, a member of the University of Zimbabwe Council. He is an ordained pastor in the Apostolic Faith Mission in Zimbabwe. He holds PhD in Intercultural Biblical Studies (Bayreuth University, Germany), Masters in Religious Studies, BA (Hons) in Religious Studies, Diploma in Project Planning and Management and a Post-Graduate Diploma in Education. His research interests are Bible and Politics, Gender, Environment, Disability and Religious Education.

Gamuchirai Gloria Rudo Masakwa is an avid reader. Her first love is Sociology. Her research interests are gender and development and resource utilization particularly in rural settlements. She holds a Master of Arts in Development Studies from Midlands State University, a BSc Honours in Sociology and Gender Development Studies from the Women's University in Africa and a Bachelor of Arts Degree in Philosophy and Religious Studies from the University of Zimbabwe.

Gift Mhlanga: BSc Hons. Economics, (University of Zimbabwe). Post-Graduate pursuing MSc, Economics and the University of Zimbabwe. Currently, he is as a Graduate Teaching Assistant in the same department. His research interests are in development economics.

Halleluah Mangombe Chirisa is holder of a BScEd dual honours in Geography and Mathematics from the Bindura University of Science Education (BUSE) and an MSc degree in Population Studies from the University of Zimbabwe (UZ). Between 2005 and 2007, she taught at Nyava and Rutope secondary schools in Shamva district and Glen View 3 High School in Harare. Currently, she is a social scientist at CeSHHAR Zimbabwe in Harare. She has also worked as an independent consultant for the Zimbabwe Statistical Agency (ZIMSTAT), involved in national census exercises. Her research interests are population issues (especially reproductive health), resources mobilisation for communities and sustainability and resilience in urban and regional areas.

Hedwig Muronzi is a Coordinator for Zimbabwe Germany Society. Currently she is involved in a number of projects, which support orphans and vulnerable children in schools and surrounding communities. She holds a MA (Development Studies) from Midlands State University, BSc (HIV/AIDS Management and Community Development) from Chinhoyi University of Technology an BSc (Psychology) from Zimbabwe Open University. Her research interests are positive parenting, climate, orphans and vulnerable children.

Henerieta Mgovo is a New Testament lecturer in the department of Theology and Religious studies at Zimbabwe Ezekiel Guti University. She holds a Master's Degree in New Testament from the University of Zimbabwe. B. A. Honours in Religious Studies from University of Zimbabwe. Diploma in Religious studies from University of Zimbabwe and Post Graduate Diploma in Education from Zimbabwe Ezekiel Guti University. Her research interests are Religion, gender and politics as well as religion and environment.

Innocent Chirisa is a Full Professor at the Department of Rural and Urban Planning, University of Zimbabwe. Currently is the Acting Dean of the Faculty of Social Studies at the University of Zimbabwe and is a Research Fellow at the Department of Urban and Regional Planning, University of the Free State, South Africa. He holds a DPhil in Social Studies, MSc (Planning), BSc Honours in Rural and Urban Planning all from the University of Zimbabwe and a postgraduate Diploma in Land Management and Informal Land Resettlement from the Institute of Housing and Urban Development Studies, Erasmus University, the Netherlands. His research interests are systems.

Joseph Francis is a Zimbabwean who is a full professor at the University of Venda. Since 2007 he has been the Director of the Institute for Rural Development. He holds DPhil and MPhil in Agriculture (majoring in Animal Science), and a BSc Agriculture Honours in Animal Science degree. All these qualifications were obtained from the University of Zimbabwe. After completing Doctoral studies, he pursued Postdoctoral studies with the Postgraduate School of Agriculture and Rural Development, University of Pretoria. His research interests include crop-livestock systems dynamics, rural development in particular citizen science, poverty studies, local governance and economic development, and higher education transformation.

Julius Musevenzi is a senior lecturer in the Department of Sociology, University of Zimbabwe. He holds a PhD in Sociology and Development Studies from the Nelson Mandela Metropolitan University in South Africa, MSc in Sociology and Social Anthropology, BSc Honours in Sociology from the University of Zimbabwe. His research interests are in rural livelihoods development and changing trends, resilience and survival strategies.

Langtone Maunganidze is a Senior Lecturer in the Faculty of Social Sciences at the Midlands State University in Zimbabwe. His academic career began at the University of Zimbabwe from where he obtained a PhD in Sociology. Dr Maunganidze has also taught at other institutions including National University of Science and Technology (NUST) in Zimbabwe and the University of Botswana. His research and teaching interest areas include Rural Livelihoods and Sustainable Development, Social Problems, Industrial Sociology, Succession Planning, Business and Society and Research Methodology. He has presented numerous conference papers at both regional and international fora and published widely on topics covering these interest areas.

Lawrence Mhandara is a Senior Lecturer in the Department of Political and Administrative Studies, University of Zimbabwe. He holds a Doctor of

Philosophy in Peace Studies from the Durban University of Technology, South Africa, MSc in International Relations, BSc in Politics and Administration both from the University of Zimbabwe. His research interest lie in the area of governance, international conflict, peace and security.

Liaison Mukarwi holds a BSc Honours Degree in Rural and Urban Planning from the University of Zimbabwe. He is currently practicing as a Town Planner at Human Settlements Experts (Pvt) Ltd in Zimbabwe. Liaison is a freelance researcher whose researches focus on Urban Management and Governance, Environmental Design, Urban Planning Practice, Housing and Community Issues and Transport and Sustainability issues. He had published more than several journal articles and book chapters. Liaison participated in various academic researches as a research assistant.

Livinia Binala is a PhD candidate in the Institute for Rural Development, University of Venda. Currently is the Senior Assistant Registrar of the Faculty of Agriculture, University of Zimbabwe. She holds an M.Ed in Adult Education, B.Ed, Adult Education, Diploma, Adult Education all from the University of Zimbabwe and a Higher National Diploma in Human Resources from the Harare Polytechnic. Her research interests are in Rural/Community Development, Food Security and Training.

McDonald Matika is an organisational psychologist mainly researching on leadership and personality in the workplace. As a positive psychologist, he is a firm believer on the need for psychology to study individual human strengths and how they promote mental health and overall wellness in the community. Psychology in Africa needs to explore, from an Afrocentric view, the individual potentials that can be measured, managed and be developed in order to fully realise the latent potential in the continent's human capital.

Milcah Mudewairi is a lecturer in the Department of Theology and Religious Studies, Zimbabwe Ezekiel Guti University. Currently she is the Department chairperson. She is a PhD student at the University of Pretoria, South Africa and also a holder of MA (Religious Studies), BA Honours (Religious Studies) all from the University of Zimbabwe and a post-graduate Diploma in Education from Zimbabwe Open University. Her research interests are Religion and Environment.

Moreen Mudenda is an Organisational Development (O.D) psychologist specialising in collaboratively assisting management to enhance their organisational performance towards effective and efficient implementation of strategic goals. This O.D work has been conducted in diverse sectors such as Finance, Health, Education, Manufacturing, Government, Transportation and Non-Profits. Dr. Mudenda has worked in Zimbabwe, South Africa, Lesotho and the USA. Dr. Mudenda's research areas include; women's leadership development, change management in Africa and innovation within industries.

Obediah Dodo (PhD) Governance and Leadership (Unilus), lectures in the Department of Peace and Governance at Bindura University, Zimbabwe. He introduced a master's degree in Leadership and Conflict Transformation at Zimbabwe Open University. Prior to his service with ZOU, he was an Evaluation and Analysis officer for 16 years in the Office of the President, Zimbabwe. Obediah's research interests are endogenous conflict resolution, youth and family violence and election management. He has published over 25 refereed papers including 2 books.

Olga Bungu is a DPhil student in Social Studies student at the University of Zimbabwe. She holds a MSc (Development Studies, Fort Hare, South Africa), B.A Honours (War and Strategic Studies, University of Zimbabwe and a Diploma in War and Strategic Studies, both from the University of Zimbabwe. Her research interests are on the issue of land (post -independence) in Zimbabwe.

Oswell Rusinga holds an MSc Population Studies (University of Zimbabwe) and a BA Honours Geography (University of Zimbabwe).

Patrick Chiroro is a Professor of Psychology who has taught at universities and conducted research studies in Zimbabwe and South Africa. He is a former lecturer at the Psychology Department and Deputy Dean for the Social Science Faculty at the University Zimbabwe. He was also a senior lecturer and professor at the University Pretoria in South Africa. He was also specialist research consultant for various state and non-state organisations in South Africa. He is also the Managing Director at Impact Research International, which operates in South Africa and Zimbabwe among other countries in Southern Africa.

Paul Goronga is a lecturer at Zimbabwe Ezekiel Guti University. He is a PhD student with the University of Pretoria. He holds a Master of Arts degree in Religious Studies, a Bachelor of Arts Honours degree and a diploma in Religious Studies all from the University of Zimbabwe and a post graduate diploma in Education from Zimbabwe Open University. His research interest includes Religion, Politics and Conflict Management in Africa, Religion and Development and New Religious Movements.

Samson Mhizha is a lecturer in Developmental Psychology, Social Psychology and Cross-Cultural Psychology at the Department of Psychology at the University of Zimbabwe. Research interests are in topics around children and youths in difficult circumstances, psychology of grief, influence of religion and culture on psychological functioning and family studies. Samson holds an MPhil and BSc Hons in Psychology from the University of Zimbabwe and is currently working on a DPhil Project on the lived experiences and resilience pathways among street children who have gone through family reunification in Zimbabwe. He has published several articles on Street Children and religious functioning.

Stanzia Moyo: PhD (University of Zimbabwe), MSc. Population Studies (University of Zimbabwe), BSc Geography and Environmental Science (Zimbabwe Open University), Diploma in Teaching (Gweru Teachers College), Certificate in Demographic Methods and Analysis (University of Groningen).

Tawanda Zinyama is the Chairman and Senior Lecturer of Public Administration in the Department of Political and Administrative Studies at the University of Zimbabwe. He received a DPhil degree from the University of Zimbabwe in Zimbabwe. His research interests include public administration and institutional governance, public policy, local government management, public-private partnerships, democratic governance and public finance management. He has supervised several MPA students in the discipline of Public Administration and Public Policy.

Tendayi Marovah is a PhD holder and an early career researcher currently teaching at the Midlands State University- Department of Applied Education. He is also a Research Fellow at the University of the Free Sate under the SARChI Chair in Higher Education and Human Development. He focuses on Curriculum and pedagogy, higher education, citizenship formation, sustainable human development and theorising using the capability approach.

Tinashe Muromo is a senior lecturer and researcher in the Department of Psychology, Faculty of Social Studies at the University of Zimbabwe. He has served as a chairperson of that department and as deputy dean and dean of the Faculty of Social Studies at the same university. He is a former High School Mathematics and Science teacher. He holds a D.Phil. in Psychology from Nelson Mandela Metropolitan University, M.Phil. Social Studies (Psychology), B.Sc. Honours in Psychology and a Diploma in Education, from the University of Zimbabwe. His research interests are in Behavioural Research, Community Health Psychology, Community Psychology and Forensic Psychology.

Toendepi Shonhe is a Research Fellow at the Thabo Mbeki African Leadership Institute based at University of South Africa. He holds a Doctor of Philosophy in Development studies from the University of KwaZulu-Natal, South Africa and a master's in public policy management from the University of Witwatersrand in South Africa. He also holds a BSc in agricultural management and a Diploma in Banking (IOBZ). His research interests are in land reform, agrarian change, rural development and food sovereignty. His current work focuses on the commercialisation of agriculture in Africa and the land reform, accumulation and food sovereignty in Africa.

Victor Muzvidziwa is a Full Professor at the Department of Sociology, University of Zimbabwe. Currently is a Vice Chancellor at the Midlands State University, Zimbabwe. He holds a PhD from University of Waikato, New Zealand, Master of Science in Sociology and Anthropology, Bachelor of Science (honours) Degree in Sociology and Anthropology all from the University of Zimbabwe. His research interests are anthropological studies of women, land.

Watch Ruparanganda is a Senior Lecturer at the Department of Sociology, University of Zimbabwe. He holds a D.Phil. in Social Studies, Master of Science in Sociology and Anthropology, Bachelor of (honours) Degree in Sociology and Anthropology all from the University of Zimbabwe. His research interests are sexuality issues, street children.

Witness Chikoko is a Senior Lecturer at the Department of Social Work, University of Zimbabwe. Currently is a Research Fellow at the Department of Social Work, University of Johannesburg, South Africa. He holds D.Phil in Social Studies, Masters of Social Work, Post Graduate Diploma in Project Planning and Management, Bachelor of (honours) Degree in Social Work all from the University of Zimbabwe. His research interests are childhood studies, social protection.

Table of Contents

Chapter 1

The Socio-Economic and Political Nuances of Sustainability and Resilience in Zimbabwe

Innocent Chirisa and Charity Manyeruke

Introduction

Zimbabwe is a signatory to the implementation of the global sustainable development goals (SDGs, 2015-2030). In line with this, the government has adopted Vision 2030 in a bid to achieving some of the sustainable development goals. Among the key aspects include social, economic and political development. Sustainable development can be taken an idea, a process and an outcome hence there is no universal conceptualisation of sustainable development. Economists, sociologists, planners, geographers, environmentalists and politicians do not share a similar notion of the idea of sustainable development. Thus, it varies across disciplines and areas. For the economists, the thrust of sustainable development is balancing the production of goods and services to the level of consumption to satisfy present consumption at the same time catering for future demands. On the other hand, sociologists focus on social equality, human capabilities and building civil society capacity to foster equality whereas the thrust of environmentalist is on conserving natural resources as inputs for economic production (Basiago, 1999). In addition, there are also differences between regions. For example, for long the concept had been strongly associated with environmental conservation in developing countries, in developed countries sustainable development refers to strategies intended to improve status of society, reduce poverty and attain the standards of modern society (Martin and Grainger, 2004).

This chapter provided an exploration into and assessment of the theory and reality of sustainable development in Zimbabwe. This was done through analysing the sustainability of developments in the social, economic and political systems from 1980 to date. Central to this is the issue of building sustainability and resilience in the system is how technology can play a role in the sustainability equation. In terms of structuring, the first part is a theoretical framework on sustainability and resilience. This is followed by an outline of the study methodology and the results of the study. After the result is a discussion and synthesis of the findings. This is followed by a conclusion to the study and policy options for enhancing sustainability of development in Zimbabwe.

Theoretical Framework

This concept of Sustainable Development has its birth in the Brutland Commission of 1987 with the intention of conserving natural resources (Enders and Remig, 2015). However, the focus has moved from natural resources to include economics, politics and culture (Enders and Remig 2015)). It now encompasses not only issues of biodiversity and environmental conservation but also provides equal importance to poverty and inequality (Enders and Remig 2015). Thus, sustainable development is trans-disciplinary (Ashford and Hall, 2011). As a process sustainable development considers strategies towards achievement of sustainable development (Enders and Remig, 2015). The strategies include economic, political or technological strategies (Ashford and Hall, 2011). As an outcome sustainable development is a condition when the social, economic and political systems of a country have attained stability and are more resilient to changes. In addition, resources are consumed in a manner that is sustainable to maintain the ecological footprint. However, this is theoretical since sustainability is difficult to attain practically.

There is no universal way of defining resilience since it can be a metaphor as well as a paradigm (Brown, 2016). Resilience entails making communities, economies and cities robust against not only environmental shocks but any other shocks (Brown, 2016). Resilience rests on the centre of the sustainable development debate. This therefore calls upon the resilience of the economic, environmental, social and political (Luks, 2015). Social resilience refers to the preparedness of communities in healthy planning, human resources and public safety and energy planning issues among others (Alibasic, Sustainability and Resilience Planning for Local Government: The Quadruple Bottom Line Strategy, 2018). In addition, social resilience also deals with how communities sustain their livelihoods and wellbeing in the face of any changes in the economy. Social resilience depends on resources and institutions available since they influence community capability to mobilise resources to support their wellbeing (Hall and Lamont, 2013). Under the social dimension good relations between citizens and administrative system is likely to produce more resilient systems. Political resilience involves empowering the change agents to take an active role in sustainable development. Hence under the political resilience greater concern is given on quality of leadership, its capacity and capabilities, and efficiency through stakeholder participation (Alibasic, 2018).

As far as sustainable development is considered resilience is the ability to provide resources that act as buffers in times of disturbance (Luks, 2015). This applies to all aspects -the economic, social and political systems. It is therefore vital to provide extra unused resources to act as a security buffer though this conflict with principles of efficiency (Luks, 2015).To ensure resilience, there is need to generate knowledge on the maximum consumption levels and the reserves needed (the reserves include resources or unused production potential). In addition, resilience also rests on the requirement for precision in calculating the risks and vulnerabilities (Luks, 2015). Resilience can be achieved through resilience planning by local authorities and communities (Alibasic, 2018).

Social development refers to the building of skills, knowledge and health essential for personal productivity (Martin and Grainger, 2004). Closely linked to social development is human development. The basic indicators of social development include access to social services (health, education, housing, social security, income) and the enjoyment of human freedoms (UNDP, 2016). In addition, social development also focuses on building capabilities and enhancing the autonomy of citizens (UNDP, 2016). Central to social development is equality, inclusiveness and human capability development (UNDP, 2018). There exist a positive correlation between good governance and the ability of citizenship to meet their human needs (social development) (Laha, 2016).

Sustainable economic growth is the eighth objective of the SDGs 2030 (World Bank, 2018). Economic growth refers to an increase in production of services and goods measured in terms of GDP output, incomes and capital investment (Martin and Grainger, 2004). On the other hand, economic development is economic growth together with improvement in well-being, education and improvement in technologies (Nafziger, 2012). Thus, economic development seeks to improve welfare of people as development subjects (Darnolff and Laakso, 2016). As a result, poverty is a critical indicator of economic development (Langdon *et al.* 2018). Measuring economic development in terms of social indicators provides a broader view of economic development rather than restricting economic development to GDP factors (Anderson, 2014). However economic growth indicators including GDP, investment, savings, trade, broad money supply, incomes and, resource endowment remain foundational (World Bank , 2012).

The political system encompasses the political regimes, systems of authority and governments capacity (Heijden, 2014). Indicators of political development include political stability, administrative structures, laws and rules, governance system, autonomy and citizenship participation (Baster, 1972). These indicators are pertinent in measuring effectiveness, stability and responsiveness of a political system. These factors shape economic and social development by determining the powers and rules for resource allocation (Nancy, 1972). Sustainable development is a political process since it involves different political interests and is subject to political conflict. It is also political in the sense that the concept is implemented by different stakeholders such as the government,

3

NGOs, research communities and the civil society among other stakeholders with different power relations (Martin and Grainger, 2004). Hence the political system is an important component for sustainable development.

Technology refers to the hardware and the skills or knowledge needed in fostering development (Grubler, 2003). By nature, technology is dynamic, and the effective technology is context specific (Arthur, 2009). The hard part of technology is the manufactured components that are used to enhance human capacity. The soft part or the skills technology is necessary in the use of the hard technologies therefore the importance of research and development (Grubler, 2003). Thus, technology can be in any specific field (social, political, economic. On the basis of its formulation, technology can be either invented or naturally evolve. A specific form of technology can emanate from the demand for it hence some form of technologies is demand driven (Arthur, 2009). As a result, there is a strong link between the economic performance and the nature of technologies in an economy since the economy evolves and re-arranges itself based on the adjustment in technologies. Since technology are hard components or new knowledge generation, technology cut across all sectors and cannot be restricted to one sector. These can be innovations in the economic, political and social systems. This section provides typical technology interventions in the three different sectors and how they can solve challenges in these sectors. For social development, information communication technologies have different and far reaching effects on improving access to education and health services (Unwin, 2009). It also has a positive implication on fostering inclusive development. ICT played a pivotal role in reaching out the disadvantaged rural children the disabled in terms of access to education in Asia. School-community media linkages in countries such as Asia, these enhanced the sustainability of education systems.

Concerning political development, ICT has an important potential to make towards democracy and effective public citizen participation. This promotes good governance which is an ingredient for effective economic development (Bhattacharya, 1997). The major advantage of e-governance is that it has the potential to boost citizenship participation and therefore build more active citizenship. As far as the costs of administration are concerned e- governance also hosts the potential to reduce costs of making government information available to the public (Niranjan and Mishra, 2008). This contributes to efficiency. Technology also has a direct link to economic performance in a country. This is through technological competitiveness and innovativeness in the different sectors such as the labour market, industry and financial markets (Steenhuis and De Bruijn, 2012). Other than the competitiveness of technology, technology management through policy has an overarching role in defining the

4

extent to which a specific technology can contribute to economic development (Steenhuis and De Bruijn, 2012). Another form of application of technology in the economic sector is adoption of a digital economy (Government of Zimbabwe, 2018). A digital economy entailed the use of IT and electronic commerce. Similarly, it is of value in business, services as well as the production of value in different economic sectors (Boccia and Leornadi, 2016). In addition, electronic commerce is regarded as a better way of reducing costs of transactions. This can stimulate entrepreneurship growth within an economy (Pfahler and Grebe, 2005).

Methodology

Secondary data from government policies and reports provided a valuable source of information on the development policies pursued from 1980 to date and their implications on development. Other than government policies, textbooks, journals, newspapers and speeches also contributed in enriching the study by providing commentaries and reviews on some of the policy achievements in social, economic and political development in Zimbabwe.

Results

Zimbabwean Socio-economic development, 1980-2017

Social development has been the emphasis of the government since independence as this is included in all of the national development policies among which such as Growth with Equity, ESAP, Millennium Development Goals and STERP. This section provides a discussion of the developments in the social field in Zimbabwe since independence.

Education is one of the key components for social development. Other than improving the human capacity and freedoms, education contributes to improve economic performance through providing human capital for economic productivity (World Bank, 2018). Education also promotes a higher citizenship engagement for community development. Through the Growth with Equity Policy there was a call to make primary education tuition free for universal access. Likewise, secondary education was subsided by government (Sibanda and Makwata, 2017). Thus, the government's education policy was mainly after quantitative increase in enrolment. Other than the government, beneficiary communities and donors also contributes in construction of education infrastructure (Darnolff and Laakso, 2016). This improved basic literacy and reading skills among the majority of its citizens.

Despite quantitative improvement, the quality of the education system is largely questioned in terms of its relevance to current labour market needs (Mihyo and Mukuna, 2015). This is despite the attempts to vocationalise the education system since the 1990s. Furthermore, withdrawal of subsidies in the education sector following liberalization resulted in marginalisation of access to education for low income households (UNICEF, 2015). Despite the improvements in literacy levels in the country, there has been a general decline in the relevance of education system to economic development and citizenship building.

Access to safe and affordable water and sanitation services is one of the critical components of social development. In line with this goal there has been a deterioration and decline in access to safe water across the nation. Between 2002 and 2012 the percentage of people with access to safe water fell from 77 to 74 % (ZIMSTAT, 2016). This has been attributed to a decline in investment in water infrastructure and a decline of NGO investment in the water and sanitation sector (ZIMSTAT, 2016). Low investment in water infrastructure affected water provision in urban and peri-urban communities (Government of Zimbabwe, 2004). Climate change has also contributed to reduce access to water. Concerning sanitation there were improvements in rural areas (owing to rural sanitation programmes) whilst for urban areas like Harare and Bulawayo the condition has worsened after 2000 (ZIMSTAT, 2016).

In terms of housing, there has been an improvement in the proportion with access to housing from 2002 to 2012 (ZIMSTAT, 2016). However, the quality of housing is poor and mainly informal and underserviced as the supply of decent housing falls below demand in most urban areas (Government of Zimbabwe, 2004). Decent housing therefore remains a challenge. Concerning access to energy, woodfuel remain the dominant source of energy in both rural and urban areas as there has been a growth in the use of woodfuel for energy in urban areas typically Harare and Bulawayo (ZIMSTAT, 2016). This points to a deterioration of the energy sector and inability to meet energy demand. This has a negative impact not only on the standards of living but on the quality of the natural environment.

Overall, there has been a strong emphasis of social development aspects soon after independence guided by the equality ideology. However, the period after 1990 to date marked a decline in social welfare as government expenditure in social services was cut back (Government of Zimbabwe 1991). Thus, provision of social services has been fragmented. Soon after independence economic policies sought to maintain the economic status inherited from British administration. Hence economic policies pursued aimed to stabilise the economy (Skalnes, 2016). The economy was state controlled and characterised by protectionist policies (Stoneman, 1990). Foreign exchange allocations to the key sectors and trade were regulated by the government. Zimbabwe had one of the most developed industrial systems in Africa (Stoneman, 1990). Furthermore, the economic system was well diversified and balanced across sectors with the agricultural sector supplementing manufacturing industries (Dashwood, 2000). For these reasons the government was pressurised to maintain the economic structure hence minimal changes were made in the 1980s.

One of the changes after independence was subsidisation of key economic sectors of the economy such as agriculture and manufacturing (Skalnes, 2016). Despite the subsidisation there were also set excessive controls on the marketing prices for such produce (Skalnes, 2016). Other than agriculture and manufacturing sectors public services (health, sanitation, and housing) were also subsidised through grants to local authorities. In line with the subsidization policy taxes were increased to finance the delivery of these social services (Skalnes, 2016). Both cooperate companies and rich individuals were taxed at 50 and 30% respectively (Dashwood, 2000). This has implications on productivity and affected different stakeholders differently.

The other change was the control of minimum wages by the state. This affected labour unions in terms of loss of control of minimum wages (Skalnes, 2016). The introduction of minimum wages negatives affected commercial agriculture production during the first decade after independence as employment within the sector fell (Stoneman, 1990). Despite the regulation on minimum wage by the state, there was a notable reduction of workers real wages towards the end of the 1990 which triggered massive strikes organised by the Zimbabwe Congress of Trade Unions (ZCTU) (Raftopoulos and Mlambo, 2009). The Zimbabwean government adopted a liberalisation of the economy in 1990. This was given way by the Framework for Economic Reform blueprint. This advocated for a reduction in government expenditure, liberalisation of public social services (Government of Zimbabwe, 1991). One of the reasons for liberalization was public sector inefficiency. In addition, the movement was also a result of self - satisfying interests among members of the international community (Skalnes, 2016).

The result was a decline in employment in the economy due to de-industrialisation. Unemployment of workers in the agricultural sector also increased in the post 2000 following the fast track land reform movement. In 1998, agriculture employed approximately 70 % of the population (Poulton et al. 2002). Approximately 60 % of these employees were laid off after land reform (Raftopoulos and Mlambo, 2009). Unemployment in urban Areas also increased from the first decade after independence as a result of limited capital investment to expand industry adopted at independence (Stoneman, 1990). Despite the growth in unemployment in agriculture and industry, there has been growth in employment in the public service sector (education, health and public administration) (Stoneman, 1990). Government related service employment rose by an estimated 4.2 % per annum between 1982 and 1984 (Dashwood, 2000). This scenario has been maintained up to present day where employment in the public sector constitute the bulk of the formal employment and Zimbabwe. As a result, the government has become the dominant formal employer. This resulting in a larger budget deficit for the country (Brett, 2005). Further the post 2000 economic policies indigenisation has made investment in Zimbabwe unattractive to foreign investors (Shari and Raftopoulos, 2009). This reduces prospects for formal employment and a growth in informal employment.

There is a strong link between political ideologies and economic development in Zimbabwe (Shari and Raftopoulos, 2009). Rather than being guided by pure economic ideologies, economic development in Zimbabwe has been shaped by political ideologies of racial equality, indigenisation and the belief in land as the basis for economic development (Raftopoulos and Mlambo, 2009).

The political system and development

There was a political economy shift from a socialist to a neoliberal political economy towards the early 1990 (Dashwood, 2000). This had an impact on resource allocation for development within the economy. There was also the arising of classes and the state elites. This saw the adoption of new public management in the 1990s in administration of public service delivery with a departure from the monopolistic government service provision. As far as the benefits of this new administration system are concerned, it has less benefits to Zimbabwe due to resentment towards the restructuring of the administrative systems, corruption and poor technology to monitor performance of local authorities (Chigudu, 2014). Weak accountability of local authorities to citizens has been a limitation posed by the political system on fostering effective service delivery (Paradza and Musandu-Nyamayaro, 1997). The other challenge is the political system is politicisation of public service delivery. This emanates from the fact that technical staff fell under the management of political structures like councillors. As a result, those technical officials responsible for public service delivery lack resources and autonomy (Zhou, 2012). This affects the operational efficiency and therefore service delivery in Zimbabwe.

The administrative structures are defined by the constitutional provisions which has been revised since independence. However, it is important to note the executive powers remain with the presidency (Government of Zimbabwe , 2013). This poses on attainment of rule of law which has been an aspiration of the government since independence. Public participation is an important component of political development. There has been widespread optimism for movement towards a democratic society since independence. This was based on the need to do away with authoritarianism structures. On a positive note provision of the right to vote in elections to all adult citizens is one of the achievements towards political participation of citizens (Makaye and Dube, 2013). In addition, there has been a growth in the role of civil society and church-based organisations participation in development. Churches and faith-based organisations have gradually adopted an increase interested in the political participation in the country. Notable is the Councils of Churches. These have been engaged as important stakeholders in shaping some of Zimbabwe's regulations and policies based on religious values and religious based development visions. One of the religious based national development visions include the Zimbabwe We want blueprint of 2007 (Churches of Zimbabwe, 2007). Not only have these been engaged as consultancies but hey have also collaborated with different parties in meeting the broader development goals of the government. A typical example is the Roman Catholic Church initiatives which provide social relief aid to help children at risk by enhancing access to education (Catholic Relief Services (CRS, 2003).

On a negative note, the degree of democracy has been critiqued informed by the existence of repressive laws on access to information and the Public Order and Security Act (POSA). These are a limitation on the free enjoyment of human rights and freedoms in decision-making (Makaye and Dube, 2013). Other initiatives to boost citizen participation include the devolution of powers to the grassroots through the Prime Minister's Directive of 1994. However, the participation of citizens in development planning remain tokenistic since municipal officials have the overall decisions (Manduna, Zinyama, & Nhema, 2015). In addition, the use of representative participation is a challenge since councillors can manipulate interests of citizens towards self-interest (Aalen and Muriaas, 2017). Furthermore, the decentralisation of participation failed to promote democratic governance as there was little engagement towards participation at local development initiatives (Makumbe, 1998).

Technology as a tying factor

As for the case of Zimbabwe, the importance of technology was emphasised as early as 2003 under the National Economic Recovery Plan (Zimbabwe Ministry of Finance and Economic Development , 2003). Technology was recognised as a necessary input in boosting the competitiveness of industry.

Strategies advocated for included the investment in research and development, promoting ICT and the inclusion of ICT education in schools (Government of Zimbabwe, 2003). Globally there are movements to integrate ICT in all aspects of development like governance, economics and social development and poverty reduction (World Bank, 2006)

Overall, technology necessary in all aspects of development since they improve efficiency and reduce costs (Ahmed and Stein, 2004). This has the potential to improve sustainable development.

November 17, 2017 into the future

Agenda 2030 in Zimbabwe is to be implemented in three phases. These include the Transitional Stabilization Programme running from 2018-2020 and two five-year plans another from 2021-2025 and the last one from 2026-2030 (Government of Zimbabwe, 2018). The Vision 2030 goals were also advocated for in the different presidential speeches such as at the United Nations Meeting and at the Inaugural on 19 November 2017. This section analyses the provision of the vision as they related to social, economic and political development for sustainability. With regard to economic development, Vision 2030 strategies include economic re-engagement, increasing domestic and foreign direct investment from the presidential mantra," Zimbabwe is open for business". The key sectors targeted are agriculture and manufacturing (President Mnangagwa Inaugural Speech, 17 November 2018). Revamping these sectors is to be achieved through revision of laws to promote competitive business environment and fighting corruption (Government of Zimbabwe, 2030). This includes the relaxation of laws on trade through statutory instrument 64 promulgated in 2016 (Government of Zimbabwe, 2017). Other than statutory instrument 216, other archaic laws are also targeted to reduce bureaucracy in business application and approvals that stifle potential investors (Government of Zimbabwe, 2017). Reducing corruption is one of the strategies for building business confidence for investment within the country (Government of Zimbabwe, 2018). Strategies to address these challenges include the use of new technology in design and administration of the taxation system. Not only has this a potential to protect investors but it is also likely to reduce financial leakages which are a loss to the economy.

For the agricultural sector, Vision 2030 seeks to address issues of landownership for the commercial and peasant farmers as well as a way of improving agricultural productivity (ZANU-PF, 2018, Government of Zimbabwe, 2018). Hence addressing the issue of land tenure for secure ownership is a central concern. (President Mnangagwa Inaugural Speech 17 November 2017). Technologies such as GIS comes into play in effective land management and tracking in conjunction with the Survey and Deeds Registry Departments hence the formulation of the Zimbabwe National Geospatial and Space Agency (ZINGSA) division (Herald, 2018). Other than improving agricultural productivity, land ownership also enhance livelihoods by transforming land into a capital asset.

The government has taken initiatives towards stimulating productive employment within the economy. On the part of gainful employment, the government has promoted youth empowerment and youth employment initiatives. For the youth, this was to be achieved through the skills for Youth and Rural Development Programmes. Other initiatives were to boost employment among women (ZVNR, 2017). Despite these attempts, the major has been a growth in informal employment which has shot to an estimated 94 % by 2014 (Government of Zimbabwe, 2017). Realigning of the national budget towards increasing capital expenditure is one of the strategies taken towards economic development under Vision 2030. Particular regard is given to the increase in capital infrastructure expenditure as opposed to expenditure on civil service wages (President Mnangagwa Inaugural Speech, 17 November, 2017). The aim is to increase development and capital expenditure from 16 to approximately a quarter of the national budget by 2020 (Government of Zimbabwe, 2018). With regard to political development , the 2030 policy thrust is on better governance and rule of law, democracy, effective citizenship participation, responsive institutions that are flexible (urban and rural councils particularly), political re-engagement (Government of Zimbabwe, 2018). Vision 2030 also seeks to improve the performance of public institutions through restructuring and the adoption of results-based management (President Mnangagwa Inaugural Speech, 17 November 2017). Other than these new institutions such as the Fiscal and Financial Stabilization Committee and a centrally controlled Monitoring Committee (Government of Zimbabwe, 2018).

Concerning social development, the policy seeks to achieve it through enhancing delivery of services in aspects of health, education, housing and social protection (Government of Zimbabwe, 2018). Targets are to be achieved through increase investment, and enhancement of quality of services for both education and health care services (Government of Zimbabwe, 2030). Concern is also given to the quality of education where to be relevant the education system has to be aligned to changes in the economic environment (Government of Zimbabwe, 2018). This has seen the review of some of the education curriculum for primary and secondary education in 2014 which has taken effect from 2015-2022(ZVNR, 2017). The aim of this revised curriculum is to promote the development of a national identity among learner and enhancing their competitiveness in Industry (ZVNR, 2017). Other than the revision of curriculums the Zimbabwean government the government has increased its expenditure on the education sector which has risen by 2% of the GDP between 2010 and 2017 from 3 to 5% by 2017(ZVNR, 2017). This includes the provisions for redevelopment of education infrastructure as part of the social infrastructure for effective education delivery at tertiary level (President Mnangagwa Inaugural Speech, 17 November 2017).

Other than access to education, the Zimbabwean government also promotes universal access to health for all. Key health consideration s include HIV and AIDS, child mortality, maternal mortality and women health (Government of Zimbabwe, 2017). The major groups targeted include infants, women and the youth (ZVRN, 2017). Resources for health were secured through cooperation and social mobilisation with private stakeholders (Government of Zimbabwe, 2017). Strategies for improving access to health include the expansion of health infrastructure (Government of Zimbabwe, 2018). Vision 2030 also provides priority to ending poverty which is the first objective of the Sustainable Development Goals, 2030 (World Bank, 2018). Strategies advocated for is the provision of a National Social Protection Policy which addresses the needs for the vulnerability groups in society (ZVNR, 2017). Special groups under the scheme include orphans, the poor and physically handicapped. Challenges identified in pursuit of this goal include increasing unemployment and a deterioration of the economy.

Discussion and Synthesis

It is important to note that aspects of social, economic development largely depend in the level of political development in a country. Economic development influences many dimensions of social well-being such as income levels, poverty and therefore access to health and education. As a result, there exist a little difference between the three aspects of development. The important of the administrative and political systems is pertinent towards sustainable development since it often requires adjustment of institutions managing the environment (Vollmer, 2011). The current Zimbabwe Vision 2030 policy bears no explicit difference from other Zimbabwe's blueprints prior to it as it has retained most of the objectives. It has retained most of the aims of development as contained in policies prior to it. This is despite the dynamics in society, population, the economy and political regimes.

With regard to resilience of these systems in the context of Zimbabwe, there has not been a stable trend in the social, economic and political system. The economic system has moved from a balanced economy towards an economy unbalanced and reduced formal employment, and incomes. As for social development, access to health, sanitation, housing and water services have been deteriorating despite the attempts to privatise these and improve efficiency back in the 1990s and the subsequent national development policies including the current Vision 2030. On the political side, there has been movements towards promoting democratic rule soon after independence. This was made through the right to vote as well as the devolution of powers to communities through the 1994 Prime Minister's Directive. Though the right to voting has been observed, there are various critiques towards the generosity of citizen political participation in Zimbabwe. Technology including both hard and the soft components bears an important implication across all these facets of sustainable development through building new inventions and interventional well as new skills and research to address new development challenges. However, emphasis should not be placed on acquisition only but on the management of the technology such that it remains relevant to address new challenges. The ability to do so improves the resilience of development.

Conclusion and Options

Generally, development in Zimbabwe has not been sustainable as shown by the dynamic trends in access to social services, and the economic system among other factors. These systems have been more vulnerable to shocks within the system such as political regime changes and population growth. The outcomes have poor access to services and a decline in formal employment among other indictors. This reflects the dire need for building resilience within the system. The following policy options are therefore suggested as a way of improving socio-economic development in Zimbabwe:

- Investment in hard technologies or devising a way to harness the existing stock of technologies to ensure they are used to achieving the Vision 2030 objectives. The other option is investment in research and development. Other than providing new ideas for development, monitor and evaluate progress of projects within the system to learn from such is important since the path to sustainable development is a learning process best defined by the contextual environment.
- Adoption a systems approach to development planning can help reduce fragmentation of efforts since in the current situation development planning is largely fragmented across sectors. This is because technologies used in different sectors need not be isolated since the challenges of economic development, social development and political development are interlinked. This calls for interdisciplinary. Thus, systems approach to development planning can be a

panacea to the problems for sustainable development in Zimbabwe. The government can also adopt of resilient plans for monitoring and correcting abnormalities towards sustainable development.

However, for all attempts that the Zimbabwe government can take, it is important to note that there is no fixed route to sustainable development as it is a learning process.

References

Churches of Zimbabwe. (2007). *The Zimbabwe We Want: Towards a National Vision for Zimbabwe* . Churches of Zimbabwe .

Aalen, L., & Muriaas, L. (2017). *Manipualting Polical Decentralization: Africa's Inclusive Autocrats,* . Taylor and Francis.

Ahmed, A., & Stein, J. ,. (2004). Science , Technology and sustainable Development: A World Review . *World Review of Science Technology and Sustainable Development, 1*(1), 5-24.

Alibasic, H. (2017). Measuring the Sustainability Impact in Local Governments Using the Quadruple Bottom Line. *The International Journal of Sustainability Policy and Practice, 13*(3), 37-45.

Alibasic, H. (2018). *Sustainability and Resilience Planning for Local Government: The Quadruple Bottom Line Strategy.* Switzerland: Springer International.

Anderson, V. (2014). *Alternative Economic Indicators.* New York: Routledge.

Arthur, B. (2009). *The Nature of Technology: What it Is and How It Evolves.* New York: Free Press.

Ashford, N., & Hall, R. (2011). *Technology, Globalisation and Sustainable Development: Transforming the Industrial State* . London: Yale University Press.

Basiago, A. (1999). Economic, Social and Environmental Sustainability in Development Theory and Urban Planning Practice. *The Environmentalist, 19,* 145-161.

Baster, N. (1972). *Measuring Development: The Role and Adequacy of Development Indicators.* (N. Baster, Ed.) London: Frank Cass and Company.

Bhattacharya, M. (1997). Conceptualising Good Governance. *Indian Journal of Public Administration*(Annual Issue), 290-291.

Boccia, F., & Leornadi, R. (2016). *The Challenge of the Digital Economy: Markets , Taxation and Appropriate Economic Models.* Switzerland: Palgrave McMillan.

Brett, E. (2005). *Crisis States Programme : From Corporatism to Liberalisation in Zimbabwe: Economic Policy Regimes and Political Crisis 1980-1997.* London: Development Research Centre.

Brown, K. (2016). *Resilience, Development and Global Change.* New York : Routledge.

Catholic Relief Services (CRS). (2003). *Report on the Mid Term Review of the Strive Project.* Catholic Relief Services.

Chigudu, D. (2014). Implementing New Public Management in Zimbabwe: Challenges and Obstacles. *Journal of Governance and Relation, 3*(2), 43-49.

Chitiyo, K., Vines, A., & Vandome, C. (2016). *The Domestic and External Implication of Zimbabwe's Economic Reform and Re-Engagemenr Agenda.* Chatham House.

Darnolf, S., & Laakso, L. (2016). *Twenty Years of Independence in Zimbabwe: From Liberation to Authoritarianism.* Palgrave McMillan. Retrieved from http://ebookcentral.proquest.com

Dashwood, H. (2000). *Zimbabwe: The Political Economy of Transformation.* University of Toronto Press.

Enders, G., & Remig, M. (2015). *Theories of Sustainable Development.* (G. Enders, & M. Remig, Eds.) New York: Routledge.

Galloping, C. (2003). *Science and Technology for Sustainable Development: A Latin American and Caribbean.Perspective.* Santiago: Sustainable Development and Human Settlement Division , Santiago.

Government of Zimbabwe . (2013). *Constitution of Zimbabwe, Amendment (No.20) Act 2013.* Harare : Parliament of Zimbabwe.

Government of Zimbabwe. (1991). *Zimbabwe: A Framework for Economic Reform ,1991-1995.* Harare: Government of Zimbabwe.

Government of Zimbabwe. (2004). *Zimbabwe Millennium Development Goals 2004: Progress Report.* Harare: Government of Zimbabwe.

Government of Zimbabwe. (2017). *Zimbabwe Voluntary National Review (ZVNR) of SDGS for High Level Political Forum.*

Government of Zimbabwe. (2018). *Transitional Stabilisation Programme: Reforms Agenda, October- December 2020: "Towards a Prosperous and Empowered Middle Income Society By 2030".* Harare: Government of Zimbabwe.

Grubler, A. (2003). *Technology and Global Change.* Cambridge: Cambridge University Press.

Hall, P., & Lamont, M. (2013). *Social Resilience in the Neoliberal Era.* Cambridge: Cambridge University Press .

Heijden, J. (2014). *Governance for Urban Sustainability and Resiliency: Responding to Climate Change and the Relevance of the Built Environment.* Cheltenham: Edward Elgar .

Herald. (2018, July 11). President Launches '30 Modernisation Agenda. *The Herald.*

Laha, A. (2016). Association between Governance and Human Development in South Asia: A Cross Country Analysis. In D. Chandra, & D. Chandra (Ed.), *Handbook of Research on Global Indicators of Economic and Political Convergence* (pp. 254- 273). USA: IGI Global.

Langdon, S., Ritter, A., & Samy, Y. (2018). *African Economic Development.* Routledge.

Luks, F. (2015). Theories of "Sustainability" and the Sustainability of Theories: For Alternatives to the Mainstream and Against Simple Solutions . In G. Enders, & M. Remig, *Theories of Sustainable Development* (pp. 80-88). New York: Routledge.

Makaye, P., & Dube, B. (2013). Zimbabwe : The Challenge of Democracy from Below, 1980-2013. *International Journal of Political Science and Development, 2*(10), 227-236.

Makumbe, J. (1998). *Development and Democracy in Zimbabwe.* SAPES Books.

Manduna, K., Zinyama, T., & Nhema, A. (2015). Local Government Participatoy Budget System in Zimbabwe: The Case of Harare City Council, 1995-2013. *Public Policy and Adminstarion Research, 5*(11), 38-60.

Martin, P., & Grainger, A. (2004). *Exploring Sustainable Development: Geographical Perspectives.* Routledge. Retrieved from http://ebookcentral.proquest.com

McKinnon, R. (2005). *Money and Capital in Economic Development.* Washington DC: Brookings Institution.

Mihyo, P., & Mukuna, T. (2015). *Urban Youth Unemployment in Eastern and Southern Africa: Features, Consequences and Cut-Back Strategies.* (P. Mihyo, & T. Mukuna, Eds.) Addis Ababa: OSSREA.

Mlambo, A., & Raftopoulos, B. (2009). *Becoming Zimbabwe: A History from Pre-Colonial Period to 2008.* (A. Mlambo, & B. Raftopoulos, Eds.) Harare: Weaver Press.

Nafziger, E. W. (2012). *Economic Development* (5th ed.). Cambridge: Cambridge University Press.

Niranjan, P., & Mishra, S. (2008). *E- Governance.* Global Media. Retrieved from http:ebookcentral.proquest.com

OCED. (2000). *Towards Sustainable Development: Indicators to Measure Progress.* Paris: Public Affairs and Communication Directorate.

Otsuki, K. (2015). *Transformative Sustainable Development: Participation, Reflection and Change.* London: Routledge.

Paradza, G., & Musandu- Nyamayaro, O. (1997). Urban Governance Outreach Program. In G. Paradza, & O. Musandu- Nyamayaro (Ed.), *Conference on Urban Governance and Management Programme in Zimbabwe* (pp. 1-98). Kadoma: University of Zimbabwe.

Pawar, M., & Cox, D. (2010). Why a Focus on Social Development in the Twenty First Century? . In M. Pawar, R. Cox, M. Pawar, & R. Cox (Eds.), *Social Development: Critical Themes and Perspectives* (pp. 1-13). New York: Routledge .

Pfahler, T., & Grebe, K. (2005). Reducing Transaction Costs by Using Electronic Commerce in Financial Services : An Institutional and Empirical Approach. In H. Kehal, & V. Singh, *Digital Economy, Impact, Influence and Challenges* (pp. 2-83). London: IDEA Group Publishing.

Poulton, C., Davies, R., Matshe, I., & Urey, I. (2002). *A Review of Agricultural Economic Policies: 1980-2000*. UK: Imperial College.

Saccheti, S., Christoforou, A., & Mosca, M. (2017). *Social Regeneration and Local Development: Cooperation, Social Economy and Public Participation*. (S. Saccheti, A. Christoforou, & M. Mosca, Eds.) Routledge.

Shari, E., & Raftopoulos, B. (2009). *Developing a Transformation Agenda for Zimbabwe*. IDASA Publishers. Retrieved from http://ebookcentral.proquest.com

Sibanda, V., & Makwata, R. (2017). *Zimbabwe Post Independence Economic Policies: A Critical Review*. Germany: Lambert Academic Publishing.

Skalnes, T. (2016). *The Politics of Economic Reform in Zimbabwe: Continuity and Change in Development*. London: McMillan Press .

Steenhuis, H., & De Bruijn, E. (2012). Technology and Economic Development: A Literature Review. *International Journal of Innovation and Technology Management, 9* (5), 1-11.

Stoneman, C. (1990). The Industrialisation of Zimbabwe: Past Present and Future. *Afrika Focus, 6* (3-4), 245-282.

Sundby, R., & Heimgartner, A. (2016). *The Welfare Society: An Aim for Social Development*. Zurich: LIT.

UNDP. (2016). *Human Development Report 2016: Human Development for Everyone*. New York: UNDP.

UNDP. (2017). *Zimbabwe Human Development Report 2017: Climate Change and Human Development: Towards Building a Climate Resilient Nation*. Harare: UNDP .

UNDP. (2018). *Human Development Indices and Indicators:2018 Statistical Update*. Washington DC: UNDP.

UNICEF . (2015). *Extended Analysis of Multiple Indicator Cluster Survey (MICS) 2014*. UNICEF.

Unwin, T. (2009). *ICT4D: Information Communication for Development*. (T. Unwin, Ed.) Cambridge: Cambridge University Press.

Vargus-Hernandez, J. G. (2016). Strategic Spatial Analysis of the Implementation of Trade Policy Opening Politics in Mexico. In D.

Chandra, & D. Chandra (Ed.), *Handbook of Research on Global Indicators of Economic and Political Convergence* (pp. 274- 313). USA: IGI Global.

Vollmer, D. (2011). *Pathways to Urban Sustainability: Lessons from the Atlan Metropolitan Region: Summary of a Workshop.* National Academic Press.

World Bank . (2012). *World Development Indicators 2012.* World Bank Publications.

World Bank. (2006). *Information and Communications for Development: Global Trends and Policies.* Washington DC: World Bank.

World Bank. (2016). *World Development Indicators 2016.* World Bank Publications.

World Bank. (2018). *Learning to Realise Education's Promise.* Washington DC: World Bank.

World Bank. (2018). *Atlas of Sustainable Development Goals: From World Development Indicators.* Washington DC : World Bank .

Zhou, G. (2012). Public Adminstration in Zimbabwe: A Framework Approach. *Journal of Public Adminstration and Governance, 2*(2), 132-150.

Zimbabwe Ministry of Finance and Economic Development . (2003). *National Economic Revival Programme: Measures to Address the Current Challenges.* Harare: Ministry of Finance and Economic Development.

ZIMSTAT. (2016). *Zimbabwe Population 2012: Living Conditions Thematic Report.* Harare: Population Census Office .

Chapter 2

Development Sustainability in the Face of Stakeholder Conflicts in Mashonaland Central Province

Obediah Dodo

Summary

This chapter is based on an explorative study conducted with three humanitarian organisations in Mashonaland Central province, Zimbabwe, was guided by an underpinning concept of good governance as defined by the World Bank vis-à-vis community development. The study sought to identify humanitarian programmes and inter-stakeholder conflicts across all the studied organisations and how the beneficiaries benefitted in the face of stakeholder conflicts. Data were collected using formal and structured interviews with participants purposively sampled from the organisations in the three development areas. In total, 16 participants were purposively sampled mainly because the study followed an anti-positivist approach which believes in depth of data rather than width. All the mobilised data were analysed using content analysis approach. The study established that most conflicts recorded in the development areas are over ownership of humanitarian aid by the beneficiaries on one side, desire to gain political mileage by some political entities on the other and finding means of embezzling the aid by the implementers. As a result of the conflicts, it is the beneficiaries and donors who lose out as aid is either diverted or government manipulates the laws and policies to the disadvantage of the targeted communities.

Introduction

The debate on sustainability and sustainable development focusing on the role of NGOs operating in Zimbabwe has fuelled conflicts involving various local communities. Since the country's independence in 1980, the development community has shifted its focus from the availability of both humanitarian and development aid to ensuring the existence of systems of accountability for resources and output. It is the establishment and enforcement of accountability systems that has seen prospective beneficiaries like rural peasants, programme implementers, host government and donors clashing and embroiled in recurrent conflicts. Each of the contenders claims ownership and responsibility and

19

demands accountability from the other. In the end, it has often been the beneficiaries and the donors who lose. The study sought to identify humanitarian programmes' sustainability in the face of recurrent stakeholder conflicts. The study findings are expected to help refine policies and institute a workable stakeholder relationship on the ground.

The study sought to identify development programmes and respective programmes' sustainability in the face of stakeholder conflicts. The study identified the following aspects: development programmes by each organisation during a ten-month period and inter-stakeholder conflicts that were experienced across all the organisations studied. The study also looked at the sustainability of respective programmes in the food security and agriculture cluster in the face of stakeholder conflicts. The chapter discusses the prevailing situation on the ground with regards to the subject of development sustainability in Zimbabwe paying attention to the historical humanitarian efforts from global down to local levels. It also looks at the historical, political, social and economic backgrounds of the districts under study. The reviewed literature paid attention to aspects around sustainable development, humanitarianism, development aid and related challenges. The chapter also outlines how data were systematically collected and analysed before presenting the results. Results presentation simply answers the research questions that sought to establish the humanitarian projects, inter-stakeholder conflicts encountered and the project sustainability. The chapter also presents the study recommendations and conclusions.

Background and Context

There are humanitarian projects in the districts of Mbire which has 17 wards and Muzarabani with 29 wards in Mashonaland Central province. Mashonaland Central province lies in the northern part of Zimbabwe (Figure 2.1). The province is made up of eight administrative districts including Mbire and Muzarabani. The districts lie in the semi-arid and hot ecological region five and four. They are therefore exposed to droughts and hunger which subsequently lead to poverty and diseases (Mahaja, 2008). The districts lie in a low altitude area with high temperatures ranging from 20° – 40°C and receive poor annual rainfall of less than 500mm. During the rainy season, floods occur causing diseases, destroying crops, roads, and bridges (Mahaja, 2008). Because of semi-aridity, the only suitable activity in the districts is livestock production and drought resistant and short season crop cultivation. To alleviate poverty, hunger and diseases, there are various non-governmental organisations working in the districts. However, for the purpose of this study, only three organisations were selected, namely World Vision (WV) in Mbire, Lower Guruve Development

Association (LGDA) in Muzarabani, and Adventist Development and Relief Agency (ADRA) in Mbire. Amongst the organisations' various development and humanitarian projects, the study only focused on the food security and agriculture cluster.

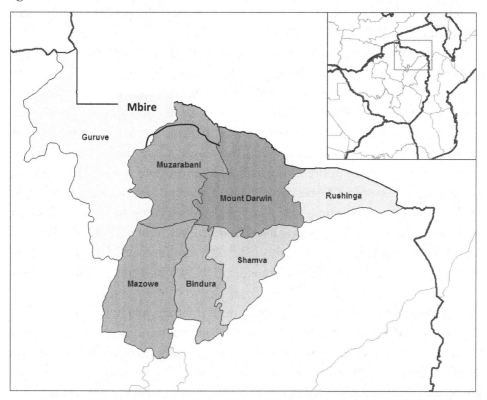

Figure 2.1 Mashonaland Central Province (Provincial Statistics Department Mashonaland, Bindura, 2006)

Problems of poverty, hunger, diseases, water and sanitation hygiene, health and nutrition and education have always been subjects of concern from the global perspective with the developed world seeking to help vulnerable and less developed countries (Simpson and Doré, 2009, World Bank, 2016). However, all efforts towards humanitarian assistance have long been tainted by allegations and counter allegations of poor management of the projects and misappropriation of project resources (Rieff, 2002, Cohen, 2004, Ravich *et al.* 2016). The international donor community has established a Humanitarian Response Plan (HRP) to attend to the problems (Nafziger, 2000). The HRP serves as a tracking tool for donor financers monitoring the effective use of the resources. There are systems that help monitor the effectiveness and accountability of humanitarian programmes. Some of the legislative tools include Private Voluntary Organisations Act [Chapter 17:05], the Cooperative

Societies Act [Chapter 24:05], Unlawful Organizations Act [Chapter 11:13], Public Order Security Act [Chapter 11:17], Deeds Registries Act (2009), and the District Development Committee by-laws. Besides, the local security services also get involved in the implementation of the projects by sitting in the District Development Committees as a way of plugging loopholes (Dodo and Mabvurira, 2012).

The donor community from the developed world realises that some of the challenges affecting the developing world are largely the results of climate change effects, to which they contribute enormously (Le Billon *et al.* 2000). Some donors also attribute poverty and under-development in the developing world to lack of opportunities perpetuated by colonial legacies and lack of innovation. Therefore, as mitigatory measures, there have been various interventions meant to address the challenges and create some balance in the world economic system (World Bank, 2008). These interventions are at different levels, legally and structurally. Some of the interventions have been through summits, treaties and declarations like The Earth Summit of 1992, the Bretton Woods conference of 1994, the Rio+20 Conference, United Nations Conference on Sustainable Development (UNCSD) and the Greenhouse Gas Protocol (Simpson and Doré, 2009).

To support the above cited efforts, various international financial and policy institutions led by the Bretton Woods institutions have also crafted various means through which they are promoting the development of the developing world. Some of the interventions addressing climate change effects include the World Bank which is involved in low-carbon growth projects, energy efficiency, and renewable energy development, which all seek to reduce destructive gas emissions. Similarly, United Nations and World Bank fund adaptation and alleviation activities that assist the poor develop their way out of poverty (Le Billon *et al.* 2000, WB, 2008).

Some international non-governmental organisations invested different efforts against hunger in Zimbabwe. There was the United States of America International Development (USAID)-funded Famine Early Warning Systems Network (FEWSNET) that played a significant role in identifying communities that needed humanitarian support. USAID also funded the Consortium for Southern Africa Food Emergency (C-SAFE) and through its Office of Foreign Disaster Assistance (OFDA), it availed maize for consumption to the needy communities (FAO/WFP, 2008). The Department for International Development (DFID)'s Protracted Relief Programme (PRP) also directed its assistance to drought stricken rural communities (DFID, 2005).

There have been various blue-prints and policies also directed at alleviating food poverty and instigating growth and economic development at local level in Zimbabwe. The Fast Track Land Resettlement Programme in 2000, the Zimbabwe Agenda for Sustainable Socio-Economic Agenda (ZimAsset), Operation *Maguta*, Indigenisation and Economic Empowerment Act of 2007 (Dodo, 2013) and Command Agriculture are some of the investments in food security in Zimbabwe. The Agriculture Sector Productivity Enhancement Facility (ASPEF) of 2005 was meant to fund agriculture. The Short-Term Emergency Recovery Programme (STERP) mobilised the international donor community to support its Crop Input Pack Scheme for vulnerable smallholder farmers during the 2009/10 farming season.

Theoretical Perspectives

The study was guided by an underpinning concept of good governance as defined by the World Bank (WB) vis-à-vis community development. Good governance 'is the appropriate allocation of services to the needy without prejudicing others' (World Bank, 2016:2) It contends that humanitarian assistance should be directed to the needy communities without unfair conditionalities detrimental to the anticipated development. Good governance recognises that needy communities are in such conditions of poverty and inadequate resource supply because of circumstances beyond their control hence deserve both humanitarian and development assistance.

Sustainable development is efficient use of resources in a carefully planned manner to provide both instant and long-term benefits for humanity and the earth allowing future use of the same resources (World Bank, 2008, Simpson and Dore, 2009). The efficient use and planning of resources requires a meticulous identification and prioritisation of the minerals and their processing in a manner that does not deplete them and harm humanity and the environment. However, development sustainability is efficient establishment and roll-out of community projects meant to up-lift local communities in a manner that ensures the survival and continued positive contribution of the projects to the intended groups (World Bank, 2008). Sustainable development is sustained by three pillars, which are environmental stewardship, economic growth, and social inclusion (World Bank, 2008). The pillars require that all natural resources be appropriately extracted and efficiently used for the development of local communities and the world at large. The pillars also require that from the extraction of resources to their use, local communities must be included so that they also benefit and protect them. As a result of institutional failures such as lack of effective laws and political will at state level, the earth's natural resources like uranium and other valuable minerals have been extracted and used in an economically inefficient and wasteful manner without looking at the consequences. The world is in a dilemma with the adverse effects of nuclear weapons and other cancer enhancing materials. The burning of fossil fuels like coal and oil accelerated world's growth unfortunately leaving the effects of climate change threatening to rewind decades of development (Simpson and Doré, 2009).

Development trends have also left several other people behind, especially in the developing world, with an estimated 1.2 billion still lacking access to electricity, 870 million being malnourished, and 780 million still without access to safe, clean drinking water (World Bank, 2016). In Zimbabwe, poverty levels are still alarmingly high with over 9 million in need of clean and safe water, 10.1 million yet to access electricity (ZIMSTATS, 2015), and 96% unemployment rate (Dodo and Dodo, 2014). There has been an increase in poverty with the number of people living below the Total Consumption Poverty Line (TCPL) at 72.3% in 2014, as a result of a decline in formal employment (MDGR, 2015). According to the Beijing +20 Report (2015), urban and rural population in Zimbabwe stands at 33% and 67% respectively. It therefore means that over 67% of Zimbabwean population faces poverty and in need of clean and safe water.

Humanitarianism is a concept that has of late gained popularity with institutions that want to gain access to areas otherwise traditionally known as sacred. It is a duty to offer help unconditionally, wherever and whenever it is required. The concept derives from the belief that the strong and the rich have a moral duty to help the weak and those in need (Branczik, 2004). According to Adam Smith, this obligation is inherent in human nature (Rieff, 2002). Aid distribution and the provision of other essential amenities may help those in leadership to manipulate the locals for their benefit. In the case of politicians, they may use humanitarian aid to mobilise votes whereas in war situations, they may sell aid to finance wars. According to Luttwak (1999), humanitarian aid has been accused of precipitating war economies and protracting conflict by availing help, openly or indirectly. They are similarly blamed for continued poor agricultural production and hunger in areas that usually receive assistance. Humanitarian work applies the principles of independence and impartiality (Oxfam, 2000). Impartiality suggests that the desires of people are evaluated and attended to without looking at their political or religious belief, origin, race or gender, amongst others. This then calls for the humanitarian organisations to be independent from religious, political or ethnic influence. However, the principle of impartiality has not been strictly adhered to owing to the influences of the financiers.

The idea of having development and humanitarian institutions accounting for their actions and resource usage is a recent one, having been promoted in the 1990s as a response to the rapid growth of humanitarian organisations, the advent of democracy, crisis of legitimacy, increased funding and the presence of a stronger voice (Cohen, 2004, Kovach, 2003). The drive for humanitarian organisations' accountability has come from several sectors, the general public, media, government and other conservative institutions. The NGO community has also added its voice on the need for accountability. In basic terms, accountability implies that an organisation explains its use of resources to both the financier and the targeted beneficiary by way of either verbal or written reports (Lee, 2004). The targeted community also plays a vital role in the production of a good and credible report.

All over the world, there are organisations that focus on the welfare of communities, rendering assistance after realizing that there are conflicts and wars that have often interrupted people's lives and their development progress. The forms of intervention are either humanitarian or development assistance. Humanitarian assistance is a response to complex crises that prolonged conflicts produce. Its main goal is averting human fatalities and ensuring access to the essentials for survival, water, food, shelter, sanitation, and health care (Boyce, 2002, Branczik, 2004). It also supports relief efforts by way of availing food, water and other vital social services, stops the spread of conflict by ensuring democracy and allowing for peace to prevail, and organise rehabilitation through rebuilding destroyed infrastructure and social relationships. Development aid is often external support for the reconstruction of a country's infrastructure, institutions, and economy, usually after war. This form of aid ensures that the specific community sectors develop, instead of gliding back into conflict (Branczik, 2004). Ideally, it looks at democratisation, reconstruction and economic development though such objectives are oftentimes not met. While humanitarian assistance is meant to prevent conflicts in societies emanating from hunger, poverty and idleness, development aid can stimulate conflict if it is managed without bearing in mind social and political circumstances. Therefore, in the case of two studied areas, while the aid is largely development oriented, there are also aspects of humanitarianism as the programmes on the ground also seek to relieve communities from a humanitarian crisis that was experienced following a drought in 2014 and 2015 agricultural seasons.

Effective coordination of both development and humanitarian relief efforts is particularly significant in order to reduce duplication of work and contradictory activities. The greatest difficulties for humanitarian and development assistance are achieving effectiveness, efficiency and the ability to delineate economic, political, and social effects linked with them. According to some researchers, it has turned out to be more and clearer that aid is not a solution (Rieff, 1997, Branczik, 2004). Though externally administered, humanitarian and development assistance programmes usually assume responsibilities within the crisis and in the communities in which they operate.

Ensuring successful development and humanitarian programmes from the least available resources has been observed by various scholars as a major challenge in delivering aid to the need communities. In regions with poor infrastructure, it is often problematic and unsafe for humanitarian organisations to provide assistance (Boyce, 2002). Effective management and coordination are made difficult to attain by the organisations' failure to obtain accurate information, the increasing number of organisations on the ground and the unpredictability of humanitarian emergencies. In other situations, humanitarian aid escalates conflicts, undermining its eventual objective of saving lives. This is especially so when there is a calculated interference by political players who might be having ulterior motives (Muchabaiwa *et al.* 2010). The provision of assistance can give civilians a false sense of safety and protection by the international community with catastrophic results (Rieff, 1997). The false sense and protection come in that communities tend to relax as they survive on the provided assistance, sometimes failing to plan for their future. Therefore, benefitting communities should be equipped for sustainable livelihoods well after the assistance has gone.

It has been observed, especially in Africa, that non-governmental organisations operate as they wish with little or no accountability. For example, in Zimbabwe, national laws such as Private Voluntary Organisations Act (Chapter 17:05) 2007 (GoZ, 2013), and local authority by-laws governing the operations of NGOs are weak and porous allowing these organisations to abuse aid and even the intended beneficiaries. The Zimbabwean laws and policies governing the operations of non-governmental organisations lack strict and water-tight provisions that can scrutinise the latter's operations. In some instances, according to Dodo and Mabvurira (2012), forums and relevant government departments that craft the laws are funded by the donor community such that laws end up coming from the non-governmental organisations. According to some scholars, both the communities and the local authorities are too poor to question whatever they see on the ground (Rieff, 1997, Dodo and Mabvurira, 2012) as they will be expecting to benefit from the aid.

Methodology

The study utilised a qualitative approach using open-ended questionnaires in order to understand the experiences and views of the target communities in

Mbire and Muzarabani districts. This was based on the understanding that participants from whom data is sought are experts who understand themselves and their situations better than any other person. Ravitch and Carl (2016) note that fieldwork in qualitative research entails the process of collecting data in a natural setting. Data were collected using both formal and informal interviews with participants purposively sampled from the World Vision (WV), Lower Guruve Development Association (LGDA) and Adventist Development and Relief Agency (ADRA) and local communities in Mbire and Muzarabani. Two policy designer participants opted to respond through e-mail while one responded by telephone. In total, 16 participants were purposively sampled mainly because the study followed an anti-positivist approach which believes in depth of data rather than width. With anti-positivism, Walsh (2003) and Hellstrom (2008) argue that in qualitative methodology, sample size is not relevant as samples are measured based on the ability to provide vital and valuable information. From each organisation, one policy designer and one field officer were selected (6 participants), eight community beneficiaries (4 in Muzarabani and 4 in Mbire) and two key participants (1 Muzarabani and 1 Mbire), two traditional leaders were also sampled. All the raw data were analysed using both Latent and Manifest Content Analysis approach which allowed a systematic identification of like themes and similarities in behaviours, activities and meanings from messages (Patton, 2002). The study also satisfied all the basic research ethical requirements.

Results and Discussion

Running development projects

All three participants drawn from the implementing agencies' policy design explained the projects that each of the organisations was running, identifying other stakeholders involved. World Vision (WV) is involved in large-scale programmes known as Area Development Programmes (ADPs) assisting communities build robust and healthier relationships. WV is into learners' retention in schools and restoring access to safe and sufficient water and improving hygiene practices in Mbire district. Its two projects were focused on food security and agriculture and water and sanitation hygiene (WASH). The projects are in 15 wards comprising over 5500 households. There are over 2 000 pupils who are supported with stationery and supplementary food at school to encourage retention of learners in schools. The project also supports households with agricultural inputs as a way of ensuring some harvest that can sustain them.

Lower Guruve Development Association (LGDA) is involved in drought emergency response and recovery programme in 19 Wards of the 29 Wards in Muzarabani District that were most affected by the 2015/2016 El Nino induced drought with targeted food assistance and starter packs for agricultural inputs. Its projects fall in the food security and agriculture cluster. Over 5000 households are involved in this project. The project avails seed packs of short seasoned variety small grains and relevant fertilizers to ensure that the targeted households reap something for their sustenance.

Adventist Development and Relief Agency (ADRA) is into the 2015/2016 El Nino induced drought emergency response, integrated management of acute malnutrition in drought affected areas and WASH emergency assistance to drought affected communities in Mbire district. Its projects fall within the clusters of food security and agriculture, nutrition and health and WASH. In total, ADRA is working with over 5000 households. ADRA is carrying out a project that distributes agricultural inputs to selected households to mitigate hunger. According to participants, all projects are funded externally, especially from the West. The donors expect to see some changes on the lives of the concerned communities over time. Therefore, while the recipients are getting agricultural inputs packs, they are supposed to kick-start the lives of the communities. They do not have to worry about food matters. Rather, they spend their energies on other developmental areas.

Inter-stakeholder conflicts

Usually when some of the aid agencies move into an area for aid work, there are some gatekeepers who wield most of the influence in as far as decisions are concerned. In the event that an organisation moves in and fails to recognise that structural arrangement, conflicts manifest. Often, there is a conflict between project implementers and local community leadership over coordination of the project management. According to two key participants who were also traditional leaders, all organisations that moved into their communities had immediately abandoned the respect for local leadership and respective cultural beliefs. They indicated that since the two districts are steeped in their culture, there was need for implementing agencies to strictly adhere to the laid down rules, especially around the dress code and personal conduct. These attitudes, according to the participants were affecting the implementation of humanitarian projects as local people were no longer taking them seriously. One traditional leader remarked:

'Dambudziko nderekuti vakomana vedevelopment ava havakoshese tsika dzedu. Ndinoona sevanotosiya vauraya hunhu muvana vedu vachitorwa moyo nemazimota avanofamba nawo aya'

(The problem is that these field officers do not recognise our cultural practices. They have contaminated our children who just admire their lifestyles).

The study observed that in Muzarabani district, there was a lot of political influence supported by the President's Office, where a single individual has a tendency of overriding all local authorities' decisions. This usually applies where food aid is supposed to be distributed to the communities in need. What often happens is that the individual makes his demands for personal benefit and in some cases, for the benefit of some political party members. These demands will be despite the qualification of the people to benefit.

In Muzarabani district, two community respondents and one field officer accused some political elements for hijacking the food security and agriculture project by LGDA where over 5000 households stood to benefit. It was revealed that of the 19 targeted wards, only 16 had effectively received all inputs due to repeated interference by both politicians and security agents. Similarly, three community participants and one field officer in Mbire, reported that politicians were creating unnecessary bureaucracy in project implementation which was impacting on the intended outcomes. One community participant said,

'*Zvinoitwa nevakuru zvirikutokanganisa maprojects. Vakauya vanotora zvese zvimwe vachipa vanhu vanevana naana baba vanoshanda*' (These leaders actually interfere with progress. When they come, they take all the resources, giving some to undeserving people).

There have always been reports, though unsubstantiated, about the politicisation of aid for the benefit of a small community section. This problem has stalled progress in some instances, especially where emergencies are involved. Some of the aid ends up going towards some political programmes that are not in any way related to food security and agriculture.

Two key participants (1 from each of the 2 districts) revealed that there were some communities, especially in Muzarabani, that were opposed to the identification of the selected beneficiaries as poor communities. They said the term poor communities was stigmatizing to the involved children. Therefore, because of that perception, some families were just receiving goods and not fully participating in the rest of the projects because they did not want to be associated with poverty. That eventually impacted on the projects. The participants also demanded ownership of projects through involvement from inception to implementation. According to seven community beneficiaries (4 from Mbire and 3 from Muzarabani), the communities have always wanted to propose projects that interest them, that transform their lives, that are culturally acceptable and implementable than those imposed from Harare. Participants indicated that their increased involvement could then serve as a monitoring and regulatory mechanism against pilferage, misappropriation and corruption. In Mbire, these sentiments were prominent around Mahuwe, Chitsungo, Mushumbi and Nyambudzi wards. Three of the four community participants in Muzarabani pointed out that LGDA project was being run like a personal project with some executives enriching themselves from the resources. They proposed a change of management for efficiency and effectiveness purposes. These sentiments were common in five wards. On the other hand, two of the three field officers indicated that it was difficult for them to allow communities to take ownership of the projects because of various reasons, lack of technical expertise, lack of management and that they were prone to abusing the resources.

What is evident in this is a conflict over the control of resources which, according to the communities, are being abused before they reach the targeted beneficiaries. On the other hand, the implementing agencies feel the communities are just an illiterate and lazy lot with no capacity to think and administer their welfare hence keep control of the projects. Communities also feel that some organisations are using their plight to secure resources from the donors, which they use for personal benefit. In Muzarabani, there was a strong voice against the manner in which some LGDA executives were personalising project resources. Similar concerns were also raised against ADRA in Mbire (in 3 wards). Closely akin to the above conflict was the question about alleged embezzlement of project resources by the implementing agencies. Generally, all t three organisations were accused of delivering inadequate materials as a result of theft along the way.

All the eight community participants and two key participants indicated that it was worrisome to note that each time there was a humanitarian project in progress, people faced more challenges. What happened, according to 10 participants, is that as soon as resources were received on the ground, they were pilfered to a secret market where the targeted communities did not have access to them. It was revealed that there were instances when senior officials in the projects would connive to under-deliver resources and share the spoils. Five community participants (3 Muzarabani and 2 Mbire) indicated that some underserving households also benefited unscrupulously. The eventual shortage in the aid often resulted in conflicts. In Mbire, ADRA project aid shortage resulted in a conflict that eventually turned ethnic with villages around Sangojena like Chafesuka, Mondo and Mharamasaka claiming to be original Korekore accusing some Karanga villages, namely Mazikana, Mpofu, Zihanzu, Marova and Pasi of hijacking a project meant for Mbire people who are originally of the Korekore tribe. According to the field officer, the ethnic conflict existed since time immemorial and had often affected most projects which required collectivity. What usually happened, according to the participant, was that programmes that required collective effort usually had groups constituted along ethnic lines and always characterised by serious suspicions. The participant said,

> 'Development in this part of the district is a nightmare. I don't think we are making any headway in as far as sustainable poverty alleviation is concerned'

Sustainability of development work

The causes for the unsustainability of development are multifarious. Among other things, they involve gender, lack of local participation, climate, and public policy. Distorted government policies, lack of project ownership and abandoned rural infrastructure, are also some of the main contributors to the failure of most humanitarian projects in the remote rural areas. Most of the roads, bridges and service facilities in these rural communities were long fallen in a derelict state so much so that effective implementation of the projects was a challenge given that mobility and communication are slow. The study observed that accessing areas like Chitima, Chapoto, Kanongo and Gonono in Mbire and Chadereka and Kairezi, Chiwenga, Dambakurima, Hoya, and Maungaunga in Muzarabani was difficult. Besides, agricultural extension officers, who are supposed to promote and supervise local communities in these agricultural projects, were not available in these two communities. Implementing organisations' field officers were inadequate for meaningful hands-on supervision. Therefore, from the outset, there is poor policy implementation on the part of the central government while there is no proper coordination between Rural District Councils and humanitarian agencies on the deployment of extension officers who are respected by locals and who are knowledgeable on the local systems.

It was reported that, despite pursuing the same objective of food security, especially in Mbire where two organisations were running parallel projects, there was an element of competition between them. While competition might be good for maximum productivity, in this case, the field officers tended to pull each other down. According to one key participant, one of the observed cases was where a field officer may notice problems in the crop fields sponsored by another organisation and, instead of giving help, the field officer would not assist hoping to prove to the communities that the rival organisation was incompetent. This situation seriously affected crop germination in some wards in Mbire (Kanongo, Chitima, Angwa and Gonono) where another organisation, whose vehicle could not navigate rough terrain, had its project crops failing.

In Mbire District, according to three participants, ADRA project was reported to be discriminating against women. Female headed households were being denied access and that approach was causing problems with some sympathisers beginning to adopt a lukewarm attitude. According to participants, single women were being asked to prove that they were family people.

Some projects fail to reach sustainability levels because of various circumstances like cultural systems and history. For example, according to three community participants, implementers of all the three projects in Muzarabani and Mbire might have failed to appreciate the importance placed in cultural systems like working in the fields on Fridays or engaging in any economic activity on this day. Culturally, the people in the two districts believe that Friday is a sacred day meant for resting. All traditional leaders ensured that people abstained from working in the fields on Fridays, including travelling to collect some of the inputs from Mushumbi business centre and Mazarabani business centre in Mbire and Muzarabani districts respectively. According to the field officers and some community participants, this was in direct contrast to the spirit of hardworking and production which require people to work as much as possible. With regards to food security and agriculture projects, beneficiaries are expected to work in the fields and ensure that they produce high yields. This requires working in the fields almost daily, if need be. Therefore, there are conflicts between project implementers and targeted beneficiaries over recognition of some cultural systems in the two districts.

Ten participants (2 key participants, 1 field officer and 7 community participants) reported that lack of consistent by both parties as a result of poor relations that would have been created during the implementation stage had contributed towards unsustainability in development. Whenever one party saw a retrogressive element, there was no intervening effort so as to prove the other party wrong. This might have emanated from a previous clash over the implementation strategy by stakeholders. One key participant said,

'Ndikaona zvabhenda, ndinosiya nekuti ndinenge ndakambotaura vanhu vakaramba' (If there is a problem, I do not intervene because some people would have rejected my advice)

The projects were also affected by the exodus of most able-bodied youth to urban areas in search of jobs and better opportunities. The need for employment on the part of most of the youth forced them to relocate to urban areas and, in the process, taking away most of the labour for the agricultural fields. The study realised that the implementing agencies, namely World Vision, Lower Guruve Development Association and Adventist Development and

Relief Agency were never paying attention to the exodus of labour leaving the aged, frail and sick having to attend to the requirements of the crop fields. This adversely affected all the three projects.

Humanitarian projects confer benefits on individuals through looting, that is, what Collier and Hoeffler (2000) called private motivation hypothesis. Where alternative prospects are limited because of low earnings and poor employment, and the opportunities of enrichment through humanitarian project resources are great, the frequency and extent of human induced crises and poverty are likely to be greater. Crises and poverty may be described as human induced when elements of an effective alleviation approach would have deliberately been sabotaged as a way of allowing the crisis to persist. This is what two participants alleged to have been done by some officials in LGDA as a way of keeping such food security projects relevant and running. This is also the work of corrupt politicians and rent-seeking public bureaucracies.

Closely related to the above is the problem of implicit taxation of the targeted beneficiaries in order to get registered. Two participants in Muzarabani and three in Mbire indicated that officials from World Vision and Lower Guruve Development Association were asking some potential beneficiaries to pay for what they termed 'administrative costs' before they registered. According to participants, this extortionist corrupt approach towards the project was adversely affecting the reputations of the implementing agencies and eventually derailing noble initiatives of alleviating hunger. However, the study notes that all the projects will continue running to some extent, not because of their successes but due to the fact that some stakeholders (implementing agencies and local leaders) will be benefitting directly, hence their desire to keep the hen that lays the eggs alive.

Policy Options and Practical Recommendations

The need-based approach implies formulation of projects on the basis of need by communities, therefore, programmes must follow what communities feel is relevant to address their concerns. As indicated by some participants, there is need for the donor agencies to understand the lifestyles of the local communities before they craft humanitarian projects. These should be accepted by the community and development oriented. A disregard for this explains why the same communities are in perpetual poverty and humanitarian crises throughout their lives. The donors, in liaison with the authorities, should understand that some of the challenges have to do with ecological issues such as the aridity of the region, and the cultural context, for example, the religious beliefs of people. The needs-based approach also encourages social inclusion of stakeholders so that there is both commitment and peer review during the management of the project. Social inclusion also inculcates a spirit of transparency and accountability in how programmes are run and how resources are used.

There is need to share information of programme activities, developments and accomplishments to make all participants answerable and reduce conflicts. This also builds ownership amongst all development parties as alluded to by community participants. Closer to this recommendation is the question of endogenous development. The study recommends the adoption of endogenous-oriented development and humanitarian initiatives which imply prioritising people's values and visions of development instead of forcing people to take part in externally crafted development and humanitarian initiatives. The study proposes a diagrammatic conceptual framework of an ideal situation on the ground where the three key stakeholders therefore play an almost equally important role towards humanitarian projects on the ground.

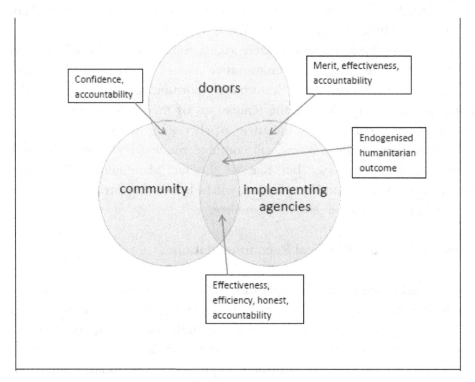

Figure 2.2 Humanitarian Stakeholder interaction
(Source: Own)

The efforts by the three players produce an endogenised outcome which is culturally acceptable and community embedded. The conceptual framework presents the interaction between the implementing agency and donor that is characterised by meritocracy, effectiveness and accountability. It also shows the implementing agency and community relationship based on effectiveness, efficiency, honesty and accountability. The third dimension of the donor and the community relationship is based on confidence and accountability. At the centre of the tripod is an endogenised humanitarian outcome. This outcome is expected to be acceptable to almost the entire beneficiary community on account of its values, founding principles and cultural foundations. The study strongly believes that endogenous humanitarian projects yield better results than externally driven ones.

To address recurrent allegations that project implementers and community leaders misappropriate and abuse humanitarian aid, the study recommends an improvement and broadening of a direct project cost (DPC) tool which is used by the international donor community to track and audit their resource usage on the ground. This tool instils some accountability in the implementing agencies so much so that they hesitate to abuse resources. The results of this tracking tool must also be widely disseminated for effective deterrence and policing. Achieving agricultural development by applying new technologies is one of the most important ways to reduce rural poverty. However, it is important to appreciate local climatic and ecological conditions which are not favourable to some of these modern agricultural approaches. The study rather recommends that rural people, especially in Mbire and Muzarabani, be assisted to develop farming strategies which thrive under their climatic conditions for commercial production. Promotion of commercial goat and cattle rearing are some of the agricultural practices that have not been explored as a way of alleviating poverty and hunger in the two districts.

Conclusion

The study realises that, while every international effort may be directed towards the success of humanitarian projects in the rural areas, there must also be support through the provision of infrastructure which facilitates the movement of resources. It is the study's conclusion that lack of appropriate infrastructure in the form of policies, adequate agricultural extension services and farming equipment on the ground has also contributed towards the collapse of humanitarian projects in Mbire and Muzarabani districts during the 2015/2016 and 2016/2017 agricultural seasons. The sustainability of the projects is therefore threatened due to inconsistent provision of resources and monitoring of the progress on the ground. The study notes that there are several community leaders and non-governmental organisations officials, both at implementing agency level and at beneficiary community level, who have sustained their livelihoods through humanitarian work by engaging in corrupt activities and diverting development resources to personal use. They long to see crises so that they earn a living. Some of these corrupt individuals have also been seen hindering some well-intended poverty and hunger alleviation programmes so that the projects keep running while they also keep looting. The study therefore concludes that for as long as a culture of self-enrichment and dishonesty within the stakeholders remains unattended, it will be ages before humanitarian assistance produces the desired outcome. It is also concluded that inter-stakeholder conflicts, especially between implementing agencies and local traditional leadership, have negatively impacted on the projects. Furthermore, political interference in the three projects also affected their smooth roll-out. Unfortunately, the fear of continued interference by politicians who may be canvassing for support may discourage some stakeholders from committing themselves thereby threatening the sustainability of community development projects. Similarly, it is ideal that there be local ownership and effective participation of the communities on the ground. The form of participation should be, though difficult to achieve, at the individual level as much as possible to avoid imposed and representative participation.

References

Beijing +20 Report. (2015). *Zimbabwe Government Beijing +20 Review report*, Government Printers, Harare.

Boyce J.K. (2002). *Investing in Peace, Aid and Conditionality after Civil Wars*, Adelphi Paper 351, New York: Oxford University Press.

Branczik, A. (2004). Humanitarian Aid and Development Assistance. (Eds). Guy Burgess and Heidi Burgess. *Conflict Information Consortium*, University of Colorado, Boulder.

Cohen, J. (2004). *Governance by and of NGOs*. London, AccountAbility

Collier: and Hoeffler A. (2000). *Greed and Grievance in Civil War*. Washington DC, World Bank.

DFID. (2005). *Growth and poverty reduction: the role of agriculture*. DFID Policy Paper.

Dodo, O. (2013). Economic Empowerment a Panacea to Conflicts: A Case of Mashonaland Central Province, 1999 to 2012. *Kenya Studies Review*, 6(4), 19-38.

Dodo, O. and Mabvurira V. (2012). Politicisation of Aid in Zimbabwe, Post-Independence. *International Journal of Asian Social Sciences*, 2(10): 1867-1876.

Dodo, T.R. and Dodo O. (2014). Unemployment and Conflict in Zimbabwe: An Analysis and Resolution in *Development Policy and Practice: Making Use of Population Census Data in Zimbabwe Eds*, IDA, Harare: 19-54.

FAO/WFP. (2008). *Zimbabwe: Crop and Food Supply Assessment*. Special Report by the Food and Agriculture Organisation and the World Food Programme, Rome.

Government of Zimbabwe (GoZ). (2013). *Constitution of Zimbabwe*, Government Printers, Harare.

Hellstrom, T. (2008). Transferability and Naturalistic Generalisation: New Generalisability Concept for Social Science or old Wine in New Bottles? *Quality and Quantity*, 42, 321-337.

ICNL. (2009). *NGO Law Monitor, Zimbabwe*. Washington D.C: Publisher.

Kovach, H., Neligan, C. and S. Burall, 2003. *The Global Accountability Report: Power without Accountability?* London, One World Trust.

Le Billon: , Macrae, J., Leader, N. and East, R. (2000). *The Political Economy of War: What Relief Agencies Need to know*. London: Relief and Rehabilitation Network.

Lee, J. (2004). *NGO Accountability: Rights and Responsibilities*, CASIN, Geneva, Switzerland

Luttwak, E.N. (1999). Give War a Chance, *Foreign Affairs*, 78(4), 43.

Mahaja, T. (2008). Improving Livestock Management and Feeding Practices for Vulnerable Communities in Mbire District. *Baseline Survey Report, 32*.

Millennium Development Goals Report. (2015). *Millennium Development Goals Progress Report*. NY: UN.

Muchabaiwa, B., Chiminya, J. and Dodo O. (2010). *Strategies and Politics of Development* (DS104). Harare: ZOU.

Nafziger, E.W., Stewart F. and Vayrynen R. (2000). *War, Hunger and Displacement: the Origin of Humanitarian Emergencies*. Oxford: Oxford University Press.

Oxfam. (2000). *Briefing Paper: An End to Forgotten Emergencies?* Oxford: Oxfam.

Patton, M.Q. (2002). *Qualitative Research and Evaluation Methods*. Thousand Oaks, CA: Sage Publications.

Provincial Statistics Department Mashonaland. (2006). Mashonaland Central Province, Bindura. Bindura: Provincial Statistics Department Mashonaland.

Ravitch M.S. and Carl, N. (2016). *Qualitative Research: Bridging the Conceptual, Theoretical, and Methodological*. Thousand Oaks: Sage Pub.

Rieff, D. (1997). Charity on the Rampage: The Business of Foreign Aid. *Foreign Affairs*, 58(3), 29-41.

Rieff, D. (2002). *A Bed for the Night: Humanitarianism in Crisis*. New York: Simon and Schuster.

Simpson, M. and D. Doré. (2009). *International Aid and its Management: Some Insights for Zimbabwe in the Context of Re-engagement.* Comprehensive Economic Recovery in Zimbabwe, Working Paper Series No.2. UNDP-Zimbabwe, Harare.

Walsh, K. (2003). Qualitative Research: Advancing the Science and Practice Hospitality. *Cornell Hotel and Restaurant Administration Quarterly*, 2, 66-74.

World Bank (WB). (2008). *World Development Report: Agriculture for Development.* Washington, DC: The World Bank.

World Bank (WB). (2016). *World Development Report: Poverty and Development.* Washington, DC: The World Bank.

Zimbabwe National Statistical Agency (ZIMSTATS). (2012). Women and men in Zimbabwe, Harare: ZIMSTATS.

Zimbabwe National Statistical Agency (ZIMSTATS). (2015) Compendium of Statistics: 2014. Harare: ZIMSTATS.

Chapter 3

Religion and Sustainable Socio-Economic Development in Zimbabwe

Abraham R. Matamanda and Gamuchirai G.R. Masakwa

Summary

The aim of this chapter is to examine the role religion plays in promoting sustainable socio-economic development in Zimbabwe. In this study, religion will be limited to Christianity, Islam and African traditional religion (ATR). This study is framed within the context of the Protestant work ethic theory by Weber. The hypothesis of the study is that religion contributes to socio-economic sustainable development in Zimbabwe. Data was collected using both secondary and primary data sources. Primary data was collected through in-depth interviews while secondary data was collected through documentary review which included religious texts. The data collected was qualitative in nature, hence, content and textual analyses were then used to analyse the data. Ethical issues were observed as respondents participated out of their own free will without coercion or intimidation. From the findings of the study, it emerges that religion helps to strengthen human capital development as it inculcates the notion of Ubuntu/hunhu[1]in the citizens which is one of the cornerstones of sustainable development. Secondly, religion helps to promote social cohesion which enhances participatory development as well as social capital where ideas, as well as social and financial resources are shared to enhance social development. Thirdly, religion has been found to play a role in provision and support of health, education and humanitarian needs of society. Fourthly, working ethos and entrepreneurial spirit is advocated for in religion thus helping in promoting sustainable socio-economic development. However, the chapter also finds that religion may stifle sustainable development in some instances where the proliferation of religious groups and politicisation of the same by the major rival political parties in Zimbabwe has effectively fragmented society. The chapter concludes by giving recommendations on how religious values and practices can be incorporated in development policies to foster sustained socio-economic developments in Zimbabwe.

---

[1] The essence of being human seen through consideration of others, social responsibility among other things

Introduction and Background

It is beyond doubt that societies around the world, especially in the Global South, are currently bedevilled by various socio-economic challenges. Unemployment, poverty, hunger and inequality seem to be on the increase in most parts of sub-Saharan-Africa. The International Labour Organization projects that unemployment in sub-Saharan Africa was at 7.2% in 2017 (Ofori-Boateng, 2017). Other challenges include poor governance and economic mismanagement, corruption and misappropriation of public funds (Olarinmoye, 2011). Furthermore, inequitable distribution of resources characterised by a few politically powerful individuals benefiting from resources meant to benefit society, that is, elite capture, is evident in many countries. The result is that the poor become poorer while the rich get richer (Alatas *et al.* 2013). According to a 2012 study by Oxfam, the net worth of India's billionaires would be sufficient to eliminate absolute poverty in the country. Many of the rich made their fortunes through government's privatisation programmes. The government underfunds social spending for low income groups in areas like health. As a result, inequality in the country has increased (Bahree, 2014). Zimbabwe is no exception because it is one such country that is experiencing multiple socio-economic challenges that include poverty, inequality, corruption, rising unemployment and hunger among many other problems (Hove *et al.* 2013). Such problems jeopardise sustainable socio-economic development since they fragment its pillars.

Sustainable development is a multi-dimensional concept. Its meaning is highly contested and has been evolving from the time it was conceptualised in the Brutland Report (Mitlin and Satterthwaite, 2013, Osborn *et al.* 2015). In broad terms, sustainable development can be thought of as a blueprint for addressing the challenges that most populations face to include poverty, pollution, stratified societies and climate change and land degradation (United Nations, 2013:2-5, Tausch, 2012). Human beings are at the centre of concerns for sustainable development as it aims to afford them life enhancing opportunities as well as health and safety resources (Hove *et al.* 2013, Rio Declaration19[th]Meeting, 1992). In the Brutland Report sustainable development is defined as development that meets the needs of the present generation without compromising the needs of the future generations (World Commission on Environment and Development, 1987:5). Kahle and Gurel-Atay (2014) support the foregoing definition and argue that sustainable development provides a way of assessing our current situation, setting goals that will produce better results and making the right choices about the direction we want to take. In its totality, sustainable development is premised on three pillars which are

40

environmental, social and economic. These three pillars work in unison and often complement each other. Hence, when looking at one pillar of sustainable development, say economic, this must not be achieved at the expense of the other two pillars (Cobbinah *et al.* 2015). Another key consideration in sustainable development is the issue of equity which ought to be upheld such that the individuals within a particular system all benefit equally from the socio-economic development. Goal 10 calls for reduction of inequalities within countries particularly income inequalities (United Nations, 2013).

Sustainable development is guided by what are known as sustainable development goals (SDGs). These are a set of seventeen global goals with 169 targets among them. A broad range of sustainable development issues are covered by the goals (UN, 2015). These include improving health and education, ending poverty, resolving food insecurity, fighting climate change and creating more sustainable human settlements. The goals are important because they enable a focused and coherent action on sustainable development (Fan and Polman, 2014, Cobbinah *et al.* 2015). Regarding these goals, each government is encouraged to set its own national targets guided by the global level of ambition but taking into account national circumstances and levels of development (Kattumuri, 2015). The question of whether sustainable development is something that can be attained or is it at all applicable in developing countries has been raised (Amoateng *et al.* 2015, Cobbinah *et al.* 2011). The SDGs are criticized for being too many and therefore difficult to conceptualise and requiring financial resources which may not be there. The recommendation is to focus on Goal one- "ending poverty in all its forms everywhere" which they claim all the other goals are founded on (Cobbinah *et al.* 2011, Perez-Carmona, 2013).

The accomplishment of sustainable development is as equally difficult as it is to define the concept. Although certain indicators tend to be used, it remains elusive as to which components (pillars) are critical to consider if any meaningful sustainable development is to be talked of. Should we just look at only one of the three pillars? In this regard, indicators make it possible to measure sustainable development. They also provide information on the changes that would have occurred regarding achieving sustainability (Tausch, 2012). Economic indicators such as GDP and per capita income can be used to measure progress towards sustainable development. The economic factor is a pillar of sustainable development, that is, high GDP is an indication of sustainability (Miller, 2012, Hendler and Smeddler, 2009). Equity is also an indicator. It is about impartiality and fairness in resource distribution to all social groups in a community. This helps do away with stratified societies where there are wide gaps between the rich and poor. According to UN (2014:7), sustainable development can be about:

- Making sure that there is equitable distribution of economic growth to all citizens,
- Revitalising brownfields through greening the environment and ecologically sensitive projects
- Equating and increasing educational opportunities for youths (girls and boys),
- adopting more energy-efficient and less polluting industrial processes,
- promoting citizen participation in policy-making processes
- eradication of poverty
- Increasing citizens' access to basic services such as water facilities, health care and livelihoods.

Religion is among such initiatives that seek to promote human well-being and achieve sustainable development by creating a just social order and providing health and education facilities (Olanrimoye, 2011). However, the effectiveness of religion in achieving sustainable socio-economic development is highly contested. Some scholars argue that religion plays a critical role in improving human well-being by creating closely knit communities, helping the needy and creating respect for the natural environment (Eum, 2011, Chibango, 2016). However, other scholars argue that religion can create conflict in society though the conflict may not necessarily be violent, and it may also serve to oppress certain social groups like women (Beyers, 2010, Opoku, Manu and Wiafe, 2015). Questions thus emerge and remain unanswered as to the role of religion in achieving and promoting sustainable socio-economic development (Mkenda, 2010, Amoateng *et al.* 2015). This chapter looks at the following questions: What role does religion in Zimbabwe play towards achieving sustainable socio-economic development? What are the constraints of religion are with regards achieving sustainable socio-economic development? Is there a place for religion in national sustainable development agenda? This chapter examines the opportunities and constraints of religion in relation to achieving the social, environmental and economic aspects of sustainable development. Using the three religions with the highest following in the country, that is ATR, Christianity and Islam as points of departure, the chapter looks at how their teachings and practices contribute to the social, environmental and economic aspects of sustainable development.

Theoretical Framing

The view that religion can instil the importance of hard work leading to economic prosperity is presented in *The Protestant Ethic and the Spirit of Capitalism* (Weber, 1930). Weber argued that capitalism in northern Europe resulted from the Protestant ethic which influenced large numbers of people to engage in work in the secular world. The people were developing their own enterprises and engaging in trade and the accumulation of wealth for investment (Ryken, 2010). This means the Protestant work ethic was an important force behind the unplanned and uncoordinated emergence of modern capitalism (Grytten, 2013). Weber defined the spirit of capitalism as the rational pursuit of economic gain. Protestants saw hard work and success as a sign that one was saved. According to new Protestant religions, an individual was religiously compelled to follow a secular occupation and work hard at it, the result was that people would accumulate a lot of money. Furthermore, Protestant religions like Calvinism also effectively forbade wastefully using hard earned money and identified the purchase of luxuries as sin. Laziness was seen as failure by an individual to glorify God (Mckinnon, 2010). People would therefore work hard and invest wealth earned rather than spend it extravagantly. A study by American sociologist, Lenski, supports Weber's assertion. Lenski notes that the contribution of Protestantism to material progress due to traits such as diligence and hard work was unintended (Grytten, 2013). However, it has also been argued that policies such as promoting literacy in these societies rather than Protestantism itself promoted capitalism and so religion cannot be directly linked to the rise of capitalism (Gregg, 2013).

In contemporary times some sociologists such as Peter Berger also agree that religion can contribute to development (Bowyer, 2017). Berger argues that there are social preconditions to economic development (Fan and Polman, 2014). These include a people's work ethic, their beliefs towards utilising resources and the wealth created from these resources. The way a society operates is important in regard to how prosperous that society can become. This is largely a matter of culture which refers to a people's way of life, what they consider to be of importance and how they express it. For most of the world, culture basically means religion (Bowyer, 2017). According to the Pew Research Institute, 91% of Nigerian Muslims agree that their religion rather than their nationality or ethnicity as an important part of their identity. This view was shared by 76% of Christians (Pew Research Centre, 2007). Religion drives culture, culture drives social forms, and social forms drive development (Bowyer, 2017).

Literature Review

Religion is an elusive and contested term. Its definition is contextual. Hence, several definitions for religion have been proffered, the majority of these are premised on the notion of shared belief systems guiding everyday life. For Marxists, religion serves to perpetuate the status quo at the same time helping the poor to accept their lot in life (Eggers, 2015). Durkheim (1915) defines religion as a system of beliefs, values and practices concerning sacred things, that is to say, things set apart and practices which unite all those who adhere to them (Sperber, 2013). Durkheim (1915) further argues that religion is about community: it binds people together and offers strength for people during life's tragedies. Focusing on ATR, Mbiti (1969) observes that religion and man's everyday existence cannot be separated (Beyers, 2010). Man asks God to protect him and his loved ones, finds comfort in the idea of an afterlife when death strikes and tries to conduct business in scrupulous ways that will bring blessings upon him. This means religion influences family and social aspects, the work and economic sphere.

This study adopts a hybrid of Durkheim's and Mbiti's definitions of religion since these two definitions bring out both the power of religion to organize society into a single entity and how it continues to influence every aspect of that entity. In this respect, religion therefore refers to a deep embedded conviction in a transcendent power responsible for ordering the universe and directing man's behaviour. This conviction results in man wanting to live a life which conforms to what has been prescribed by the higher being which includes honest and hard work as well as charity. This conduct will encompass all facets of life including the social and economic domains.

Religion manifests through practices and rituals such as praying, ancestor veneration in ATR, alms giving in Islam and Christianity and moral uprightness (Beyers, 2010). African traditional religion (ATR), Christianity and Islam are the religions that inform this study because these three have the most followers in Zimbabwe. According to a 2010-2011 demographic survey in Zimbabwe, Christianity constitutes 87%, ATR 3.8% and Islam 0.9% (ZIMSTAT 2012). Most indigenous black people in the country who identify as Christians or Muslims also incorporate beliefs and practises from ATR in their everyday lives. For instance, practices like *kurova guva*[2] are even practised by some indigenous black Christians and Muslims.

The role of religion in sustainable development in this study emerged from the teachings and doctrines of the religions examined and how they are put into practice. These teachings can be summarised as honest and hard work, love, the

---

[2] Bringing back the spirit of a deceased family member

importance of community and a profound respect for creation. It also emerged that religion creates a great awareness of the part individual plays in promoting the greater good. Zimbabwe is a country that is faced by extreme poverty (Hove *et al.* 2013). Interviewees agreed that in order to reduce poverty and propel the country towards sustainable development, various means had to be harnessed, religion included. One development practitioner stated that religion can both promote and undermine development so its place in sustainable development will always be contested. This sentiment was also echoed by all 10 adherents of Christianity who were interviewed. They pointed out that, although religion largely promotes the greater good, sometimes it has been used as a vehicle for siphoning resources from unsuspecting congregants. The 10 adherents of Islam were emphatic that pure and true belief in God results in a strong sense of social responsibility, a condition which is essential in sustainable development. The majority of those interviewed agreed that religion has always had a place in socio-economic development issues.

Role of religion in sustainable socio-economic development

Religion creates an environment conducive to sustainable development by creating social solidarity and helping channel resources to the needy (Opoku *et al.* 2015, Avevor, 2012). Christian faith-based organisations (FBOs) such as the Christian Association of Nigeria (CAN) and Muslim FBOs that include Nigeria Supreme Council of Islamic Affairs (NSCIA) provide health services through their hospitals. They also own economic institutions such as hotels and mass media companies. These institutions have been instrumental in creating employment and improving the standard of living of Nigerians (Olarinmoye, 2011). It can be argued therefore that religion presents itself as a pathway to sustainable development as it directly or indirectly affects the economy and social well-being in a positive way (Siebert, 2007). In India, churches have established health care services mostly in rural areas with centres for mental health, leprosy and those affected by HIV/AIDS. For example, the coordinating agency for the Catholic Church in India, Caritas India has initiated water harvesting and self-help projects (Avevor, 2012). In the USA, faith-based organisations have promoted healthcare, especially among low-income people who usually do not have health insurance. The National Congregations study revealed that about 57% of congregations take part in various social service delivery projects including food and clothing, providing shelter for the homeless and employment (DeHaven *et al.* 2004).

In several countries' religion has upheld education, thus promoting sustainable development. Goal four of the sustainable development goals spells out the importance of inclusive and equitable education and lifelong learning opportunities in sustainable development. Religion therefore plays a crucial role in national development through education. Education is most often considered to be the backbone of development. Opoku, Manu and Wiafe (2015) argue that religion and formal education are inseparable aspects wherever they are found in every human society. In Ghana, for example, the coming of the missionaries saw the birth of the formal education system. Christianity and Islam contributed immensely to the development of education and the provision of resources to that effect. This is seen in the hundreds of educational institutions established and financed by Christianity and Islam in the country which support government efforts to remove gender disparities and produce an empowered citizenry (Opoku *et al.* 2015). Islam also places a lot of emphasis on education in the country in order to fulfil the obligation of seeking knowledge placed on them by Prophet Muhammad. According to Avevor (2012), as of 2010, the Catholic Church in Ghana had 9 colleges of education, 11 tertiary institutions and 58 vocational training centres. Over the years, the result has been a significant increase of citizens trained from basic to tertiary level.

Although religion plays a pivotal role in creating just societies, there are instances where it has been held responsible for numerous challenges and conflicts. Examples are the raging wars in the Middle East, West Africa and Somalia as well as the chronic bombings in Europe which are all done in the name of religion (Robinson, 2016). In this regard, every major religion has at some point been held responsible for starting violent conflicts. In contemporary times, the percentage of countries with high levels of acts of religious hostility increased in 2015 from 23% to 27% (Pew Research Centre, 2017). However, the role of religion in such conflicts tends to be oversimplified as religion is not usually the primary and sole cause of conflict (Smock, 2008). The role that religion plays in peace-making, conflict resolution and creating just societies cannot be overlooked (Johnston, 2014). A case in point is the Truth and Reconciliation Commission in South Africa where Christianity was used to foster personal, communal and national truth telling and reconciliation.

The history of Christianity as contained in the Prophetic tradition shows religious figures called not only to call people to monotheism but to also create a just social order (Davis, 2017). They acted as the voices of the voiceless, checking the power which kings sometimes abused by introducing draconian laws (Davis, 2017). Religion has been a platform in championing just societies. The role of religion in *motivating people to work for positive social change cannot be understated.* Freeland (2006) explains that the southern USA civil rights movement a few decades ago owes much of its success to religion which played a central role in its development. Religious beliefs motivated Martin Luther

King Jr. and other civil rights activists to risk their lives to desegregate the south Black churches in the South USA. Religion also served as settings in which the civil rights movement held meetings, recruited new members, and raised reservations money. According to Makari (2009), the revolution in Iran championed by Imam Khomeini signifies how religion is instrumental in transforming society. Islam was used to unite people and act as a weapon for transforming Iranian community. Religion can thus create equity, justice and respect for human rights which are preconditions to sustainable development. Religion therefore can act as a powerful voice which is readily heard and accepted by members due to its normative integration (Avevor, 2012). Attempts to transform society and possibly introduce socio-economic development policies and programmes have to consider religion as it is more legitimate than most organisations. Due to the moral influence of religious leaders, they are best placed as influential figures in society through which dialogue can be fostered as well as setting priorities for community members based on the teachings of morality and justice (Olarinmoye, 2011).

By promoting a peaceful and tranquil environment, religion creates an environment conducive to economic and social growth. On the economic front, a stable society will attract and protect investment (Strauss-Khan, 2009, UN, 2015). The Canadian Council of Churches, for example, sponsors Project Ploughshares which is concerned with the prevention of war, disarmament of weapons and peace building. It has promoted peace in the Horn of Africa, among other initiatives (Siebert, 2007). Social unrest and turmoil stand at loggerheads with development in general and with sustainable development in particular. The World Development Report (2011) suggests that the main constraint on development these days may not be poverty trap but violence trap. No poor violent country has achieved a single sustainable development goal. Until 1990, Burundi and Burkina Faso had similar rates of growth and levels of income. But in late 1993, a civil war erupted in Burundi, peaceful Burkina Faso became two and a half times richer (The Economist, 2011, Mitlin and Satterthwaite, 2013). Protecting the environment and ending poverty are virtually impossible in politically unstable scenarios. Goal 16 of the Sustainable Development Goals emphasises peace, justice and strong institutions. These promote peaceful and inclusive societies for sustainable development.

Resource distribution is one way by which religion contributes to sustainable development. Sharing, especially with the less fortunate members of society, is a crucial element of most religions. Distribution of wealth and income is practised in different ways in different religions, but all religions acknowledge the relevance of this as tithe, alms giving and *zakat* to sustain the poor. In Islam, social justice is a cornerstone of the faith. *Zakat and Sadaqa'h* are intended to bridge the gap between the affluent and needy thereby promoting a more just society (Hallaq, 2013, Saleem, 2014). The Qur'an considers charity as one of the most virtuous deeds because it challenges social inequalities (Mamoun and Phillips, 2009).

In ATR, the natural environment is viewed as a sacred space (Beyers, 2010). This view helps to preserve the environment. ATR has strong ties with the natural environment and promotes conservation of natural resources. Eneji *et al.* (2012) points out that, although ATR has intrinsic environment conservation values, it is often left out of environmental initiatives. Plants, animals and other living beings are respected as part of God's creation and His way of providing for man's needs like food and medicine. Mkenda (2010) cites the Chagga of Tanzania who view mountains (Mt Kilimanjaro in particular) and forests as sacred places of worship. In traditional Chagga society, when the weather was good people felt to be at peace with nature, the ancestors and God. Every member of society had a religious and moral responsibility towards the environment. The realisation that sustainable development ought to be anchored in the worldviews of its intended beneficiaries has resulted in increased efforts to incorporate religious values in the financial world (Barthel-Bouchier, 2012). Ethiopia is a predominantly Muslim country. For a long time, there were no financial institutions catering for the large population requiring Islamic-compliant products. As a result, only 14% of the adult population has access to formal credit and savings products (Salehi, 2014). Islamic banking, which is also known as interest free banking, is being built up in Ethiopia. It is banking activity that is consistent with the principles of Sharia law. No one can charge or pay interest or invest in items that Islam forbids such as alcohol or gambling (Salehi, 2014, Hallaq, 2013). The increase of such banking services will translate to an increase in the number of Muslim people who have access to financial amenities.

Methodology

This study is qualitative in nature. Consequently, it takes into consideration multiple viewpoints, perspectives and standpoints concerning the role of religion in sustainable socio-economic development in Zimbabwe (Johnson and Christenen, 2014, Berg, 2012). Data was collected using both secondary and primary data sources. Primary data was collected through in-depth interviews while secondary data was collected through documentary review which included religious texts. Considering that each religion has various followers in Zimbabwe, purposive sampling was used to select participants for the interviews. Purposive sampling, also known as selective sampling, was used in

48

specifically selecting adherents of the three religions in order to get insight on how they consider their religions relevant to sustainable development (Crossman, 2017, Creamer, 2017). In this way, a total of 50 participants were involved in the research and these include:

- 12 key informants comprising 4 religious leaders from each religion,
- an official from the Zimbabwe Association of Church Related Hospitals (ZACH),
- 7 development practitioners from NGOs around the country, and
- 10 followers from each religion.

The sampling frame was based on the argument by Creswell (2013) who postulates that participants in in-depth interviews may be between 1 and 20. The sample for this study is therefore statistically justified (Creswell, 2013). Ethical issues were observed as participants were involved in the study out of their own volition, i.e. without coercion or intimidation. Before engaging with participants, informed consent was sought so that all respondents were aware about the nature of the study. In addition, they were informed that the study was for academic purposes only. Pseudonyms have been used to keep the identity of participants anonymous. The data collected was qualitative in nature, hence, content and textual analyses were then used to analyse the data.

Results

This section presents the findings of the study. It contains what was obtained from interviews with key informants who included development practitioners, religious leaders and adherents of ATR, Islam and Christianity in Zimbabwe. The questions asked were premised on if and how religion contributes to sustainable development. The interviews were substantiated by religious texts in the case of Islam and Christianity.

Christianity and sustainable socio-economic development in Zimbabwe

From the findings of the study, it emerged that Zimbabwe has benefitted much from the initiatives by religious organisations who have invested in the education and health sectors. A significant number of those interviewed were of the opinion that Zimbabwe has benefited much from the efforts of religious organisations in key areas such as education and health. An officer in the Ministry of Public Service, Labour and Social Welfare stated that religious institutions play an important role in service provision in Zimbabwe. In a challenged economy, they have done much in terms of providing social services to citizens particularly the poor. This was supported by an official at The Zimbabwe Association of Church Related Hospitals (ZACH) who explained that:

> The association has 126-member institutions providing health care to the most poverty-stricken groups in the country. Church owned medical institutions like Karanda Mission Hospital and Howard Hospital are well known throughout Zimbabwe for providing affordable and much needed health care which is sometimes not available at state run institutions.

A member of staff interviewed at Karanda Mission hospital said that the hospital's sphere of influence was now the entire country as people come from all over Zimbabwe for services. The hospital, as was the case with all church owned hospitals, treated everyone regardless of religious affiliation. Quite a number of those interviewed in Harare and Chinhoyi had been treated or had relatives and friends from different parts of the country who had been treated at these institutions, some after being referred from state hospitals. They stated that it was necessary for them to go to mission hospitals as state run institutions had failed to adequately deal with their cases. From the information obtained in the course of the study, given the choice, most people preferred church owned hospitals to government hospitals. This is not peculiar to Zimbabwe but is true of many African countries. Health is an essential service which determines, among other things, the quality of life in a country.

A trainee pastor whose area of interest is church history in Zimbabwe, pointed out that in the field of education has benefited much from the efforts of Christian denominations. Dating from the colonial period, church owned schools have a significant presence in Zimbabwe. Every region in the country has benefited from these. African Independent Churches like the Zion Christian Church (ZCC) and ZAOGA have established schools in many parts of the country. ZAOGA also has vocational training centres offering dressmaking and cooking courses among others. These have assisted many people in securing employment or starting their own businesses. Some universities in the country are church owned. For example, ZEGU is a ZAOGA university, the United Methodist Church runs Africa University, while Solusi University falls under the auspices of the Seventh Day Adventist. The Reformed Church in Zimbabwe has a school for the deaf and dumb at Morgenster as well as the Margaretha Hugo School for the blind. A visually impaired interviewee – a former student at Margaretha Hugo who is now a teacher explained that the area of education for people with special needs is one in which government lags behind, therefore the efforts by religious groups should be commended.

The study revealed that churches like the United Church of Christ are also involved in enhancing agriculture which happens to be an important economic activity in the country. The United Church of Christ in Zimbabwe is active in rural development. The church facilitated the establishment of Nyanyadzi irrigation scheme in Manicaland. The scheme, despite facing several challenges, has played a role in improving agricultural productivity and increasing rural income. Trumpet Call Agriculture is an initiative of the Evangelical Fellowship of Zimbabwe and Foundations for Farming. It teaches sustainable agriculture with the aim of reducing hunger and creating food security in communities. In this study, it emerged that religious doctrine has an impact on people's work ethic thus contributing to the accumulation of wealth by individuals and enhancing standards of living. Some African independent churches in Zimbabwe such as the Johanne Marange and ZAOGA teach and urge entrepreneurship among their members. Virtue is placed on using one's hands to generate income. This has resulted in a rigorous work ethic and self-sufficiency among members. Indeed, entrepreneurship has become synonymous with these churches. One sociologist pointed out that:

> The "vapostori" have impressive business acumen. Trading in household items like pots and metal cans has been their preserve for a long time. Women are especially encouraged to empower themselves so they can become financially independent.

An interview by a church elder revealed that the biblical concept of talents is put into practice in ZAOGA, and members are encouraged to take on incoming generating projects. Some members interviewed attested to having developed savings and uplifted themselves and their families by putting this into practice. Bayers (2010) asserts that religion can define worthwhile objectives oriented to this world or the afterlife and provide tools for the development of savings and investment strategies driving the economy to great heights. This supports Weber's (1905) argument that religion can impart to its followers the value of hard work. A pastor in charge of an orphanage belonging to a Pentecostal church in Harare observed that:

> In contemporary Zimbabwe the church is responsible for stepping up to care for children where the family has failed to do so. Issues like migration, economic hardship and HIV/AIDS have contributed to the breakdown of the family unit.

A considerable number of orphanages and old people's homes are run by churches. Orphanages step in to raise abandoned children or those who might find themselves without a guardian in the absence of a biological parent. This brings out the principle of *hunhu/ubuntu*. Makumbi Mission Children's Home, Emerald Hill Children's Home, The Mother of Peace Community as well as St Marcelline Children's Village and Matthew Rusike are some of the church run orphanages in the country. Children are cared for in a family environment and get life enhancing opportunities like education. There was consensus among those interviewed that these orphanages help cushion children from extreme poverty and protect them from life on the streets. Capernaum Trust is another Christian organisation giving assistance to orphaned children operating in all the country's ten provinces. It assists the children with scholarships up to tertiary level as well as career guidance.

The Christian faith forms part of an active civil society. It has acted as a watchdog of the state, speaking against human rights abuses. Rather than remain aloof, the church has involved itself in the political issues of the day. The Catholic Commission for Justice and Peace Zimbabwe (CCJPZ) is a commission of the Zimbabwe Catholic Bishops' Conference. Some of its aims include to make people aware of their rights and duties as citizens and to investigate allegations of injustice which it considers to merit attention and to take appropriate action. It also encourages citizens to live their lives in greater awareness of Christian justice and to work for a more just society (Zimbabwe Human Rights NGO Forum, undated). The Catholic organisation was critical of the draconian laws that were put in place by the state in the form of AIPA and POSA which violated citizens' freedom of expression. It was also critical of the political violence that was being experienced in the country, especially during the Mugabe era. This brought international attention to what was happening in the country. Eppel (2006) states that, while the official picture is bleak, it has been possible in certain moments for civil society in Zimbabwe to find spaces in which to promote truth telling and peace building initiatives. The CCJP together with The Legal Resources Foundation (LRF) sponsored the researching and writing of a report that documented the state sponsored massacres, also known as Gukurahundi massacres, of the 1980s in Matabeleland and parts of the Midlands Provinces. An interviewee belonging to one mainstream church said it was nothing new for the church to involve itself in the political issues affecting societies. During the second Chimurenga (anti-colonial war) some churches criticized minority rule and supported the struggle. The Catholic Church at the time spoke out against oppression of the people in publications like *MOTO*.

Islam and sustainable socio-economic development in Zimbabwe

Islam in Zimbabwe has contributed to improving welfare of the people. It has done this through several organisations such as the Majlisul Ulama Zimbabwe. This is a registered Islamic welfare organisation that was founded in 1975. The organisation provides social and humanitarian services. A Sheik who is employed by the organisation explained that:

"There is a drought relief programme that assists those who are affected by drought and other disasters. In addition, the organisation also helps orphans, widows and the needs where basically focus is on livelihoods and human well-being."

Zimbabwe has been affected by El Niño resulting in recurring droughts in some parts of the country, notably the dry southern districts. Such environmental disasters greatly compromise sustainable development, hence the initiatives by religious organisations help citizens to adapt and cope in such times thus enhancing sustainable development. A Sheikh associated with the Islamic Supreme Council of Zimbabwe said young people in the country were getting scholarships to pursue their studies in Islamic states. School going children from underprivileged backgrounds were assisted with school supplies including stationery.

The Clinic of Red Crescent Society of The Islamic Republic of Iran in Zimbabwe was established with the aim of providing health services to the poor. It offers consultation as well as treatment facilities at a low cost. Another Muslim health provision initiative is the Islamic Medical Association of Zimbabwe. The association has conducted free eye operations. To date, 280 cataracts have been performed. In addition, the association is in the process of having a free medical aid card for the poor which allows them to receive free medical care at any of the association's clinics.

Zimbabwe is faced by high rates of unemployment (Hove *et al.* 2013). In order to help Muslim families affected by unemployment, a small businesses programme was launched. This program is supported by a rotating fund from which soft loans can be obtained for those interested in starting income generating projects. Successful projects are granted further capital injection should they wish to expand. Furthermore, the needs of particular Muslim communities are identified and, where possible, assistance is given. The help can be in the form of stationery for school children.

Islam emphasises caring for one's neighbour (Salehi, 2014). The believers are protectors of one another so those in need, such as orphans and widows, should be cared for. And for the love of Allah, they feed the poor, the orphan and the captive… (Soorah al- Insaan, 8). This is why the Iqra Ilm Centre was established in Harare. The centre, apart from housing many Islamic activities, has a centre for orphans. One Islam Imam said the prophet was an orphan, so orphans hold a special place in Islam. Anyone chosen by Allah to be the guardian of an orphan must take good care of that child.

ATR and sustainable socio-economic development in Zimbabwe

The majority of participants belonging to either Islam or Christianity brought out that despite adherence to the aforementioned religions, a great number of people in the country kept beliefs as well as rituals belonging to ATR. The religion is deeply entrenched in the culture of the country's majority although variations may exist in methods and rituals. However, one traditionalist from a shrine in Chitungwiza pointed out that colonialism sullied ATR in Zimbabwe as is the case in many African countries. His assertion was supported by the fact that when asked, several interviewees could not find the relevance of ATR in sustainable development in these times. An elderly woman also bemoaned that colonialism had an overwhelming effect on the destruction of traditional religion and culture. People were removed from the mountains and their land and driven into the reserves. This destroyed the communication between the people and the spirits as the mountains were the sacred places to do so. The result of the colonial period was the extreme dilapidation of cultural values and beliefs and the physical degradation of sacred places and biodiversity leading to famine, unnecessary drought and spread of diseases (Arnalte, 2006).

In Shona traditional religion, there is a strong belief in God as the all-powerful being who provides for creation. ATR adherents view the community and family as important units. An elderly man who is a renowned herbalist owning a stall in Mbare's Mupedzanhamo Market stated that rituals and solutions to life's problems like drought, illness or bareness are done by the family and the community. Whatever good is done is said to benefit the individual and ultimately society. This means ATR promotes cohesion and social responsibility. Cohesion is essential for development (Keitumetse, 2016). It is the duty of the community to cushion those who might find themselves in need. This applies to issues of food security. *Zunderamambo*[3] was a traditional social security arrangement designed to mitigate food insecurity. People were mobilised to work in the designated fields on a voluntary basis. After harvesting the crops were stored in granaries and kept as food reserves at the chief's homestead. Access to the grain reserves of *zunderamambo* prioritised older people, widows, orphans and people with disabilities. Under Chief Makoni in

---

[3] Fields belonging to a community for which the chief is custodian of both fields and produce. The entire community provides labour

Chiendambuya, the mechanism continues up to this day. In recent times, the concept is finding new support. The Food and Agricultural Organisation-FAO acknowledged in one of its reports that the chief's granary (*zunderamambo*) could be an important mechanism in improving nutrition security (*The Financial Gazette*, 2013, July 11). The practice is sustainable in as far as it is in the hands of the community who feel that it belongs to them. Ending hunger and achieving food security is Goal 2 of the sustainable development goals.

The natural environment has an important place in traditional life. It represents the presence of God and is also his way of providing for the whole creation. One religious studies lecturer at a local university stated that forests and mountains in Shona culture are sacred places. They are where people communicate with the spirits and God. Their wildlife and vegetation ought to be conserved and valued. Rituals such as "*mukwerera*" or the rain-making ceremony are held in sacred areas. Goal 15 of the Sustainable Development Goals emphasises the protection, restoration and promotion of sustainable use of terrestrial ecosystems and sustainably managing forests and to halt biodiversity loss as well as land degradation (UN, 2015). The study identified several practices inherent in the African traditional religion in Zimbabwe which contribute to environmental conservation. These include setting apart sacred places. These are mostly forests and certain trees which are sanctified. It is in these forests or under these trees where rituals are conducted and where people make known their supplications to God and ancestors. Nationally, this has helped preserve forests like Chirinda, the Nyanga Mountains. Anyone who desecrates these spaces is punished by ancestors. They may wander for all eternity never to be found. Use of traditional medicines also results in preservation of plant species and afforestation in order to procure herbs.

Discussion

The foregoing paragraphs suggest that religion is a building block of socio-economic development. Often discussions on socio-economic development seem to cast a blind eye on religion, side-lining it, yet, it is an intrinsic part of the seemingly complex and scientific process. Thus, religion should be at the fore of socio-economic development policies and programmes since it offers opportunities for social networking, social control and promote social stability. Building on arguments posited by Durkheim (1915) and Weber (1905), religion thus constitutes the life blood of sustained socio-economic development due to its normativeness and the way it upholds morality, justice and ethical behaviour and conduct among individuals and communities. It is an undeniable fact that social values are best shaped through religion. Religion promotes responsible behaviour that respects the dignity and sanctity of all life. Once religious values are inculcated in the socio-economic development framework of a community, there is a likely propensity towards morality and dignity associated with the community. Islamic Republic of Iran epitomizes the functionality of embracing religion in socio-economic development with remarkable results being achieved.

Six lessons can be drawn from the chapter. The first is that sustained socio-economic development is enhanced by a system that recognises and includes religion as an ingredient towards development goals. Second lesson is that religion is all-embracing and addresses almost all aspects of man's daily life. This means t it is imperative to include religion in socio-economic development since religion has a package which also focuses on socio-economic development, hence the need to unravel those aspects of religion that link up with the socio-economic development aspects. The third lesson is that the integration of religion in the realm of society helps to promote social stability, social cohesion as well as social justice. It has been established that religion creates opportunities for social interaction and provide social support and social networking. The fourth lesson is that religion promotes economic well-being in society through encouraging hard work, thriftiness and business ethics that are conducive to sustained economic development. An economic system found on religious teachings and practices has a lot of potential to excel since people may place much faith in it. The fifth lesson is the fact that religion, through religious leaders and institutions, effectively acts as an echo chamber since people often recognise the voice of religious leaders more than any other authorities in society. Lastly, all religions place emphasis on giving to those in need and looking out for the less fortunate. This helps in eradicating extreme poverty. To this end, religion has to be used as a pathway in instances where social transformation is required or when the community is resistant to social change.

Conclusion

Religion in Zimbabwe complements the three pillars of sustainable development. It does this through its teachings which emphasise social cohesion, environmental conservation and economic growth resulting from honest work. It also emphasises the attainment of education which leads to economic development at individual and national level. From the study, it emerged that religion continually strives to address problems faced by society which include resource inequality and social injustice. It was also established that the efficacy of religion as a social force may have declined in some cases. For example, some participants could not identify the relevance of ATR in sustainable development. Despite this, concrete cases in which religion is championing health delivery, education, and environmental conservation, distribution of resources to the marginalised and social justice were clearly identified and made this study worthwhile.

References

Alatas, V., Banerjee, A., Rema, H., Olken, B.A., Purnamasari, R., and Wai-Poi, M. (2013). *Local elites and targeted welfare programmes in Indonesia.* Available online: economics.mit.edu/files/8567 [Accessed 3 September 2017].

Cobbinah, P. B., Erdiaw-Kwasie, M. O., and Amoateng, P. (2015). Africa's urbanisation: Implications for sustainable development. *Cities, 47,* 62-72.

Arnalte, L. (2006). *Recovering our sacred mountains.* Available online: base.d-p-h.info/en/fiches/dph/fiche-dph-7067.html [Accessed 28 March 2017].

Avevor, D. (2012, September). *Strengthening church-state partnership in education.* Ghana Catholic Bishops Conference. Available online: https://www.modernghana.com/news/415646/1/strenghthening-church-state-partnership-in-educatio.html [Accessed 30 April 2017].

Bahree, M. (2014). Who's to blame for the increasing gap between the rich and the poor? Market policies, says the new report. Available online: forbes.com/sites/meghabahree/2014/11/05/whos-to-blame-for-the-increasing-gap between-the-rich-and-the-poor-market-economy-says-new-report/#27fb6dff2c77 [Accessed 3 September 2017].

Berg, B. L. (2012). *Qualitative research methods for the social sciences.* Boston, MA: Allyn and Bacon

Beyers, J. (2010). What is religion? An African understanding. *HTS Teologiese Studies/Theological Studies,* 66(1): 1-8.

Cobbinah, P. B., Erdiaw-Kwasie, M. O., and Amoateng, P. (2015). Rethinking sustainable development within the framework of poverty and urbanisation in developing countries. *Environmental Development,* 1(3), 18-32.

Cobbinah: B., Black, R. and Thwaites, R. (2011). Reflections on six decades of the concept of development: Evaluation and future research. *Journal of Sustainable Development in Africa,* 13(7), 134-149.

Creamer, E.G. (2017). *An introduction to fully integrated mixed methods research.* Thousand Oaks CA: Sage.

Davis, A. (2017). *Exalting Jesus in Isaiah.* Broadman and Holman.

Eggers, W. (Ed.). (2015). *Lessons of the five classics of Marxism-Leninism on religion.* Comintern (SH).

Eppel, S. (2006). *"Healing the dead": Exhumation and reburial as a tool to truth telling and reclaiming the past in rural Zimbabwe.* Indiana: University of Notre Dame Press.

Fan, S. and Polman, A (2014). An ambitious development goal: Ending hunger and under nutrition by 2025. In: Marble, A and H. Fritschel, H. (Ed.), *Global food policy report* (pp. 15-28). International Food Policy Research Institute (IFPRI).

Freeland, G. (2006). Lutherans and the southern civil rights movement. *Journal of Lutheran Ethics,* 6(11), 23-32.

Grytten, O.H. (2013). The Protestant ethic and the spirit of capitalism: Entrepreneurship of the Norwegian Puritan leader Hans Nielsen, Hauge. *Review of European Studies, 5*(1), 10.

Hallaq, W. (2013). *The impossible state: Islam, politics and modernity's moral predicament.* New York: Columbia University Press.

Hendler: and Thompson-Smeddler, L. (2009). *Indicators and performance areas for sustainable human settlement.* The Southern African Housing Foundation, Regional housing conference and exhibition, 9-11 July 2009. Swakompund, Namibia.

Hove, M., Ngwerume, E.T. and Muchemwa, C. (2013). The urban crisis in sub-Saharan Africa: A threat to human security and sustainable development. *Stability, 2*(1). 1-14.

Johnson, R.B and Christensen, L.B. (2014). *Educational research: Qualitative, quantitative and mixed approaches.* London: Sage.

Kahle, L.R. and Gurel-Atay, E. (2014). *Communicating sustainable development for the green economy.* New York: M.E Sharp.

Keitumetse, S.O. (2016). *African cultural heritage conservation and management.* Basel, Switzerland: Springer International Publishing.

Mckinnon, A.M. (2010). Elective affinities of the Protestant Ethic: Weber and the chemistry of capitalism. *Sociological Theory, 28*(1), 108-126.

Miller, E. (2012). *Gender issue guide: Urban planning and design.* Nairobi: UNHABITAT

Mitlin, D. and Satterthwaite, D. (2013). *Urban poverty in the Global South: Scale nature.* New York: Routledge.

Ofori-Boateng. (2017). *Unemployment rate in sub-Saharan African: Africa forecast to be 7.2% in 2017.* Available online: ghanabusinessnews.com/2017/01/15/unemployment-rate-insub-saharan-africa-forecast-to-be-7-2-in-2017[Accessed 3 September 2017].

Olarinmoye, O. (2011). *Accountability in faith-based development organisations in Nigeria: Preliminary explorations.* Global Economic Governance Programme. GEG Working Paper.

Pew Research Centre. (2017). *Global restrictions on religion rise modestly in 2015, reversing downward trend.* Available online: pewforum.org/2017/04/11/global-restrictions-on-religion-rise-modestly-in-2015-reversing-downward-trend, [Accessed 2 September 2017]

Pew Research Centre. (2007). *Nigerian Muslims first identify with their religion.* Available online: pewresearch.org/fact-tank/2007/04/16/Nigerian-muslims-self-identity-first-with-their-religion, [Accessed on 3 September 2017]

Robinson, C. (2016). Revisiting the rise and fall of the Somali Armed Forces 1960-2012. *Defense and Security Analysis,* 32(3), 237-252.

Ryken, L. (2010). *Worldly saints: The Puritans as they really were.* Harper Collins.

Salehi, M. (2014). A study on the influence of Islamic values on Iranian accounting practice and development. *Journal of Islamic Economics, Banking and Finance,* 10(2), 154-182.

Smock, D. (2008). *Religion in world affairs: It's role in conflict and peace.* Available online: usip.org/pubs/specialreports/sr201.pdf, [Accessed 1 September 2017].

Sperber, J. (2013). *Karl Marx: A nineteenth century life.* Liveright Publishing Corporation.

Strauss-Khan, D. (2009). *Economic stability, economic cooperation and peace: The role of the IMF.* Speech presented at IMF Forum, Oslo 23 October 2009.

United Nations. (2013). *World economic and social survey 2013: Sustainable development challenges.* New York: Department of Economic and Social Affairs.

Zimbabwe Human Rights NGO Forum. (2013). Catholic Commission for Justice and Peace in Zimbabwe. Available online: www.hrforumzim.org/members/catholic-commission-for-justice-and-peace-in-zimbabwe/ [Accessed 5 April 2017].

Chapter 4

The Bible and Ecology: A Re-reading of the Pentateuchal Laws in Safeguarding the Natural Environment in Zimbabwe

Milcah Mudewairi

Summary

Environmental degradation continues to be one of the topical challenges of sustainable development in Zimbabwe. The chapter seeks to demonstrate the applicability of the Old Testament Pentateuchal laws in protecting and preserving the natural environment in Zimbabwe. The chapter is based on a study which evaluated the impact of environmental degradation in Zimbabwe using a Pentateuchal scriptural approach. The study utilised the survey approach to examine the extent to which the Pentateuchal laws can be utilised as a panacea to environmental problems in Zimbabwe. The problem that justified this research is the continuous ravaging of the environment in Zimbabwe despite the maximum effort by scientists and environmentalists to restore order. The bottom line is that natural environmental degradation in Zimbabwe is a reality hence there is need for collective and collaborative research to root out its causes that are threatening the livelihoods of people and animals. The study yields that the Bible can also complement science in minimising the destruction of the natural environment since scriptures assert that God commanded humanity an interdependency relationship with nature. It is recommended that the biblical message can be utilised too in the endeavour to end the destruction of the natural environment.

Introduction

The destruction of the natural environment in Zimbabwe is evidenced by deforestation in the rural areas, mining areas and the resettlement areas, especially among the beneficiaries of the land reform programme. In addition, there is the contamination of vital water sources especially in the urban areas where illegal settlers are constructing houses in wetlands and also clearing woodlands for settlement purposes. Furthermore, the extinction of animal and bird species, climate change, and unnecessary veld fires, as well as, the continuous land ruin by the illegal miners continue to threaten the present and future generations of Zimbabwe. The natural environment is the life supporting hub for both people and animals hence there is a need to implement collective and innovative strategies to avoid risking the depletion of the natural environment. The Environmental Management Agency (EMA) advocates for the protection of the natural environment through environmental awareness campaigns as well as prosecution of those destroying the environment. Environmental degradation continues, though EMA is working tirelessly to preserve the natural environment.

This study traced the nexus between the Old Testament and the protection of the natural environment with special reference to civil, criminal, military and ritualistic Pentateuchal laws. The laws were coined for the effective management of society as they offer insights on how the Old Testament Jews were to co-exist with the natural environment. An interpretation of the Pentateuchal laws can be relevant in aiming for sustainable development in Zimbabwe since the nation is battling with environmental degradation. This research considered the relevance of the Pentateuchal laws as the possible avenue to mitigate the problems of the destruction of trees, animals, land, pollution problems as well as veld fires. In this study, the civil, criminal, religious and military laws are referred to as the Pentateuchal laws. The study traces the historical background of the civil, military, criminal and religious laws to examine the extent to which these laws can provide a protective measure to the natural environment in Zimbabwe.

The research explored the contributions of the civil, criminal, military and religious Pentateuchal laws of the Old Testament Jews in protecting the natural environment with special reference to Zimbabwe. In the Old Testament, these laws controlled human activities in the effective use of the environment without destroying or causing damage to it. The objectives of the study were to;

- Justify the relevance of the Old Testament scholarship in environmental protection platforms.
- Establish the magnitude of the damage of the natural environment in Zimbabwe.
- Find out the viability of the civil, criminal, military and religious laws of the Pentateuch in sustaining the natural environment in Zimbabwe.

Background and context

Christianity and ecological theology
Christians are also victims of the destruction of the natural environment therefore scripture should be relevant in responding to the needs of our time. Ecological theology is the branch of contextual theology that seeks to retrieve

the ecological wisdom in Christianity as a response to environmental threats and injustices (Conradie, 2006:3). This literature asserts on the need to rediscover and renew the Christian tradition in the light of the challenges posed by the environmental crisis to humanity, animals, land, trees and water. This study is concerned with how biblical scriptures address environmental concerns. The destruction of the natural environment in Zimbabwe is a reality and this research traces the feasibility of applying Pentateuchal laws to the Zimbabwean context for the safe use and keeping of the trees, animals, birds, water sources, soil and other natural objects.

The Old Testament and the natural environment

Wenham (1999: 86) supports the need to dig deeper the extent to which the Old Testament people were actively involved in the natural environment. The relationship between human beings and the natural environment around them was to a less extent also perceived as potentially harmful to humanity. This observation is very crucial as it is connected to the problem under investigation because the civil and criminal laws of the Pentateuch also point to the 'greening' of the natural environment. However, there is need to trace the connection of the cited laws to the current Zimbabwean problem of the destruction of the natural environment.

The genesis of the Pentateuchal laws

The term Pentateuch refers to the first five books of the Old Testament which are Genesis, Exodus, Leviticus, Numbers and Deuteronomy. The Hebrew term for the Pentateuch is *Torah* referring to law or instruction (Nicholson, 2006:2). The Pentateuch is a collection of laws meant to govern and regulate the Israelite community when they settled in their promised land-Canaan. The Pentateuchal laws can be grouped into civil, criminal religious and military laws. The laws were given to the Israelites in the form of the covenant and there were the first to gain the canonical status in the Old Testament because of their importance (Noth, 2006:3). The focal point of these laws can be traced back to Israel's earliest settlement in Canaan when Yahweh sealed a covenant with Israel as a nation. The covenant had terms and conditions that if people observe and keep the laws of God and obey them, then they will live and prosper, but if they forget and disobey, they will not prosper. To obey is life, to disobey, death, "So, choose life in order that you may live, you and your descendants!" (Deuteronomy 30v19). By protecting and preserving the natural environment in a sustainable way the Israelites would yield more from the Promised Land. The Israelites obeyed the laws and commandments of Yahweh concerning their relationship with the environment. This study sought to apply

63

the same laws for the natural environment management to the current situation of environmental degradation in Zimbabwe.

The biblical world and the contemporary world

Olson (2013:266) appeals to the Pentateuch to establish Christian ethics. For Christians to perfectly co-exist with the natural environment, there is also a need to consider the Pentateuch as it has a section on the civil laws that offered a favourable living environment to the Old Testament Jews. Although the author is referring to Christian ethics, literature has a bearing to this discussion since the same civil laws also point to the protection of the natural environment in the Pentateuch. This research is delimiting the application of the Pentateuch to the contemporary problems of the natural environmental degradation in Zimbabwe.

Van Heerden (2009:697) surveys the Old Testament scholarship publications on natural environment degradation and asserts the need for assessing the applicability of the Old Testament scriptures to our very different world. The survey traces the extent to which the Old Testament can contribute to the contemporary debates given the different time frame and the living environment. The work concludes that the Old Testament Jews lived in contact with the natural environment for survival purposes and this is still applicable to the contemporary world. The land, animals, water and trees are essential to the modern Zimbabweans and the Old Testament Jews hence the need to trace how the Pentateuch protected these essential commodities for the survival of humanity.

Van Dyk (2009:186) also reacts to the publication by White (1967) that the Bible is hostile to the environment basing on Genesis 1v28. White misses the argument by pointing out that humanity was given powers to dominate the natural world hence it is their right to ravage the land, plants, animals and water. However, a close analysis of the cited biblical scripture reveals that God instructed humanity to protect the natural environment against degradation. Conradie (2004:126) articulates that the ecological approach to the study of the Bible indicates that the scriptures can offer ecological wisdom, but this has remained hidden until the publication of the accusations by White. If God pointed on the need to take care of the natural environment why is it that in Zimbabwe there is the problems of deforestation, contamination of water sources, serious pollution, damaging of the soil and may more? This research seeks to find out how best Zimbabweans can utilise the Pentateuchal laws in safeguarding the natural environment.

Ecological biblical hermeneutics

Conradie (2006:3) reviews the five-volume work of the earth Bible project with the view of establishing its significance towards the development of an ecological biblical hermeneutics. The project recommends reading the scriptures through ecological lenses and asserts that the Bible is against the violation of the ecosystem. An ecological interpretation of the Bible shows that the natural environment is liberated in the scriptures. However, the natural environment is oppressed in Zimbabwe and therefore there is a need to note the ecological wisdom spelt out in the Pentateuchal laws on the preservation of nature.

Moskala (2011:3) interprets the ecological degradation in the scriptures by appropriating the significance of biblical texts for a particular contemporary context. This research targets the analysis of the ways in which the meaning, significance, value and the relevance of the civil, criminal, military and religious Pentateuchal laws can be appropriated in the context of the depletion of the natural environment in Zimbabwe. In other words, this research linked the Pentateuchal laws to the reality of the natural environmental challenges in Zimbabwe. The eco-theologians traced the appropriateness of biblical scriptures to the problems of environmental dilapidation and similarly this research considered the Pentateuch to the Zimbabwean scenario.

Environmental stewardship in the Old Testament

Calvin (2012:18) insists on the biological egalitarianism of equal rights of all forms in the hope that human beings will have respect for the earth. Humanity is therefore to blame for environmental degradation. For Calvin, environmental stewardship implies that we are morally accountable for the safe keeping of the natural environment since the earth is divine. The theory of equality in terms of importance between human beings and the natural environment, so as to note how it can help in protecting the natural environment in Zimbabwe, is the focus of this chapter.

Currently humanity is yet to consider the natural environment on equal footing with them hence the problems of environmental degradation for us and the future generations. Graham (2017:3) supports that human beings are trustees of God's creation who should not abuse or neglect nature. The argument is that there is need to take care of the natural environment since it is vital to the present people and the next generations. It is to this extent that this chapter considers the Pentateuchal laws in protecting the trees, animals, water sources and land in Zimbabwe.

Causes and effects of the environmental degradation in Zimbabwe

The degradation of the natural environment refers to any change in the condition of the natural environment which reduces its productive potential, the quality of the land, especially deterioration of the top soil affecting vegetation growth and population, the pollution of water resources and the extinction of the birds and animal species (EMA, 2016). Major causes of the depletion of the natural environment include the extreme or unsuitable utilisation of natural resources, especially by human activities like veld fires, deforestation, water pollution, and overgrazing. These activities degrade the quality of the natural environment. Furthermore, the inappropriate use of the marginal land, poaching, illegal mining and unauthorised fishing are also driving forces of the destruction of the natural environment. Effects of the destruction of the natural environment include the increased risk of floods and erosion leading to the washing away of the topsoil and the formation of gullies. The loss of soil fertility results in poor crop yields, loss of vegetation cover, shortage of local surface water resources, increased levels of ground water and loss of vegetation which plays a major role in determining the biological composition of the soil (EMA, 2016). There is need for more mitigating measures to be put in place so as to reduce the destruction of the natural environment in Zimbabwe since the Environment Management Agency also needs collective support even outside the realm of scientific knowledge.

Theoretical Framework

The study was informed by the eco-theology perspective of interpreting biblical texts in the light of ecological degradation. The eco-theologians argue that the Bible can also participate in the natural environment protection platforms. This study interprets Pentateuchal laws by tracing the effectiveness of eco-theology amidst the natural environmental degradation in Zimbabwe. The destruction of the natural environment continues in Zimbabwe regardless of the effort by the Environment Management Agency to minimise forests destruction, water pollution, veld fires, poaching, illegal mining and the general land degradation. This research considered the Pentateuchal laws as part of the greening of the environment to curb ecological crisis in Zimbabwe. This theoretical framework enabled the researcher to have ample time in engaging with Bible and the environment, particularly the contributions of the Pentateuchal laws for sustaining the natural environment for developmental purposes in Zimbabwe. The depletion of the natural environment is one of the huge setbacks for sustainable development in Zimbabwe. This is because trees that are randomly destroyed cannot grow over a night, yet they are important in providing the oxygen, medicinal herbs, construction timber, home for wild animals, wind breaks as well as the water cycle.

The severe shortage of clean water due to pollution is also costly to the economy of Zimbabwe. Wild animals are reduced in numbers due to the destruction of forests. Some wild animals are killed, and others migrate due to the clearing of forests and veld fires. Eco-theology brings the contributions of the biblical scriptures to today's problems and this research is limited to the contribution of Pentateuchal laws to the protecting of the natural environment in Zimbabwe. According to historical criticism, the biblical texts were directed to ancient recipients to solve issues peculiar to them. This means any attempt to apply biblical texts to the modern times is forcing texts to respond to issues with no parallels to them. In overcoming the cited limitations, the author asserts that the Bible is a timeless document that can be consulted to solve the burdens of the hour. In other words, although the Bible is an ancient text, its message is valid and not limited by a time frame, hence the sacredness and uniqueness of this ancient book in the contemporary world.

Methodology

A survey of the selected Pentateuchal laws underlies the data gathering of this research. The criminal, civil military and religious laws related to the protection of the natural environment were purposively sampled. The selected laws were analysed and interpreted through biblical exegesis with the aim of deducing the extent to which the laws can be a panacea to the degradation of the natural environmental in Zimbabwe. Biblical exegesis refers to the interpretation of biblical texts by tracing the original meaning to the intended recipients and at the same time drawing a modern meaning of the ancient biblical texts to the contemporary problems. The Pentateuchal survey is the appropriate methodology for this study because it enables the researcher to have an in-depth study of the selected laws through analysis and interpretation as well as linking them to the contemporary problem. The original life setting (*stiz-em leben*) of the laws was also taken into consideration in tracing the modern meaning for Zimbabweans to preserve and protect the natural environment. The historical background of the origins of the laws enabled the investigator to trace how 'green' were Pentateuchal laws.

Results and discussion

The applicability of the Pentateuchal laws in protecting the environment

The Levitical food laws

The Levitical food law of clean and unclean animals has a concern for animal life. These laws are classified as religious ritualistic laws. The Israelites were to meticulously observe these food laws for their sacrifices to be accepted by Yahweh. The book of Leviticus has a comprehensive list of clean and unclean animals. The unclean animals were not to be offered to Yahweh as sacrifice. Milgrom (2004:13) purports that, although the primary purpose of the food laws seems to be ritualistic activities, a close analysis of the laws reviews that animal life was given an upper hand by the Levitical priests. If the animals were to be randomly slaughtered for sacrifice, there was a danger of extinction of other species. The Levites were very much aware of the need to protect animal species hence the limitations on the type of animals to be offered was a greater advantage on the side of the preservation of the animals. The fauna in Zimbabwe is very important for the survival of human beings. Animals provide meat, important skins, medicinal elements, and are a source of wealth, a means of transport and tourist attraction, thus they should be protected. The laws of the Levitical food laws also point to the need for the protection of the animals and birds in the biblical period and this is still relevant in the present-day Zimbabwe. The extinction of the animal species can be minimised if humanity considers the part of the Levitical food laws aimed at the protection of animals

Complementing faith and reason

Moskala (2011:3) considers faith and reason as complements. According to the civil laws in the book of Deuteronomy there will be human accountability on the judgement day to Yahweh for being stewards of the earth. In Deuteronomy17v14-20, the laws specify that Christians view the rulers of any nation as God ordained to execute justice. Justice in this case implies the respect of the natural environment by the mere application of reason. Human beings who promote the destruction of the natural environment will receive punishment for failing to take care of the earth as spelt out in Genesis 2v15 in which Adam was put in the Garden of Eden to take good care of it so that it yields the desired fruits. For the natural environment to efficiently perform its purpose according to its creator, the human beings must provide favourable conditions and stay away from the habit of destroying the environment. Humanity should note that civil laws of the Pentateuch indicate that creation belongs to God and we are only trustees of God's creation and it is a gross criminal act to abuse or even neglect nature. Human beings are failing to take into cognisance that the earth belongs to Yahweh hence they are becoming greed and this egocentric view is creating problems for people today and generations to come.

Bridging the gap between humanity and nature

Bergstrom (2014:23) argues that God created all elements of the natural environment to fit and function together in an orderly and unique fashion as attested by the creation stories in the book of Genesis chapters one and three. The earth was created in such a way that none can function on its own but for common purpose. The physical world is not destined for destruction and this is attested by the Noaic covenant in Genesis 9v8. An analysis of the covenant shows that God valued living creatures and God even vowed to never destroy the earth with severe floods (Butkus, 2002:73). An analysis of the relationship between human beings and nature can lead one to consider that the environmental creatures need one another for survival purposes. As a result, the destruction of some of the elements of nature affects the dependency chain that connects all the components of the natural environment.

Legal portions on animals

The Pentateuchal civil laws also regulate on how best the Old Testament Jews would make use of the environment without threatening it for themselves and the future generations. The laws prohibit various forms of activities which would involve cruelty to animals. For instance, the cross breeding of the unusual species of animals is not allowed. The law is also clear in pointing out that one may not harness together animals of different strength or even by passing an animal that would have collapsed under its load (Leviticus 19v19). It is a criminal offence to slaughter the mother bird or animal and its young one on the same day or even taking the eggs while the mother bird hovers over them (Deuteronomy 22v26). An interpretation of the cited criminal laws reminds people that all of God's creation are entitled to protection from any form of harm or destruction and human beings should take the role of the protector. The eggs and the young ones of animals represent the future generation of the animal and bird species. The veld fires and deforestation are destroying large hectares of forests that harbour the birds and animals in Zimbabwe. The beneficiaries of the land reform programme are also clearing land for agricultural purposes and this is threatening the livelihood of plants and animals. A revisit of the legal sections of the Pentateuch may minimise the destruction of the flora and fauna in Zimbabwe.

The Pentateuchal legal expectations from human beings

The Levitical religious and civil laws also state the importance of protecting our fellow humans as attested by that one should not stand idle by the blood of your neighbour, it was a criminal offence for an Old Testament Jew to fail to intervene in rescuing an innocent person from injury or death (Levitucus 19v6). The care for humanity also is extended to property because to treat the nonhuman as private property or as source of material wealth is immoral. The shedding of the innocent blood was prohibited by Yahweh. However, human cruelty to fellow human is increasing in Zimbabwe. The criminal laws cited in the Pentateuch encourage people to value human beings as they are part of the balance of nature. There is a need for mitigating measures to reduce the threat to human life in Zimbabwe due to the destruction of the environment. Awareness of the value of human blood as attested in the Pentateuch can be applied in this case.

Linking nature and revelation

Natural revelation is one of the sources of theology whereby God revealed himself to humanity (Brown, Charles and Samuel, 2000:126). The natural world is sufficient to guarantee the existence of God. By mere observation of nature, it suffices human beings to salute God as the creator of the universe through his wisdom. Nature also points out that the ultimate mystery of God's creation can be traced from the perspective of nature hence human beings should treat and protect nature with sensitivity it deserves as it symbolises the mighty works of Yahweh (Wenham, 1999:87). The Pentateuchal religious laws consider nature as sacred and any threat to it will not be tolerated. For instance, the random cutting down of trees, illegal hunting, unauthorised mining, unnecessary veld fires and illegal settlements can be controlled if humanity view nature as a symbol of the creator. The importance of nature as part of God's revelation is an added value in protecting the natural environment in Zimbabwe.

Legal notes on the protection and planting of *trees*

The scriptures assert that when you besiege a city for many days to wage war and capture it, you shall not destroy its trees by wielding an axe against them, for you may eat from them, but you shall not cut them down (Deuteronomy 20v19-20). This scripture reveals that people should not cut down trees even in times of war. Though war times disturb the normal economic activities of society, people can survive on fruit trees during such precarious times. In addition, fruit trees take a long time to reach maturity stage hence unnecessary destruction of them will have severe impact. This message on the preservation of the trees is so fundamental that it has become the basis of the teaching against overall prohibition of needless destruction. The commentaries on the military Pentateuchal laws lamented that the life is hinged on a tree therefore we should not cut down some trees rather we should protect them from destruction and damage, and take benefit from it (Habel, 2000:77).

The first thing that the Israelites were commanded to do when they entered the Promised Land was to plant trees (Leviticus 19v23). It can be added that the Pentateuch is also against the disturbance of the environmental conditions like soil, sunlight and water necessary for the trees to grow. The overall protection of the necessary environmental conditions ought to aid to the general strategies to control environmental degradation resulting in sustainable development in Zimbabwe. The trees are not enemies to humanity, we have no right to destroy or make them suffer or even exert aggression on them. The first activity the Israelites did when they occupied the promised land of Canaan was to plant trees. This was an indication that trees are vital for human beings although they take long to grow.

Trees play a key role in sustaining life on earth through the process of photosynthesis and its indispensable role in the water cycle (Wenham, 1999:86). The Pentateuch values trees and it is therefore imperative to protect the trees. Human beings found this world already provided with trees, and our ancestors domesticated some of them for us, so we too have mandate to take care of them for our descendants. Planting trees is a long-term investment which may not bear fruit immediately. The instruction to plant trees is thus a lesson to think beyond the present moment to the needs of the future. When one is settling in a new land, one might have other more pressing needs than "planting trees!" but the Pentateuchal military laws encourage us to give first preference to trees (Regenstein, 2017:1). By encouraging us to think of the long-term needs of our children and future generations, trees thus represent the ecological principle of sustainability.

Environmental degradation and economic problems

The research established that the major cause of environmental degradation is the economic hardship in Zimbabwe. the majority of people, especially the youth, are unemployed hence they are resorting to environmental degradation for survival. For instance, illegal mining, unauthorised hunting, deforestation for firewood and clearing the land are some of the activities that cause land degradation in Zimbabwe. The Pentateuchal laws do not condone this kind of destruction because the environment sustains life. Such kind of destructions engender more problems and the mitigating measures are costly to affected generations.

Conclusion and recommendations

The research has generated information on how Zimbabweans can utilise the Pentateuchal laws to reduce degradation of the natural environment. The study illustrated how Pentateuchal laws can be used to complement science in securing the natural environment in Zimbabwe. In addition, this chapter used Pentateuchal laws to contend that trees, water sources, animals, human beings and the soil also have naturally enshrined rights to be protected since they all share for a symbiotic existence. The research submits that human activities are largely contributing to the destruction of the natural environment. It can also be pointed out that, even amidst economic hardships in Zimbabwe, the exploitation of the natural environment is not the solution as this engenders more problems than before. There is need for multidisciplinary approaches to minimise the destruction of the natural environment and this research has brought Pentateuchal laws into consideration. The laws worked effectively as a preventative measure to the ancient Jewish communities as there no reported evidence of degradation of the environment in the scriptures.

References

Bergstrom, J. C. (2014). *Subdue the earth: What the Bible say about the environment.* Available online: arcapologetics.org.

Brown, F., Samuel, R. and Charles, A. (2000). *Enhanced Brown-Driver-Briggs Hebrew and English lexicon* (Electronic edn.). Oak Harbor: Logos Research Systems.

Butkus, R. A. (1999). *Sustainability: An eco-theological analysis.* In O.P. Carol Dempsey and R. A. Butkus (Eds.), *All creation is groaning.* Collegeville: Liturgical Press.

Calvin, J. (2012). *Public policy environmental stewardship in the Judeo-Christian Tradition: Jewish Catholic and Protestant wisdom on the environment.* Florida: Knox Theological Seminary.

Conradie, E.M. (2004). Toward an ecological biblical hermeneutics: A review essay on the Earth Bible Project. *Scriptura,* 85(1), 123-135.

EMA. (2016). Environmental Impact Assessment in Zimbabwe. Available online: www.ema.co.zw/indexphp.

Graham, B. (2017). *Christianity and environment: Should Christians work to protect the environment.* Charlotte: Billgraham.org.

Habel, N.C. (2000b). *Guiding eco-justice principles in reading from the perspective of the bible.* Sheffield: Sheffield Academic Press.

Makala, J. (2011). *Categorisation and Evaluation of different kinds of interpretation of the laws of clean and unclean animals in Leviticus 11.* Sheffield: Sheffield Academic Press.

Milgrom, J. (2004). *Leviticus: A book of ritual and ethics.* Minneapolis: Augsburg Fortress.

Nicholson, E. (2006). *The Pentateuch in the 20th century: The legacy of Julius Wellhausen.* Oxford: Oxford University Press.

Noth, M. (1967). *The laws in the Pentateuch and other studies.* Fortress Press: Edinburgh.

Olson, R.E. (2013). *The Old Testament and contemporary Christian ethics.* Available online: patheos.com.

Regenstein, L. (2017*). Animals, religion and the environment: The Bible's teaching on protecting animals and nature.* Available online: all creatures.org.

Van Dyk: (2009). *Challenges in the search for an eco-theology:* Old Testament essays. Mine Apolis: Fortress Press.

Van Heerden, S. W. (2009). Taking stock of Old Testament scholarship on environmental issues in South Africa: The main contributions and challenges. *Old Testament Essays,* 22(3), 695-718.

Wenham, G. *(*1999). *Transformation: The Old Testament and the environment: A response to Chris Wright.* Cheltenham and Gloucester: SPCA.

White, L. (1967). The historical roots of our ecologic crisis. *Science, 155*(March), *pages.*

Wright, D. (1990). *Observations on the ethical foundations on the Biblical dietary laws: A response to Jacob Milgrom.* Winona Lake: Eisenbrauns.

Chapter 5

The Significance Shona Religious Value System in Ecological Conservation

Henrietta Mgovo and Dudzirai Chimeri

Summary

The research examines the significance of the Shona value system in African traditional ecological conservation. The study argues that fear of ancestral spirits, totems and taboos are a vital force to implement the Shona environmental ethic. The research rests upon a qualitative paradigm and a case study approach was adopted for this study. Bindura town was the case and Manhenga community was the unity of investigation. Interview guides were used to collect primary data. The research revealed that fear of ancestors, totems and taboos were regulating authorities in traditional Shona society. This fear ensured environmental conservation in the ecological system. Taboos were the 'Environmental Management Agency' of the time while ancestral and territorial spirits were endowed with power to impose the taboos. The research reveals that the Judeo-Christian view that nature is for human use was and still is strange to the Shona religious value system that accords respect to ancestors as owners and guardians of the land. The results indicate that fear of ancestral spirit was and is still a key lever to enforce an environmental ethic that can impose limits on human freedom of action in relation to nature. The research therefore recommends that environmental policy implementers can learn something from Shona traditional ecological conservation program in the fight against environmental crisis and in promoting sustainable development.

Introduction

The debate whether Shona beliefs and practices support religious environmentalism is still a bone of contention. Beliefs refer to convictions that are generally accepted to be true. These ingrained beliefs influence our values, attitudes and behaviour. Practices refer to the long-held beliefs now put into practice. Taringa (2006) cites the ambiguity of Shona beliefs and practices, for Shona people portray a mixed paradoxical attitude towards nature. This means that the Shona beliefs and practices can be found to conserve nature and at the same time found to be harmful to nature. At one time, their practices and beliefs reveal a long pattern of environmental degradation whereby hunter gatherers armed with stone tipped spears and arrows, snares and traps would be portrayed. This may show that the Shona played a key role in global extinction of animals and species (Polycarp, 2014:7). On the other hand, Shona practices and beliefs, according to Schoffeleers (1997:5), reveal a worldview that is profoundly ecological, especially the fear of ancestral spirits as owners of the land and custodians of morality including environmental ethics. By environment we mean humanity, the surrounding including the life support provided by the air, water, land animals and the entire ecosystem of which humanity is but a part (Osuntokun, 2001:293. Ethics is a normative study of the principles of human conduct in relation to justice and injustice, good and evil right and wrong. It questions what ought to be done and the extent to which there is justification for a past action that has been done. Ethics has something meaningful to do with the environment, it questions humanity's relationship to the environment, its understanding and responsibility to nature and its obligation to leave some of nature's resources to prosperity (Pojman, 1997:1-2) Environmental ethic is therefore a field of applied ethics that ask fundamental questions about humans and the environment. It examines the moral basis of environmental responsibility (Ogungbemi Tangwa 2011).

The ancestral spirit guardian functions in areas of soil conservation, veld fires, conservation of water sources and legislation against wanton chopping down of trees and this belief bear evidence of a strong African environmentalism. The potential is exhibited in Shona totems and taboos that clearly say if one is found to have cut down a tree, he/she will pay two goats to the chief and if one is responsible for starting a veld fire, he/she pays three goats. These penalties were imposed because it was believed trees and vegetation belonged to ancestors, and one would have grieved the ancestors and therefore must pay for the damage.

Taringa (2006:191) argues that the Shona people were not environmentally friendly, but their ecological attitude was based more on "fear or respect of ancestral spirits". The question is: What is it that Taringa calls "fear of ancestral spirits" in African ecological conservation? The chapter therefore examines Shona value system, especially that which Taringa (2006) described as "fear of ancestral spirit", totems and taboos to find out their significance in African ecological conservation.

The aim of this research is to examine the Shona value system, particularly the significance of "fear of ancestral and territorial spirits,' totems and taboos in African ecological conservation among the Shona people of Zimbabwe. To obtain data for the above aim, this chapter examines the following objectives: First, examine the Shona world view and its environmental implications.

Secondly, to explore the significance of totems and taboo in Shona ecological conservation. Thirdly, to formulate an environmental ethic that is embedded in Shona culture which can be shared by the global village. The research hypothesis is: "Fear of ancestral spirits,' totem and taboos are a strong force which can impose limits on human action in relationship to nature.

Background to the study

Chemhuru and Masaka (2010) argue that Shona people made use of taboos (*zviera*) which are avoidance rules enforced by the ancestral (*midzimu*) and territorial (*mhondoro*) spirits to protect the environment. Taboos forbid the Shona people from performing certain actions that were cruel to nature in fear of certain unpalatable consequences. Violators of these taboos were believed to invite wrath of the ancestral or territorial spirits (*mhondoro*). Everyone would try as much as possible to observe certain rules in fear or respect of these spirits to avoid punishment which came in form of disease, bad luck (*munyama*) or death (Chemhuru and Masaka, 2010:123). Thus, the observance of taboos promote life that fosters a desirable environment ethic, while breaking the taboos led the moral agent to a vicious life that disregards not only the moral standing but also its sustainability. The argument is whether this Shona value system can be improved and incorporated as an environmental ethic that can impose limitations on human freedom of action in relationship to nature.

Taboos such as '*Ukaitira tsvina munzira unoita mamota pamagaro/ magaro anosvuuka*' (If you excrete along a path you will develop boils on your bottom/ your bottom will become sore). These taboos were meant to discourage people from polluting water sources from behaviour which can lead to diseases (Chemhuru and Masaka 2010:127). It was believed that these taboos were enforced by ancestral and territorial spirits. The taboos represent African casuistic laws comparable to casuistic laws of the Old Testament. Casuistic laws are conditional in nature with the conjunction if. They encouraged human relations among the Israelites, for example, in Exodus 22, 23, and Leviticus 1-6. The punishment appended to the participial formulation is also characteristic of the casuistic style in contrast to the apodictic ones which generally do not have a punitive clause (Alt, cited in Weinfeld, 1973:63-75). Curse laws also begin with a conditional clause which begins with if or suppose that and then. Alt keep his eyes on the conditional conjunctive 'If' which is the first characteristic of the casuistic laws. The curse laws are a series of conditional sentences. Thus Deuteronomy 27:16 'If a man dishonours his father and mother then he will be cursed' compares very well with the Shona taboo which says if you scold or beat your mother you will be punished (*kutanda botso*). Taboos enforced by ancestors are also conditional in nature and compare very well with Israelite casuistic laws and can be called African casuistic laws. These can be utilised in conservation of natural resources and environmental stewardship.

Among the Shona people, anyone who breaks a taboo is a threat to the wellbeing of others. Taboos acted as African casuistic laws enforced by ancestral or territorial spirits who were feared for punishing moral deviants. The taboos were believed to help reduce environmental problems such as erratic rainfall patterns, and other activities such as wanton cutting down of trees, siltation and global veld fires. They also helped conservation of water sources, particularly marsh lands. These traditional ways of environmental conservation maintained a balance in the ecological system and still can be improved and utilised. Taboos were the legislation of the time while ancestral and territorial spirits were endowed with power to impose them.

The research is significant in as far as it tries to draw insights from Shona value system to help reduce the environmental global crisis. Furthermore, the research is important in as far as it tries to exhume the long lost African casuistic laws embedded in Shona culture which were written in the hearts of the Shona people and transmitted orally and were enforced through taboos as efforts to reduce environmental degradation. The research is also important as a search for an environmental ethic found in African cultural heritage, which could be of much help in ecological policy formulation. This chapter posit that such an environmental ethic ought to be improved in order contribute in reducing environmental degradation in Zimbabwe as well as the global village.

Literature review

According to Leedy (2004), the purpose of literature review is to explore what has already been written on the topic, what has not been written and how the current researcher's inquiry addressed the 'gap', silence or weakness in the existing knowledge base. According to McNill (1990), every researcher of whatever status should spend time reading what other people have written about the topic under research. This section thus provides a review of the relevant literature on the Shona religious value system which includes role of ancestral and territorial spirits, totems and taboos which contribute to the protection of the environment. This will assist in identifying gaps and strengthens the research. It is however not possible to review every piece of work that has been produced on this topic since it has been an issue debated over a long time.

The context of the environmental crisis

The environmental crisis debate can be traced from the 1960s through works by Western scholars up to the 21st century when African scholars contributed to the discussion. The questioning and rethinking of the relationship of human beings with nature reflect an already widespread perception in the 1960s. The historical roots of the environmental crisis, as argued by the historian White (1967), was the main strand of Judeo-Christian thinking and had encouraged the exploitation of nature by maintaining the superiority of humanity over all other forms of life on earth and by depicting all elements of nature as created for the use of humans. White (1967:1205-6) argues that even the Bible supports the anthropocentric view (Genesis 1:27-28). Anthropocentricism sees nature and resources as things available for humanity's use. Their exploitation would therefore be acceptable if it did not lead to negative consequences for human beings. Here dominion is taken to mean that humanity may utilise and consume everything else to their advantage without any injustice for they are superior to all other creatures. According to White, religious cosmologies had a hand for the destructive alliance of science, technology and democracy that now threatens the earth. He further contends that Western Christianity's world view influenced Europeans to view themselves as separate from all other creatures which they could dominate. After White had traced the roots of ecological crisis in religious cosmologies, some researchers attempted to find the remedy therein. The obligation left was to recover an ecological world view centred on nature's value rather than on human transcendence.

Environmental crisis is a dramatic unexpected and irreversible worsening of the environment leading to significant welfare losses (Taylor, 2009). This ecological crisis has become a pressing concern of our planet at the turn of the 21st century. It became a global phenomenon that no society is totally immune against the threat and danger which it poses to humanity and to the ecosystem. Researchers sought therefore to run away from ethical theories grounded in Western perspectives and experiences. Ogungbemi and Tangwa (1997:204) pioneered the philosophical discussions on environmental ethics from an African perspective. These African authors contributed to the consolidation of an African environmental ethics and effective environmental management. There are yet many Zimbabwean scholars whose works reflect extensive effort on the contribution of African religion in reducing the environmental crisis. These include Taringa (2006), Masaka and Chemhuru (2010), Taringa (2014), Mangena (2014) and Godwin and Makaudze (2015), just to mention a few. All these contributed immensely to how the Shona taboos can contribute in reducing the environmental crisis.

Of interest, however, is the work of Taringa (2006:191) who critically examined how Shona people seem to be environmentally friendly, especially the beliefs in ancestral spirits, pan-vitalism, kinship, totems and taboos (Taring, 2006). He examined the beliefs of the Shona people based on Tomalin's observation about Hinduism. Tomalin laments attitudes of romanticizing or venerating the past as a recurring theme in most literature on religion and the environment. This view, according to her, tends to essentialise the lifestyle and values of the tribal peasant's non-industrial societies as if there existed an eco-golden age at some point in the past. Taringa (2006) therefore examined Shona attitudes to nature considering Tomalin's remarks. He exhumed the paradoxical and ambiguous nature of attitude and practices of Shona people. He said their attitude bears positive and negative implications on the environment. He draws the conclusion that Shona attitudes to nature are not environmentally friendly. Taringa highlighted that African practices and attitude towards nature are more based on "fear of ancestral spirits" than respect for nature itself. He advocates for an examination of Shona attitudes to nature if African religion is to re-emerge as a stronger environmental force in Zimbabwe and the world at large.

This research therefore attempts to examine the Shona value system, particularly that which Taringa (2006) calls "fear or respect for ancestors", to find out its significance in African ecological conservation. The research is a recovery, revival and deliberate reconstruction of an environmental ethic from the raw materials of indigenous African Shona culture to re-emerge with an environmental ethic to be utilised in environmental sustainability in Zimbabwe and the global village in general. To understand this long held Shona indigenous environmental ethic, it is important to first highlight the traditional Shona cosmology in terms of the place of God, territorial and ancestral spirits in their spiritual hierarchy. This will in turn help us understand how totems and taboos help to mitigate environmental crisis among the Shona people of Zimbabwe and the ecological implications.

God (Mwari)

The Shona people believe in one ultimate reality, the creator, whom they call *Mwari*. The God of the Shona is active and involved, existing not only in the mythical past of creation, but also present among the Shona people even today. Because God is the final authority, God regulates fertility both of humanity and agricultural proceeds as the ultimate source of rain. God's help is thus sought, not only in times of drought, but also when other crises take place.

Ancestral/ territorial spirits custodian of ecological survival

Below God (Mwari) are the territorial spirits *(mhondoro)*, that is, the lion spirits which are concerned chiefly with the welfare of the community or nation. As Daneel (1971) observes, their involvement in the lives of the people is of multiple significance. There are the ones who are believed to be guardians of Shona environment. Schoffleers (1978:2) sums up this ecological value of Shona religion in this manner:

In Africa, concern with ecological matters is distributed through a number of religious institutions. According to Daneel 1971:93, *Mhondoro* are custodians of ecological survival and their responsibility is to mediate between God (*Mwari*) and the community when rain is needed, or other national issues need to be addressed. Klostermaier (1973:134) argues that Shona beliefs have a very significant ecological element. This is evidenced in how the Shona attitude towards nature determines the use people made of the environment. According to Klostermaier (1973:136), Shona people live with the environment as if it were a living being with feelings. They see themselves as part of it but respect it greatly, because they sense something mysterious about the environment. There is a wholeness and togetherness in all parts of the environment because the land, the mountains, rivers and forests are linked closely to God *(Mwari)* and the Territorial Lineage cults, having to do among other things with the holding of stock and land obviously have an ecological dimension and so do the professional cults of hunters, fishermen and others. Throughout Africa there exist a type idea or understanding which function for the whole of the community rather than for sections within it and which is at the same time profoundly ecological. It is this type of held view we have in mind when we speak of territorial Spirits. Characteristic activities of territorial Spirits are rituals to counteract droughts, floods blights, pests and epidemic diseases afflicting cattle and man. Put positively the territorial Spirits function in respect of the well-being of the community, its fields, livestock, fishing, hunting and general economic interests. Apart from engaging in ritual action, they also issue and enforce directives with regard to a community's use of its environment. Finally, they provide scheme of thought in which myths, rituals and directive for actions appear as part of a coherent worldview. What sets territorial Spirits apart from other religious institutions is the combination of communal and ecological concerns and they are primarily accorded these concerns.

Totems and taboos which contribute to ecological conservation

One way of protecting the environment against extinction was via the practice of *mutupo* (totemism). A totem is an animal, or part of an animal which is considered taboo and thus cannot be eaten or killed by people of that totem.

81

The totemic animal had a taboo attached to it or to part of its carcass such that the totem bearer is forbidden to eat it. Infringement of this taboo had certain consequences or magical sanctions. It was taboo for anyone to kill or eat an animal of their totem. The Shona taboo states '*Ukadya mutupo unobva mazino*' (If you eat your totem all your teeth will fall off). Aschwanden (1982:120) adds that eating a totem was committing a crime like incest, whose punishment was severe. It was strongly believed that those who ate their totems also developed a rash all over their bodies, went blind, or became sterile, and these were punishments imposed by ancestral spirits (Aschwanden 1982:120). Shona religious observance of totems and taboos work for the preservation of the environment. The Shona totem system is based on wildlife and it regulates their social life such as who to marry and food which they may eat as well as their succession to Chieftainship. Sabahire (1990:71) asserts

By Totemism we mean the belief in the relationship between an animal or vegetal species and a kinship group, the clan. Belief in totems seems to us to be symptomatic of a remarkable fact. That is man to identify himself/herself as a group, projects himself in nature which has become his/her mirror, thus recognising that he/she shares the basic biological attributes. One of the Consequences is that he/she feels obligated to respect this same nature. In Shona world view it means that one is forbidden to kill and eat certain species with whom he enjoys a quasi-ontological relationship. Everyone has a totem animal, bird, or part of an animal, which is one's totem (mutupo). This Totem (mutupo) gives identity and provides collective aspirations. The Shona totem system is paternal. Eating totem animal (mutupo) is believed to leave one vulnerable to misfortunes.

Tobayiwa (1985:229-236) reminds us that it is never done (*zvinoera*) meaning to say it is a taboo. Most totem animals exhibit elegance, dignity, strength or other positive features. The totem system is friendly to the environment as certain game is protected. Taking into consideration the duty played by ancestors in this whole drama of imposing limits of human action to nature, one is tempted to see this fear or respect of ancestors as a much-needed environmental ethic that can impose limits on human action in relationship to the environment.

Forestry ethic

Every youth in Shona society was taught how to behave in the forests. Forests were not supposed to be angered otherwise one would be vulnerable to wildlife or get lost in the jungles. It was also a taboo to despise the animals one encountered and the fruits one gathered or ate in the forest because no one should despise what the ancestral spirits had given. Cruelty to animals was prohibited. It was a taboo to kill animals such as baboons while in their natural habitat (*chiro*). The same was true of snakes. It is in hunting and fishing that we see clear ecological concerns. There were ritual ordinances which regulate those activities. Can those Shona values be revived and help reduce environmental degradation?

There were forests people were prohibited from cutting trees. These included holy groves (*masango anoera*) dedicated to local ancestral spirits. It was also a taboo to hunt or cut trees in these sacred groves. This helped to maintain a natural preserve where traditional plants and wildlife survived unhampered and undisturbed. There were also certain sacred mountains, caves and wells dedicated to spirits of local chiefs and other high-ranking people believed to reside in animals, such as lions (*mhondoro*) and others. These animals, which were supposed to be harmless, were believed to drink from sacred wells. As a result, the use of certain containers such as metallic ones or pots with soot to fetch water from such sacred places was prohibited. Only traditional containers were permitted.

During the war independence war (second *Chimurenga*), the ancestral spirits were believed to give security to people who hid in certain mountains. The mountains were always covered with mist (*mhute*) and hence enemies were confused and lost direction. Certain herbs and grass were also protected. People were discouraged from pulling uprooting plants and thus destroying wild plants. Those who uprooted plants were warned that they will be struck by lightning if they continued to destroy Mother Nature. Certain trees were not to be cut, especially those providing landmarks (*muhacha, muonde and muchakata*). Such trees were not to be cut down because their evergreen foliage was a symbol of protection by ancestors for animals and people. Important community gatherings were held under such trees. Certain trees were prohibited from being used as firewood, especially the *mushozhowa* tree which was used to exorcise spirits. Using it as firewood was believed to result in the homecoming of the exorcised spirits.

The Shona were not just sensitive to the welfare of animal only but even to that of plants. It was considered taboo to destroy fruit trees and to use them as firewood. Most trees that produced fruits feeding people, for example, *mutsubvu, muchakata, etc.*, were thus spared. Certain trees were also not considered suitable for firewood, for example, *muora muzeze*, because some of these trees were used for medicine (*miti inorapa haiveswi*). To the researcher, this seems to be a sound environmental ethic embedded in Shona culture.

Hunting ethic

Poaching elephants for ivory is a direct result of colonialism and capitalism. Africans never engaged in hunting for sports even those who buy ivory and ivory products from poached animals are not Africans (Polycarp, 2014:17). The problem with modernity is that poaching has substituted totemism and traditional selective hunting because poachers do not identify with any animal. Any animal can be killed for as long as it fetches a good price on the market despite that it may be the poacher's totemic animal. However, there were certain animals which were not considered edible by the Shona, for example, lion, python, elephant, zebra, baboon, monkey, and other bird species like rain bird, crow, owl, and the stoke bird (Godwin and Makaudze, 2015). Birds that built their nests around the homestead were considered part of the homestead and were not trapped.

Fishing ethic

If fishermen dragged big and small fish in a net, the traditional Shona value system dictated that the smaller fish ought to be thrown back into the pool and the bigger ones collected for a meal. This would help conserve species from extinction and traditional fishermen would do this in fear or respect of ancestors as custodians of morality including environmental mores (Godwin and Makaudze, 2015). Besides, water is a habitat of aquatic creatures like fish that must be protected because urine contains nitrates which are dangerous to aquatic life. Taboos were also used to promote existence of plant life in water sources that were most likely to be affected by unbecoming human behaviour (Mangena, 2014:8). The above taboos vindicate the Shona as very hygienic people, contrary to what colonialists propagated.

Sacred sites ethic

Mountains evoke the sacred among the Shona people as they inspire the people to experience the wholly others. Mountains always arouse feelings of overwhelming devotion, awaken an overwhelming sense of the sacred and embody and reflect the ultimate and most central values of religion. Though mountains are now losing most of their sanctity, the Shona people believed that they were the very presence of divine power. What gives these sacred sites their intrinsic worthy is that they are spaces that links the dead and the living (Source, 2014:355). The Shona believed that sacred sites like rocks (Matonjeni/Zame), caves (Chinhoyi caves), mountains (Inyanga and Buchwa) and rivers (Zambezi and Save) are places where territorial spirits resided as they did their job of protecting the environment through the enforcement of moral behaviour. Shona people believed there were certain sanctions which befell those people who failed to revere these sacred sites. Many parents had their children disappear because of failing to observe moral codes that guide and regulate behaviour during tours at these sites. Mangena (2014) alludes to an occasion when a tourist disappeared after visiting Inyanga Mountain. All these Shona mysteries would induce fear in people to stop tempering with the environment.

Water and hygienic ethics

The Shona people also had ways of ensuring a clean environment and atmosphere. Taboos such as '*Ukawetera mumvura hauzozvari*' (If you urinate into water you will not sire children). Such beliefs were meant to discourage people from polluting water sources from behaviour which can lead to diseases. The Shona society had built very responsible citizens through respect or fear of ancestors as a strong force and so they did not hesitate to drink from most sources. Water sources, the forest and the air were all kept clean. Waste of whatever kind would barely find its way into water sources and other surroundings. The people dug pits where solid waste was thrown into, and then burnt. As Gelfand (1968:46) notes, "The African is inherently clean and the village and huts I have visited are neat and tidy. The yard is well swept." Among the Shona people, it is believed even today that '*Ukacheresa mvura nehari ine matsito tsime rinopwa*' (If you fetch water using a pot with soot, the well dries up). The Shona had a saying '*Mvura haina n'anga*', that is, water has no purifier. The statement shows the conviction in the cleanliness of water which people drew from most sources.

Disease control ethic

The other given taboos centre on cleanliness of the environment. The Shona people did not tolerate throwing of litter anywhere. Writing about his experiences among the Shona, Gelfand (1968:48) says, "I have never observed dirt in the villages of Africa, certainly nothing that is seen in a city slum". Shona citizens were responsible enough to make sure that dirt is not scattered all over the place. Bath water, especially that of babies, usually has a lot of dirt because children at tender ages may relieve themselves in their clothing. This water, if thrown everywhere, was a sure way of inviting flies and threats of disease outbreaks hence it was poured in pits and covered with soil (Godwin and Makaudze, 2015). Today one would see baby diapers (pampers) scattered everywhere. People were so hygienic as to cover their waste with soil each time they relieved themselves in the bush. This is unlike today where people sometimes gather for church occasions under trees and away from ablution facilities and leave dirty is thus scattered all over and this has resulted in cholera outbreaks in many places in recent years.

Farming ethic

Polycarp (2014:16) highlights that traditional peasants were organic farmers. Transformation of peasant farming into commercial farming led to the destruction of large acres of forests. Traditional African peasant farmers did not use fertilizers and chemicals. They preserved farmlands by making them fallow for years to allow soil to acquire nutrients organically before going back to farm it again. In contrast, mechanical farming uses fertilizers, insecticides fungicides and herbicides which have not only killed the soil but polluted ground water, rivers and lakes. The research does not want to underestimate the positive side of commercial farming that is producing more food for the people. However, this can be done while recognising the moral conservation attitude of peasant farmers. Kelbassa (2006:24-29) argues that contemporary environmentalists can learn something from the traditional conservation practices and moral attitudes of Africans.

Educational ethic

Modern Western systems of education, religion and medicine have had negative impact on the environment. The modern Western beliefs were inconsistent with the traditional indigenous social, cultural practices and moral norms that sought to conserve natural resources and preserve the environment. The examples given were relevant to European context and not adaptable to African situation. Western education taught Africans to see nature as an objective reality that must be exploited for human needs. There was lack of phenomenological or empathetic mode of enquiry conducive to preservation of the environment. Colonial education, with its emphasis on science, led Africans to throw away their traditional modes of healing because they were deemed to be incompatible with the Western mode of healing brought by colonialism (Polycarp, 2014). By getting rid of their traditional healing of using herbs, they did not see any need for leaves, plants, roots and barks of trees and the need to preserve them. Thus, they sought to exploit them for economic gains. The contemporary Africans lost all that was African including the fear or respect of ancestors since it was deemed demonic by the colonisers resulting in environmental degradation.

Policy formulation ethic

The government that emerged from colonialism did not have sound moral foundation to guide people's attitude and formulation of public policies regarding the environment. Indigenous moral values had been destroyed by colonialism. Political leaders relied on Europe on moral values that led the government to make environmental policies that were consistent with

European moral attitudes, such as exploitation as opposed to conservation of the environment (Polycarp 2013) This explains in part why African governments have not been able to develop comprehensive environmental policies and why there are no systematic efforts to prevent the destruction of the environment. Fear or respect of ancestors is no more a legal enforcer as it was in pre-colonial Shona society.

Godwin and Makaudze (2015) maintain that traditional Shona societies jealously guarded against the devastation of the environment and other natural resources. They would not only exploit the environment for their benefit but would safeguard it against extinction or pollution.

Today in Zimbabwe, environmental management agencies safeguard and punish those who threaten the environment while the police enforce the law. In the past, it was taboos that fought wars against environmental degradation. They minimised excessive firewood collection, emission of toxic substances into the water, air or land (Godwin and Makaudze 2015). They were the environmental police who maintained order and peaceful existence between people, the flora and the fauna. Unlike the relations between the environmentalists and society today, which is like the hunter and the hunted, with taboos, they were part and parcel of the art, education and day to day living of the indigenous people (Godwin and Makaudze, 2015). It is ironic in Zimbabwe that while safety belts in a car is worn for safety of the individual person one would just wear a belt when he or she sees the police (Dimingu, 2014).

Methodology

A case study approach was adopted for this research. Case study research enables the investigation of important topics not easily covered by other methods (Yin, 2004). Bindura town was the case with Manhenga community as unit for investigation. Robson (2002) defines a case study as a strategy for doing research which involves an empirical investigation of a contemporary phenomenon within its real-life context using multiple of evidence. It is a qualitative research method used to examine contemporary real-life situations and province the basis for the application of ideas and extension of methods. Magwa and Magwa (2015) submit that a case study probes deeply and analyses intensively so as to establish generalization about a wider population to which that population belongs. It attempts to describe the subject's entire range of behaviours to the subject's history and environment. The researcher chose this approach because of its considerable ability to generate answers to "why" as well the "what" and "how" questions. A case study design was also chosen because the researcher intends to have a closer and detailed analysis of the

Shona ecological values. Qualitative research focuses on collection and analysis of full and rich data about a phenomenon, as a result, data collection is not limited to numerical facts but includes data obtained through observation, interview and participation (Leedy, 2004). Witzel (2000) defines the target population as all possible cases of interest in a study. He further defines a population is a group which the researcher is interested in a study. From Manhenga community in Bindura 20 people, that is, 10 males and 10 females, were purposively selected for face-to-face interviews. The use of purposive sampling in the study was also supported by Krathwoh (1996) when he says that there would be occasions when a researcher wants to interview specific types of people who can supply the researcher with important information.

Research instruments

The researcher used interview guides to collect primary data from Manhenga community in Bindura. Face-to-face interviews were conducted with the residents in Manhenga. According to Leedy and Ormrod (2001), face-to-face interviews have a distinct advantage of enabling the researcher to establish rapport with participants and therefore gain their cooperation. The strength of an interview is that it has highest response rate unlike questionnaires. With face-to-face interviews, the researcher could seek clarity from respondents on ambiguous answers and when appropriate probe further. Collins *et al.* (2000:176) suggest that interviews see the centrality of human interaction for knowledge production and emphasises the social situations of research (Magwa S. and Magwa W. 2015). The interview was thus a reliable instrument of obtaining information and gaining insights into the Shona people's value system with regards to the conservation of natural resources.

The interview method, however, has its own weakness. In an interview a respondent, according to Witzel A. (2000), must cooperate when given questions. A frequent problem with interviews was that answers given tend to be verbose. Another disadvantage was that an interview tends to be biased because of face-to-face interaction. This would be clear on issue whereby the manner the gestures exhibited by the interviewer might direct the interviewee in his or her answering. To minimise this problem when preparing interviews, the researcher was analytic and applied the criteria to what extent a question influences the respondent's answer. An interview guide was used to solicit qualitative primary data from respondents. Mainly open-ended and probing questions were used in the guide. The open-ended questions aimed to collect respondents, feelings, opinions and worldviews about the Shona ecological values. The researcher recorded interviewee responses on manuscripts for analysis.

Advantages of interview guides are that interviewer and interviewees had the chance to both clarify questions and ideas. The researcher asked questions that were consistent with the research objectives and used probing questions to get further clarification of ideas by interviewees. The main advantage of an interview as a data collection tool was that open-ended questions made interviewees to give a whole lot of details and the researcher had to take pains to sift through and note only what was relevant to the study Some respondents who answered questionnaires were in a hurry for other business and could have rushed through the questionnaire without putting careful thought. To mitigate the weaknesses, the researcher had to triangulate interview data with questionnaire data to improve the validity, credibility and reliability of the results.

Research ethics were considered. Issues of informed consent have significant ethical weight in qualitative research (Leedy and Ormrod, 2001). The researcher sought the consent of participants before they could participate in the study. The researcher began by explaining the purpose of the research before inviting participants to take part in the study. The researcher, to protect participants and to ensure confidentiality, made sure that the identities of respondents have not been disclosed anywhere in this study. The findings of the study will only be used for academic purposes and the results will be shared with participants upon request.

This section described the methodology. It also examined research instruments and procedures to be used by the researcher to collect data. The use of interview guides in face-to-face interview were discussed. The section also discussed the techniques employed by the researcher to deal with the ethical issues in research. The following section will present, analyse and discuss the findings of the study.

Results and discussion

The research has been a revival and deliberate reconstruction of an environmental ethic from the raw materials of indigenous Shona culture based on the role of ancestral and territorial spirits as enforcers of an environmental ethic for the future of Zimbabwe and the global village. The research revealed that fear of ancestors/territorial spirits is a vital force that is missing in the contemporary world to come up with an environmental ethic that can impose limitations on human activities in the environment. The majority of the respondents (95%) revealed that before debating Shona religion one should first understand Shona attitudes to nature from their own traditional, social cultural and political perspective rather than through Western spectacles and potential ethnocentric bias of most African theologies. The research also discovered that Euro-Americans assume they know it all and that Africans have nothing to offer as efforts to solve environmental problems. This problem is underscored by efforts to teach Africans Western environmental values. For instance, Western science had demonized African traditional food and medicine but now there is a drive to use herbs and traditional foods that had been condemned before (Polycarp, 2014:17).

A majority of respondents (85%) agreed that taboos are African casuistic/conditional laws enforced by ancestors and written in the hearts of Africans and handed down from generation to generation. This is comparable to the Old Testament casuistic laws handed down to the Israelites from Moses, their ancestor. Most respondents (99%) revealed that indigenous Zimbabweans have a cosmology that is different from Europeans in relation to the environment. Among the Shona people, nature was represented as inspirited and was therefore the direct object of reverence. There is an element of the superiority of the spirit world (ancestral or territorial spirits) to the human world that acts as the driving force to accord the spiritual world with authority to reward good behaviour and punish errant behaviour. African ecological ethics are spiritually anchored hence appeal to taboos enforced by ancestral or territorial spirits and this leads to protection of nature. In this research, it was established that taboos are mostly interested in the preservation of endangered species.

The study discovered the existence of culturally evolved and integrated environmental ethics that served to limit destructive environmental impacts in pre-industrial Shona technologies. Shona people believed that nature was created by God and thus was to be used with care and passed on intact to the next generation. Ancestral and territorial spirits regulated the use of nature through totems, taboos and different environmental ethics. The research discovered the presence of environmental degradation also in pre- industrial period. However, industrial civilization intensified environmental harm already afoot in the activities of pre-industrial people and has gone further to pollute the environment with synthetic toxic chemicals. The research discovered possible reasons why governments are not able to stop or control poaching of elephants for ivory or deforestation for lumber. It is due to economic dependency in which African states must survive on earnings from exports. Making environmentally sensitive policies such as hunting or trade and educational policies that limit outsiders from hunting, etc., will imply economic doom for the respective governments.

Recently many Africans are starting to see that the contemporary environmentalist views represent traditional African beliefs, ways of life and moral views that have been rejected by Europeans (Polycarp, 2014:16). These are the beliefs which, due to modernity, Africans have shunned as bad and uncivilized. Africans now must further embrace their lost old traditional way of life and values which they had previously regarded as uncivilized due to modernity. Even in health issues, people are encouraged to use the once discarded herbal medicine and are advised to eat traditional foods and diet. Several respondents (80%) revealed that environmentalists who have sought the implementation of a sustainable development are promoting values that seem to have been borrowed from Africans ecological conservation programmes. They seem to have taken a leaf from African ecological conservation without acknowledging it. They seem to have plagiarized African environmental ethics already known to Africans but had been lost due to colonialism and modernity.

Conclusion and Recommendations

The research examined the Shona value system particularly the fear of ancestral and territorial spirits in African ecological conservation among the Shona people of Zimbabwe. The chapter argues that fear of ancestral and territorial spirits was a vital force to enforce an environmental ethic that could impose limitation on human activities on natural resources. Fear of ancestors and territorial spirits was the regulating authority in traditional Shona society. The traditional ways of environmental conservation maintained a balance in the ecological system. Taboos and totems were the legislation and the environmental management agencies of the time while ancestral spirits or territorial spirits were endowed with power to impose them. In Zimbabwe, environmental management agencies now safeguard and punish those who threaten the being of the environment while the police enforce the law. In the past, it was taboos that fought wars against environmental degradation. Fear of ancestral or territorial spirit is that respect and reverence owed to the living timeless by the living. Fear of ancestors/territorial spirits was an environmental legal enforcer to ensure observance of taboos associated with an environmental ethic that could impose limitation on human freedom of action in relationship to nature and environmental sustainability in Zimbabwe and the global village. The researcher submits that there are both negative and positive practices in African traditional ecological ethics for no culture is perfect. However, it should be observed as a sign of mature reasoning to detect what is good from what is negative. The research therefore recommends Africans to treasure their rich traditional world view, traditional education and traditional medicine. It also recommends researchers to study Africans from a phenomenological point of view to appreciate the role of ancestral spirits in African ecological conservation.

Scholars do not need to underestimate African ecological conservation programmes that have tremendous future potential because of their embeddedness in Shona culture. The research also recommends environmentalists to take a leaf from African ecological conservation and fashion it in a way a contemporary person can comprehend for use in ecological conservation.

References

Aschwanden, H. (1982). *Symbols of life: An analysis of the consciousness of the Karanga.* Gweru: Mambo Press.

Chemhuru, M. and Masaka, D. (2010). Taboos as sources of Shona people's environmental ethics. *Journal of Sustainable Development in Africa,* 12(7), 121-133.

Daneel, M.L. (2001). *African earthkeepers: Wholistic interfaith mission.* New York: Orbis Books.

Dimingu, W. (2014). The preferential option for the poor: a contextual reading of John Wesley's social ethics in contemporary Zimbabwe. Gweru: Unpublished Bachelor Theology and Religious Studies, Midlands State University

Gelfand, M. (1968). *African crucible: An ethno-religious study with special reference to the Shona-speaking people.* Cape Town: Juta and Company.

Leedy P. (Ed.). (2004) *Practical research: Planning and design.* New York, MacMillan.

Leedy: and Ormrod, J. (2001). *Practical research: Planning and design* (7ᵗʰ edn.). Thousand Oaks: SAGE Publications

MacNeil: (1990). *Research methods.* London: Routledge.

Makaudze, G. (2015). Sex and the female body in Shona society. *Journal of Pan African Studies,* 7(8), 140-153.

Mangena, F. (2014). Environmental policy, management and ethics in Zimbabwe, 2000-2008. *Journal of Pan African Studies,* 6(10), 224-240.

Mbiti, J.S. (1969). *African religions and philosophy.* London: Heinemann.

Ojomo: A. (2011). Environmental ethics: an African understanding. *African journal of environmental science and technology,* 5(8), 572-578.

Polycarp, A.I. (2014). Traditional African environmental ethics and colonial legacy. *International Journal of Philosophy and Theology,* 2(4), 1-21.

Robson, C. (2002). *Real world research.* London: Blackwell.

Schoffeleers, J.M. (Ed.). (1979). *Guardians of the land: Essays on Central African territorial cults.* Gweru: Mambo Press.

Taringa, N. (2006). How environmental is African traditional religion? *Exchange*, 35(2), 191-214.

Taringa, N., and Mangena, F. (2015). Shona Religion in Zimbabwe's Land Reform Program: Is a Sustainable Shona Ecological Ethic Possible? *Philosophy in African Traditions and Cultures*, 41-54.Mangena, F. Chimuka, T.A. and Mabiri F. (Eds.). *The Council for Research in Values and Philosophy*. Washington DC.

Tomalin, E. (2004). Bio-divinity and biodiversity: Perspectives on religion and environmental conservation in India. *Numen 51*(3), 265-295.

White Jr, L. (1967). The historical roots of our ecological crisis. *Science, 155*(3767), 1203-1207.

Yin, R. (2004). *The case study anthology*. Thousand Oaks: SAGE.

Chapter 6

Rural Livelihoods Diversification in Semi-Arid Districts of Zimbabwe

Julius Musevenzi and Benjamin Gweru

Summary

This chapter assesses the sustainability of livelihood diversification in reducing poverty particularly in marginal areas under politically charged environments. The chapter brings out the available opportunities and challenges for the rural poor in environmentally degraded areas for improved livelihood diversification to reduce their vulnerability. The question is: Are these diversification opportunities withstanding the external shocks in marginal areas? Dry and marginal areas are confronted with the problem of increasing poverty and insecure livelihoods. Livelihood diversification has over the years been adopted as an appropriate strategy to reduce poverty and the vulnerability of the rural poor. Using interviews and selected participatory methods with the rural poor in selected districts, the study shows that poverty remains and in fact continues to increase as the natural environment struggles to support the multiple sources of livelihoods despite having access to multiple sources of livelihood. The politically charged environment in marginal areas reverses some of the gains made by livelihood diversification to reduce poverty. The chapter concludes that sustainable livelihood diversification to reduce rural poverty in marginal areas under politically charged environments is limited and poverty continues to increase.

Introduction

This chapter brings out questions around the sustainability of livelihood diversification in semi-arid districts (Gokwe, Muzarabani and Mwenezi) of Zimbabwe under a politically charged environment. The study brings out the diversification strategies by the vulnerable poor and the role played by external players in the context of sustainability. The chapter acknowledges that rural livelihood diversification and poverty reduction strategies have yielded mixed results that are better tested using the lens of sustainability. Despite the vulnerability of semi-arid districts to external shocks such as drought, climate change, economic melt-down and political challenges the adopted responding strategies seem to be failing to sustainability tests and this is the focus of this chapter.

Bryceson (1999:3) contends that rural livelihoods in southern Africa are in crisis in sharp contrast to a few decades ago when the region was the breadbasket of the continent, economic reforms were generating growth and investment, and hopes of the democratic transition were expected to show quick dividends. However, during those years of economic development, the region was hit by its worst food crisis in memory, particularly in the early 1990s, with over 14 million people reported to be at risk (Bryceson, 1999). Southern Africa in the main has not benefited from economic reforms and globalisation, and evidence from several studies on livelihoods in the region raises questions about the nature of the current livelihood crisis, its origin and potential solutions, many of which remain unanswered (Institute of Development Studies, 2008). Most of this literature is linked to global changes without considering political dynamics at a local level, and this is the gap that this study seeks to fill by looking at livelihood changes under politically charged conditions.

Zimbabwe was one of the countries that showed promise in the 1980s as the 'breadbasket' of southern Africa, but it was faced with several challenges that brought rural livelihoods into crisis. Research findings by the Institute of Development Studies at the University of Zimbabwe (2006) relate livelihood changes to the dynamics of power politics and policy changes, and to challenges in finding solutions in management and technical support. Global level changes including economic reforms, market trends and climate change pushed the semi-arid districts of the country, already poverty-stricken, into further crisis. Poverty in these districts is pervasive and seems to be on the increase. Past prescriptions appear not to be working, and new offerings, though acknowledging some of the failings of past efforts, have been criticised for not being radical enough to confront the enormity of the rural livelihood challenges in dry districts of Zimbabwe. This has thrust rural development policy into crisis.

Theoretical Framework

Sustainable livelihoods framework (SLF)

Discourses and development frameworks have histories and Sustainable Livelihoods Framework (SLF) has a history based in the academic disciplines of anthropology, sociology and geography, and in applied research of governments and aid agencies. Those engaged in agrarian studies justifiably claim a long engagement with rural livelihoods (Batterbury, 2008).

As argued by Chambers and Conway (1992:23), the livelihood framework that emerged from the debate on sustainable rural development is useful in analysing rural development practices in marginalised areas as actively constructed household strategies. Among the many theories of rural development, the sustainable livelihoods framework (SLF) is appropriate for studies of this kind as it provides an overview of the evolving inter-relationships between capabilities and capital that exist at household level and the institutions and measures that interact with them and the wider political, economic and social context. It is a theoretical tool which accommodates analysis of both the economy (at household level) and institutional context within which households function.

The use of the SLF thus contributes to the progression within development theory from the 'modernisation model' of the past to an understanding of the multi-level, multi-actor and multi-faceted nature of development. It contributes to an understanding of how mono-functional households are being transformed into multi-functional enterprises. Chambers and Conway (1992) argue that the modernisation paradigm has reached its intellectual and practical limits. This study contributes to the understanding of sustainable livelihoods as a heuristic device that represents a search for new futures and reflects the agency of the rural population. It goes beyond modernisation theory, according to which problems of agriculture were considered 'resolved' by technology.

The study contributes specifically to an understanding of Zimbabwe's political economy, the type of rural livelihoods that can develop in politically charged environments, and how some groups of rural people in Zimbabwe react and behave in an endeavour to survive. This brings to the fore the issue of sustainable development. The use of the sustainable livelihoods framework potentially addresses the deficiencies of traditional approaches to rural development and broadens our understanding of how rural people in marginal areas make a living.

Methodology

The participatory rural appraisal (PRA) methodology, which uses a variety of techniques or tools, was used. Selected were ranking techniques such as preference ranking and scoring, pair-wise ranking. Time trends analysis was also used during the study particularly calendars such as seasonal and historical seasonal calendars. Plenary presentations kick-started the process in all study areas where objectives of the process were explained to people, as well as how the process was going to be handled until the end. Plenary presentations were used for people to understand the process and for them to be involved and participating, and that formed the basis for other methods that followed.

Participants began by identifying different livelihood activities they depended on in their specific community in no particular order of importance. This technique generated basic information about livelihood activities, sources of food for different people, income generated, available support services, opportunities available for both women and men, and how people allocate time for labour and ownership of property, both movable and immovable.

Pair wise ranking was used to rearrange the listed livelihood activities in order of importance. This technique reorganised livelihood activities according to their importance, with the most important at the top and down to the least important at the bottom. Some of the activities were not even accorded a ranking, showing that they were very peripheral to the rural livelihoods of people in that area.

Timelines were used to determine patterns and trends for each livelihood activity listed and prioritised by the community members throughout the ten-year period. Participants easily remembered what happened in 2008 and 2009 by each season and month. The technique generated data on rainfall distribution patterns and how livelihoods were affected, food availability focusing on own production savings and food aid, agricultural production patterns, income generation by local people, health problems, and human development.

Literature Review

According to the United Nations Development Programme:

> Poverty is a human condition characterised by the sustained or chronic deprivation of the resources, capabilities, choices, security and power necessary for the enjoyment of an adequate standard of living and other civil, cultural, economic, political and social rights (UNDP, 1987:23).

Scoones (1998:118) contends that in poverty reduction and livelihood diversification, the household is the basic economic decision-making unit in rural society. For the purposes of this study it is defined as:

> ... a group of people who live and eat together and typically engage in joint economic activity. This group is usually based on kinship, and normally comprised of nuclear or extended family (Scoones, 1998).

Ellis's (1998a:105) studies in India demonstrate that rural livelihood diversification has been promoted in recent years as a rural development strategy for poverty reduction. This diversification happens under conditions and influencing factors particular to each area. Ellis (1998:109) defines rural livelihood diversification as "the process by which households construct a diverse portfolio of activities and social support capabilities for survival and in order to improve their standard of living". This implies that this can happen under normal conditions as well as when facing severe economic and political challenges. Ellis (*ibid.*) points out that a diverse portfolio of activities contributes to the sustainability of a rural livelihood because it improves its resilience in the long run in the face of adverse trends or sudden shocks. His research does not indicate whether the same argument applies under conditions of severe socio-economic challenges and political instability.

Boras (2006:7) argues that rural livelihood diversification in southern Africa is potentially one of the best strategies for reducing poverty, especially among the rural poor. This belief saw an increase in rural livelihood development and diversification interventions in the region, particularly in countries facing political and economic challenges and armed conflict. His study looks at livelihood diversification in post-war Angola. However, it cannot be assumed that the same results would be achieved in rural Zimbabwe, which has not been involved in armed conflict since 1980 and faces different socio-economic, climatic and political challenges.

Chambers (1997:56) argues that responses to poverty are better understood at an individual or community level, as poverty levels vary within a community. In other words, people living in the same village are economically different because they employ different strategies and may possess different levels of potential. Although different macro theories are used to understand poverty reduction strategies and policies, very little attention has been paid, according to Chekole (2006:3), to trying to understand what happens at the micro level in responding to poverty in southern Africa, and particularly in Zimbabwe, under severe socio-economic and political conditions.

If rural livelihood diversification happens under normal conditions, it is regarded as broadly beneficial for the poor and rich alike, reducing poverty among the poor (Ellis,1999). However, Reardon (1992:65) notes that the desperation-led diversification of the very poor may sometimes result from the accumulation-led diversification of the rich, where the poor would want to increase their opportunities of accumulation in an endeavour to catch up with the rich. Such a diversification has challenges as it widens the inequality gap and may not be sustainable in the long run as it may not be supported by maximum access to and control of resources by the poor, as compared to their rich counterparts.

Development agencies complement government efforts to improve livelihoods in rural Zimbabwe in the face of the country's economic challenges. Some of the initiatives in livelihood diversification were initiated by external development agencies, and this study shows how they contributed to livelihood diversification and improvement. For successful reduction of poverty among rural people, it is necessary to understand their levels of access to and control of resources, how external interventions were designed, and the role played by rural people in the interventions.

The capability to diversify income streams is critical for the survival of the rural poor. This is especially true in semi-arid districts which are vulnerable to seasonal and other risk factors. Different groups among the very poor have different methods and strategies of responding to seasonal and annual risk factors under different conditions. As an actor group, they have limited access to and control of assets such as land, finance, education and skills, and possess little or no livestock. Without the capability to produce enough food, the poor are left with only the option to diversify income sources in order to survive and reduce poverty (Nareh and Titi, 1994).

Hussein and Nelson (2008:12-14) observe that diversification is an important strategy by which rural people may work to achieve sustainable livelihoods rather than an end in itself. DFID defines a sustainable livelihood as one that:

> Can cope with and recover from stresses and shocks, maintain or enhance its capabilities and assets both now and in the future, while not undermining the natural resource base (DFID 1999:12).

Chambers (1997:23) observes that a livelihood should be sustainable because it comprises people, their capabilities and their means of living, including food, income and assets – both environmentally sustainable in that it should maintain or enhance the local and global assets on which livelihoods depend, as well as have net beneficial effects on other livelihoods, and socially sustainable in that it should be able to cope with and recover from stresses and shocks and still provide for future generations. This suggests that, whatever types of livelihood poor people engage in, they have to be sustainable to cope with stresses and shocks.

Cole and Carney (1999:15) observe that the concept of sustainable livelihoods was developed after decades of limited success in eliminating poverty and, as a result, new ideas about development emerged. They argue that the concept of sustainable livelihoods was adopted to reduce poverty in the most effective way. Hussein and Nelson (1998) go one step further and point out that, since livelihood diversification is aimed at achieving sustainable livelihoods, the end goal of sustainable livelihoods through portfolio diversification is to reduce poverty. They further show that livelihood diversification operates in conjunction with other strategies that contribute to the sustainability of livelihoods.

Reardon's (1997:49) focus on agricultural intensification as a strategy to combine with diversification makes a useful contribution to the literature with the observation that increased average inputs of labour or capital on a smallholding, either cultivated land alone or on cultivated and grazing land, increases the value of output per hectare. Reardon (1997:53) further argues that the effectiveness of agricultural intensification is affected by market proximity and these markets can help farmers generate farm and non-farm income from a wide range of sources, or in other words, to diversify. A study by Delgado (1989:73-4) in Central Africa concludes that crop and livestock integration is one form of diversification that can also be used in conjunction with non-farm livelihood diversification, a complex strategy that enables the construction of sustainable livelihoods.

In her study of rural Mali, Cavan (1992:234-251) established that livelihood diversification may take place when poor peasants change the composition of their agricultural produce. Hussein and Nelson (1998) concluded too that poor rural farmers or producers with low levels of capital may be able to restructure their production mix more easily than investing in non-agricultural areas. The strategy of crop-livestock integration is one level of livelihood diversification that can help peasants to maintain fertility through incorporation of manure into the soil, and the animals themselves provide other assets and can also act as liquid assets that can easily be sold. This level of diversification helps to build up or maintain agricultural production and reduce risk. This argument differs from a concept of de-agrarianisation that emphasises branching out from agriculture into non-farm economic activities as the main form of livelihood diversification, with diversification within farm activities (crop + animal livelihoods) as secondary and farm activities that can lead to non-farm activities as third.

Change from farm to non-farm activity is a level of diversification, according to Liedholm et al. (1994:177). Many of these non-agricultural activities involve micro-enterprises that generate employment and income in rural areas. Liedhold et al. (1994:144) flag past empirical studies showing that micro-enterprises provide an estimated 20% to 45% of full-time employment and 30% to 50% of rural household income in sub-Saharan Africa. De Janvry (1994) argues that pursuing non-farm activity represents a risk minimisation strategy to achieve basic household subsistence needs. These scholars contribute to the understanding that livelihood diversification is at different levels and this has a bearing in this study. Another crucial point is that, although diversification has different push-and-pull factors, it also has external and internal supports.

Results and discussion

Rural livelihoods in semi-arid districts of Zimbabwe

The overall findings on rural livelihood activities show that crop production and livestock rearing were the dominant livelihood activities during the period under study. The commonly grown crops are cotton, maize, sorghum, cowpeas, millet, rapoko and groundnuts, with watermelons and pumpkins among other supplementary crops. As agricultural production declined, smallholder farmers fell back on increased selling of livestock for survival, in addition to milk production and selling of meat for household consumption. For smallholder farmers with livestock, it became a source of survival during periods of adverse shocks and trends as indicated in timeline analysis findings.

All study areas are conducive to livestock production of both small and large livestock such as goats, sheep, chickens and donkeys. However, in Gokwe and Muzarabani livestock is prone to diseases and populations declined as the government failed to provide dipping chemicals to rural areas. In Mwenezi, both small and large livestock populations decreased due to persistent droughts peculiar to the district. Animals were sold for cash and bartered also for maize grain. During the period of severe food shortages, particularly between 2008 and 2013, selling of livestock in all study areas became a lucrative business for middlemen buyers from urban areas. During these years a single goat was exchanged for 12kg of maize meal, and a beast was exchanged for 50-250kg depending on its size and the district. Barter of livestock had market value calculations based on visual estimations and there were no hard and fast rules for it in any of the districts during the period of food scarcity. Households with small herds sold all their livestock for survival and were left with no assets, increasing their vulnerability.

The government and non-governmental organisations (NGOs) provided interventions to target communities. These interventions targeted the poor and vulnerable groups in each district to increase livelihood diversification in both farm and non-farm activities. Small grain production, vegetable gardening, open pollinated seed varieties, agricultural input distribution, agricultural mechanisation support, vocational skills training, irrigation schemes, small dam rehabilitation, commercialisation of non-timber forest products, establishment of community-based enterprises and food aid have been introduced in semi-arid districts since the year 2005, just after the FTLRP.

The commercialisation of mopane worms during the decade under study saw an increased number of people engaged in the harvesting. This resulted in privatisation of mopane trees. Local authorities now control the way this local resource is marketed to middlemen, who in turn sell to regional and international markets. As a result of the commercialisation, the local authority passed local by-laws to regulate the harvesting and marketing of local products as they are the custodians of all communally owned resources.

The role of natural resources, especially non-timber forest products, became more noticeable during periods of food shortages, particularly the period 2007-2013. Considerable income is generated from various commercialised products such as baobab pulp and oil, marula jam and oil, mopane worms and *masau* jam. Income is used to purchase maize grain and other basic goods for food security and rural livelihoods. Rehabilitation of small dams was an intervention specific to Mwenezi because of limited water sources whilst rehabilitation of irrigation schemes took place in both Muzarabani and Mwenezi. The same districts also benefited from vocational skills training centres established for training youths in skills such as building, welding, carpentry and dressmaking. Based on these prioritised livelihood activities, rural people were able to diversify their livelihood portfolios in a politically charged environment. Although contract labour is not a new livelihood activity in all study areas, it declined during the period under study along, with a decline in commercial agricultural production after the FTLRP.

Gold panning emerged as a growing livelihood activity in both Muzarabani and Mwenezi. There was also gold panning in Gokwe though it was not listed as an important livelihood activity. Poaching was more pronounced in Gokwe and Muzarabani because of the proximity of wildlife reserve areas. Theft emerged as a surprising livelihood strategy, ranked at the middle level in Muzarabani, where it was discussed as a desperate livelihood by unemployed youths. However, theft also took place in all study areas although it was not openly discussed in the other two. As contract workers were made redundant, there was a sharp decline in contract work in all study areas after the FTLRP. Some people engaged in political violence in an endeavour to forcibly take property from others in their respective communities.

Evidence of livelihoods diversification in semi-arid districts of Zimbabwe

The study findings identified three sets of rural livelihood activities. These are traditional activities (crop farming, livestock and contract labour), external interventions (different projects, food aid and buying and selling), and local initiatives (gold panning, wildlife poaching, remittances, theft, harvesting wild fruits). Although these activities responded to the pressures of the period's shocks, they also showed continuity with earlier trends studied by Bryceson (1998) and Berkvens (1997). However, clear differences with other scholars emerged in how external interventions were implemented, how target beneficiaries responded and, most importantly, what local strategies were employed by rural people.

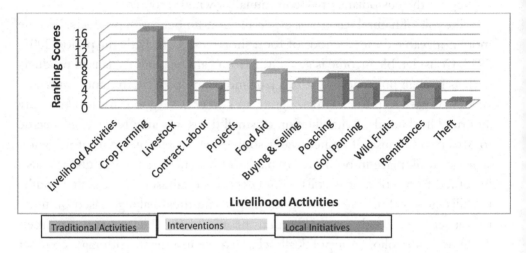

Figure 6.1: Dominant Rural Livelihood Activities in Semi-Arid Districts (Adapted from the livelihood pairwise ranking excercise)

From the bar graph the study shows that crop production, livestock rearing and contract labour (green bars), which are considered traditional activities, form the dominant set. As argued by Berkvens (1997), agriculture is a way of life that rural people do not easily abandon. In other words, there is evidence that, despite the crises of political turbulence, economic hardship and extreme weather conditions in the period under study, agriculture remained dominant. However, there was some branching out from agriculture into non-farm activities and diversification of portfolios in all study areas.

In the sustainable livelihoods framework (SLF), people are at the centre of a network of factors that affect how they create their livelihoods. These factors could be natural resources around them and other assets they have, for example, technology, skills, health status, social networks and infrastructure. Their vulnerability context takes into account wider trends such as global and national economics and shocks such as floods and disease outbreaks, and thus the vulnerability context partly determines people's access to resources. Smallholder farmers, as actors, seem reluctant to completely change rural livelihood activities, despite threats to their output posed by adverse trends and shocks. In the three districts in this study, the natural resources on hand such as land and water lent themselves to agriculture, which may be a major reason for its dominance.

Scoones (1998) argues that engaging in other non-farm activities together with agriculture can be a strategy for reducing risk and this is indeed what occurred in the districts under study-livelihoods diversification did take place. However, sustaining this diversification was threatened by the continuing vulnerability context of political tension, extreme weather conditions and economic hardship. The continued dominance of agriculture in the study areas, despite these challenges, could indicate that attractive non-farm activities such as developing rural industries were not that easily accessible. The study shows that despite a definite de-agrarianisation trend, semi-arid areas remained largely engaged in agricultural production. From another angle the continued dominance of agriculture can be attributed to the large number of external interventions that supported it. In other words, organisations supported agriculture as a livelihood strategy despite how adversely it was affected by exogenous trends such as droughts, diseases and the economic crisis.

The second on the graph category (yellow bars) is intervention activities by the government and NGOs. The interventions on the bar graph indicated as (projects, buying and selling) as per field work findings are in two subcategories, namely agricultural support, off-farm activities the third category is food assistance. In this discussion, projects are unpacked as both agricultural and non-farm support to all study areas.

As argued above, the increase in agricultural support through projects may be attributable to limited opportunities outside agriculture. NGOs as actors wanted an intervention that would be easily accepted and adopted, so they focused on crops that were responsive to the climate and on rehabilitating irrigation infrastructure. In other words, they identified land, dams and irrigation equipment as assets of the smallholders and facilitated their rehabilitation, an intervention that was enthusiastically adopted by smallholders. These farmers were then able to diversify their livelihood portfolios and further increase their asset bases and strategies such as conservation agriculture and adoption of crops suitable for arid areas promoted sustainable land use. The dominance of agriculture was also influenced by government support for smallholder farmers as part of its rural development policy including the promotion of cotton farming. In SLF terms, the mediating role played by external organisations was thus aimed at identifying appropriate strategies for livelihood diversification. This signified a re-agrarianisation strategy in semi-arid districts to counter the decline of agriculture in the face of climatic conditions, political crises, economic sanctions, a general rural to urban migration, shortages of agricultural inputs and the impact of structural adjustment programmes.

Food handouts were aimed at supporting the immediate needs of the most vulnerable people in semi-arid areas. This intervention was an externally fostered survival strategy to avert a famine as agricultural production came to an almost complete halt in some areas during a part of the period under study. As discussed in Chapter 5, this intervention reached the highest number of beneficiaries. Inability to produce enough food in semi-arid areas during the period drove people to diversify but food aid became an external option. Although the sustainability of this intervention is doubtful, it contributed towards food availability. However, the intervention is criticised for suffocating innovation and creating dependency on food aid. The SLF accommodates conflicting outcomes and perhaps it is sufficient to say the short-term gain of preventing starvation was accompanied by the negative consequence of increased dependency on an intervention that is neither sustainable nor long-term.

The interventions also focused on several non-farm livelihood activities captured as projects as well and buying and selling by respondents such as skills training, rural enterprise development and marketing of produced products. These interventions branched out from agriculture to take advantage of natural resources available in semi-arid areas such as non-timber forest products, fish and timber for carpentry products. People therefore remained engaged in agriculture but added new activities to complement it. The increased portfolio of asset combinations indicates successful diversification although sustainability was limited by the vulnerability context. As indicated in previous sections, cash income generated from non-farm activities was usually channelled towards agricultural support, so it can be argued that no one livelihood strategy was adequate on its own. The argument is that changes in agriculture in the decade studied influenced other assets such as social and financial capital and how they were used.

The third category (red bars) on the bar graph constitutes initiatives by rural people as desperate measures for survival. This set represents other locally initiated non-farm activities. Poaching, gold and diamond panning, wood carving, property theft and, lastly, labour migration presented as remittances in the graph are some of the ways people branched out from agriculture as determined by the capability of each household. Access to available natural resources became an opportunity to diversify rural livelihoods in the face of failing crops, inadequate support from other external interventions and increasing vulnerability in an environment characterised by crisis. The cash income generated from this set of livelihood activities was invested in agricultural production. Engagement in these activities depicts rural people as innovators rather than docile recipients of external interventions. Although they received external support, they also initiated their own activities for survival and sustainability.

The combinations of these three categories show that despite the dominance of agriculture in rural livelihoods, it became a component of the largely reorganised set of rural livelihoods that included external interventions and locally based initiatives. Diversification within each identified set of livelihoods is reflected. Within external interventions, households benefited from agricultural support, non-farm activities and food assistance. In agriculture some households engaged in different crop production together with livestock rearing whilst others engaged in contract work. The livelihood activities identified in this study show a complex set of portfolios. Different households diversified differently despite having access to similar resources. The actor-oriented approach acknowledges that different actors respond differently to similar structural circumstances depending on how the operating context has determined their accessibility to livelihood assets. As a result, people as social actors were able to choose from at least two options, and this selection both determined and were determined by the capabilities in each household besides the exogenous trends making up the vulnerability context.

External interventions overlapped with existing agricultural production by providing agricultural inputs, rehabilitating agricultural infrastructure and creating vegetable gardens. Similarly, external interventions in enterprise development and commercialisation of non-timber forest products overlapped with local initiatives by commercialising wild fruit harvesting through technology development, product development and improved marketing, regularising illegal fishing and reducing property theft by creating community income generating projects. In SLF terms, this juggling of assets is mediated through different community level structures and processes and it reflects asset transferability and capital switching by rural people. Switching from agriculture to non-farm activities and back became a survival strategy but the livelihood outcomes were limited by the politically charged environment and the economic meltdown during the period studied.

External interventions played a critical role in aiding local initiatives and reviving agricultural production in semi-arid districts. It can be argued that unaided, agriculture and local initiatives during the period under study would not have supported rural livelihoods to the same levels. The study therefore shows a variety of livelihood activities that were both externally fostered and locally initiated, and the combination contributed to a diversification of portfolios that improved many people's ability to make a living. The changing trend in these various intertwined activities is the increase in externally fostered activities and the role they played in livelihood diversification. It is difficult to analyse the identified livelihood sets independent of each other due to these complex overlaps. The interrelationships between the three sets enabled rural people to survive during the period under study. However, an increased number of interventions do not necessarily translate into greater effectiveness or sustainability because the capability to effectively use the external support depended on each beneficiary household based on its composition in terms of size and the gender, age, health and skills of its members. Some interventions targeted the elderly who could no longer do manual labour. It was not only the operating context that determined access to assets but also the way institutions and organisations mediated the access.

The three sets of livelihood activities identified in this study contributed differently towards people's survival and interventions by NGOs, government and the private sector were different in nature and size. The pie chart below shows that 58% of the interventions came from NGOs, 28% from the private sector and 14% from the government. The chart is an indication of the levels of investment by the government, private sector and NGOs based on the number and size of interventions.

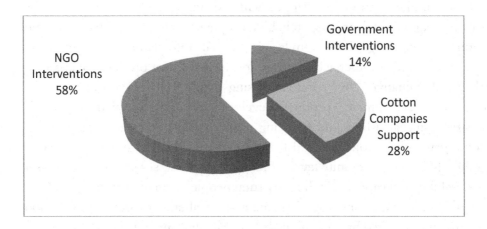

Figure 6.2: Proportion of Interventions by External Actors

NGOs reached a higher number of beneficiary households than the state or cotton companies due to the availability of donor funding. Government support is ranked low because of the economic crisis, targeted sanctions and staff shortages. Although the extent of interventions does not automatically correspond with the level of success of the outcomes, by reaching high numbers of people, the NGO support became one of the major sources of livelihoods despite being ranked behind agricultural production. The following pie chart also shows the total reach of different intervening institutions.

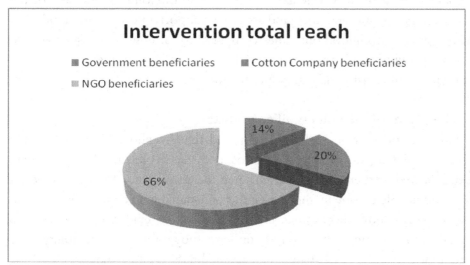

Figure 6.3: Reach of External Interventions

The above pie chart shows that the number of interventions can be linked to the number of people they reach. Of the total households reached by external interventions, 66% benefited from NGOs, 14% from government and 20% from the private sector. It was clear that there was private sector, government and NGO support for agriculture in various ways, making agricultural production, as a traditional livelihood activity, a major beneficiary of external support during the period under study. However, the success of external interventions in improving livelihoods is determined both by their own systemic weaknesses and external threats to their implementation. Despite having an increased number of interventions such as agricultural input distribution, food distribution and rural enterprises development, the politically charged operating context and the economic crisis limited the livelihood outcomes and compromised the sustainability of the activities.

Although diversification does not necessarily lead to improved quality of life, this study found that, based on accumulated assets, households that engaged in agricultural activities and external non-farm support improved their rural livelihoods compared to households that engaged in local initiatives and agricultural production only, although sustainability was limited in both cases. Households that benefited from irrigation schemes only also had better chances because of the long-term and widespread results of the intervention. However, not all crop production, coupled with other activities, resulted in positive livelihood outcomes because under dry land agriculture not all households had good yields. Only households that engaged in successful crop production together with other activities had a better chance of improving quality of life.

Although it is difficult to calculate the livelihood outcomes from each of the activities, agricultural activities and external support interventions tended to show improved livelihood outcomes compared to local initiatives such as gold panning, poaching and wood carving, which involved a number of challenges of illegality, safety risks and difficulties in entry.

The extent of the vulnerability context

Hussein and Nelson (1998:144) contend that livelihood diversification is aimed at achieving sustainable livelihoods, and that people are the first human asset, followed by their capabilities and their means of living. Whatever types of livelihood people engage in, they ought to be sustainable to cope with stress and shocks. This study shows that, although there is evidence of livelihood diversification during the period under study, their sustainability was undermined by the extent of the vulnerability context characterised by economic collapse, climatic challenges, political tension, poor road infrastructure, the remoteness of semi-arid districts, the government regulation of foreign currency use in the country and undeveloped markets, among other factors.

Rehabilitating water sources and irrigation schemes, establishing vegetable gardens, introducing crop production technologies, distributing agricultural inputs and setting up a contract farming system were all attempts to construct sustainable livelihoods, but they were affected by the poorly developed market for the products. Chambers (1994:177) notes that markets for both farm and non-farm products help smallholder farmers to generate income from a wide range of sources.

The study found that, despite having products from a variety of sources, both farm and non-farm, generating income from them was constrained by the limitations of the market, the remoteness of the areas studied, poorly developed roads, distorted prices for goods and services, depleted soils, limited access to education, low wealth status and small household size. This was further worsened by the politically charged environment, stringent market regulations particularly for livestock and grain products, and global economic changes. Smallholder farmers who were closer to the rural centres were slightly more able to diversify their livelihoods than those further from town as the latter could not transport fresh produce to the market in time.

Crop livestock integration was also another diversification strategy adopted during the period under study that was affected by poorly developed markets and this even deteriorated further due to the economic crisis. The opportunities for livelihood diversification fostered by external organisations did not have the institutional and policy support needed to ensure sustainability of the livelihood outcomes. The major livelihood outcomes realised from agricultural production intensification were related to food provision and security, but they failed to build on other assets important for constructing sustainable livelihoods such as financial capital and human capital.

The use of 'open eye' judgment for assessing the value of assets in the barter economy was a major limitation in all semi-arid areas as it distorted the actual value of exchanged assets and goods, usually at the expense of smallholders, as discussed earlier. Although the re-emergence of the barter system played an important role in facilitating livelihood diversification and asset holding by the poor, it failed to facilitate the construction of sustainable livelihoods in the long term.

In the case of non-timber forest products, strict foreign currency regulations by central government constrained income from international markets. For marula and baobab products, there was no ready local market but international markets, whilst for mopane worms and *masau* products, they had a local market that was poorly developed and affected by the political and socio-economic crisis. Although international and regional markets helped build financial capital, the market and the community enterprises were detached and the logistical arrangements for shipping and paying became prohibitive. In addition, although community based non-timber forest enterprises were an important cash income livelihood strategy with potential to generate even more cash income, they were negatively affected by the stringent government monetary policies that prohibited foreign currency transactions without authority from the Reserve bank of Zimbabwe. The study therefore found that the positive livelihood outcomes from the non-farm livelihood diversification strategy were constrained by government policies and regulations. It took a long time for community producers to access the cash payments from international markets and this adversely affected production as people needed quick returns for survival. The following graph shows the total quantity ordered by the market and the total quantities supplied.

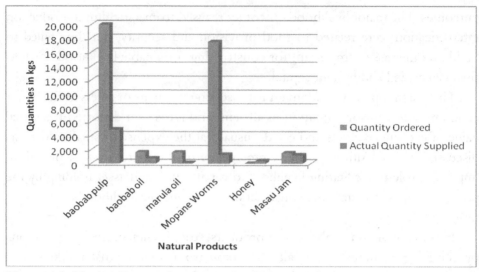

Figure 6.4: Market Demand and Supply of Natural Products

The bar graph shows that the emerging rural industry has viable markets, but producers failed to meet the demand. This failure can be attributed to operational and production challenges, limited capacity by rural producers and technological challenges. The study found that limited production adversely affected the potential for income generation to build the asset base of producers, thus making the enterprise less sustainable. Sustainability was further compromised by high costs involved in production and marketing. Although quantities ordered remained very high compared to quantities supplied, the following graph shows income generated from the little that was supplied was relatively high, indicating the strong livelihood potential in this rural industry if impediments were removed.

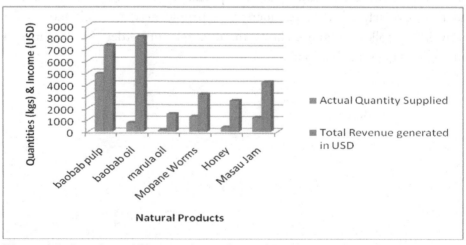

Figure 6.5: Supply and Income from Natural Products

Although the graph shows that there is high income from the sale of limited quantities from international markets, the operational costs, which are almost as high, are not reflected. Once production and shipment costs are deducted, the actual income generated is minimal. Since foreign currency transactions were highly regulated by the central bank, there are levies on foreign currency handling and this reduced income for the community producers even further. Direct payments to communities were also not possible because they have no access to bank accounts and these services are far away from the producing communities. As a result, the construction of sustainable livelihoods from this strategy became constrained. However, challenges related to marketing logistics and late payments resulted in increased consumption of some of the products such as baobab oil and pulp, marula oil and cake, mopane worms and honey.

An analysis of the initiatives by local people, as actors engaging in a wide array of activities to diversify livelihoods, shows that they also fell short of constructing sustainable livelihoods. Chambers (1994:66) argues that, to be environmentally sustainable, a livelihood has to maintain or enhance the local assets on which it depends, and to have net beneficial effects on other livelihoods. Woodcarving, gold and diamond panning contributed to environmental depletion in already degraded semi-arid areas, as discussed previously. Although remittances as immediate outcomes of migrant labour did not cause environmental degradation, the construction of sustainable livelihoods from both cash and material remittances did not take place. Cash remittances were directed towards agricultural production and, in the period studied, crops also succumbed to external trends like the socio-economic challenges and shocks like droughts and floods. Despite having cash, people lost access to agricultural inputs and this meant most of the remittances were directed at meeting basic household needs without building assets. As a result, the complex vulnerability context during the studied period constrained the sustainable construction of livelihoods in semi-arid areas.

Conclusion

The chapter concludes that despite positive outcomes of livelihood diversification in semi-arid districts to reduce poverty, the gains are reversed by the politically charged environment that continues to perpetuate economic melt-down and economic crisis. The sustainability of the livelihood diversification outcomes is very limited and does not last long as the shocks such as drought and climate change are worsened by the socio-economic and political challenges associated with a politically charged environment.

113

Livelihood diversification in semi-arid areas under politically charged environments thus faces sustainability limitations and outcomes are short lived.

References

Lebert, T. (2006). An introduction to land and agrarian reform in Zimbabwe. In P. Rosseet, R. Patel and M. Carvile (Eds.), *Promised land: Competing visions of agrarian reform.* Pretoria: Land Research Action Network.

Liedholm, C. (1990). Small scale industry in Africa: Dynamic issues and the role of policy. *LD' A-QEH Working Papers.* Oxford: Queen Elizabeth House

Lipton, M. (1987). Limits of price policy for agriculture: Which way for the World Bank?. *Development Policy Review, 5*(2), 197-215.

Kappor, I. (2002). The devils' in the theory: A critical assessment of Robert Chambers work on participatory development. *Third World Quarterly, 23,*101-117.

Keeley, J. (2001). *Influencing policy processes for sustainable livelihoods: Strategies for change.* Brighton, UK: Institute of Development Studies.

Kinsey, B., Burger, K. and Gunning, J.W. (1998). Coping with drought in Zimbabwe: Survey evidence on responses of rural households to risk. *World Development, 26*(1), 89-110.

Roth, F. and Gonese, M. (2003). *Delivering land and securing rural livelihoods: Post independence land reform and resettlement in Zimbabwe.* New York: Amazon Books.

Rugube, L. and Chambati, W. (2001). *Land redistribution in Zimbabwe: Five census surveys of farmland transactions, 1996-2000. Broadening access and strengthening input market systems.* University of Wisconsin-Madison, USA.

Chapter 7

Rural Livelihoods Diversification in Marginal Areas of Zimbabwe

Julius Musevenzi

Summary

Rural poverty reduction and income distribution are affected by policies that promote or downgrade alternative income generating activities. Appropriate rural development policy is the entry point for poverty reduction and rural livelihood development in marginal areas. This chapter unravels what has been going wrong in rural development policy in relation to livelihood diversification and poverty reduction. Despite continuous formulation of rural development policy, rural poverty is on the increase as the poor remain underprivileged and increase in number. Marginal areas are confronted with the problem of increasing poverty and insecure livelihoods and rural development policy is not adequately providing answers. Using interviews and focus group discussions with the rural poor in selected districts, the findings show that most rural development policy is not helping the poor by reducing poverty but rather perpetuating their vulnerability. Most policies are a replication of the old and failed and this is not helping either. Livelihood diversification efforts by the poor are frustrated or curtailed by the ill-conceived rural development policy, particularly in areas with limited opportunities. The chapter concludes that not all rural development policies are aimed at poverty reduction and income distribution achieves the desired outcome but, in some cases, constrain the poor.

Introduction

This chapter brings out the policy challenges and problems adversely affecting rural livelihoods diversification and poverty reduction in selected semi-arid districts, namely Gokwe Muzarabani and Mwenezi. The study also brings out the policy inconsistencies and unreliability particularly under politically charged environments, and how they affect livelihood diversification and poverty reduction by the poor. For the past 15 years, rural livelihood diversification and poverty reduction strategies have not yielded positive results due to policy constraints and political interference in some cases. Despite the vulnerability of semi-arid districts to climate change and dry conditions, poor policy development and policy inconsistencies further worsened the vulnerability of smallholder farmers in semi-arid districts and this is the focus of this chapter.

Background and Overview

In the year 2000, the United Nations made poverty reduction the first goal of the Millennium Development Goals to be achieved by 2015 by the international community. Ellis (1998a:61) contends that the high incidence of poverty in southern Africa is a result of a combination of factors including unemployment levels, limited access to resources such as land and capital, unresponsive rural development policies, poor governance systems, urban biased policies that leave rural areas looking less attractive, and economic policies that do not generate economic growth. This argument by Ellis (1998) has been generalised for the southern African region, where poverty is ranked the highest by the World Bank (2006:13). Chambers (1997:56) argues that responses to poverty are better understood at an individual or community level, as poverty levels vary within a community. In other words, people living in the same village are economically different because they employ different strategies and may possess different levels of potential even if they are affected by the same policies. Although different macro theories are used to understand poverty reduction strategies and policies, very little attention has been paid, according to Chekole (2006:3), to trying to understand what happens at the micro level in responding to poverty in southern Africa, and particularly in Zimbabwe, under severe socio-economic and political conditions that determines inconsistent policy development.

Theoretical Framework

The sustainable livelihoods framework (SLF) has a history based in the academic disciplines of anthropology, sociology and geography, and in applied research of governments and aid agencies. Those engaged in agrarian studies justifiably claim a long engagement with rural livelihoods (Batterbury, 2008). Baumann (2000:16) points out that the SLF was not intended to be a sophisticated model for theoretical analysis, but one oriented towards a comprehensive and practically focused understanding of grounded realities that could directly or indirectly inform development interventions. Chambers (1995:321), who introduced the concept of sustainable livelihoods in a 1987 paper, indicates that the SLF approach facilitates a holistic view of what resources, or combination of resources, are important for the poor, including not only physical and natural resources but social and human capital as well.

Scoones (1998:37) shows that central to the SLF is an analysis of the range of formal and informal institutional factors that influence sustainable livelihood outcomes. It helps to show micro-institutions that function daily to mediate access to the combination of resources necessary to maintain the livelihoods of smallholder farmer households. Its strong focus on the processes of negotiation that take place within local and non-local institutions to mediate access to resources makes it useful for analysing how households engage each other and organisations in accessing resources in semi-arid areas of Zimbabwe. Its focus on micro-level outcomes of individuals and households shows how the context might influence poverty outcomes and how policies and institutional processes and structures affect different groups of the poor.

Literature Review

Overview of policy development and rural livelihoods in Zimbabwe

Rural poverty reduction and income distribution are affected by policies that promote or downgrade alternative income generating activities (Arnold, 1998). Reardon (2004:109) and Rukuni (1999:53) note that an appropriate rural development policy is the entry point for poverty reduction and rural livelihood development. Such a policy should create clear institutional ownership for vulnerable groups, invest in sustainable rural financial systems that can reach previously excluded sub-populations of the rural community and encourage increasing investment in the physical and institutional infrastructure necessary to make markets accessible to all. Rural livelihoods in Zimbabwe need to be understood in a historical context that shows changing trends in policy. According to Wright (2000), policy is located in political and bureaucratic contexts. Wright (2000) points to particular histories and the balance of state and society forces as shaping the emergence of any given policy path, and argues that policy is often contested, substantially reshaped or even initiated from a range of places or points between macro and micro levels. This chapter seeks to understand how national policy impacted on semi-arid areas since the government shifted its focus to new resettlement areas since the year 2000. But first, it is important to place post-colonial rural development policies in the context of colonial policy.

Colonial policy and rural livelihoods in Zimbabwe

Colonial marketing policies were highly restrictive, preventing competition, encouraging unidirectional trade and causing low rates of economic growth in communal areas (Bruce, 1990:72). They created barriers to entry and discouraged the emergence of rural markets and private traders. Various marketing and controlling boards were established to control the marketing of agricultural products. The Grain Marketing Board of 1931 controlled maize and the products were increased to sorghum (1950), groundnuts (1952), soya beans (1969) and wheat (1970). Rukuni (1994) shows how the Cotton Marketing Board, established in 1969, had monopoly in the purchase, processing and export of all cotton products. However, of greater concern to Rukuni (1994:68) was the discriminatory producer price policy. The producer prices were set at levels aimed at protecting white farmer producers, whilst prices to urban consumers were subsidised in a bid to keep down wages and buy political favour. In addition, cotton and groundnut farmers, who were largely peasant farmers, tended to be taxed, thereby reducing income to rural peasants and limiting their livelihood options, whereas wheat and other capital-intensive commodities produced by white farmers were heavily subsidised (Rukuni 1994:74). This analysis has helped show that rural livelihoods in rural communities of Zimbabwe remained highly restricted and livelihood opportunities declined due to the highly restrictive policy environment.

Post-colonial policies and implications on livelihoods

Agriculture and the rural sector remain of considerable importance to the Zimbabwean economy today. The success of the agricultural sector, which supports over 73% of the total population in Zimbabwe, hinges on rural policy development. Zimbabwe's agriculture sector is highly dualistic, consisting of the densely populated smallholder sector and a modern, large-scale commercial sector (UNDP, 2002). It is therefore important to analyse the policy shifts that came with the new political dispensation after the transition to the post-colonial era. The government of Zimbabwe (1982:114) stressed that it had a key development policy challenge of promoting re-distributive strategies to reduce the colonial racial inequality and poverty, broaden the base of economic growth and focus on domestic needs, particularly of the poor.

Moyo's (2004:56) analysis of Zimbabwe's post-independence rural development policies shows that they did not change much as they were modelled along the heavily interventionist and essentially inward-looking domestic policy lines that were implemented after the Unilateral Declaration of Independence (UDI) in 1965. Direct controls on imports, foreign exchange, investment, agricultural marketing and prices were maintained. The state intervened extensively in communal area agriculture by putting in place prime movers necessary for an agricultural take-off to serve smallholder farmers. These included setting up parastatals, marketing boards for agricultural products, extension services and easy loan facilities, and providing free seeds and fertilisers (Rukuni, 1994). These early policy reforms combined, led to an agricultural mini-miracle and peasants produced about 60% of the maize and 90% of the cotton in the country between 1980 and 1984. However, in semi-arid communal areas the policies only worked well for cotton production whilst other crops did well in communal areas in non-semi-arid areas.

To Berkes (2003:21) such 'old' policies significantly expanded social investment and government support for smallholder agriculture in Zimbabwe, including land purchases for resettlement of smallholder households that were implemented similarly to the UDI days when there was support for resettled farmers. However, Moyo (2003:26) notes that continued land disparities were also observed in policy development that did not prioritise land redistribution. Large-scale farms enjoyed the same support they enjoyed during the colonial period because they were protected by the Lancaster House Constitution. He contends that, although communal people were supported through the input provision, access to land was the major question that needed to be addressed. This shows that the two parts of the dualistic agricultural system were not equally supported by government policy, commercial farmers benefited at the expense of smallholder farmers despite input support to communal farmers.

Moyo (2004:94) reveals that rural livelihoods in semi-arid areas remained unchanged despite a new political order in 1980. Drinkwater (1989:38-43), in a similar vein, observes a remarkable policy consistency between the colonial and post-colonial eras in terms of actual policies and styles of governance. Despite intensive support to communal areas, the policy pivot remained supporting of smallholder farmers in the same colonially designed, degraded communal areas, albeit with new support services. As a result, departures from the colonial policy were minor and that is why Zimbabwe's agricultural boom lasted for a very short time and was already in decline by 1984.

Moore (2001:23), in his studies of agrarian change in Zimbabwe, observes that despite failures by the colonial state to destroy the worker-peasantry, the new state spent decades attempting to resurrect the colonial master farmer, remould the rural sector and incorporate peasant households into the capitalist mode of production through translocation and resettlement. Colonial agrarian policies played an important part in moulding the rural landscape and have left legacies that continue to shape rural livelihoods and households' behaviour today. This suggests that there were no significant policy shifts to assist the improvement of rural livelihoods after independence in Zimbabwe. Thebe (2010:29-31) concurs and is deeply critical of the continuation of a policy that failed during the colonial period. He argues that the strategy was geared at creating a rural peasantry after the ZANU-PF led government adopted a peasantisation rural development policy no different from the colonial policy.

Impact of the ESAP on rural livelihoods

Mustapha (1999:101) notes that Zimbabwe's adoption of structural adjustment programmes from 1991 was another turning point in rural livelihoods of people in communal areas. Because the state was weakened through restructuring and retrenchment, external players or non-state actors such as international financial institutions (IFI), NGOs, bilateral donors and the private sector such as fertiliser companies, seed companies, civil society actors and even churches began to have greater influence on the state in policy discussions. Bryceson (1999:12-19) shows that the subsequent removal of subsidies on improved inputs such as fertilisers, seeds and chemicals, introduced just after independence in 1980, drastically undermined most peasants' capitalised production and threatened the viability of their market-oriented production.

The adjustment largely dismantled the African marketing boards and parastatals that had serviced peasants' input requirements, enforced commodity standards and provided single-channel marketing facilities and controlled prices. Scoones and Keeley (2000:59) show that it resulted in increased migration reversal from urban to rural areas, creating further crises of lost cash income from urban employment and re-congestion of rural areas. This triggered a huge, unplanned income diversification response in rural communities. Peasants found themselves straddling an active search for viable new income sources and their declining or unsupported subsistence agriculture.

Moyo (2005:167) argues that during the 1990s, the agrarian policies were dramatically redirected by the adjustments with far-reaching anti-poor effects on land use, land markets and land redistribution. The state's retreat from subsidising agriculture was widely supported and private traders were allowed to compete, reversing the late 1980s trends of increased smallholder profitability and affordable food. The state budget contracted, and this led to reduced extension services, input support and credit for smallholders, which eroded farm incomes (Moyo, 2005).

Implications of government policy changes on rural livelihoods in Zimbabwe

Barret (2001:15-17) argues that rural livelihood development policies aim to improve the asset holdings of the poor by endowing them with additional financial, fixed, human, natural or social assets, by increasing the productivity of the assets they already hold, or both. The post-ESAP period was characterised by another policy shift in favour of creating an indigenous black commercial farming class (Sachikonye, 2003, 2005).

Policy questions related to land tenure are central at both national and local levels (Matondi, 2008). Moyo (2005:118) indicates that profound tenurial insecurity in Zimbabwe's communal lands continued during the post-colonial period including the post-2000 period. This has resulted in even lower productivity and unsustainable agricultural practices. Moyo (2005:78) observes that from 2000 Zimbabwe saw a gradual return to a dirigiste and heterodox macro-economic policy framework alongside the execution of extensive land reform in a context of increasing economic decline and international isolation after the FTLRP.

Moyo (2005:67) notes that the government policy transformed after 2000 when the agricultural sector was reorganised through the FTLRP. Despite numerous studies on the effects of the FTLRP, these studies did not reveal how rural livelihoods in dry communities were affected by agricultural policies that were largely focused on large-scale farms. The argument by Matondi (2009) that communal areas remained congested because many beneficiaries came from urban areas was supported by Sachikonye (2003) who gave a statistical analysis showing that in total, only 1.3 million from communal areas and 52 000 from commercial farming areas were resettled on 11 million hectares but there are no exact figures for those who came from urban areas. In terms of policy analysis this is a serious gap because more smallholder farmers remained in communal areas created by the Land Apportionment Act of 1930 than those who were relocated.

Methodology

A triangulation of qualitative research methods was used for the study. Sampling of the target study participants was purposive and convenient. The study purposively targeted officials from various stakeholders as key informants whilst at the community level discussions were held with smallholder farmers who were conveniently mobilised by the local leadership. In-depth interviews were carried out with twelve officers from the Department of Agritex, six officers from the Department of Irrigation and Mechanisation, fifteen officers from the NGO sector (Plan International, SAFIRE, Care International, Mwenezi Development and Training Centre, World Vision, Concern World Wide and LED), three officers from Mwenezi, Muzarabani and Gokwe Rural District Councils and seven councillors. Interviews were also conducted with two officers from the Irrigation Department, one officer from ZINWA as well as 17 village heads and headmen. A total of 12 focus group discussions (four FGDs in two wards per district and FGD with an average number of 15 participants were conducted largely with community members}, particularly

121

small holder farmers to understand their local livelihood diversification, and poverty reduction strategies, interests, perceptions, needs and proposals regarding the national and local level policies. Group discussions produced data and insights into the priorities of each household and community, livelihood activities, policy challenges, constraints and limitations to their livelihood diversification efforts. Participants in FGDs also suggested what they think could be done differently for their communities to reduce poverty and improve food security.

Results and Discussion

Rural livelihood trends in semi-arid districts of Zimbabwe

Study findings show that crop production and livestock rearing were the dominant livelihood activities during the period under study. The commonly grown crops are cotton, maize, sorghum, cowpeas, millet, rapoko and groundnuts, with watermelons and pumpkins among other supplementary crops. However, of all the crops, cotton and maize production trended downwards during the period.

As maize and cotton production declined, small grain and vegetable gardening increased. Smallholder farmers fell back on livestock for survival through increased selling, milk production and meat for household consumption. For smallholder farmers with livestock, it became a source of survival during periods of adverse shocks and trends.

In Mwenezi, both small and large livestock populations decreased due to persistent droughts that were peculiar to the district. Animals were sold for cash and bartered for maize grain in the district in 2008. A single goat was exchanged for 12kg of maize meal, and a cow or ox was exchanged for 50-250kg depending on its size. The study shows that barter of livestock had market value calculations based on visual estimations and there were no hard and fast rules for it in any of the districts during the period of food scarcity. Households with small herds sold all their livestock for survival and were left with no assets, increasing their vulnerability.

The government and donors started increased interventions, and these interventions targeted the poor and vulnerable groups to increase livelihood diversification, in both farm and non-farm activities. Small grain production, vegetable gardening, open pollinated seed varieties, agricultural input distribution, agricultural mechanisation support, vocational skills training, irrigation schemes, small dam rehabilitation, commercialisation of non-timber forest products, establishment of community-based enterprises and food aid were introduced in semi-arid districts since the year 2005, just after the FTLRP.

Mopane worm harvesting and processing for income generation became one of the non-farm activities in which rural people were trained in sustainable harvesting, processing and marketing in Mwenezi district. Harvesting the worms for local consumption is a traditional activity but it was not seen as an important livelihood activity until commercialisation. This resulted in privatisation of mopane trees. Rural District Councils as local authorities control the way this local resource is marketed to middlemen, who in turn sell to regional and international markets. As a result of the commercialisation, local authorities passed local by-laws to regulate the harvesting and marketing of the local products. The local authorities are the custodians of all communally owned resources.

As in Mwenezi, the local authority in Muzarabani placed *masau* under regulation in an endeavour to also benefit from the local communally owned resources. The endowment of dry communities with natural resources or non-timber forest products played a role in the establishment of community-based enterprises for processing of natural products in study areas. Rehabilitation of small dams was an intervention specific to Mwenezi because of limited water sources whilst rehabilitation of irrigation schemes took place in both Muzarabani and Mwenezi. The same districts also benefited from vocational skills training centres established for training youths in skills such as building, welding, carpentry and dressmaking. Based on these prioritised livelihood activities, rural people were able to diversify their livelihood portfolios in a politically charged environment.

Livelihood development interventions in semi-arid districts of Zimbabwe

Small grain production

As indicated by Manyani (2010), the impact of persistent drought in the study period influenced a shift from maize to small grain production in Gwanda. Small grain crops grown are sorghum, millet, rapoko, cowpeas, groundnuts, sunflowers and open pollinated varieties of maize that are more drought and heat resistant. The promotion of small grain varieties aimed to cushion smallholder farmers during drought years. However, the government had no financial support for the programme, and this is the gap taken over by NGOs.

Figure 7.1: Sorghum and Millet crops under irrigation in Mwenezi district
Source: (Musevenzi, August 2015)

NGOs conducted research in semi-arid areas aimed at ascertaining appropriate crop varieties that would guarantee food security in these areas. Since 2005, NGOs introduced and promoted increased production of small grains for food security at the expense of cotton and maize. This became a reversal of a vigorous promotion of maize production in semi-arid areas undertaken since 1980. This previous policy did not take into account the unsuitability of maize varieties in agro-ecological region four. Based on the study on food security the food deficit in most semi-arid areas over the years was worsened by the government's policy focus on increased cotton production as a cash crop at the expense of cereal crops.

Despite increased small grains production, switching people from maize to small grain production was a challenge as smallholder farmers believe in maize production as a staple and food security crop for livelihoods. Berkvens (1997) also found that smallholder farmers in rural Zimbabwe stuck to maize production as a cultural activity that they are used to. Despite efforts to promote small grain production, NGOs were also sceptical about the success associated with its production.

After five years of small grain intervention, each beneficiary household produced an average of 21 bags of white Macia sorghum for consumption. Based on World Food Programme calculations of 10kg of maize meal per person per month, such a harvest provides food security for a household of seven people for nine months, leaving a deficit of three months in a year. It was found out that before the intervention sorghum production levels were very low because not all smallholder farmers produced the crop. The intervention increased small grain output by 60-100%.

Table 7.1: Small Grain Production Hectarage: The Ten-Year Trend in Muzarabani District

Agricultural season	Hectares under sorghum	Hectares under cowpeas	Hectares under maize
2000-2005	Below 200	Below 100	Above 18 000
2006-2008	600	100	19 000
2009-2010	800	300	16 000
2010-2011	1 300	700	14 000
2011-2012	14 151	1 200	10 000
2012-2013	11 954	1 500	7 000
2013-2014	20 000	2 083	5 000

Source: World Vision, 2015

The increase in sorghum and cowpea production is attributed to small grain production advocacy by NGOs and increased free distribution of inputs. NGOs mostly distributed more small grain inputs compared to maize in all study areas. This is reflected by a sharp increase of hectarage in 2008 due to drought predicted in 2007. Based on calculations for an average household of six people, 300kg of sorghum could last for about six months and for about four months for a household of eight people if it is consumed daily with no major alternatives.

Small grains marketing

Despite an increase in small grain production, particularly white sorghum, the most promoted crop does not have a well-developed market in Zimbabwe. Although small grains were meant for food security, people's consumption levels of the product were very low in all study areas. The crop was widely adopted, but it has not filled the food security gap left by maize production. Rural people failed to consume small grains on a daily basis, and as a result people remained with large stocks of white sorghum that could not be sustainably consumed. The option of selling the surplus for cash was not available as there was no market for it. The effort put into the promotion of small grains did not equal the benefits, in other words, it has not reduced food insecurity. The large reserves of white sorghum observed in semi-arid rural communities show that it was an ill-advised intervention that missed its intended objective. Small grains have failed to meet the requirements for improving rural livelihoods in semi-arid districts of Zimbabwe, despite their increased production.

Cotton production under contract farming

Cotton contract farming was a common intervention spearheaded by the cotton private sector. Promoting cotton production in semi-arid areas became a government policy aimed at improving rural livelihoods. This was guided by the export-oriented government policy inherited from the colonial period. The government-controlled cotton production through Cottco until the liberalisation of the sector to private players in 1999. Since 1999 a number of private cotton companies have supported cotton production. This created competition among cotton companies and to counter this, Cottco initiated contract farming in order to guarantee its supply. However, the competition among cotton companies for the product was replaced by the competition to register smallholder farmers as contractors. Contract farming only targets farmers with property they can use as collateral. Monopolisation of cotton inputs after the introduction of contract farming worsened the situation for smallholder farmers as cotton inputs are no longer found on the open market.

Most rural farmers faced funding challenges because they could not borrow from financial institutions as they used to do before the national economic crisis. Although cotton is the major cash crop in semi-arid areas, farmers had no access to inputs and their cotton was sold at low prices. During the 2011-2014 seasons cotton farmers withheld their cotton in protest at prices as low as US $0.33 per kg. Cotton smallholder farmers in all study areas complained that they are subsidising the government and cotton companies instead of vice versa. Cotton hectarage declined in all study areas and this was attributed to food shortages and intensified advocacy by NGOs for increased small grain production for food security. However, during the same period the government encouraged rural farmers to engage in contract farming for improved cotton production to generate cash income for multiple livelihood activities.

The table indicates that there was an increase in cotton production between 2006 and 2010 in all the districts. This was attributed to increased cotton buyers and contract farming that was slowly being adopted by farmers. During the 2011-2012 cropping season, support to cotton smallholder farmers was cut back and the number of farmers who produced cotton declined, resulting in lower production.

Table 7.2: Declining Cotton Production Hectarage in Muzarabani District

Agricultural Season	Hectares Under Cotton		
	Gokwe	Muzarabani	Mwenezi
1999-2003	16 000	10 000	1 000
2004-2005	16 000	12 000	3 000
2005-2006	17 000	14 000	7 000
2006-2007	19 000	16 000	9 000
2007-2008	35 000	29 000	11 000
2008-2009	27 000	21 000	15 000
2009-2010	22 000	21 000	16 000
2010-2011	17 000	17 000	17 000
2011-2012	13 000	15 000	11 000
2013-2014	11 000	13 000	9 000
2014-2015	10 000	7 000	5 000

Source: World Vision, Care and CWW 2015

NGOs also supported the contract farming model targeting the young and newly married poor farmers without collateral since 2009. Their policy saw the emergence of free cotton farmers who were trained in the use of conservation technologies that improved their production and could choose who they sold to. However, this undermined the hold that contracting companies had on the smallholders. In 2009 the Agricultural Marketing Authority (AMA) passed new legislation requiring all cotton farmers in Zimbabwe to register with a cotton company of their choice before they could access inputs. Farmers had to register every year and pay a registration fee of about US$50, but this has contributed to a sharp decline in cotton production as smallholder farmers could not afford the fees. This legislation was aimed at reducing competition among cotton companies. As this was made mandatory, it prompted NGOs to assist free cotton farmers to produce cotton without being tied to any particular company and sell it to buyers of their choice and increase profit. However, the number of free cotton farmers who benefited was very low (157 households in total in the three districts).

Cotton marketing

Despite its downward trend, cotton remained the largest cash crop in all semi-arid areas under study. Prices for cotton are determined on the international market, therefore, price bargaining by smallholder farmers is limited. With a fall in the global price, smallholder farmers do not get the expected returns, prompting many to partially abandon cotton farming as a non-viable crop. Cottco is the largest local market for cotton. However, the market for cotton remained very poor despite the establishment of cotton buying centres in all study areas. Cotton prices have ranged over the past decade from US$0.30 to US$0.85 per kg depending on its quality and grade which are determined by the buyer. Smallholder farmers complained that, in most cases, they are forced by desperate poverty to sell their cotton at low prices.

Small irrigation schemes development

This intervention revolves around the rehabilitation of colonial irrigation infrastructure that became derelict. In most cases, the intervention is a joint venture between the government and NGOs because the government owns the infrastructure. NGOs financed and managed development and crop production, but the government owns the old and new infrastructure through its community structures.

Figure 7.2: Rehabilitated canals with irrigation water in Manjinji irrigation scheme in Mwenezi (Musevenzi August 2014)

After independence in 1980, productivity in small irrigation schemes in semi-arid districts declined due to poor management of irrigation equipment and other resources as well as poor management systems and structures. The government policy in the early 1980s did not value small irrigation schemes and irrigation infrastructure in semi-arid districts collapsed due to increased focus on prime land crop production on large commercial farms. In 2006 the

128

government realised the importance of small irrigation schemes in rural semi-arid districts of the country for improved food security but had no financial resources to rehabilitate them. This is the gap covered by NGOs.

Three irrigation schemes, namely Dinhe, Murove and Manjinji, lay idle for almost over 15 years after the infrastructure collapsed in 1994. This intervention rebuilt infrastructure such as canals and night water storage dams, improved crop production and moreover, established a viable, community-based irrigation scheme management committee and systems to ensure sustainable management.

Farmers accessed pieces of land within the irrigation schemes whilst more than 7 000 farmers indirectly benefited through labour provision and access to the products of the labour for food security. Crop production focused on maize, cowpeas, beans, wheat, vegetables, cabbage and tomatoes for both food security and income generation. Mariwo (2010), in her study of women's empowerment in rural Mutoko district, east of Zimbabwe, argues that NGOs create stereotypes of rural women as vulnerable and so come up with petty projects that fail to address the real issues of women. However, community participants indicated that the intervention resulted in crop diversification and livelihood improvement in semi-arid areas affected by perennial droughts and severe food deficits. It was observed that some farmers are doing well compared to others in the scheme. Some competent farmers increased their maize harvest to the extent that they could exchange surplus for both small and large livestock. This indicates some degree of livelihood diversification.

Changing policy and institutional arrangements

Institutional arrangements and policies were discussed to ascertain how they enabled or inhibited rural livelihood development during the past fifteen years. Rural people at community level were critical of the institutional arrangements and some of the policy changes that restricted their livelihood options. This resulted in increasing emergence of informal livelihood activities.

The centralisation of rural district councils

Rural District Councils are run according to the Rural District Councils Act of 1980 (amended in 1981, 1982, 1989 and 2005) as it is applied to communal lands. Although the Rural District Council has authority and general powers relating to the administration of a local government authority and legislation regarding rural development, this has not happened as expected, particularly during the past decade or so. Since independence there have been important institutional changes that broadly favour decentralisation to ensure development of the neglected former tribal trust lands. However, this was accompanied by lack of financial autonomy, limited influence of the local authorities over their development plans, limited powers of taxation and the dominance of the central government, limiting the enabling role of this institution to foster rural development in the communities in its jurisdiction.

Selected policies and district by-laws affecting livelihoods in Zimbabwe

The Grain Marketing Act of 1991

The Grain Marketing Board (GMB) was established to regulate the production, storage and marketing of all cereal and non-cereal agricultural products in the country. The act empowers the relevant minister to declare any agricultural product a controlled product, and the GMB to declare a monopoly over the purchase and sale of any controlled product. The GMB's extensive powers have had different implications for the livelihoods of people in semi-arid districts of the country during the past years.

In 2007 most smallholder farmers growing maize were unable to sell it because it was declared a controlled product due to national food shortages. The GMB's powers include setting prices and forbidding people to store any grain declared a controlled product, as well as outlawing the sale of the product to any institution other than the board itself. Transactions among rural people were restricted to two bags, or 100kg. All purchases in excess of this were confiscated by the police. This exacerbated the food crisis in most semi-arid areas. The GMB's absolute control over the movement, sale and purchase of the nation's staple diet made it a powerful weapon, and one which was abused to control the livelihoods of rural people in semi-arid and marginal areas.

Reviving and Tightening the Agricultural Marketing Act of 1989

The Agricultural Marketing Act of 1989 regulates and administers the marketing of all agricultural products. It is mandated to promote contract farming of crops considered strategic by the minister. In September 2009, the Agricultural Marketing Authority (AMA) amended the Agricultural Marketing Act to focus more closely on cotton products. The move was intended to regulate the entire cotton production chain from crop production to marketing as a way to encourage the growth of the cotton industry in the country again after its decline in the latter half of the decade. However, changes made benefited the cotton companies at the expense of the cotton smallholder farmers.

New policies were aimed at stopping contracted farmers from selling undeclared cotton to companies offering higher prices. Through the AMA, uniform cotton prices were introduced across the board by different cotton buyers and free farming was abolished as smallholder farmers now had to register with a cotton company to access inputs. The amended act thus empowers contracting companies to manipulate cotton farming at the expense of poor rural smallholder farmers. Bringing together cotton contracting companies weakened the position of smallholders in terms of price negotiation and, as a result, NGOs encouraged smallholder cotton farmers to concentrate more on food security production as cotton became less viable.

Rural institutional arrangements and implications for rural livelihood development

The institutional focus of sustainable livelihoods framework enables the location of policy spaces where useful interventions can be made. This institutional analysis further shows how people in semi-arid areas secured access to resources they needed to construct sustainable livelihoods. The study established that various formal and informal institutional factors influenced the extent of livelihood diversification and sustainability of strategies adopted by people in a politically charged environment. At a local level, micro-institutions function on a day-to-day basis and mediate access to the combination of resources necessary to maintain livelihoods. At the district level institutional structures both enabled and inhibited livelihood diversification and construction of sustainable livelihoods.

In politically charged environments, local institutions and institutional arrangements become more centralised and politicised. For example, the local institutions became a vehicle for patronage as well as a conduit for silencing dissenting voices against the then-ruling ZANU-PF, whose legitimacy had waned during the period under study. Its role of gatekeeper in all development work in the districts constrained both the operations of existing NGO interventions and the number of organisations as some NGOs were denied entry. The ZANU-PF government feared that an increased number of NGOs would increase the dissemination of the 'regime change' agenda that would encourage people to vote for the opposition. To control NGOs, the Rural District Councils tightly monitored and regulated their operations in each community.

Institutional arrangements became more politically oriented, they also contributed to increased social differentiation based on political affiliation, ethnic identities, familial networks and religion connections. Local institutions determined who accessed land, inputs and other services and resources important for livelihood diversification and sustainable construction of livelihoods. Small minority tribal and ethnic identities such as the Tonga, the

131

Tavara, the Shangwe, the Pfumbi and partly the Shangani were largely excluded from the FTLRP as they were labelled 'politically incorrect'. Moyo and Yeros (2005) similarly argue that through the operations of local authorities in semi-arid districts the FTLRP reconstructed ethno-regional identities in land holding and a new class formation was created aimed at establishing black capitalist farmers from the favoured tribes and new peasant farmers through the re-peasantisation A1 resettlement scheme model. This meant that marginalised tribes largely remained in degraded semi-arid areas that were remote and climatically challenged, with poor infrastructure.

The mutual suspicion between government and NGOs adversely impacted on the extent of diversification and sustainability of rural livelihoods. As a result, potential investment in semi-arid areas of Zimbabwe was withdrawn. Had these various development agencies been freely allowed to support rural communities, the livelihood outcomes and extent of livelihood diversification and improvement could have been different.

Implications of policy development on rural livelihood diversification and improvement

In the context of the politically charged environment of Zimbabwe of the past fifteen years, public pronouncements by political leaders became policies for development. They were not written and approved as per the linear policy development procedure, and their implementation process was not well thought through. As a result, policy development constrained rather than facilitated improved rural livelihoods in semi-arid areas. Policy development in the period under review favoured particular interest groups which did not include the rural poor. Structural and policy changes thus constrained and limited human independence, innovation and creativity as local people adopted different non-farm activities in partial shifts from agricultural production. To a great extent, policies created from announcements made during political rallies were pushed through for authorisation, without adequate analysis to understand how they would enable or inhibit rural development and impact on different social groups of people in a particular area. As a result, uncertainty affected rural people as they adopted various livelihood strategies to construct sustainable livelihoods.

Livelihood diversification and improvement was influenced and constrained by the institutional arrangements in study areas. The formal and informal institutional arrangements were heavily politicised and militarised, to the extent that relations between the government of Zimbabwe and NGOs were constrained by mutual suspicion. Government interference and surveillance of individual people and of the operations of NGOs increased as simultaneously its grip on local institutions was tightened. This limited the potential of rural development in all study areas. Policy development was transferred from the legislature to ZANU-PF as a political party and there was no separation between ZANU-PF as a political party and the government. This became a hindrance to livelihood diversification and rural development in all study areas. The politically charged environment distorted policy development and the functionality of institutional arrangements, thus impeding the construction of sustainable livelihoods.

Conclusion

The chapter concludes that rural livelihood diversification in semi-arid districts aimed at reducing poverty is adversely affected by poor policy development that is characterised by inconsistency, lack of innovation and originality. Policy development procedures are not followed and, as a result, fail to respond to the rural development challenges in semi-arid districts. The livelihood diversification outcomes are affected by poor policy development under a politically charged environment. Livelihood diversification in semi-arid areas under politically charged environments thus faces policy constraints and limitations that inhibit access to resources for maximum diversification.

References

Ahmed, I. and Lipton, M. (1989). Impact of structural adjustment on sustainable rural development. *IDS Working Paper 62*.

Barret, C. (2001). *Heterogeneous constraints, Incentives and income diversification strategies in rural Africa, London:* Edinburgh University Press.

Baterbury, S.C.E. (2002). *Top-down meets bottom-up: Institutional performance and the evaluation/monitoring of the EU's SME policies in Galacia and Sardinia* (Unpublished DPhil Thesis). University of Sussex

Baumann: (2000). Sustainable livelihoods and political capital: Arguments and evidence from decentralisation and natural resource management in India. *ODI Working Paper 136*. London: ODI.

Bebbington, A. (1999). Capitals and capabilities: A framework from analysing peasant viability and rural livelihoods and poverty. *World Development, Great Britain: Elsner Science*, 27(12), 2021-2044.

Berkes, F., Colding, B. and Folke, F. (Eds.). (2003). *Navigating social systems: Building resilience for complexity and change.* Cambridge: Cambridge University Press.

Berkvens, R. (1997). Backing two horses: Interaction of agricultural and non-agricultural household activities in a Zimbabwean communal area. *Working paper 24*. Leiden: Africa Studies Centre.

Berry, R.A (1989). Agricultural and rural policies for the poor. In M. Lepert Richard and H. McLeod Susan (Eds.). *Government policy and the poor in developing countries,* Toronto: University of Toronto Press.

Chambers, R. (2004). Poverty and livelihoods: Whose realities count? *IDS paper 347*. Brighton: IDS.

Chambers, R. and Conway, G. (1992). Sustainable rural livelihoods: Practical concepts for the 21st century. *IDS Discussion Paper No. 296*. Falmer Sussex: Institute of Development Studies.

Chaumba, J., Scoones, I. and Wolmer, W. (2003b). New politics, new livelihoods: Changes in the Zimbabwean lowveld since farm occupations of 2000. *SLSA Research paper 3*. Brighton: IDS.

Chapter 8

Harurwa: For Food Security and Sustainable Livelihoods in Nerumedzo, Bikita District

Elmond Bandauko and Johannes Bhanye

Summary

Harurwa is an insect found in Nerumedzo in Bikita. The whole value food chain of harurwa is associated with traditional and customary beliefs which sociologists and anthropologists have not adequately examined. As a forest resource, harurwa contributes significantly to the lives and livelihoods of the people of Nerumedzo and nearby communities in Bikita District. The local community has gone to commercialise the commodity to the local market, especially at Nyika growth point and in major towns and cities. The additional revenue from such sales is used to buy farm inputs that also boost their agricultural productivity, hence food security. The Jiri forests in Nerumedzo are of religious significance to the surrounding communities and they play a significant role in the conservation of natural forests. The wild forests are a major natural resource for rural livelihoods. This chapter explores the ecology and management of harurwa for sustainable livelihoods in Nerumedzo, Bikita. We adopt an interpretive inductive approach. We draw information from secondary literature, archives, newspaper articles and perceptions from informal discussions with community members. We apply the interface between ecology and the sustainable livelihoods framework as our basis for analysis. We argue that harurwa continues to play an important role as a source of livelihoods for the people of Nerumedzo. The sociological and cultural beliefs associated with harurwa also continue to be a leading factor in environmental conversation of the forests. However, our analysis also reveals that ecological sustainability is under threat due to unstainable forest harvesting techniques, gradual changes in cultural practices and loss of traditional values. With minimal barriers to entry into both the collection and trade of harurwa in Nerumedzo, coupled with an increasing incidence of poverty in the area, overexploitation is currently increasing while selective harvesting is decreasing. The chapter recommends sustainable harvesting practices of harurwa to be developed and implemented.

Introduction

The United Nations projects that there will be about 9 billion people living in the world by 2050. This development exerts massive pressure on the capacity of food production and presents a major threat to food security (Food and Agricultural Organization of the United Nations, 2016). Researchers have proposed various strategies to improve food security and reduce environmental impact on food supply (Burchi and De Muro, 2016). In this regard, FAO has proposed the promotion of insects as a viable option to feed both humans and animals (van Huis *et al.* 2013). This is mainly because edible insects provide significant nutritional benefits (protein, vitamins and amino acids), and reduce the environmental footprint stemming from food production. It is further argued that edible insects provide more sustainable economic opportunities, especially to disadvantaged communities (van Huis *et al.* 2013, Han *et al.* 2017). In many societies, insects are not only considered as food or feed but also medicine and spiritual symbols (van Huis *et al.* 2013). However, conservation policy can often fail to integrate biological and cultural conservation (Correal *et al.* 2009). Giving an example from the African continent, De Prins (2014) notes in her review of *Edible insects: prospects for food and feed security*, that there is a conflict of interest between those who protect the tropical biodiversity and those who have the ingenuous wish to improve the agricultural economy in Africa (De Prins, 2014, pg. 1). This chapter examines the ecology and management of *harurwa* for sustainable livelihoods in Nerumedzo in Bikita District. Our main research question for this study is: To what extent does *harurwa* contribute to sustainable livelihoods at the same time conserving natural ecosystems? Other sub-questions include: What local structures exist for ecological management of forest resources like *harurwa*? What options can be adopted for sustainable management of this resource in Nerumedzo? We apply an interpretive inductive approach. This is a qualitative study that draws largely from secondary literature, newspaper articles and perceptions from informal *harurwa* traders at Nyika Growth Point. The following section characterises the case study, followed by a literature review. This will lead into the results, discussion and concluding remarks.

The Case Study: Nerumedzo Community in Bikita District

Nerumedzo community is administered under Chief Mazungunye. The Headman is Nerumedzo. Nerumedzo is in Bikita District in Masvingo Province. It is about 30 kilometres south east of Nyika Growth Point. Administratively,

Nerumedzo is in Ward 15 of Bikita District. According to the Census of 2012, the population size of this ward is about 6 662 (Census ZIMSTATS, 2012).

The major educational facilities include Nerumedzo Primary School and Machirara Secondary School. Households from Nerumedzo rely heavily on subsistence farming and informal trading activities at Nyika Growth Point. The local community practice small scale irrigation farming where crops such as wheat are grown. Vast tracts of the area are characterised by red clay soils. The local communities grow drought resistant crop varieties such as rapoko, sorghum and finger millet. Nerumedzo is in agro-ecological region IV, which receives 450-650mm of rainfall per year, and endowed with natural timber forests. This region is also characterised by seasonal droughts and is unsuitable for crop production without irrigation (Mandima, 1995). Tambara rural service centre provides the community with their basic commodities such as mealie meal, salt, sugar and others. For health services, Nerumedzo rely on the nearby Silveira Mission Hospital. Boreholes and deep wells are the major sources of water in Nerumedzo. Nerumedzo is highly mountainous, with thick forests, locally referred to as the '*machiri Jiri'*. The forests have wild fruit trees. The area is renowned for its vast forest resources including wild fruits and edible insects.

Literature Review

The literature review focuses on the livelihood framework, forest resources and their contribution to rural livelihoods as well as the ecology and management of locally available natural resources. These concepts form the basis upon which our analysis of the Nerumedzo case is based on the livelihood strategy of a rural household. The livelihood approach (de Sherbinin *et al.* 2008; Soltani *et al.* 2012) is used in this chapter as a conceptual framework describing the livelihood activity choices (Nguyen *et al.* 2015) and the factors determining these choices (Nguyen *et al.* 2010; Wunder *et al.* 2014). A livelihood is defined as the capabilities, assets, and activities of a means of living (Ashley and Carney, 1999). A livelihood comprises the assets (natural, physical, human, financial and social capital), the activities, and the access to these (mediated by institutions and social relations) that together determine the living gained by the individual or household." (Ellis, 2000, p.10). A livelihood is sustainable when it can cope with and recover from stresses and shocks and maintain or enhance its capabilities and assets both now and in the future, while not undermining the natural resource base (DFID, 1999). When applied to developing countries, a rural household in this framework is considered the basic decision-making unit regarding production and consumption (Ellis, 2000). In most developing countries, the livelihood of a rural household is linked to environmental resources since the income from agriculture and other sources might not be adequate (Nguyen *et al.* 2015). The sustainable livelihood framework includes three closely connected components: livelihood platforms, livelihood strategies and livelihood outcomes (see Figure 8.1). The livelihood platforms consist of environmental resources as part of the natural capital (Van den Berg, 2010) and household capital (Ellis, 2000). The natural capital is defined as the natural ecosystems available to the household and provides a flow of valuable ecosystem goods and services (Turner and Daily, 2008). However, the household might not legally own the respective land, even though it can extract certain types of goods from this capital. In several developing regions, forest and water resources are open access or communally owned (Angelsen *et al.* 2014). The household therefore does not have full control over this capital, but only the limited right to use it (Nguyen, 2008, 2012). The household capital is classified into physical capital (e.g., tractors), human capital (e.g., education), financial capital (e.g., remittances), and social capital (e.g., social network integration). Brown *et al.* (2006) argue that these different types of capital are platforms for a household to choose its livelihood strategy as a combination of assets and activities. A household can allocate its assets to different activity choices, for example, extraction of environmental resources (e.g., collecting forest products and fishing), agricultural production (e.g., crop production and livestock rearing), non-farm self-employment (e.g., cottage industry or small-scale trade), and permanent or temporary off-farm wage employment. Each livelihood strategy selected by the household leads to a set of livelihood outcomes such as the sustainable or unsustainable use of environmental resources (Nguyen *et al.* 2015).

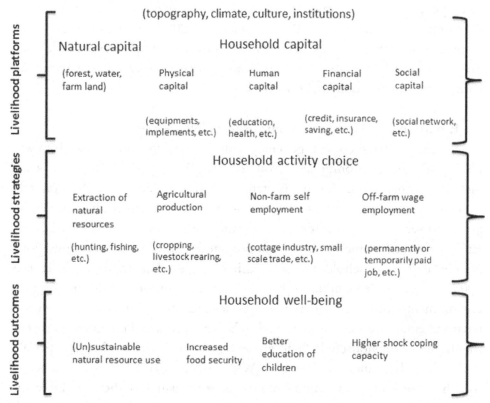

Physical and socio-economic infrastructure

(topography, climate, culture, institutions)

Livelihood platforms

Natural capital   Household capital

(forest, water,   Physical   Human   Financial   Social
farm land)   capital   capital   capital   capital

                       (equipments,   (education,   (credit, insurance, (social network,
                       implements, etc.) health, etc.) saving, etc.)   etc.)

Livelihood strategies

Household activity choice

Extraction of   Agricultural   Non-farm self   Off-farm wage
natural   production   employment   employment
resources

(hunting, fishing, (cropping,   (cottage industry, small   (permanently or
etc.)   livestock rearing, scale trade, etc.)   temporarily paid
                 etc.)   job, etc.)

Livelihood outcomes

Household well-being

(Un)sustainable   Increased   Better   Higher shock coping
natural resource use food security education of   capacity
                                    children

Figure 8.1: A Conceptual Framework for analysing livelihoods (de Sherbinini *et al.* 2008, Ashely and Carney, 1999)

Forest resources and their use in rural communities

Harurwa is just but one by-product of natural forests in Zimbabwe. In this section, we discuss the relationship between forest resources and rural livelihoods, environmental income as part of rural livelihoods and the ecology and management of these resources.

Forests and rural livelihoods

Harurwa do not exist in isolation. Rather, mountain forests play a significant role in rural livelihoods. Wild insects are a by-product of forests. Literature suggest that several disciplines, including the environmental, conservation, economics and development fields appreciate that forests and forest products add to the well-being and, at times, the very survival of millions of rural poor throughout the world (World Bank, 2002, Kaimowitz, 2003, Sunderlin *et al.* 2005). In developing countries forest products are a crucial component of the livelihoods of most rural households and a lower, although not insignificant, proportion of urban households (Shackleton *et al.* 2007). Rural households rely heavily on natural resources. Meta studies indicate that as much as 20–25% of rural people's income may be derived from environmental resources in developing countries (WRI, 2005, Vedeld *et al.* 2007). Kamanga *et al.* (2009) argue that forest resources help alleviate poverty among rural households. Forest resources are also an important source of environmental income particularly among poor rural households.

Environmental income as part of rural livelihoods

Environmental income is generally defined as the income earned from wild or uncultivated environmental resources (Angelsen *et al.* 2014). It does not include income from forest plantations and agricultural fields. Naturally generated forests or surrounding water systems providing readily harvestable goods or services are sources of environmental income (Sjaastad *et al.* 2005). Environmental income can be very important for rural low-income households who have little household capital for other livelihood alternatives (Cavendish, 2000). A clear understanding of how low-income households depend on their environment is fundamental in shaping policies aiming to safeguard and develop environmental assets for these households. Environmental income may sustain the livelihood of households and act as a safety net against shocks especially during periods of income shortages (Wunder *et al.* 2014). The dependence of rural households on environmental income is mediated by the availability and mobility of household capital under various specific physical and socio-economic factors (Babigumira *et al.* 2014). A better understanding of the factors determining the environmental dependence of rural households may help to formulate rural development strategies aimed at economic development and nature conservation (Clements *et al.* 2014, Thondhlana and Muchapondwa, 2014).

Ecology and Management of Forest products

Forest management practices are not identical to natural disturbance, but forestry professionals are able to mimic natural disturbances in many ways through the use of silvicultural practices (Nyland, 1996). For example, recent advances in forest ecology research have revealed that many of the natural forest types are adapted to periodic cycles of landscape-scale disturbance such as by wildfires. Understanding of some of these processes has resulted in the application of harvesting practices and/or regimes that address issues of sustainable forest management. We focus on harvesting methods and traditional management systems these are more applicable to the case of Nerumedzo.

Harvesting of non-timber forest products

Scholars have argued that products that are seasonally available, such as fruits, do not require harvesting limits and that, provided no damage is done to the trees during harvesting, the impact of fruit removal is minimal (Shackleton and Clarke, 2007). However, harvesting of bark for various products including medicine, rope fibre and for making beehives can be highly destructive and result in increased tree mortality (Chidumayo *et al.* 1996). Several methods for reducing the negative impacts of bark harvesting have been proposed and tested, notably by using improved harvesting methods that prevent ring barking and reduce fungal infestation and the use of leaves to obtain medicinal products instead of bark (Geldenhuys *et al.* 2006).

Traditional management systems

Traditional management systems or local institutions play a crucial role in the management of locally available natural resources. A study conducted by Campbell, Luckert and Scoones in Jinga and Matendeudze villages in Mutambara communal area in the eastern Zimbabwe reveal the role of traditional institutional structures in regulating the use of local resources. In both villages, there are traditional institutional structures. The traditional chief for both villages is Chief Mutambara, and both village headmen are of his lineage. The study indicates that in Jinga, the chief, through the headman and three aides, makes the rules and passes them down to the villagers, with the deposition of violators by aides through the hierarchy. These controls are said to be very effective such that only warnings have been issued to offenders without need for fines (Campbell, Luckert and Scoones, 1997). Most of the conservation practices that are used today have been in place as long as anyone can remember, although a few additional rules have been introduced. The existing practices and rules include prohibiting the cutting of live trees for household cooking, dry wood and off-cuts from poles, crafts and other implements used for firewood, sale of firewood and poles without permission is prohibited, cutting of wild fruit trees and certain special trees is not allowed, permission for brick making is granted by the village leader and people are only allowed to lop branches rather than cut entire trees for brick burning, when cutting trees for a permitted purpose, people should selectively cut from within the woodlands, rather than clear-cutting. This applies to the use and harvesting of wild edible insects. The quantity harvested can also be largely monitored. Control of use is also sometimes governed by traditional cultural practices. In Zimbabwe, trees growing scared forests such as Jiri in Nerumedzo may not be felled for fear of spiritual misfortune (van Rijsoort, 2000).

Results

We compile and discuss results based on livelihoods interpretation of *harurwa*, commercialisation of *harurwa*, role of traditional institutions in conversation and emerging threats to sustainability in Nerumedzo community.

Livelihood interpretations of harurwa

Some studies indicate that *harurwa* is an important source of rural livelihoods in Nerumedzo community (Sithole and Muchapondwa, 1999). *Harurwa* is regarded as an important food source. This resource contributes to local economies and household food security in Nerumedzo, Bikita. They are not only sold widely in the village markets, but they have managed to penetrate urban markets. Community members raise income which they can use to supplement their food supplies, especially during drought periods. Zvidzai *et al.* (2014) argue that *harurwa* an important source of income in parts of Zimbabwe. When harvested and stored appropriately, the edible stink bug or *harurwa* has the potential to be an important source of nutrients in the diets of Nerumedzo community which is often dominated by cereals that may lack some essential amino acids and nutrients. Aside from their nutritional and environmental benefits, experts see considerable opportunity for edible insects to provide income and jobs for rural people who capture, rear, process, and transport and market insects as food. These prospects can be enhanced through promotion and adoption of modern food technology standards to ensure that the insects are safe and attractive for human consumption. *Harurwa* contribute greatly to rural incomes. Most of the people from this area sell *harurwa in* the nearby growth point, Silveira Mission, other rural centres and to areas as far as Harare. A small packet of *harurwa* is sold at $1 dollar. One dollar may seem small for urban dwellers, but it is a significant amount given the high poverty levels in the rural areas. Informal discussions with *harurwa* traders at Nyika reveal that a seller can make an average of $10 per day. These sales are usually used to complement household basics such as sugar, and meeting other family needs like paying school fees. Though insects like *harurwa* are unlikely to make major contributions to the world's food supply in the near term, but the idea that insects might help overcome hunger, food insecurity and malnutrition is not as farfetched as it might first seem. Insects offer significant advantages in food production, especially when compared with traditional livestock production. Realising the commercial or economic potential of edible forest insects like *harurwa* must go hand-in-hand with one or more of the following: 1) increased production of wild edible insects through expansion or intensification of the harvests, 2) adoption of forest management practices to enhance productivity, 3) steps toward insect ranching and domestication.

Commercialisation and barter trade

During the drought period, *harurwa* can be exchanged for food products such as mealie-meal. One of the *harurwa* dealers, Jacob Zhou had this to say:

> Most areas where the insects are found are inaccessible by road. During the harurwa season I go to these areas with grain and other commodities and do barter trade. For a 10kg of mealie meal, I get a bucket of the insects... (Sithole, 2012).

Barter trade is therefore contributing to the reduction of rural poverty given the multiple roles that *harurwa* play in the provision of food and income generation. *Harurwa* play a critical role in terms of food security as well as socio-economic well-being of the rural communities. Another women vendor at Nyika Growth had this to say about her *harurwa* business:

> My son, these harurwa really helps us. Now there is a very big drought and we sometimes go to people who had better harvests and exchange with maize. With this money you have given me through the sale of *harurwa*, I will buy sugar for my children at home and life goes on).

The above statements indicate that the local community is benefiting greatly through the commercialisation of *harurwa*. The commodity is sold to both local and external markets, hence income is generated to sustain household livelihoods.

The role of tradition institutions in conserving the Jiri

Like any other rural community, Nerumedzo has its own local traditional structures to manage the use of natural resources. In Nerumedzo community, there exists what are referred to as the *harurwa* policemen. These are responsible for ensuring that traditional rules and regulations are adhered to so as to ensure preservation of the forests for sustainability. Those who violate the tradition of the land are usually brought before the chief's council. Moreover, the people in the community usually hold traditional ceremonies to honour their ancestral spirits they believe are the owners of these indigenous resources which sustain their livelihoods. The organisational structure for the management of the forest resources derives from the locally known and accepted myth that the forest is home to the then four eyed Nerumedzo ancestor, who is believed to have been murdered by his own people. The traditionally inspired management system by the Nerumedzo people is applicable in those areas where traditional beliefs and practices are still upheld, and there are many such places where spirit mediums command the respect of the people. In the past, fear-based traditions sufficed for sustainable environmental management, but as communities develop, knowledge-based adaptive management where the benefits of biodiversity and ecosystems are acknowledged will be needed to prevent environmental degradation and ensure the survival of stinkbugs and associated indigenous plants and animals.

The forest resources have several socio-economic benefits to the rural households in Nerumedzo area. The local people thus attach traditional and cultural beliefs in conserving the forests. The Jiri is considered sacred. There is a general belief among the Nerumedzo villagers that there are certain practices that are not allowed in these areas. These include smoking, cutting down of trees, unauthorised exploitation of the indigenous resources. The local communities believe that these sacred forests actually belong to their "ancestral spirits". In the past, the Nerumedzo Community was confronted by a serious tragedy when *harurwa* failed to appear as a result of failure to respect tradition. Moreover, the violation of the above-mentioned rules and restrictions by an individual will result in serious charges by chiefs and other traditional leaders. In terms of government policy, the National Museums and Monuments of Zimbabwe (NMMZ) is working tirelessly to declare the sacred forests in Nerumedzo a national heritage site because of the importance of *harurwa*, which is found in the forest (Siamonga, 2014).

Value chain of harurwa (indigenous food system)

The *harurwa* insect has its own value chain in the indigenous sense. For example, the value chain starts right from the ritual ceremonies, then harvesting, to processing or preparation, storage and finally marketing or commercialisation (see Figure 8.2).

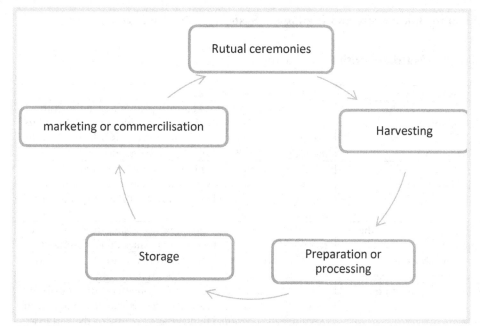

Figure 8.2: The Value Chain of Harurwa (Indigenous Food system)
Source: Authors (2015)

Figure 8.3: Harvesting and Processing Of Harurwa

Threat to Biodiversity and Ecological Systems in Nerumedzo

Table 8.1: Matrix of critical observations

Key Aspect	Critical Observation
Role of Traditional values and norms	Traditional values and norms play a pivotal role in the conservation of the sacred forests. People are not allowed to cut down trees. The spirit of Nerumedzo is believed to be in the forest and is responsible for its protection.
Commercialisation and Barter Trade	Harurwa is being sold to boost rural incomes which can be used to buy supplementary food supplies, hence food security. Harurwa can be exchanged with other goods such as maize meal and chickens.
Organisation of the community	Nerumedzo has a traditional leadership structure that is responsible for upholding cultural values in the community.
Livelihoods interpretation of Harurwa	Harurwa has significant contribution to the livelihoods of the people of Nerumedzo community.
Government policy	The National Museums and Monuments of Zimbabwe (NMMZ) is working tirelessly to declare the sacred forests in Nerumedzo, a national heritage site because of the harurwa in the forest.

Discussion

This chapter has discovered that indeed the sustainable livelihoods Framework (SLF) is applicable to the case of *harurwa* in Nerumedzo. There are transforming structures such as the traditional leadership structures with cultural norms and values to uphold in Nerumedzo. The structures regulate the use of natural resource base, in this case the *harurwa* or stinkbugs. The key aspects of the framework such as social capital, physical capital, financial capital and natural capital reflect very well in the Nerumedzo community. Social capital is being created when people do exchange deals and financial capital is generated through the marketing and commercialisation of the commodity while natural capital depicts the vast forest resources in the area. These include improved food security, reduced vulnerability to hunger and drought, improved well-being and more income being raised to supplement the available food basket. However, the SLF fall short when it fails to include critical aspects such as the spiritual capital being enjoyed by the people of Nerumedzo. It is therefore critical to modify the model so that it can actually accommodate such issues in the indigenous food systems in Zimbabwe.

Religious groups are of the view that the harvesting and consumption of *harurwa* is associated with rituals and spiritism which they do not believe. Such groups do not consume edible insects, hence face hunger amidst plenty. It is therefore critical to harmonise tradition and modernity through evidence-based researches which can inform the making of policies and decision-making by communities. The market of *harurwa* has not been fully broadened to reach the international and regional markets. It is against this notion that the government and other stakeholders should explore alternative ways of promotion, marketing and advertising of *harurwa* so that the rural households can be able to generate higher incomes which they can use to boost their food security since *harurwa* is a seasonal commodity. The traditional methods of natural resources management concur with modern ones such as those advocated for by the Environmental Management Agency (EMA). What needs to be done is to harmonise whatever legislation exists for the sustainable management of resources found in indigenous forests. Communities with similar forest resources also need to draw lessons from the Nerumedzo case study. There is need for awareness training so as to educate people of the social, economic and environmental benefits that can be derived from insects such as *harurwa*.

Table 8.2: Key Constituents of the Sustainable Livelihoods Framework and Ways They Can Be Enhanced

Capital/Asset	Key Constituents	Ways to Revamp/Enhance the assets
Physical capital	Infrastructure (roads, rail etc.)	Rehabilitating roads to improve accessibility to the markets
Financial capital	Income	Lining the harurwa harvesters to the wider markets
Social capital	Social networks, relationships between humans	The need for recognition of possible tensions between different 'social capitals' e.g. between the modern and traditional social capitals.
Human capital	Human skills	Research and Development, training the community on marketing and advertising
Natural capital	Natural Resources such as forests, land, sea and air	Policies and strategies that enhance natural resource management
Political capital	Goodwill of politician and policymakers	Political will to introduce policy reforms
Spiritual capital	Moral and psychological beliefs and practices of a society	Recognising moral beliefs key aspects of human welfare and life.

Conclusion

This chapter has explored the contribution of *harurwa* to sustainable rural livelihoods in Nerumedzo community. Our findings reveal that environmental income is a significant contribution to household income and a sustainer of household food security. The level of environmental resource extraction is influenced by the human, physical, social, and financial capital, and by the shocks and village characteristics. Our findings confirm the notion that rural households are highly dependent on environmental resources for their livelihoods, even though the level of dependence differs. Despite their significant contribution, forests in Nerumedzo are under threat due to unsustainable harvesting practices. Given the importance of environmental resources to household income and the fact that the extraction is mainly undertaken in open access areas, we recommend that the access to environmental resources should be effectively regulated in order to prevent their over-extraction. This will promote sustainable use of natural resources.

References

Adams. W. M. (2006). The future of sustainability: Re-thinking environment and development in the twenty-first century. Report of the IUCN Renowned Thinkers Meeting, 29-31 January 2006.

Allison. E. H. (2010). Potential applications of a 'sustainable livelihoods approach' to management and policy development for European Inshore Fisheries. *School of Development Studies*. Norwich: University of East Anglia.

Barrett, C.B. (2002). Food security and food assistance programmes. Gardner, B.L. and Rausser, G.C. (EdS.). *Handbook of Agricultural Economics Volume 2*, Part B, pp.2103-2190

Bayliss-Smith, T. (1991). Food security and agricultural sustainability in the New Guinea Highlands: Vulnerable people, vulnerable places. *IDS Bulletin*, 2(2), 5-11.

Bookchin, M. (2005). *The ecology of freedom*: The emergence and dissolution of hierarchy. Oakland: AK Press.

Bookchin, M. (2007). What is social ecology? From social ecology and communalism. Oakland: AK Press.

Clay, E. (2002). Food security: Concepts and measurement. FAO Expert Consultation on Trade and Food Security.

Conway, G.R. (1985). Agro ecosystem analysis. *Agricultural Administration*, 20(2), 31-55.

Conway, G.R. (1987). The properties of agro ecosystems. *Agricultural Systems* 24(1), 95-117.

DFID. (1999). *Sustainable livelihoods guidance sheets*. London: DFID.

Durst, B., Johnson, D.V, Leslie, R. N. and Shono, K. (2010). Forest insects as food: Human fight back. *Proceedings of the Asia-Pacific Resources and their potential for development.* Bangkok: Food and Agricultural OrganisOrganisation (FAO).

Ellis, F. (2000). *Rural livelihoods and diversity in developing countries.* Oxford: Oxford University Press.

Environmental Defenders Office. (2009). Ecological sustainability: The purpose of the sustainable planning act. Available online: http://www.edonq.org.au/documents/ Fact_Sheets_(Active)/Planning%20-%20Overview/11.03- Factsheet2%20(Matilda).pdf (accessed 31/01/2017)

FAO. (2000). The state of food insecurity in the world. Rome: FAO.

FAO. (2008). An introduction to basic concepts of food security. Available on http//www.foodsec.org/docs/concepts_guide.pdf (Accessed 28/02/15).

Holling, C.S. (1973). Resilience and stability of ecological systems. *Annual Review of Ecology and Systematics,* 4(2), 1-23.

Ignowski, E.A. (2012). Two essays on food security in Zimbabwe (Unpublished MSc thesis). Agricultural and Applied Economics in the Graduate College of the University of Illinois at Urbana-Champaign, Urbana, Illinois.

Musundire, R., Zvidzai , J.C. and Chidewe, C. (2014). Bio-active compounds composition in edible stinkbugs consumed. *International Journal of Biology,* 6(3), 36-45.

Pangaribowo, E.N., Gerber, N. and Torero, N. (2013). Food and nutrition security indicators: A review. Available online: https://www.econstor.eu/bitstream/10419/88378/1/773397795.pdf

Siamonga, E. (2014). Stinkbugs that saved a forest from deforestation. Available online: www.chronicle.co.zw. (Accessed 02/06/15).

Sithole , Z. (2012). Harurwa: Insects boost rural incomes. Available online: www.thezimbabwean.co. (Accessed 27/05/15).

Sithole, M. and Muchapondwa, B.N. (1999). *Disaster risk reduction (DRR) through harvesting encosternum delegorguei insect (Harurwa) in Nerumedzo, Bikita district, Zimbabwe.* Water Academy of Science, Engineering .

Thin, N. (2002). *Social progress and sustainable development.* Bloomfield: Kumarian Press.

Food and Agricultural Organization of the United Nations. (2016). Insects for food and feed. Available from URL: http://www.fao.org/edible-insects/en/ (Accessed 26 October 2017).

Burchi, F. and De Muro: (2016). From food availability to nutritional capabilities: Advancing food security analysis. *Food Policy,* 60(4), 10–19.

van Huis, A., Van Itterbeeck, J. and Klunder, H. *et al.* (2013). Edible insects. Rome, Italy: Food and Agriculture Organization of the United Nations.

Han, R., Shin, J.T., Kim, J., Choi, Y.S. and Kim, Y.W. (2017). An overview of the South Korean edible insect food industry: Challenges and future pricing/promotion strategies. *Entomological Research*, 4(7), 141–151.

De Prins, J. (2014). Book review on edible insects: future prospects for food and feed security. *Advances in Entomology*, 2(1), 47–48.

Correal, C., Zuluaga, G., Madrigal, L., Caicedo, S., Plotkin, M. and Kuhnlein, H. *et al.* (2009). Ingano traditional food and health: Phase 1, 2004–2005. In: Kuhnlein, H.V., Erasmus, B, Spigelski, D. (Eds.), *Indigenous people's food systems: The many dimensions of culture, diversity and environment for nutrition and health* (pp. 83–108). Rome: CINE/FAO.

Chirwa: W., Syampungani, S. and Geldenhuys, C.J. (2008). The ecology and management of the Miombo woodlands for sustainable livelihoods in southern Africa: The case for non-timber forest products. *Southern Forests: A Journal of Forest Science*, 70(3), 237-245,

Rijsoort, J. (2000). *Non-timber forest products (NTFPs): Their role in sustainable forest management in the tropics.* Wageningen: National Reference Centre for Nature Management, International Agricultural Centre.

Campbell, B.M., Luckert, M. and Scoones, I. (1997). Local-level valuation of Savanna resources. A case study from Zimbabwe. *Economic Botany*, 51(1), 59-77.

World Bank. (2002). A revised forest strategy for the World Bank Group. Washington DC: World Bank.

Kaimowitz, D. (2003). Not by bread alone forests and rural livelihoods in sub-Saharan Africa. In T. Oksanen, B. Pajari and T. Tuomasjakka (Eds.), *Forests in poverty reduction strategies: Capturing the potential* (pp. 45 – 63). Torikatu:

Sunderlin, W.D., Angelsen, A., Belcher, B., Burgers: , Nasi, R., Santoso, L. and Wunder, S. 2005. Livelihoods, forests and conservation in developing countries: an overview. *World Development*, 3(3), 1383 – 1402.

Shackleton, C. M., Shackleton, S. E., Buiten, E., and Bird, N. (2007). The importance of dry woodlands and forests in rural livelihoods and poverty alleviation in South Africa. *Forest policy and economics*, 9(5), 558-577.

Kamanga: , Vedeld: and Sjaastad, E. (2009). Forest incomes and rural livelihoods in Chiradzulu District, Malawi. *Ecological Economics*, 6(8), 613 – 624.

World Resources Institute (2005). The wealth of the poor: Managing ecosystems to fight poverty. Washington, DC: WRI.

Vedeld: , Angelsen, A., Bojö, J., Sjaastad, E., and Berg, G. K. (2007). Forest environmental incomes and the rural poor. *Forest Policy and Economics*, 9(7), 869-879.

Halloran, A., Vantomme: and Hanboonsong, H. (2015). Regulating edible insects: The challenge of addressing food security, nature conservation, and the erosion of traditional food culture. *Food Security, 7,* 739-746.

Nguyen, T.T., Lam, D., Bühler, D., Hartje, R. and Grote, U. (2015). Rural livelihoods and environmental resource dependence in Cambodia. *Ecological Economics,* 1(20), 282–295.

Wunder, S., Börner, S., Shively, G. and Wyman, M. (2014). Safety nets, gap filling and forests: A global-comparative perspective. *World Development,* 6(4), 29–42.

Soltani, A., Angelsen, A., Eid, T., Naieni, M. and Shamekhi, T. (2012). Poverty, sustainability, and household livelihood strategies in Zagros, Iran. *Ecological Economics,* 7(9), 60–70.

Ashley, C. and Carney, D. (1999). *Sustainable livelihoods: Lessons from early experience.* London: DFID.

de Sherbinin, A., VanWey, L.K., McSweeney, K., Aggarwal, R., Barbieri, A., Henry, S., Hunter, L.M., Twine, W. and Walker, R. (2008). Rural household demographics, livelihoods and the environment. *Global Environmental Change,* 1(8), 38–53.

Brown, D., Stephens, E.C., Ouma, J.O., Murithi, F.M. and Barret, C.B. (2006). Livelihood strategies in the rural Kenyan highlands. African *Journal of Agricultural and Resource Economics,* 1(5), 21–36.

Angelsen, A., Jagger: , Babigumira, R., Belcher, B., Hogarth, N.J., Bauch, S., Börner, J., Smith-Hall, C. and Wunder, S., (2014). Environmental income and rural livelihoods: A global-comparative analysis. *World Development,* 6(4), 12–28.

Turner, R.K. and Daily, G.C. (2008). The ecosystem services framework and natural capital conservation. *Environmental Resource Economics,* 3(9), 25–35.

Chapter 9

Peace, Democracy and Social Justice in Zimbabwe since 1890

Paul Goronga

Summary

The issue of land distribution in Zimbabwe is complex and has remained controversial since independence. The study argues that the socio-economic causes of the land conflict in Zimbabwe can be traced back to the pre-colonial era and these hinged on the question of social justice. This study, therefore, sought to demonstrate that democracy and peace cannot be achieved without ensuring social justice. It focused on the socio-economic imbalances that have bedevilled the country and proffers measures of managing these conflicts effectively. The country used to be the main source of food for southern Africa but now faces challenges of meeting its own food needs. The study used a descriptive survey approach and data is qualitatively presented and quantitatively transformed into tables and graphs. The research instruments used were interviews and questionnaires, and these were employed to collect data from a random sample of sixty participants. Document analysis complemented the data collected through interviews and questionnaires. Ethical considerations were taken into account. The findings of the study indicate that representation of the ordinary people and accountability of land reallocation need to be improved. The study recommends reassessment of gender issues, citizenship and consideration of high-density residents in the land redistribution if further conflicts are to be reduced. The study concludes that national healing is necessary to address historical imbalances and human rights issues committed over the past century.

Introduction

After independence in 1980, Zimbabwe's main economic sectors, particularly agriculture, remained in the hands of the minority white farmers, one percent of the white population owned seventy percent of the arable land. This was part of the Lancaster House Agreement in 1979 which involved the United States of America and Britain. In this agreement Britain had promised to subsidise the buyout of these farmers but did not provide funds to pay them (Palmer, 1990:1). As a result, most Africans remained marginalised until the situation became unbearable. The war veterans invaded the white farms in the year 2000 in what came to be called the 'Third Chimurenga'. This chapter seeks to explore whether peace and democracy are attainable amid social injustice. The first section traces the history of the land conflict in Zimbabwe and subsequently examines how the issue can be resolved. Finally, the conclusions are drawn from the findings of the discussion.

The main objective of this chapter is to help Zimbabweans to achieve democracy and freedom from exploitative and oppressive regimes. The chapter seeks to identify and analyse the cause of land conflict by tracing the history of colonialism in Zimbabwe. It is also hoped that it will stimulate debate among academics, political and community leaders. The research questions are:

- What is the nature of the conflict in Zimbabwe?
- Why are there so many protracted social, economic and political conflicts in the country?
- Do we have effective mechanisms to manage these conflicts in this country?

Methodology

The descriptive survey has been selected to help in providing answers to the questions of how, what, when, where and who was associated with the land conflict in Zimbabwe. The qualitative approach establishes the source of the land question (Babie 1983) from the colonial era up to present. Interviews were conducted to determine how the communities around Chinhoyi experienced oppression in Zimbabwe. This research used sixty political and community leaders from a possible total of two hundred leaders in Mashonaland West Province. Shumbayaonda (2006:74) suggest that the sample size for surveys should be more than thirty percent of the total population. Simple random sampling was used in Coldstream, Chikonohono, Alaska, Mhangura and Murombedzi area. In as far as data collection is concerned the researcher used self-administration to conduct interviews and questionnaires to community leaders in Chinhoyi and those surrounding the urban centre. Data was then qualitatively processed and summarised into tables and graphs. Ethical considerations were taken into account by using pseudonyms since this is a politically sensitive issue.

Background of the Study

For about one hundred and fifty years, land has played a vital role in the history of people in Zimbabwe. When put to good use, it has been a source of life and sustenance, hope, freedom and redemption. But where humans have been unable to make use of it fruitfully, they have experienced curses, exploitation, dispossession, disillusionment, captivity, and even death (Bakare, 1993: 1). From the biblical story, when Cain murdered his brother Abel, the Lord cursed him from the land, which had his brother's blood (Genesis 4: 11-12). Cain became a wanderer and a vagabond on earth. To exploit someone is to take unfair advantage of them. Exploitation can be transactional or structural. In the former case, the unfairness is a property of a discrete transaction between two or more individuals. A pharmaceutical research firm that test drugs on poor subjects in the developing world might be said to exploit others in this sense. Exploitation can also be structural, a property of institutions or systems in which the "rule of the game" unfairly benefit one group of people to the detriment of another. Some feminists have argued that the institution of traditional marriage is exploitative in so far as it preys upon and reinforces pernicious forms of inequality between men and women (Sample, 2003: Ch 4). Dispossession is the act of depriving someone of land, property or other possessions. During colonisation in Zimbabwe millions of black farmers were dispossessed. The black population was deliberately marginalised by a system of state managed repression, segregation and violence. Disillusionment is a state of being freed from belief, conviction, idealism or illusion. In other words, disappointment is when you realise that something you thought was good is not as good as you believed it was. Captivity is the state of being confirmed or forced submission to control by others. Consequently, when Nehanda Charwe Nyakasikana organised revolts against the hut tax imposed in 1894, in what became known as the first Chimurenga or second Matabele war, she was captured and hanged in 1897. In China, peasants pay about 40% to 50% of their farm produce in rent to landowners (Bakare, 1993: 1). On the other hand, in India, the Muslim and Hindu ruling elite also demand about a third to a half of the crops from peasants. The ruling elite also demand about a third to a half of the crops from their peasants. The ruling elite not only depend on the landless to work their land but also to carry out their corvee projects. Peasants are often obliged to work for the ruling class for so many days a week, and sometimes even for longer periods, especially when there is crop failure caused by drought or other natural disaster. The great majority of the political elite exploit the energies of the peasantry to the full, while depriving them of all but the necessities of life (Lenski, 1984: 266). The indigenous people have been marginalised for a long time before and after independence. Although a lot has been written about the land question, new perceptions continue to trickle in today.

Precolonial importance of land in Zimbabwe

It is necessary to have a look at the precolonial period to trace the issue of land conflict in Zimbabwe. The history of Zimbabwe is marked by a series of wars of resistance against foreign invaders. The first resistance occurred in 1572 against the Portuguese under Francisco de Barreto. It took two Zimbabwean kings (Mutapa and Changamire), in an alliance, to fight the enemy. The Portuguese were defeated in 1693. Zimbabwe experienced relative peace for the next 150 years. There were isolated attacks and excursions from some hunters and land speculators, but they were too insignificant to warrant a war. It was not until the 1880s that the country was faced with a new invasion, this time from British colonialists (Bakare, 1993: 40).

The Ndebele King, Lobengula, was misled into signing a mining 'concession' which effectively granted Cecil Rhodes the right to occupy Zimbabwe (Douglas, 1984: 182). The British government was thereby persuaded to grant a Royal Charter which delegated the functions of government in this region to Rhodes' British South Africa (BSA) Company (Oliver and Fage, 1988: 164). The area of present-day Zimbabwe and Zambia was ceded to the company in 1891 and named 'Rhodesia' in 1895. Settlers, many of whom had been urban South Africans in search of gold, demanded land and the labour to work it. This sparked wars which left the Shona and the Ndebele people with enormous casualties (Oliver and Fage, 1988:193, Palmer and Birch, 1992). Conflict between white ruled Mashonaland and the independent black state of Matabeleland culminated in the Anglo-Ndebele war of 1893-94 which added Matabeleland in the British South Africa Company's territories (Douglas, 1984:184). The settler helped themselves to the best land by dispossessing the original inhabitants and pushed them out into less fertile areas (Douglas, 1984:137). The indigenous population had to pay rent and taxes to the BSA Company of what remained of their land and property. A louse policy of setting aside reserves for Africans following the South Africa policy began in the 1890s but became regularised and intensified in the 1920s. In 1922, the settlers voted to run the country (by then Southern Rhodesia) themselves with only limited supervision by the British Government. Southern Rhodesia became a self-governing British colony the following year (Douglas, 1984:184).

The Land Apportionment Act of 1930 'allocated fixed reserves – generally poor, remote and inadequate to the African people (Douglas, 1984: 137). The alienated lands of Africans became 'European areas' (Elich, 2002). During the subsequent 30 years the new government concentrated all its policies on the promotion of further white settlement and consolidation of its power and economic predominance (Oliver and Fage, 1988:189). Through immigration, the number of white settlers increased from 80 000 to 220 000 from 1945 to 1960 (Palmer and Birch, 1992).

Up to the 1950s there was wholesale forced removal of African people to make room for white farming (Cliffe, 2000:36). Black people continued to be forced from their land right up to the 1970s (McGreal, 2002). While labour was thereby 'reproduced' in the African reserves, now re-labelled 'communal areas' (CAs), competition in the market from African smallholders was prohibited (Clife, 2000: 36, Jane and Jones, 1997). The older generation who are still alive have passed some of these painful memories to the younger generation.

The Struggle for Majority Rule (Second Chimurenga)

On November 11, 1965, the settler regime declared unilateral independence from the British government. This was done to prevent majority rule, a movement sweeping the rest of the continent of Africa, particularly in southern Africa. Neighbourhood countries like Malawi and Zambia had already attained their independence. The so-called declaration of independence was intended to give settlers unlimited powers to safeguard their political power and to maintain the control of the Africans. According to Palmer (1990: 166), "the number of landless peasants increased while the number of landed settlers increased. It is against such a background of the impoverishment of the African peasantry in Rhodesia that the remarkable prosperity enjoyed by many Shona farmers in the early years of the century was ended by a combination of factors". Bakare (1993:44) argues that "to be a peasant is bad enough, but to be a landless peasant is to be like a ship without a rudder destined to destruction". Prior to the declaration of independence, the government intended to give settlers unlimited powers to safeguard their political power and to maintain the control of Africans. In addition, a series of repressive land acts had been passed one after another, to keep Africans in the designated reserves in the same period. Poverty and a sense of hopelessness were becoming unbearable among them (Bakare, 1993: 44).

When Zimbabwe attained independence in 1980, the country inherited a strikingly unequal racially distorted agricultural system. Approximately 6,000 white commercial farmers owned 15.5 million hectares of 47% of the country's agricultural land, while 8000 black small – scale commercial farmers owned or leased 1,4 million hectares, and 700,000 peasant households occupied 16,4 million hectares under communal tenure (Shaw, 2003:78). Between 1980 and 1999, there was a consensus that these were inequalities should be redressed, but in a way that would avoid damaging Zimbabwe's economically crucial commercial farm sector (Shaw, 2003:78).

The Importance of Land to Africans in Zimbabwe

Bakare gives several meanings of the term "land" in Zimbabwean culture. These meanings contribute to an understanding of it as a cultural reality. He says that "land" may mean:

> A community or territory. People may identify themselves with the *dunhu* (land) they come from. For many Zimbabweans *kumusha* (home) means a village, district, province, or country. Land (home) therefore, is a place of connection with mother earth, where one's roots are, where one's umbilical cord has been buried, where one's ancestors are deposited, a place of connection and orientation (Bakare 1991:54).

Sometimes people often identify themselves with the land they come from or were born in. For others, land may mean an allocated plot on which to build a house or a field for farming purposes, or an inherited piece of land reserved for special purposes, such as a burial site. Consequently, land includes mountains, hills, trees, birds, animals, and even air and weather.

The quote above shows how Zimbabweans are attached to the land. On the other hand, for Rhodes and his Pioneer Column, inspired from early childhood by traditional legends such as Robin Hood and his band of merry men, there was nothing morally wrong with the idea of fighting for land, even if it was land already belonging to others. Robin Hood is a heroic fugitive in English folklore who was a highly skilled swordsman. Alongside his band of merry men in Sherwood Forest and against the Sheriff of Nottingham, he became a popular folk figure in the late Middle Ages. He continues to be widely represented in literature, film and television (Dixon, 2006). The British South Africa Company's desire, under Rhodes' leadership, to invade Zimbabwe to occupy it and plunder its mineral resources was within the context of British culture, and an acceptable thing to do (Richardson, 1984:40). Apparently, the white settlers showed signs of egocentricism and arrogance as they invaded the country. The term *'egocentricism'* implies that settlers were self-centred, they had little regard for beliefs and interests of the indigenous people.

The removal of Africans from their traditional communal land was not seen as terrible thing by the settlers, indeed, the African traditional concept of ownership was taken advantage of. Communal land had been neither fenced nor plots clearly marked, for the British unmarked land meant that it was not owned. Eviction exercises were carried out without compensating the Africans for the loss of their homes. No transport was offered to carry the dispossessed or their belongings to the newly designated reserves which were sometimes as far as 150 kilometres away. The evacuees walked to their destination like refugees fleeing a battle front (Richardson, 1984:40). This explains why some of the indigenous people still have bitterness against the white settlers even up to this day.

As a commodity, land was marketable and classified as cheap or expensive. Settlers were not bound to the land in the same way as Africans. They stood over it, exploiting it and later abandoning it when its mineral wealth was depleted (Bakare, 1991:51). Bruggemann reminds us that land has its own rights over human beings and even its own existence. "To treat it as a mere commodity is to fail to understand and appreciate its original purpose as a gift from God" (Bruggemann, 19: 64). I concur with Bakare that the principal thread of Zimbabwe's history must do with the history of land, land as a home which has to be protected against invaders, where access to land is a birth right worth fighting and dying for.

Most Zimbabweans still have bitter memories about the war and an individual or regime which deprives them of it by amassing land is regarded as the people's enemy. Brueggemann (1977: 61) says: "Only the landed are tempted to forget. Only the well-off and seemingly satiated are tempted to forget the history of barrenness and slavery, of hunger and manna, of gifts and promises kept beyond all human expectation". Apparently, some of the white settlers never seem to comprehend how the Africans suffered and remained marginalised before and after independence.

The Policy of Reconciliation

Soon after 1980 general election victory by the Zimbabwe African National Union Patriotic Front (ZANU-PF), a policy statement on reconciliation was made by the then former Prime Minister of Zimbabwe, Robert Gabriel Mugabe. The statement was made to avoid scaring the white settlers, particularly large-scale farmers, most of whom were aware of the unjust land tenure system they had created in the country (Bakare, 1991:58). The white settlers feared retaliation and were therefore reassured by the new government that no revenge would be taken against them. The past was to be forgotten and buried, and a new era ushered in where all persons, regardless of colour or creed, would live together equally and in harmony. What this statement achieved in real practical terms was to allow the settlers on large farms to remain where they were, the majority African population to continue in their overcrowded reserves, and the newly established elite to consolidate its position, thereby further depriving the landless peasants of their livelihood (Bakare, 1991:58). The new black ruling elite also benefitted because its position was consolidated. According to Bakare

(1991:58), "it has joined hands with the settlers as it has amassed large tracts of land for itself". This means that the poor people remained oppressed but from different masters.

It is interesting to note that the two parties never shook hands on the newly promulgated friendship. Attitudes and hostile feelings remained unchanged. This was clearly demonstrated by the President of the Commercial Farmers' Union (CFU) when he responded to the statement by the Minister of Lands of December 12, 1991 on land policy. He said that:

> ... the Union has spent some time with the Ministry of Justice, Legal and Parliamentary Affairs to establish what constitutional amendments might be effected to enable the government to acquire land whenever and wherever it wants it for resettlement purpose (Bakare 1991:59).

For Bakare (1991:60), the settlers never accepted that their parents simply took away land from the African without paying for it. Africans had been driven away from their traditional settlements by use of settlers' tenure law. In fact, the settlers claimed to have more land rights than Africans whose ancestors had lived on the land for centuries (Bakare, 1991:59). Apparently, for Zimbabweans land offers them identity, history, and livelihood. They inherited it from their ancestors and continue to use it for farming, grazing and at times hunting.

During the 1990s, however, the pace of land redistribution programme slowed down, and disenchantment grew as meaningful and economically viable land turned out to be more difficult and more expensive than expected. Such land redistribution as did occur was widely seen as marred by cronyism, corruption and incompetence. By 1999 the economic situation deteriorated, and this saw the rise of political opposition.

The Svosve people arrived in what is now Marondera District (Mashonaland East) from the north in the mid-eighteenth century (Beach 1994). Commissioners' reports from the 1920s to the 1940s observed that 75% of the Svosve cattle were grazing on neighbouring farmland designated for European use (Elliot, 1989). The destocking and population removals of the 1940s were the first serious efforts by the administration of Southern Rhodesia to compel Svosve residents to live within new boundaries (Chimhowu and Woodhouse, 2010: 25). It is not surprising that Chief Svosve of Marondera led people from several villages in the communal areas in an occupation of Izava, Daskop, Nurenzi and Eirene farms on 18 June 1998 (*The Herald*, 1998). The war veterans subsequently occupied the White owned farms. It is unfortunate that neither the British government nor the government of Zimbabwe was prepared to compensate the white farmers. On one hand, people were resettled without facilities or infrastructure. For Shaw (2003:78), the exercise was wholly cynical exercise, sacrificing the good of the nation for short term political expediency. Newly resettled farmers saw Mugabe as having genuine desires to inaugurate a new and profound stage of decolonisation before he exited the political stage.

Shaw (2003:79), however, argues that it may be useful to examine the public rationale that Mugabe's party provides for expropriating white farms. Zimbabwe's rulers do claim the moral high ground for pressing ahead with radical and redistribution in a country where everyone, including not only the opposition Movement for Democratic Change (MDC) but also the commercial Farmers Union (CFU) agrees that land reform is necessary. ZANU-PF has been able to set the framework of debate, with opponents reduced to cavilling about the extra-legal methods used, about the chaotic and under financed character of redistribution or about cronyism in the process (Shaw, 2003:79). Given this scenario, it becomes difficult to condemn Mugabe's land policies. The main political parties (MDC and ZANU-PF) understand the need for resettlement.

From a socio-political point of view, an ethical critique of any political programme may seem idle because political actors are not driven by moral theories. But people's ideas at least partly explain their behaviour and those ideas include their notions of what is right and wrong, just and unjust (Shaw, 2003:80). Shaw (2003:80) gives three arguments why the government expropriated white farms. The first one is that peasants needed land. Counting farm workers and their families in 1999, Zimbabwe's 4,500 or so white owned commercial farms supported around a million and half people. By contrast over six million people are crowded in Zimbabwe's communal areas (the former so called tribal trust lands) which, although representing a somewhat larger area, are generally inferior, often significantly inferior in agricultural quality to the commercial land, partly for natural reasons and partly because white farmers have had the resources, which black peasant have lacked, to irrigate, fertilise to enhance the productivity of their soil. Shaw (2003: 80) also argues that Zimbabwe communal areas were not always overcrowded, but its rural black population has grown dramatically from no more than 881,000 in the 1920s to its current levels. This is contrary to the current situation in areas surrounding Chinhoyi area. People are still crowded around Chinhoyi rural areas and Murombedzi growth point.

Figure 9.1: Map of Zimbabwe

Chinhoyi and the Surrounding Areas

Chinhoyi is in Mashonaland West Province in central Northern Zimbabwe. It lies about 120 kilometres northwest of Harare, the capital city of Zimbabwe. It is the provincial capital of Mashonaand West Province. It is also the district headquarters of Makonde District.

Alaska

Alaska is a small town in central northern Zimbabwe in Makonde District, Mashonaland West Province.

Figure 9,2: Map of Areas around Chinhoyi

Mhangura

Mhangura (formerly Mangula) is a small town and former mining community in the Doma District of Mashonaland, in northern Zimbabwe.

Murombedzi

Murombedzi is also known as Murombedzi Growth Point. It is a small town in Zvimba district, Mashonaland West Province, in Central Northern Zimbabwe. The town lies 110 kilometres west of Harare, the capital city of Zimbabwe. Farming of both crops and animals is the main economic activity in the areas that surround the town.

A shortage of good agricultural land is not the only problem peasants face. Poor infrastructure and insufficient capital investment both of which handicap peasant productivity, still bedevil the newly resettled farmers (Shaw, 2003: 79). It is difficult for communal farmers to borrow money without private ownership of the land just like commercial farmers around the world do. Shaw (2003: 79) contends that moving away from a system of communal land rights would have serious social repercussions, because it would inevitably remove from many Zimbabweans little bit of economic security they have. In any case, peasants and the landless poor would undoubtedly benefit from being given land. Furthermore, Shaw (2003: 79) argues that poor Zimbabweans want land or believe they need it only because they see themselves as lacking any better options for providing for themselves lacking any better options for providing for themselves and their families. However, Shaw's argument that it is the poor who need land does not hold water. Both the rich and the poor need land. Be

163

that as it maybe, I concur with him when he says that poverty alleviation is a moral imperative in countries like Zimbabwe. Enhancing the wellbeing of Zimbabwe's citizens may require profound changes in the nation's social and economic structure.

Secondly, Shaw (2003: 80) posits that Zimbabweans refer to the armed struggle against the Smith regime as 'the Second Chimurenga'. By establishing a connection between the struggle and the 1896 uprising (Chimurenga) against early colonial occupation, the nationalist movement of the 1970s created a powerful historical consciousness that helped to win it legitimacy and to lay the ideological basis for the emerging nation of Zimbabwe. Shaw (2003: 81) also raises the argument of the historical question of whether the war was really fought over land, as ZANU-PF says it was. He argues that the desire of blacks was to establish majority rule and self-determination to end discrimination and the injustices of Rhodesian style apartheid, to promote black social and economic advancement, and to enhance generally the welfare of the population were more significant causes and goals of the struggle than was the desire to seize white farmland (Shaw, (2003). Shaw's argument cannot go unchallenged. Surely the land question cannot be ignored among the chief reasons for the struggle of independence among the Zimbabweans as they were displaced into Gwai and Shangani reserves. Resettlement was thus inevitable. The government of Zimbabwe had to exercise patience and diplomacy in 1980. For that reason, the then Prime Minister of Zimbabwe, Robert Gabriel Mugabe instilled a sense of unity between the blacks and whites in 1980 by declaring the policy of reconciliation. This was welcomed by many Zimbabweans and the international community.

Shaw (2003:80) talks of the entitlement theory of justice in his third argument. It states that a society's distribution of holdings is just "if and only if each person is entitled to his or her holdings". This theory's approach is historical other than structural. One is entitled to a holding only if one has acquired it by means of a just initial acquisition of a previously unowned resource. The entitlement theory of justice has no interest in what the resulting pattern of holdings happens to look like, for example, whether there is inequality or not – or what its consequences are, if the distribution of holdings that exists developed in accord with the theory's historically oriented principles. This fits into Zimbabwe's history when the farms were occupied during the 'Third Chimurenga'.

Shaw (2003:81) also argues that 'our land' also excludes black Zimbabweans whose ethnic ancestry traces to neighbouring countries – such as Zambia, Malawi or Mozambique and possibly the majority of people living and working on commercial farms. However, this is not true as the people who used to work around farms in around Chinhoyi, in places such as Mhangura and Ridziwi were resettled in the same area they were employed. There are people who came from Malawi, Zambia or Mozambique who became citizens by birth. This also applies to the white settlers whose children were born in this country. However, Shaw (2003:82) admits that the entitlement theory is complex and may require the input of historians and archaeologists. The principles that underlie the entitlement argument entail that someone who purchased or inherited it from a thief, depriving him of the farm now, in the name of rectification, creates another injustice, which cannot be ignored. After all the current owner loses something, he paid money for and, in the case of Zimbabwe, which he purchased with the consent or at least the acquiescence of the government. So, on whom, then does the burden of rectification fall? The answer would seem to be the original thief or his estate. What if he cannot be brought to book? Nozick (1974: 30) seems to assume that the state will compensate victims from taxes paid by its citizens (Trebble, 2001:93).

Moreover, officials within the Zimbabwean government involved in the resettlement programme have generally been self-critical both privately and publicly about the initial problems and about the lack of adequate ongoing infrastructural and staffing support for it (Palmer, 1990: 167). However, resettlement made little impact in alleviating problems in the communal areas, some settlers had benefitted far more than others, the position of some women gave cause for concern, and insufficient productive services had been provided to settlers. There is greater need to revisit the land reform programme to cater for all marginalised groups.

Democracy and Peace

The Lancaster constitution of Zimbabwe represents a social contract among the people of Zimbabwe, terms of which could not be altered. The constitutional negotiations at Lancaster House occurred within the context of a ceasefire settlement (Horn, 1994: 161). No constituent assembly was elected or selected with a view towards representing the interests of various groups in society. Apparently, the Lancaster constitution was not approved by the people of Zimbabwe. The amendment provision itself, that is, its requirement of a special parliamentary majority, demonstrates the compromise intended by the drafters about the appropriate rigidity and flexibility of the constituency's provisions parliament's power to amend the declaration of rights, but was specifically negotiated during its drafting (Horn, 1994: 162). All parties to the Lancaster House negotiations agreed on the importance of a justifiable declaration of rights, but consensus on parliament's power to amend it was achieved with greater difficulty. In the end, the delegations consented to an effective, ten-year entrenchment of the declaration of rights (Horn, 1994:163). This temporary entrenchment provided stability needed to gain the consent of the Smith-Muzorewa delegation and the flexibility to allow a new government to govern the people while abiding by the law of the constitution that was required by the Patriotic Front delegation. The addition of a substantive limitation to parliament's power of amendment, by way of the "essential features" doctrine, would alter this balance between rigidity and flexibility achieved by the farmers in the amendment provision. Parliament's amendment power is as much a part of the constitution as the protection of property from compulsory acquisition without fair compensation (Horn, 1994:163). Section 48 of the amended constitution arguably is itself a basic term of the social contract in the birth and life of the constitution of Zimbabwe.

Constitutional conventions play important role. They provide the "spirit of cooperation" necessary to adapt the structure of the constitution to its function (Horn, 1994: 161). The purpose of most conventions is to ensure that public affairs are conducted in accordance with the wishes of most of the electorate. For instance, the conventions of an institutionalised opposition and of a public mandate or referendum for fundamental (or constitutional) policy changes promote political activity and foster public debate. These conventions are not transcribed in the constitution of Zimbabwe, but it presupposes their existence. Their absence has resulted in the accretion of executive power (Horn, 1994: 161). By neglecting these conventions, the government has easily circumvented the checks on its power. Most African countries lack the political culture to support and engender these conventions and constitutions which in many cases give rise to one party rule. However, like the British constitution with its conventions, the constitution of Zimbabwe expresses a commitment to both democracy and multi-party politics within the democracy. For example, section 58 of the amended constitution (2013) guarantees the rights to associate and assemble and to form and belong to political parties.

The task of constitutional government is also to insulate some values from the ordinary political process. In the constitution of Zimbabwe, the amending process is deliberately distinguished from the ordinary law-making process by the requirement of a special majority (Horn, 1994: 161). This section supplies textual evidence of the importance of broad public support for constitutional amendments. Although the public was involved in the amendment of the constitution in Zimbabwe, more could have been done to promote awareness.

On the other hand, peace can be defined as absence of violence. Others like to call it atmosphere of unity, harmony, or mutual respect among citizens. Justice is a fundamental sense of fairness (Horn, 1994: 161). There is a need to create a peaceful country without political violence by engaging the public. However, events in Zimbabwe did not exactly follow the seemingly noble intentions of Robert Gabriel Mugabe. They were continuing indications of disregard for good governance, probity and the rule of law. For instance, there were casualties during the so-called Third Chimurenga and the 2008 elections. It is necessary for all the people from all political parties to work together for the benefit of everyone in the country.

Social justice

The issue of land must be resolved through the broad context of development, democracy and human rights as envisaged in the millennium Africa recovery Plan (Naidoo and Uzodike, 2003: 47). Chairwoman of the SADC (Southern African Development Cooperation) foreign ministries, Lilian Patel, Malawi's foreign minister, cautioned that "the situation in Zimbabwe needs a careful and mature approach because it is complex … we would like to make it clear that we do not support sanctions" (*Mail Guardian*, 2001). Interference by other countries should be avoided. South Africa hence opted for a policy of 'quiet diplomacy' and constructive engagement in response to the Zimbabwean crisis (Naidoo and Uzodike, 2003: 47). The land reform is therefore not a legal but a social justice issue. Initially, the Lancaster House agreement had promised to fund the land reform process. There must be social justice for both the white settlers and the indigenous people. Movement for Democratic Change (MDC), a party of trade unionists, human rights activists, academics and some business owners has provided little cue on how it intends to pursue and resolve the all-important and seemingly defining land reform (Naidoo and Uzodike, 2003: 48).

Robert Gabriel Mugabe and his party, ZANU-PF, justified and supported the invasion and occupation of white farms by arguing that they were acquired by imperial conquest, not the rule of law. Under both British imperial rule and illegal white Rhodesian regime of Ian Smith, the African population was systematically stripped of the country's most productive land without compensation. So, it is a question of who grabbed land first? (Naidoo and Uzodike, 2003: 48).

Mugabe argued at the United Nations' Millennium Summit that most of Africa was still burdened by the unfinished business of the twentieth century. The same people who have denied black Zimbabweans many of their rights are now appealing to the courts for the protection of their constitutional rights (*Mail Guardian*, 2001). Naidoo and Uzodike (2003: 49) pose a central question that: Should the economic interests and human rights of white farmers supersede the human rights and economic interests of other Zimbabweans? President Robert Mugabe said that no white farmer would have to go without a farm, but with 12 million hectares of land and 30% of the entire country in the hands of just four thousand white farmers, land reform was urgent (Naidoo and Uzodike, 2003: 49). The government really needed to handle the land reform programme with great care as it was quite difficult to satisfy all stakeholders in Zimbabwe.

Discussion

Various leaders who hold key political and community positions both in the ruling party and opposition in Chinhoyi urban area, Murombedzi, farms around Mhangura Mine and Alaska Mine were asked whether Robert Mugabe had sincere desires when he launched the land reform programme.

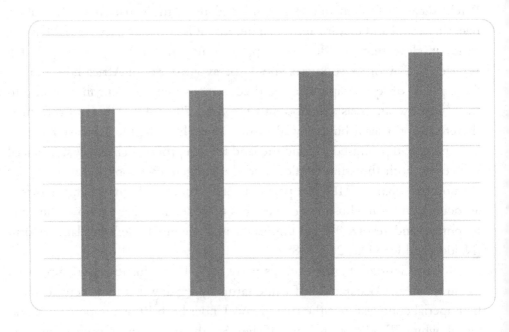

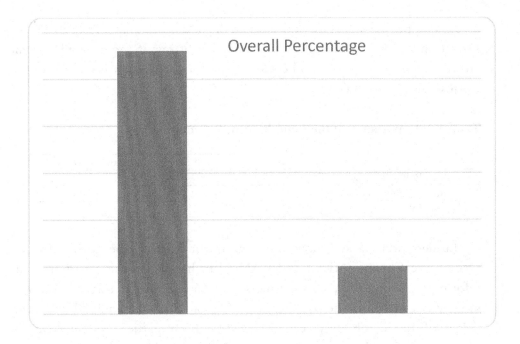

Figure 9.3: Sincerity of the Land Reform Programme

Figure 9.3 shows that 63 % of the council leaders interviewed in Chikonohono pointed out that Mugabe had genuine desires for resettling people, whereas 69 % of the council leaders in Alaska also were of the same opinion. Furthermore, 75 % of the council leaders in Mhangura thought that Mugabe was justified to resettle the people whereas 81 % of the council leaders in Murombedzi were convinced that the land resettlement programme was a noble idea. The overall percentage of those who felt that Mugabe had genuine desire for land reform was 84% as shown in Figure 9.4. However, 16% of the leaders overall felt that Mugabe did not have sincere desire to resettle people.

Most of the people felt that the people resettled should be given a chance to till the land just in the same way the whites were accorded the opportunity to farm for several years. After all, the people living on these farms are the same people who used to work for the white settlers. If given inputs, the new farmers can produce something for the nation. Mrs Huni felt that it is better to have land even in the absence of inputs since land is valuable. "The white settlers worked hand in glove with the missionaries to trick Lobengula and do not deserve our sympathy", retorted Mrs. Huni. On the other hand, some felt that land reform was rather accidental and therefore became political. This is evidenced by Chief Svosve's people who were prohibited from occupying farms on the first invasions. However, although the intention was good, the process had hiccups and turbulences. He did not have a foresight on how best people would benefit. On the hand, Gift Siyawamwaya argued that there is need to reconsider people who are squeezed in high density areas such as Mbare, Dzivarasekwa, Epworth and Highfield. It is not fair if these people remain crowded in such areas when others are in spacious areas such as in Glen Lorne, Borrowdale and Mandara.

Table 9.1: Importance of the Land Reform Programme

	No of leaders	Percentage (%)
Both Political Parties	62	94
MDC Not genuine	25	37.8
Peaceful	41	62.1

Leaders were asked how the two major parties, the Movement for Democratic Change (MDC) and ZANU-PF, handled the issue of the land reform programme. The above table shows 66 community leaders who were interviewed in Murombedzi, Chinhoyi, Alaska and Mhangura. The majority (94%) of the community leaders felt that both parties acknowledge the importance of land otherwise people would not have aligned themselves with these political parties and only 6.1 % of the community leaders begged to differ. These felt that the government needed to focus on the creation of employment particularly in industries. Apparently, most people in Mashonaland West Province unanimously support the land reform programme. However, 37.8% the community leaders felt that MDC was simply capitalising on the loopholes of the government and ZANU-PF. They are simply acting as a detour. On the other hand, 62.1 % of these leaders felt that the land reform should have been peaceful, and the whites should not have been chased away.

Although some people sympathised with the whites, others felt that some whites were selfish and did not take heed of the government's call to surrender farms which were underutilised. Those who heeded the government's call were spared and are still with us. Mrs Mawire gave an example of Kalinga who took heed of the call of the government and his farm was spared. She added that President Mugabe was under pressure from the indigenous people and had no other option except to embark on the land reform programme. "Anyone else would have reacted the same", she added. Others sympathised with whites that it was unfortunate the way the land reform was done. It could have been more peaceful. Violence was not necessary.

Leaders were also asked whether the policy of reconciliation worked or not.

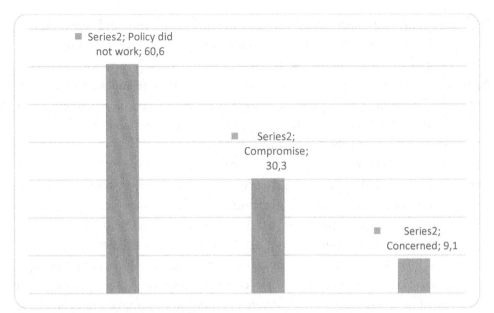

Series2; Policy did not work; 60,6

Series2; Compromise; 30,3

Series2; Concerned; 9,1

Figure 9.4: Reconciliation Policy

Figure 9.3 shows that 60. 6% of the councillors felt that reconciliation did not work. They argued that people should not cannot compromise the truth. They further added that whites were not prepared to work with others. On the hand, 30.3 % of the councillors felt that there was need to compromise for sustainable development. A few (9.1 %) of the councillors felt that it was unfortunate that some blacks have amassed more than one farm. They bemoan that, to aggravate the matter, 'cell phone farming' has also become the norm with the majority resettled of people. According to the councillors, this cannot improve the yields as country still needs to reclaim its position as the breadbasket of southern Africa. The land issue still needs to be addressed to avoid the Fourth Chimurenga. A survey conducted in many African townships also revealed that 54% of the people support Zimbabwe's land seizures (*Africa Confidential*, 2000:4). This is despite the decidedly negative slant of South African news report about events in Zimbabwe.

Conclusion and Recommendations

It is evident that both the opposition and the ruling party in Zimbabwe feel that the land reform issue is imperative. Both the indigenous people and the white settlers need land. However, this cannot be done without engaging the public. Most white settlers did not go back to their home country and are still waiting in neighbouring countries (such as Zambia and Malawi) to cease the opportunity to come back to Zimbabwe. However, the findings have shown

171

that people are still harbouring bad memories of how the land was grabbed before independence. Although the land reform seems to have been haphazard, many people feel that the people resettled need to be supported by the state. National healing is necessary to address the historical imbalances. If leaders do not carefully handle this issue, it will burst sooner or later. Government must be applauded and must continue to supply inputs for the resettled farmers as was done in 2016 using the command farming.

It must be observed that a small percentage of the people in Zimbabwe are illiterate. However, the rate of legal illiteracy is even greater, there is need to promote discussion, debate, and decision on certain issues on a village and community level. The context could require that an amendment be published, not only in the print media but on radio, television and in the meetings of village and urban organisations such as cooperatives, unions, schools, women's groups, and among chiefs and headmen. The court requires that the content of an amendment be a subject of discussion in legal education seminars in every ward or village throughout the country. The court requires that a proposed amendment be included as issue in party's election manifests. The state should engage the public for support for a general policy of land redistribution. There is need to consider some whites who were born in Zimbabwe who have the right to be Zimbabweans. As such, they also deserve the right to be considered in the land reform programme. Women too have been left out and they need to be considered in the resettlement schemes. There is need to reconsider people who are squeezed in high density areas such as Mbare, Dzivarasekwa, Mufakose and Highfield as shown by some respondents. It is not fair if these people remain crowded in such areas when others are in spacious areas such as in Glen Lorne, Borrowdale and Mandara. People therefore ought to be resettled elsewhere to avoid the Fourth Chimurenga.

References

Africa Confidential. (2000). Confidential, A. (2000). The battle for Freetown. *Africa Confidential, 41*(10), 12.

Babie, E. (1983). *The practice of social research.* Belmont: Wadsworth Publishing House.

Beach D. (1994). *A Zimbabwean past: Shona dynastic histories and oral traditions.* Gweru: Mambo Press.

Brueggemann, W. (1977). *The land.* Philadelphia: Fortress Press.

Chimhowu, A. and Woodhouse: (2010). Forbidden but mot suppressed: A 'vernacular' land market in Svosve communal lands, Zimbabwe. *Africa Journal of the International African Institute*, 80(1), 14-35.

Constitution of Zimbabwe Amendment (No. 20) Act 2013.

Davis L. (1981). Nozick entitlement theory. In J. Paul (Ed.), *Reading Nozick: Essays on anarchy, state and Utopia*. Oxford: Blackwell.

Eliade, M. (1961). *The sacred and the profane: The nature of religion*. New York: Harper and Row.

Elliot, J. (1988). *Soil erosion and conservation in Zimbabwe: Political, economy and the environment* (Unpublished PhD thesis). Loughborough University of Technology.

Elliot, J, (1996). Resettlement and the management of environment degradation in the African Farming Areas of Zimbabwe. In M. Eden and J. Parry (Eds.), *Land degradation in the topics: Environmental policy issues*. London: Pinter

Horn, V.A. (1994). Redefining property: The constitutional battle over land Redistribution in Zimbabwe. *Journal of African Law*, 38(2), 144-152

Leski, G. (1954). *Power and privilege*. London and Chapel Hill: University of North Carolina Press.

Uzodike, U. O. (2003). Between Scylla and Charybdis: Challenges Facing South African Policy on Zimbabwe. *African Journal of Political Science*, 8(2), 33-54.

Nozick, R. (1974). *Anarchy, state and Utopia*. New York: Basic Books.

Palmer, R. (1990). Land reform in Zimbabwe, 1980-1990. African Affairs, 89(355), 163-181.

Richardson, R.W. (2012). *Family ties that bind: A self-help guide to change through family of origin therapy*. Vancouver: International Self-Counsel Press.

Shaw, H. W. (2003). They stole our land'. Debating the expropriation of White farms in Zimbabwe. *Journal of Modern African Studies*, 41(1), 75-89.

Shumbayaonda, W. T. (2006). *An analysis of factors that determine teaching practice supervisions effectiveness in primary teachers colleges* (Unpublished PhD thesis). Harare: University of Zimbabwe.

Sidhu, S. K. (1984). *Methodology of research in education*. Jakandlah: Sterling Publishers.

Thomas, N. H. (2003). Land reform in Zimbabwe. *Third World Quarterly*, 24(4), 691-712.

Tebble, A. J. (2001). The tables turned: Wilt Chamberlain versus Robert Nozick on rectification. *Economics and Philosophy*, 17(1), 89-108.

Tuckman, B. W. (1994). *Conducting educational research* (4th Ed.). New York: Harcourt Brace Jovanovich.

Chapter 10

Political Conflicts and Dialogue in Glen View North Constituency, Harare

Lawrence Mhandara and Ashton Murwira

Summary

Peace building efforts after violent experiences are usually accompanied by powerful calls to embrace interventions that reduce conflicts. Yet such efforts remain elusive in most societies that have experienced destructive political conflicts. Equally, Zimbabwe, with its known history of political conflicts, is facing a similar situation despite a series of state-centred interventions. From the 1980 policy of national reconciliation to the National Peace and Reconciliation Commission (NPRC), a predictable and constant pattern of inefficacy is observed. This chapter argues for restorative-based dialogue as a tool to build capacity for reducing political conflicts in Zimbabwe. The argument is based on evidence extracted from a small sample of adult Zimbabweans who constituted an action research group that utilised facilitated dialogue to reduce political conflicts in Glen View North Constituency, Harare. The responses of the action group participants offer evidence of how restorative-focused dialogical conversations are useful in reducing conflicts. This is found to be a viable alternative to reduce conflicts in the absence of effective state responses.

Introduction

Transforming conflict is an integral component of recovery in societies emerging from or experiencing conflict. After violent conflicts, there is need for transformative efforts that target the socio-political and economic levers of society. Dialogue is one of the available mechanisms within the conflict transformation toolkit. It is an essential mechanism in repairing damaged relationships if sincerely executed. In Zimbabwe, recurring political conflicts presents a challenge to peaceful relationships. Bitter political conflicts define the history of the country from the days of Shona-Ndebele antagonism prior to colonial occupation, through to colonial and post-colonial periods. Where the government has attempted to address the effects of the conflicts, the approaches have lacked efficacy. Existing scholarly accounts concur that past and on-going attempts at conflict transformation have been mainly elite-driven

(Bratton, 2010, 2011, Bhebhe, 2013, Hapanyengwi-Chemhuru, 2013). The impact of the policies of amnesia and the various commissions set up by the government such as the Organ on National Healing, Reconciliation and Integration (ONHRI) and National Peace and Reconciliation Commission (NPRC) strengthens this observation. Ndlovu-Gatsheni (2003: 526) observes that the government may have succeeded in building the state, but it has failed to build the nation as divisions persist along race, ethnicity, regions and politics.

That Zimbabwe needs alternative models of transforming political conflicts is incontrovertible. This is especially relevant when such interventions are informal and bottom-up. This chapter aims to contribute to the alternatives discourse by proposing dialogue as a potent tool for transforming political conflicts. This is based on evidence gathered from evaluation results from an action research project implemented with a small sample of adult Zimbabweans based in Harare, Glen View North Constituency, Ward 30. The central question that motivates the chapter is: How can people affected by incessant political conflicts, but continuing to live together, participate in building their own capacity to reduce the same in the absence of effective government interventions?

Background and Overview

Conflicts motivated by power relations have a long history in Zimbabwe. The country was historically inhabited by the Bantu people who are the ancestors of the Shona, Ndebele and other groups in southern Africa (Beach, 1980: 4). The reference 'Shona' is a blanket term used to refer to all Bantu migrants who settled in Zimbabwe before the Ndebele came (Ranger, 1985). The difference between the Shona and the Ndebele relates to the arrival time in Zimbabwe. The former arrived earlier than the latter, which entered around 1839 from South Africa. The Ndebele people created their independent state in Zimbabwe through strategies such as raids, conquest, assimilation and incorporation. This shows that the Ndebele state relied on a dual strategy to pursue its nation building project that relied on both violent (raids and conquest) and non-violent approaches (assimilation and incorporation). However, most accounts characterise the relationship between the two tribes as generally antagonistic and frequently violent (Beach, 1980), with the Ndebele regarded as the perpetrator and the Shona as the victim. The dominant Shona view was represented by a definition of the Ndebele as a tribe that expanded through force. This was accompanied by a negative stereotype of the Ndebele as *madzviti* (violent strangers) who terrorised them through raiding of their livestock, grain and women. By and large, the Shona were viewed as subjects of the Ndebele Kingdom.

With the colonial occupation of Mashonaland in 1890 by the British South African Company, on behalf of the imperial power, Britain, the Shona-Ndebele antagonism worsened as the settler narrative was to justify the occupation as necessary to protect the Shona from the militant and violent Ndebele. By 1893, the occupying Company conquered Matebeleland with the help of some Shona Chiefs who were disgruntled with Ndebele domination of their ethnic group (Ndlovu-Gatsheni, 2003: 28). The Shona-Ndebele divide was thus exacerbated by colonialism although both groups were reduced to subjects who were controlled through direct and structural violence till the moment of independence. The colonialists reinforced the bifurcated ethnic belonging by the administrative division of the country into ethnic names like Matebeleland, Mashonaland, Manicaland, etc., making the process of integration between the ethnic groups herculean as each province was supposed to be homogenous in terms of language, culture and authority. Even when both ethnic groups deciphered the dangers of colonialism, tribal affiliation precluded them from forging a formidable force as inter-tribal violence took its toll. Although conscious efforts were made to promote inter-ethnic harmony through regional balance in the pioneering nationalist organisations such as Zimbabwe African People's Union (ZAPU), ethnicity was always lurking. During the movement for independence, political conflicts, especially factionalism, based on ethnicity and tribalism was rife within the nationalist movement. The split of ZAPU into Zimbabwe African National Union (ZANU) (Shona-dominated) and ZAPU (Ndebele-dominated) in 1962 was instructive. Since then, the liberation struggle was characterised by ethnic politics and tribalism, fomenting division and violence between the Shona and Ndebele (Sithole 1999).

The disconcerting reality is that the ethnic rivalry, and therefore political division, was passed onto the post-colonial dispensation that reached its crescendo during the disturbances (Operation *Gukurahundi*) witnessed in Matebeleland and Midlands during the first decade of independence. Many insightful accounts of the *Gukurahundi* conflict exist (Catholic Commission for Justice and Peace (CCJP) and Legal Resources Foundation, 1997, Ranger *et al.* 2000). Added to the historical power-driven ethnic conflicts are election-related divisions that continue to push people far apart, within and across ethnic, political, regional and racial identities as elections are construed in zero-sum terms (Sachikonye, 2012, , 2009: 92, Kriger, 2005, Ndlovu-Gatsheni, 2003). Instead of serving the purpose of free competition and participation, elections become "more a barometer of people's fears than of people's choice" (Masunungure, 2009: 97).

The impact is that there has been a negative cumulative effect on peaceful relationships among citizens of different political ideas, beliefs and affiliation. Yet, the government continues to respond in ways that have failed to promote political tolerance, typically through the ineffective policy of amnesia and commissions of inquiry (Bratton, 2011, Hapanyengwi-Chemhuru, 2013). This chapter is inspired by the empirical effect of dialogical conversations of people affected by political conflicts but still living in the same neighbourhood. Indeed, in situations of politically motivated conflicts, the effects are best addressed in the family or community contexts (Zelizer, 2008).

Literature Review

The etymology of dialogue is Greek word *dialogos*, split as *dia* (through) and *logos* (meaning). Dialogue entails meaning shared by people through words to form the basis of understanding one another (Horsfjord, 2012, Sanders, 2011). To clearly capture the essence of dialogue, its attributes ought to be identified. In dialogue, people:

- See the whole among parts
- See the connections between parts
- Inquire into assumptions for re-evaluation
- Learn through inquiry and disclosure
- Create shared meaning and explore options through deep listening to self and others.

In dialogue, people are involved in a process of sincere interaction by committing to listening to each other deeply enough and re-evaluate their positions in order to be changed by the process (Sanders, 2011). The process is underpinned by active listening, self-reflection, empathy and ultimately behaviour change in the face of destructive conflict. Dialogue is appropriate in reducing political conflict because of the strengths observed by Stain (2014: 1):

- It is dynamic, allowing people to create new relationships.
- It allows engagement of parties who cannot negotiate.
- It offers a powerful alternative for engaging with the feelings and needs of the people.

The utility of dialogue is that it facilitates people to shift their mind sets from stereotyping to genuine interest by changing the nature and process of their conversations. Dialogue is a symbolic cultural tool that enables sharing through the medium of conversation, and out of which new understanding may emerge. In that way, "Dialogue can be a powerful force for healing communities and relationships broken by divisions…" (Stain, 2014: 1). Black (2008: 93) also makes a similar observation: "… through talking and responding to personal stories, group members craft their identities and take on others' perspectives." This opens receptivity to others' stories, dilutes stereotypes and unites the heart and mind together. Eilberg (2014) thinks that heart-focusing can transform political enemies to friends. Figure 10.1 summarises reasons for choosing dialogue as a tool to reduce political conflict.

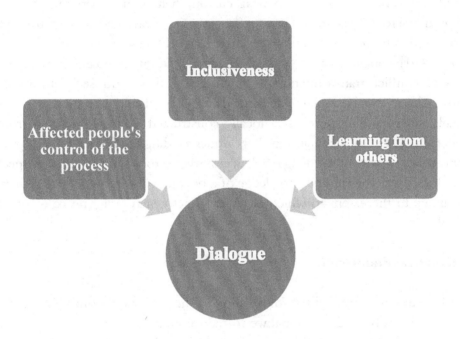

Figure 10.1: Reasons for Choosing Dialogue as an Approach to Reduce Political Conflicts
Source: Own data

Dialogue, unlike other conflict intervention tools such as negotiation, does not rely on persuading another person on the accuracy of a point of view (Brown, 2014: 48). Rather, parties engage in constructive conversations, exchanging views and perspectives. This allows for self-evaluation in relation to others' ideas. This is a conversation that conveys what people affected by political conflict want to say in the form of statements or words. Dialogue can create space to understand each other's perspectives and opinions to address political divisions. The challenge to conflict transformation is that it has to be a long-term orientation, targeting sustainable and peaceful futures. Sustainability underpins thinking about relationships (Skarlato *et al.* 2012: 39, MacGinty, 2006: 22). One dimension of sustainability is internal legitimacy which comes about through participation of affected people. Participation may come in varied forms that include dialogue, incorporating a social inclusion agenda into peacebuilding. Buchanan (2008: 405) argues that "the use of decentralised and local delivery mechanisms is crucial to a grassroots-led approach to transformation so that it gives local ownership of the process and ensures progress and success."

The transformative effect of dialogue is also culturally grounded. Dialogue is culturally understood in the African custom, helping members of a divided community to rediscover their own language of peacebuiding and become active agents in the construction of a new reality (Donais, 2006). Indeed, Funk (2012: 401) concludes that "approaches must adopt humbler attitude that regards conflict transformation as a cultural activity and seeks forms of partnership… emphasising the dynamic nature of local cultural resources." This entails understanding peace as a locally constructed reality, borrowing from Lederach (1995: 10)'s conclusion that "understanding conflict and developing appropriate models of handling it will necessarily be rooted in, and must respect and draw from, the cultural knowledge of a people." This recognises that there are limits to the extent to which an external actor may bring peace to other people.

Theoretical Framework

Two questions guided the formulation of the theoretical framework: What intervention is needed in Zimbabwe to reduce politically motivated conflicts? What would be the purpose of the intervention? Within the scope of peace building, two theories were utilised, namely restorative justice (represented by the method of dialogue) and conflict transformation. Restorative justice is reparative-centred and futuristic – privileging the dignity of the human being. Dialogue is thus a method that can be located within the restorative framework. It puts the victim and the offender as primary actors, where the needs and rights of the victim are central (Braithwaite, 2003). Offenders are encouraged to understand the harm they caused and to take responsibility for it. Clothier (2008: 18) notes in glowing terms that restorative justice recognises that conflict hurts everyone hence the voices of the victims are important: What do they need to move toward wholeness? The voices of the offenders are also important: Why did they choose destruction and what will make their behaviour change in the future? The problem is defined in relational terms as violation of people and their relationships. The three hallmarks of restorative justice are encounters between victims and offenders, the obligation to repair harm and the expectation that transformation will take place (Huyse, 2003).

The ultimate end for dialogue that is restorative-based is to transform conflict. The starting point in conflict transformation theory is that conflict is both normal and a motor of change in human relationships (Lederach, 2005: 4). While conflict and humanity are inseparable, conflict should not have destructive effects in a society. Seeking constructive change without eliminating conflict is therefore the goal of conflict transformation. Transformation views conflict as caused by relational aspects that cannot be resolved but can be transformed (Lederach, 2005). Transformation is long-term, with a clear emphasis on mitigating destructive relationships bearing in mind that conflict is a permanent feature of humans-in-relationship.

Conceptually, the answer to the question of "what" as the target of transformation is complicated by the fact that conflicts are inherently dynamic phenomena (Mitchell, 2002). However, Augsburger (1992) argues that conflict transformation occurs when there is a metamorphosis of three elements: the process first transforms attitudes by changing and redirecting negative perceptions, secondly, it transforms behaviour and, lastly, it transforms the conflict itself by seeking to discover, define and remove incompatibilities between parties concerned. Dialogue is a way of transforming conflict (Rothman, 1998). Negotiations between disputing parties often take the form of polarised debates but dialogue can create moments of transition or become vehicles for transformative insights and actions by the affected. Whether it occurs in private or in public, the major goal of dialogue is to change destructive relationships.

The theory underpinning the chapter is that dialogue allows for victim-perpetrator encounter and aims at restoring dignity in human relationships. This process has a transformative effect by reducing political conflicts through fostering empathy, interdependence, tolerance, respect, trust and a sense of security. Figure 10.2 summarises the theoretical framework.

Methodology

The research was carried out in Ward 30, Glenview North Constituency in Harare. This is a high-density urban area and was chosen because of the knowledge of the area and its history of political conflicts. Incidents of political conflicts in Zimbabwe are well documented, so are the dimensions of the violence (Research and Advocacy Unit, 2016). In recent years inter-party violence has become intensified in urban areas. Harare's high-density suburbs are sometimes turned into 'war zones', with houses destroyed, properties vandalised, people abducted or tortured (Kaulem, 2011: 79). The need for an intervention that can build capacity for reducing such destructive conflict among people from different political groups was considered essential in this context.

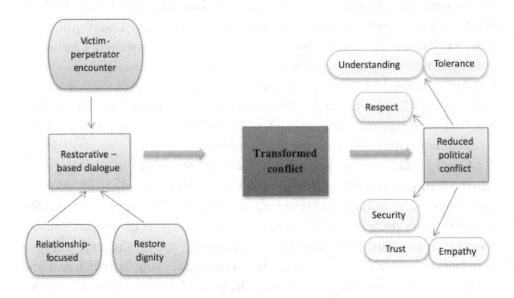

Figure 10.2: Theoretical Framework. Source: Authors' own construction

The overall research design motivating the research was action research executed within a case study context. A qualitative methodology was adopted since the problem at hand was social, involving people's experiences, feelings, perceptions and opinions. Within this paradigm, convenience sampling technique was employed to select participants. The data gathered through evaluation interviews was analysed through a thematic analytical procedure which was the basis for constructing the findings and interpretation narrative. Thirteen participants took part in the action research and their bio-data in terms of age is presented in Table 10.1.

From Table 10.1, participants within the 18-35 age range constituted 84.4% of participants in the group. The need for youths to embrace peaceful relationships that can promote reconciliation cannot be overemphasised given the demographic reality of Zimbabwe. Close to 60% of the population are youths (Zimstat, 2015). The dominance of the youth in the action group also aided the peacebuilding objective of the research since youths are more receptive to change than old age, values and attitudes acquired over time are difficult to substitute. Young people are important agents of change (Mitchell, 2011), transforming them is like sowing the seeds of future peace (Steinberg, 2013). Although unintended, it was advantageous to work with a group whose majority (11 out of 13) were young (18-35 years).

Table 10.1: Participants' Bio-data (age)

Age Range	Number of Participants	Percentage (%)
18-25	3	23
26-30	5	38.4
31-35	3	23
36-40	1	7.6
41 and above	1	7.6
Total	13	100

Source: Own data

Since the problem inspiring the study was political conflicts, it was also necessary to ascertain the political affiliation of members in the action research team. Table 10.2 summarises participants' political affiliation.

Table 10.2: Participants' Political Affiliation

Name of political party	Number of Participants	Percentage (%)
ZANU-PF	7	53.8
MDC-T	4	30.8
Zim PF	1	7.7
NCA	1	7.7
Total	13	100

Source: Own data

Table 10.2 shows that participants from ZANU-PF (7) out-numbered other parties followed by the opposition MDC-T (4), with the newly formed Zimbabwe People First (ZimPF) and National Constitutional Assembly (NCA) having one apiece. Studies on political conflicts in Zimbabwe suggest that most of the violent political conflicts, were a result of the power contests between the two major parties, ZANU-PF and MDC-T (Sachikonye, 2012). It was therefore important to have the two parties well represented in the action research group and the dialogue process to induce positive behaviour.

Four facilitated dialogue sessions involving 13 participants were held from 28 May to 25 November 2016 within the research location. The themes for the sessions focused on ice-breaking, problem analysis, determining the direction for reducing conflicts and determining the indicators of reduced conflicts. In order to determine the impact of the dialogue on the participants, a control group of 13 conveniently selected people was used to compare outcomes. It is also important to state that it is not possible to draw definite conclusions on the effectiveness of dialogue based on a small group of participants but the use of two groups was an appropriate way of measuring change. Post-dialogue questions were posed to each participant in the experiment group to allow them to reflect on how the dialogue sessions affected their perceptions, attitudes and behaviour in order to determine the extent to which they were developing the necessary capacity to reduce conflicts. On the basis of responses from the experiment group, questions were designed to evaluate perceptions, attitudes and behaviour of the 13 participants in the control group.

The post-test only method was used to compare short-term changes between the action research group (experiment group) and the control group. The evaluation method is depicted in Figure 10.3. The criteria used to detect positive contributions of dialogue was that if the experiment group reported positive changes as compared to the control group, then dialogue had resulted in positive outcome. The differences identified became the basis of conclusions on the outcome.

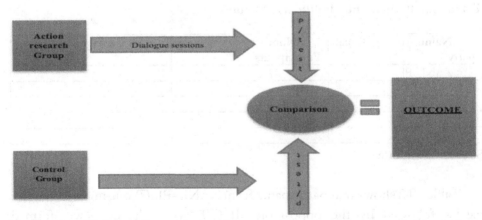

Figure 10.3: Dialogue Intervention Outcome Based on Post-test (p/test) Only Outcome
Source: Authors' own data
Results and Discussion

The four dialogue sessions involving 13 participants in the action research group were targeted at attitudes, perceptions and behaviour changes among participants divided by political conflict and capacitate them to reduce such conflicts. The behaviour change indicators were improvements in inter-personal communication, minimizing mistrust, accommodation, conflict-handling skills, collaboration, cooperation, and reduction in the use of violence and hostile language among participants.

Effect of dialogue on perceptions and attitudes

Participants in the experiment group were asked the following question: *What are your experiences with the dialogue you undertook with others in the group?* This question sought to gather feelings of individual participants and the specific ways in which the dialogue sessions had improved their perceptions and attitudes. The question had two parts: the short answer and a section providing an explanation to the short answer. Participants were asked to choose one of the following answers: 'Very helpful', 'helpful', 'somewhat helpful' and 'not helpful'. Participants' responses are shown in Figure 10.4.

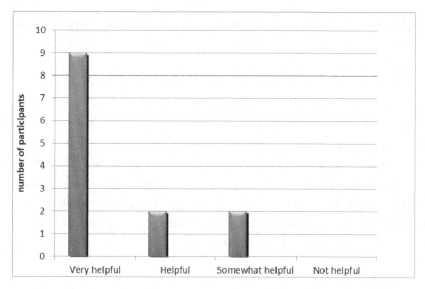

Figure 10.4: Experiment Group Participants' Experiences with Dialogue
Source: Own data

Of the 13 participants in the action group, nine (69.2%) reported to have had a very helpful experience while four (30.8%) found the experience to be either helpful or somewhat helpful. The 'not helpful' response was not reported.

Better understanding

Explanations to the short answers showed that dialogue enabled participants to discuss real issues that affected them across the political divide. They indicated that dialogue enabled them to explore issues that were affecting their relations, which could have been difficult to talk about. Participant 4 said:

> Sharing and talking about forgiveness helped me realise that we are only divided by politics but our different ethnic backgrounds have almost common values that promote forgiveness and peace.

Participant 13 also said:

> The dialogue made me realise that people are really hurt by conflicts. This is not a problem that is happening elsewhere. It's with us and I felt obligated to do something to improve the understanding of one another. I'm challenged to behave respectfully toward others even if they come from a different political background from mine.

The dialogue process provided participants on both sides an opportunity to correct perceptions about each other. This was confirmed by Participant 3:

> It was my first time to be in a conversation with people from other political identities. At first, I thought what we were doing was just to kill time but with time I began to realise that despite our differences what we discussed was really exposing our genuine interests. After three or four meetings, I began to have a little sense of being liberated and connected. My emotions were slowing down. The whole process allowed me to feel and think properly. I managed to express my feelings and emotions from deep inside and I was touched to realise people can have time to listen to me. I am also developing this habit of listening when others are talking, which I was not used to before. I felt the growing cohesion and understanding in the group.

From the above quotes, it can be surmised that dialogue allows people to engage in conversations among former opponents by giving each space to talk and listen. The process allowed for change of perceptions and mind sets toward each other. Participants who were not in talking terms or who considered others as their enemies began to connect, develop a sense of safety and fear was lessening. Relationships were beginning to be re-established as participants began to define their common interests and grow something new. New realities were beginning to emerge. The power of restoration and transformation embedded in dialogue was felt by participants. There is cause for optimism that participants were developing the necessary capacity to work toward reducing conflicts.

The attitudes and perceptions from the experiment group were compared with the control group in order to observe disparities. The following question was asked to participants in the control group: *Have you made an effort to understand someone whom you have been in conflict with?* The question had two parts. The short answer required participants to make one choice among the following phrases: 'Always', 'Almost always', 'Sometimes' and 'Not at all'. The choices were followed by an explanation. Participants' responses are shown in Figure 10.5.

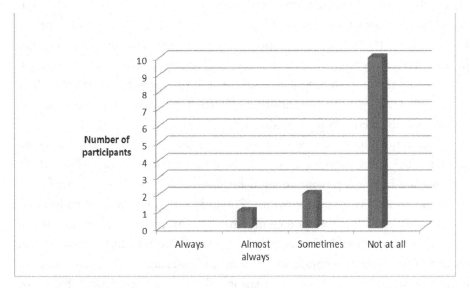

Figure 10.5: Perceptions on Understanding Opponents
Source: Own data

From the responses in the figure, understanding among participants in the control group had not improved as responses recorded showed that of the 13 participants, 10 (76.9%) reported a 'Not at all', 2 (15.4%) 'Sometimes', and one (7.7%) reported 'Almost always'. The 'Always' category was not reported. This implied that the attitude not to engage others was still rife. The explanations given to the short answers showed that use of hostile language and the tendency to justify positions were key factors sustaining the negative views on engagement. The feeling of 'us' versus 'them' was still rampant. The inability to engage one another is a sign that the person concerned can also not understand the interests of opponents. Where there is failure to understanding one another, misperceptions tend to define relationships. Yet it is fact that most of the conflicts that occur are fuelled by assumptions and misperceptions. People need

187

to improve their understanding of the other if relationships are to be transformed.

Dialogue facilitates reconciliation of interests or at least individuals achieve some level of satisfaction in their legitimate interests. As individuals engage each other, their sense of who they are in relation to others can improve. As they understand themselves better, they can also identify similarities which help to reduce conflicts with others. There is potential for unity and common identity among individuals who engage in dialogue. Dialogue tends to promote interaction at an interpersonal level and help create a new environment in which members become involved (Kartz and McNulty, 1994: 2-3). As an individual changes, other members may see the need for change as well. Through engagement, group members begin to realise their differing needs and interests which may lead to adjustment in positions that generate negative conflict. Dialogue offers opportunity to clarify the real problem that causes divisions. This is possible through sharing ideas and interaction. As individuals share their thoughts and feelings with one another, mistrust is minimised, releasing the energy previously spent on fuelling the conflict.

The conviction that one's perceptions reflect reality and that those who see things differently are wrong is part of human nature. The tendency of people to deny their own bias, even while recognising bias in others, reveals a profound shortcoming in self-awareness (Pronin, 2006: 36). People are inward-looking and are mostly subjective at perceiving their positions in relation to others. Perceptions are informed by belief, context, needs, interests and motives. Such biases can compromise accurate judgement and decision-making that lead to misunderstanding and conflict escalation. The most common form of misperception is that people tend to see themselves in a positive light even when evidence suggests otherwise. People who are the source of the conflict tend not to notice it. They tend to see their behaviour, perceptions and attitudes as justified or overly positive. Through dialogue, wrong perceptions can be corrected and promote better understanding.

Improved communication

Participants also felt that the group experience was 'very positive' or 'positive' because dialogue laid the foundation for communication among them. Communication was ostensibly made easier by the *WhatsApp* platform. Participant 7 had this to say:

> My fear was the communication we were having in the group will disappear with the end of the dialogue meetings. I have been proven wrong for now. We are

continuing to know each other better because we are talking every moment on *WhatsApp*.

The response shows the impact of dialogue where there is poor communication. Dialogue enables face-to-face encounter which encourages better understanding and communication. Through dialogue, decisions to improve communication were made. Communication in turn reduces wrong assumptions and mysteries as parties develop closer understanding and appreciation of the other. Where there is good communication, misinformation which plays a significant role in inflaming conflicts is reduced. Even if participants were not yet a united block, they were at least developing an understanding and appreciation of the other through constant communication. Experiment group participants' views were compared with the control group. Respondents in the control group were asked the following question: *Do you communicate with people who have wronged you in the past or those whom you consider enemies and how do you communicate?* The question had two parts. The short answer required participants to make one choice among the following phrases: 'Always', 'Almost always', 'Sometimes' and 'Not at all'. The choices were followed by an explanation. Responses to the question are shown in Figure 10.6.

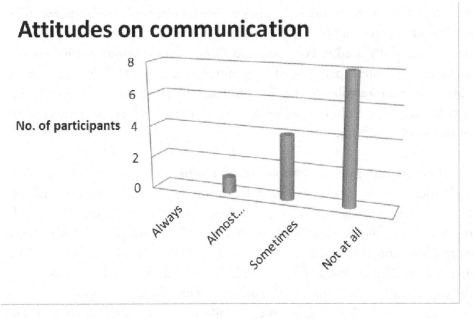

Figure 10.6: Control Group Attitude on Communication
Source: Own data

The majority of participants in the group strongly indicated no reason to communicate with people whom they considered enemies. Of the 13 participants, eight (61.5%) chose 'Not at all', four (30.8%) chose 'Sometimes', and one (7.7) chose 'Almost always'. The 'Always' category was not reported. Participants thought that establishing communication with people who had abused them was wrong as doing so will be glorifying their acts. Some said they were still overwhelmed by emotions of anger and frustration, discomfort, fear and insecurity as reasons why they were not keen on communicating with others. There were also sentiments that communicating with political opponents was not proper as participants feared censure in their own party structures. The 'Almost always' and 'Sometimes' choices were chosen because participants said they were communicating with the people who had wronged them whenever they came face- to-face because some of them had apologised. They said they were finding it hard not to talk to them because some of the people were close neighbours. Participants said communicating with their neighbours was as important as communicating with their relatives since these were the people whom they were seeing every day. This was positive since people were finding time to talk to each other without the involvement of a third party. However, the fact that the 'Always' choice was not reported suggests that where there is no understanding, communication may be difficult to establish. Participants in the experiment were beginning to establish lines of communication because the dialogue that they engaged in offered those opportunities to understand each other better, transcending the misperceptions and prejudices they had before. Results suggest that intervention strategies are meaningless if the need to communicate about issues causing negative conflict is ignored. Negative patterns of communication can often lead to greater frustration and escalation of conflict. Dealing with tense conflict situations can be challenging but embracing basic communication can increase opportunities for relationship growth.

Effect of dialogue on approaches to conflict

Participants were also asked the following question: *In what ways will your approaches to conflict change as a result of dialogue within the group?* This question sought to gather data on the specific ways in which the participants thought their approach to conflict would change to peaceful approaches as a result of the intervention. The question had two parts: the short answer and the long answer that explained the short answer. Participants were asked to choose one of the following options: 'Very significant', 'significant', 'somewhat significant' and 'not in any way'. Results showed that of the 13 participants, four (31%) found the experience 'Very significant', 6 (46%) felt the group experience was 'Significant', two (15%) regarded the experience as 'Somewhat significant' while one (8%) thought the experience not significant in terms of informing their approaches to conflict situations. The responses are shown in Figure 10.7.

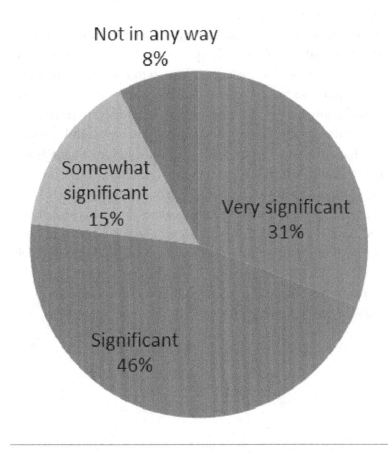

Figure 10.7: Effect of Dialogue on Approaches to Conflict (Experiment Group)
Source: Own data

In explaining of the short answers, participants who reported 'Very significant' and 'Significant' observed that, in as much as conflict was normal, they intended not to use violence as an option to resolve differences. Participants strongly felt that they were ready to embrace peaceful solutions. This commitment recognised the past experiences of witnessing destruction as a result of political violence. Participant 8 captured this commitment:

When you don't know what you are doing, the tendency is to resort to violence and the excitement of violence is misleading. You can't even realise the damage that you are causing but you come to realise that the price is too high when you have an opportunity to share those experiences like we did in the group. The persistence of conflict is so distressing. I'm realising the barbarism of violence. It's hell to see others nursing injuries of violence simply because you have failed to agree on some issue. I'm beginning to see alternative ways of resolving differences which are even better than violence. Simply talking and asking a few questions before you react can be helpful.

The response was encouraging considering that the common source of division is political violence that is frequently sponsored by powerful political actors in different. The realisation that violence is synonymous with destruction was a push factor towards non-violent solutions. The *'talking and asking a few questions before you react'* contained in the response is an indirect reference to engagement and negotiation when faced with conflict. Such peaceful ways of approaching conflict have the capacity to yield peaceful solutions that will last for long compared to violence which leaves scars that last long.

The attitudes of participants in the experiment group were compared with those from the control group. Significant differences were observed on the basis of the following question: *Would you use physical violence to resolve a conflict in which you may be involved in?* Participants were given the following choices, from which they were to pick one: 'Yes', 'Maybe' and 'No'. The choices were followed by explanations. The responses from the participants were as follows: Two reported 'Yes', three said 'Maybe' and eight said 'No'. The responses are shown in Figure 10.8.

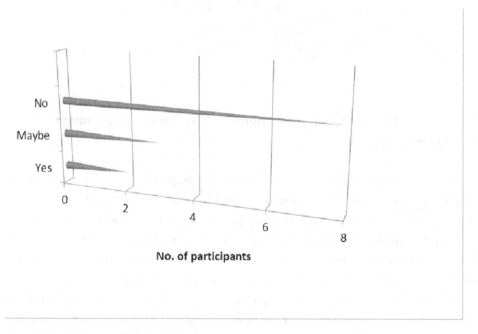

Figure 10.8: Control Group Participants' Attitudes toward Use of Violence
Source: Own Data

192

As shown in the figure, the majority of participants did not either believe in peaceful approaches to conflict (8 participants) or expressed doubt on whether they would use such approaches (3). However, a minority (2) were amenable to peaceful approaches. While the persistence of political violence was regarded as distressing by participants in the experiment group, the majority in the control group thought that violence was an important tool for communicating the message to one's political opponents. Besides, use of peaceful means was also regarded by this group as a sign of weakness, a message which they did not want to send to their opponents. The 'No' option was therefore chosen by participants who found pleasure in seeing their opponents suffer. In other words, participants were intolerant of diversity in opinions and choices. Participants who reported the 'Yes' option said they were socialised by their families not to use violence no matter how serious the argument. Participants who reported the 'Maybe' choice thought that they could use peaceful means if others were willing to do the same. Their choices were therefore driven by the principle of reciprocity. However, they were also prepared to use violence to defend themselves against violent opponents.

The efficacy and viability or superiority of nonviolent methods to attain social change is well established but was also confirmed by participants. Nonviolence is not a negative term but an effective response that focuses on love of doing well, even to the evil doer. However, it does not mean helping the evil doer to continue the wrong or tolerating it by passive acquiescence. Nonviolent emphasis is on peaceful intervention to conflict (Jeong 1999). This means presenting a peace alternative in which people act as agents seeking nonviolent solutions. Felder (1991: 13) cogently underscores this: "Peace does not mean the removal of all conflict and anger and the bringing in of love for everyone, what it does mean is that we have methods for creating balance and harmony between opposing parties."

Nonviolence is based on a culture that believes in and love of all humanity.

Dialogue and behaviour change

The last question posed to participants was: *After your experience with dialogue, in what ways do you think your behaviour will reduce political conflicts?* This question was meant for participants to state the specific ways they thought their conduct would reduce political conflicts after being part of the action group that experienced facilitated dialogue. This question sought to establish the specific behaviour traits that participants had developed. The question had a section for short answers followed by long answers, which were explanations to the short response. Participants had to make choices for their short answers from the following: 'Very significant', 'significant', 'somewhat significant' and 'not in any way'. Most participants (11 - those who chose 'Very significant' and 'Significant') stated that they would mutually encourage peaceful engagement in situations of misunderstanding in order to understand the circumstances pushing them into conflict. Figure 10.9 captures participants' short responses. Themes that emerged from the explanations to the short answers are presented and discussed in the forthcoming paragraphs.

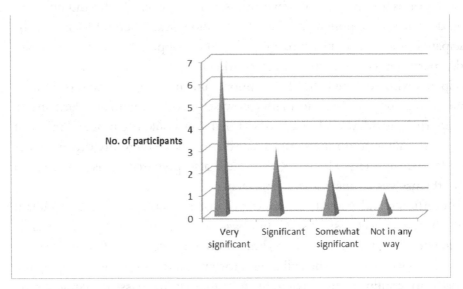

Figure 10.9: Perceptions on Behaviour Change among Participants in the Experiment Group
Source: Own data

Participants who chose the 'very significant' and 'significant' option pointed out that they would convey respect toward others to promote healthy relationships. Participant 5 emphasised that he would express respect to others first in order to be respected in return. Others emphasised that they would desist from the use of hostile language to attack opponents which they felt was a sign of disrespect. Participant 2 made a commitment to make an effort to be cautious about on what to say to others because he considered words to be a measure of respect or lack of it.

The responses were compared with those from participants in the control group. The following question was posed: *Do you think it is proper to respect people with whom you have been involved in conflict for the sake of reducing political conflicts?* The question required a two-tier response: the short answer, followed by a long answer, which was an explanation to the short answer. Participants were asked to choose one of the following short answers: 'Very proper', 'Proper', and 'Improper'. The short responses are shown in Figure 10. Of the 13 participants in the group, 10 thought it was 'Improper' to respect your opponents even if it meant that was the way to build peaceful relations, three felt it was 'Proper', while none saw it being 'Very proper'. The majority of participants who saw it improper to respect others were doing so on the basis of self-pride in that they were not willing to show kindness toward their enemies. Others said they can only respect those whom they love not their enemies. This displays rudeness and a rejection of the basic values that bind human beings together. It shows there was no love among participants and that they were self-seeking.

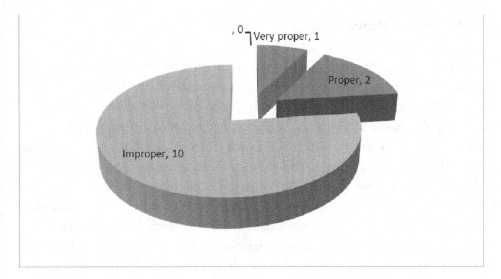

Figure 10.10: Control Group Participants' View on Respecting Opponents
Source: Own data

Action group participants' views were important in relating respect to relationship building. When respect is nurtured, people have the potential to rise above hatred, cruelty and violence. It can also lead to parties overcoming feelings of insecurity, mistrust and fear of the other, opening opportunities for building strong and long term mutually supportive relationships. Rawls (1971), a political philosopher whose vocation was social justice, opines that respect is a primary good in human relationships. He argues that justice is a public expression of people's respect for another. Others have observed that respect inhibits aggression (Pruitt and Kim, 2004). Equally, disrespect is often associated with scorn, humiliation and violence.

The responses from participants generally show that individuals involved in political conflicts possess the desire to change through engaging one another in purposeful conversations outside formal processes. There is potential for reducing conflicts through non-formal interventions. Dialogue involving people affected by social problems such as political conflicts is a powerful method of relationship transformation. Encounter between victims and perpetrators through dialogue has the capacity to facilitate relationship transformation among sworn political rivals where better understanding, improved communication, nonviolent solutions to conflicts, trust and respect are potential by-products of the process. Dialogue thus instils a sense of shared belonging which allows participants to disengage in violent acts, diminish polarisation, division, stereotypes which enhances the capacity of individuals to reduce political prejudice and tension.

Conclusion and Policy Options

In concluding the chapter, it is important to note that the action group participants endorsed the dialogue as a positive catalyst for reducing political conflict. Participants' responses offer evidence of how building capacity for reducing political conflict needs to be conceptualised through interventions that are acceptable to the people affected. In such interventions, restorative-focused dialogical conversations are useful in transforming relationships defined by political conflicts. This is found to be a viable alternative in the absence of effective government interventions. Key findings emerged from the study that can be relevant to shaping and designing non-hierarchical interventions to reduce political conflicts. This chapter reinforces the widely acknowledged fact that the impact of political conflict is still alive in Zimbabwe. The adoption of restorative-based dialogue may be a typical intervention that can build capacity for reducing political conflict because of its reported transformative effect through fostering skills of understanding, communication, nonviolence and respect. Dialogue is thus an active agent of peace in societies struggling with negative political conflicts. The attitudes, perceptions and behaviour change reported by participants who experienced dialogue makes a strong case that the intervention can make every community in Zimbabwe peaceful.

References

Augsburger, D. (1992). *Conflict mediation across cultures*. Kentucky: Westminster Press.
Beach, D. N. (1980). The Zimbabwean plateau and its peoples, 1400-1900. *Henderson Seminar 52*. University of Zimbabwe, Department of History, August 1981.

Benyera, E. (2014). *Debating the efficacy of transitional justice mechanisms: The case of national healing in Zimbabwe, 1980-2011* (Unpublished PhD thesis). University of South Africa.

Black, L. (2008). Deliberation, story-telling and dialogic moments. *Communication theory*, 1(8), 93-116.

Braithwaite, J. (2003). Restorative justice and a better future. In G. Johnstone (Ed.), *A restorative justice reader: Texts, sources, context*. Cullompton: Devon.

Bratton, M. (2011). Violence, partisanship and transitional justice in Zimbabwe. *Journal of Modern African Studies* (online), 49(3), 353-380. Available: search.proquest.com (Accessed 1 August 2015).

Brown, V. N. (2008). Reconciliation in Rwanda: Building Peace through Dialogue. *Conflict Trends*, 8(1), 48-53.

Buchanan, S. (2008). Transforming conflict in Northern Ireland and the Border countries: some lessons from the peace programmes on valuing participative democracy. *Irish Political Studies*, 23(3), 397-417.

Catholic Commission for Justice and Peace in Zimbabwe (CCJPZ) and Legal Resources Foundation (LRF). (2008). *Breaking the silence, building true: A report on the disturbances in Matabeleland and Midlands 1980 to 1988*. Harare: CCJPZ.

Clothier, D. (2008). Restorative justice: what's that then? *Criminal Justice Matters* (online), 65(1): 18-34. Available: www.tandfonline.com (Accessed 11 February 2015).

Donais, T. (2006). Empowerment or imposition? Dilemmas of local ownership in post-conflict peacebuilding processes. *Peace and change*, 34(1), 3-26.

Eilberg, A. (2014). *From enemy to friend: Jewish wisdom and the pursuit of peace*. Maryknoll, NY: Orbis.

Felder, D.W. (1999). *How to work for peace*. Tellahassee: Florida Press.

Funk, C. (2012). Building on what's already there: valuing the local in international peacebuilding. *International Journal* (online), 67(2), 391-408. Available: www.jstor.org (Accessed 29 March 2017).

Galtung, J. (1995). Conflict resolution as conflict transformation: the first law of thermodynamics revisited. In K. Rupesinghe (Ed.), *Conflict transformation*. New York: St. Martin's Press.

Hapanyengwi-Chemhuru, O. (2013). Reconciliation, Conciliation, integration and National Healing: Possibilities and Challenges in Zimbabwe. *African Journal on Conflict Resolution*, 13(1), 79-99.

Horfsjord, V. (2012). Dialogue as speech act and discourse: methods to understand what interreligious dialogue does with reference to a common word between us and you. *Journal of Enumenical studies*, 48(3), 289-298.

Huyse, L. (2003). Offenders. In D. Bloomfield T. Barnes and L. Huyse (Eds.), *Reconciliation after violent conflict: A handbook* (online). Available: www.un.org/ (Accessed 16 August 2016): 68-76.

Jeong, Ho-won. (Ed.). (1999). *The new agenda for peace research.* London: Boulder.

Kartz, N. and McNulty, K. (1994). *Reflective listening* (online). Available: https://www.maxwell.syr.edu (Accessed 11 June 2017).

Kaulem, D. (2011). *Enduring violence in Zimbabwe.* Harare: Konrad-Adenauer-Stiftung.

Kriger, N. (2005). ZANU-PF strategies in general elections, 1980-2000: discourse and coercion. *African Affairs* (online), 104(414), 1-34. Lederach. J.P. (2005). *The little book of conflict transformation.* USA: Good books.

MacGinty, R. (2006). *No war, no peace: The rejuvenation of stalled peace process and peace accords.* New York: Palgrave Macmillan.

Machakanja: (2010). *National healing and reconciliation in Zimbabwe: Challenges and opportunities.* South Africa: Institute for Justice and Reconciliation.

Masunungure, E.V. (2009). A militarised election: The June 27 presidential run-off. In E.V. Masunugure (Ed.), *Defying the winds of change.* Harare: Weaver Press.

Mitchell, C. (2002). Beyond resolution: What does conflict transformation actually transform? *Peace and Conflict Studies*, 9(1), 1-23.

Ndlovu-Gatsheni, S.J. (2003). The post-colonial state and Matebeleland regional perceptions of civil military relations, 1980-2002. In R. Williams G. Cawthra and D.O. Abrahams (Eds.), *Ourselves to know: Civil-military relations and defence transformation in Southern Africa.* Pretoria: Institute of Security Studies.

Pronin, E. (2006). Perception and misperception of bias in human judgement. *Trends in Cognitive Sciences*, 11(1), 36-43.

Pruitt, D. G. and Kim, S. H. (2004). *Social conflict: Escalation, stalemate and settlement.* McGraw-Hill: New York.

Ranger, T., Alexander, J. and McGregor, J. (2000). *Violence and memory.* Oxford: James Currey publishers.

Ranger. T.O. (1985). *The invention of tribalism in Zimbabwe.* Gweru: Mambo press.

Research and Advocacy Unit. (2016). *Conflict or collapse? Zimbabwe in 2016* (online). Available: researchandadvocacyunit.org/.../ (Accessed 27 December 2016).

Sachikonye, L. (2012). *Zimbabwe's lost decade: Politics, development and society.* Aukland Park: Jacana.

Sanders, H. H. (2005). *Politics is about relationships: A blueprint for citizens' century.* New York: Macmillan.

Sithole, M. 1999. *Zimbabwe: Struggles within the struggle* (2nd edn.). Harare: Rujeko Publishers.

Skarlato, D. (2012). *Building sustainable peace through education*. New York: UNESCO Publishing.

Stain, R.R. Jnr. (2014). Repairing the breach: The power of dialogue to heal relationships and communities. *Journal of Public Deliberation (online)*, 10(1), 1-7.

Steinberg, G.M. (2013). The limits of peacebuilding theory. In R. Ginty-Mac (Ed.), *Routledge handbook of peacebuilding* (pp.35-53). New York: Routledge.

Zelizer, C. (2008, December). Trauma-sensitive peacebuilding: lessons for theory and practice. *Africa Peace and Conflict Journal*, 1(1), 81-94.

Zimstat. (2015). *Population projections thematic report* (online). Available: www.zimstat.co.zw/.../population_... (Accessed 2 June 2017).

Chapter 11

The Political Economy of Peasant Agriculture and Climate Change in Zimbabwe in the Post Fast Track Land Reform Era

Toendepi Shonhe

Summary

The chapter examines how power and political hegemony interface with social and biophysical vulnerabilities caused by climate change in the post fast track land reform programme era in Zimbabwe. Although knowledge on climate change and the effect of de-forestation caused by tobacco production in Zimbabwe is poor, however, contemporary agricultural practices must incorporate innovation, climate change adaptation and mitigation for sustainable development. The chapter centres on a study of the political economy of peasant agricultural practices and climate change in Zimbabwe. The study used a mixed methods approach to collect data from 230 peasant households in Hwedza District. The main finding of this chapter is that national and global economic and political elite interests shape and constrain responses to climate change in Hwedza District. The study also reveals high levels of farmers' awareness and adaptation to climate change, yet mitigation remains low in rural Zimbabwe. The chapter contributes to ongoing debate on both climate and agrarian change under the changing agrarian relations aiding policy development in Zimbabwe, southern Africa and the periphery.

Introduction

The chapter examines how power and political hegemony interface with social and biophysical vulnerabilities caused by climate change. Within the realm of global change, driven by multiple variables involving shifting "meaning, paradigms, lifestyle, economy, energy, land use and climate change" (Ahamer, 2013: 273), this remains "one of the most urgent and complex challenges for societies and economies" today (Corner, Whitmarsh and Xenias, 2012, Giddens, 2009, United Nations Development Programme, 2007).

There are varied definitions of climate change by different authors and policy bodies. Brazier (2015, x) defines climate change as the long-term shift "in the earth's climate caused by the release of greenhouse gases – such as carbon dioxide [CO_2] and methane [CH_4] – which trap heat in the atmosphere, causing the planet to become hotter (global warming)". The IPCC (2007a) defines climate change as an alteration in the state of the climate which can be identified, for example, using statistical calculations. These changes are identified "in the mean and/or the variability of its properties and that persists for an extended period, typically decades or longer", whether attributable to natural causes or human activity (IPCC, 2007a, 30). This definition differs from that of the United Nations Framework for Convention on Climate Change (UNFCCC) where it is suggested that climate change refers to altering of climate which is attributable directly and/or indirectly to human activity over and above that which is caused by natural variability observed over a comparable period (*ibid.*). Whereas the IPCC definition is compelling, the focus here is on responses to and not sources of climate change, and therefore no effort is made to carefully select which definition to apply.

As Brazier (2015) elaborates, human activities release greenhouse gases (GHGs) from fossil fuels such as coal, oil and natural gases, and from commercial agriculture and deforestation. Climate change accounts for "[l]ong term shifts in annual averages and seasonal patterns of precipitation, temperature, and humidity", while "more erratic and extreme weather events leading to increased risk of floods, drought, and fire are anticipated in the future" (Coumou and Rahmstorf, 2012, Hatfield *et al.* 2011, cited in Arbuckle *et al.* 2015). Brazier (2015, x) observed that "climate change will cause average temperature to rise by about 3°C by the end of this century. Annual rainfall could decline by between 5% and 18%, especially in the south", with greater rainfall variability and increase in floods, droughts and storms. In the 2016/17 rain season, variations in precipitations resulted in heavy rains that reportedly killed 250 people, left about 2 000 people homeless and displaced 900 people, and with 72 dams bursting in Zimbabwe (*NewZimbabwe.com*, 20 March 2017).

The Environmental Protection Agency [EPA] (2015) identified the main greenhouse gas as carbon dioxide, with fossil fuel use contributing 57%, deforestation and decay of biomass 17%, methane 14%, nitrous oxide 8%, and fluorinated gases 1%. Due to climate change, developing countries face increasingly complex challenges of poverty (Hassan, 2010, Hope, 2009), underdevelopment and unemployment leading to difficulties in achieving the sustainable development goals (SDGs) set by the World Bank in 2015 (SDGs, 2015). Climate change has a significant negative effect on agriculture and therefore affects food security, agriculture-led economic growth and development, and the livelihoods of the population. Yet, the nexus between agricultural commodity production patterns, capital accumulation trends and climate change remain understudied. Most studies on Zimbabwe's agrarian

202

change tend to eschew the effects of climate change and instead focus on food and cash crop production patterns, emphasising their effect on social reproduction and capital accumulation (see Zamchiya, 2012, Scoones *et al.* 2010, Shonhe, 2017). A political economy analysis aids in revealing the nexus between capital, power dynamics and climate and how hegemonic blocs undermine the earth system and sustainable development.

The sub-Saharan African region faces greater vulnerability to climate change due to poorly developed transport networks, and energy, information and communication systems (Hameso, 2016, see also Hassan and Nhemachena, 2008, World Bank, 2009). Yet, around 80% of Africa's population depends on smallholder non-irrigated and low-level investment agriculture as a source of livelihoods (Sonwa *et al.* 2016). Moreover, in Zimbabwe, 68.3% of the population resides in rural areas (50% in communal areas and 17.7% in commercial farms and resettled areas) and depend on agriculture for livelihoods, while 31.7% reside in urban areas (Zimstats, PICES, 2013). In some provinces such as Mashonaland East, 89.2% reside in rural areas and 10.8% reside in urban areas (*ibid.*). Failure to emphasise research and policy design on climate change therefore poses insurmountable risk on the greater population groups residing in rural areas.

Knowledge on climate change and the effect of deforestation caused by tobacco production in rural Zimbabwe remains limited yet farmers' agricultural practices must incorporate innovation, climate change adaptation, resilience and mitigation which are keys for sustainable development, as this chapter reveals. Moreover, farmers are also experiencing losses in value as the quality of the crops are being affected by too much rain and in some cases long dry spells. As Mr Elias Magwenzi, a farmer from Karoi observed:

> I hope this year prices will be better because there is not much tobacco out there after farmers lost their crop through hail as well as the mid-season dry spell that affected the dry land crop. We also hear that in Malawi there is not much tobacco after the floods that destroyed the crop there (*The Sunday Mail*, 26 February 2016)

Similarly, the Tobacco Research Board annual report for 2014 observed:

> The 2013/2014 growing season was a challenging one as heavy rains received in January affected both the early and late planted crops. At Kutsaga, 34% of the seasonal total of 755 mm of rain fell in January alone. To compound the problem, the rainy season then ended prematurely. This presented many growers with the challenge of severe leaching of nutrients leading to elevated fertilizer use,

premature ripening of the leaf and a substantially higher labour requirement. The effect of this was a reduction in the quality of most of the crops, particularly in the case of small-scale tobacco growers. This culminated in growers receiving lower average prices on sale of their crops. (TRB, 2015:7).

As Hameso (2017) observed, left unchecked, climate change poses great potential to reverse progress in development and presents a hazard to the well-being of current and future generations. It is therefore opportune for communities, spaces and diverse disciplines to gain greater understanding of the subject of climate change as part of a broader array of strategies to adapt and mitigate the effects of global change. Yet smallholder farmers' knowledge of climate change is hardly known nor identified as a priority. Notwithstanding, agriculture is both vulnerable to and a source of the GHGs responsible for climate shifts (Intergovernmental Panel on Climate Change [IPCC], 2007, Beddington *et al.* 2012, National Research Council [NRC], 2010), highlighting the need for urgent action towards mitigation, informed by localised and relevant research. As Munanga (2014) pointed out, tobacco-related deforestation is estimated at 15.9% of annual total deforestation, while over 138 million m^3 of firewood was used to cure part of the 127 million kg produced in the 2010/11 season.

What then is the gap in knowledge? Many studies focussed on climate change in Zimbabwe eschew the political economy issues and therefore tend to miss out on issues of power, politics, traditions, age and gender. As a result, research on anthropogenic climate change has concentrated on social-ecological systems comprising of the human-social and ecological elements (Berks and Folke, 1998) and misses the political dynamism of social economic systems in crisis and the capacity to surprise endowed in climate shift (Phelan *et al.* 2013). The major research question in the Zimbabwean context is: How have different stakeholders responded to climate change in Zimbabwe? To answer this question, there is a need to ask a political economy question: How are stakeholders' responses to climate change shaped in Zimbabwe?

The chapter hypothesises that even though farmers and agro-industrial merchants are aware of the hazards caused by climate change, their response remains in the confines of adaptation as they are unwilling to engage in mitigation responses. To be sure, responses to climate change have tended to focus on how communities adapt to the emerging hazardous circumstances rather than how the shift in climate can be minimised through mitigatory measures. The perverse resilience propagated by the dominant bloc within the earth system tends to undermine efforts towards climate adaptation, mitigation and resilience in its bid to advance the hegemonic interests through various disguises (Levy and Newell, 2005).

Background

Given that climate change is an increasingly serious threat to human societies and that it poses great danger to biodiversity and the earth system as a whole (Phelan *et al.* 2013), the subject has gained currency and become immensely contested. Bond (2016:1) argues that a "billion residents of Africa are amongst the most vulnerable to climate change in coming decades besides being the hardest hit by war, economic looting and socio-political unrest." At a global level, leading polluting countries which include the United States of America (US) and China remain reluctant to take mitigation action to keep temperature increases below 1.5 degrees Celsius, whence runaway climate change hazards are likely to take off (Bond, 2012, Klein, 2014). China remains the biggest polluter of the environment contributing 12% of greenhouse gas emissions mainly from the use of coal, followed by the US which contributes up to 12%. Excluding South Africa and Nigeria, Africa contributes a paltry 4.6% in greenhouse gas emissions (see Figure 11.1).

Instead of slowing down on emissions, corporations in the developed countries have exported production centres to the semi-periphery countries (IPCC, 2007a), where CO_2 emissions from fossil fuel combustion is released for the production of goods to be exported back to the developed countries (Bond, 2016). The adoption of the carbon markets by countries such Brazil, Russia, India, China and South Africa (BRICS), provided scope for capitalists to trade in carbon allowances, also referred to as emission credits, and therefore permit strategies for offsetting local emissions. On the whole, Europe appears to be more committed to reduction of GHG emissions, with a 40% reduction promise from the 1990s levels by 2030, compared to 15% reduction by China and the US by 2015. To this end, the world systems theory and primitive accumulation as articulated by Luxemburg (1968), Harvey (2005) and its twin sister of export finance under the monopoly stage of imperialism exposed by Lenin (1964) with the attendant extraction of super profits through super-exploitation of cheap resources and cheap labour comes into play.

For Africa, the annual UNFCCC Conference of the Parties held in 2009 in Copenhagen (COP15) heralded the beginning of major problems regarding climate change. As Bond (2016) observed, five leaders from the United States of America and a group of countries – Brazil, South Africa, India, and China (BASIC) – signed a separate deal called the Copenhagen Accord which delivered a blow to the hope for a decarbonised global economy initially placed on the

BRICS bloc of countries. The voluntary arrangement set up under the Copenhagen Accord in 2009 with the objective of limiting emissions to levels that limit temperature rises are not being met by most polluting countries and some cases some countries (Japan, Russia, Canada, and Australia) have withdrawn from the Kyoto Protocol (Bond, 2016).

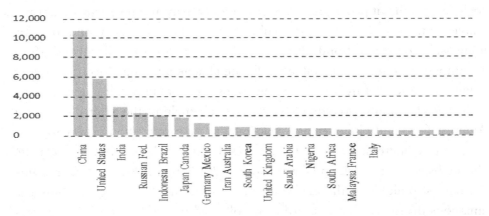

Figure 11.1: Total greenhouse gas emissions (MtCO$_2$ equivalent) in 2012 for the top 20 countries
Source: Adapted from World Resources Unit 2015, cited in Brazier (2015).

Predominantly, climate change has been funded through carbon markets at the behest of capital thus allowing polluting corporates to buy the right to pollute at low cost as opposed to reliance on state control which would lead to deep cuts in emissions. As a result, Africa is still footing the bill of environmental damage caused by profit extracting corporates and GHG-emitting capital with headquarters in the Western and Eastern capitals. In addition, as Brazier (2015) argues, it is unjustifiable that developed countries insist that developing countries must stop developing as a means to reduce GHG emissions or that they should pay fines in terms of agreed treaties when they did not contribute to the damage to the environment to date.

Meanwhile, studies on the impact of ongoing damage in Africa show catastrophic hazards to human societies and the ecological systems. For instance, a climate change and adaptation in Africa (CCAA) study programme, from Central Africa, East Africa, North Africa, Southern Africa, and West Africa evaluated by Sonwa *et al.* (2016) shows that the impact of the climate shifts has been devastating on social and biophysical vulnerability. Table 11.1 illustrates the hazards, impacts, social vulnerabilities, biophysical vulnerabilities and opportunities that exist for adaptation in response to climate change. In southern Africa, the study covered Zambia and Zimbabwe with farmers, agricultural extension staff, university students and staff and national research organisations being the main respondents. However, the study was silent on mitigation efforts that were being undertaken across the five regions in Africa.

Table 11.1: Summary of the Five Elements of Risk for the CCAA Project
Source: Sonwa et al. (2016)

Hazards	Impacts	Social vulnerability	Biophysical vulnerability	Opportunities for adaptation
Heavy rainfall (1)	weak agricultural productivity, crop failure and losses	remoteness of populations from urban centres (1)	Intercropping is generally considered to be more resilient than mono-cropping (1)	Livelihood Diversification and innovation within and beyond agricultural systems (1,2,3,4,5)
Heavy rainfall for a short period (1,3,4,6)	Decrease in animal performances and number (3)	Poor transport network Limited access to markets (2)	Continuous change in the cropping system as varieties, species, and farming practices try to adapt (3)	Diversification – from pastoralism to agro-pastoralism, increase in permanent settlement from nomadism lifestyle, increase in Remittances from the diaspora, increase in Women-headed households, increase in ownership of smaller livestock (goats and sheep) (2)
Stone rains which destroy annual crops (6)	Crop pest infestations (1,4)	Limited access to information (2)	Increase in loss of biodiversity and deforestation (3)	Crop and farming diversification; Expansion of new cash crops using excessive water during summer time; Increased intercropping using more than two species (woody and herbaceous) ; Activity and income diversification (3)
Irregular rainfall (3)	Etiolating (rapid elongation) of rain-fed rice, peanuts, and corn (1)	Sense of hopelessness (2)	Decline in vegetation cover (5)	Crop diversification and growing of short-season varieties in years that are predicted to be below normal and medium season varieties in years that are predicted to be above normal (4)
Erratic rainfall (5)	withdrawal of wild game during pockets of severe drought (1)	Increased jobless population and poverty (3)	Reduced vegetation for grazing (2)	More producers pool together to exploit land (5)
Occasional rainfall during dry season (1)	loss of flowers of cocoa, branches of multipurpose trees (1)	Increased female and child vulnerability Changes in gender roles (2)	Frequency in the occurrence of drought (2)	Improved deep tillage practices using deep tillage implements; Used early maturing crop varieties of annual and tree crops; Improved application of organic fertilizers, particularly compost manures and animal farmyard manure; Improved and engaged local agricultural innovation systems; (6)
Low rainfall during the year (1,3)	fewer edible caterpillars, mushrooms, and fish (1)	Differentiation of vulnerability by gender (1,4)	Increase in soil degradation and losses (3,4,5,6)	Change of crop types and varieties; more livestock rearing such as poultry and livestock; crafting as alternative activity (woody and non-woody items) (5)
Droughts (2,4,5)	increased animal, livestock, and human morbidity (1)	Food insecurity (2,4,6)	Increase in soil desertification as result of non-adopted agricultural practices and overgrazing (3)	Hard sizes reduction in animal husbandry transformations (3)
Severe Frequent drought (3)	increased bushfires (1,2)	Introduction of new crops Increase in conflicts (2)	Increase in the occurrence of flash floods (2)	Abandon of some traditional practices (5,6)
Early and late season droughts (1,2)	Migration (1,6)	Increase in conflict around water, grazing land, and land tenure (3)	Increased water loss and decreased water use efficiency (5)	More people drop rain-fed agriculture to turn to gardening (5)
Punctual droughts during rainy season (1,4)	Abandon of agricultural activities in some areas (5)	Increase in conflict between crops and livestock keepers (6)	Increase in water salinity as deep water is over exploited (3)	Increased access to deep water tables (3)
High temperatures (6)	Increase in livestock theft (5)	Disintegration of local institutions and organizations (3)	Sedimentation (4)	Improvement of irrigation systems and water management (5)
Heat waves during dry season (2)	Decrease in the snowbelt (3)	Weak extension services (1,3)	Poor infrastructures (2)	Increased state investments in water catchment and harvesting; New policies and investment for water economy and water use efficiency (3)
Strong winds (1)	Soil degradation and loss (3)	Unfavourable government policies hindering the survival of pastoralism system		Migration from rural to urban or other areas (2,3,4,5,6)
Excessive wind in semi-arid areas (6)	Soil erosion or formation of hard pans (3,6)	poor performance of national institutions and international aid agencies as drivers of vulnerability (1,3)		
Floods (4,6)	Decrease in the water table (3,5)	xx		
Occasional heavy flooding storms (3)	Disappearance of long-term growing crop such as maize and sorghum (6)			

1: Project 1 (Cofcca: Congo Basin Forest and Climate Change) [Central Africa].
2: Project 2 (Enhancing Adaptive Capacity of Pastoralists to Climate Change: Induced Vulnerability in Northern Kenya) [East Africa].
3: Project 3: Adaptation Mechanisms to Climate Changes of local communities of two contrasted ecosystems of Morocco: arid plain and High Atlas Mountain [North Africa].
4: Project 4: Building adaptive capacity to cope with increasing vulnerability due to climate change [Southern Africa].
5: Project 5: InfoClim (Platform for Helping Vulnerable Communities Adapt to Climate Change) [West Africa].
6: Project 6. Strengthening Local Agriculture Innovation Systems to Adapt to Climate Change in Tanzania and Malawi [Cross-Regional: East and Southern Africa].

In these countries, the study revealed weakened agricultural productivity, crop failure and losses, and increased crop pest manifestation that resulted in differentiated vulnerability by gender and on food security threats. In terms of biophysical vulnerability, the study found an increase in soil degradation and losses as well as sedimentation. However, opportunities exist for livelihood diversification and innovation, within and outside the agrarian economy. Within the agrarian economy, opportunities exist for the simulation of short season varieties, while migration from rural to urban areas and the diaspora constituted non-agrarian approaches to resilience. As Brazier (2015) observes, urban drift and cross-border migration have increased due to increased climate change that triggered rural poverty. Regarding Zimbabwe, Murwira (unpublished, cited in Brown 2012), highlights the various projected impacts of climate change on agriculture, water, health, forestry and biodiversity, rangelands, human settlements and tourism.

While the area suitable for cash crops, such as cotton, is projected to increase, a possible reduction in the area suitable for food crops, such as maize, by 2080, is likely to negatively affect the food security situation for Zimbabwe (Murwra, unpublished). In addition, it is predicted that temperatures will warm by a margin of 2^0C by 2080. Available water will decrease in the country and will mostly affect the northern and eastern parts of the country (*ibid.*). Such a scenario will affect biodiversity and human settlement and eco-tourism, which will affect the economic well-being of citizens relying on this enterprise for livelihoods. In Zimbabwe, climate change hazards are mainly influenced by "El Niño-Southern Oscillation, which originates in the Pacific Ocean", which is characterised by tropical cyclones, thunderstorms, hailstorms, floods and long (3-5 years) and frequent droughts (every 5-7 years) (Brazier, 2015:6). An increase in drought occurrence since the 1990s was observed, while increases in average temperature have resulted in increases in hot days, including heat waves, droughts and storms (*ibid.*)

The impact included yield reduction which gradually became more pronounced, defined by increased intensity as one moves from agro-ecological region 5 to agro-ecological region 1, implying that wetter areas will incur higher yield reductions. This has a significant effect on national food security, capital accumulation by farming households, rural livelihoods and the performance of the agro-industrial companies involved in the inputs and output markets. Ahlenius (2006) posits that the rate of economic growth is correlated to annual precipitation since 60% of the population is employed in agriculture and the sector contributes to 15% of the gross domestic product (GDP). In addition, crops with a larger yield response factor suffer a larger percentage yield reduction as Table 11.2 illustrates. Maize has a yield response factor of 1.25 compared to millet, sorghum and tobacco, all at 0.9.

The Zimbabwean agrarian economy is defined by an increase in the production of tobacco following an initial slump after the fast track land reform program (FTLRP). Whilst Africa increased its tobacco production to approximately 500 million kg (ZTA, 2013), SADC countries (Malawi, Tanzania and Zimbabwe) produce 90% of the crop (Munanga, 2014) and Zimbabwe produces approximately 29% of the total production. Whereas maize is the staple food in Zimbabwe and is grown by most farmers, the production of tobacco has experienced phenomenal growth since 2004.

Table 11.2: Impact of Climate Change on Yield of Major Rain-Fed Crops in Zimbabwe

Crop	Season length (days)	Yield response factor	% yield reduction per agro-ecological region					
			5	4	3	2b	2a	1
Cotton	190	0.85	8.5	10.5	11.0	12.0	10.6	13.5
Millet	110	0.9	9.7	11.8	12.5	14.0	12.3	16.4
Sorghum	120	0.9	9.7	11.8	12.5	14.0	12.3	16.4
Soya beans	135	0.85	9.1	11.2	13.9	13.3	11.6	15.5
Tobacco	200	0.9	8.9	10.9	11.4	12.3	11.0	13.8
Maize 150	150	1.25	13.4	16.4	17.3	19.4	17.0	22.6
Maize 135	135	1.25	13.4	16.4	20.4	19.5	17.1	22.8
Maize 120	120	1.25	13.4	16.4	17.4	19.5	17.1	22.8

Source: World Bank report, unpublished.

The tri-modal agrarian structure that emerged following the FTLRP (Moyo, 2011) also resulted in changes in agricultural commodity production patterns (Shonhe, 2017) where smallholder producers now account for 54.6% percent of the total tobacco produced in 2015 (TIMB, 2015). As Figure 11.5 shows, communal farmers now constitute the highest number of producers (35,253), followed by A1 farmers (27,282), together representing 82.9% of the growers. These changes have broadened the rural economy to include more peasants in global commodity circuits through the introduction of contract farming which constituted 76.4% of the production in 2015, however, most farmers rely on firewood for curing of tobacco, contributing to GHG emissions.

Even though contract farming promotes the use of coal in place of firewood, coal is accountable for huge emissions of GHGs in Zimbabwe, at the behest of tobacco merchants as highlighted in Figure 11.2. It is within this context that climate justice emerges as a critical issue for study and advocacy in

Zimbabwe, even though the tobacco merchants are said to be promoting a re-afforestation program in areas where they have contracted tobacco farmers.

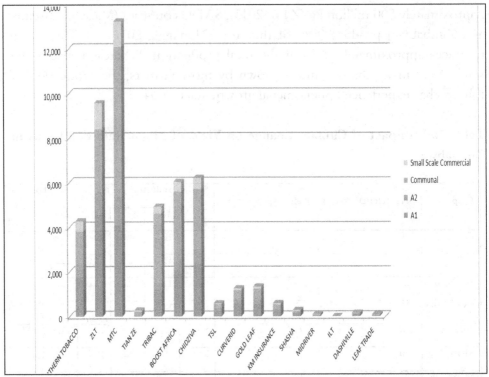

Figure 11.2: Contracted Number of Growers by Sector and Merchant for 2014/2015
Source: TIMB, 2015.

At a local level, Hwedza experienced increased incidences of drought, reduced rainfall, unpredictable wind movements associated with cyclones, changes in seasonal temperatures, prolonged winters, delayed onset of the rain season, alternating floods and droughts, often within the same season, and declining water reservoirs (Brown *et al.* 2012). These were observed to be caused by deforestation, poor farming practices, industrial emissions, veld fires, and disregard of traditional cultural and religious values, as Table 11.3 shows.

Table 11.3: Smallholder Farmer's Perceptions of Climate Change in Hwedza

Indicators	Causes
• Increased drought incidences	• Deforestation
• Reduced rainfall and shortening of rainy seasons	• Poor farming practices destroying soil ¿ water resources
• Unpredictable wind movements resulting in 'cyclones'	• The rise of industries, towns and cities
	• Increasing incidences of veld/wild fires
• Changes in seasonal temperature regimes (very hot summers and very cold winters)	• Lack of respect of traditional cultural ¿ religious values (e.g. violation of sac places, cutting down of sacred trees, n performance of rain-making ceremonies
• Prolonged winter seasons	
• Marked delays in onset of rainy seasons	
• Alternating floods and droughts within same seasons	• Unexplained natural forces
• Disappearance of wetlands and declining water reservoirs	

Source: Brown *et al.* 2012

A study by Mapfumo *et al.* (2010) established that rainfall variability was the major problem causing the vulnerabilities to women, children and those living with HIV and Aids. Mapfumo *et al.*'s (2010) study also reveals that "[t]he majority of maize cultivars are susceptible to soil moistures stress and are therefore vulnerable to frequent droughts and prolonged mid-season dry spells, which are increasingly coming to characterise Zimbabwe's rainfall". How then, should we conceptualise these developments? The following section reveals a political economy approach which will help shed light onto dynamics underlying climate change.

Theoretical Framework

Adopting a neo-Gramscian international political economy (IPE) theory advanced by Levy and Newell (2005) reveals human-social elements of the earth system to political dynamism of the social-ecological systems in crisis (Phelan *et al.* 2013). This approach places the dynamism of how the global economy functions in a way that is inconsistent with the limits of the earth system. (Hansen *et al.* 2005: Rockstrom *et al.* 2009). According to Berkes and Folke (1998:65, cited in Phelan *et al.* 2013): "The earth system can be conceptualised as a social-ecological system, that is, a complex adaptive system comprising human-social and ecological elements". The social-ecological system can be disrupted by the global economy, itself a component nest in the Earth system (Phelan *et al.* 2011a), one such is through the anthropogenic climate change (IPCC, 2007b) resulting in a sustainability paradox (Phelan *et al.* 2013).

To maintain the stability of the social-ecological system and to ensure that "ongoing viability of human society's ecological foundations" are sustained, excesses of the anthropogenic climate change must be curtailed, even if a radical societal change has to be adopted (Phelan *et al.* 2013, Schneider, 1976, Daly, 1982, Meadows *et al.* 2004). A radical critical political economy analysis of the global economy which focuses on how it works with the social-ecological systems across domains and scales, beyond resilience approaches, is appropriate for this study. This approach aids investigation as to how polluters have adopted perverse resilience which is "socially unjust, inconsistent with ecosystem health or threatens overall system viability" (see Waltner-Toews, 2004:79, School of Environmental Design and Rural Development 2005:7, Albrecht, 2009). The writers observe that resilience approaches are generally criticised for their "bloodless treatment" of power dynamics associated with human societies, because "[g]roups of humans in political economic systems often have interests and values that are contradictory, even incompatible, and in conflict with maintaining the familiar stability of the earth system" (Phelan *et al.* 2013). The political economy framework therefore considers the weaknesses of the resilience approaches and thus places "the political economic dynamism within human-social systems" to ensure that "options for mitigation responses reflect political as well as Earth system constraints" (Phelan *et al.* 2013).

The IPE advanced by Levy and Newell (2005) enables the consideration of multiple actors and their interests beyond that of the state in the contexts of corporates and business management which is often decontextualised from state power. For instance, perverse resilience by the hegemonic bloc whose interests are often impartible and even irreconcilable with the social-ecological system as they are driven by the resource and profit extraction, despite which, the environment that accompany the process can be placed at the centre of the analysis. In Levy and Newell's (2005) view, such hegemonic stability is rooted in a set of interests established as the general interests of an alliance of actors and groupings. This enables the analysis to capture political economic dynamism within human-social systems, or to provide options for mitigation responses that fully reflect political as well as earth system constraints. Phelan *et al.* (2013) therefore propose to combine the neo-Gramscian IPE approach with resilience approaches to create an integrated social-ecological system framework which pays attention to the dynamics of power and politics in social-ecological systems. At a planetary level, the integrated socio-ecological system framework adopts the neo-Gramscian IPE's cross scale analytical capabilities and therefore enables an analysis of the global hegemonic bloc powers and interests enmeshed with local political and economic dynamism to reveal how global capital resorts to perverse resilience rather than confronting mitigating approaches in a more radical fashion.

Literature Review

Much of the literature on climate change focuses on the impacts, farmers' awareness, adaptation, resilience and mitigation strategies in space and time. Scholars are generally agreed that climate change redistributes water availability and compromises its quality, increases soil erosion, and decreases crop productivity (Howden *et al.* 2007, McCarl, 2010, cited in Arbuckle *et al.* 2015). Some writers observe changes in that length and success of agricultural farming seasons, and the changes in rainfall patterns as well as increases in the mean and extreme temperatures affect water resources on which agriculture depends, often leading to increased drought (e.g., Cook and Vizy, 2013, Lott, Christidis and Stott, 2013) and resulting in reduced crop productivity (Battisti and Naylor, 2009, Lobell, Banziger, Magorokosho and Vivek, 2011). Sonwa *et al.* (2016) also observe that climate variations and changes also lead to crop failure, household income reductions, food insecurity, and livelihood collapse among the human society.

Some scholars have sought to highlight farmers' awareness and perceptions about climate change. For instance, levels of awareness and perceptions about climate change vary despite existing indigenous and scientific knowledge across space and time (see Maibach, Roser-Renouf and Leiserowitz, 2009, Weber, 2010). It is, however, generally observed that perceptions about climate change are shaped by worldviews and values more than they are by objective data (Weber and Stern, 2011), and these views are influenced by personal experiences and manipulation by actors and groupings with disparate interests (Kahan *et al.* 2011, McCright and Dunlap, 2010, Weber and Stern, 2011). This often leads to reduced commitment to reduction in GHGs as farmers are less committed to mitigation initiatives proposed by policy-makers (Arbucke *et al.* 2015). Regarding anthropogenic climate change, Shonhe (2017) observed that most farmers (95.6 percent) confirmed awareness, yet farmers have adapted to new farming methods in response to changing climatic conditions, and not necessarily engaged in mitigation approaches.

The IPCC (2007a) emphasises the adaptive capacity of the human society to short-, medium- and long-term changes and variations in the climate. Such adaptive capacity must be contingent on a collection of factors linked to "(i) knowledge, preparedness, and ability to act, (ii) the role of institutions (formal and informal, including social networks) in facilitating or constraining action/innovation, (iii) access to resources including natural resources, technology, and financial resources, (iv) mobility (closely related to access to resources), and (v) cultural factors, perceptions, and beliefs that affect the willingness to take (or not take) certain actions" (Sonwa *et al.* 2016:3). A study in six centres in Africa established that adaptive capacity varies with spaces and time (Sonwa *et al.* 2016). Regarding resilience, Walker and Salt (2006, cited in Phelan *et al.* 2013) believe that this is important in bringing about social-ecological systems by focusing on maintaining system function and stability.

Scholars on climate change have however generally not emphasised mitigation approaches to reduce the impact of climate change. Galaz *et al.* (2006) assert that climate change and its mitigation are anthropogenic and anchored in human-social systems of the earth system, across domains and scales, where political dynamism becomes a critical factor. However, Paterson (2001) posits that effective mitigation for anthropogenic climate change connected to the political economy is yet to be achieved. Yet, the political economy approach to anthropogenic climate change analysis draws insights into how hegemonic formations undermine the familiar stability of the earth system (Phelan *et al.* 2013), exposing the system to social and biophysical vulnerability (Sonwa *et al.* 2016). The historical bloc (government, monopoly finance, corporates and industry) which constitutes the hegemonic dominance, is a result of societal commitment to carbon-based economic growth that is underpinned by increasing reliance on fossil fuels (see Newell and Paterson, 1998).

Figure 11.3: Use of Firewood in Tobacco Curing, Hwedza District
Source: Author.

Quite often, the resistance to mitigation and resorting to perverse resilience is a consequence of the fossil fuel historical bloc's lack of commitment to carbon-based economy (Daly, 1982). To this extent, the production of tobacco led by merchants through contract farming must be viewed from the perspective of the fossil fuel historical bloc and hegemonic formations where globally connected peasants commit to the use of coal and firewood aiding the emissions of GHGs, at the behest of global monopoly capital. At a local level, it is therefore crucial to establish how Zimbabwean farmers have refrained from mitigation, preferring adaptation in spite of high levels of awareness. This chapter establishes the nuanced undercurrents leading to reduced mitigation preference by farmers.

Study area

Using a case study of Hwedza District, located in region IIa, IIb, III and IV where people are relying on mixed crop-livestock production in Zimbabwe (see Map 11.1), a study on climate change was undertaken.

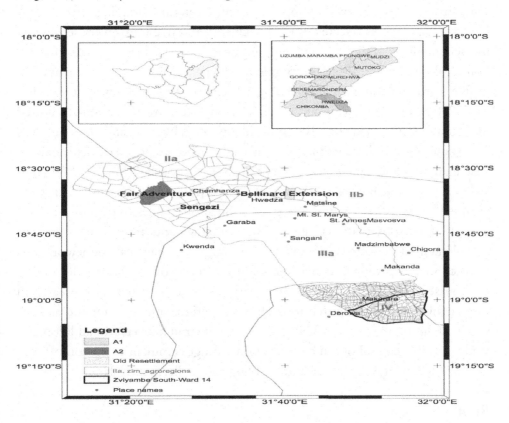

Map 11.1: Hwedza District - Agro-ecological Regions and Settlement Sectors Studied.

Hwedza District is situated 127 kilometres south of Harare and has a total population of 70,968. Hwedza District has sandy loam soils, suitable for tobacco and cereal crop farming. Most recently the people have begun to diversify into tobacco production in response to the liberalisation of the marketing mechanism, particularly after 2000. The district is susceptible to frequent droughts. The yield reduction is gradually more pronounced as one moves from agro-ecological region 5 to agro-ecological region 1, implying that wetter areas will incur higher yield reductions. In addition, a crop with a larger yield response factor suffers a larger percentage yield reduction.

Methodology

Quantitative and qualitative data on smallholder farmers' perceptions on climate change were collected using a structured questionnaire and through semi-structured interviews. In applying multi-clustering sampling in the study, Hwedza District was selected as the big cluster, and five wards were selected in the second stage while random sampling was used within the wards to select households within villages as respondents. The study was therefore carried out in five wards, one in each agro-ecological region and settlement sector and in total, 250 respondents were surveyed, 50 from each ward. The semi-structured interviews were used on 10 respondents in Hwedza and the relevant government and civil society actors. The study relied on the use of yield analysis, spatial analysis and agricultural systems analysis approaches (Smit *et al.* 1988) to allow for the integration of community perceptions. Quantitative data were analysed using SPSS to develop cross tabulations tables and graphs to aid analysis. Field observations, documentary analysis and archival data analysis complemented collected data to give meaning. An analytical framework was adopted to aid drawing of conclusions and proffering of new knowledge during the course of the study. Political instability is a major constraint to research in rural Zimbabwe. The research took electoral periods into account and as such was held during the period when elections were far in between. In addition, the study was also carried out in collaboration with government extension officers easing access to the study area and enabling ease collection of data.

Results

Whereas awareness of climate change was generally high across the resettlement models in Hwedza District, the same could not be established for

216

conservation agriculture. As Figure 11.4 shows, there were more A2 farmers and CA farmers who had not adapted conservation agriculture compared to other sectors. This was unexpected given that A2 farmers are expected to be informed people who work in government and the private sector. The A2 farmers fall in region IIa which receives high rainfall appropriate for intensive agriculture. As one A2 farmer observed: "We are situated in region IIa, in the main watershed and as such, the area hardly experiences any drought conditions" (Interview AM, 26 July 2016). With regard to CA farmers, these are situated in region IIb and are experiencing land shortages resulting in most farmers not engaging in meaningful agricultural activities other than market gardening and the produce sold through vending at Hwedza growth point and within the villages.

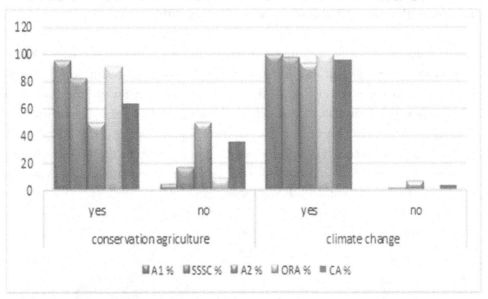

Figure 11.4: Awareness to Soil Conservation and Climate Change, 2016
Source: Author, compiled from own survey data, 2016

Efforts towards ensuring climate change awareness differ across stakeholders. For instance, 88.7% of the households who professed awareness of climate change revealed that they learnt about it from the government, compared to 2.5% who learnt about it through contracting companies and 3.4% from other farmers. Table 11.4 shows climate adaptation and sources of information.

Table 11.4: Climate Change Adaptation and Sources of Information

Are you aware of climate change? * If yes, how did you learn about the CC situation? Crosstabulation

Are you aware of climate change?		If yes, how did you learn about the CC situation?				Total
		govenrment	contracting companies	other farmers	others (specify)	
yes	Count	180	5	7	10	203
	Expected Count	180.2	5.0	6.9	9.9	203.0
	% within	88.7%	2.5%	3.4%	4.9%	100.0%
	% within If yes, how did you learn about the CC situation?	98.9%	100.0%	100.0%	100.0%	99.0%
	% of Total	87.8%	2.4%	3.4%	4.9%	99.0%
no	Count	0	0	0	0	2
	Expected Count	1.8	.0	.1	.1	2.0
	% within	100.0%	0.0%	0.0%	0.0%	100.0%
	% of Total	1.0%	0.0%	0.0%	0.0%	1.0%
Total	Count	182	5	7	10	205
	% of Total	88.8%	2.4%	3.4%	4.9%	100.0%

Source: Author, compiled from own survey data, 2016

The government is engaging farmers as groups, with all the departments responsible for agricultural extension, irrigation and technology, natural resources and forestry relying on this approach more than others. As Figure 11.5 shows, the individual approach was used mainly by the Department of Irrigation and Technology, with the Agritex Department and the Department of Natural Resources relying on this mode of engagement the least. Engaging farmers in groups limits the scope for deliberation on climate change issues, as the process often turns into token appearances.

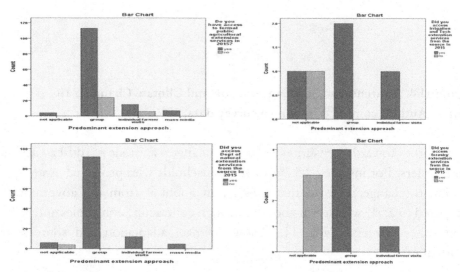

Figure 11.5: Predominant Departmental Extension Approach
Source: Author, compiled from own survey data, 2016

At least 91.8% (198 households) of the farmers confirmed that they had adopted new farming methods in response to the climate change compared to 4.3% who never adopted and 4.3% who had discontinued. The need to grow staple foods and often the inability to buy certified drought-resistant crops by farmers lead to failure to adopt new crops and resorting to old varieties. In some cases, farmers rely on government input supply schemes where the varieties are decided by the government and often depend on available seed varieties on the market thus limiting the scope for farmers to choose appropriate varieties. An interview with an Agricultural Extension Officer revealed that the quality of extension advice rendered was weak as the extension officers were unaware of what recommendations to proffer to the farmers regarding timing for planting of the crop. Table 11.5 shows current levels of adaptation to new cropping programmes by the farmers in Hwedza District.

Table 11.5: Level of Adaptation to Climate Change

What is the current status on CC adoption * if adopted, have you changed your cropping programme? Cross-tabulation

What is the current status on CC adoption		if adopted, have you changed your cropping programme?	
		yes	no
n/a	Count	0	1
	% within	0.0%	100.0%
	% within if adopted, have you changed your cropping programme?	0.0%	2.7%
	% of Total	0.0%	0.4%
never adopted	Count	1	0
	% within	4.3%	0%
	% within if adopted, have you changed your cropping programme?	0.5%	59.5%
	% of Total	0.4%	9.7%
discontinued it	Count	8	0
	% within	100.0%	0.0%
	% within if adopted, have you changed your cropping programme?	4.3%	0.0%
	% of Total	3.5%	0.0%
current adopter	Count	198	15
	% within	91.8%	7.7%
	% within if adopted, have you changed your cropping programme?	95.2%	37.8%
	% of Total	79.2%	6.6%
Total	Count	188	38
	% within	83.2%	16.8%
	% within if adopted, have you changed your cropping programme?	100.0%	100.0%
	% of Total	83.2%	16.8%

Source: Author, compiled from own survey data, 2016

Adaptations, mainly through changed cropping patterns and conservation agriculture, were observed in Hwedza District. Farmers were involved in reclaiming gulleys under the government's food for work programmes apropos conservation agriculture. In addition, the Environmental Management Agency (EMA) enforced reduction of burning of forestry, management of cattle stocks and improved crop management (crop rotation and use of composts and mulching) and these were coordinated by the agriculture extension officers. As Figure 11.6 shows, changes to cropping programmes was differentiated by settlement models.

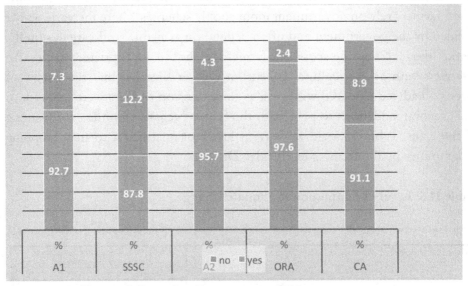

Figure 11.6: Changed Cropping Programme, 2016
Source: Author, compiled from own survey data, 2016

The highest percentage (97.6%) of changes was identified in the ORA while the lowest was observed in the SSSC sector (87.8%). These results show that high rainfall areas have a greater response to climate change (ORA – region IIb and A2 – region IIb) compared to dry regions (SSSC – region IV) in Hwedza District.

Over 98% of the households interviewed confirmed that they had not undertaken mitigation responses to climate change, notwithstanding the high levels of awareness and significantly high levels of adaptation responses to climate change. What explains this phenomenon? Empirical evidence gathered shows that four government departments are involved in the climate change awareness campaigns and natural resource management in rural Zimbabwe, namely the Department of Agricultural Extension Services, the Department of Irrigation and Mechanisation (Technology), the Department of Natural Resources and the Department of Forestry. However, the quality of engagement and information shared appears to remain poor and unhelpful given that the farmers exhibited high-level misperceptions of the causes of climate change. As shown in Table 11.6, 47.7% professed ignorance while 6.3% of the households assigned God's wishes or punishment to climate change. Furthermore, 18.5%

and 10.8%, respectively regarded Europeans and industry as being responsible. As little as five percent of the interviewed households suggested farmers were responsible for climate change. Given the high level of misperception about the causes of climate change, it is conceivable that farmers' responses exclude mitigation action as the Hwedza District survey case shows.

Table 11.6: Responsibility over Climate Change

Are you aware of climate change? * Who would you think is responsible for changes in the climate Crosstabulation

Are you aware of climate change?		Who would you think is responsible for changes in the climate						Total
		Don't know	farmers	government	industries	Europeans	God's wishes	
yes	Count	106	11	26	24	41	14	222
	% within	47.7%	5.0%	11.7%	10.8%	18.5%	6.3%	100.0%
	% within Who would you think is responsible for changes in the climate	93.8%	100.0%	100.0%	100.0%	97.6%	100.0%	96.5%
	% of Total	46.1%	4.8%	11.3%	10.4%	17.8%	6.1%	96.5%
no	Count	7	0	0	0	1	0	8
	% within	87.5%	0.0%	0.0%	0.0%	12.5%	0.0%	100.0%
	% within	6.2%	0.0%	0.0%	0.0%	2.4%	0.0%	3.5%
	% of Total	3.0%	0.0%	0.0%	0.0%	0.4%	0.0%	3.5%
Total	Count	113	11	26	24	42	14	230
	% within	49.1%	4.8%	11.3%	10.4%	18.3%	6.1%	100.0%
	% within Who would you think is responsible for changes in the climate	100.0%	100.0%	100.0%	100.0%	100.0%	100.0%	100.0%
	% of Total	49.1%	4.8%	11.3%	10.4%	18.3%	6.1%	100.0%

Source: Author, compiled from own survey data, 2016

As Table 11.6 shows, there are other sources of information, including tobacco merchants, mass media and other farmers, however, their prevalence remains quite low in Hwedza District. The quality of engagement with the various departments of government is important as it impacts on farmers' understanding of climate change dynamics. Figure 11.6 shows that those who access Agritex services from the Department of Agricultural and Extension services viewed the service as either poor or very poor, with only a few suggesting it was good, while at least 60% confirmed not having accessed the service at all.

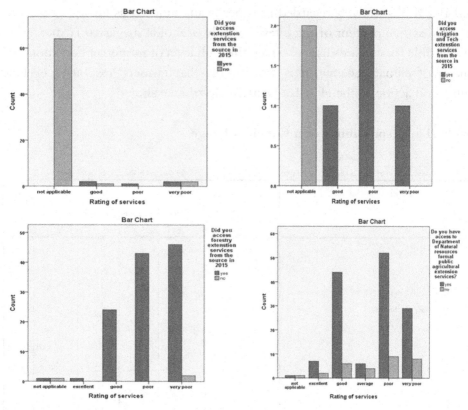

Figure 11.7: Rating of Services from Government Departments
Source: Author survey 2016

Asked for a similar rating, the majority of the farmers who accessed services from the Department of Irrigation and Technical (Mechanisation) Service felt it was poor or very poor. Many more did not access the service at all. Most farmers confirmed interfacing with the Department of Forestry, mainly through EMA and felt that the service was overly poor with some suggesting it was very poor. The same was observed for the Department for Natural Resources, even though a significant number felt the service was good.

The bid to minimise the future impact of climate change by reducing greenhouse gas emissions has resulted in decades of negotiations and agreements, protocols and treaties. The UNFCCC is the main treaty to which Zimbabwe is a signatory. The treaty obliges developing countries to commit resources to reduction of GHG emissions, poverty reduction and social development through sustainable agriculture and industrial development. The 1997 agreement (COP7) included that countries receive funding for national adaptation programmes of action (NAPAs) and the "reduced emissions from deforestation and forest degradation" (REDD) (see Brazier, 2015), however, as revealed by an expert in climate change developments in Zimbabwe, the government has not benefitted from these international treaties.

Zimbabwe has obligations in terms of the Intended Nationally Determined Contributions (INDCs) (see Brazier, 2015) developed during the period leading to COP21. In part, the reliance on renewable energy technology such as solar, wind and wave energy, hydroelectricity and biofuels have been given priority at a global level. Zimbabwe is involved in several initiatives in these areas. For instance, several solar and biofuel projects have been established. For example, the Tobacco Research Board has developed a solar barn (Kutsaga barn rocket barn) which has a 50 percent fuel saving capacity and reducing curing fuel consumption amount from conventional barn coal use of 1700kg to 800kgs and curing time from 7-9 days to 5-6 days, with no adverse effect on the quality of the leaf (Munanga, 2014). Private companies such as Robison Engineering Pvt Ltd and Carbon Green Investment (CGI) have also been involved in the building of solar barns. The CGI "barn code named 'smart barn' will result in the decline of cutting down of trees as farmers will stop the use of firewood for curing" (AllAfrica.com, 2011) and reduced reliance on coal and firewood (CFU, 2015). Figure 11.8 shows the Rocket barn developed at Kutsaga TRB station.

Figure 11.8: Rocket Barn Developed by Tobacco Research Board
Source: Munanga, 2014

However, agriculture continues to contribute to GHG emissions with 20.8% of national emissions. Even though this remains lower than that of power generation (60.7%), it is higher than industry (16.6%). Zimbabwe is also implementing REDDS with projects covering 750 000ha in Binga, Mbire, Nyaminyami and Hurungwe districts, promoting awareness, fire prevention and conservation-based programmes and projects.

Conclusion

This chapter has revealed how global and national interests and grouping determine climate change adaptation and mitigation with a focus on peasant agriculture and tobacco farming in rural Zimbabwe. The political economy approach allows us to reveal the forces, interests and groupings pushing varied policy directions on climate change in Zimbabwe at local and national levels. Whereas the study was confined to one district, which presents a weakness for generalisation, and data were collected in a politically unstable area, the findings of this chapter are worth outlining. The effects of climate change in Zimbabwe include rising average temperatures, declining rainfall, variations in the onset of the rain season, increasing mid-season dry spells and increased occurrence of extreme droughts, floods and storms. All these changes affect water supply for domestic and agriculture use and result in the degradation of natural resources, including soil, natural vegetation and livestock, and therefore have a negative impact on food security for the country.

Although there is a high level of awareness and adaptation, the poor quality of knowledge prevents farmers from adopting mitigation programmes on their farms and within their communities. The merchants involved in tobacco production and responsible for an increase in GHG emissions have not taken any significant action towards mitigation at a local level. Economic interests prevent the merchants from taking mitigation action and instead choose to employ adaptation programmes, which enables continued exploitation of natural resources in very unsustainable ways. Even though the government appears engaged in climate change issues at local and national level, the quality of engagement is seriously unsatisfactory. The quality of education and awareness programmes remains wobbly and inadequate given the high levels of misperceptions at a local level. Farmers are mostly either ignorant or blame other stakeholders for the changes in climate and as such do not see the need to undertake mitigation action at the local level. At a national level, the government is involved in climate change mitigation in line with various protocols and treaties, but the country has been excluded from arrangements with potential for funding for climate change adaptation programmes. Reflecting on theoretical issues requires a reconsideration of the forms of knowledge on climate change dominant among the farmers. Evidence seems to point to the fact that indigenous knowledge systems (IKS) may not be able to draw the farmers' attention to the required mitigation requirements but may be capable of enabling adaptation responses. The infusion of Western scientific knowledge with IKS within the political economy/ecology paradigm (see Levy and Newell, 2005) will deepen the scope for theoretical reframing.

Recommendations

Lack of participation in key global climate change programmes limits Zimbabwe's capacity to implement critical awareness, adaptation and mitigation programmes. Moreover, the Zimbabwean government has not benefited from international protocols to the desired extent, signifying the need to strengthen its representation during negotiation at international forums. The exclusion of the country from NAPAs and other programmes with potential for funding indicates that the country needs to strengthen its representation in international climate change negotiations in order to secure technical and funding support for adaptation and mitigation.

There is a need to review the education and awareness programmes beginning with the training of Agritex officers and enacting of laws that ensure that companies in extractive industries and those engaged in emission of gases are made accountable. Given that farmers are poorly educated on climate change issues, there is a need to review extension services approaches. Evidence shows that extension officers are not very knowledgeable on climate change issues. Government extension officers ought to be educated more extensively than is currently the case so that they are able to educate farmers on adaptation and mitigation approaches.

Efforts towards cleaner and sustainable energies such as solar, wind, waves, and biofuels must be promoted through incentives for private sector participation. These programmes, including REDDS, must take a national outlook to attain a deeper contribution to reduction in GHG emissions. Currently REDD+ is being implemented on 750 000ha of forest in Binga, Mbire, Nyaminyami and Hurungwe and provides communities with support for conservation agriculture, sustainable honey production, fire prevention campaigns and alternative low-emission brick-making production methods. A REDD+ programme covering the entire estimated 15.6 million hectares would enable Zimbabwe to go beyond mitigation to revenue generation. The forest is currently valued between USD1 billion and USD4 billion. A new forestry policy that also focuses on broadening the sources of fuel sources for rural communities must therefore be promoted at a national level.

Given the predominance of tobacco merchants from the USA, China and the United Kingdom, there is a real possibility that these countries are evading the carbon trading arrangements by producing in a developing country such as

Zimbabwe where national contribution to global emissions remain low (1.3%) and therefore avoid the cost in carbon trading. The government of Zimbabwe must establish laws that ensure that companies involved in tobacco production and other natural resource extraction are involved in climate change adaptation and mitigation programmes in a significant and compensating manner. Moreover, given the increasing role of tobacco farming across farming sectors, the country should consider the development of natural gas-heated barns to replace coal-fired power, given the vast methane deposits that the country is endowed with. The adoption of solar as a renewable source of energy will also be useful for Zimbabwe given that the cost of solar appliances has been declining steadily. In addition, solar farms could also be built as the cost of construction has declined by over 80% in the recent past.

Whereas natural resource extraction is a major source of revenue for Zimbabwe, however, no cost is placed on the effect of such extraction on the environment. The budgeting framework must take into account the cost of environmental damage in coming up with GDP and growth projections. Such an approach will enable the country to begin to consider the issue of sustainable development in a more practical sense, at the core of public policy-making. Civic society engagements with climate change need to zoom in on mitigation and begin to speak truth to real power – which is located in global monopoly capital. Currently the voice of civil society is muddled and hardly visible in public policy-making. This requires a united front by farmers mobilised from below, through unions and cooperatives.

References

Ahamer, G. (2013). *Game, not fight: Change climate change!* Salzburg, Austria: Austrian Academy of Sciences, GIScience.

Arbucle Jr., J. G, Morton, L.W. and Hobbs, J. (2015). *Understanding farmer perspectives on climate change adaptation and mitigation: The roles of trust in sources of climate information, climate change beliefs, and perceived risk.* SAGE Publications

Battisti, D. S. and Naylor, R.L. (2009). Historical warnings of future food insecurity with unprecedented seasonal heat. *Science,* 323(5911), 240–244.

Beddington, J., Asaduzzaman, M., Clark, M. Fernández, A., Guillou, M., Jahn, M. and Wakhungu, J. (2012). *Achieving food security in the face of climate change: Final report from the Commission on Sustainable Agriculture and Climate Change.* Copenhagen, Denmark: CGIAR Research Program on Climate Change, Agriculture and Food Security (CCAFS).

Brazier, A. (2015). *Climate change in Zimbabwe: Facts for planners and decision-makers.* Berlin: Konrad-Adenauer-Stiftung, Harare: Sable Press.

Brown, D., Chanakira, R., Chatiza, K., Dhliwayo, M., Dodman, D., Masiiwa, M., Muchadenyika, D., Mugabe: and Zvigadza, S. (2012). *Climate change impacts, vulnerability and adaptation in Zimbabwe.* IIED Climate Change Working Paper 3, October 2012. Available online http://pubs.iied.org/pdfs/10034IIED.pdf, accessed August 2015.

CFU. (2015). *New tobacco barns.* Available online http://www.cfuzim.org/index.php/ agriculture/5263-new-tobacco-curing-system-unveiled.

Cook, K.H. and Vizy, E.K. (2013). Projected changes in East African rainy seasons. *Journal of Climate.* 26:5931–5948.

Corner, A., Whitmarsh, L. and Xenias, D. (2012). Uncertainty, scepticism and attitudes towards climate change: biased assimilation and attitude polarisation. *Climatic Change,* 114(3/4), 463–478.

Coumou, D. and Rahmstorf, S. (2012). A decade of weather extremes. *Nature Climate Change, 2,* 491-496.

Daly, H. (1982). The steady state economy: what, why and how? In R. Birrell, D. Hill and J. Stanley (Eds.), *Quarry Australia? Social and environmental perspectives on managing the nation's resources* (pp.251–60.) Melbourne: Oxford University Press.

Environmental Protection Agency (EPA). (2015). *Global greenhouse gas emissions data.* Available online www.epa.gov/climatechange/ghgemissions/global.html, accessed August 2015.

Giddens, A. (2009). *The politics of climate change.* Malden: Polity.

Government of Zimbabwe. (2013). *Zimstats poverty income consumption and expenditure survey, 2011/12 Report.* Harare.

Hansen, J., Nazarenko, L., Ruedy, R., Sato, M., Willis, J., Del Genio, A., and Novakov, T. (2005). Earth's energy imbalance: Confirmation and implications. *science,* 308(5727), 1431-1435.

Hassan, R. and Nhemachena, C. (2008). Determinants of climate adaptation strategies of African farmers: multinomial choice analysis. *African Journal of Agricultural and Resource Economics,* 2(8), 83–104.

Hassan, R. (2010). The double challenge of adapting to climate change while accelerating development in sub-Saharan Africa. *Environment and Development Economics, 15,* 661–685.

Hatfield, J.L., Ort, D., Thomson, A.M., Wolfe, D., Izaurralde, R.C., Kimball, B. and Ziska, L. H. (2011). Climate impacts on agriculture: Implications for crop production. *Agronomy Journal,* 10(3), 351-370.

Hope, K.R. (2009). Climate change and poverty in Africa. *International Journal of Sustainable Development and World Ecology, 16*(6), 451–461.

Howden, S.M., Soussana, J.-F., Tubiello, F.N., Chhetri, N., Dunlop, M. and Meinke, H. (2007). Adapting agriculture to climate change. *Proceedings of the National Academy of Sciences,* 10(4), 19691-19696.

European Association of Tobacco Research. (2011). *Solar barn on test.* Available online http://www.aeret.eu/en/contents/news/ShowNews/zimbabwe-solar-barn-on-test-61

IPCC. (2007a). Climate change 2007: Mitigation. In B. Metz, O.R. Davidson: R. Bosch, R. Dave and L.A. Meyer (Eds.), *Contribution of Working Group III to the Fourth of the Intergovernmental Panel on Climate Change* Cambridge, UK, New York, NY: Cambridge University Press.

IPCC. (2007b). *Climate change 2007: Synthesis report.* Contribution of Working Groups I, II and III to the Fourth Assessment Report of the Intergovernmental Panel on Climate Change. Cambridge and New York: Cambridge University Press).

Kahan, D. M., Jenkins-Smith, H. and Braman, D. 2011. Cultural cognition of scientific consensus. *Journal of Risk Research,* 1(4), 147-174.

Levy, D. L. and Newell: J. (2005). A neo-Gramscian approach to business in international environmental politics: an interdisciplinary, multilevel framework. In Levy, D.L. and Newell: J. (Eds.), *The business of global environmental governance* (pp.47–69). Cambridge and London: The MIT Press.

Phelan, L., Henderson-Sellers, A. and Taplin, R. (2013). The political economy of addressing the climate crisis in the earth system: undermining perverse resilience. *New Political Economy,* 18(2), 198-226.

Lobell, D.B., Banziger, M., Magorokosho, C. and Vivek, B. (2011). Nonlinear heat effects on African maize as evidenced by historical yield trials. *Nature Climate Change,* 1(1), 42–45.

Lott, F.C., Christidis, N. and Stott: A. (2013). Can the 2011 East African drought be attributed to human-induced climate change? *Geophysical Research Letters, 40,* 1177–1181.

Maibach, E., Roser-Renouf, C. and Leiserowitz, A. (2009). *Global warming's six Americas 2009: An audience segmentation analysis.* New Haven, CT: Yale Project on Climate Change Communication.

Mapfumo, P, Chikowo, R. and Mtambanengwe: , (2010). *Lack of resilience in African smallholder farming: exploring measures to enhance the adaptive capacity of local communities to pressures of climate change.* A Project Final Technical Report submitted to the International Development Research Centre (IDRC) Climate Change Adaptation in Africa (CCAA) program. October 2010.

McCarl, B.A. (2010). Analysis of climate change implications for agriculture and forestry: an interdisciplinary effort. *Climatic Change*, 100(1), 119-124.

McCright, A. M., and Dunlap, R. E. (2010). Anti-reflexivity. *Theory, Culture & Society*, 27(2-3), 100-133.

.Munanga, W. (2014). In pursuit of greener curing methods: use of the rocket barn for tobacco curing in Zimbabwe. Coresta Congress 2014. Tobacco Research Board Kutsaga.

Murwira, A., Masocha, M., Gwitira, I., Shekede, M.D., Manatsa, D. and Mugandhani, R. (Unpublished). Zimbabwe vulnerability and adaptation assessment. Draft report.

Murwira, A. (Unpublished). Climate change in Zimbabwe: opportunities for adaptation and mitigation through Africa. Biocarbon Initiative Draft Report submitted to Centre For International Forestry Research.

National Research Council. (2010). *Advancing the science of climate change: America's climate choices*. Washington, DC: National Academies Press.

Newell: and Paterson, M. (1998). A climate for business: global warming, the state and capital. *Review of International Political Economy*, 5(4), 679–703.

Paterson, M. (2001). Risky business: insurance companies in global warming politics. *Global Environmental Politics*. 1(4), 18–42.

Rockström, J. *et al.* (2009). A safe operating space for humanity. *Nature*, 4(61), 472–75.

TRB. (2015). *Tobacco Research Board annual report for 2014*. Harare: Government of Zimbabwe.

Walker, B. and Salt, D. (2006). *Resilience thinking: Sustaining ecosystems and people in a changing world*. Washington, DC: Island Press.

Waltner-Toews, D. (2004). *Ecosystem sustainability and health: A practical approach*. Cambridge: Cambridge University Press.

Weber, E.U. (2010). What shapes perceptions of climate change? *Wiley Interdisciplinary Reviews: Climate Change*, 1(6), 332-342.

Weber, E. U. and Stern: C. (2011). Public understanding of climate change in the United States. *American Psychologist*, 6(6), 315-328.

World Resources Unit (WRU). (2015). *CAIT historical emissions data*. Available online www.wri.org/resources/data-sets/cait-historical-emissionsdata-countries-us-states-unfccc, accessed August 2015.

Chapter 12

Substance Abuse among Children Living in the Streets in Harare Central Business District

Witness Chikoko, Emelia Chikoko, Watch Ruparanganda and Victor. N. Muzvidziwa

Summary

The chapter examines the relationship between heterosexual behaviours and substance abuse among children living in the streets in Harare Central Business District. The conceptual frameworks of children's rights and child agency perspectives were used to analyse the lives of street children. The findings of the study suggest that the heterosexual behaviours and substance abuse among street children of the Harare Central Business District demonstrate agency of these children. The actions or behaviours involving substance abuse and heterosexual behaviours of the street children could also be viewed as the only viable options of these children thus thin agency. However, the behaviours could be viewed as part of the ambiguity of agency and or self-destructive agency. Drawing from a child rights perspective, the heterosexual behaviours and substance abuse among street children illustrate significant violations of child rights on the streets of the Harare Central Business District. The qualitative methodology that included street ethnography spanning more than twelve months was used in this study. The chapter concludes by lobbying the government of Zimbabwe and other stakeholders to implement the laws policies and programmes pertaining to child rights in order to reduce the risks associated with heterosexual behaviours and substance abuse among street children in Harare Central Business District.

Introduction

Substance abuse and heterosexual behaviours are some of the serious problems affecting adolescents including those living on the streets. Little is known about the multi-dimensional nature of heterosexual behaviour and substance abuse among the street children of the Harare Central Business District. Ruparanganda (2008) and Beazley (2003) maintain that children, including those in street situations, are sexual beings. The terms sexual beings denote that adolescent children living in the streets practise various sexual behaviours. In addition, scholars such as Ruparanganda (2008), Mhizha (2010), Chikoko (2014 and 2017) seem to agree that the children living in the streets of the Harare Central Business District, as sexual beings engage or indulge in heterosexual behaviours, sodomy, unprotected sex, multiple sexual relationships among others. Scholars such as Chikoko (2014 and 2017), Mayock *et al.* (2013) and Blais *et al.* (2012) observed that some of the children living in the streets also abuse substances. Makaruse (2010) defines substance abuse as taking too much of a drug, taking a drug too often or taking drugs or substances for wrong reasons. For example, taking on substances such as cough syrup with the intention of getting drunk could be considered as substance abuse. Alleyne- Green *et al.* (2012) submit that sexual violence is a serious health problem among African American and Hispanic adolescents in the United States of America. Alleyne-Green *et al.* (2012) assert that, due to dating violence adolescents had their abilities to negotiate for safer sexual behaviour are compromised thereby becoming vulnerable to contracting sexually transmitted diseases such as HIV and AIDS. Furthermore, Alleyne-Green *et al.* (2012) also maintain that adolescents, including those on the streets, are vulnerable to unintended pregnancy, sexually transmitted diseases, substance abuse and suicidal behaviours among others. Asante *et al.* (2014), in their study of children living in the streets in Accra, Ghana, state that substance abuse increased the likelihood of adolescent children living in the streets to engage in risky sexual behaviours such as unprotected sex, multiple sexual relationships that put them at the risk of contracting sexually transmitted diseases including HIV and AIDS.

This chapter examines the interrelatedness between heterosexual behaviours and substance abuse among the children living in the streets in Harare Central Business District. However, previous studies by Bourdillon (1984, 1994, 1999, 2003, 2009), Mhizha (2015), Mella (2012), Wakatama (2007), Ruparanganda (2008), Chirwa (2007), Chirwa and Wakatama (2000) have been limited in articulating the complex or multi-dimensional relationship between abuse of substances and heterosexual behaviours among children living in the streets of the Harare Central Business District in Zimbabwe. In other words, there is paucity of literature on the interrelatedness of heterosexual behaviours with the abuse of substances by children living in the streets. In addition, none of the earlier studies looked at the lives of children living in the streets of the Harare Central Business District from child rights and child agency perspectives. For example, Ruparanganda (2008)'s studies looked at the lives of the children living in the streets of Harare from a social constructionist perspective whereas Mhizha also adopted psychological theories.

Theoretical Perspectives

Ruparanganda (2008) established that children living in the streets of Harare were practising heterosexual sex as one of the sexual behaviours. He observed that street girls had heterosexual relationship with both the street boys and boys or men from the mainstream society. For example, Ruparanganda cited a case of girls living in the streets that had heterosexual relationship with patrons from night clubs and on the other hand having sex with street boys. In a similar vein, he observed that these girls had sex in Harare gardens or from motor vehicles of their clients, among other places.

Ruparanganda also noted that the street boys were also practising heterosexual relationship with sex workers as well as street girls in Harare. Similarly, Montanez (2011) observed that the majority of boys living in the streets of Pretoria, South Africa, were having sexual relationships with their girlfriends living in the streets as well as prostitutes or sex workers. Ruparanganda observed that street girls had challenges with initiating heterosexual relationships with the street boys. This could have been due to gender socialization. Floyd and Brown (2012) observed that female children living in the streets were having sexual partnerships with drug dealers. The authors observed that the behaviours of heterosexual relationship between female children living in the streets and drug dealers could be responsible for heterosexual transmission of HIV and other sexually transmitted diseases such as syphilis, among others.

Ruparanganda's observations on heterosexual behaviours among children living in the streets were somehow limited in terms of articulating the relationship between substance abuse and sexual behaviours. For example, one would have expected that, as a result of substance abuse, children living in the streets (boys and girls) had challenges initiating heterosexual relationship. Alternatively, as a result of substance abuse, children living in the streets had more confidence in heterosexual relationships, among other issues. The children living in the streets exercised their agency through heterosexual relationships. Through heterosexual relationships, they were able to survive on the streets of Harare. As observed by Floyd and Brown (2012), the street girls were able to raise resources for survival by having heterosexual relationships with drug dealers. The use of substances also made these girls to cope with the demands of heterosexual relationship, thus, being resilient. However, such kind of agency is unconventional or ambiguous as observed by Bordonaro (2012). Gigengack (2006, 2008) referred to the behaviours as self-destructive agency. Tisdall and Punch (2012) also viewed the behaviours as 'thin agency' considering the limitedness of viable options at their disposal.

The heterosexual behaviours and abuse or misuse of substances among children living in the streets also illustrates child rights violation. The practices contravene the provisions of the United Nations Convention on the Rights of a Child (1989), particularly article three thus the best interest of the child principle. The Children's Act Chapter (5:06) refers to these children as 'in need of care.' They are considered as children in need of care because of the level of vulnerabilities they are exposed. As observed by Floyd and Brown (2012), as a result of heterosexual relationships and use of substances, some of the girls living in the streets were vulnerable to sexually transmitted diseases including HIV and AIDS. In addition, the fact that these children indulge in heterosexual relationships and abuse substances also shows that the government of Zimbabwe, as the primary duty bearer, has failed to provide protection services to vulnerable children living in the streets of Harare.

Drawing from qualitative research design scholars, Montgomery (2007) used life history interviews, among other data collection tools, for children involved in prostitution in Thailand. Taft (2015) also used ethnography that includes in-depth interviews as part of the data collection tools on working children in Peru. Godoy (1999) also used in-depth interviews for a study on children living in the streets of Guatemala City. Scholars such as Chikoko (2014), Chikoko et al. (2016), Mizen and Ofosu-Kusi (2010), Ruparanganda (2008) adopted in-depth interviews, informal conversations, and life history interviews to generate data from street children's lives

Child agency

Butler (2009) observes that the new social studies of childhood as an emerging paradigm consider that childhood is socially constructed. The author also added that the child agency theory has challenged the universalization of childhood which has dominated several Euro-American conceptualisations of childhood. Davies (2008) viewed children living in the streets as social actors in a subculture that has influence over their lives through creating strong group support networks. The author adds that through demonstrating their agency, the children living in the streets were able to survive on the streets. Agency is therefore about the abilities, and capabilities of individuals to survive or cope with their situations (Ansell, 2015, Ritzer, 1992). According to Andrea and Godin (2014), the children in Katanga area in Democratic Republic of Congo demonstrated their agency as social actors through contributing towards household income. The authors added that the children exercised their agency in artisanal mining sector besides growing international pressure that the activities were part of the 'worst forms of child labour.' Tisdall and Punch (2012) also argue that thin agency as when there are limited survival options of young people in a constraining environment. The heterosexual behaviours and abusing of substance could be regarded as part of the notion of thin agency. Bordonaro and Payne (2012) also argue that agency sometimes becomes ambiguous. The authors add that ambiguity of agency is when it clashes with societal values. For example, Chikoko (2014) submits that the behaviours or actions of children living in the streets involved in abusing substances and also heterosexual behaviours could be regarded as ambiguity of agency. The author observes that the behaviours are seen as threatening moral values of Zimbabwean society. In addition, the abuse of substances and heterosexual behaviours also threaten the well-being of these children.

Child rights

The United Nations Convention on the Rights of a Child (1989) defines child rights under four principles, namely the best interest of the child, the right of a child to participation, non-discrimination and the right of a child to survival and development. Save the Children (2002) also submit that a child rights perspective recognises the relationship between the duty bearer and the rights holders. Chikoko (2014) observes that the child rights perspective could be seen as social contract that exists between the rights holders and the duty bearers. Nhenga (2008) maintains that, in an effort to domesticate the provisions of the United Nations Convention on the Rights of a Child (1989) and the African Charter on the Rights and Welfare of Children (1999), the government of Zimbabwe has enacted a number of child rights laws, policies and programmes. Chikoko (2014) also notes that some of the laws, policies and programmes include the Children's Act (5:06), the Criminal Law (Codification and Reform) Act (9:23) and the Multi-Sectoral Response to Child Sexual Abuse and the National Action Plan for Orphans and Other Vulnerable Children (2016-2020), among others. However, a number of critics or flaws have been raised against the United Nations Convention on the Rights of a Child. Scholars such as Nhenga (2009), Bourdillon (2009), Morrow and Pells (2012) posit that the United Nations Convention on the Rights of a Child is seen or viewed as a Western conceptualisation of childhood. In addition, Morrow and Pells (2012: 04) assert that "the United Nations Convention on the Rights of a Child does not contain specific rights relating to poverty and does not define the term." The vulnerability of the children is explained when some of the children living in the streets of the Harare Central Business District contract sexually transmitted diseases and abuse substances. In addition, the behaviours are inconsistent with the provisions of the United Nations Convention on the Rights of a Child, the African Charter on the Rights and Welfare of Children and some of the national child rights laws, policies and programmes. The

235

behaviours demonstrate huge child rights violations prevalent on the streets of the Harare Central Business District.

Methodology

The study was purely qualitative. Convenience sampling was used to select eight (8) participants for the study. Specifically, four (4) in-depth interviews were conducted with adolescent children living in the streets to solicit their narratives on regarding heterosexual behaviours and substance abuse on the streets. In addition, through four (4) life history interviews, the study gathered data regarding street children's lived experiences of heterosexual behaviours and substance abuse. Four (4) key informant interviews were also undertaken with officials from Cesvi, Oasis, Streets Ahead and Department of Social Services. As key informants who interact with children living in the streets on a daily basis, they provided valuable data on the heterosexual behaviours and substance abuse of these children. Neuman (2011) argues that convenience sampling is ideal when working with difficult or hidden populations such as children living in the streets or sex workers. The author submits that, through convenience sampling, it becomes easy to identify and recruit participants in a study. Qualitative data were analysed through thematic content analysis. The data analysis focused on themes and sub-themes that emerged from the study. For example, some of the themes and sub-themes include use of aphrodisiac substances and use of psycho active substances to gain confidence to engage in heterosexual behaviours. As other studies have shown, thematic content analysis is very ideal for children living in the streets (see McAlinden and Maruna, 2016, Garland, Richard and Cooney, 2010, Mizen and Ofosu-Kusi, 2010, Mhizha, 2010, 2014, 2015, Mhizha and Muromo, 2013, Chikoko, 2014, Chikoko *et al.* 2016, Ruparanganda, 2008).

Results and Discussion

The perceptions and attitudes of children living in the streets of the Harare Central Business District suggested that the escalation of heterosexual behaviours is linked to substance abuse. On one of the Saturday afternoons, the researcher visited the *Majubheki*[4] area accompanied by one of the street boys called Kheda. The *Majubheki* area of Mbare Township (a high-density residential area) is characterised by mushrooming of shebeens and the selling of sex and substances, among other vices. When the researcher and Kheda arrived at one

---

[4]*Majubhek*i is an area around Mbare high density area

236

of the shebeens, called *Ambuya*[5] Dorcas, the patrons were very uncomfortable as they thought the researcher was part of police undercover agents However, since Kheda was known by some of the patrons of the , including sex workers and other hardcore criminals, he had to introduce the researcher as one of his uncles. At *Ambuya* Dorcas shebeen, a host of activities were happening. For example, some of the people were busy smoking *mbanje*[6] or *chamba*[7] and drinking *kachasu*[8], while others were playing *njuga*[9]. Some sex workers were also milling around the place, soliciting for clients. After a while, Kheda joined his colleagues in drinking *kachasu*[10] and *chitongo*[11] substances, among others. At a time when Kheda started to show signs of being heavily intoxicated, he went to the dancing floor with one of the sex workers, dancing to Tocky Vibes' (a well-known local artist) music. Later on, Kheda disappeared for a while and eventually came back to the researcher and said:

> Elder, are you not interested in some of the ladies that are around? Elder, just go and have a short time[12]. I have already had short time[13] with that lady. She is very good in sex.

During the life history interviews, one of the street girls confessed that she engages in heterosexual behaviours. The girl added that she engages in heterosexual behaviours with both some of the boys living in the streets and other *mhenes*[14] from the mainstream society, including the municipal policemen. The narrative shows how children living in the streets exercised their agency through heterosexual and abuse of substances. The behaviours could be considered as ambiguous agency as observed by Bordonaro and Payne (2012), for heterosexual relationships among minors clashes with societal values. The ambiguity of agency is also the context when the action threatens the wellbeing of citizens and community (Bordonaro, 2012). The engagement in heterosexual relationship by girls living in the streets is therefore seen as threatening the interests of these girls. Children, including those in the street situations, are not expected to engage in substance abuse and heterosexual relationships in the

---

[5] *Ambuya* is a grand mother
[6] *Mbanje* is cannabis or marijuana
[7] *Chamba* is cannabis or marijuana
[8] *Kachasu* is highly intoxicating psycho active substances
[9] *Njuga* is gambling
[10] *Kachasu* is highly intoxicating psycho active substances
[11] *Chitongo* is another highly intoxicating psycho active substances
[12] Short time is referred as a quickie or short time session of sex
[13] Short time is referred as a quickie or short time session of sex
[14] *Mhenes* are male clients

Shona culture in Zimbabwe. Tisdall and Punch (2012) also refers to the behaviours of these children as 'thin agency' as heterosexual relationships and substance abuse might have been the only viable options at their disposal. The thin agency is explained as few available options for survival for these children. The abuse of substances and heterosexual relationship could be the only few available opportunities, thus, survival options for the girls living in the streets of the Harare Central Business District. Scholars such as Gigengack (2006 and 2008) viewed such behaviours as self-destructive agency. The self-destructive agency is also explained when the children living in the streets engage in substance abuse and subsequent heterosexual relationship because there are a number of risks associated with the actions (Gigengack, 2008). Some of the risks could be contracting sexually transmitted diseases including HIV and AIDS, gonorrhoea, syphilis, and genital warts, among others. These risks could even lead to death of children living in the streets.

The narratives also illustrate sexual abuse, violence and exploitation. For example, the involvement of *Kheda* in sexual intercourse and abuse of intoxicating substances contravenes the provisions of the child rights laws, policies and programmes. The behaviour contravenes the provisions of the United Nations Convention on the Rights of a Child Article 3, in the best interest of a child. *Kheda* is also a child 'in need of care' in terms of the Children's Act (5:06). One becomes worried about children living in the streets having sexual intercourse with commercial sex workers when they are under the influence of intoxicating substances. This could expose the street boys to several risks such as unprotected sex or contracting sexually transmitted diseases.

Ruparanganda (2008) established that both boys and girls living in the streets had heterosexual sex as one of their sexual behaviours on the streets. He observed that girls living in the streets could have heterosexual relationships with both boys living in the streets and men from the mainstream society. For example, Ruparanganda cited a case of a girl living in the streets who had heterosexual relationships with men who were patrons of night clubs and, on the other hand, had sex with boys living in the streets. In addition, Ruparanganda observed that these girls had sex in Harare Gardens or motor vehicles of their clients, among other places. Ruparanganda also observed that the boys were also practising heterosexual relationships with sex workers as well as girls living in the streets. Montanez (2011) observed that the majority of boys living in the streets of Pretoria, South Africa, were having sexual relationships with their girlfriends living in the streets as well as prostitutes.

Ruparanganda noted that girls living in the streets had challenges with initiating heterosexual relationships boys. According to Ruparanganda, this could have been due to gender socialisation. Floyd and Brown (2012) established that the female children living in the streets were having sexual partnerships with drug dealers. The authors observed that such kind of heterosexual relationships between female children living in the streets and drug dealers was regarded as responsible for heterosexual transmission of HIV and high cases of sexually transmitted diseases.

Use of aphrodisiac substances

It is evident that the heterosexual behaviours of some of the children living in the streets of the Harare Central Business District could be associated with the use of aphrodisiac substances. During the in-depth interviews, one of the boys living in the streets revealed that he uses some of the aphrodisiac substances such as wild horse or seven hours and then engages in sexual intercourse with some of the sex workers. He had this to say:

> Elder, I abuse aphrodisiac substances such as wild horse or seven hours. I buy these tablets on the streets for 50 rand. When I take these tablets, I sometimes have short time[15] with some of the sex workers in the Avenues area. There is a certain sex worker who prefers short time with street boys, and she charges one dollar for a quickie. The prices of sex have gone down these days among sex workers around Avenues area. These days you negotiate with what you have because getting cash is a toll order. When I have taken on wild horse, I have strength for a heavy sex not a joke. However, the use of some of these tablets poses problems. One can get migraine or having a running stomach or stomachache. Some also get severe nose bleeding as a result of using the tablets. Sometimes it depends with users or individuals.

During the in-depth interviews, some of the girls living in the streets that trade in prostitution also revealed that some of their counterparts and boys living in the streets engage in heterosexual behaviours and use aphrodisiac substances. One of them had this to say:

> Elder, many of us enjoy sex. Our boy friends of the streets, they enjoy sex. They abuse sex drugs and if you slacken yourself, they would have heavy sex with you until you defecate. One of the days I had heavy sex with a guy who had taken some of these tablets. I did not enjoy the sex sessions as I developed some bruises on my vulva or vagina.

---

[15] Short time is referred as a quickie or a quick session of sex

During the key informant interviews, one of the sex workers also confirmed that some of their clients that include boys living in the streets were using aphrodisiac substances. She said the following:

> When I have sex with some of the street boys, I would have taken some of the sex drugs. One would realise that as the boys would demand several sessions of sex as a result of continuous penile erection. Some of the boys have very big penis that may shock you. One of the days I had sex with a street boy who had taken on aphrodisiac substances. He took time to ejaculate and I demanded for more money as I was threatening to end the sex session. These tablets enhance the sexual prowess of the young boys.

The narrative demonstrates that the children living in the streets in Harare Central Business District are social actors who engage in heterosexual behaviours and substance abuse. The heterosexual behaviours and abuse of sex drugs could be explained with the context of thin agency (Tisdall and Punch, 2012) as the actions could be the only viable options of these children. The thin agency in the context of behaviours of children living in the streets using sex drugs and engaging in heterosexual relationships was their survival or coping mechanisms. The actions or decisions of the children living in the streets could have been influenced by few survival options in an environment characterized with harsh survival options. The actions or behaviours could be viewed as part of the notions of ambiguity of agency (Bordonaro and Payne, 2012) as heterosexual behaviours and substance abuse threatens existing societal values. As noted, before, in the Shona culture children are not expected to engage in heterosexual relationship, but rather encouraged to abstain from pre-marital sex. The involvement in heterosexual relationships and substance abuse is seen as part of moral decadence. In addition, the actions could also be regarded as self-destructive agency (Gigengack, 2006, 2008) considering several risks associated with heterosexual behaviours and abuse of aphrodisiac substances among these children. Some of the risks could be a severe headache and or death, among others. For example, one of the boys in the interview above had a severe headache after using some of the aphrodisiac substances.

The heterosexual behaviours and misuse of substances among the children living in the streets of the Harare Central Business District demonstrate the level of their vulnerability. The behaviours illustrate alarming child rights violations on the streets of the Harare Central Business District. The actions and behaviours are inconsistent with the provisions of the international, regional and local child rights laws, policies and programmes. For example, heterosexual behaviours and substance abuse among the children living in the streets of the

Harare Central Business District is viewed as inconsistent with Chapter 3 of the United Nations Convention on the Rights of a Child (1989), that is, in the best interest of the child principle. In other words, the heterosexual relationships involving minors is seen as a form of sexual violence and exploitation. The children that engage in heterosexual relationships and substance abuse should get protection services from the duty bearers.

Use of psycho-active substances to gain confidence to engage in heterosexual behaviours

The study also observed that some of the street boys use psycho-active substances so as to gain confidence to sustain behaviours associated with heterosexual relations. During the life history interviews, one of the street boys revealed that substances such as *chapomba*[16] or *chamba*[17] made him to have confidence to engage in heterosexual relations. He had this to say:

> When I am drunk, I gain confidence to initiate sex. I am able to talk with the girls as compared when I am sober because initiating such talks would be difficult for me. Also, when I am intoxicated, I enjoy having sex, I fantasize a lot, elder.

One of the sex workers who trade in commercial sex working at the Fife Avenue base also added that some of the boys living in the streets abuse psycho-active substances to have confidence to approach girls. She added that such boys have low self-esteem, so they abuse substances to gain confidence to negotiate sex with girls. She had this to say:

> Some of the small boys particularly *magunduru*[18] would approach you for sex when they are heavily intoxicated by substances to gain confidence of talking with sex workers. When they are drunk, they are not shy, and they are able to even initiate sex discussion including negotiating for better or cheaper prices.

During the informal conversations, one of the street girls called Tara also indicated that substance abuse made her to have confidence to engage in heterosexual behaviours. She added that when she is drunk, she does not think of many issues to an extent that she has confidence of even approaching males for sex. Tara revealed that through the use of *chamba*[19] or *maragada*[20], she engages

---

[16] Chapomba is highly intoxicating substances that include brandy, chateau etc
[17] Chamba is cannabis
[18] Magunduru are children on and of the streets
[19] Chamba is cannabis
[20] Maragada are tablets used for the treatment of mental patients

in heterosexual relationships with some of the boys living in the streets and men from mainstream society for various reasons that include raising money for survival and also for funny. She had this to say,

Elder, when I am intoxicated by *bhurongo*[21] and or *chamba*[22] I get enough confidence of even approach male clients for sex. When I am drunk, I enjoy having sex. There are street boys including those from the mainstream society who come for sex with me. Some of them would pay me money to buy *sadza*[23].

The intricate relationship between the use of psycho-active substances and heterosexual behaviours among the children living in the streets of the Harare Central Business District illustrates thin agency of these children (Tisdall and Punch, 2012). It is within the context of thin agency because of the multiplicity of constrains characterizing the streets of the Harare Central Business District. The children living in the streets of Harare Central Business District find it extremely difficult to survive and they end up engaging in substance abuse and heterosexual relationships. In addition, the behaviours could be explained with the context of ambiguity of agency (Bordonaro and Payne, 2012) as the behaviours threaten or clash with societal values. Substance abuse and heterosexual behaviours also threaten the wellbeing of the children living in the streets as this increases their vulnerabilities to sexual abuse and exploitation, among others. The behaviours involving substance abuse and sexual behaviours among children living in the streets are seen as abomination among the Shona culture in Zimbabwe.

The behaviours of substance abuse and heterosexual relationships among the children living in the streets are also part of the concept of self-destructive agency (Gigengack, 2006 and 2008). The self-destructive agency is within the context of risks that are associated with use of psycho-active substances and heterosexual relationships associated with the children living in the streets. Some of the risks could be death and contracting several life-threatening diseases. The narratives also confirm that there are severe child rights violations on the streets of Harare Central Business District. The behaviours are inconsistent with international, regional and local child rights laws, policies and programmes. The actions of these children show that they are very vulnerable to abuse, violence and exploitation, for example, having sex under the influence of drugs. The phenomena of substance abuse and heterosexual relationships

---

[21] Bhurongo is cough syrup
[22] Chamba is cannabis
[23] Sadza is a staple food in Zimbabwe

among the children living in the streets in Harare Central Business District demonstrate that the duty bearers, for example, the City of Harare and government through the Ministry of Social Services and as well as the Ministry of Health and Child Welfare, are not providing adequate protection services to these vulnerable children. Some of the protection services could include raising awareness of substance abuse and heterosexual relationships among the children living in the streets.

Conclusion and Recommendations

As discussed above, there is an intricate relationship between heterosexual behaviours and substance abuse among the children living in the streets of the Harare Central Business District. Through abuse of psycho-active substances, some of the boys living in the streets gain confidence to approach and engage in heterosexual behaviour relationships. Furthermore, some of the boys engaged in heterosexual relationships are exposed to aphrodisiac substances. In addition, some of the children living in the streets abuse or misuse psycho-active substances to engage in heterosexual relationships with sex workers in shebeens, among others place. Nevertheless, the behaviours could be explained within the context of ambiguity of agency as the actions clashed with societal values (Bordonaro and Payne, 2012, Bordonaro, 2012). The heterosexual relationships and substance abuse involving children living in the streets is strongly condemned in Zimbabwean society. In other words, heterosexual relationships and abuse of substances among children are viewed as abomination in the Shona culture in Zimbabwe. On the other hand, Zimbabwean society ought to take the blame for producing such citizens or children who engage in heterosexual behaviours and substance abuse. The Zimbabwean society has failed to provide protection to children living in the streets who indulge in substance abuse and heterosexual behaviours. Their actions or behaviours could therefore be referred as thin agency as they were the most viable options in a constraining environment (Tisdall Punch, 2012). In addition, the behaviours could also be regarded as part of the notion of self-destructive agency (Gigengack, 2006, 2008). For example, through the excessive use of substances and heterosexual behaviours, the children living in the streets increase their vulnerabilities to sexual exploitation and drug abuse, among other exploitations. The heterosexual relationships and abuse of substances by the children living in the streets of the Harare Central Business District demonstrate child rights violations. The behaviours are inconsistent with the international, regional and local child rights laws, policies and programmes.

243

Several recommendations have been proffered by this chapter so as to reduce the risks associated with heterosexual behaviour and abuse of substances among the children living in the streets of the Harare Central Business District. Some of the recommendations include lobbying and advocating for full implementation of child rights laws, policies and programmes. This will go a long way in terms of arresting abuse of substances and heterosexual relationships among these children. In addition, there is a need to arrest all drug peddlers on the streets of the Harare Central Business District. This will also reduce the flow of substances on the streets. In addition, this will reduce easy accessibility of substances to the children living in the streets. There is a need to raise awareness on heterosexual relationship, substance abuse and sexuality issues among the children living in the streets of the Harare Central Business District. The awareness campaigns on heterosexual relationships and substance abuse could empower children living in the streets with information about sexuality issues and substance abuse, among others. The government of Zimbabwe's programmes such as National Action Plan for Orphans and Other Vulnerable Children should specifically target children living in the streets. Such programming may empower children living in the streets and also reduce their vulnerability to childhood poverty. For example, there is a need to initiate and implement social protection programmes targeting children living on the streets with the view to address childhood poverty. Furthermore, there is a need to increase access to contraceptive methods such as condoms among the children living in the streets of the Harare Central Business District so as to reduce risks associated with unsafe sex, among other unsafe behaviours.

References

Alleyne-Green, B., Coleman-Cowger, V.H. and Henry, D.B. (2012) Dating violence perpetration and/ or victimization and associated sexual risk behaviours among a sample of inner city African American and Hispanic adolescent females. *Journal of Interpersonal Violence*, 27(8), 1457- 1473.

Andrea, G. and Godin, M. (2014). Child labour, agency and family dynamics: The case of mining in Katanga (DRC). *Childhood*, 21(2), 161- 174.

Ansell, N. (2016). 'Once upon a time…': Orphanhood, childhood studies and the depoliticisation of childhood poverty in southern Africa. *Childhood*, 23(2), 162-177.

Asante, K.O., Meyer-Weitz, A. and Petersen, I. (2014). Substance abuse and risky sexual behaviours among street connected children and youth in Accra, Ghana. *Substance Abuse Treatment, Prevention and Policy*, 9(1), 45.

Beazley, H. (2003). The sexual lives of street children in Yogyakarta, Indonesia. *Review of Indonesian and Malaysia Affairs, 37*(1), 17-44.

Blais, M., Cote: B., Manseau, H., Martel, M. and Provencher, M.A. (2012). Love without a home: A portrait of romantic and couple relationship among street involved young adults Montreal. *Journal of Youth Studies,* 15(4), 403-420.

Butler, U. M. (2009). Freedom, Revolt and Citizenship' Three pillars of identity for youngsters living on the streets of Rio de Janeiro. *Childhood,* 16(1), 11-29.

Chikoko, W. (2014). Commercial 'Sex Work' and substance abuse among adolescent street children of Harare Central Business District. *Journal of Social Development in Africa,* 29(2), 57-80.

Chikoko, W. (2017). *Substance abuse among the street children of Harare: The case of Harare Central Business District, Zimbabwe* (Unpublished DPhil thesis). Department of Social Work, University of Zimbabwe, Harare.

Chikokoa, W., Chikokob, E., Muzvidziwa, V. N., and Ruparanganda, W. (2016). Non-governmental organisations' response to substance abuse and sexual behaviours of adolescent street children of Harare central business district. *African Journal of Social Work,* 6(2), 58-64.

Davies, M. (2008). A childish culture? Shared understandings, agency and intervention: An anthropological study of street children in northwest Kenya. *Childhood,* 15(3), 309-330.

Dickson-Gomez, J., Bodnar, G., Gueverra, A., Rodriguez, K. and Gaborit, M. (2006). Childhood Sexual Abuse and HIV risk among crack-using commercial sex workers in San Salvador, EL Salvador: A qualitative analysis. *Medical Anthropology,* 20(4), 545-574.

Gigengack, R. (2014). "My body breaks. I take solution." Inhalant use in Delhi as pleasure seeking at a cost. *International Journal of Drug Policy, 25*(4), 810-818.

Godoy, A. S. (1999). Our Right is the Right to Be Killed' Making Rights Real on the Streets of Guatemala City. *Childhood,* 6(4), 423-442.

Kagan, S., Deardorff, J., McCright, J., Lightfoot, M., Lahiff, M. and Lippman, S. (2012). Hopelessness and sexual risk behaviour among adolescent African-American males in a low-income urban community. *American Journal of Men's Health,* 6(5): 395- 399

Katsulis, Y. and Durfee, A. (2012). Prevalence and correlates of sexual risk among male and female sex workers in Tijuana, Mexico. *Global Public Health: An International Journal for Research, Policy and Practice,* 7(4), 367-383.

Makaruse, T. (2010). *Substance abuse among school children: A case study of Pafiwa High School in Mutasa* (Unpublished Master of Social Work dissertation). School of Social Work, University of Zimbabwe, Harare.

Mayock: , Corr, M.L. and O'Sullivan, E. (2013). Moving on, not out: when young people remain homeless. *Journal of Youth Studies,* 16(4), 441- 459.

Mhizha, S. (2010). *The self-image of adolescent street children in Harare* (Unpublished MPhil thesis). Department of Psychology, University of Zimbabwe, Harare.

Mhizha, S. (2014). Religious self-beliefs and coping vending adolescent in Harare. *Journal of Religion and Health,* 53, 1487-1487.

Mhizha, S. (2015). The religious-spiritual self-image and behaviours among adolescent street children in Harare, Zimbabwe. *Journal of Religion and Health,* 54, 187-201.

Mhizha, S. and Muromo, S. (2013). An exploratory study on the school related challenges faced by street children in Harare. *Zimbabwe Journal of Educational Research,* 25(3), 23-34.

Mizen: and Ofosu-Kusi, Y. (2010). Asking, giving, receiving: Friendship as survival strategy among Accra's street children. *Childhood, 17*(4), 441- 454

Montgomery, H. (2007). Working with child prostitutes in Thailand: Problems of practice and interpretation. *Childhood, 14*(4), 415-430.

Morrow, V., and Pells, K. (2012). Integrating children's human rights and child poverty debates: Examples from young lives in Ethiopia and India. *Sociology, 46*(5), 906-920.

Rurevo, R., and Bourdillon, M. (2003a). Girls: the less visible street children of Zimbabwe. *Children Youth and Environments,* 13(1), 150-166.

Rurevo, R. and Bourdillon, M. F. C. (2003b). *Girls on the street.* Harare: Weaver Press.

Ruparanganda, W. (2008). *The sexual behaviour patterns of street youth of Harare Zimbabwe in the era of the HIV and AIDS pandemic* (Unpublished DPhil thesis). Sociology Department, University of Zimbabwe, Harare.

Sundin E.C. and Baguley, T. (2015). Prevalence of childhood abuse among people who are homeless in Western countries: A systematic review and meta-analysis. *Social Psychiatry Epidemiology,* 50, 183- 194.

Taft, J. K. (2015). "Adults talk too much": Intergenerational dialogue and power in the Peruvian movement of working children. *Childhood,* 22(4), 460- 473.

Thompson, S. J., Rew, L., Barczyk, A., McCoy: , and Mi-Sedhi, A. (2009). Social estrangement: Factors associated with alcohol or drug dependency among homeless, street-involved young adults. *Journal of Drug Issues,* 39(4), 905-929.

United Nations. (1989). *The United Nations Convention on the Rights of a Child* (Unpublished report). Geneva.

Chapter 13

Succession Planning and the Sustainability of the Land Reform Programme in Zimbabwe

Vupenyu Dzingirai and Langtone Maunganidze

Summary

The role played by leadership succession in influencing long-term sustainability of organisations has been widely acknowledged globally. However, scholarly work on succession in farms allocated to indigenous farmers under the different land reform programmes in Zimbabwe has remained scanty. In the context of the fast track land resettlement programme, this chapter examines the factors influencing succession in the newly resettled farms in general and the implications for a sustainable land reform programme. Data were collected following an interpretive cross-sectional multi-case study design focusing on the experiences of purposively selected farms in Seke Rural District in Mashonaland East province. Seke Rural District lies about 50 kilometres south east of the capital of Zimbabwe, Harare. The study considered both A1 and A2 model farms. One of the major observations was that most farms have become derelict following the departure of the founders. The chapter contends that, although some indigenous African farmers practised some planning, this has overall often been neglected due to political and cultural reasons. Notwithstanding other structural and institutional constraints, lack of readiness by farm settlers to embrace modern versions of succession planning, and the politics of survival pose a serious threat to the sustainability of the land reform programme.

Introduction

The land question has been a dominant feature of the political and economic dynamics of resource distribution and utilisation in Zimbabwe. In the context of the fast track land resettlement programme, this chapter examines the factors influencing succession in the newly resettled farms in general and the implications for a sustainable land reform programme. For an organisation's long-term stability, survival and growth, it is imperative for founders to always look beyond the incumbent leader, develop strategies and create conditions for a smooth succession (Chrisman, Chua and Sharma, 2003, Irefin and Hammed,

2012). The founder in this chapter refers to the first beneficiaries of fast track land reform programme (FTLRP). The critical role played by leadership succession in influencing the long-term sustainability of organisations, especially small-scale enterprises is widely acknowledged.

This chapter is motivated by the fact that, while there are numerous studies on succession in black owned businesses, particularly family-controlled ones, evidence of similar works on newly acquired farms in Zimbabwe is scanty. While extant literature is intimate with the significant contribution of land reform programmes to poverty reduction and the empowerment of local communities (Scoones *et al.* 2010, Chingarande, Mugabe, Kujinga and Magaisa, 2012: 79-80), there has not been much scholarly attention paid to the survival of the farms beyond the lives of the "founders". This is perhaps unsurprising because farms in Zimbabwe have hardly been considered business entities. In addition, studies of farm succession planning focusing on the experiences of the developed parts of the world such as Australia, United States of America, and United Kingdom are abundant while they are almost entirely absent in poor rural agrarian contexts such as Zimbabwe. Furthermore, even in the developed economies, experiences of both inter-generational transitions and land reforms programmes have not been adequately interrogated. This is the gap this chapter seeks to address and therefore providing a timely contribution to the volume.

In this chapter, we also draw insights from experiences of black owned farms previously known as the 'purchase areas' before attainment of independence in 1980. Such farms, in some cases, became derelict even though they had been legally passed on to the next holder. The chapter also examines how the different panning practices adopted by the newly resettled farmers or land occupants influence farm continuity and consequently sustainability of the land reform programme. We advance the argument that while there is, on the part of some resettled farmers, some form of succession planning taking place, the practice overall has often been neglected for various reasons relating to cultural and political legitimacy. For example, the steady involvement by women in the programme has reconfigured power dynamics making the succession puzzle even more complex.

Background and context

On the attainment of political independence in 1980, the ruling party, Zimbabwe African National Union-Patriotic Front (ZANU-PF) initiated various land acquisition programmes for redistribution to the historically disadvantaged black citizens particularly the rural people. In doing so, the party was delivering on wartime promises for land reform at independence and equally considered the land reform as part of a broad strategy to build a socialist state in which the means of production were socialised (Moyo, 1995, Matondi, 2012). This was the policy that directed the country's political economy in the first ten years of independence.

In the late 1990s the government of Zimbabwe state abandoned its neoliberal land reform in favour of a more radical land reform. The justification for radicalism was, it is argued by Moyo (1995) and de Villiers (2003), motivated by the failed or slow progress of the market-driven 'willing-buyer and willing-seller' model. Further to this, the failed economic restructuring programme (ESAP) triggered high levels of unemployment and poverty across the country (Ncube, 2000, Nherera, 2005). As a way of dealing with opposition party, the Movement for Democratic Change (MDC), civil society and white commercial farmers, a swift and drastic land reform that delivered land to the people was found most appropriate. In the year 2000, these forces mobilised voters against a proposed new constitution that sought to support compulsory land acquisition and redistribution (Chitsike, 2003). The result of the 2000 general elections in which for the first time ZANU-PF lost most of its urban and some rural support to the MDC, triggered massive land invasions and occupations led by veterans of the liberation struggle who, with the support of ZANU-PF structures, considered themselves champions and custodians of the new revolution. While it was reluctant to bless the land reform in its radical character, the government launched the accelerated land reform and resettlement programme commonly known as the 'fast track' land resettlement programme (FTLRP). Its main objective was to accelerate both compulsory land acquisition and redistribution (Zikhali, 2008). The shift from "land reform" to "land invasions" attracted a lot of media attention and condemnation particularly in South Africa where a similar land revolt was feared (Lahiff and Cousins, 2001). Another key characteristic of this programme was that most of the land occupants and their kin or close associates were either unskilled or without any requisite resources and experience to engage in productive farming. This posed structural challenges for post-founder sustainability. It is important to note that the pioneers of this new "revolution" coined the programme the Third Chimurenga (Third Revolution) or *'hondo yeminda'* (war for the land) or *'jambanja'* (for its chaotic and violent disregard for rules or law) (Harrison, 2006, Magosvongwe, 2013, Matondi, 2012). They also targeted white commercial farms that were adjacent to cities and towns.

The fast track resettlement programme followed two models, namely the A1 and A2 models, labels echoing early independence land zoning or modelling. The farms were classified based on what seems to have been a rational arrangement relating to equity and growth (Zikhali, 2008, Matondi and Dekker,

2011, Moyo, 1995, Mutondi, 2012). The A1 model targeted the rural landless and small holder farmers who were resettled in villages or self-contained small plots of about 5-6 hectares. Majority of these were family controlled or managed. The A2 model is an elite commercial farming land-use model. It targets the elite in the Zimbabwean society, for example, top military leadership, civil senior bureaucrats and established businessmen. The motive was to create a new class of producers rooted in Zimbabwe. The whole model is based on full-cost recovery with the beneficiaries having an option to purchase the land within the 99-year lease period (Masiiwa, 2004). There different types of the A2 Model are shown in Table 13.1 below.

Table 13.1: A2 Model Land-use Types

| Type of Farm | Maximum Farm Size per Agro-Ecological Zone | | | | | |
	1	IIa	IIb	III	IV	V
Peri-Urban	2 - 50 ha	2 - 50	2 - 50	2 - 50	2 - 50	2 - 50
Small Scale Commercial	20	30	40	60	120	240
Medium Scale Commercial	100	200	250	300	**700**	**1000**
Large Scale Commercial	250	350	400	500	1500	2000

Source: Government of Zimbabwe (2001) (in Masiiwa 2004:16)

Lack of security of tenure and uncertainty surrounding the fast track land reform programme triggered dual residence, that is, people moving to newly acquired farms while at the same keeping their urban houses or communal homesteads. As a result, land occupants constructed temporary structures on the farms while other family members continued to reside in nearby towns or remained in their original rural villages.

Global context

Comparisons with international experience in land reform, such as in India, Australia, New Zealand, Malaysia and Brazil, show that effective land reform is not only very complicated, but that it also takes many years and extensive resources to accomplish (de Villiers, 2003). Studies on land reform programmes and also issues of succession among small or family-controlled businesses have been widely discussed both within and outside Africa. A few studies looking at the intergenerational transfer of managerial control in the family-farm business have been conducted in the England, France and Canada (Errington, 1998), the UK and in Pennsylvania (Pitts *et al.* 2009) that intimate the vital role played by succession planning in family-farm businesses. The authors concur that, though succession planning was vital for the farm survival, many founders failed to take necessary succession planning actions.

Regional context

The sustainability of land reform programmes has already been discussed elsewhere in southern Africa. For example, while the land reform in Zimbabwe sought to speed up redressing land ownership disparities inherited from colonial system, the challenge for countries such as Namibia was not only to speed up the process but also to prevent the high risk of failure after new farmers have been resettled (de Villiers, 2003: 42). All the other countries that have pursued land reform programmes, South Africa, Namibia and Malawi have adopted a claims-based approach. All these presented very little threat to the white commercial famers as had been experienced in Zimbabwe.

The land reform policy of the independent South African government comprised three elements (set out in more than 22 statutes), namely tenure reform, redistribution, and restitution (Cousins, 2000, de Villiers, 2003: 49). The issue of redistributing land without addressing ownership dynamics has been a challenge. One of the challenges of the land reform in South Africa was poor implementation and lack of protection for the rights of farm workers and farm dwellers (Binswanger-Mkhize, 2014: 262), and lack of land ownership by victims of dispossession during the apartheid era (Ramutsindela and Mogashoa, 2013: 314). Tenure reform was the most difficult to implement due to lack of supporting legislation (*ibid.* 310). The Zimbabwean land reform was more of a political approach rather than a strategic developmental initiative for arresting poverty, unemployment creation and inequality. In South Africa, entrepreneurs, including those in farming, have turned seemingly 'hopeless' situations into profitable business ventures, while very viable and productive farms in Zimbabwe have been left desolate and derelict.

Theoretical Framework

Given the complexity of the issues under investigation, the chapter combines ideas from Flora and Flora's (2008) community capital framework Model (Figure 1) and Amartya Sen's (1992) capability approach (Figure 13.2) as analytical techniques for exploring issues relating to succession and their influence on the sustainability of the land reform programme. The community capitals framework was developed (CCF) (Emery, Fey and Flora, 2005) as an expansion to the systems approach to poverty reduction, effective natural resources management and social equity. As shown in Figure 13.1, the framework contains seven capitals: human, social, cultural, political, built, financial and natural. Central to the model is social inclusion and empowerment, which are all critical aspects resonating well with the dynamics of the land reform programme. Flora and Flora (2008) put a case for the understanding of the interdependence, interaction and synergy among capitals. It is critical to maintain a balance between the capitals to avoid decapitalisation (Mary, Guiterrez-Montes and Fernandez-Baca, 2013). Decapitalisation refers to over-emphasis of one capital at the expense of others. During the implementation of the fast track land reform programme political interests superseded all other capitals.

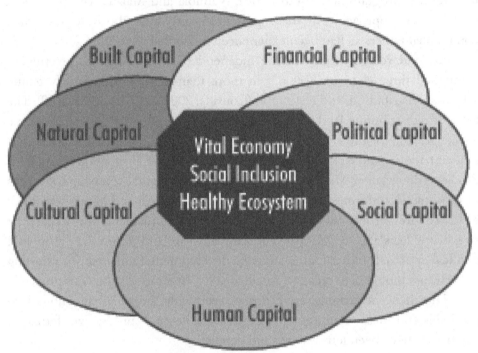

Figure 13.1: Flora and Flora's (2008) Community Capital Framework Model (adapted from Gauvin, 2011)

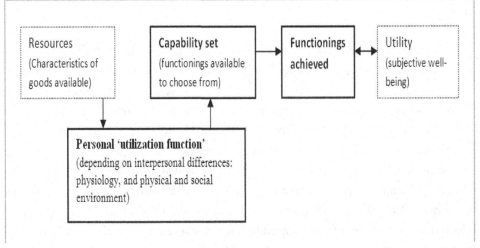

Figure 13.2: Core relationships of Sen's Capability Approach. (htt://www.iep.utm.edu/sen-cap)

For purposes of examining the dynamics of the fast track land reform programme and the succession issues that arise, the capabilities approach plays a complimentary role to the community capitals framework. According to Sen (1999), development is a matter of expanding the capabilities that people have reason to choose and value. However, this depends on what institutions exist to contribute to that freedom (Stewart and Deneulin, 2002: 67) because "... The expansion of freedom both as the primary end and as the principle means of development" is central to the approach. Human development is viewed as a process of expanding the real freedoms that people enjoy, expressed as their capabilities in doing so (Alkire, 2005: 120-121). As shown in Figure 13.2, transforming resources or capitals into capabilities also depends on the 'personal utilisation function'. In the case of the fast track land reform programme, it was important to identify capitals that were central for coping and adaptation. For example, a social capital aspect, particularly the family dimension which is a critical driver of intergenerational transitions, was neglected. Majority of A1 settlers occupied the land as families. Social capital and by extension cultural capital weave through both the community capitals and capabilities and any neglect of this aspect would threaten the sustainability of any rural system (Bowler, Bryant and Cocklin, 2002). While the fast track land reform programme sought to speed up the process of redressing of inequalities and providing freedoms to landless majority, it neglected the aspect of balancing the various community capitals which was essential to achieve real freedom.

Methodology

The study followed a qualitative research approach and used a cross-sectional multi-case study design. Case studies have been used in similar situations and found to be very useful as they allowed investigations to retain the holistic and meaningful characteristics of real-life events (Yin, 1994, Wild, 1997, Maphosa, 1999, Maunganidze, 2011). The choice of this design also emanated from "the desire to understand complex social phenomena" on the basis that "the case study method allows investigators to retain the holistic and meaningful characteristics of real-life events" as they unfold in their complexity as a whole (Yin, 2003:2). The study focused on the experiences of purposively selected occupants of a farm located in Seke Rural District in Mashonaland East province. Seke Rural District lies about 50 kilometres south east of the capital Harare as shown in Figure13.3.

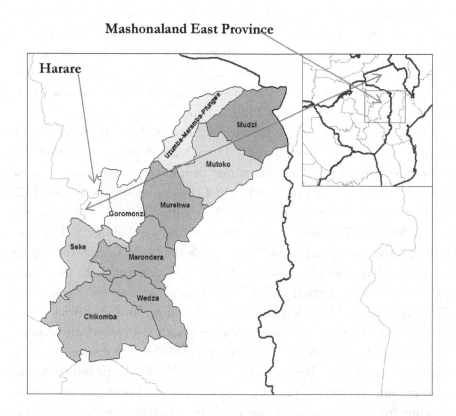

Figure 13.3: Seke District, Mashonaland East Province
Source: zim.gov.zw

The study focused on the A1 and A2 models, specifically the villagised or self-contained plots and the small holder commercial farms respectively. Sampling was both convenient and purposive. Five A1 and other five A2 occupants were selected on an availability basis. Both groups settled in two large commercial farms and had been on the land for a minimum of ten years. All occupants under the A2 originated from the nearby city, Harare, while the A1 settlers were resettled from rural areas as far as Masvingo provinces and happened to have contacts in the area as previous labourers in the nearby commercial farms. This sampling strategy was adopted for two main reasons. First, one of the researchers' familiarity and previous contact with key informants from the target population particularly A1 occupants facilitated easy access. The use of acquaintances has been found useful for collecting qualitative data such as narrating one's lived experiences (Etikan, Musa and Alikassim, 2016). Secondly, key informants were chosen on the basis of their willingness to provide information by virtue of knowledge and experience (Creswell and Plano Clark, 2011). Such key informants included the veterans of the liberation struggle and village committee members. This ensured provision of credible data given their intimate knowledge of events leading to and during the execution of the programme.

Data were collected using a combination of unstructured interviews, informal discussions involving historical narratives of lived experiences and direct observations. The qualitative interview and intense dialogue are at the centre of the data collection methodology (Ryen, 2002). This was complemented by documentary survey of previous studies on fast track land reform programme in Zimbabwe. This approach recognises the value of the complementarity of various techniques in collecting information related to people's views, observations and interpretations (Kottak, 2006). Data were thematically analysed using a combination of pattern matching and illustrative multi-case analytical techniques in line with theoretical frameworks used for the study (Newman, 2000). Data collection procedure was ethically informed as participation was voluntary and participants were assured of confidentiality and protection relating to the information they provided.

Results and Discussion

Social capital and challenges of succession

One of the findings of our study was that social capital in the form of social networks, trust, collaboration and linkages was critical for agricultural production at farm level and, by extension, farm longevity. According to Flora and Flora (2008), social capital can be divided into two parts, namely bonding social capitals and bridging social capitals. Bonding social capitals refer to connections that occur among homogenous individuals and groups, while bridging social capital describes diverse groups of individual bonded together to pursue specific ends. These definitions are important in this case given that most of the occupants originated from same area or were recruited to the farms via the same social or political networks. When the bonding and bridging of social capitals are high effective community action is realised together with the creation of an entrepreneurial social infrastructure (Gauvin, n.d). This supports Portes (1998) and Wolz *et al.* (20005), observations that social capital, when well institutionalised provides sufficient investment to transform ordinary households into viable firms. Preparation for leadership take over, therefore, could be more effective when it becomes part of the whole community, support groups, and associations. Saidapur (2012) observes that entrepreneurs organised groups or working networks which allow them to overcome obstacles and conflicts easily. This is one of the missing links in the Zimbabwean case. Furthermore, Kabir *et al.* (2012) contend that leadership skills are also acquired during social networks. They further note that, even though not everybody can be a leader, entrepreneurs can be assisted to achieve such kind of ability through proper training and guidance. In this study, these were hardly visible.

The challenge with the fast track land reform programme was the fact it was not only fast, rapid, radical and potentially disruptive to social capital but was overly political. Occupants and their dependants were expected to be more connected to the ruling party structures than other social capital dimensions. In essence, social capital was an underappreciated factor of production and, as a consequent; the issue of transfer management (succession) did not feature on the agenda. The land reform programme was reduced to a patronage dispensing instrument (Maunganidze, 2016.) and acted also as a hot bed for rent seeking or predation (Fine, 2003). Drawing insights from the community capitals framework, we advance the argument that the overemphasis on the political dimension of the process or alternatively decapitalisation of social capital (Mary, Guiterrez-Montes and Fernandez-Baca, 2013) diffuses family social capital which is a critical driver for inter-generational transition and succession. This observation is consistent with other scholarly works elsewhere (Coeurderoy and Lwango, 2012) which found out that the dilution of the social capital associated with the traditional African family system in the management of the newly acquired farms, handicapped the firm in the long run. The fast track land reform programme destroys social capital because it tears away existing institutions. First, the land was owned by the state and, secondly, often solely managed by the occupant, which is in most cases was the male war-veteran or collaborator. The absence of spouse (wife) involvement does not necessarily exclude them from being part of the personal contact network (Poza, 2001). However, consistent with patriarchy they were effectively excluded from succession on the basis of primogeniture. The same personal contact network has been regarded as a business resource (Carter and Jones-Evans, 2000) as networks assist small firms in their acquisition of information and advice (Shaw, 1997).

The two conditions that are critical for sustaining family social capital are missing across the cases, the condition of power with respect to the family's predominance in terms of ownership, and the condition of involvement which is directly linked to management control by family members. For example, in the absence of written succession plans, the sons' active involvement in the management of the farm could provide sufficient preparation for the possible takeover in the event that the founder retires or dies. The lack or absence of succession plans can also be explained with the use of concepts of social and cultural capital (Flora and Flora, 2008). Although the land reform programme did not directly reconfigure new class formations, the three dimensions of capital, economic, social and cultural capital (Siisiainen, 2000) were manifest, particularly under both the A2 and A1 models.

The paradox of individualisation and the politics of survival

Debate around the issue of individualisation as an enablement and constraint to a successful reform programme has not been conclusive. The individualisation of land rights under both the A1 and A2 models has far reaching implications for both agricultural investments and productivity. The family dimension is frequently neglected. The findings of this study are similar to what Matondi (2005) (cited by Chingarande *et al.* 2012), observed elsewhere in the same region regarding how fast track land reform programme provided individual women with alternative means of accessing land unlike under the customary communal system. Consistent with Sen's capabilities (or freedom) approach, although the programme did not originally seek to redress gender imbalances, the overall outcome empowered women. As one key informant intimated,

> We might not be the owners of the land as women but at least have direct control on the produce and jointly make decisions regarding land utilisation and the incomes from sales particularly tobacco.

Guided by the community capitals framework, this chapter makes a case for considering the aspect of community level participation and empowerment to facilitate durable succession and sustainability of the programme. Taking cognisance of women input or participation as a key resource and central for sustainable development helps to avoid land being derelict on the departure of the founder. However, individualisation also comes with costs. It disrupts social relations and norms of reciprocity characteristic of the kin-based communal land households. The fast track land reform programme had little regard for the family fabric through its promotion of mobility of men to take up new farmland thus splitting families (Nyawo, 2016). The new social networks and the accompanying interactions are transactions more driven by political interests and parochial economic sectional interests. They are very fragile and often fail to build solidarity among communities. Our study found out the existence of a combination of both communalized and individualised households under both the A1 and A2 models. A negation of balanced community capitals as espoused by Flora and Flora (2003), through the ruling party and the government's preoccupation with political survival led to decapitalisation which consequently suppressed agricultural productivity. The new settlers or occupants have not only remained subsistent or "tenant farmers" nearly two decades after, but subservient and dependent on both the State and ruling party structures. The fast track land reform programme has been reduced to a harvesting rod and an idiom of accumulating political capital (Maunganidze, 2016). Basing on informal discussions and lived experiences of various occupants, one discerns that land occupations were just a new form of political mobilisation. There is very little attention paid to ensuring that individual capabilities were created before resettlement as, people rushed to the farms with no one taking stock of their capabilities.

As elaborated in the next section, for the ruling party and State, security of tenure was not a priority. As at the beginning of 2017, A1 occupants in this study had not been issued occupation offer letters or permits. They continued to be regarded illegal settlers or 'squatters'. Drawing insights from both the community capitals (Flora, 2008) and capabilities approach (Sen, 1992, 1999) to development, it is observed that, while the fast track land reform programme may have granted the landless rural people rights to use land, lack of requisite farming skills and experience, appropriate infrastructure and other capitals necessary to create capabilities to transform their livelihoods denied them ultimate freedom. They have remained dependent on State handouts.

The politics of survival as observed elsewhere (Portes, 1998:15) has negatives such as "exclusion of outsiders, excess claims on group members and restrictions on individual freedoms". At present, it would seem the government is fixated on the survival of the ruling party with very little attention paid to building individual capabilities. While the programme has some attraction from a political perspective, it has turned out to be problematic and complicated as

258

there are already incidents of some occupants who have abandoned their plots and relocated to the city or migrated to neighbouring countries.

Security of tenure and succession

While family social capital generates benefits in the short term, in the long run there are non-economic compensatory costs with an equally economic impact (Chrisman, Chua and Sharma, 2003). The influence of the nexus between land rights security and investments in agriculture has implications for succession. In the absence of any significant initial individual investment (sunk costs), the pursuit of entrepreneurial initiatives for farm survival beyond one's generation was scanty. The land reform beneficiaries have not invested much so as to warrant any serious concern for its survival beyond their time. Unlike with 'owned' properties where the founder and successors would seek to preserve the family legacy, under the fast track land reform programme, land was held on a lease or permit basis subject to review at the discretion of government. However, given the claims-based or entitlement nature of the land reform programme, occupants, particularly war-veterans, did not find the arrangement inordinate and maintained that,

> Although we did not pay any cash for the land it is our legitimate inheritance. Blood was spilled to gain the right to access the use of the land. So, this land is not for free.

Our study confirms that any land reform programme cannot exist independent of property rights and the institutions and ideologies that sustain it (Fine, 2003). These constrain the founder's social capacity to delegate or transfer responsibility and control (Zuern, 2003). Occupants in these two models were starkly different with the later often dependent on the farmer as casual labourers on the A2 farms. The communal dimension of the A1 model was also not attractive to the younger generation and most occupants and potential successors agreed that lack of land ownership was a huge disincentive. The ownership was only legitimised through the mediation of political capital. The rights were only extended to land use (usufruct) and not extended to ownership or disposal. Ownership and control over the land was thus effectively symbolic and sentimental. The apparent insecurity and inadequate sizes allocated under the programme did not allow subdivisions to sons particularly when they came of age. This has far –reaching implications for succession. This is important given that the son preference for property inheritance is still dominant even among women. Our findings agree with earlier studies in other parts of Zimbabwe (Chingarande *et al.* 2012, Matondi, 2005) which observed more security in the traditional customary or communal land tenure system than in the new resettlement programme. The new occupants have thus been effectively reduced to "tenant" farmers. As a result, there are numerous cases of resident and non–resident farmers. Resident farmers put up some structures on the land and also brought with them livestock while the non-resident group puts up temporary structures and only on-site during farming season or operating from nearby towns or cities or even in the diaspora particularly those working in foreign missions. It is quite evident that some form of delegation occurs on the farms allocated to non-resident farmers although not enough to prepare someone for permanent take over. A case in point is that of one of the war collaborators in the area who has been on the farm since 2004. As of the beginning of 2017, he had not been issued an offer letter, permit or lease agreement to stay on the land. He is therefore forced to maintain a foot in his previous communal village as 'insurance' in the event of dispossession. As he intimated,

> Split households make succession difficult as families spread their risk through maintaining dual farming households as fall back if ever, they were evicted.

As a result, temporary structures have become a common feature. Figure 13.4: depicts the typical common structure on A1 plots.

Figure: 13.4. Typical Common Structure on an A1 Plot in Zimbabwe (authors' photo shoot)

Entrepreneurial capabilities, gender and patriarchy

Entrepreneurial intensity is critical for the success of the land reform programme in Zimbabwe. One of the major findings of this study is that most land occupants lacked sufficient entrepreneurial capabilities and attitudes to pursue business ventures. Although factors such as age, gender, experience and education, as well as the "social positions, worldviews and dispositions", have been found to predict whether someone becomes an entrepreneur or not, the chaotic and political character of the programme did not allow the nurturing of entrepreneurship. The claims-based approach and the entitlement orientation associated with the programme did not motivate the occupants to pursue any economic agendas particularly under the A1 model. Further to this, there was no immediate capacity building to prepare the new farmer. For most war-veterans, particularly those who originated from the city, land invasions provided an opportunity to 'own' land to build a home. The failure of the farmers to transform their new plots into viable entrepreneurial or commercial ventures remains a threat to their own livelihoods and sustainability of the programme.

Patriarchal rules of inheritance and property rights in Zimbabwe have had a significant bearing on the nature and extent of the succession process (Maunganidze, 2013, Maphosa, 1999, Mbiba, 1999). Although land occupants appreciated the need to appoint successors on the basis of knowledge and experience in farm management, they still argued that, for the sake of family legacy, sisters and daughters were the least preferred heirs as they could be married out of the family. This would create an additional problem as their spouses and siblings would also expect to benefit from any succession arrangement. Previous studies elsewhere (Cole, 1997, Stavrou, 1999, Vera and Dean, 2005) support this observation. Any form of succession, if it ever occurred, would follow the primogeniture route, which dictates inheritance on the basis of birth order and gender. Knowledge of family history, birth order and gender were identified as the key successor attributes. Gerontocratic and patriarchal values that are deeply entrenched in the family (Birley, 1986, Cheater, 1986, Wild, 1997) impacted greatly on the character of succession. It is therefore not only the characteristic of the founder and incumbent leader which significantly influenced the character of the firm in the next generation but 'gendered habitus'. Very few females would have received the 'basic leadership apprenticeships' (Mulholland, 2003) that is needed to prepare them for succession. Even among the previous owners, white commercial farmers, there was no evidence or literature supporting direct participation or involvement of female heirs or siblings. Land was allocated unevenly to men and women. In most cases, it is men whose names appear on the 'offer letters', or the permits.

Women, however, were important players in the land invasions, providing support to the base camps during the '*jambanja*' period, and subsequently investing in the development of new homes and farms (Scoones *et al.* 2010). There are however few instances when women as wives or in their own right were allocated some plots, particularly under the A1 self-contained model. To some extent, the fast track land reform saw the death of women 'invisibility' and hiddenness (Ogbor, 2000, Cole, 1997).

Conclusions, Policy Options and Recommendations

This chapter sought to examine the factors influencing succession in the farms acquired under the fast track land reform programme and the implications for sustainability of the programme. One of the key findings was the interweaving connections between social, cultural and political capitals relating to inheritance, land rights security and investments in agricultural production. The programme execution was also disruptive to family social capital which rendered planning for leadership transfer problematic. The fast track land reform programme also disrupted numerous kin-based social institutions and practices such as the patriarchal control of communal property and heirship.

We also conclude that most of the land occupants did not pursue any deliberate strategies to transform their plots into entrepreneurial entities. This could be attributed to the lack of investment in training and mentoring to prepare farmers for the new challenges. Beyond the variants of cultural and social capital, there are also the political and legal frameworks circumscribing the control and management of the land. The uncertainty surrounding security of tenure and the overly-partisan system of land allocations were thus sufficient to scare away any potential successors, especially the youth. It is apparent that the State and the governing ZANU-PF were more concerned about political survival than productivity on the farms. Preoccupation with accumulation and consolidation of political capital at the expense of other community capitals generates a condition of decapitalisation (Mary, Guiterrez-Montes and Fernandez-Baca, 2013, Flora and Flora, 2003) thus threatening the potential of the programme to create capabilities and freedoms on the part of individuals (Alkire, 2005). Consequently, most plots have become derelict following the departure of the founder and have been reduced to nothing more than 'just new homes'. The new settlers or occupants have not only remained subsistent or "tenant farmers" nearly two decades after occupation but have continued to be subservient and dependent on both the State and ruling party structures.

The chapter contends that, although some resettled farmers engaged in some form planning, the practice overall has often been neglected due to both cultural and political reasons. It may be too early to say the point, but there is no evidence of deliberate succession strategies put in place at individual, community and institutional levels. The absence of succession planning has the potential to threaten the sustainability of the land reform programme.

The failure of the fast track land reform programme to engender a new culture of both individual and collective entrepreneurship remains a challenge to both development researchers and practitioners. This chapter, with the support from extant literature and conceptual frameworks, highlighted how individual entrepreneurship has struggled to take root in the newly resettled areas. It is critical for both State and non-state actors to recognise the need for balancing political, social, human and economic interests to avoid decapitalisation. It is important to target both the rural and urban youth, particularly university graduates, for capacity building and repositioning the land reform programme as a strategic option for employment creation.

Given the newly created social and political formations arising from the programme, perhaps the State, in collaboration with universities and non-state actors, could promote the growth of team entrepreneurship in order to widen the pool of successors beyond the boundary of kinship and family tree. As informed by Sen's capabilities approach, the ability of people to convert bundles of resources into valuable capabilities depends on their personal utilisation function (Sen, 1992, 1999). Further research is recommended in order to take stock of the 'community capitals' and the accompanying reconfigurations in order to mutate the politicization of the programme. It is important to recognise the heterogeneity of land occupants not only in terms of their capacities to engage in commercial farming but also in terms of attitudes towards farming. To facilitate recovery and transformation of capitals there is a need for designing and putting into practice community-based monitoring and evaluating strategies accompanying any future land reform programme.

References

Alkire, S. (2005). Why the capability approach? *Journal of Human Development*, 6(1), 115-133.

Binswanger-Mkhize, H.P. (2014). From failure to success in South African land reform. *African Journal of Agricultural and Resource Economics*, 9(4), 253-269.

Birley, S. (1986). Succession in the family firm: The inheritor's view. *Journal of Small Business Management*, 24(3), 36-43.

Bowler, I. R., Bryant, C. R., and Cocklin, C. (2002). *The sustainability of rural systems: Geographical interpretations*. London: Kluwer Academic Publishers.

Carter, S. and Jones-Evans, D. (2000). *Enterprise and small business*. London: Prentice-Hall.

Cheater, A. (1986). *An introduction to social anthropology*. London: Penguin Books.

Chingarande, S.D., Mugabe: H., Kujinga, K. and Magaisa, E. (2012). Struggles within the struggle: Gender and land reform experiences in Chimanimani District, Zimbabwe. *Journal of Social Development in Africa*, 27(1), 57-84.

Chitsike, F. (2003). A critical analysis of the land reform programme in Zimbabwe. 2nd FIG Regional Conference, Marrakech, Morocco, December 2-5, 2003.

Chrisman, J.J., Chua, J.H. and Sharma: (2003). *Current trends and future directions in family business management studies: Towards a theory of the family firm*. Colman White Paper. Calgary: University of Calgary.

Coeurderoy, R. and Lwango, A. (2012). Social capital of family firms and organisational efficiency: Theoretical proposals for a transmission model through bureaucratic costs. *Management*, 15(4), 415-439.

Cole: M. (1997). Women in family business. *Family Business Review*, 10(4), 353-371.

Cousins, B. (2000). *At the crossroads: Land and agrarian reform in South Africa into the 21st Century*. Bellville: Programme for Land and Agrarian Studies.

Creswell, J.W. and Plano Clark, V. L. (2011). *Designing and conducting mixed methods*. London, Thousand Oaks: Sage Publishing.

de Villiers, B. (2003). *Land reform: Issues and challenges, A comparative overview of experiences in Zimbabwe, Namibia, South Africa and Australia*. Johannesburg: ICAS, Konrad Adenauer Foundation, Stiftung.

Emery, M., Fey, S. and Flora, C. (2005). Using community capitals to develop assets for positive community change. Community Capitals Framework: Research, Evaluation and Practice Conference, Ames, Iowa.

Errington, A. (1998). The intergenerational transfer of managerial control in the farm-family business: A comparative study of England, France and Canada. *The Journal of Agricultural Education and Extension*, 5(2), 123-136.

Etikan, I., Musa, S.A. and Alikassim, R.S. (2016). Comparison of convenient and purposive sampling. *American Journal of Theoretical and Applied Statistics*, 5(1), 1-4.

Fine, B. (2003). Social capital for Africa? *Transformation*, 5(3), 29-52.

Flora, C.B. and Flora, J.L. (2008). *Rural communities, legacy and change*. Boulder, CO, USA: Westview Press.

Gasson, R., Crow, G., Errington, A., Hutson, J. and Marsden, T. (1988). The farm as a family business: A review. *Journal of Agricultural Economics*, 39(1), 1–41.

Gauvin, T. (2011). *Community capitals framework and sustainable development.* Fort Kent, ME.

Gauvin, T. (n.d). *Community capitals framework and rural sustainable development.* Orone, ME: School of Economics, University of Maine, https://core.ac.uk/download/pdf/6625486.pdf

Harrison, E. (2006). *Jambanja.* Harare: Maioio Publishers.

Irefin, I.A. and Hammand, O.G. (2012). Effect of culture on entrepreneur successor. *British Journal of Arts and Social Sciences,* 7(2), 168-177.

Kabir, M.S., Hou, X., Akther, R., Wang, J. and Wang, L. (2012). Impact of small entrepreneurship on sustainable livelihood assets of rural poor women in Bangladesh. *International Journal of Economics and Finance,* 4(3), 265-280.

Kottak, C. (2006). *Mirror for humanity.* New York. McGraw-Hill

Lahiff, E. and Cousins, B. (2001). The land crisis in Zimbabwe viewed from South of the Limpopo. *Journal of Agrarian Change,* 1(4), 652-666.

Magosvongwe, R. (2013). *Land and identity in Zimbabwean fiction writings in English from 2000 to 2010: A critical analysis* (Unpublished PhD thesis). Cape Town: University of Cape Town.

Maphosa, F. (1999). Leadership Succession: A recalcitrant problem in the indigenization of African economies. *Zambezia,* 26(2), 169-80.

Mary, E., Guiterrez-Montes, I. and Fernandez-Baca, E. (2013). *Sustainable rural development: Sustainable livelihoods and the community capitals framework.* London: Routledge.

Masiiwa M. (2004) *Land reform programme in Zimbabwe: Disparity between Policy Design and Implementation.* Harare: Institute of Development Studies, University of Zimbabwe.

Masiiwa, M. (2003) *The agrarian reform in Zimbabwe: Sustainability and empowerment of rural communities.* Harare: Institute of Development Studies, University of Zimbabwe.

Matondi: B. (2005). *Mazowe District Report: Findings of land reform* (Volume 11) (Unpublished). Harare.

Matondi: B. and Dekker, M. (2011). Land rights and tenure security in Zimbabwe's post fast track land reform programme: A synthesis report for land acquisition. Project ID WS.320005.1.3

Matondi: B. (2012). *Zimbabwe's fast track land reform.* London: Zed Books.

Maunganidze, L. (2011). Succession planning and business survival at crossroads: The Case of selected family-controlled businesses in Harare succession, Zimbabwe. *Zambezia, Journal of Humanities of the University of Zimbabwe,* XXXVIII(ii), 45-74.

Maunganidze, L. (2013). 'Invisible' and 'hidden' actors: A gendered discourse on participation in family-controlled businesses. *Alternation* (Special Issue), 20(2), 52-74.

Maunganidze, L. (2016). Zimbabwe: Institutionalized corruption and state fragility. In D. Olowu and C. Paulos (Eds.), *State fragility and state building in Africa: Cases from Eastern and Southern Africa* (pp.39-60). London: Springer. ISBN-13: 9783319206417.

Mbiba, B. (1999). *Urban property ownership and the maintenance of communal land rights in Zimbabwe* (Unpublished PhD thesis). London: Oxfam, UK.

Moyo, S. (1995). *The land question in Zimbabwe*. Harare, Zimbabwe: SAPES Books,

Mulholland, K. (2003). *Class, gender and the family business*. New York: Palgrave Macmillan.

Ncube, M. (2000). Employment, unemployment and the evolution of labour policy in Zimbabwe. *Zambezia*, xxvii (ii),

Nherera, C.M. (2005). Shifts in the livelihood structure of Zimbabwe following economic liberalisation. Report Number 15, Institute of Education, University of London

Nyawo, V.Z. (2016). Families divided: Disruptions of the family in Zimbabwe's fast track land resettlement programme. *American Journal of Social Science, 1*(1), A18-27.

Ogbor, J. O. (2000). Mythicising and reification in entrepreneurial discourse: Ideology-critique of entrepreneurial studies. *Journal of Management,* 37(5): 605-635.

Pitts, M. J., Fowler, C., Kaplan, M. S., Nussbaum, J. and Becker, J. C. (2009). Dialectical tensions underpinning family farm succession planning. *Journal of Applied Communication Research,* 37(1), 59-79.

Poza, E.J. (2001). Spousal leadership and continuity in the family firms. *Family Business Review,* 14(1), 25-26.

Ramutsindela, M. and Mogashoa, M. (2013). The people's choice: Options for land ownership in South Africa's land reform. *Social Dynamics,* 39(2), 308-316.

Ryen, A. (2002). Cross cultural interviewing, In J.F. Gubrium and J.A. Holstein (Ed.), *Handbook of interview research.* London: Sage Publications.

Saidapur, S. (2012). Informal brick industry in the North Karnataka: Flourish or perish. *Asian Journal of Economics and Management,* 1(8), 87-97.

Scoones, I., Maringwe, N., Mavenzenge, B., Murimbarimba, F., Mahenehene, J. Sukume, C. (2010). *Zimbabwe's land reform: Myths and realities.* Harare: Weaver Press.

Sen, A.K. (1999). *Development as freedom.* New York: Knopf Press.

Shaw, E. (1997). The real networks of small firms. In D Deakins *et al.* (Ed.), *Small Firms: Entrepreneurship in the 1990s.* London: Paul Chapman Publishing

Siisiainen, M. (2000). *Two concepts of social capital: Bourdieu vs Putman.* Paper presented at ISTR Fourth International Conference "The third Sector: For what and for whom?" July 5-8, 2000, Dublin, Trinity College, Ireland.

Stewart, F. and Deneulin, S. (2002). Amartya Sen's contribution to development thinking. *Studies in Comparative International Development,* 37(2), 61-70.

Stavrou, E.T. (1999). Succession in family business: Exploring the effects of demographic factors on offspring intentions to join and take over the business. *Journal of Small Business Management,* 37(3), 43-61.

Vera, C.F. and Dean, M.A. (2005). An examining of the challenges daughters face in family business succession. *Family Business Review,* 18(4), 321-345.

Wild, V. (1997). *Profit not for profit's sake: History and business culture of African Entrepreneurs in Zimbabwe.* Harare: Baobab Books.

Wolz, A., Fritzsch, J. and Reinsberg, K. (2005). *The impact of social capital on farm and household: Results of survey among individual farmers in Poland.* IAMO, Institute of Agricultural Development in Central and Eastern Europe.

Yin, R.K. (1994). *Case study research: Design and methods.* London: Sage Publications.

Yin, R.K. (2003). *Case study research: Design and methods.* Thousand Oaks: Sage.

Zikhali: (2008). Fast track land reform and agricultural productivity in Zimbabwe. *Environment Development. Discussion Paper Series, 2008, 8-30.*

Zuern, E.K. (2003). Debate: Social capital and modernity. *Transformation,* 5(3), 69-75.

Chapter 14

A Study of Agency and Women's Livelihoods in Post Fast-Track Land Reform Programme in Zimbabwe

Olga Bungu and Charity Manyeruke

Summary

Most literature on land reform shows that women in Africa face various challenges of accessing land. These challenges usually emanate from the collusion of both traditional and colonial institutional power structures that discriminated against women. Even in countries such as Uganda, Kenya, Zimbabwe where land reforms have been conducted, most studies focus on patriarchal structures that affect women's access to land. For instance, following Zimbabwe's fast track land reform programme (FTLRP) some studies point to the limited number of women who accessed land. However, after the FTLRP, about 12% and 18% of women accessed land under the A1 and A2 farming models respectively. Empirical evidence from the study conducted in Mashonaland East, Mashonaland Central, Manicaland and Matabeleland provinces of Zimbabwe among resettled A1 and A2 women farmers indicate agency and improved livelihoods among these resettled farmers. The objective of the chapter is to examine the contributions of A1 and A2 women farmers to the national economy and to their family livelihoods. The chapter adopts a liberal feminist theory which posits that sex should not be used as a tool to discriminate women in accessing productive resources including land. Empowerment concept is also used as a framework of analysis. The chapter uses secondary data and mainly primary data obtained from interviews that were conducted with A1 and A2 women farmers in the above-mentioned provinces.

Introduction

Women in agriculture are often described as "invisible" yet they are not "invisible", but it is the officials both policy-makers and development planners who do not appreciate them (ISIS, 1983). The causes of this situation go a long way back into history when traditional and colonial social structures in Africa discriminated against women. Women in colonial Zimbabwe were thus historically considered as second-class citizens and were subjected to double discrimination on account of colour and sex both in the world of work and in society (Mzingi and Kamidza, 2011: 323). Waged labour forced men to migrate to towns leaving women as active farmers - albeit with limited decision-making powers over the crops they were producing and use of profits (Goebel, 2006). African women's unequal access to power and resources caused by colonial capitalism and local patriarchal control has been the fundamental locus of African women's oppression and invisibility in agriculture. This impacted negatively on their potential to access land. Women's access to land and other productive resources in society has consequently been through their relations with men either husbands or sons.

Although women have been denied direct access to land in colonial Zimbabwe and other African countries, their contributions in agriculture are important both for economic growth and ensuring food security. The FTLRP in Zimbabwe opened spaces for women to access land. Under the FTLRP, about 18% of women accessed land in the A1 farming models and 12% in the A2 farming models (The Utete Report, 2003: 25). According to Mgugu and Chimonyo (2004: 150), the question of land and gender is closely related to survival matters in Zimbabwe as 86% of women in Zimbabwe depend on land for their livelihoods. Agriculture contributes between 15-20% to the gross domestic product (GDP), over 40% to exports, 60% of raw materials to agro-industries and providing livelihood to over 70% of the population and employment to one-third of those in the formal labour force (Zimbabwe Brief, 2009: 3). Agriculture in Zimbabwe is therefore important for improving economic growth and reducing poverty.

The challenge which the dominant literature on women in agriculture presents is that women are taken as a monolithic group with limited access to land even under land reforms such as the fast-track land reform programme (FTLRP) in Zimbabwe (Goebel, 2005a: 16, Gaidzanwa, 2011: 8, Njaya, 2014: 32). This generalization on women's access to land, while historically applicable, simplifies the complicated picture after the FTLRP. There are different categories that differentiates women. These categories include marital status, professions and wealth. Generally, professionals and wealthier women have better opportunities to access land. This chapter examines the contributions of women beneficiaries under the FTLRP to the national economy and their livelihoods. The various ways through which women accessed land under the land reform programme are also examined. Contextualising agricultural production and marketing by A1 and A2 women farmers in Zimbabwe is important as pathways to development and empowerment prospects. The population of Zimbabwe is estimated to be 13.061 million (2012 census) with 52% being female.

Zimbabwe attained independence from Britain on 18 April 1980. Land redistribution was among the unresolved contentious issues from the country's liberation struggle (UN, 2014). However, during the first decade of independence, land redistribution was slow due to the 'willing seller, willing buyer' clause as per the 1979 Lancaster House Constitution (UN, 2014). Even in the second phase of land reform, the programme was slow again. By 1997, only a total of 71 000 households had been resettled on 3.6 million hectares from the original target of 162 000 households (UN, 2014: 10). Due to the failure of the donor conference in 1999 and the sporadic land invasions or *jambanja* which had started around 1997, the government launched the FTLRP in 2000. Agriculture is one of the major foreign currency earners in the country with a contribution of about 19% to the country's gross domestic product (GDP) (ZimStat, 2013: 32). The contributions of women, who constitute 52% of the population, is therefore important in alleviating poverty and spurring economic growth in mainstream economic activities including agriculture.

Conceptual Framework

This chapter was guided by the "liberal feminist theory" (Jaggar, 1983: 27, Bearsley, 1999: 16) and the "concept of "empowerment" (Kabeer, 1991, Mehra, 1997). Liberal feminism draws back to the Enlightenment period of the late 17th and 18th centuries which emphasised individual autonomy. Mainstream liberalism in the eighteenth and nineteenth centuries offered a form of thought borrowed from the Enlightenment concept of an 'individual' as a product of an autonomous rational being and political equality is associated with that ability to reason (Bearsley, 2005: 30). Liberal feminism is based on the premise that "the sense of male superiority and entitlement is deeply embedded in cultural and social systems throughout the world and has set up the hierarchy of power between men and women" (Riley, 2008: 3). Gender, the social construction of roles between the sexes, is therefore a power laden concept which reinforces and mirrors the power dynamics in society which discriminates against women. African women have therefore been faced with many challenges in accessing productive resources such as land and agricultural inputs such as seeds and fertilizers. Yet the central argument proposed by liberal feminists such as Mary Wollstonecraft (1792) and John Stuart Mill (1988), is that custom should not be used as a tool of discriminating the sexes and, as such, men and women must not be treated differently under the law. Women empowerment is therefore necessary to uplift women in society and promote their access to resources and participation in the public domain including the national economy.

271

Empowerment can be understood as both a process and the outcome of the process. As a process, Whitmore (1988: 13) defines empowerment as

> ... an interactive process through which people experience personal and social change, enabling them to take action to achieve influence of the organisations and institutions which affect their lives and the communities in which they live (as cited in Lord 1993: 4).

Kabeer (2005: 13) concurs by noting that "... people who exercise a great deal of choice in their lives maybe very powerful, but they are not empowered, because they were never disempowered in the first place." Empowerment therefore "refers to the processes by which those who have been denied the ability to make choices acquire such an ability" (Kabeer, 2005: 13). Empowerment as an outcome emphasises "achievements" (Kabeer, 2005: 14) made through exercising autonomy in making decisions. The notion of agency as an important element of empowerment emphasises that women themselves must be significant actors in the process of change that is being described (Sen, 1993, Mehra, 1997). Kabeer observed that empowerment also implies 'thinking outside the system' and challenging the status quo (as cited in Malhotra *et al.* 2002: 6). The various ways through which women exercised agency and accessed land under the A1 and A2 farming models is therefore important as empowerment processes meant to reduce poverty.

Methodology

The chapter used primary and secondary data. Primary data was gathered through interviews that were conducted with A1 and A2 women farmers and officials from different ministries. The key stakeholders that were interviewed for the study include officials from the Ministry of Finance and Economic Development, Ministry of Women Affairs, Gender and Community Development, Ministry of Lands and Rural Resettlement, and the Agricultural Marketing Authority. These stakeholders provided key policy issues on women farmers in Zimbabwe.

The table 14.1 below highlights the various provinces and districts in Zimbabwe where interviews were conducted with A1 and A2 women farmers,

Table 14.1: Targeted Provinces and Districts in the Study

Province	District	A1 women farmers	A2 women farmers
Mashonaland East	Marondera	25	2
	Murewa	2	2
	Goromonzi	2	2
	Seke	2	2
Mashonaland Central	Guruve	2	2
	Mazowe	2	2
	Muzarabani	2	2
	Shamva	2	2
Manicaland	Makoni	2	2
	Mutare	2	2
	Mutasa	2	2
	Nyanga	2	2
Matabeleland South	Beitbridge	2	2
	Gwanda	2	2
	Insiza	2	2
	Umzingwane	2	2
Total		55	32

Source: Authors' Own Compilation (2016)

The table indicates the 4 provinces and 16 districts where interviews were conducted with A1 and A2 women farmers. A total of 87 A1 and A2 women farmers were interviewed, 55 A1 and 32 A2 farmers. In Marondera district under Mashonaland East province, 25 A1 women farmers were interviewed. Almost 23 more A1 women farmers were interviewed compared to 2, the targeted number for A1 women farmers per district. A comparative analysis was done on the production trends of 10 A1 women farmers who joined Machiki Irrigation Scheme, a cooperative farming scheme, and 13 others who did not. The study found the production per hectare for A1 women farmers under the scheme was 5.8 tonnes compared to 1.02 tonnes for women who did not join the scheme. However, a detailed discussion of this comparative analysis is beyond the scope of this chapter.

Different farming activities undertaken by women farmers in the target provinces allowed the study to fulfil the objective of the chapter which sought to establish the contributions of women beneficiaries of the FTLRP to the national economy and their livelihoods. These farming activities include cereal production, especially of maize in the Mashonaland East and Central provinces.

McNairn (2014: 5) observed that cereal production in Zimbabwe is generally highest in the three Mashonaland provinces, Mashonaland East, Mashonaland Central and Mashonaland West. Manicaland province and Matabeleland South were chosen for the specialized production of agricultural commodities such as potatoes and livestock and small grains respectively. Land is a political issue in Zimbabwe thus the study ensured anonymity of women respondents and did not include their names in the study. Instead, the study used pseudonyms to represent women respondents.

The Study Area

Zimbabwe is a land-locked country that is located in southern Africa and has a total land area of 390, 757 square kilometres (United Nations, 2014). The following map of Zimbabwe shows the administrative provinces and districts that were visited during the study.

Figure 14.1: Study Area
Source: Authors' Own Compilation (2016)

Zimbabwe is divided into 10 administrative provinces, but the study targeted the four provinces of Mashonaland East, Mashonaland Central, Manicaland and Matabeleland South. The various districts that were visited under each province are also shown on the map. Zimbabwe is bordered by Mozambique to the east, South Africa to the south, Botswana to the west and Zambia to the north.

Results

Women, agency and agricultural production after the fast track land reform *programme*

The fast track land reform programme resulted in new patterns of land ownership among women. While power structures are most often unequal, they are not static. Under the fast track, women managed to access land, both in the A1 and A2 farming models. Several studies found different statistics on the number of women beneficiaries to the program. During the FTLR, women were allocated land but, in fact, a lot more women benefitted indirectly as wives and through being part of a family (Mutopo *et al.* 2014: 51). Chingarande (2008) and WLZ (2007) point that women who accessed land range between 10% and 28% of the total (as cited in Moyo, 2011: 504). However, the Utete Presidential Land Review Committee Report (2003) observed that about 18% of women benefitted land under the A1 model and 12% in the A2 model. These women managed to access land without male intermediaries as was the case during the colonial period (Gaidzanwa, 2011: 4). The findings of this study, therefore, indicate women's agency on land access under the fast track land reform programme and points to the opportunities that land presents to their livelihoods. They also discuss the power struggles that are inherent in the A1 and A2 farms within the local and international domain and how they have been impacting on women's productivity.

Women's land access under the FTLRP

The study found that women emerged as landowners despite their marital status. The table 14.2 below shows the various ways through which women who responded to the study accessed land.

Table 14.2: Land Ownership among A1 and A2 Women Farmers from the Sample

Farmer type	Self	Child	Husband	Joint	In laws	Total
A1	32 (58.2%)	1 (1.8%)	17 (30.9%)	3 (5.5%)	2 (3.6%)	65
A2	27 (84.4%)	0 (0.0%)	4 (12.5%)	1 (3.1%)	0 (0.0%)	22
Total	59 (67.7%)	1 (1.1%)	21 (24.1%)	4 (4.6%)	2 (2.3%)	87

Source: Author's Compilation from Interview Data (2016)

From the table, most women respondents (67.7%) managed to access land in both the A1 and A2 models. Among the sampled provinces, for the A2 farmers, Manicaland and Matabeleland South had 25% each of women beneficiaries, Mashonaland Central had 18.75% and the least was Mashonaland Central with 15.62% (the sum total of these percentages is equal to 84.37%). For the A1 women farmers, the number of beneficiaries for women who accessed land per province was 29.09% for Mashonaland East province, followed by both Mashonaland Central and Manicaland each with 10.9%, and Matabeleland had 7.27%. For the 'self' category, some women had participated in the farm invasions, while some had accessed the farms after the death of their spouses and changed ownership.

The study, as shown on the table also found de facto women landowners. These are women who were actively working on the land without legal entitlement to the land they were working on. These women constituted about 24.1%. Widows who were yet to change land ownership and married women comprised members of this group. The third category that emerged was joint ownership, and this was about 4.6% of the population. As a matter of policy, the Ministry of Lands and Rural Resettlement now insists that if, for instance, a man wants to be issued with an offer letter, lease or permit, enquiries are made as to whether he is or not married. If he is married, then an offer letter is issued jointly to him and his spouse respectively (Ministry of Lands and Rural Resettlement official during an interview, 2016).

Women are not a monolithic group. They assume different identities and roles within society. Each identity that a woman assumes, for example, wife, police officer, nurse, and war veteran, come with a different level of power. Women within the sample had different roles and occupations. These roles had an impact on the various ways through which women accessed land.

From the table, about 63.2% of women respondents took farming as their main occupation, followed by 19.5% of different professions which include police, teaching and nursing, 5.7% were war veterans, 9.1 % were cross border traders followed by 2.3% who were a councillor and a headwoman respectively. All these women were found in all the various provinces in the sampled provinces. The councillor and the head woman (*sabhuku*) were found in Guruve and Insiza respectively. The various modes of accessing land used by the women respondents include participating in the *jambanja* (sporadic) invasions, networking and applying for the farms. Women's roles and positions in society influenced their access to land.

Table: 14.3 Occupations of the A1 and A2 Women Farmers

Occupation	Frequency	Percentage (%)
Farmer (former communal farmers, farm workers, Non-farmers)	55	63.2%
Professional (Police officers, teachers, nurses, registrar, agronomist)	17	19.5%
War veterans and spouses of war veterans	5	5.7%
Councillor and Head woman	2	2.3%
Cross border traders and tuckshop owners	8	9.1%
Total	**87**	**99.8%**

Source: Author's Own Compilation from Interview Data (2016)

This study confirms Matondi's (2012) study, *Zimbabwe's fast-track land resettlement* that,

> … women who were ex-combatants or civil servants accessed land in both the A1 and A2 schemes. Many of them confirmed that they used their privileged positions to gain access to land, and would not have been successful as ordinary women. Therefore, networking, understanding the processes and having connections were important factors influencing their access to land.

However, what Matondi misses is that some women managed to access land through participation in farm invasions even though they did not have influential positions. In Marondera, where the study interviewed 23 more A1 women farmers than any other sampled district, about 39% were former farm workers (n=23). These women therefore showed agency by actively participating in farm invasions and succeeded in accessing land despite being ordinary women. The following are some of the narratives showing agency in participating and making decisions to access land:

Mary (not her real name), an A2 farmer from Muzarabani said:
While we were still applying for the farms, my husband did not take it seriously and did not take farming as a well-paying economic activity. He only began to assist

me in buying seeds and taking farming seriously after seeing the money that I had made from growing tobacco.

Grace (not her real name), an A1 farmer from Machiki said:

We were camped here during the *jambanja* period". Previously, she was a farm worker at Dosemary farm, near Machiki in Marondera district.

Susan, an A1 farmer from Machiki said:

As a war collaborator, when it was announced that those who wanted farms come and apply, I came whilst others were watching us.

Several analyses on gender and the fast track land reform programme in Zimbabwe pointing to women's vulnerability under different forms of power structures (Gaidzanwa, 2011, Njaya, 2014), miss the point for taking women as a homogenous group. This results in an assumption of women as an always constituted group, one which has been labelled 'powerless', 'exploited', and sexually harassed (Mohanty, 1984: 337). Different categories of women including married, teachers, war veterans opened up opportunities for them to access land. Each category led to a certain level of power which allowed the woman to exercise autonomy in making her strategic life choices. As underscored by agency, previously disempowered people must have the 'power to' define their own life-choices and to pursue their life goals even in the face of opposition from others (Kabeer, 1999). Some married women also relentlessly pursued their goals and successfully fought for land access in a male dominated area.

Crop production among resettled women farmers

The division of agricultural labour based on gender in Africa led to the conclusion that men engage in cash cropping while women produce food crops (Carretta and Bryceson, 2002, Boserup, 1970), yet such binary categorisation miss women's agency in growing cash crops. In Zimbabwe, crops are divided among the following groups: food grain crops- maize, wheat and small grains (sorghum and millets), oil seed crop mainly soya beans, and the third category includes the main export crops which are tobacco and cotton and livestock commodities (Anseeuw *et al.* 2012). The following is a figure 14.2 on the variety of crops that women beneficiaries of the land reform are growing,

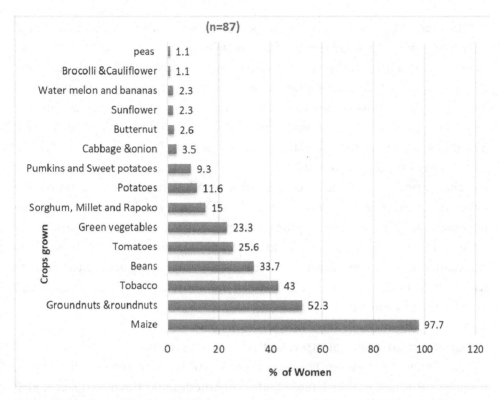

(n=87)

Crop	% of Women
peas	1.1
Brocolli &Cauliflower	1.1
Water melon and bananas	2.3
Sunflower	2.3
Butternut	2.6
Cabbage &onion	3.5
Pumkins and Sweet potatoes	9.3
Potatoes	11.6
Sorghum, Millet and Rapoko	15
Green vegetables	23.3
Tomatoes	25.6
Beans	33.7
Tobacco	43
Groundnuts &roundnuts	52.3
Maize	97.7

Figure 14.2: Crop Production among the Resettled A1 and A2 Women Farmers
Source: Authors' compilation from interview data (2016)

The figure 14.2 indicates the various crops that are grown by resettled A1 and A2 women farmers. These resettled women farmers were involved in the production of food grain crops, including, maize (97.7 %), small grains including, sorghum, rapoko and millet (15%). About 43% of women in the targeted group were producing tobacco, one of the main export crops in Zimbabwe. A significant number of women were also into horticultural production, growing tomatoes (20.9%), and green vegetables (18.6 %). Another important crop grown by women farmers both for diet and cash was beans (33.7%). About 11% of women farmers are into potato production. Women potato growers were mainly found in Nyanga district in Manicaland province, with the exception of some women farmers in Mazowe who were also into potato production. The study found that the least grown crops among targeted women farmers were bananas, peas, broccoli, cauliflower and watermelons. Choice of crop, especially for the least grown crops, was determined by inherited farm infrastructures which supported the production of these crops. The integration of women's contribution in the production of both these cash and food crops is important for economic growth and poverty reduction.

Traditionally, women have been associated with subsistence farming, that is, mainly growing food crops for household consumption. Research in Mashonaland East, Mashonaland Central and Manicaland in Zimbabwe after the fast track land reform programme revealed that A1 and A2 women farmers are increasingly growing tobacco. However, A1 women farmers are mostly viewed in the lenses of communal farming characterised by subsistence farming. Yet this study supports MacNain's study, *Zimbabwe Food Security Brief* (2014), which indicated that smallholder farmers, most of whom are women, have switched from maize to tobacco production. While his study focused on the implications of this shift on food self-sufficiency in Zimbabwe, this also questions gender stereotyping on women as subsistence food producers. Resettled women farmers thus continuously fight gender stereotyping which is still manifest as they are inherently looked down upon as subsistence farmers with limited potential to venture into higher value crops such as tobacco and even livestock production.

Contract farming among resettled women farmers

According to Women Tobacco Report (2016), Zimbabwe is the largest producer of tobacco after United States of America and Brazil. Tobacco, also known as the 'golden leaf', has become a lucrative business for the new farmers including women. Some of the companies that contract A1 and A2 women farmers include Boost Africa, Mid River, Tobacco Coverage Industries, Progressive Union, Dutch Veil, Zimbabwe Leaf Tobacco, Salt Lakes, Tianze and BAT. Tobacco production is attractive for newly resettled farmers in the A1 and A2 farming models because, unlike other agricultural commodities, there are more contractors that are easily accessible to farmers in both models than any other crop. Through contract farming, women also get access to seeds, inputs and chemicals, important productive factors which women usually have a difficulty in accessing because of their sex. According to the Agribusiness Marketing Specialist from the Ministry of Agriculture, contract farming is beneficial because women farmers have a secure market for their products and have access to technical expertise (human capital, and monitoring and extension advice). In addition, contract farming is good for women farmers because they have access to finance without collateral (Agricultural Marketing Authority Director, during an interview, 2016). Tobacco today is one of the sources of income for women in agriculture in Zimbabwe. Furthermore, on the market, tobacco tends to pay more than maize, the traditional crop that most women farmers grew.

In Zimbabwe today, tobacco farming through contracting is a sub sector in agriculture which is power laden and presents both opportunities and challenges for women farmers. The challenges that women face mainly emanate from the exploitative nature of contract farming. While it is believed that contract farming is good because farmers have access to extension services and inputs, and are assured of a ready market (USAID, 2009), interviews with women farmers and other stakeholders indicated the opposite. For instance, it was widely pointed out by women farmers that, through contract farming, women farmers are usually short-changed by contractors. Some of the issues raised by women farmers is that of low buying prices. A woman farmer from Guruve said, "I was contracted by Chidziva, but I saw that they were paying less than Boka in Harare". This was also supported by the Agricultural Marketing Authority (AMA) director who indicated during an interview in 2016 that contract farming usually is characterized by low and unviable producer prices. Without market information, women farmers in remote areas are vulnerable to contractors who take advantage of the distance between farmers and main tobacco floors which are usually located in the distant urban areas. The chances of improved livelihoods through farming for women farmers thus will be reduced and their living standards would still remain poor.

Although input provision under contract farming is attractive to farmers, this may be meant to hide the exploitative nature of the relationship which however manifests itself during marketing. According to Sarah (not her real name), an A2 woman farmer from Mutare in Manicaland Province, the contractors usually have an excuse of buying one's tobacco at a low price. For instance, they can indicate that "… your tobacco has no weight therefore it is spoiled". They buy the crop at a low price such as at 80 cents/kg. This is clear exploitation because tobacco has the potential of paying more. In 2012, Zimbabwe got US$771 million from tobacco exports at an average price of US$5.94. Compared to what a farmer can get when her tobacco has been labelled as, "spoiled" contract farming can thus be viewed as a form of neo-colonialism meant to short-change farmers from enjoying the fruits of their labour. Women farmers under tobacco production are therefore constantly faced with capitalist exploitation in the form of various international contracting companies.

Contract farming appears to be more beneficial to the contractors because they have guaranteed access to the produce despite weather conditions and usually, they are mostly highly placed in the agricultural value chain (Ministry of Agriculture, Agribusiness Marketing Specialist during an interview, 2016). For instance, in the local market, National Foods (one of the largest manufacturers and marketers of food products in Zimbabwe and southern African region), is involved in various activities which include stock feeds, mealie meal and flour. These are value added commodities which pay more in the agricultural value chain as opposed to the contracted farmer who mainly participates at the production level. The same horse-rider relationship in contract farming also applies to international companies like Tianze and other bigger players in the market from overseas. An official from the Ministry of Finance also observed that, since contractors buy inputs in bulk, they get them at lower prices, yet they inflate the prices to the farmers. In contract farming cycle, women farmers therefore appear at the bottom end of the value chain, yet they are the critical actors in the production of tobacco.

In response to the exploitative nature of contract farming, some women farmers devised coping mechanisms to ensure that they eke out a living out of tobacco production. One such strategy is contract marketing. Contract marketing is when the farmers uses her own inputs and engages the contractor as the potential buyer of her commodity. The farmer can benefit from farming experience from the contractor, but she retains her autonomy to choose another buyer if she does not agree with the price being offered by the initial engaged contractor. Through contract marketing, women farmers retain the independence of selling their tobacco to any market of their choice in such cases where contractors label their tobacco as *"spoiled"* in order to buy it at low prices. Other women farmers indicated cases where the contractor sought to buy tobacco at low prices, and they sold it to informal traders. This is the narrative of Winnie (not her real name), an A1 farmer from Marondera,

> Tobacco needs to be grown by wise farmers in order for one to benefit from it. Most people in Marondera are no longer growing it because the contracting made them loses. What I do when I go to sell my tobacco is that when I realize that it is being sold at a low price, I will get out of the auction floor holding my receipts. Outside there would be informal traders and once they see you holding your receipts, they will ask you the amount you will be willing to sell your tobacco, we will negotiate, and they usually buy at a higher price than the contractor. Whilst walking out I would have shouted at the contractor even if he is a white man that I laboured alone while growing my tobacco.

Another coping strategy that women have developed is side marketing. This can be done in two ways. First, farmers avoid selling tobacco to the contractor but use their friends' contract numbers to sell to other contractors or tobacco auction floors. Secondly, they may only send a few bales of tobacco to the contractor and sell the remainder to other buyers. As such, the experience of women farmers in tobacco production indicates that women are not only victims of the exploitative tobacco marketing industry, but some are autonomous agents who are constantly negotiating and challenging the power structures to ensure that they benefit from their agricultural work. Land access on its own is therefore not enough for women farmers if the exploitative power structures that seek to exploit and diminish the work of women farmers remains intact.

Livelihoods after the fast-track land reform programme

Land access among women farmers enabled them to carve land-based livelihood activities through crop production, including tobacco farming. Through farming, most women farmers have managed to accumulate assets. This is shown in Figure 14.3.

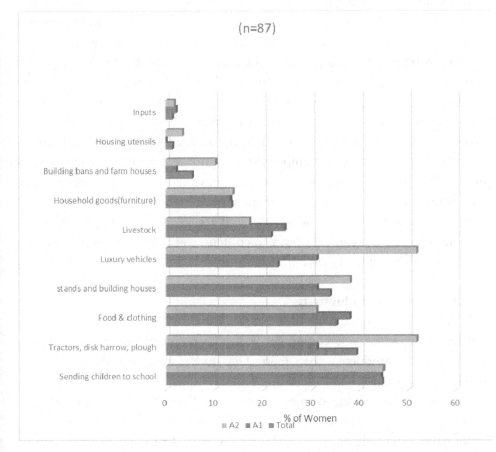

Figure 14.3: Successes Recorded by A1 and A2 Women through their Agricultural Work
Source: Author's Compilation from Interview Data (2016)

Figure 14.3 shows various assets and investments which A1 and A2 women farmers managed to accumulate through their diverse agricultural work. The total percentages for the various successes recorded for both the A1 and A2 farmers were include sending children to school 44.6%, purchasing tractors, and other farm equipment 39.2 %, food and clothing 35.1%, purchasing of luxury vehicles 23%, buying stands and building houses 33.8% and livestock 21.6%. Findings as shown in Figure 3 indicate that the highest successful investment made by women was sending their children to school (44.6%). This supports the findings of other studies that when they have an income, women farmers tend to spend their income on sending children to school and ensuring their household welfare (Ashby *et al.* 2009, Verhart *et al.* 2016).

Land access not only resulted in asset and wealth accumulation among women farmers, but it also empowered them to make strategic life choices that even result in challenging their spouses. The study found that Queen (not her real name), an A2 farmer in Seke was able to challenge her cheating husband because, as a farmer, she was economically empowered to stand up against her abusive husband. She indicated that the reason for her divorce was that she realized that her husband used their income from tobacco production to buy his girlfriend a car. Queen indicated that she was fortunate in that "from the time I got the farm, it was registered in my name. When I got divorced after discovering that my husband had bought his girlfriend a car, I ordered him to '*March and go*!'". In terms of empowerment and independence, women who previously had the least access to economic activities outside of domestic work have therefore gained economic independence with increase in power and authority over the use of their incomes. Land access and the ability to carve out a livelihood give a woman the power to contend with power structures that are abusive and discriminatory even in marriages.

Challenges to productivity

Challenges to productivity rooted at the farm level relate to access to inputs such as seeds and farming equipment. It has been argued that women farmers usually are less productive than men. The study found that about 16% (14 women) among the A1 and A2 women farmers from the sample had tractors. Tractor ownership among women farmers was highest in Mashonaland East where 6 women had tractors followed by Manicaland where they were four, Mashonaland Central had 3, with Matabeleland South having only one. From the 16 percent of women who had tractors, only 1 farmer was an A1 farmer from Murewa in Mashonaland East Province. About of 17% women owned disk harrow, cart and ploughs. The findings therefore point to lack of farming equipment as a major challenge for increased productivity among women farmers. Although agriculture is an important engine of growth and poverty reduction, chances of making headway are limited if women farmers continue working with limited farming equipment. Women empowerment through mechanization programmes would ensure equal opportunities between men and women and this is important for increased productivity among A1 and A2 women farmers.

Although women farmers indicated that they had been applying for farming equipment such as tractors under different programmes they indicated that they witnessed only male farmers benefiting from the programmes. Some of the mechanisation programmes that were undertaken by the government of Zimbabwe include, More Food for Africa Programme Phase 1. The program involved the supply of US$38 million worth of mechanisation and irrigation equipment from Brazil under a facility of US$98 million in 2015 (Ministry of Agriculture, Mechanisation and Irrigation Development, 2017: 18). Nomagugu (not her real name), an A2 farmer from Gwanda, indicated that they were trained on how to use the tractors after applying for tractors, yet the tractors were given to chiefs who had not been trained. Zanelle, also an A2 farmer from Macheke, indicated that she was not aware of the mechanization program being undertaken by the government, she only came to know about it after those who were delivering a tractor to a male beneficiary were lost and came to her farm instead. Women farmers therefore continue to face difficulties in accessing farm equipment. This affects their productivity, reduces their potential to have improved livelihoods and affects national economic growth.

While liberal feminists call for women empowerment through the inclusion of women in the economic domain, inclusion and the increase in numbers of women beneficiaries on land reform programmes must be matched with the productive resources, especially inputs and equipment availed to women. Zimbabwean feminists have been critiqued for relying too much on the state to support change (Moyo, 1995), a reliance that refers to the state as a rational engine of social reform. However, the reason why equal opportunities remain a call from women farmers and feminists both in Africa and Zimbabwe is that 'the state' is enmeshed in, rather than distinct from 'society' (Wolby, 2001). The state hence perpetuates and promotes male's dominance in the allocation of resources.

Conclusions

Agriculture is a contested terrain where women's access to land has been limited because it is dominated by powerful male actors. Such a position has been created and perpetuated by male dominance in the indigenous and colonial patriarchal structures. This chapter has shown that during the colonial period in southern Africa, the imposition of hut taxes and male waged labour resulted in male migration with females left as de facto communal farmers. The structures

285

that discriminates women in agriculture are still manifest today even in countries where land reforms have been done. For instance, although women managed to access land on the A1 and A2 model farming schemes in Zimbabwe, they still have to fight for their rights in the production and marketing of their crops. The study found that only 16% women out of a sample of 87 women farmers had tractors. In addition, contract farming is a challenge to women, especially when they market their tobacco. Women respondents indicated that contractors were paying low prices, for example, Chidziva in Guruve. Furthermore, from the interviews conducted at the Ministry of Finance, it was observed that contactors buy inputs in bulk and get them at low prices, but they inflate the prices to farmers. Carretta and Bryceson (2014) therefore cautioned that the word 'negotiate' for inclusion in land reforms by women may not entail substantial marked changes on gender power structures.

Exploitation is too evident in tobacco production, especially under contract farming. Some women farmers were losing out to contractors, for example, their tobacco is bought at low prices as the case in Guruve under Chidziva. However, other women farmers have devised strategies to counter the exploitative nature of contract farming. For instance, Winnie from Marondera contends that tobacco production requires wise farmers who can walk out negotiate with informal traders outside auction floors for higher prices. The chapter concludes that women are not a monolithic group. There are different categories among women including professionals, teachers, nurses, police offices, war veterans, widowed and married. Each identity that a woman assumes presents both opportunities and challenges. Professional women, war veterans and former farm workers managed to access land under the fast track land reform programme. There is a need for government intervention to meet the financial and technical requirements of the diverse groups of women farmers for increased productivity.

The study recommends that, for genuine transformation in agriculture to take place, there is a need for a change of attitudes and structures that oppress and look down upon women. For example, some women respondents indicated that though they applied for tractors, only their male counterparts benefitted, among them chiefs who did not even undertake the necessary training. Liberal feminists should move away from their call for equality which mainly emphasises on numbers because women's empowerment is not a game of numbers only but also of transforming society and how it views women. The study found diverse categories of women who accessed land under the A1 and A2 farming models and established various ways through which they are responding to male domination. This means that development is possible if the role of women in agriculture, both in food and cash crop production, is integrated in national development projects.

References

Anseeuw, W., Kapuya, T., and Saruchera, D. (2012). Zimbabwe's agricultural reconstruction: Present state, ongoing projects and prospects for reinvestment. *Development Bank of Southern Africa, 32,* 1-5.

Bearsley, C. (1999). *What is feminism? An introduction to feminist theory.* UK: Sage Publications.

Bearsley, C. (2005). *Modernist emancipatory feminism-Wollstonecraft to Wolf. Gender & Sexuality: Critical Theories, Critical Thinkers,* 1(3): 1-28.

Boserup, E. (1970). *Women's role in economic development.* London: George Allen and Unwin Limited.

Caretta, M. A., and Börjeson, L. (2015). Local gender contract and adaptive capacity in smallholder irrigation farming: a case study from the Kenyan drylands. *Gender, Place & Culture,* 22(5), 644-661.

Chingarande, S. (2008). Gender and the struggle for land equity. In S. Moyo, K. Helliker and T. Murisa (Eds.), *Contested terrain: Land reform and civil society in contemporary Zimbabwe* (pp. 275–304). Pietermaritzburg, South Africa: S and S Publishers.

Gaidzanwa, R. B. (2011, April). Women and land in Zimbabwe. In *conference on Why Women Matter in Agriculture, Sweden* 1(9): 4-8.

Goebel, A. (2005a). *Gender and land reform: The Zimbabwe experience.* McGill-Queen's University Press.

Goebel, A. (2005). Zimbabwe's 'fast track' land reform: What about women? *Gender, Place & Culture,* 12(2), 145-172.

ISIS Women's International Information and Communication Service. (1984). *Women in development: A resource guide for organization and action.* Philadelphia: New Society Publishers.

Jaggar, A.M. (1983). *Feminist politics and human nature.* New York: Rowman and Littlefield Publishers.

Kabeer, N. (1999). Resources, agency, achievements: Reflections on the measurement of women's empowerment. *Development and change, 30*(3), 435-464.

Kabeer, N. (2005). Gender equality and women's empowerment: A critical analysis of the third millennium development goal 1. *Gender & Development,* 13(1), 13-24.

Kumar, K. (1989). *Conducting key informant interviews in developing countries.* Washington DC: Agency for International Development press.

Lord, J., and Hutchison, P. (2009). The process of empowerment: Implications for theory and practice. *Canadian Journal of Community Mental Health*, 12(1), 5-22.

MacNairn, I. (2014). *Zimbabwe food security brief.* Available at: http://www.fews.net/sites/default/files/documents/reports/Zimbabwe_Food_Security_Brief_2014_0.pdf. [Accessed: 25 April 2017]

Made, J. (1997). *Financing smallholder farmers.* Available at: http://afraca.org/?wpfb_dl=58. [Accessed: 25 April 2017].

Malhotra, A., Schuler, S.R. and Boender, C. (2002). *Measuring women's empowerment as a variable in international development.* Washington DC: The World Bank.

Matondi: B. (2012). *Zimbabwe's fast-track land resettlement.* London, New York: Zed Books.

Mazinga, L. and Kamidza, R. (2011). *Inequality in Zimbabwe.* Available at: http://www.osisa.org/sites/default/files/sup_files/chapter_5 _-_zimbabwe.pdf. [Accessed: 20 October 2017].

Mehra, R. (1997). Women, empowerment, and economic development. *The Annals of the Academy*, 5(54), 136-149.

Mill, J.S. (1988). *The subjection of women.* New York: D. Appleton and Company.

Mohanty, C. T. (1984). Under Western eyes: Feminist scholarship and colonial discourses. *Boundary 2*, 333-358.

Moyo, S. (1995). A gendered perspective of the land question. *Southern African Feminist Review (SAFERE)*, 1(2):13-31.

Mushunje, M. T. (2001). Women's land rights in Zimbabwe. *Broadening Access and Strengthening Input Market Systems (BASIS): Madison, WI, USA.*

Mutopo, P., Manjengwa, J., and Chiweshe, M. (2014). Shifting gender dimensions and rural livelihoods after Zimbabwe's fast-track land reform programme. *Agrarian South: Journal of Political Economy*, 3(1), 45-61.

Njaya, T. (2014). Closing gender asset gap in land access and control in A1 schemes in Zimbabwe.

Riley, M. O. P. (2008). *A feminist political economic framework.* Available at: https://www.coc.org/files/Riley%20-%20FPE0.pdf . [Accessed: 25 April 2017]

Schimdt, E. (1992). *Peasants, traders, and wives: Shona women in the history of Zimbabwe, 1870-1939.* London: Baobab Books.

Sen, G. (1993). *Women's empowerment and human rights: The challenge to policy.* Paper presented at the Population Summit of the World's Scientific Academies.

288

United Nations. (2014). *Country profile, Zimbabwe.* Available at: www.zw.one.un.org/uninzimbabwe-country-profile. [Accessed: 25 April 2017].

Utete Presidential Land Review Committee. (2003). Available at: http://www.sarpn.org/documents/d0000746/P840-Utete_Report_August2003.pdf. [Accessed: 28 June 2017].

Women Tobacco Farmers Report. (2016). *The experience of women tobacco farmers at the tobacco auction floors in Zimbabwe.* Available at: http://www.wag.org.zw/wp-content/uploads/2016/05/Women-Tobacco-Farmers-Report.pdf. [Accessed: 25 April 2017].

Worby, E. (2001). A redivided land? New agrarian conflicts and questions in Zimbabwe. *Journal of Agrarian change*, 1(4), 475-509.

ZimStat. (2012). *Census for national report.* Available at: http://www.zimstart.co.zw/dmdocuments/Census/CensusResults2012/ National _Report.pdf. [Accessed: 25 April 2017].

ZimStat. (2013). *Women and men in Zimbabwe Report, 2012.* Available at: http://www.zimstat.co.zw/sites/default/files/img/publications/Gender/Report2012.pdf. [Accessed: 25 April 2017].

Chapter 15

Corporate Social Responsibility and Spirituality in the Zimbabwean Context

Mehluli Pius Mlilo and Linda Maidei Mabwe

Summary

Despite previous explorations on African perspectives on corporate social responsibility (CSR), little is known about the connection between spirituality/spiritualities and corporate social responsibility within the Zimbabwean context. This chapter proposes spirituality or ontology as a CSR sustainability strategy for Zimbabwe. Spirituality is a form of ethical contribution to business. The CSR conceptions are contentious and vital in the debate of development in Zimbabwe. It critiques contributions of spirituality in the business world and discuss how this can enable and nurture business practices. There is a constant need to interrogate how ethical behaviour can be understood in the CSR debate in the limelight of sustainable development. The chapter proffers that there is a need for a renewal of African philosophical identity in spirituality, and transformation of social reciprocity (contemporary moral virtues).

Introduction

One of the most contentious subjects in the twenty-first century is that the utmost obligation of commerce is to sustain society. It debates how there could be no need to abrogate the social good of contemporary CSR, but augment spirituality with respect to tentative changes and challenges in the business context of Zimbabwe. CSR is argued to enable the functions of business, while this is not entirely the case. Later, the chapter revisits the African philosophical assumptions of *ubuntu* and groundings that it offers to contemporary CSR perspective. The history of commerce within this country has shown that livelihoods are sustained by commercial transactions, hence, corporates do not solely operate for the sole purpose of profit but do so as a means to an to end to sustain individuals within a society. The chapter shall re-examine the relationship of human and market behaviours, in this particular case, how spirituality predisposition influences corporate social responsibility to sustainable development. Despite this CSR priority, it has been found that the corporate world has failed to wield pecuniary stimulus for civic or community purposes. Hence, the common deceptive move by corporates towards sustainable development is fraud or rent-seeking (Friedman, 1970). This illusory practice is part of a strategic business initiative by many corporations to make huge profits. Corporates have devised corporate social responsibility with intention to gain competitive advantage at the expense of sustainable development within economies. This is much evident in Third World economies where policies lack in the face of investment and revenue.

This chapter offers spirituality or an ontological grounding as a partial remedy to sustainable developmental complexities. Conversely, innumerable retributive agencies and codes of practices have been employed to govern the Western CSR view and processes, and they have done so little to ameliorate corrupt practices in the world over. This chapter suggests a response to why employers should be ethical in their business practices. It offers an alternative view of CSR (spirituality) how it can curb complications and corrupt practices in the corporate world (Bornstein, 2005, Stambach, 2004). This chapter suggests that there is insufficient response to problems or malpractices, if these malpractices or difficulties are secularised (working without spirituality), then this might be one of the reasons why the contemporary CSR view has failed (Crane, McWilliams, Matten, Moon and Siegel, 2008). For example, a plethora of orthodox CSR failures is illustrated by environmentally degradation in the mining ventures in parts of Africa and local cases in Zimbabwe, the destruction of Mvuma area near Chicken Slice and Innscor Chicken Inn, and inhuman or exploitative labour practices in third world economies, in the name of low wage labour and low cost excavations (Christian Aid, 2004, Malan, 2005).

Further examples of CSR failures include the contamination of water sources that surround Bindura due to the mines that encircle the town and the seepage of poisonous mineral extraction chemicals into the final water for consumption. Similarly, the local government and Harare Municipality have failed to manage the case of waste from industry trickling into Lake Chivero. These are sensitive, and yet practical examples of how industries emit dangerous substances into the air and ground, and how these inhumane acts can be treated by the corporate community and much by government in the face of sustainable development.

Many examples from abroad abound, but the surrounding examples suggest a different view of what and how environment degradation is and how local authorities respond. The exercise of new approaches that respond to this should be foreseeable and pragmatic. Ethical considerations in business ventures seemed to clash because of insufficient policies to buttress the reclaiming and protection of the environment. However, the thrust of self-interested organisations has given birth to corrupt practices in relation to disposal of waste from industries in cities into nearby rivers. The partial solution is a bilateral and multilateral strategic resolution of state and non-state agencies. This move depends on how local government police various industries in the conservation of the environment. Furthermore, local authorities should extend research on pollution and degradation of the environment as a developmental malady. The contemporary solutions of CSR seem to provide tentative remedies hence this chapter's call for the spirituality effort.

Theoretical and Conceptual Framework

The concept of CSR arose in the 1960s, although business throughout commercial history has been a vital socio-political activity before the birth of orthodox CSR. CSR has been used a business strategy to manage government tax remittances (tax revenue exemptions), a marketing tool and passing on the additional cost of producing a good (Crane, McWilliams, Matten, Moon and Siegel, 2008). According to Carroll (1983), "corporate social responsibility involves the conduct of a business so that it is economically profitable, law abiding, ethical and socially supportive. To be socially responsible then means that profitability and obedience to the law are foremost conditions when discussing the firm's ethics and the extent to which it supports society in which it exists with contributions of money, time and talent" (p.608). The relationship of communities and businesses or corporates was vague, for there was no clear understanding of how business was to respond to communities' values towards the environment (Carroll, 2008). In Zimbabwe, this case of responsibility was vaguely treated because of economic hardships that fell upon the economy. For example, the much-publicized Look East Policy is mainly premised on Zimbabwe-China relations that have been built over the years but reached a crescendo with the beginning of mammoth economic problems in Zimbabwe around 2000 (Makwerere and Chipaike,2012).

Methodology

A purposive sampling frame guided the study. The study triangulated the quantitative and qualitative methods of documentary reviews. A review of key documents on Zimbabwe's corporate governance was conducted. Corporate governance pronouncements, government publications, various texts, journals, articles and archived documents were instrumental in examining the trends, patterns, fluctuations, inconsistencies and imbalances in the formulation and implementation of Zimbabwe's corporate social responsibility (CSR). In addition, the history, normative values, structures, and legacies that have shaped African and Zimbabwe's corporate social responsibility options were examined using documentary review. Key informants from Zimbabwe's Ministry of Local Government were also instrumental in providing insights on the shift of Zimbabwe's corporate social responsibility, particularly its deliberate focus on environmental strategic and sustainable development issues.

Historical Overview of Orthodox CSR to Zimbabwe Corporate Social Responsibility

Zimbabwe is a young nation in terms of corporate governance and in the development of CSR due to international sanctions and its quest seeking investment at the same time. There have been clashes between investment and sustainable development in Third World economies in relation to the environment. There is no direct contribution of laws or codes (earlier the National Code of Corporate Governance for Zimbabwe (NCGZ) in 2011 to the ZIMCODE in year 2014) on how corporates are to deal with social responsibilities of the community (corporate organisation functions are not to be confused with Company Law inferences). The emergence of the ZIMCODE should suggest therefore exploits to understand how spirituality can augment the contemporary exercised view. The triple bottom line of people, planet, profit lacks ethics of conduct (Carroll, 2008).

Ethical schools of thought contribute and interpret CSR differently just as much as spirituality would. Kantian or deontological school would argue that practical reason of any rational being understands the categorical imperative (CI) to be: "Act only according to that maxim whereby you can at the same time will that it should become a universal law" (Kant, 1996). This is contrary to corporate actions for they act deceptively and in secrecy in the conduct of their business dealings, hence, this principle would be insufficient to explain practical dealings with community. Competition is not fair and just, and hence these Kantian morals do not respond fairly to business. Corporates in Zimbabwe would struggle with obligations and hence the development of community is a political tool of manipulation by the same.

Ethical views that can inform CSR and challenges

Deontological principles and CSR
Kant went further and offered the "formula of the end in itself" as: "Act in such a way that you treat humanity, whether in your own person or in the person of another, always at the same time as an end and never simply as a means

"(Kant, 1996). This too would be insufficient for business entities because they act to achieve profit and, in turn, people are a means to achieve the goal of profit.

How spirituality can be thought of in CSR

However, a human being is an ontological being and cannot divorce physical actions from spiritual needs for there is a juxtaposition of the two. An action by an individual is both a figurative and non-figurative composition and product, hence, one cannot argue that spirituality does not play a role in the development of human surroundings. Development cannot only be understood to address material needs merely, but likewise the meta-realities that shape the sphere of man. Emergence of CSR without ethereal considerations is invalid and just as the idea of sustaining or much later sustainable development. Why sustain? Why develop and much for whom? These questions are in the physical domain. However, continuity of man develops with careful considerations and suggests that man "hopes and believes" in the better. The 'hope for a better' is a metaphysical reality, for one cannot exhibit empirical evidence of the future reality. However, the low academic contributions should not discourage the spirituality proposition that there is a need for related spirituality-CSR evolution. Some scholars argue for common and ecological justice, human development and spiritual value (Price, 1997). Human development suggests man to be centre of activity, and thus too, the profit seeking facet of corporates should not be manipulated for material gains. This fact leads to be a bi-polarity view of optimists and pragmatists who argue for different realities in the study of CSR and development.

Optimists argue that corporates have a caring affinity towards business and community as long as the company makes gains (Freeman, 2005, Wood, 1991). However, pagmatists contend that business as a 'going-concern' and an entity in a community ought to work with the community to develop (Davis, 1975, Jones, 1980). In this view, businesses should not compromise their endeavours but should aid community where possible. This begs the question: Who operates the business? The personification or distinct character of a business suggests foul play by those who mediates corrupt practices or the good name (goodwill) on behalf of the business. If individuals act in the interest of the business, then the conceptualisation of private limited persona of business is a dubious play or strategic move to protect the corporate. Goodwill as a conceptualisation term of business activity thus suggests a meta-reality as this begs the question: How can dealings of a business be termed 'good' in a moral capacity when it is certain that human beings operate it? This idea suggests 'situational morality' in business operations (Whitehouse, 2006). Why should business choose how they act and when to act in the interests of its survival and to what extent does survival mean a compromise of individuals? The measure of business survival is to act in whatever manner in which it does not publicly destroy its good name. Although in secret it manipulates the world around it and gives a false picture of things, no one can understand its nature without knowing its subsistence mission.

Goodness or business sophistry as means of survival

The conviction that business survives to protect their sovereign existence means that they act only to protect their interest and make profit. Ethical considerations of goodness are not much of a concern, for being 'good' means to make profit despite how it was made. The 'going concern' principle of a business has the four following elements: (1) competitive advantage (2) risk minimisation (3) status and legitimacy, and (4) innovation, and none of these reflect ethical considerations (Kurucz, Colbert and Wheeler, 2008). Competitive advantage is about winning the consumer and the survival of the firm, hence in the words of Sun Tzu,

> War is a matter of vital importance to the state, a matter of life and death, the road either to survival or to ruin.

Competitive advantage hence serves as a survival tactic. Competition in business presents a structure of a battlefield, business behaviour should therefore be meticulously studied (Michaelson and Michaelson, 2010:4). The future concerns of survival of a firm are utmost to that of the community. Rational behaviour is a business conduit strategy not much of moral actions, hence, business behaviour is a situational action (Maignan and Ralston, 2002). This rational behaviour by the corporate fraternity should be reflected in the way it relates to ethical considerations and how business responds to environmental degradation in the quest for high profits. Spirituality suggests that man ought to act in a way to edify human dignity and work. While the secular view would suggest legitimacy and legality as means to justify orthodox corporate behaviour.

Legitimacy versus spirituality

Suchman (1995) contends that legitimacy is a comprehensive insight or hypothesis that activities of a subject depend on whether the subject or corporate body in this case are appropriate within some collective paradigm of standards, customs, principles, philosophies, and characterisations. CSR is perceived by the corporate world as an underlying assumption of making enormous profits and ploughing back to the community as a goodwill strategic advantage. It is subtle that legitimacy is evidence enough to support the actions in business for appropriateness in subject to self-interests. For example, Zimbabweans are rightfully entitled to their earthly endowments, but that does not give them the right to plunder or much damage the environment so much as others not to benefit in the immediate future. The hypothetical case would be: How much is appropriate and what quantity not damage? Apportionment of resources is problematic in practical situations just as much as fairness and justice would be in any debate. Spirituality as a resolute response to contemporary CSR would argue that 'rightfulness" should only improve the work ethic and treatment of individuals. Religious wisdom in any circumstance should remind human beings that man is a steward of earthly resources.

There is a difference between goodwill and legitimacy in that legitimacy is an assumption to success while goodwill is the practice of this success assumption. Corporates take legitimacy to suffice since the entity needs to be in proximity with the community it supports, and thus this propinquity gives it the quintessence and authentic right of survival. Legitimacy concerns itself with the perceptiveness of the common good and the proficiency of the communication networks used by the organisation. The development of the "legitimacy theory" hence necessitates business entities to unremittingly inspect whether their existence is helping the community (Mobus, 2005). Legitimacy suggests that it is the community that governs the beneficial aspect of the business – what they anticipate from the entity and what they actual achieve (Haron *et al.* 2007). This should serve as a reminder that an entity being legitimate does not guarantee it being altruistic in its functions. The legitimacy of organisations does not extend to acting in a rational manner constantly. This area of study has fostered how corporates perceive themselves in relation to injustices practices faced by labour, labour rights and child labour (Pallazo and Scherer, 2006, Dijken, 2007). Legitimacy has no spiritual support of the community it relates with and some argue that it would be incorrect to encompass the spiritual needs of a community (Vallance, 1993).

The legitimacy view seems to be insufficient where spiritual bodies like churches have engaged in business activities. It has been realised that entities governed by churches follow spiritual or religious principles for survival and these practices have made these entities survive longer than some secular organisations. Schools and hospitals owned by the Catholic and Pentecostal churches in Zimbabwe serve as examples of how spiritual principles can enable longevity and survival of an organisation. However, business choices are political and social in nature rather than the perceived economic goals and hence a drastic and all-inclusive approach should be formulated (Mintzberg, 1983).

For example, the business drive has much associated itself with political entrepreneurship which often leads to corruption cases, examples arise everywhere.

The purpose of business is meticulously examined throughout its existence. Various questions abound, for example: How should business be understood? Does business operate only for its purpose? What is that purpose? If it harms the collective, does it still suffice to be an integral entity of community? (Duska and Ragatz, 2008). Moral obligations ought to supersede the legitimacy of actions by a business entity. If capitalistic views support business integrity and harm societal norms, then business should cease its purpose. The purpose of business is not to harm society, but to support and integrate individuals. Capitalism as a mode of economic system should support life not to end it, and hence spiritual values permeate capitalism principles, namely love, respect, hope and dignity. All these cannot be understood in their entirety without a metaphysical appreciation. Spirituality therefore responds adequately to the purpose of business. However, some argue that legitimate corporates cannot prosper in dwindling political economies (Wade, 2005). For example, Zimbabwe is a Third World country where much of the industry is highly informal and this means CSR has to be understood differently from the First world. The conduct of CSR in Zimbabwe can therefore be applied differently from the conventional CSR in the developed economies. CSR should not mean only community involvement but a sincere approach to community.

Legality of CSR

The purpose of business in capitalism is to increase the profits of the firm (Friedman, 1962). This neat conceptualisation by Milton Friedman has directly influenced CSR and hence formal businesses act only in their interest, so the community is not a direct priority. Some critics therefore argue that CSR is a form of rent-seeking for it supports capitalism and abuses the dignity of individuals. Legality of something does not suffice it being ethical, there is no best construed view that legality extends to ethical considerations. For example, the social benefits of business ought to exceed social costs of engaging in any business activity, but the case is not as simple as that. Business ought to consider other variables in the equation like the common good and the environment sustainability considerations. Some impediments can occur, and, in some cases, they are inevitable but may not result in the collapse of the entrepreneurial activity. For example, gas emissions by business may not undermine its core-business. However, the realities that surround the subject are politically and economically sensitive and the business may be tempted to give false information highlighting the social benefits and ignore any knowledge of the negative repercussions of gas emissions. More often research and development lobby groups also regulate and manipulate quality of knowledge to pass on to the public.

This argument of legality also should surround the argument of whether CSR should be made a law and whether it should be aligned with national constitutions. Some argue that CSR should have limitations on how this concept can be understood in relation to the market (Vogel, 2005). On an extreme angle, legality introduces lobbying for regulations that regulate market disequilibrium. If corporations achieve CSR targets within law limits, then are doing so for the sake of shareholders? Then there are unsaid rules about CSR legality and binding regulations. For example: Who decides and what is lobbied for and how is it decided? Organisations cannot be told what to do be responsible for when it comes to what they give to community and that is unregulated by government. In Zimbabwe, company law is composed of the civil code and some special laws on business societies, yet this does not prove to be enough for there are lacking facets to this company law as it cannot be extended to corporate governance. There should be an instrument on commercial law on capital markets for those companies allotting securities. The gaps in the development of capital market laws and commercial law may not be necessary because of the huge chunk of the informal economy. This begs the question what CSR is in an informal economy. There are no obligatory responsibilities or duty of corporations to carry out this social welfare in Third World economies such as Zimbabwe. There is no way administering CSR in developing countries because of the laxity of laws, for example the company law in Zimbabwe. There is no way to administer CSR for most firms are indigenous and struggling to make profits and hence CSR is not an immediate reality. Legality does not protect labour and the environment. Why would the shift to community be positive when the corporates do not treat their first customers well? CSR should go beyond legality but provide a spiritual contentment. CSR can be beneficial if the aspect of spirituality is taken seriously as part of business creation and sustainability. Another intuitive and local conceptualisation of CSR should therefore be employed using the African concept of *ubuntu*, "I am because we are" or "*umuntu ngumuntu ngabantu*". From its ontology, this multi-faceted concept of *ubuntu* exemplifies the spirit of communality, hence, some scholars suggest it to be spirituality at work. For example, UBUNTU is a 3.0 technological computer program that suggests more than the orthodox.

CSR in African economies

From the pre-independence era, African economies did not practise commerce in the conventional manner as the West, hence, business was to progress communities and not individuals like in the West. The concept of *ubuntu/unhu* within some of the African contexts explains why some African communities practised commerce this way. The exchange of goods was a social tool for purposes of the wellbeing of the community. This communitarianism spirit brought some sense of accountability and responsibility. Undoubtedly, there existed a lot of instances of commercial connivance of political corruption, ecological devastation, workforce manipulation and societal disorder as far as 100 years ago (Christian Aid, 2004, Malan, 2005). However, commercial activity was to sustain livelihoods within the community in the traditional setup, but this has changed with the introduction of conventional concept of CSR as illustrated in Carroll's pyramid.

Defining CSR and sustainable development

According to Carroll (1983), "corporate social responsibility involves the conduct of a business so that it is economically profitable, law abiding, ethical and socially supportive. To be socially responsible then means that profitability and obedience to the law are foremost conditions when discussing the firm's ethics and the extent to which it supports the society in which it exists with contributions of money, time and talent" (p.608). There are contending questions to this definition: Why should business be economically profitable and why not super normal profits? This affects the livelihoods that are directly involved in obeisance to the cost of production, hence the cheap labour, and poor living standards for individuals in least developing countries, e.g., Zimbabwe. Amartya Sen argues that human development is centred on expansion of individuals' capabilities and freedoms, and that income is not the alternative measure of development (Selwyn, 2011:69). Development ought to be human centred to be termed sustainable. Similarly, for CSR to be sustaining it ought to value humans as a vital element of the sustainable development chain. Human life is sacred and considered vital in all aspects of development. If conventional CSR does not give freedoms and capabilities, then it is not enhancing the lives that it seeks to bestow dignity.

Sustainable development is "development that meets the needs of the present without compromising the ability of future generations to meet their own needs" (World Commission on Environment and Development, 1987). The first document to call for sustainable development by means of conserving our living resources was the World Conservation Strategy (IUCN *et al.* 1980). However, some define sustainable development as "Improvement in the quality of human life within the carrying capacity of supporting ecosystems" (World Wildlife Fund, 1993). Presently, the term has been presented in three facets, that is, 'Triple P – People, Planet, Profit'. This manifest definition has come to be

300

understood as a people centred definition though this may beg to define what is "human development" in the face of the latter. Human development is at the heart of sustainable development (Sen, 1994). The idea of sustainable development arose essentially from concerns relating to the overexploitation of natural and environmental resources (Sen and Anand, 1994). To refer to well-known example, the company 3M used a hypnotic phrase of 3-P (Pollution Prevention Pays) program and in the process saved hundreds of millions. None of the efforts were either legislatively mandated nor a matter of social custom or contract. Yet 3M raised the bar and is finding both economic and ecological benefits in the process. Consequently, win-win situations for the atmosphere and political economy can be taken through developments which moderate contamination or degradation in creation procedures (Porter and van der Linde, 1999). Effective governance means effective use of resources and thus capacitating sustainable development connections and avoidance of inefficient use of resources (Dernbach, 1998). In the present day, there are growing complexities in understanding CSR and sustainable development with impositions of conceptualisation not applicable in some cases because of environmental dynamism (Wohlgemuth, Carlsson and Kifle, 1998).

CSR, law and sustainable development

There is undoubtedly an argument that something can be unethical while it is legal. The conventional understanding of CSR is least ethical in practice because of the fruits it has given birth to, while it is legal within the business fraternity. Conventional CSR is therefore unethical if it is used by business to manipulate the individual or community. Not even the commitment to CSR stops large corporations in the industrialized world from violating price and competition laws which in return affects their customers (Freyer, 2006). CSR and sustainable development definitions also differ according to economic, social, governance and environmental structures in which they are positioned. For example, CSR may not carry the same agenda sustainable development has in case of the four mentioned spheres. At times, environmental degradation may be an issue so much as to hamper the development. The comparative nature of development depends from country to country, for there are no set standards in this case. The complexities of sustainable development may not align with the economic, legal, ethical and philanthropic responsibilities.

If corporations are drivers of sustainable development, then how do they balance the CSR agendas? This related idea questions the role of CSR in development and how it should be understood. Governments address problems by meeting common prospects. If corporations assist governments to govern in the area of industry and commerce, then how do they engage the subject of socially responsibility and development since they may clash on the subject of either? In some cases, sustainable development financially issues are run by corporations so much that governments have no say since they have no finance or research facilities to facilitate development.

Globalisation has presented complexities for both sustainable development and CSR since tentative and ever-changing knowledge systems inform either differently; hence alignment with either concept is difficult. Some argue that a crucial driver of resource and know-how development is the natural environment (Hart, 1995). The economic question can end up being: Marginal benefits greater than marginal costs. If marginal costs are less than benefits, then it is deemed a go-zone for sustainable development efforts, but this may not agree with the CSR agenda. At times government systems or institutions have so much influence on the subject of sustainable development and inadvertently neglect CSR issues. For example, sustainable development is an issue in Zimbabwe in the mining industry but this clashes with CSR interests (for example, small-scale artisanal miners around the country). There is a need of hexes between the CSR and sustainable development conceptualisations in national building. There are conflicting interests in CSR investments, foreign direct investments (FDIs), sustainable development and corporate sustainability, all these may have conflicting interests relating to politics and economics of the day. For example, in the ways it deals with international trade, the Zimbabwean indigenisation programme has brought CSR complexities in understanding sustainable development since the economy is young and under sanctions and hence most of the local corporates have not grown much to address the obligations of CSR and sustainable development.

Sustainable efficiencies have a competitive advantage, but this entails that business ought to be creative and innovative. Responsible business is necessary but not enough for sustainable development. Sustainable development is not a necessity of CSR and vice versa. Globalisation and religious influences are incoherent cultures of influence on both CSR and sustainable development, although spirituality is offered as a transcendent phenomenon which unifies coherent beliefs and submits to the unanimity of governments and communities as a solution. Spirituality also counteracts the unanimity of choices made by corporate bodies and government. Christianity breeds a new bureaucracy that controls sustainable development and norms of CSR. There is non-negotiable character and variance of sustainable development and CSR, and if both fail to give dignity to the human character then they are void in human development and much understandings of corporate behaviour. Authenticity of spirituality needs communal experience that helps sustainable development and CSR. If both CSR and sustainable development do not support each other then there is a missing link and hence spirituality may be a border line of connectivity.

Sustainability, spirituality and CSR

Spirituality is derived from the Latin word *spiritus* meaning spirit, ultimate or immaterial reality or inner path, the essential part of the person (Piles, 1990) which 'controls the mind and the mind controls the body' (Neuman, 1995:48). The term spirituality has its own fascinating history but is generally used to denote "certain positive inward qualities and perceptions (Wulff, 1996: 47). These suppositions point that a human being is fully human when he integrates all capabilities. Spirituality is capability to achieve goals, and examples include the church-related schools and hospitals which have led way in development. These articulate skills employed by these trans-state organisations to shape how CSR can be understood. If leaders continue to inspire the spirit of workmanship for the better, that form of spirituality inspires the individual to do better hence the development of his or her surroundings. For example, the Zimbabwe Republic Police repositioned its mandate to the public and in 2017 it included in its annual theme the word, "grace". As an organisation, its members are encouraged to pray before work. Spirituality permeates to motivate all aspects of business if humans act from desires of the spirit.

Conclusion, Recommendations and Practical Implications

Corporate social responsibility of any given country is influenced by the domestic and external environment. It is not in the interests of any one nation in a multipolar framework, to focus on one part of the globe and condemn the other. Zimbabwe therefore needs to engage with all progressive nations of the world if it is to experience economic recovery and growth. Environment sensitivity and sustainable development are linked to the subject of CSR. There is a need to re-conceptualise CSR from a foreign policy to state it in the local context. Foreign conceptualisation clashes with the local political economy situation. African spirituality offers a personification of CSR and application of sustainable development goals (SDGs) in Africa and Zimbabwe. The integration of spirituality in organisations can integrate CSR facilitation and processes. Organisations should operate beyond profit making and avaricious interests. The indigenisation policies, with respect to ZIMASSET, would therefore be applicable directly. There is a need to improve understanding of the position of industry and commerce vis-à-vis community they operate in. Research should be carried out on the impact of indigenisation policies in line with an informal economy. Operations of business ought to be considerate to

303

the environment, customers and employees. The achievement of community responsibilities is the integral utility of spirituality in a workplace. The simple practices of mission and vision within a workplace reflects the spirituality imbued in the organisation to achieve its ultimate goal. It has been established that non-government organisations such as church-related schools reflect spirituality at use in Zimbabwe. However, corporations in Zimbabwe continue to demonstrate the metaphysical origins of CSR permeating the secular views but this does not mean that spirituality has no place in this regard. Control or management reflects the priorities of individuals. Spirituality presents a view that care is also a belief that change is inevitable. The formulation of CSR systems must be decentralised, and government should be involved in establishing a corporate governance code that offer binding regulations.

References

Anand, S. and Sen, A. (1994). _Sustainable human development: Concepts and priorities. Cambridge: Harvard University Press.

Ashar, H. and Lane-Maher, M. (2004). Success and spirituality in the new business paradigm. *Journal of Management Inquiry, 13*(3), 249–260.

Bornstein, E. (2005). *The spirit of development: Protestant NGOs, morality, and economics in Zimbabwe*. Stanford: Stanford University Press.

Davis, K. (1975). Five propositions for social responsibility. *Business Horizons, 18*(3), 19-24.

Dawes, J., Dolley, J. and Isaksen, I. (2005). *The quest: Exploring a sense of soul.* Ropley: O-Books.

Dernbach, J.C. (1998). Sustainable development as a framework for national governance. *Case Western Reserve Law Review,* 57(1),1-103.

Duska, R., & Ragatz, J. A. (2008). How losing soul leads to ethical corruption in business. In *Leadership and business ethics* (pp. 151-163). Springer, Dordrecht.

Forman, R. (2004). *Grassroots spirituality: What it is, why it is there, where it is going?* Exeter: Imprint Academic.

Frederick, W.C. (1998). Moving to CSR4: What to pack for the trip. *Business and Society, 37*(1), 40–59.

Freeman, R.E. (2005). A stakeholder theory of the modern corporation. In L.P. Hartman (Ed.), *Perspectives in business ethics* (3rd edn.) New York: McGrawHill.

Friedman, M. (1970, September 13). The social responsibility of business is to increase its profits. *New York Times Magazine.* Available at http://www.rohan.sdsu.edu/faculty/dunnweb/rprnts.friedman.html.

Fry, L.W. (2005). Toward a theory of ethical and spiritual well-being, and corporate social responsibility through spiritual leadership. In R.A. Giacalone, C.L. Jurkiewicz and C. Dunn (Eds.), *Positive psychology in business ethics and corporate responsibility* (pp. 47–83). Greenwich: IAP.

Giacalone, R.A. and Jurkiewicz, C.L. (Eds.). (2003). *Handbook of workplace spirituality and organisational performance*. Armonk: M.E. Sharpe.

Guillory, W.A. (2001). *The living organisation: Spirituality in the workplace* (2nd edn.). Salt Lake City: Innovations International.

Hart, S. (1995). A natural-resource-based view of the firm. *Academy of Management Review, 20*(4), 986–1014.

Jones, T.M. (1980). Corporate social responsibility revisited, redefined. *California Management Review,* 22(2), 59-67.

Kant, I. (1996). The metaphysics of morals, ed. Mary Gregor. *Cambridge, UK: Cambridge University Press,* 9(1), 42-43.

Lips-Wiersma, M. and Nilakant, V. (2008). Practical compassion: Toward a critical spiritual foundation for corporate responsibility. In J. Biberman and L. Tischler (Eds.), *Spirituality in business: Theory, practice, and future directions* (51–72). New York: Palgrave Macmillan.

Makoshori, S. (2013, June 13). Scandal rocks Sedco. Retrieved from [http://www.financialgazette.co.zw/scandal-rocks-sedco/] Accessed: 08 April 2017.

Makwerere. D. and Chipaike, R. (2012). China and the United States of America in Africa: A new scramble or a new cold war?' *International Journal of Humanities and Social Science,* 2(17): 1-9.

Michaelson, G. A., & Michaelson, S. W. (2010). *Sun Tzu-The Art of War for Managers: 50 Strategic Rules Updated for Today's Business.* Simon and Schuster.

Mintzberg, H. (1983) The case for corporate social responsibility. *Journal of Business Strategy,* 4(2), 3-15.

Mitroff, I.I. and Denton, E.A. (1999). *A spiritual audit of corporate America: A hard look at spirituality, religion and values in the workplace.* San Francisco: Jossey-Bass.

Mobus, J.L. (2005). Mandatory environmental disclosure in a legitimacy theory context. *Accounting, Auditing and Accountability Journal, 18,* 492-517.

Neuman, B. (1995). *The Neuman system model* (3rd edn.). Norwalk: Appleton and Lange.

Porter, M.E. and Mark, R.K. (2006). Strategy and society: The link between competitive advantage and corporate social responsibility. *Harv. Bus. Rev, 78,* 88-89.

Porter, M. E., & Van der Linde, C. (1995). Toward a new conception of the environment-competitiveness relationship. *Journal of economic perspectives, 9*(4), 97-118.

Price, A. (1997. *In search of legitimation: Payback and practice.* Paper presented at the meeting of the EBEN-UK Business Ethics: Principles and Practice, Newcastle.

Stambach, A. (2004). Faith in schools: Toward an ethnography of education, religion and the state. *Social Analysis,* 48(3), 90–107.

Suchman, M. (1995). Managing legitimacy: Strategic and institutional approaches. *Academy of Management Review,* 20(3), 571–610.

Tullock, G. (1967). The welfare costs of tariffs, monopolies and theft. *Western Economic Journal,* 5(3), 224-332.

Visser, W. (2005). Is South Africa world class in corporate citizenship? In A. Freemantle (Ed.), *The good corporate citizen.* Johannesburg: Trialogue

Vallance, E. (1993). What is business for? Ethics and the aim of business. *Business Strategy Review,* 4(1), 45-52.

Vogel, D. J. (2005). Is there a market for virtue?: The business case for corporate social responsibility. *California management review,* 47(4), 19-45.

Whitehouse, L. (2006). Corporate social responsibility: Views from the frontline. *Journal of Business Ethics,* 63(3), 279-296.

Wohlgemuth, L., Carlsson, J. and Kifle, H. (Eds.). (1998). *Institution building and leadership in Africa.* Uppsala: Nordiska Afrikainstitutet.

Wood, D.J. (1991). Corporate social performance revisited. *Academy of Management Review,* 16(4), 691-718.

Wulff, D.M. (1996). The psychology of religion: An overview. In E.P. Shapraspse (Ed.), *Religion and the clinical practice of psychology* (pp.43-70). Washington DC: American Psychological Association.

Zsolnai, L. (Ed.). (2004). *Spirituality and ethics in management.* Dordrecht: Kluwer.

Chapter 16

Leadership Derailment: A Threat to Workplace Sustainability in Zimbabwe

McDonald Matika and Moreen Mudenda

Summary

Very few issues derail organisations such as ineffective leaders. Understanding leadership derailment requires a holistic approach including the recruitment and selection processes, performance management, leadership development opportunities and succession planning. Leadership derailment, as observed through organisational failures occurs when leaders make questionable ethical choices or when they lack the competence to steer organisations effectively. In order for leadership to be effective, there is need for confidence to be instilled in the followers. Those in leading positions need to make the correct and ethical choices that promote the strategic realisation of an organisation's goals faced with a very challenging external environment. Leaders who make decisions that compromise the integrity of the organisation run the risk of losing the faith of employees, clients and other key stakeholders. Once this confidence is lost, the organisation's sustainability and contribution to national development is in danger of not being realised. This exploratory study employed a qualitative paradigm using mixed methods in an attempt to show the missing dimensions in leadership development through investigating the serious gaps in the leadership value chain which are crucial to promoting sustainability. In addition, a case study and focus group discussions were conducted to gain insight into leadership derailment. This study suggests revisiting leadership training and development programmes with a view to better understand and in the process counter the factors that result in derailment.

Introduction

The world of work in Zimbabwe and indeed across the globe is not a place for the faint-hearted. Many competing job or situational demands are placed on individuals and organisational systems. Failure to manage these demands can result in organisational failure. This has serious negative consequences for the formerly employed, particularly in a difficult macro-economic environment as has been experienced in Zimbabwe since the turn of the century. For sustainability in organisations to be realised, competent and ethical leadership becomes a necessity as the entity must continue to exist and effectively discharge its mission. Leadership is that function charged with enhancing organisational effectiveness, and it is therefore important to identify the pertinent factors associated with both good and bad leadership. Leadership has been one of the most observed, yet least understood phenomenon in organisational management. Effective leadership is at the centre of well-managed operations and is the difference between organisational survival and death. Organisations must generally operate in a manner that instils confidence about their survival today and into their future. The sustainability question for organisations is invariably intertwined with committed and able leadership.

However, there has been a preoccupation with understanding and studying good leadership suggesting that bad leadership was a rare phenomenon. The reality is that derailed leadership is at the crux of failed and dying organisations. Leader derailment is multifaceted and becomes apparent when organisations are forced to close operations due to bad decisions by the chief executive officer. Organisational failure hence becomes a consequence of leader derailment which is characterised by low levels of competency and the failure to make ethical choices. Attention to the principles of good leadership has been the apparent reality with most management and leadership training schools concentrating on how to be a good and effective leader. Most postgraduate business programmes in the local universities and, indeed the region, have no component on bad leadership. However, bad leadership has been observed to be responsible for the failure of most corporate entities and continues to be a factor in organisational collapse in Zimbabwe and across the globe.

Over 50% of documented organisational failures are purely a result of leadership derailment. Even in the face of daily reports of voluntary and forced company closures resulting from bad judgement by leaders, the bias in understanding and teaching good leadership continues unabated in many management and leadership development programmes. It is in this vein that this chapter intends to re-examine the popular notion that assumes only good leadership should be taught. This realisation necessitates the need to mainstream into management literature that there indeed exists a 'dark side' of leadership which must be understood, just as much as effective and good leadership. This is important for sustainable organisations to be realised. There also exists a big and thriving industry promoting the idea that leadership is similar to any skill and ought to be taught to anyone. This has consequently given support to the idea that good leaders can simply be churned out. This thinking ought to be revisited as evidenced from documented organisational failures in Zimbabwe's public and private sectors. Indeed, organisations have folded with otherwise competent leadership at the helm in most parts across the world. The cases of Enron in the United States and bank failures in Zimbabwe are results of derailed leadership at their core.

It is not enough for a leader to have the knowledge, skills and attitude as laid out in job descriptions for the position of the chief executive officer. There is more to it and organisational psychologists ought to be concerned with the need to expand or search for leadership factors that have a relationship with success and failure. The pertinent factors associated with derailment need to be figured out in order to improve the overall performance and impact of current and future leaders. With sound leadership, sustainability is better ensured and can be demonstrated through the organisation being left to be taken over by others.

The chapter seeks to detail and unpack the leadership question in relation to sustainability with particular reference to Zimbabwe. Effective leadership is often a missing dimension or is treated as an afterthought of sustainability question. An understanding of the evolution of leadership derailment meaningfully contributes to the contemporary understanding of ethical and effective leadership. This chapter argues that derailed leadership is an important predictor of the organisational failure matrix. It is important for management students and practitioners to benefit from empirical understanding bad leadership just as much as from the success stories (Clements and Washbush, 1999). By continuing to pretend that there is no 'dark side' to leadership, which is a clear and present danger to sustainability, there is a real threat to the development of good leaders in the quest for sustainability as outlined by Hogan, Curphy and Hogan (1994).

The chapter is a result of the realisation that it is simply not enough to explore the question of sustainability whilst being blind to the leadership and management question. Any organisation and arguably, any nation, is a reflection of the culture as set out by the leaders. In the literature section, the chapter questions the essence of leadership training and the impact of management on the sustainability of institutions through examining both derailed and effective leadership examples. These are not two sides of the same coin. Successful and failed leadership must be viewed from different perspectives. For organisations following the path that leads to derailment, it is important to audit their management and operational systems and search for that path to effectiveness.

Literature Review

Organisational derailment

Derailment of organisations is evidenced by death, bankruptcy, decline, downsizing and overall system collapse. Downsizing and retrenchment are normally excluded as they been associated with breathing life into organisations and indeed have some association with success (Greenhalgh, Lawrance and Sutton, 1988). Retrenchment has since graduated into a legitimate and common strategic tool used by managers in growth or change periods. Some have argued bankruptcy as not enough to consider an organisation derailed as it is only but a symptom of other causes. This also resonates with the idea that leadership style is most predictive of organisational failure. Organisations failing to sustain market presence have depleted operational resources within them. This in turn results in failure to turn them around. The failure to sustain operations quickens their exit from the market altogether. Freeman (2010) outlines that when sound leadership exists, an organisation stands a better chance to recover from loss of market share, a negative balance sheet and eroded legitimacy.

The leadership and organisational failure nexus

The industry life cycle (ILC) theory posits that all institutions follow a predetermined sequence which is independent of strategy and leadership (Klepper, 1997). The theory intimates that failure is inevitable and is a natural and expected consequence. In other words, individuals, institutions, nations and civilisations all follow the inexorable path towards the reality of death and that the history of any firm or individual is characterised by a rise and then the expected extinction. However, there is need to realise that the cyclical nature of both living beings and organisations needs to be managed or overcome. Failure is not simply a result of the setting in of diminishing returns, running out of supplies or new technology supplanting the existing means of production. In Zimbabwe, the environment is littered with institutions that have gone into extinction in both the private and public entities. A cursory glance will reveal that mining was worst affected with the asbestos mines in Zvishavane and Mashava, the copper mines in Mhangura and Lion's Den. The once prosperous Cold Storage Commission (CSC) and the National Railways of Zimbabwe (NRZ), both government-owned entities have been teetering on the brink of total collapse for over a decade, yet in their heyday they were premier organisations with skilled well motivated workforces. There are also examples of organisations that have continued to thrive well after the pioneers or the people who set them up have left to leave them in the hands of effective managers. The correlation between death and leadership type then arises as the

310

quality of leadership and the type of decisions made resonate with when and how fast an organisation will inevitably meet its end.

Leadership derailment

Derailment has, in most instances, been viewed from the lenses of leadership and management failure. For the purposes of this chapter, the terms leadership and management will be used interchangeably. Derailment in leadership is argued to be poor individual performance that fails to cope with ever-changing market demands. It could also be outright failure to perform at or above the expected performance levels. Burke (2006) proposes a framework for derailment which holds across many cultures including the Zimbabwean environment:

- Failed leaders were incompetent: However, most leaders in Zimbabwe were appointed on the basis of the considerable knowledge and skills they possessed for the industry.
- Failed leaders were victims to events beyond their control: However, there is not much empirical evidence to support this notion. Proponents point to the industry life cycle theory outlining that death was inevitable for organisations as much as for living entities. In Zimbabwe, there has been a sense that managers in some state-owned institutions were captive to political directives and could not be held wholly accountable for failure to turn around operations.
- Failing leaders were slow in implementation: However, implementation is a result of the macroeconomic environment which must be supportive of such initiatives.
- Failing leaders did not try hard enough: Organisations grapple with internal integration and external adaptation forces.
- Failing leaders did not have leadership ability: However, many leaders were able, in practice, to manage operations and actions as planned.
- The organisation did not have enough resources: In practice, leaders need to be carefully when allocating meagre resources.
- The failing leaders were just common thieves who had somehow risen to the top echelons of organisations: The reality in Zimbabwe was that most leaders had reached their positions on merit.

The foregoing framework however is simply not enough to unpack the commonly reported failures that have been experienced in the Zimbabwean context. Many company executive managers have often been seen as savvy, smart, hardworking individuals who rose to the top echelons through a combination of talent and a work commitment. However, some of them experienced derailment in the organisations they have led. Many of the entities were just not small organisations but were major corporations that employed many people. The number of banks in Zimbabwe that have been forced to go into judicial management is quite telling on this matter. Most state-owned enterprises have been struggling to stay afloat and survived mostly on injections from the national treasury. Government has been rightfully unwilling to allow them to collapse due to their strategic nature and national importance. There is a common thread running through all the failed organisations and that identifier is leadership derailment. Kellerman (2004) outlined the two types of leaders associated with derailment. They were often ineffective and unethical individuals, and this is the question this chapter seeks to highlight.

This study also identified patterns of behaviours based on local realities that ultimately lead to derailment. The following are often correlates of leadership and organisational derailment:

- *Incompetence*: These leaders lack the knowledge, skills and attitude required by a leader to foster citizenship or the required change within the organisation. One just has to visit the leadership or management value chain to discern how the individual would have been appointed to that position in the first place. Oftentimes one is faced with fake qualifications having been used to secure the top position. The selection procedure would also have been heavily compromised, and, in most instances, other candidates would just be called in for interviews or selections as a cover for an already flawed process.

- *Inflexibility*: Such leaders are simply not able to adapt to the ever-changing dictates of the marketplace and hold on to old traditions which might have worked for them or the organisation before.
- *Temperament*: Failure to control or manage emotions.
- *Bullying*: Doing psychological and or physical harm in a callous manner showing the leader is divorced from the feelings and needs of his/her subordinates.
- *Nest feathering*: They are not sensitive to the needs of those outside their circle and only interested in maximising personal benefits to the detriment of the group.
- *Corrupt*: The leader will cheat, lie, steal and will consider the needs and wants of himself or herself and their close connections only. Merit becomes an anathema as resources and privileges are given to members of the inner circle.

The incompetent, inflexible and temperamental leader in general, is just incompetent. However, the worst kind of derailment is when the leader is not only corrupt but also possesses a trait of nest feathering. Unethical behaviours become a natural extension of such corrupt and insensitive individuals. The incompetent leader is the least problematic while the corrupt thieving leader holds the greatest threat to any organisation.

Theories of Leadership

Are leaders born or made

The age-old question has been whether leaders are born or made. There exists a general consensus on the idea that good leaders are actually made and do not have ascribed status (Hannah, 2013). Bass and Bass (2008) outline that developing effective leaders, who are unlikely to derail is thus an iterative process and constantly evolves self-appraisal, education, training and the accumulation of relevant experience. Effective leaders are able to learn from their experiences and draw important lessons that will enable them to make decisions which will result in the existence of the organisation post their period at the helm. Over the years, management researchers have proposed different styles of leadership as there is no universal style that would be appropriate in all situations. Despite the existence of many leadership styles, an effective leader inspires subordinates and motivates them in a manner that ensures that units and people within the organisation are working towards meeting the set strategic and operational goals. Such leaders are very clear on the direction and the type of skills required to meet particular goals. On the other hand, the leader who is derailed cannot contribute to the organisation's success. In effect, such a leader is actually harmful to the very existence of the organisation and can detract efforts towards accomplishing the organisation's goals.

Methodology

A common tendency among scholars of leadership failure is to adhere to one strict method, level of analysis and a set of assumptions as guided by the research design. The lack of consensus on the appropriate research design for understanding leadership failure has resulted in a dearth of studies employing mixed methods approaches. Industrial/organisational psychologists are likely to employ large survey designs while organisational strategists will favour using case studies. The result has been a tendency to dismiss the results of either approach by practitioners and researchers alike. This has been counterproductive to the conceptualisation of leadership and organisational failure in the Zimbabwean context.

The study employed a mixed methods approach to explore factors underlying organisational failure in the context of the current political and economic situation in Zimbabwe from the turn of the century. The mixed methods approach within the qualitative paradigm was intended to bridge the gap between the organisational strategist and organisational psychology approaches. The aim was to come up with a comprehensive picture of leader cognitions, actions and the external adaptation strategies within which organisational failure was experienced. The focus group discussions were meant to tap the perceptions of management students on organisational failure in the local context. Documentary research was also carried out with particular emphasis on organisations that had derailed such as Kingstons Private Limited and the struggling government owned entities such as Ziscosteel in Kwekwe and the National Railways of Zimbabwe.

As local empirical data is sparse on the subject, it became crucial to employ the mixed methods approach. This allowed for the collection of a large body of information that would otherwise have not been possible with a unitary quantitative approach. To achieve the aim of understanding leadership failure in relation to sustainability, the researchers first established that they needed to undertake desk research on the selected organisations that had failed or were barely operational. The documentary search was guided by sampling a domain specifying that leadership and organisational derailment had a positive relationship.

There was a detailed analysis of failures in both private and public institutions in Zimbabwe with a special focus on Zimbabwe's banking institutions that went into liquidation such as Time Bank, Trust Bank and Kingdom Bank. Government owned entities such as the Cold Storage Commission, the National Railways of Zimbabwe, Ziscosteel and to some extent Air Zimbabwe where also included in the leadership-organisational-derailment matrix. The methods were focused on investigating how organisational failure was related to leadership derailment. The methods involved the identification of the failed institutions and the actions of the leadership before and after the collapse of the organisations they had previously led. For banks, the researchers consulted primary sources such as central bank reports and the periodic monetary policy statements, secondary sources such as journals, working papers, consultative reports, and running records as historical evidence. The authors searched databases for archival data on failed organisations within Zimbabwe. They then used the information to develop an interview guide with which they then used to collect data from students in a

314

Master of Business Administration class. The interview guide had questions related to the impact of leadership on organisational failure and whether indeed failed leadership was a reality in both local and international contexts. The researchers then used a case study approach as guided by the sampling domain of the selected institutions. The intention was to investigate if any link existed between organisational failure and leadership.

Results

The results summarised below are put into themes. This analysis is a summary of the themes and emerging patterns as arising from the case study, focus group discussions and desk research.

Organisational failure and leadership derailment in Zimbabwe: A case study of the collapsed of indigenous owned banks during the period 2003-2015

The major causes of the Zimbabwe financial crisis and the subsequent collapse of some indigenous banking institutions since 2003 was largely a result of poor corporate governance. In addition, there were also poorly constituted boards of directors, weak board oversight and ineffective leadership. Management in the failed institutions was accused of poor risk management and weak financial management systems. Speculative non-core activities, where financial institutions would invest in areas outside of their core business resulted in poor balance sheets with depositors failing to access their funds, which had been locked in assets that could not be easily liquidated. Such assets included cars, purchase of future production lines for cement, bricks and other building materials. When depositors then sought to withdraw funds, the money would simply not be there as it was tied up in assets which had been purchased with the intention of being sold later. There were also creative accounting activities through the creation of fictitious financial positions and failure to declare losses through creating non-existent assets and by creating non-existent assets and under-declaration of expenses and liabilities (RBZ, 2012). Liquidators also observed the overstatement of capital positions through the hiding of nonperforming loans, use of depositors' and borrowed funds to create adequate capitalization. The high levels of non-performing insider loans were particularly devastating as management would borrow large sums of money and raise salaries and in the process offset the borrowed funds to the disadvantage of the depositing stakeholders (RBZ, 2012). Some of these loans were eventually written off. Corporate governance had in essence collapsed. The unsustainable earnings seen in the balance sheets were through high paper profits resulting from a revaluation of assets. The rot was eventually seen through the never-ending liquidity problems with some depositors failing to access their funds.

The selection and development value chain

To be effective, a leader needs to have a clear vision with performance targets and show the desire to have competent and committed followers. Failure through mistakes was observed by participants as a human trait of leadership and the analysis showed the nature of common issues that are a clear and present threat to the sustainability of organisations. A question that often arose was on the selection processes where in most cases have robust systems appeared to be in place, particularly for the private sector. However, lack of transparency was an issue in the appointment of executives in public entities. The respondents argued that some of the appointments were political and the beneficiaries had failed to lead the organisations.

Unethical and corrupt options

Leadership and eventual organisational derailment are quickened by bad ethical and corrupt choices. For leaders to be effective, they need to be trusted by followers. Leaders in the habit of lying, cheating and stealing for their own benefit will have a hard time in the effort to inspire their followers in operations that are crucial to the strategic goals of the organisation. The respondents advised that faced with a leader they viewed as corrupt, the levels of counterproductive behaviours also rose. In the same vein, when senior management makes operational decisions that are detrimental and contrary to the ethics of the industry, their employees, customers and financiers rapidly lose faith with such an organisation. This was seen through the run on deposits in all the indigenous banks such as Time Bank which eventually collapsed. Air Zimbabwe was also constantly grappling with loss of confidence among suppliers and customers due to allegations of corruption on the airline's insurance tender. Investigations eventually led to the prosecution and eventual incarceration of the former chief executive officer, Mr Peter Chikumba, and company secretary Grace Pfumbidzayi for seven year (Burns, 1998).

Failure to delegate effectively

An effective leader does not make all decisions independently or complete all the important operational tasks on his or her own. A good leader will delegate tasks to those most skilled and equipped to perform them. However, one must put in place an effective performance monitoring and evaluation system. Micromanaging will result in low morale and poor organisational commitment due to the assumed lack of input on the operators. If those tasked with

316

operations have the leader always second-guessing and questioning all their decisions, morale and distrust will often be the result. Organisational climate survey results conducted at selected financial services institutions in Harare showed that leaders who did not delegate had poor leader-member exchange patterns.

Talent management

The participants outlined that talent management was crucial for profitable organisations. Hiring, training and compensation must be geared at enabling employees to reach their optimum potential. Failure in any aspect of the human capital management chain is linked to leadership derailment. In the competitive private sector, human capital that is not constantly trained in line with the strategic thrust of the entity will result in their organisation lagging behind the competition. There is a need to constantly undertake skills audits and determine the current and future skills required by the organisation. The knowledge and skills of the employees must constantly be upgraded in order to ensure survival of the organisation. Employees are also generally in search of growth opportunities and through coaching and development, the quality of the leader-membership exchanges can be greatly improved.

External adaptation

Sustainable organisations respond effectively to the ever-changing industry factors and the economic environment. The leader must have the knowledge, skills and attitude to make the correct business decisions. The personality also comes into play and high levels of emotional intelligence become crucial in navigating the organisation through the treacherous maze of survival. Derailed leaders will quickly experience burnout. There is need for rapid and logical decision-making in line with the evolving trends. It came out during the discussion that a derailed leader was likely to be indecisive and would potentially frustrate employees. This could even eventually result in counterproductive work behaviours due to poor leader-member exchange patterns.

Corporate social responsibility, transparency and sustainability

Whatever the size of the company, there is still a need to think about the type of business an organisation is involved in and explore ways how its operations can benefit the community. This is taking a sustainable view of the entity. There is evidence that indicates that, for example, after the case of Enron, socially responsible companies are generally longer lasting and more sustainable. Because such entities are transparent, the public has more confidence in them. In addition, such organisations take criticism in their stride and in true democratic fashion, then take steps towards changing their operations in line with stakeholder concerns. While the majority of shareholders are generally interested with returns on their investment, the trend, however, indicates that there is an increasing number who are concerned about the ethical impact of their investments. In the United States, for example, it has been estimated that such stakeholders are moving towards investing in Ethical Investment Funds which have been rapidly growing. According to the latest figures, 150 billion - 1 trillion US dollars of investments are going into Ethical Funds in the United States alone (Freeman, 2010).

Organisations that are the most socially responsible have turned out to be the most transparent as well. This enables anyone to find out what is taking place in their operations. Such windows into their operations enable the anticipation of any challenges that could arise in their operations. As organisations become more transparent, the more appealing they become to the investing public and private funds.

Discussion

The ethical leadership framework to mitigate leadership and organisational derailment

This study suggests a clear leadership ethical framework development. From the aforementioned patterns of derailment, it is possible to draw out a short list of ethical guidelines that institutions could follow in order to limit leadership derailment:

i) First, it appears that an optimum level of transparency is crucial. Transparent corporations, as observed, particularly those with active and knowledgeable boards, seem to be longer-lasting, are internally more democratic, have better fits social needs and the organisations are often more respectful of legal responsibilities.

ii) Secondly, the creation of a code of conduct or a code of ethics becomes a vehicle for respecting those "non-business" demands. The code needs to be widely distributed to all employees including the top management. Importantly, there needs to be training and workshops about the contents and how it should be applied across all levels of the organisation.

iii) Thirdly, a controversial issue the authors suggest is the creation of an expert ethical manager post responsible for all corporation ethical issues. If this is not possible, the organisation can seriously consider expanding the responsibilities of the human capital and culture managers.

The Chartered Institute of Management Accounts (CIMA) has global ethics standards and it serves as a suitable framework that resonates with sustainable leadership and organisations. The principles are universally applied and normally set out the responsibilities for auditors but, in principle, they serve to combat unethical behaviours which may result in leadership derailment.

- *Principle 1* – "Integrity": A leader must behave with integrity in all professional and business relationships. Integrity implies not merely honesty but fair dealing and truthfulness. A member's advice and work must be uncorrupted by self-interest and not be influenced by the interests of other parties.
- *Principle 2* – "Objectivity": A leader should strive for objectivity in all professional and business judgements. Objectivity is the state of mind which has regard for all considerations relevant to the task but no other.
- *Principle 3* – "Competence": A leader should undertake professional work only where he or she has the necessary competence required to carry out that work, supplemented where necessary by appropriate assistance or consultation.
- *Principle 4* – "Performance": A leader should carry out professional work with due skill, care, diligence and expedition and with proper regard for the technical and professional standards expected of them as a member.
- *Principle 5* – "Courtesy": A leader should conduct himself or herself with courtesy and consideration towards all with those whom he or she meets during the course of performing work.

The above principles consequently represent the minimum ethical standards to which all leaders should conform. These principles enable leaders to tackle many ethical dilemmas. They serve as the conceptual framework in resolving such dilemmas which can quicken the pace to derailment should the parties involved ignore them.

Transformational leadership: The link with sustainability

James MacGregor Burns writing in his book, '*Leadership*', was the first to put forward the concept of "transforming leadership". According to Burns, transforming leadership "is a relationship of mutual stimulation and elevation that converts followers into leaders and may convert leaders into moral agents" (Burns, 1998). Burns draws upon the humanistic psychology movement in his writings on 'transforming leadership' by proposing that a transforming leader shapes, alters, and elevates the motives, values and goals of followers achieving significant change in the process. He argues for the existence of a special power imbued within the transforming leadership saying such individuals were armed with principles ultimately transforming them and their followers into a group that jointly adhere to modal values and end-values.

Burns saw the power of transforming leadership as more refined and different from that of charismatic leadership, which he termed as 'heroic'. Despite this, it is surprising that most of the application of Burns' work has been in the aforementioned two types of leadership. Bass (1990) developed Burns' concept of transforming leadership in '*Leadership and performance beyond expectations*' into 'transformational leadership' with the leader transforming the followers. For Bass, the direction of influence was thus one-way, unlike Burns who saw an interaction that was bi-directional. However, Bass goes further and touches on a transformational style of executive leadership which incorporated social change, a facet missing from Burns' work.

For Bass 'transformational leaders' may:
* expand a follower's portfolio of needs through job enrichment or job enlargement
* transform a follower's self-interest and in the end be more likely to engage in citizenship behaviours
* increase the confidence of followers through ethical leadership
* elevate followers' expectations by demonstrating and championing sustainability initiatives
* heighten the value of the leader's intended outcomes for the follower
* encourage behavioural change through a culture shift.

Tichy and Devanna (1986), in their treatise on 'transformational leadership' developed further the work of Burns and Bass in organisational and work contexts. They described the hybrid nature of transformational leadership as not resultant from charisma but argued it to be a behavioural process that could be learned. Bass and Avolia (1994) suggested that transformational leadership was similar to the prototype of leadership that people thought of when they described ideal leaders. Such leaders were largely seen as role models whom subordinates desired to identify with. Transactional leadership has been the usual model of leadership with its roots in the organisational or business perspective centred on profit maximisation. Covey (1991) in '*Principle-centred leadership*' suggests that transformational leadership focuses more on organisational objectives. However, servant leadership for our purposes will better guarantee sustainability through the high levels of trust within the work groups, empowerment of employees and empathy as demonstrated by the managers.

Conclusion

Zimbabwean management trainers and, indeed, across the globe, must shoulder some of the blame for leadership derailments that have been experienced. Academics have often distanced themselves from the failures that would be taking place in the service and manufacturing sectors. It is quite easy for them to dissociate themselves from the sins of managers in failed banks, government owned and private entities, arguing that they only teach good management and leadership practices. The university environment appears a world away from the cut-throat business environment where the thinking and culture is an obsession with market domination and the desire to exterminate the competition. Excessive executive entitlement has often been commonplace with devastating consequences for the lower level workers. These issues must be given prominence in the teaching and development of effective leaders. Effective and competent leadership is, arguably, interlinked with sustainability.

References

Bass, B. M., and Avolio, B. J. (1994). Introduction. In B.M. Bass and B.J. Avolio (Eds.), *Improving organisational effectiveness through transformational leadership* (1-38). Thousand Oaks, CA: Sage Publications.

Bass, B.M. (1990). From transactional to transformational leadership: Learning to share the vision. *Organisational Dynamics*, 18(3), 19-31.

Bass, B. M., Bass, R. and Bass, B.M. (2008). *The Bass handbook of leadership: Theory, research, and managerial applications*. New York: Free Press.

Burke, R. J. (2006). Why leaders fail: Exploring the darkside. *International Journal of Manpower*, 27(1), 91-100.

Burns, J. M. (1998). Transactional and transforming leadership. In G.R. Hickman (Ed.), *Leading organisations* (pp. 133-4). Thousand Oaks, CA,: Sage Publications.

Clements, C. and Washbush, J.B. (1999). The two faces of leadership: Considering the dark side of leader-follower dynamics. *Journal of Workplace Learning*, 4(3), 146-8

Covey, S. R. (1991). *Principle-centered leadership*. New York: Summit Books.

Devine, K., Reay, T., Stainton, L., and Collins-Nakai, R. (2003). Downsizing outcomes: Better a victim than a survivor. *Human Resource Management*, 42(2), 109-124.

Freeman, R.E. (2010). Managing for stakeholders: Trade–offs or value chain. *Journal of Business* Ethics, 9(6), 7–9.

Greenhalgh, L., Lawrance, A. and Sutton, R. (1988). Determinates of workforce reduction strategies in declining organisations. *The Academy of Management Review.* 13(2), 241-254.

Hannah, S. (2013). The psychological and neurological bases of leader self-complexity and effects of adaptive decision-making. *Journal of Applied Psychology*, 98(3), 393-411.

Hogan, R., Curphy, G.J. and Hogan, J. (1994). What we know about leadership: effectiveness and personality. *American Psychologist, 49*(6), 493-504.

Hunt, J. G. (1991), *Leadership: A new synthesis.* Newbury Park, CA: Sage Publications.

Kellerman, B. (2004). Thinking about... leadership. Warts and all. *Harvard Business Review, 82*(1), 40-5.

Reserve Bank of Zimbabwe. (2012). *Midterm monetary policy statement.* Harare: Reserve Bank of Zimbabwe.

Tichy, N. M. and Devanna, M. A. (1986). *The transformational leader: The key to global competitiveness.* New York, NY. John Wiley and Sons, Inc.

Websites

Air Zimbabwe Executive Jailed. Downloaded from:
https://www.southerneye.co.zw/2015/04/10/former-air-zimbabwe-executives-jailed-for-fraud/ on 27 March 2017

Leadership Theory. Downloaded from: http://www.strategies-for-managing-change.com/support-files/leadershiptheoryexeteruniversity.pdf on 30 March 2017.

Ethics Code at a Glance. Downloaded from:
http://www.cimaglobal.com/Professionalism/Ethics/CIMAs-code-at-a-glance/

The financial stability report. Downloaded from:
http://www.rbz.co.zw/assets/financial-stability-report-june-2014.pdf on 3 April 2017.

Chapter 17

Sustainability of Family Reunification among Street Children in Zimbabwe

Samson Mhizha, Patrick Chiroro and Tinashe Muromo

Summary

The primary goal of interventions on the street children by services providers logically involves reunification with biological families. The objective for the current study was to explore the family reunification experiences of street children in Zimbabwe. This study was conducted out of the researchers' conviction that research on the reunification of street children with their families in Zimbabwe has not been sufficiently exhausted. The Juconi model of family reunification underpins the current study. The model advances that sustainable street children reunification should be anchored on livelihood support, schooling and rehabilitation to heal the attachment breakdown. Key informant interviews were the data collection methods. A total of 11 participants took part in this study. The key informant interviewees were staff at NGOs that assist to reunify the children, social welfare officers from government, former street children, and staff members from international agencies that deal with children and officials from Harare City Council. The respondents were recruited using the purposive sampling method. An interpretive phenomenological analysis was used to analyse data. The family reunification experiences for the street children included successful family reunification by agencies, re-entry into the streets, rejection by families and schools, return to school, being led to wrong homes and reunification with alternative relatives. The challenges for family reunification that emerged included poor budgets, stigma in the families and communities, poor coordination and policies for family reunification and non-resolution of the factors that led the child into the streets. In terms of recommendations, the government through the Department of Social Services and various other stakeholders, should devise better policies and programmes for family reunification, impart vocational and life skills to the children, ensure thorough family tracing and reunification together with rehabilitation of the children, counselling of the guardians and train parents and guardians on appropriate parenting skills.

Introduction

Scholarly studies on the sustainability of the interventions on street children in Zimbabwe have not exhaustively researched this contemporary issue. The primary concern in this chapter is the sustainability of family reunification efforts street children in Zimbabwe. The phenomenon of street children punctuating the cityscape of many urban areas is global, disquieting and escalating (Mhizha, 2010). Though the exact numbers of street children are elusive (Thomas de Benitez and Hiddlestone, 2011), and impossible to quantify (UNICEF, 2005, Thomas de Benitez and Hiddlestone, 2011), the figure almost certainly runs into tens of millions globally (UNICEF, 2005). It is indubitable that the challenge of youths in the twenty-first century is more acute in Africa than elsewhere (Biaya, 2005). In Zimbabwe, the media and scholars alike have lamented the increase in population and menace of street children seen as 'uncouth' for their antisocial tendencies (Mhizha, 2010, Muchini, 2001, Ruparanganda, 2008). Ruparanganda (2008) warns that these street children may eventually emerge in growth points and rural villages in Zimbabwe. The objective of the current study was to examine the experiences of street children who go through family reunification.

Background and Overview

According to Nieuwenhuys (2001:551), the term 'street children' has been part of a discourse constructed around the children of the urban poor, which has become very powerful in appealing to the 'international charity market'. Nieuwenhuys (1999) argues that these children, represented as urgently in need of help but competent enough to take charge of their own lives, have been the perfect allies for NGOs in their bids to raise funds and gain legitimacy. Ennew (1994) states that governments tend to abstain from developing policies for street children in favour of funding, and encouraging NGOs engaged in actions to combat the problems, particularly actions which diminish the visibility of children on the streets. Saunders-Adams (2011) argues that the major goal of programmatic interventions on street children is to achieve rehabilitation yet there is paucity in academic literature concerning family reunification particularly the outcomes of reunification and the factors for its sustainability. Conticini (2008) argues that getting the child off the streets through family reunification activities is not easy. What if the child's decision to leave the family home and move on to the street was the best option available? There is a general perception that the child or youngster needs to be rescued from street life in order to restore a childhood that is supposedly absent in the street. The insistence of removing children from the street and integrating them into the family rests in the idea that childhood is synonymous with domesticity (Conticini, 2008).

Family Reunification for Street Children

Family reunification of street children is based on The Universal Declaration of Human Rights by the United Nations in 1948, Article 16.3 which holds the family as the fundamental and natural social unit which should be protected by society and the state (Feeny, 2005). The Convention on the Rights of the Child (1990) echoes the same thinking saying that the family is the basic environment for the harmonious and full development of the personality of the children. Thomas de Benitez (2007) has observed that family reunification of street children only succeeds if there is rehabilitation of street children from drug abuse. It has been reported that street children abuse drugs frequently and they need to be rehabilitated from drug abuse for reunification to succeed. Service providers should thus precede their social interventions with child rehabilitation and resolution of the causative factors for the street childhood before the actual reunification.

For Feeny (2005), it is important to ascertain the incompatibility of street children with family life, and the need to 'erase' the 'street' from the child to help facilitate a smoother reunification. Nonetheless, Feeny (2005) argues while it may be true that some children need time and support in readapting to a family environment, role and responsibilities, the idea that the children should fundamentally seek to change themselves is worrying. On the one hand, the approach serves to further vilify and stigmatise the nature of street children as 'deviant', while on the other it may encourage feelings of guilt and fear in the child that the perceived 'failure' of their reunification is solely their fault. Indeed, the stigma attached to street children is one of the challenges, especially for those who have been involved in sex work as this may mean that their reunification could nearly be impossible (Feeny, 2005). The negative images and assumptions of street children as 'diseased' and 'delinquent criminals' dominate many societies around the world and pose a significant challenge to family reunification and reintegration. Street children are negatively perceived as having high sexual indulgence and equally high risk of contracting HIV/AIDS in the absence of contraception (Feeny, 2005). Although most children on the street do not have access to medical services that could diagnose HIV/AIDS or other STDs, a small number sometimes find out they are infected through other means, such as NGO health clinics.

Literature shows that there are some preferred street children groups when it comes to reunification. Feeny (2005) has observed that some organisations concentrate reunification efforts on street-living children over street-working children. This bias does not imply that street-working children are any fewer worthy targets for reunification interventions than street-living children. In fact, the distinction between the two is in many contexts very slight. Rather, it is argued that reunification is more 'significant' or 'necessary' in the lives of the latter group because of the greater distance between themselves and their family. However, for Feeny (2005), there is no reason why *any* child who is on the streets should not be able to seek help in returning to their family, and agencies should ideally avoid predetermining which groups of street children they intend to target for reunification using as guidance the particular circumstances of each individual child instead.

Feeny (2005) write about reunification windows which are points in street life when street children consider going home, or at least changing their environment. These times include particular events such as fights with friends, episodes of abuse and/or harassment and periods of isolation which can be morally, emotionally and physically exhausting. Mhizha (2010) has observed that some street children seek reunification with their biological families when they are ill. It is often at these points that children decide to seek the help of an NGO or similar authority for support. This act is not to be confused with the child 'giving up' on their street life as this is usually a much longer and gradual process of withdrawal (Feeny, 2005). Reunification windows are not predictable though they depend on two critical factors: the age of the child and the length of time they have spent on the street. Most organisations target younger, pre-adolescent street children for reunification in the belief that children of this age group are less independent and/or suspicious of adults (and thus easier to persuade), are more likely to fear the street and miss their family, are most in need of adult supervision and care and are not likely to have had the time to become deeply assimilated into the street lifestyle. Some scholars believe that children who have been in the streets for more than a year find it difficult to stay at home again. The child may miss their friends in the streets and are likely to return (Beazley, 2003).

Family Tracing for Reunification

Family tracing involves the implementing agency contacting the family and assessing their suitability and reciprocal interest in receiving the child again (Feeny, 2005). Depending on the length of time and geographical distance that have separated these two, tracing the family can pose quite a challenge. Magagula (2009) has observed that not all parents can be located because some street children might not permit the reunifying officials to approach their homes. Sometimes the parents themselves can reject the reunification with their child. Some children may not reunify with their parents because, for example, their mothers may still be staying with stepfathers who may not have forgiven the children for offences they committed before running away from home. It has also been shown that some biological parents prefer boyfriends as opposed to their own flesh and blood. Magagula (2009) further has observed that parents need training in parenting skills so that they learn how to interact with children and how to nurture them in a family environment.

Sometimes children and their guardians could be having different perspectives on issues that separated them. One study in Botswana (Campbell and Ntsabane, 1995) found that parents and guardians blamed their children's life on the streets as 'juvenile delinquency', while the children maintained it was parental negligence. Interestingly, over 60% of the parents/guardians interviewed were not aware of any symptom related to the child's decision to run away, suggesting that they were unable to correctly assess the needs or desires of their children before they ran away (Campbell and Ntsabane, 1995). According to Feeny (2005), family reunification also entails assessing the suitability of the family for reunification. NGOs are in a hurry to reunite as many children as possible and may not take the time to consider the circumstances thoroughly. It can involve assessing the social, economic and emotional suitability of the family in welcoming back the child. Similarly, the Convention on the Rights of the Child (CRC), while providing children with the right to reunification, does not give any specific indication beyond the vague notion that it should be carried out only if it is in the child's 'best interests' (Feeny, 2005).

The Reunification Kits

As the Convention on the Rights of the Child makes clear, families should be afforded the 'necessary protection and assistance so that it can fully assume its responsibilities within the community', and most organisations interpret this as an obligation to provide some material or financial package to help the family cope with the challenges of (re)absorbing an extra member to feed, clothe and educate. Such 'reunification kits' may also act symbolically as a gift associated with the child that helps them to be accepted and to feel just a little less of a burden to the family (Feeny, 2005). Although the composition of these kits more often reflects the individual organisation's budget rather than the family's actual needs, it nevertheless ranges from basic foodstuffs, clothes, school materials and tools to more sustainable items such as bicycles, livestock and pieces of land. Deciding which are the most appropriate and effective combinations for a particular family will once again draw heavily on the assessment conducted prior to reunification and, to ascertain, may require considerable flexibility from an organisation over time. This may involve helping the family set up a small business to improve their sustenance. Magagula (2009) has observed that when there is not enough continued support from the organisation is when the reunification is said to be unsuccessful. There must be continued support and communication between the child, the family, and the organisation to ensure the child does not abscond again. This includes assisting the family with basic needs (food, school fees, and the like) and what also may be important is teaching them basic life skills (i.e., budgeting, a trade, or gardening) (Magagula, 2009).

Reunification Follow-Up

Feeny (2005) has observed that reunification is not the end of an organisation's involvement with the child, rather, it is the beginning of a new stage that requires further support and monitoring. There have been too many instances where, following reunification and the termination of an organisation's involvement, the child could be beaten or abused as punishment for having run away, only to then return to the streets weeks later (Feeny, 2005). Given the considerable resource strain that most organisations conducting reunification programmes for street children find themselves under, the idea of carrying out a further set of follow-up visits may seem exhausting and not particularly time or cost-effective. However, monitoring the progress of reunified children through these visits offers numerous benefits, not just to the child, but to the organisation as well. Monitoring enables the worker to assess the success of the reunification (necessary for inclusion in the end of project reporting to donors), it acts to prevent some problems, since both the family and the child expect that their situation will be followed up, it offers reassurance to the child that someone cares about them outside the family, it offers protection to the child when bad things happen as they have someone they know to approach for support who will be on their side, it offers feedback to the reunification programmes on which elements need strengthening or improving (Feeny, 2005).

Conceptualising Sustainability

Feeny (2005) has observed that organisations conducting family reunification programmes with street children normally give quantitative figures to prove the success of reunification without actually revealing the criteria on which such claims are based. The sustainability claims are therefore from partial and limited perspectives such as the length of time a child remains with the family following reunification, be it two years, one year or even a matter of

328

months. Others simply aim for a certain target number of children to be returned each year. Neither approach tells us anything about how a child has qualitatively experienced reunification and can actually hide instances of abuse or other serious issues affecting their welfare that would directly contradict such claims of 'success'. Feeny (2005) observes that it is more prudent to measure the child's circumstances more holistically following reunification. That would include whether the child has not lost weight. Studies have shown that during follow-up visits, there would be changes in the children's appearance, with the children not wearing the clothes they would have been given but putting on rags (Bonnerjea, 1994). Many of the families would be extremely poor and even resort to selling such clothes to buy food. Sometimes children may be taken back to the orphanage to make sure they do not die of hunger (Bonnerjea, 1994).

One way to measure sustainability is through the rates of absconding. Reunified children sometimes return to the streets after reunification. Rurevo and Bourdillon (2003) has observed that, although street children repeatedly complain of the hardships of life on the streets, for instance, the cold in winter, the lack of regular meals and proper sleep, attempts to reunify them have rarely succeeded. One street child was reconciled with her aunt with promises of support for education. Soon after the tensions and mistreatment which caused the girl to leave in the first place returned and she was back on the streets again. Even those that were placed in a training institute outside Harare, where they were given food, accommodation and education complained of food shortages and poor treatment by staff. As a result, a group of children absconded and returned to the streets of Harare. In her study, Thomas de Benitez (2007) observed that among street children participants who had been returned to their families, the majority had subsequently returned to living on the streets.

Government Policy and Capacity on Street Children

The government of Zimbabwe faces the challenge of resources to conduct family tracing, escorting, reunification and reintegration with continued monitoring (MoLSS and UNICEF, 2010). The Department of Social Services (DSS) which deals with street children and their reunification is one of the least funded departments by the national treasury. In an institutional capacity assessment that was conducted in 2010, the MLSS and UNICEF observed with concern that the DSS is under resourced to meet its obligations. Its shortcomings ranged from unavailability of adequate qualified staff and shortage of vehicles needed for family tracing and reunification of children with their families. The report observed that the DSS depended more on non-state actors and donors to discharge its duties than the state itself. This resulted in the DSS providing patchy services around the country to the children needing support. The report further observed that the ratio of children to social workers in Zimbabwe was 49,587:1, compared with 1,867:1 in Botswana and 4,300:1 in Namibia (MoLSS and UNICEF, 2010). This ratio means that children in need of care will not be able to access the services of a probation officer timeously. In order to address this challenge, the government then resorted to recruiting staff who were not social workers such as sociologists and psychologists without systematic orientation on how to discharge social work responsibilities (MoLSS and UNICEF, 2010).

Not only does the Zimbabwe government lack resources for reunifying children with their families, it also seems to lack a sound policy on this duty. Wakatama (2007) and Ndlovu (2015) agree that Zimbabwe does not have any meaningful rehabilitative policy on street children. The default reaction has been to round up the street children with the intention of putting them into the so-called institutions of safety which are themselves 'mini-prisons.' The traditional response to street children by the government of Zimbabwe has been of repression which does not solve the issue of street children. In other words, the government of Zimbabwe has failed to take appropriate measures to promote physical, psychological recovery and social reintegration of street children who are victims of neglect, abuse, exploitation and inhuman degrading treatment or punishment. The government is in a clear violation of Article 39 which requires the state to provide rehabilitative care to children who are victims of torture, maltreatment and exploitation (Wakatama, 2007).

Theoretical Framework

The current study employs the Juconi model as the theoretical framework used to implement and evaluate schooling among former street children in Mexico. Juconi is derived from *Junto con los Niños* meaning 'Together with the Children' and as a model has been employed on children who lived and worked on the streets and their families for over 20 years (Schrader McMillan and Herrera, 2014). Thomas de Benitez (2008) asserted that the Juconi provide personalized, family-based, livelihood support, integral educational and psychotherapeutic services for sustainability. The first step is preparation, which includes intensive and regular contact with children, recreational activities, and preparing street children for life away from the street. The second step is intensive change, which could include living in a residential home and attending some formal schooling or working with a child's family. The final stage is a follow-up or tracking, which helps graduates integrate back into society through home visits, work visits, and continued counselling. The model incorporates key stakeholders on the lives of the children, and these include teachers, employers, neighbours, and the wider community (Thomas de Benitez, 2007).

Schrader McMillan and Herrera (2014) analysed the Juconi theoretical framework incorporating both attachment and trauma theories. The model holds that for reunification gains to be sustained, it is essential first to heal the effects of trauma. The model assumed that street childhood emerged from factors such as painful losses, neglect, and engagement in family violence with the children as victims, perpetrators or witnesses. Symptoms for the trauma may include risky behaviours, substance abuse, poor relationships, poor and difficult emotional expressions and nightmares or night terrors. Without sufficient rehabilitation on the children, there can be reunification challenges (Thomas de Benitez, 2008). The model creates environments where the children can identify, recognise, interpret and express their own emotions and loss involving the children reflecting on their suffering caused by traumatic experiences and grief, and coping with such losses, and having the children imagine and plan for their future.

The Juconi model appreciates the significance of the stepparents in street childhood and subsequent reunification. Indeed, the presence of a loathed, generally but not always violent stepfather (or a succession of 'stepfathers') is one of the reasons why many children leave their homes in the first place (Thomas de Benitez, 2008). The Juconi model works with such families to resolve the strained relationships and sometimes reach a pragmatic compromise as parents can decide to continue their relationship with their partner, but not share the same family home. JUCONI respects that family reunification can certainly involve extended family hence it is essential to keep several options open and respond flexibly to each situation (Thomas de Benitez, 2008).The Juconi model was employed by the Railway Children in East Africa focusing on psycho-social support, livelihood support and emotional healing. Furthermore, the Juconi model has been employed sustainably in Afghanistan, Ecuador, Brazil, Chile, Mexico, Kenya, Tanzania and South Africa (Railway Children, 2015). Thomas de Benitez (2008) argues that the model can work in a politically unstable and low-income country environment where there is no public funding and educational support for street children while parental support is limited.

Methodology

The current explorative study employs a qualitative research approach as the research design. In addition, qualitative methods approach is used to generate data on how the street children eked a living in the streets. The present study employed key informant interviews to collect the data. Interviews remain emblematic of qualitative research, affording participants the opportunity to talk more or less expansively about their lives (Ennew, 2003). This approach is qualitative and phenomenological. It involves detailed analysis of the lifeworld of the respondents, it endeavours to explore personal and subjective experiences and focusses on the individual respondent's personal account and perception of a phenomenon which is different from attempts to give objective views of the phenomenon itself. All in all, there were 11 participants who were all key informant interviewees. The key informant interviewees included adult street dwellers, officials from a drop-in centre for street children, social welfare officers and community services officers from Harare City Council. The researchers felt that they would exhaust the various categories and dimensions in the current study after interviewing 11 participants.

The study employed purposive sampling in recruiting participants for the current study. Purposive sampling is influenced by multiple dimensions, like time or availability (Strauss and Corbin, 1998), and at times, from the nature of the topic, the scope of the study, or the amount of useful information obtained from each participant (Morse, 1994). The 11 participants ensured that theoretical sampling was reached (Charmaz, 2014). Data for the current study were collected using key informant interviews.

The goals of the researchers were to analyse in detail how participants perceive and make sense of their experiences. It therefore required a flexible data collection instrument. The recognition of key informant interviews is based on the argument that they are a primary means by which participants make sense of their experiences. Consent was sought from gatekeepers of the street children who include the Ministry of Social Welfare, the Harare City Council and drop-in centre officials. Informed consent from the participants was obtained from respondents and involved assuring them that they could terminate the interview at any time. Confidentiality and anonymity were spelt out and adhered to. The data analysis method was used in the current study is the interpretive phenomenological analysis. In this method, the researchers learnt about the respondents' psychological world in the form of constructs and beliefs that were given by participants (Smith, 1996). The data analysis focused upon the generation of explanation and common themes that arose from the transcripts. Codes were assigned to the themes which reflected the shared perceptions among respondents of the investigated phenomena (in this case, the reunification experiences for the reunified former street children).

Results

Family tracing and assessment

Family tracing involves going to the family to assess whether the family knows the particular child, whether they know the context involving the child leaving the family and if they are available to the resolution of the said factors and whether they have the capacity to resolve the factors. Interviewee #1, who was a director at an organisation that provided services to street children in Harare revealed that family tracing was included in reunification processes in Zimbabwe after they were in a trip with officials from the Ministry of Public Service, Social Welfare and Labour and the UNICEF Country Representative. Interviewee #1 said:

> We wanted to have them see the importance of family tracing. We went to Murehwa. We took 5 children for reunification. We arrived at one homestead. The family head openly declared that he could not take that child. He asked if we were serious that we wanted him to prepare another plate of sadza for that child. He told us that if hell is there with its flaming fire, he would rather enter it than taking that child. He told us point blank that he could not take that child. There were 10 orphans there and the child we had escorted was the 11ᵗʰ orphan. That is when the Ministry started insisting on family tracing.

It emerged from the data that family tracing was important and had to be pursued. The challenges faced by children were due to funding due to organisations failing to follow family reunification properly. It turned out that some officials from reunifying agencies did not travel for the family tracing as they merely phoned to verify with nearby officials if the homestead for the child can sustain the reunification. Interviewee #3, was a programme officer at a drop-in-centre in Harare, decried that some officials merely engage in what he called 'phone family tracing,' which is not thorough. Still on family tracing, Interviewee #2, who was a director of an organisation that provided services to vulnerable children in the whole of Zimbabwe including street children, decried that modern-day social workers just go around homesteads and note that there are cattle and goats at the homestead and then write down their reports and claim to have done family tracing. He decried that modern-day social workers are not interviewing the village heads as is per guidelines to assess whether the family can care for the child. He observed that family tracing is not done properly with ramifications on the reunified child. Thus, if family tracing is not done satisfactorily, the resultant family reunification will be faulty and unsustainable.

Reaction of the family and community

A significant factor was the reaction of the family and community to family reunification of the child. Sometimes the child is accepted by both the family and community and such reunification can be sustainable. Interviewee #10, who was a maternal aunt to a street child who was reunified from the streets revealed that she had to take the child when all relatives and families members including the biological father had refused to take the child. Nonetheless, she accepted the child on conditions that the reunifying organisation was to provide school fees and uniforms. Interviewee #1 narrated a story in which a paternal aunt rejected her niece who was ill with AIDS in Rusape touching the female street child's leg saying, 'this is AIDS you are bringing here,' whilst shaking that leg. He returned with the child to the streets and the child died 3 months later. Rejection by stepparents was cited as another impediment to reunification with key informants citing rivalry between the stepparents and the stepchildren. Interviewee #11, who was a stepmother to a street child who was reunified, revealed that she initially had rejected the reunification efforts and that her husband would not have managed to force her to accept the child and only accepted when the police intervened.

Sometimes it needs the community for reunification to succeed. Interviewee #4, was social protection officer at a drop-in-centre in Harare, narrated a story of a child who was only accepted after the village head was informed and had to call for a village meeting to ask if the village would agree to child coming back. Interviewee #1 further related an incident in which reunification succeeded when he managed to have a village meeting with members of a village including a school head as the community was stigmatizing a member of child-headed household after reunification. After educating the community about the ills of stigmatising the child only did the reunification succeed. Interviewee #4 and interviewee #1 revealed that it has been very difficult for former street children to adjust at schools where they are placed by reunifying agencies. These two informants narrated cases of children who got into serious trouble with communities for stealing goats and food from fields as they complained of late provision of food by the sponsoring organisations. The children were later named goat thieves.

Non-resolution of the causal factors

A critical factor for the success of family reunification is the resolution of the factor that had thrown the child into the streets. Without the resolution the reunification process ends up as merely returning the child back home. Interviewee #1 narrated an instance when a street child they wanted to reunify fled back to the streets when his grandmother started narrating the reasons why he initially left for the streets. The grandmother had revealed to them that the grandchild was tasked to give guests food. The guests were housed in a different room in the homestead. On the way, the child ate all the food and replaced it with his faeces and handed that to the guests. During family tracing that issue was not raised, only to be raised during reunification and the child fled for good. It therefore emerged that children were reunified without any attempts to resolve the issues that had made them go into the streets. The factors included poverty, delinquency, poor parenting practices and family discord. Indeed, the respondents asserted that most reunifications were merely processes of returning children home and this was done by different actors who included social workers, police officers, pastors, the children themselves, the guardians and relatives who used different approaches but most of them did not clearly seek to resolve the contributing factors. The practice involved the reunifying agents apologising for the children in their absence such that the guardians would not recognise any need for change in parenting of the returning child. Interviewee #11, who was a stepmother to a street child who was reunified, revealed that she would never forgive the reunified child for the delinquent behaviours he had exhibited.

Reunification windows

Reunification windows occur when children offer themselves for reunification probably after realising that life in the street has no future. Sometimes it is because of negative events which they may not like. Sometimes these children just become homesick after realising that they are lonely when their peers had returned home or sent to institutions. These children normally live in groups to protect each other from other groups which can abuse or bully them. If they are left on their own, their safety would be compromised. Some children choose to be reunified with their families after misdemeanours, for example, fleeing from a conned drug lord. Others may want to leave the streets when they feel overwhelmed by extreme cold weather, especially if there are reunification grants during the winter season. The children may agree to go back home during winter only to return by September. Children wanted by the police for petty crimes such as breaking into cars may decide to go home and return when their case would have been closed or forgotten, say, after four months.

Reunification kits and family strengthening

Reunification kits

The data revealed that the children are given different items as reunification kits. These include money, which is referred to as settlement fees, and sometimes they are given livestock and groceries. Sometimes it is just the process of reunifying the child with the family without any reunification kit. The reunification kits do ensure sustainability of family reunification. Interviewee #8, who was a social welfare officer with the Ministry of Social Welfare, Labour and Public Services, revealed that sometimes they have nothing to provide for the family and that they sometimes leave a small settlement fee they get from NGOs. The settlement fee is normally given once and sometimes can hardly be enough to buy groceries and school uniforms. Interviewee #9, a social welfare officer with the Ministry of Social Welfare, Labour and Public Services, echoed the same sentiments and narrated that they once reunified a certain child with her grandmother in Gokwe Nembudziya area. She said that she had just $10 to hand to the family which could only be used to buy a packet of mealie meal and cooking oil. That particular child absconded, possibly after the mealie meal was used up. Interviewee #1 commented that he once initiated a reunification livelihood project involving goats. He indicated that some families are faced by food insecurity and they only accept the child if provided with something. He narrated an incident when he bought 2 goats for a child he was reunifying. The whole family could benefit from the reunification kit and the child will have few issues with adjustment.

Rehabilitation

A significant theme that emerged regarding the sustainability of family reunification was rehabilitation of street children. The respondents agreed that without rehabilitation of the street children, family reunification can hardly succeed. Indeed, it emerged that the children had assumed behaviours in the streets which would not fit at home. The lifestyles involved substance abuse, fighting, stealing and sexual permissiveness. Interviewee #1 revealed that, when reunifying street children, he tells the receiving family that they should hide their money in safe places as the children may have developed a proclivity to stealing. Interviewee #1 further narrated that they also tell the receiving families that the returning child may be prone to use obscene words such as 'musatanyoko' (referring to mother's genitals or one who has sexual intercourse with his mother). The families which receive street children may therefore need to tolerate such vulgar language if the reunification is to be sustainable. Interviewee #7, himself a former street child, revealed that its normal to hear street children shouting among themselves or at people passing by using vulgar words such as 'your penis', 'you bullshit,' 'your ass' and 'mind your stale vagina'. Such words may be taboos at home but, for the street children, they are part of their language. Interviewee #1 revealed that he once made a follow-up on the children he had reunified in Mutoko and found a female reunified child daring to beat up her

336

father with a hoe handle after he had questioned her about the multiple relationships she was having at school. The family was able to tolerate her, but she later dropped out of school and got married. The problem is that some female children survive on sexual activities in the streets and, when reunified, it becomes difficult to drop that lifestyle. Interviewee #2 narrated the case of a former street child who was having multiple and concurrent with her teachers that they started fighting amongst themselves. When they tried to counsel her, she frankly told them that she was finding it very difficult to stop her sexual behaviours.

Reunification framework

A worrying observation was that Zimbabwe does not seem to have a framework or model to guide interventions on street children. The interventions were said to be uncoordinated, haphazard and not grounded in a sound framework. Interviewee #3 narrated that in most cases the reunification is sponsored under short-term funding terms and sometimes without even opportunities for follow-up. Interviewee #9 underscored that they hardly made follow-up visits due to staff shortage, funding challenges and lack of vehicles. At some point each district was manned by only about two officials when they were supposed to make three follow-up visits for each child reunified. Interviewee #1 decried that, whereas the numbers of street children in Zimbabwe is increasing, the challenges affecting them have not been addressed yet nationally there is no framework put in place to cushion these children. He went on further to say that the Children's Act does not properly provide intervention strategies on these children as is there no policy that directly speaks to street children issues. It emerged from the data that in Zimbabwe, there are no transit centres to hold the children during family tracing, there are hardly night outreach visits due to funding constraints and that there is no clear model to follow when reunifying children.

Discussion

The data revealed that family reunification in Zimbabwe is beset with many challenges that affects its sustainability. The challenges include poor family tracing, funding challenges, lack of rehabilitation, absence of a clear policy, non-resolution of causal factors and rejection by families and communities These factors make the family reunification unsustainable. The factors tally with the observations by Wakatama (2007), Ndlovu (2015) and Mhizha (2010), that Zimbabwe lacks a clear policy on rehabilitation of street children in Zimbabwe and that any attempts to reunify them have been haphazard and uncoordinated.

337

The findings resonate with what researchers such as Feeny (2005) and Schrader McMillan and Herrera (2014) observed regarding the family reunification which should be supported by psychological interventions and livelihood support. Furthermore, former street children need individualised, well-supported interventions which should involve family members, schooling officials and other community members (Feeny, 2005, Schrader McMillan and Herrera, 2014). The fact that former street children may stop schooling after being withdrawn by their family members seem to be a novel finding since it was not observed from the reviewed studies.

Conclusion, Policy Options and Recommendations

This paper interrogated the sustainability of family reunification for street children in Zimbabwe. The writers suggest that a clear and well-grounded policy based on research be formulated on family reunification of street children in Zimbabwe. Attention should also focus on factors that push children into the streets. The factors include the economic meltdown exacerbated by high unemployment levels and poverty levels. Orphanhood is high also due to the HIV and AIDS scourge. Many children have dropped out of school as families fail to pay for the schooling costs. There is also a rise in child abuse, especially child sexual abuse which has reached epidemic levels due to the economic crisis. In reunifying the children, it is important to repair the strained relationships between parents and children first. The paper recommends that the government of Zimbabwe and other stakeholders increase efforts to ease socio-economic challenges in the country, especially to help the children who seem to bear the brunt of the crises. More so, there should be a framework to help families and guardians to better provide emotional and economic care for their children. Such education ought to equip children with training in life skills and vocational training as well as decision-making, interpersonal skills, stress and coping with it, health literacy and emotional intelligence. Regarding vocational skills, the individual street children and former street children be free to select courses they want from an array including mechanics, welding, farming, sewing, embroidery, brickwork, carpentry, computer literacy and programming among many others. The government and interested stakeholders should avail funding for such education. Perhaps more importantly, the government should provide rehabilitation and therapeutic services to street children to help them deal with the adverse psychological and emotional experiences both at home and in the streets. There should be advocacy to deal with stigma, labelling and stereotype the street children face in schools and communities. Parents, families and communities should also be trained in provision of care and positive parenting for children which should help them prevent, mitigate and detect the cases of street childhood. The training should make the parents aware of the negative and traumatizing effects of the behaviours that throw the children into the streets. Thus, it is imperative to arrest the human factor decay that is manifested in the factors that cause children to leave families due to the traumatic experiences at home.

References

Beazley, H. (2003). The construction and protection of individual and collective identities by street children and youth in Indonesia. *Children, Youth and Environments,* 13(1), 899-902.

Biaya, T. K. (2005). Youth and street culture in urban Africa: Addis Ababa, Dakar and Kinshasa. In A. Honwana and F. De Boeck (Eds.), *Makers and breakers: Children and youth in postcolonial Africa* (pp.215–228). Oxford: James Currey, Trenton: Africa World Press, Dakar: Codesria.

Campbell, E. K. and Ntsabane, T. (1996). Health risk practices among street children in Gaborone, Botswana. *CHASA Journal of Comprehensive Health,* 7(1), 23-33.

Charmaz, K.C. (2014). *Constructing grounded theory* (2ⁿᵈ ed.). Thousand Oaks, CA: Sage.

Conticini, A. (2008). Surfing in the air: A grounded theory of the dynamics of street life and its policy implications. *Journal of International Development,* 20, 413-436.

Drane, M. (2010). Street children as unaccompanied minors with specialized needs: deserving recognition as a particular social group. *New England Law Review,* Summer.

Ennew, J. (2003). Difficult circumstances: Some reflections on 'street children' in Africa. *Children, Youth and Environments,* 13(1), 128-146.

Feeny, T. (2005). *In best or vested interests? An exploration of the concept and practice of family reunification for street children.* London, UK: The Consortium for Street Children.

Magagula, S. J. (2009). *Evaluation of reunification programmes rendered by service providers in respect of street children with their families/households* (Unpublished master's thesis). University of Zululand, South Africa

Mhizha, S. (2010). *The self-image of adolescent street children in Harare* (Unpublished master's thesis). University of Zimbabwe, Harare, Zimbabwe.

MoLSS and UNICEF. (2010). Institutional capacity assessment. Harare: Ministry of Labour and Social Services and UNICEF.

Morse, J. M. (1994). Designing funded qualitative research. In N.K. Denzin and Y.S. Lincoln (Eds.), *Handbook of qualitative research* (pp. 220-235). Thousand Oaks, CA: Sage.

Muchini, B. (2001). A study on street children in Zimbabwe. *Retrieved February, 6*, 2007.

Ndlovu, I. (2015). *Life experiences of street children in Bulawayo: Implications for policy and practice* Unpublished PhD thesis.) The Open University.

Nieuwenhuys, O. (2001). By the sweat of their brow? 'Street children,' NGOs and Children Rights in Addis Ababa Africa. *Journal of the International African Institute* 71(4), 539-557

Railway Children. (2015). *Intensive family work to Suppet Street: Connected children in Nairobi, Kenya.* Nairobi, Kenya: Kibera Slums press.

Ruparanganda, W. (2008) *The tragedy of procrastinating? A case study of sexual behaviour patterns of street youth of Harare, Zimbabwe in the era of HIV and AIDS pandemic* (Unpublished doctoral thesis). University of Zimbabwe, Harare, Zimbabwe.

Rurevo, R. and Bourdillon, M. (2003). *Girls on the street.* Harare: Weaver Press.

Saunders-Adams, S. M. (2011). *Reunification and reentry in child welfare: A systematic review and meta-analysis* (Doctoral dissertation, The Ohio State University).

Schrader McMillan, A. and Herrera, E. (2014). *Strategies to ensure the sustainable reintegration of children without parental care: JUCONI, Mexico.* Retrieved from http://www.familyforeverychild.org/wp-content/uploads/2014/01/Children-s_Reintegration_in_Mexico.pdf.

Smith, J. A. (1996). Beyond the divide between cognition and discourse: Using interpretative phenomenological analysis in health psychology. *Psychology and health, 11*(2), 261-271.

Thomas de Benitez, S. and Hiddleston, T. (2011). *Research paper on the promotion and protection of the rights of children working and/or living on the street: OHCHR 2011 global study.* Geneva: OHCHR

Thomas de Benitez, S. (2007). *State of the world's street children: Violence.* London: Consortium for Street Children.

Thomas de Benítez, S. (2008). *Square holes for round pegs: "Street" children's experiences of social policy processes 2002-2005 in Puebla City, Mexico* (Unpublished doctoral dissertation). Department of Social Policy, LSE.

United Nations Children's Fund. (2005). *State of the world's children 2006: Excluded and invisible.* New York: UNICEF.

Wakatama, M. (2007). *The situation of street children in Zimbabwe? A violation of the United Nations Convention on the rights of the child (1989)* (Unpublished PhD thesis). University of Leicester.

Chapter 18

Malthus and Sustainability of the Food Security Sphere in Zimbabwe

Halleluah Chirisa, Stanzia Moyo, Gift Mhlanga,
Oswell Rusinga and Alfred Zvoushe

Summary

The exploration of the nexus between population growth and food supply dates back to the 18th century. At global, regional and national levels, population growth almost doubled between 1980 and 2015. However, a holistic perspective regarding the applicability of Malthus' propositions and postulations in agricultural economies of developing nations, and Zimbabwe in particular, has remained a grey area in academic research. Utilising triangulated qualitative research approach through the use of strategic documents, reports, reviews, book chapters and journal articles, the chapter sought to establish the link between population growth and food supply in Zimbabwe. Another main objective of the study was to establish other underlying factors, besides the Malthusian perspective, which contribute to food insecurity in Zimbabwe. The study revealed that, contrary to Malthus' postulation of an inverse relationship between population growth and food supply, the strategic grain reserves in Zimbabwe allowed for a positive relationship between population growth and food security. In addition, it was revealed that the major factors which lead to food insecurity in Zimbabwe may be categorised into ecological, economic and political. This invalidates the Malthusian argument that the main cause of food insecurity for a particular country is due to overpopulation. In this regard, the study recommends financial commitment to the agricultural sector as agreed upon at the Maputo Declaration in 2003. Furthermore, the involvement of all key ministries and implementing partners is also important in food production if Zimbabwe is to regain the lost status of being the 'breadbasket of Southern African Development Community' earned during the first decade of independence.

Introduction

Despite the Malthusian postulations in the 18th century about the inverse relationship between population growth and food supply, the theory seems to be less applicable in the 21st century, especially in developing countries. Focusing on Zimbabwe, Zipperer (1987) claims that the country was the breadbasket of Africa from 1980 to 2000 regardless of the growing population (Zipperer, 1987). In this regard, the regression of the country into a basket-case is not owed to overpopulation effects but to a socio-economic breakdown (Chitongo, 2013, Mutondi, 2011). The ability of Zimbabwe to produce sufficient food for its population in the 1980s made it possible for it to be responsible for food security in the SADC region. However, given the economic meltdown, compounded by political and environmental factors, food insecurity was compounded (Chitongo, *ibid.*). Thus, the nexus between population growth and food insecurity is missing in the Zimbabwean case. This discourse explores the significance of this Malthusian aspect in relationship to food situation in Zimbabwe.

Specifically, the chapter seeks to establish the levels and trends of food security in Zimbabwe from 1980 to 2015. In addition, the factors underlying the observed levels and trends of food security in Zimbabwe are analysed and interpreted in the context of Malthusian theory. This implies that the answers to the sustainability of the food question should be derived from looking closely not only at the Malthusian perspective, but also at the various dimensions of the historical and contemporary facets. Thus environmental, political, economic and technological aspects should also be explored so as to ascertain their contribution to food insecurity in Zimbabwe.

The Malthusian theory

Thomas Robert Malthus enunciated his views about population in the article entitled, "Essay on the Principle of Population as it affects the Future Improvement of Society", published in 1798. Specifically, the theory explains the relationship between the growth in food supply and in population. It claims that population increases faster than food supply upon which the former grows exponentially while the latter increases geometrically. Resultantly, if nature does not intervene through a strong check on population, namely the difficulty of acquiring food, vice or misery will inevitably occur. From this analysis, it is evident that Malthus was one sided in his perspective. The theory anchors on the view that natural disasters are a way for the earth to shed away excess population.

Background and Overview

The world's population has increased by 64%, from an estimated 4.5billion to 7.4 billion between 1980 and 2016 (United Nations [UN], 2015, 2016). However, developing countries constitute at least 83% of the global population (UN, 2016). The population in sub-Saharan Africa has increased by 149% from an estimated 390 million in 1980 to 974 million in 2016 (UN, 2015, 2016). The global population growth rate decreased from 1.8% in 1980 to 1.1% in 2016 (UN, 2016). While the growth rate for developed nations has declined to the current 0.4%, the overall growth rate for developing countries is 4 times higher than that of the developed nations. Similarly, while developed nations' growth rates are showing a declining trend since 1980, substantial differences remain across countries and regions. For instance, while Western Europe annual growth rate is close to a zero, sub-Saharan Africa has rates that are still higher than the 3% that was recorded for the world at the beginning of the 1960s (Roser and Ortiz-Ospina, 2016).

The population of Zimbabwe increased by 71%, from 7 608 432 in 1982 to 13 061 239 in 2012 (Central Statistics Office, 1982: Zimbabwe National Statistics Agency [ZIMSTAT], 2012, World Fact Book, 2014). The Zimbabwean population pyramid is broad based, with the under 15 population consistently constituting at least 40% of the population from 1980 to 2012 (Central Statistics Office, 1982: ZIMSTAT 2012: Central Intelligence Agency, 2014). This implies that food sustainability in Zimbabwe needs proper planning and implementation given the relationship between population growth and food supply.

Given an imploding world population, it is of paramount importance to consider the questions of global and regional food security. Bremner (2012), the World Food Programme (2013) and United Nations (2015) assert that at least 12% of the world population suffered from severe food insecurity which was characterised by chronic hunger and inability to live active lives between 1980 and 2015. However, food insecurity is higher in developing countries compared to their developed counterparts. This disparity could be primarily because developing countries rely on agriculture as an economic base. For example, 60% of the world population experiencing food insecurity are in the developing continents of Africa and Asia (Frimpong, 2016). In spite of the decreasing food insecurity and nutrition status in Africa, the proportion of food insecurity in Africa to the global food insecurity has constantly remained high, at least 35%, from 1980 to 2016 (UN, 2015: Frimpong, 2016). In sub-Saharan Africa, at least 26% of the population suffered from food insecurity between 1980 and 2015 (UN, 2015, Frimpong, 2016).

Although the Malthusian model is of the view that food insecurity and famine are a result of nature reacting to overpopulation, it is not always the case in Africa (Smith *et al.* (2000). In other words, there are several underlying factors that explain food insecurity in developing countries. According to Sasson (2012) and Sadza *et al.* (2015), climatic change and weather vagaries contribute to food insecurity in these countries. For example, severe droughts, especially to the "horn" of Africa (Somalia, Ethiopia and North Eastern Kenya), and catastrophic floods are observed to have inflicted heavy damage to ecosystems and agro-ecosystems, thereby threatening food security of people in these areas (Sasson, *ibid.*).

Moreover, inadequate funding, a factor not envisaged by Malthus, also contributes to food insecurity and poverty. Accordingly, Jayne *et al.* (2006), assert that there has been inadequate funding for the implementation of agricultural policies and strategies in developing countries. Contrastingly, this is against the background that there is a positive relationship between government expenditure in agriculture, agricultural growth and poverty reduction especially in rural areas (Akroyd and Smith, 2007). However, if there are inadequate funds for agricultural subsidies and inputs, for example, food insecurity crops in. Nonetheless, as a continent, Africa has some guiding policies pertaining to the production of food. For example, the 2003 Maputo Declaration on Agriculture and Food Security in Africa drafted some strategies to support agricultural investment. In this vein, among other important decisions regarding agriculture was the commitment by African governments to allocate at least 10% of national budgetary resources to agriculture and rural development policy. Subsequently, agriculture expenditure in Africa increased by 103%, from 7.3% in 1980 to 14.8% in 2005. On the other hand, Africa enjoys relief donations from nongovernmental organizations and international organizations such as World Food Programme (WFP) and United States Agency for International Development. Looking at these helping arms at local, regional, and international levels, the Malthusian cataclysm in food insecurity is therefore far-fetched.

Inappropriate agricultural policies have been observed as another contributing factor to food insecurity in Africa. For instance, Sasson (2012) asserts that the structural adjustments policies which typically dominated Africa during the past two decades to some extent contributed to food insecurity in the region. Specifically, Akroyd and Smith (2007) state that the structural adjustments loans (SALs) and the conditions agreed as part of the loan packages triggered temporary and sometimes permanent postponement of trachea releases and changes in commitments from other donors that further destabilised the levels of agriculture, especially in Africa.

344

Internationally, governments are aware of the intricate relationship between population growth, poverty, food insecurity and nutrition bearing in mind Malthus' (1798) proposition on the relationship between population growth and food supply. However, contrary to the preventative checks to population growth alluded to by Malthus, the importance of planning for food security in terms of availability, accessibility and adequacy, has been espoused as a human right in international legal frameworks which include, inter alia, Article 25 of the 1948 Universal Declaration of Human Rights, Article 11 of the 1976 International Covenant on Economic, Social and Cultural Rights, Article 27 of the 1979 Convention on the Elimination of Discrimination Against Women, Article 27 of the 1989 United Nations Convention on the Rights of the Child, and, The Convention on the Rights of Persons with Disabilities. In Africa, African Union treaties, and Southern African Development Community (SADC), where Zimbabwe also subscribes to, have declarations which emphasise the need for provision of food security and nutrition. The African Union commitments to the right of food and nutrition are observed in the following instruments: The 1987 African Charter on Human and People's Rights, The 1999 African Charter on the Rights and Welfare of the Child, The 2001 Abuja Declaration, The 2003 Maputo Declaration on Agriculture and Food Security in Africa, The 2003 Comprehensive African Agriculture Development Programme, The 2005 Protocol to the African Charter on Human and People's Rights on the Rights of Women in Africa, The 2008 African Union Summit, and The 2014 Malabo Declaration on Accelerated Agricultural Growth and Transformation for Share Prosperity and Improved Livelihoods.

In Zimbabwe, the government adopted the United Nations Declaration where the need to eradicate hunger and poverty by 2015 was the first goal of the 2002 Millennium Development Goals (MDGs) and the second goal of 2015 to 2030 Sustainable Development Goal (SDGs) which aims at '… eradicating hunger, achieve food security and improved nutrition and promote sustainable agriculture'. The importance of food security and sustainability is also enshrined in the 2013 Constitution of Zimbabwe Amendment 26 Act, Section 15 and 17. Specifically, Section 15 states that, 'The State must encourage people to grow and store adequate food, secure the establishment of adequate food reserves, and encourage and promote adequate and proper nutrition through mass education and other appropriate means', while Section 17 among other issues enshrines the right to '….sufficient food….within the limits of the resources available to it'.

Notwithstanding, the growing importance of the international and regional relationships between population growth and food insecurity using the

Malthusian lens as highlighted above, there is a lacuna of scholarly inquisition of such a relationship in Zimbabwe. Scholars such as Stanning (1985), Rukuni and Eicher (1994), Mudimu (2003), Shumba and Whingiri (2006), Jayne *et al.* (2006), USAID (2014) and Sadza *et al.* (2015) have carried out studies about agricultural production and the subsequent food security situation in Zimbabwe. Nonetheless, the trends of the food security situation in Zimbabwe and the factors underlying the observed trends from the abovementioned studies are not only piecemeal, but also devoid of the analysis using the Malthusian perspective. This chapter therefore explores the trends of food production and insecurity in Zimbabwe from 1980 to 2014 while highlighting the underlying factors from the Malthusian lens.

Methodology

The study used a desk study approach to gather and analyse the information concerning food security. This is an approach which is basically involved in collecting data from existing resources. In this regard, it is considered to be a low-cost technique as compared to field research since there are no transport costs, for example. However, just like in any other study approach, the required information may not be readily available. This mostly occurs when one is researching on relatively sensitive issues which require governmental consent to be availed. In this study, the researchers used online research as well as documents, journals, as well as governmental publications in hard copy form. It is significant to note that for one to be efficient using online research, there is need to be information specific while fetching out this information since there are billions of pages available on internet.

The study was purely a literature review study whereby existing information was analysed. This involved the review of literature on the relationship between population growth and food supply as published in the various strategic documents, reports, reviews, book chapters and peer reviewed journal articles which were considered under this research. This kind of wide exploration in literature was important given that it helped establish the levels and trends of food insecurity in Zimbabwe. Subsequently, data were analysed using content or thematic analysis. The authors created a coding tree anticipating key themes that would emerge. The processed data were then read in order to identify key themes related to the levels and trends of food insecurity in Zimbabwe from 1980 to 2015 and the factors underlying. Consequently, a coding tree was revised with new themes added and other themes from the initial coding tree dropped. Information regarding each of the following themes: levels and trend of food insecurity, economic, environmental, policies and strategies were then subsequently grouped together.

Results and Discussion

Although the Zimbabwean population is on the rise, a notable increase in food production was observed (Mudimu, 2003). In this vein, Shumba and Whingiri (2006) note that the overall crop production of cereals such as maize groundnuts, sorghum cotton and burley increased by 13% from 2 198 000 metric tonnes in 1980 to 2 486 000 metric tonnes in 2000. Stanning (1985) also notes that agricultural production of cereals by communal farmers increased from 4.7% in 1980 to 65% in 1989-1990 season. Consequently, Rukuni and Eicher (1994) have termed this food production a success, particularly the increase in output of maize during the aforementioned period as Zimbabwe's smallholder revolution. Commercial grain production increased by 284%, that is, from 675 000 to 2 594 000 tonnes between 1992 and 2000 (Mudimu, 2003).

Furthermore, between 1980 and 2000, Zimbabwe had a sound strategic grain reserve which enhanced the food security situation. For instance, Jayne *et al.* (2006) note that in 1985, grain self-sufficiency in Zimbabwe was 212% and this earned the country the responsibility of heading the food security sector of the Southern African Development Community. In particular, the strategic grain reserve cushioned some of the country's districts in Matabeleland North and South, Manicaland, Masvingo and Mashonaland East and Central from food insecurity effects of the droughts in 1987, 1992 and 1995 (Jayne *et al.* 2006). In addition, the strategic grain reserve enabled Zimbabwe to export surplus maize to countries such as Mozambique, Malawi, Zambia and Ethiopia in the 1980s (Sanning, 1986). The factors underlying food security in Zimbabwe during the period 1980-2000 hinged on governmental political will and commitment (Eicher and Rukuni, 1994). In this regard, Jayne *et al.* (2006) elaborates that governmental policies increased agricultural production by both the communal and large-scale farmers. Examples of such policies included producer prizes for food and cash crops, credit extension and then agricultural research. This proves that effective agricultural planning by governments can help to maintain an equilibrium between population growth and food supply, invalidating the Malthusian perspective.

Nonetheless, according to USAID (2014), there was a declining trend in cereal production between 2002 and 2015 in Zimbabwe, a scenario which triggered a recurrent food insecurity in the country. To elaborate further, USAID (*ibid.*) notes that maize production in Zimbabwe has been on the declined since 2002 and has never fully recovered. For instance, Jayne *et al.*

347

(2006) stipulate that between 2002 and 2003, all districts in Zimbabwe were identified as food insecure. Furthermore, maize production declined by 43%, from 1.4 million to 800000 metric tonnes in 2011 and 2013 UN, 2014). Consequently, between 11% and 40% of the Zimbabwean population were food insecure between 2006 and 2014 (UN, *ibid.*). Figure 18.1 depicts that food insecurity was highest in 2008/2009 agricultural season when about 5.2 million people (almost 40% of the population) needed food aid. Sadza *et al.* (2015: 17) note that there are ten districts which are prone to recurrent food insecurity and these are Kariba, Mudzi, Umzingwane, Nkayi, Bulilima, Tsholotsho, Gokwe North, Zvishavane, Buhera and Mangwe. These districts recorded food insecurity levels of between 10% and 52% in January to March of 2013 (Sadza *et al. ibid.*). In addition, the Zimbabwe Vulnerable Assessment Committee (2014) also highlights that between January and March of 2014, 25% of the population in Zimbabwe needed food assistance.

Moreover, the role played by technology improvements such as use of fertilisers and genetically modified seeds not only defy the Malthusian proposition of an autarky state, but also his postulation on the preventative checks to population growth and the resulting hunger. In this vein, the well-planned and implemented strategic grain reserve in Zimbabwe between 1980 and 2000 not only enhanced the food security situation in the country, but also at regional level. This is largely because Zimbabwe was the main exporter of food to hunger stricken countries such as Mozambique, Ethiopia and Zambia. Nonetheless, Makumbe (2009) and the Famine Early System Network (2014) reveal that from 2000 up to the mid-2000s, economic hardships, compounded by climatic and environmental factors, have seen Zimbabwe depending on international food aid, as aforesaid.

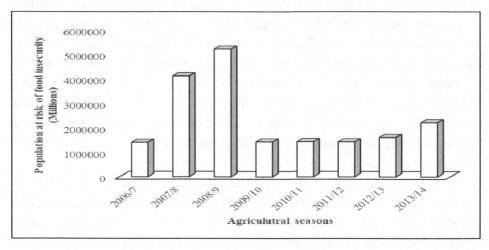

Figure 18.1: The Zimbabwean Population at Risk of Food Insecurity (UN, 2014)

Zimbabwe is prone to suffer from natural disasters, such as the 1982, 1987, 1992, 2002 and 2007 droughts and 2000 Cyclone Eline, and these have contributed to food insecurity in the country. Noteworthy is the fact that the natural disasters are contrary to Malthus's postulation that overpopulation leads to natural disasters, implying them as the direct results from overpopulation. From Malthus' perspective, natural disasters are natural checks to mitigate the adverse effects of overpopulation and their consequences are to curtail the population to maintain the balance between population growth and food production. However, according to WFP (2017), the periodic droughts are due to global warming, not overpopulation. On the other hand, Cyclone Eline was observed to have led to food insecurity in Zimbabwe in early 2000. The cyclone left in its wake hunger and starvation as it had destroyed the planted crops by the excessive rains. This was compounded by the early termination of rains, another evidence of climatic change. Consequently, the reduction in crop yield resulted in a 70% shortfall in production to meet the country's annual food requirements, marking it the largest deficit in its food production history since 1980 (WFP, 2002).

The impact of environmental factors to the food security discourse in Zimbabwe mirrors findings by Smith, Obeid and Jensen (2000), Jayne *et al.* (2006), Sasson (2012) and Sadza *et al.* (2015) for the entire African continent. However, Anseeuw *et al.* (2012) argue that insufficient funding, research and dissemination of agricultural information not only leads to limited transfer of productive farm technologies, but also lack of commercial farming skills. Similarly, the Ministry of Environment, Water and Climate is responsible for promoting sound environmental and sustainable development and utilisation of natural and water resources. Nonetheless, Gwimbi (2007) notes that the absence of preparedness plans for evacuation and overdependence on rain-fed agriculture by locals hamper the implementation of early warning systems. In addition, Chimanikire (2011) posits that limited development of programmes that aim to develop best practices to enhance carbon sequestration and reduce carbon emissions exacerbate the consequences of climatic change. Furthermore, Sadza *et al.* (2015) points out that lack of regional integration on climate change also contributes to the adverse effects of climatic change. Thus, in this analysis, it is evident that measures to reduce overpopulation, such as family planning are not put forward. This infers that the effects of overpopulation on food security may be evident at household level, whereby it becomes one variable among many which affect household food security.

In addition, the economic crises in Zimbabwe have largely been responsible for food insecurity since 2002. Specifically, the country's economy encountered severe challenges from 2002 to 2010. The Ministry of Finance and Economic Planning (2011: 230) notes that by July 2008, Zimbabwe's gross domestic product had declined by over 50% and inflation had peaked at 231 million percent. Moreover, capacity utilisation in industry had fallen below 10% by July 2009. Consequently, severe food and foreign currency shortages were experienced due to the crippled economy. These observations were echoed by Shumba and Whingwiri (2006: 6) who argue that the declining economy from the early 2000s led to high levels of unemployment, and hence food insecurity in Zimbabwe. Moreover, Fan and Anuja (2012) point out that the proportion allocated to the agricultural sector had dwindled between 2002 and 2015. For example, the proportion of the budget allocated to agriculture was reduced by 0.7%, from 8.3% in 2002 to 7.7% in 2005. Noteworthy is the fact that during the same period, countries such as Burkina Faso, Ethiopia, Malawi and Mali allocated at least 10% of their national budgets to the agricultural sector (Fan and Anuja, *ibid.*).

Inadequate funding has also affected the pivotal role played by the Grain Marketing Board and the Agricultural Bank of Zimbabwe (Agribank) in preventing food insecurity in Zimbabwe. The Grain Marketing Board (GMB) in Zimbabwe has the mandate to maintain strategic grain reserves in the country and pegging crop prices. However, Sadza *et al.* (2015) argue that GMB parastatal has limited capacity to carry out its mandate due to lack of financial resources. Late payments, which have become typically common of GMB, have been asserted by World Food Programme (2017) to be one of the factors underlying the shift to cash crop farming like tobacco by most communal farmers. This directly reduces the amount of food crops grown hence hunger and poverty (*ibid.*). Similarly, Agribank has, among other issues, the mandate to provide sustainable agricultural development through financing farmers. According to Sadza *et al.* (2015:34), Agribank "…. contributes towards national agricultural development, food security, increased output and productivity, and the generation of foreign currency, particularly for farming and rural communities". Nonetheless, the economic decline had its toll on these institutions and hence the mandate is rarely put into practice (Kapuya, 2010). In other words, the aforementioned challenges have resulted in limited access of working capital and difficulties in accessing agricultural finance among the farmers. However, although inadequate finding was not envisaged by Malthus as an underlying factor to poverty and food insecurity, it is critical to note that, unless the issue of agricultural funding is seriously taken on board, the achievement of agricultural policies, programmes and production will always remain a pipeline dream.

Unlike Malthus's proposition that overpopulation results in poverty and food insecurity, structural adjustment policies undertaken by governments can have a negative impact on the nation's food security. The 1991 Economic Structural Adjustment Programme (ESAP) had a negative impact on food production (Matondi, 2011). This observation corroborates findings by Akroyd and Smith (2007) and Sasson (2012) about the African continent. According to Kanyenze (2011), one objective of ESAP in relation to agriculture was "… the production of enough food for the population…" (*ibid*: 26). However, the Zimbabwe Congress of Trade Unions (ZCTU, 1996), points out that the government made the wrong assumptions that the agricultural sector was homogeneous, where both commercial and communal farmers would uniformly benefit from the liberalized agricultural sector. Furthermore, the governmental budget cuts in the sector resulted in less expenditure by the government on extension services, research, subsidies and market outlets (*ibid*.). Thus, the small-scale, communal, farmers were left to fend for themselves in an environment, which was highly competitive. Resultantly, Rukuni (2006) points out that the average yields per hectare in the communal agriculture declined due to this programme. Matondi (2008: 18) notes that "… the 1990s witnessed a growth in both poverty and vulnerability in rural areas, rather than the expected economic growth." Consequently, food security was at stack due to the economic adjustment programme. Therefore, as explained before, food security in Zimbabwe is affected by various factors, including the socio-economic environment.

Stack and Sukume (2006) argue that between 1990 and 2001, up to 57% of the population in Communal Lands was classified as having, on average, insufficient food entitlements to ensure basic food security at some point in time. Consequently, although the commercial produce continued to flourish from irrigation development, infrastructural renewal, and new market streams, the communal people were languishing in abject poverty. Had it not been for the strategic grain reserve, the entire national food insecurity was going to be at threatened given that at least 65% of the population was based in rural areas. The foregoing findings show that there is need for proper planning of agricultural programmes if the food insecurity problem in any country is to be abated.

The fast track land reform programme had also adverse effects on the Zimbabwean food security. In this regard, Anseew *et al.* (2012) note that prior to 2000, the commercial sector consisted of 1.3 million people (including farm owners and farmworker households) who lived on 4660 large commercial farms, covering 15 million hectares, while the small-scale sector consisted of over a million households (5.6 million people) subsisting on 16 million hectares.

As aforementioned, this status quo had positive results in food production. However, FAO and WFP (2009) reveal that over two million Zimbabweans were food insecure in 2008 and one factor attributed to this is the FTLRP (Utete, 2003, Madhuku, 2004, Matondi, 2011). According to Rodrik (2000), for a new policy to be functional and operational, its implementation should be smooth and well-planned beforehand. Thus, the violence associated with the programme, the poor planning, and the unfair redistribution of land to politicians and elites within the ruling ZANU (PF) party deepened the sharp differences. This suggests that, instead of the land program being a national concern, it was now a partisan issue. The direct result of this was on how the land was distributed. Madhuku (2004) claims that the government did not follow the legal route on how the land was parcelled as some constitutional and legal imperatives were suspended in the process. To elaborate on this, Matondi (2011) argues that the A2 model is labelled as a "…sanctuary for the political elites…" (*ibid.* p28). In other words, the FTLRP exacerbated food insecurity in Zimbabwe due to the inconsistencies in land allocation and the subsequent drying out of expertise in agriculture.

Moreover, during the FTLRP, the government concentrated its limited financial input to the new farmers, seemingly forgetting the communal and old resettlement areas. The farmers in these two areas had previously relied on the government to provide for their inputs and this governmental intervention benefited the nation at large since they contributed to the national food produce. In this regard, the irony of the land reform program was that, instead of the government continuing to offer the input packs to these seasoned farmers, it now directed its efforts on the new, mostly inexperienced, farmers. This led to the decline of agricultural productivity as Sukume and Guveya (2009) state that the overall agriculture production declined by 30% between the period 2000 and 2008. Some areas which were usually known to be food-reliant in Mashonaland, for instance, , needed food relief even in the best farming seasons (FAO and WFP, 2009). Resultantly, once known as the breadbasket of the Southern African Development Community (SADC) region, Zimbabwe was now characterised by chronic food insecurity (Makumbe, 2009). To date, WFP (2017) notes that due to the FTLRP, 98% of the farmers in Zimbabwe are smallholders working on 73% of agricultural land. In this regard, WFP (*ibid.*) asserts that low productivity, limited access to markets, lack of competitiveness and exposure to adverse weather patterns are typically common attributes which contribute to the overall food insecurity in Zimbabwe. Noteworthy is the view that demographic issues, as attributed by Malthus, are far-fetched in this discourse.

In addition, policies have been formulated both at national and local levels in Zimbabwe to ensure an equilibrium between population growth and food production. Note that the policies and strategies are contrary to the Malthusian postulation that an equilibrium between overpopulation and resources can only be achieved through checks such as epidemics, wars and famine. Among the policies and strategies at national level are the 1991 Economic Structural Adjustment Programme (ESAP), the 1995-2020 Zimbabwe Agriculture Policy Framework, the 2005 National Land Policy, the 2007 Zimbabwe Agriculture Policy, the 2013 Zimbabwe Agenda for Sustainable Socio-Economic Transformation, the 2013 Food and Nutrition Security Policy (Government of Zimbabwe and Food and Nutrition Council, 2013), the 2014-2018 Zimbabwe National Nutrition Strategy, the 2014-2018 National Food Fortification Strategy, the 2011-2015 Zimbabwe National HIV and AIDS Strategic Plan, and Social Transfer Policy Framework. On the other hand, ZIMASSET aims to '...create a self-sufficient food surplus economy and focuses on crop and livestock production and marketing, infrastructure development' while anchored on indigenisation, empowerment and employment creation (Government of Zimbabwe, 2013, Sadza *et al.* 2015: 24). On the other hand, community-based food security strategies have been developed to ensure food sustainability. These include the Food Deficit Mitigation Strategy, the Public Works Programme, the 1987 Community Food and Nutrition Programme, the 1996 *Zunde raMambo*, the 2012-2032 Draft Agricultural Policy Framework, the 2013-2017 Zimbabwe Agricultural Investment Plan, the 2010-2015 Conservation Agriculture Strategy, the 2011 Agricultural Inputs Programme, the 2009 Environmental Policy Strategies, the 2013-2017 National Gender Policy, and Zimbabwe United Nations Development Assistance Framework. However, Sadza *et al.* (2015) argue that the *Zunde raMambo* initiative was affected by droughts where the majority of households were food insecure and the grain reserves were not sufficient for all needy households. Furthermore, the Conservation Agriculture Strategy was not fully embraced by all stakeholders, while inputs sometimes reach farmers late for the impact to be realised during the Agricultural Inputs Programme (*ibid.*). Notwithstanding the importance of the challenges outlined before, the strategies to maintain the equilibrium between population growth and food supply are very different from the Malthusian positive checks to population growth. However, what needs to be done by the government for the success of the strategies, is to ascertain full participation of all stakeholders and that inputs are distributed early.

Unlike the preventative checks to maintain equilibrium between population growth and food supply articulated by Malthus, a multi-sectoral approach has been implemented in Zimbabwe to curtail the food insecurity problem. There is coordination of the implementation of food security programmes through various ministries such as the Ministry of Public Service, Labour and Social Welfare, Ministry of Health and Child Care, Ministry of Primary and Secondary Education, Ministry of Women Affairs, Gender and Community Development, Ministry of Agriculture, Mechanisation and Irrigation, Ministry Environment, Water and Climate, Ministry of Local Government, Public Works and National Housing. In addition, the Food and Nutrition Council, Agricultural and Technical and Extension Services (AGRITEX), Grain Marketing Board (GMB), Agricultural Bank of Zimbabwe (Agribank) and Conservation Agriculture Working Group also play crucial roles in implementing food security programmes in Zimbabwe. International Development Agencies such as World Food Programme, Food and Agriculture Organisation, United Nations Children's Fund, United Nations Women, World Health Organisation, European Union, United States Agency for International Development and the Department for International Development United Kingdom also play pivotal roles in financing the implementation of food security programmes in Zimbabwe. It is important to note that Ministry of Health and Child Care is on the forefront of the implementation of nutrition-based programmes which have witnessed among other successes, the reduction in health indicators such as wasting and stunting by 167% and 18% respectively, between 1999 and 2014 as observed by World Food Programme (2017).

Conclusions

Zimbabwe witnessed an increase in population from 1980 to 2015. However, contrary to Malthus's postulation that population growth always results in food insecurity, the Zimbabwean case proved otherwise between the period 1980 and 2000 since food security was stable. This was largely because of the strategic grain reserve which not only cushioned the country from the effects of the 1987, 1992 and 1995 droughts, but also earned the country the title of the breadbasket of SADC. In this regard, the Malthusian population theory is limited in that it does not put into consideration mitigating interventions from the government and non-governmental organizations. Moreover, technology has boosted food production as the application of fertilisers allows for increased and better yields, which are above the geometric predictions of Malthus.

Although the country became food insecure from 2000 to 2015, environmental, economic and political factors underpinned the food insecurity problem instead of population increase. This implies that food insecurity cannot only be explained by excessive rapid population growth over food production.

This myopic trait in the Malthusian theory renders it inapplicable in contemporary societies. In addition, the preventative checks to population growth and the subsequent equilibrium with food supply, as postulated by Malthus, were different from the mitigating measures that were implemented in Zimbabwe. Policies, strategies, trade, and a multi-sectoral approach involving all key stakeholders in different ministries and international cooperation, though facing some challenges, were adopted and implemented in Zimbabwe to help maintain a relative balance between population growth and food security. What ought to be done by the government is to find lasting solutions to the economic, environmental and political challenges inhibiting the smooth implementation of policies and strategies that are aimed at ensuring constant food security in Zimbabwe. For instance, the government must have a committee to ensure that the budget for agriculture is at least 10% as per the 2003 Maputo target. Similarly, the government of Zimbabwe should have sustainable ways of warnings in periods of looming natural disasters like floods, cyclones and droughts. This implies that the metrological department should be furnished with modern technology which would accurately forecast the weather patterns. In this case, the weather forecast should not be falsified to suite parochial agendas. Moreover, state media like the national television and newspapers should be used effectively in this regard. The government should also establish a well-defined food security policy. Since the food security issue is of paramount importance for the development of the nation, the policy should be a stand-alone development, not being a sub-theme in any other policy or blueprint like the current ZIMASSET. More so, the policy should neither be an instrument of politics nor a mere drafted paper to be discarded away at the whims of a politician or a technocrat, but rather it should be drafted and implemented

References

Akroyd, S. and Smith, L. (2007). *The decline in public spending to agriculture – does it matter? Briefing Note, No. 2.* Oxford: Oxford Policy Management Institute.

Anseeuw, W, Kapuya, T. and Saruchera, D. (2012). *Zimbabwe's agriculture reconstruction: Present state, ongoing projects and prospects for reinvestment.* Midrand: Development Planning Division and Development Bank of Southern Africa.

Anseeuw, W, Kapuya, T. and Saruchera, D. (2012). *Zimbabwe's agricultural reconstruction: Present state, ongoing projects and prospects for reinvestment.* Midrand: Development Planning Division and Development Bank of Southern Africa Limited.

Bremner, J. (2012). *Population and food security: Africa's challenge.* New York: Population Reference Bureau

Central Intelligence Agency. (2014). *World fact book.* New York: Central Intelligence Agency.

Central Statistics Office. (1982). 1982 *Census report.* Harare: Central Statistics Office.

Chimanikire, D.P. (2011). *Mitigation and national and sub-national response to climate change institutional architecture in southern Africa. The case of Zimbabwe.* Tokyo: Global Industrial and Social Progress Research Institute.

Chitongo, L. (2013). *The contribution of non-governmental organisations to rural development: The case of Catholic Relief Services protecting vulnerable livelihoods programme in Zimbabwe.* Oyama: Leena and Luna International.

Community Working Group. (2014). *National budget analysis report.* Harare: Community Working Group.

Famine Early System Network. (2014). *Zimbabwe food security brief.* Harare: Famine Early System Network

Fan, S. and Anuja, S. (2010). *Tracking agriculture spending for agricultural growth and poverty reduction in Africa.* Washington: Regional Strategic Analysis and Knowledge Support Systems.

Fan, S. and Saukar, A. (2006). *Public spending in developing countries: Trends, determination and impact.* Mimeo. The International Food Policy Research Institute.

FAO and WFP (2009). *Special report: FAO/WFP crop and food security assessment mission to Zimbabwe, 22 June 2009.* Rome: FAO.

Frimpong, J. (2016). *Food insecurity in Africa.* Accra: The Lead International Company.

Government of Zimbabwe and Food and Nutrition Council. (2013). *National food and nutrition security policy (NFNSP) for Zimbabwe: Promoting food and nutrition security in Zimbabwe in the context of economic growth and development.* Harare. Government of Zimbabwe.

Government of Zimbabwe and Ministry of Finance and Economic Planning. (2011*). Zimbabwe medium term plan 2011-2015.* Harare: Government of Zimbabwe

Gwimbi. (2007). The effectiveness of early warning systems for the reduction of flood disasters: Some experiences from cyclone induced floods in Zimbabwe. *North Carolina Journal of Sustainable Development in Africa,* 19(4), 152-169.

Jayne, T.S and Chisvo, M. (2006). Zimbabwe food insecurity paradox. In M. Rukuni: Tawonezvi, C. Eicher M. Munyuki-Hungwe and P. Matondi (Eds.),

Zimbabwe agricultural revolution revisited (pp 525-541). Harare: University of Zimbabwe Publications.

Kanyenze, G. (Ed.). (2011). *Beyond the enclave: Towards a pro-poor and inclusive development strategy for Zimbabwe.* African Books Collective.

Kapuya, T., Saruchera, D., Jongwe, A., Mucheri, T., Mujeyi, K., Ndobongo, L. T., & Meyer, F. H. (2010). The grain industry value chain in Zimbabwe. *Unpublished draft prepared for the Food and Agricultural Organization (FAO). www. fao. org/fileadmin/templates/est/AAACP/eastafrica/UnvPretoria_GrainChainZimbabwe_2010_1_. pdf.*

Madhuku, L. (2004). Law, politics and the land reform process in Zimbabwe. In M. Masiiwa (Ed.), *Post-independence land reform in Zimbabwe: Controversies and impact on the economy.* Harare: Friedrich Ebert Stiftung.

Makumbe, J. (2009). *The impact of democracy in Zimbabwe: Assessing political, social and economic developments since the dawn of democracy.* Harare: Centre for Policy Studies (CPS) Research Report 119, University of Zimbabwe.

Malthus, T. (1798.) *An essay on the principle of population.* Oxford: Oxford University Press.

Matondi, B. (2011). Institutional and policy issues in the context of the land reform and resettlement programme in Zimbabwe. In, C.T. Kazembe and L.R. Ndlovu (Ed.), *The livestock sector after the fast track land reform in Zimbabwe.* Harare: Institute of Rural Technologies.

Ministry of Finance and Economic Development. (2011). *The 2012 national budget statement: Shared economy, shared development, shared transformation "Creating the fair economy".* Harare: Ministry of Finance and Economic Development.

Ministry of Finance and Economic Development. (2012). *The 2013 national budget statement. Beyond the enclave: Unleashing Zimbabwe's economic growth potential.* Harare: Ministry of Finance and Economic Development.

Ministry of Finance and Economic Development. (2013). *The 2014 national budget statement: Towards an empowered society and a growing economy.* Harare: Ministry of Finance and Economic Development.

Mudimu, G (2003). *Zimbabwe food security issues paper.* Forum for Food Security in Southern Africa. London: Overseas Development Institute.

Novak, T.P. (1996). *Secondary data analysis lecture notes.* Marketing Research, Vanderbilt University.

Riely, F. (2002). *Pilot food aids needs assessment (FANA) methodology: A step-by-step guide.* Rome: World Food Programme.

Rodrik, D. (2000). Growth versus poverty reduction: A hollow debate. *Finance and Development,* 37(4), 8-9.

Roser, M. and Ortiz-Ospina, E. (2016). *World population growth*. Varna: University of Iowa. Rukuni, M. and Eicher, C. (1994). *Zimbabwe agricultural revolution*. Harare: University of Zimbabwe Publications.

Rukuni, M. (2006). The evolution of agricultural policy: 1980-1990. In M. Rukuni P. Tawonezvi, C. Eicher, M. Munyuki-Hungwe and P. Matondi (Eds.), *Zimbabwe agricultural revolution revisited* (15-29). Harare: University of Zimbabwe Publications.

Sadza, H.C. *et al.* (2015). *Zimbabwe zero hunger strategic review*. Harare: Women's University in Africa.

Sasson, A. (2012). Food security for Africa: An urgent global challenge. *Agriculture and Food Security*, 1(2), 1-8.

Shumba, E.A. and Whingwiri, E.E. (2006). Commercialisation of smallholder agriculture. In M. Rukuni: Tawonezvi, C. Eicher M. Munyuki-Hungwe and P. Matondi (Eds.), *Zimbabwe agricultural revolution revisited* (pp.577-591). Harare: University of Zimbabwe Publications.

Smith, L.C, Obeid, A.E.E. and Jensen, H.H. (2000). The Geography and Causes of Food Insecurity in Developing Countries. *Agricultural Economics*, 22, p199-215.

Stack, J. and Sukume, C. (2006). Rural Poverty: Challenges and Opportunities. In M. Rukuni: Tawonezvi, C. Eicher M. Munyuki-Hungwe and P. Matondi (Eds.), *Zimbabwe agricultural revolution revisited* (pp.557-576). Harare: University of Zimbabwe Publications.

Stanning, J. L. (1985). *Constraints of smallholder agriculture to marketed output in Zimbabwe. 1970-1985: Recent experiences and some future issues*. Harare: Department of Agricultural Economics and Extension, University of Zimbabwe.

Sukume, C. and Guveya, E, 2009. *Improving input and output markets for smallholder farmers in Zimbabwe*. Unpublished report.

Tickner, V. (1979). *From Rhodesia to Zimbabwe: The food problem*. Cambridge, Landon.

UN. (2015). *World population data sheet -2015*. New York: Population Reference Bureau

UN. (2016) *World population data sheet -2016*. New York: Population Reference Bureau

UNICEF. (2016). *Zimbabwe 2016 health and childcare budget brief*. Harare: UNICEF.

United Nations Zimbabwe. (2010). *Country analysis report for Zimbabwe*. Harare: Government of Zimbabwe.

USAID. (2014). *Zimbabwe food security brief*. New York: USAID.

Utete (2003), *Report on the presidential land reform committee on the implementation of the fast-track land reform programme, 2000-2002*. Harare: Government of Zimbabwe.

WFP. (2002). *WFP annual report*. Rome: World Food Programme.

World Bank and Government of Zimbabwe. (2010). *Zimbabwe agricultural assessment study. Final report. December 2010*. Harare: PricewaterhouseCoopers.

World Food Programme. (2013). *World food programme annual report*. Rome: World Food Programme.

World Food Programme. (2017). *Zimbabwe country strategic plan 2017-2021*. Rome: World Food Programme.

Zimbabwe Congress of Trade Unions. (1996). *Beyond ESAP: Framework for a long-term development strategy in Zimbabwe beyond the Economic Structural Adjustment Programme*. Harare: Zimbabwe Congress of Trade Union.

Zimbabwe Economic Policy Analysis and Research Unit. (2006). *Zimbabwe national health sector budget analysis and equity issues*. Harare: Zimbabwe Economic Policy Analysis and Research Unit and Training and Research Support Centre (TARSC) Zimbabwe.

Zimbabwe Government. (1991). *Second five-year national development plan, 1991-1995*. Harare: Ministry of Finance, Economic Planning and Development.

Zimbabwe Vulnerable Assessment Committee. (2014). *Rural livelihoods assessment*. Harare: Food and Nutrition Council.

ZIMSTAT. (2012). *Census 2012: National report*. Harare: ZIMSTAT.

Zipperer, S. (1987). *Food security agricultural policy and hunger*. Harare: ZIMFEP.

Chapter 19

Farmer Training Needs in Smallholder Irrigation Schemes in Mashonaland Central Province

Livinia Binala, Joseph Francis, Thomas Mupetesi
and Benjamine Hanyani-Mlambo

Summary

The chapter explains the dynamics of farmer training in smallholder irrigation schemes at Chimhanda, Eben and Negomo in Mashonaland Central, Zimbabwe. In most countries in the sub-Saharan Africa food security through agricultural production is a central government concern. Farmers and agricultural extension officers are critical players in the agricultural sector. Extension agents provide an avenue for dissemination of advice and information critical for farmers' production and marketing decisions. This facilitates best and viable resource utilisation, which contributes directly to solving issues of food security, unemployment, income generation and rural poverty. Smallholder irrigation schemes in southern Africa have continuously been performing poorly. This could be attributed to limited farmer participation, limited knowledge of various cropping systems and ineffective extension services. There is no one agricultural extension method that suits every situation as approaches need to be adapted to suit different settings like the terrain and soils of the area. In view of the current climate changes responsible for major droughts and land degradation dating back to the 1970s, there is a need to review the training needs of the smallholder farmers and the knowledge of extension officers imparting farming skills. The purpose of the review is to help Zimbabwe as a country to revert to its breadbasket status through irrigation rehabilitation. The study discussed in the chapter was based on desk methodology with an extensive review of secondary data using a systematic search. Agricultural extension interventions have been in existence since the establishment of the irrigation schemes. There are emerging agricultural extension approaches that need to be availed to farmers for better technological adoption and adaption in view of the current climatic changes basing on the cognitive, affective and psychomotor taxonomies of learning domains.

Introduction

The study examined the extent to which learning domains have been applied to the training maize farmers on three small-scale irrigation schemes in Mashonaland Central province of Zimbabwe (see Figure 1.2). Three contextual aspects, notably human resources development, land water resources and food security are the focus of the chapter. Smallholder farmers in Zimbabwe, as in most sub-Saharan Africa (SSA), face extreme weather variations. As a result, the livelihoods of these farmers are ruined with possible increase in poverty (Chazovachii, 2012). However, smallholder farmers can achieve remarkable increases in agricultural production given the necessary support to become resilient in the face of weather changes. Traditionally, these farmers had to wait for the summer rainy season before planting. If the rains are late, then the country's staple maize crop is affected causing food insecurity for the farming households. It is in this context that most African governments and policy-makers ought to be action-based rather than being rhetoric in order to effectively support smallholder farmer development in the sub-region.

Facing climate variability and dwindling land resources, most governments in poor African countries such as Zimbabwe have introduced smallholder irrigation schemes (SIS) in communal areas so that smallholder farmers do not have to rely on dryland farming. Such government policy measures seek to help rural households improve their living standards and production capacity by maximum utilisation of the existing resources (Mupaso et al. 2014). Irrigation agriculture can be referred to as the artificial watering of land. Methods of applying water include free-flooding of entire areas from canals and ditches, ridges or furrow methods. There are also methods like the surface-pipe method, sprinklers, centre pivots and trickle systems (The Columbia Electronic Encyclopaedia, 2013). This form of agriculture was and is still viewed as the most viable means of reducing crop failure, hunger and malnutrition in Africa. Although irrigation development is considered as a farming method to increase agricultural productivity, household and national food security (Feeler et al. 1985, Nhundu and Mushunje, 2010, Chazovachii, 2012), its development has been a major challenge in many poor countries.

In many countries, a significant gap is evident between actual farmer practices and advanced agricultural technologies. The programmes that focus on the delivery of inputs and farming practices have been initiated as an attempt to close the existing gap. In view of the land reform programme initiated by the government of Zimbabwe in 2000, there is a need to review the training needs of those newly resettled farmers and the knowledge of extension officers imparting the skills. These are newly resettled farmers with little or no knowledge of major agricultural activities to boost maize production for increased food security in households as well as feeding into the economy of the country (Scoones, 2013). Although some of the smallholder famers in the schemes have received some form of agricultural training there is need to view if the domains of learning (cognitive, affective and psychomotor) were linked to the training sessions starting with the facilitator or teacher to the learner himself. The aim of the review is to help Zimbabwe retain its breadbasket status through farmer training in irrigated maize schemes. The review is also necessary considering the current climate change causing major droughts and land degradation dating back to the 1970s.

A desk methodology was adopted for this study. Information from various sources was accessed for the compilation of data for the document. Extensive review of secondary data was engaged as part of the methodology. The data was then organised and interpreted. Key words such as training needs, agricultural extension, domains of learning, irrigation, poverty and climate change were used to search for relevant data using Google Scholar. Each scheme was investigated as a standalone case.

Description of the Study Area

Zimbabwe is a landlocked country situated in the southern Africa surrounded by Mozambique, South Africa, Zambia and Botswana. The country lies on longitude of 33.050 and latitude of 15.610. Its total coverage is 390,757 square kilometres. Of the area, 386,847 square kilometres is land, and water covers 3,910 square metres (ZimAtlas, 2016). Zimbabwe is the 61st largest country in the world. Mashonaland Central Province has a total population of 1152 520. This is made up of 567 140 males and 585 380 females (ZIMSTATS, 2012), which is about 8.5% of the total Zimbabwean population. It is within 17°00'S and 31°00'E. The total area of the province covers 28,347 km^2 (see Figure 1.2). The province falls in natural region II, III and IV. Natural region II receives 700-1050 mm rainfall per year in summer (FAO, 2000) (see Figure 1.1). Flue-cured tobacco, maize, cotton, sugar beans and coffee can be grown. Small grains and various horticultural crops are also grown in natural region II. Smallholder farmers occupy only 21% of the area in this productive region. Natural region III is a semi-intensive farming area with rainfall ranging from 650-800 mm (see Figure 19.1). There are prolonged seasonal droughts and unreliable start of the rainy season. In this region, irrigation plays a very important role in the sustainability of crop production. Natural region IV is a semi-extensive farming region. The region is too dry for crop production without irrigation (Vincent and Thomas, 1961, Rukuni and Eicher, 1994). Low rainfall is experienced in the 450-650 mm range (see figure 19.1). Farmers occupy 50% of the area.

Out of those who are employed, the highest proportion (69%) is engaged in agriculture related occupations which include the irrigation schemes investigated in this study. This high agricultural production justifies why Mashonaland Central is considered the breadbasket for the country. The study areas are communal irrigation schemes in Mashonaland Central that produce maize. The study areas chosen were Shamva (Eben) and Mazowe (Negomo), Rushinga (Chimhanda) (see Figure 19.2). The three community-owned smallholder irrigation schemes were purposively selected for the study. The SIS fall under natural regions II and IV. Negomo has 296 beneficiaries on 394 ha whilst Eben has 40 plot holders covering 20 ha of land. Chimhanda hosts 134 beneficiaries on 67 ha of land. Negomo and Chimhanda were purposively selected after considering the size of the scheme and that they were established in the pre-land reform programme which is before 2000. Distance from urban settings was also considered in the selection of Chimhanda Irrigation Scheme. Eben, with 40 plot holders covering 20 ha of land, was chosen on the basis of proximity to Harare, the capital city, and that it was established in the post land reform programme period. The distances of the irrigation schemes range from 90 km to 250km from Harare, the largest city of Zimbabwe. (MoAMID, 2014). The regions have red and sandy soils but, generally, there is degradation from fairly rich to poor soils as we go further. MoAMID (2014) further asserts that some farmers have received training in operation and maintenance (OandM) and training for transformation training (TFT) to date though others have not. This entails that there is a gap to be filled by farmer training sessions to cater for those who have not received the other part of training. Literature reveals that plot holders who work on the schemes are full-time as well as part-time owners who have other pieces of land outside the scheme where they do dryland farming in summer.

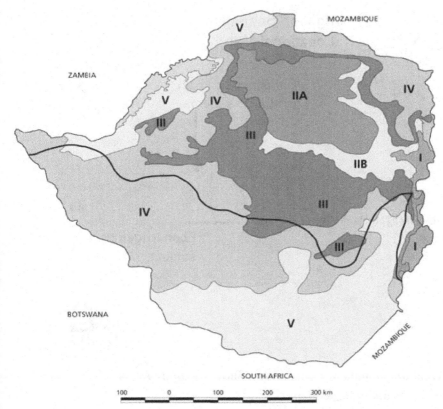

Figure 19.1. Zimbabwe Ecological Zones. (Google Maps, 2015)

KEY: Natural Regions

I	Specialised and Diversified Farming Region
IIA	Intensive Farming Region
IIB	Intensive Farming Region
III	Semi-Intensive Farming Region
IV	Semi-Extensive Farming Region
V	Extensive Farming Region

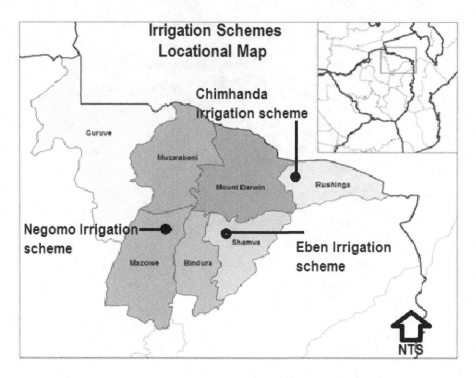

Figure 19. 2: Mashonaland Central Map Showing Study Areas.
Source: authors and google maps

Theoretical Framework

The chapter sought to explore the suitability of extension services offered to farmers basing on Bloom's taxonomy of learning domains theory that consist of cognitive, affective and psychomotor domains (Bloom, 1956, Anderson *et al.* 2000). Randall (2011) posits that a cognitive domain encompasses mental skills, that is, using the head or knowledge. The domain helps in the comprehension and remembering of aspects by individuals after training or learning new experiences. It takes form of participation by members in workshops or exercises provided as well as learning through lecture method. Affective domain makes use of the heart that causes change of attitude. The domain involves how people value what they have been taught or presented as new material. Change of attitude only occurs if an individual sees the worth of the material considered as relevant to him or her. The smallholder farmers are adults who need education for immediate use and not for banking. The level of adoption depends on the value attached to the new experience. Psychomotor deals with manipulative skills using the hands. It mainly refers to manual physical skills. Operation and maintenance in the irrigation schemes reviewed entailed repairing of irrigation equipment and other farm implements. The activity makes use of the ability to use hands by the participants. The three domains cannot be separated from each other as they are interlinked. They start from the knowledge retention to change of attitude and then applying the learnt skills.

Conceptual Framework

The trainers start by identifying the goals and objectives of the learning situation, that is, the problem at hand. The objectives determine the audience to be targeted. Agricultural extension officers decide on the best methods to be used during the training sessions. Due consideration should be afforded when choosing the agricultural approach which best suits the audience and the problem to be solved for better learning to take place. Teaching methods should be harmonised in order to effectively address the concerns of the participants. It should be an approach that facilitates comprehension, enables connectivity and putting to use the taught experiences. Participants, in this case smallholder farmers, were expected to put to good use the three levels of the mind using the cognitive, affective and psychomotor domains. As a result, better agricultural production could be realised as participants remember and value the information obtained. The conceptual components of domain-based farmer training are depicted in Figure 19.3.

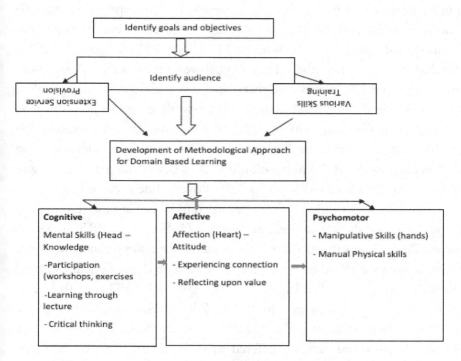

Figure 19.3: Domain Based Learning for Farmer Training
(Source: Author, 2017)

367

Literature Review

Extensive literature review of secondary data on poverty, climate change, irrigation, agricultural extension, training needs and domains of learning were sought for this study. This was done to assess the farmer training needs in smallholder irrigation schemes using the three levels of the mind as depicted in Figure 19.3. The fact that these farmers are failing to produce to the expected standards despite having received various trainings necessitated this assessment on farmer training needs and the agricultural interventions that can be used for various problems encountered by farmers. This has resulted in hunger and poverty in the households of most farmers. If farmers manage to produce reasonably, they can afford schools, health facilities improve their living conditions. The chapter tries to unravel why farmers fail to produce agricultural yields as expected, and whether this failure is related to the training they get.

Poverty

Poverty is described as hunger, lack of shelter and not being able to access better health facilities, and inability to afford schools (Government of New Brunswick (GNB), 2015). Poverty is defined by contexts as it varies from place to place. Most people live in absolute poverty as they are not able to acquire meaningful standard of living. Poverty is therefore a concept that cannot be easily defined as observed by Aryeetey *et al.* (2013). Rural poverty in Zimbabwe is still widespread marked with 63% in 2013 to 76% in 2014 (Zhangazha, 2014) mainly due to poor harvests. The Zimbabwe Vulnerability Assessment Committee (ZimVac, 2014) reported that 6% of the rural population, equivalent to 565 000 people needed food assistance to take them through to the next harvesting period. The same author argues that the country was ranked at 156 out of 187 countries, which are low-income, and food deficit countries in the world. The proportion of the population that lives below the national poverty line of less than US$1.25 a day stood at 72%. Poverty line is considered as the margin which families or individuals are regarded to be lacking the resources to meet the basic needs for a healthy living (ZIMSTATS, 2015, Business Dictionary, 2016). Food Poverty line is the minimum consumption expenditure that each household member could consume in a day. In Zimbabwe, total consumption poverty line (TCPL) (ZIMSTATS, 2015, ZIMATLAS, 2015) as of June 2015 was $98.96 compared to $99 in July. Mashonaland Central had poverty prevalence rate of 73% (ZIMSTATS, 2015). This justifies the importance to assess the training offered to maize farmers in the irrigation schemes that are failing to perform effectively and efficiently.

The insufficient food production could be attributed to many factors such as droughts, lack of inputs, equipment or draught power to use. Those who are extremely poor in rural areas are pegged at 30% compared to 6% in urban areas (ZIMSTATS, 2015). Increased crop production and increases in household incomes contributes to improving households' access to food (Zhangazha, 2014). SDG1 is still a major challenge to the Zimbabwean government as poverty is not declining as expected. Many workers are engaged in poorly remunerated informal jobs hence have direct bearing on both poverty and hunger statistics.

Climate Change and Food Security

Climate change refers to "any significant change in the measures of climate lasting for an extended period of time. In other words, climate change includes major changes in temperature, precipitation, or wind patterns, among other effects, that occur over several decades or longer" (US EPA, 2016). In simple terms, it is the rise in surface temperatures on earth. There is clear evidence that climate change is happening as reflected by changes in rainfall that results in flooding, intense rain, droughts as well as heat waves. Southern Africa faces a new set of challenges caused by climate change. The problem is that, while the continent affected by effects of climate change, it is ill-prepared for the risks and natural hazards which negatively affect crop production. Key agricultural activities, such as maize production, are affected with countries like Mozambique, Swaziland and Zimbabwe cited as being most vulnerable. This entails that cultivation practices need to be improved in accordance with particular agronomic researches.

As a form of information dissemination, ICT is playing a crucial role in agriculture in view of the current state of weather patterns. SPORE (2015) indicates that some organisations in Ghana use ICTs apart from interactive radio that helps to provide information needed by farmers. Both methods afford farmers the opportunity to create links with markets and also ways of improving their farming activities in light of the climate change. In Zimbabwe Eco-farmer is a programme that has been initiated by a local mobile phone service provider, Econet Training of farmers to understand what is entailed in climate change and its effects is therefore necessary to curb famine in households and nations at large. Using ICTs requires someone who is enlightened, and farmers therefore still need to be trained to know how to retrieve messages on the mobile phones. The practice helps farmers to understand improved farming methods and be prepared on their farms for the next season. This is where extensionists come into play through helping the local farmers retrieve useful information. Important information should always be available in times of disasters and emergencies. This is a key element in disaster risk management. This can be achieved if training needs are assessed to have an insight of the gaps that exists within the farmers. Human competence offers the opportunity to be compatible with technological changes and systems in the new agrarian system. The advantage of needs-based training helps individuals to contribute to improved food supply in homesteads and Zimbabwe at large.

Food shortages continue to plague Zimbabwe (ZimVAC, 2011, 2012, 2013, 2014). There are increased droughts and flooding that require a shift in crops and farming practices. Policy-makers should consider training and retraining of personnel in the agricultural sector. The domains of learning should be considered as these involve attitudes and skills for the people involved to accept and adopt new farming practices. Poverty is more intense in semi-arid regions where climatic extremes like droughts can lead to famine and result in acute food insecurity, or millions of people (SPORE, 2015). Despite all efforts to address hunger and poverty, food shortages continue to plague Zimbabwe. The principal problem is that many people still do not have sufficient income to purchase enough food. At the peak of the lean season about 4.1 million people are estimated to be food-insecure because of the erratic rains, increased climate change leading to droughts and poor harvests (WFP, 2014). Poverty therefore fuels the levels of hunger in households (World Bank, 2015). Climate change is also increasingly becoming a current and future cause of hunger and poverty.

The unreliable and erratic rainfall makes dryland cultivation a risky venture. The success rate of rain-fed agriculture in the regions (iv and v), according to Mutambara and Munodawafa (2014) and Rukuni and Eicher (1994), is one good harvest in every four to five years. Zimbabwe secured a loan of $200 million Africa Export and Import Bank to import 700,000 tonnes of maize to avert hunger following the drought caused by El Nino that resulted in poor harvests. The food shortages have continued from the 2015 harvest period as it was half the annual consumption due to another drought. The poor harvests cause food deficits in Zimbabwe as farmers relying on dryland farming cannot not produce to add into the breadbasket of the country. Government of Zimbabwe (2013) concurred that due to poor rain season, the percentage of food-insecure rural households was expected to rise sharply reflecting Zimbabwe's reliance on rain-fed agriculture. If the country had functional smallholder irrigation schemes, then most households would be food secure.

Food scarcity exists whenever the availability of nutritionally adequate and safe foods or the ability to acquire acceptable foods in socially acceptable ways is limited or uncertain. Food insecurity refers to the social and economic problem of lack of food due to resource or other constraints, not voluntary fasting, dieting or for other reasons. Food security is said to be the availability of food, access to food and food utilisation (Zwane, 2012, Jongwe, 2010). According to FAO (1996), food security is defined as a situation when all people at all times have physical and economic access to sufficient, safe and nutritious food to meet their dietary needs for an active health life. Food is available through household production, importation or food assistance. Poverty oriented programmes that are initiated do not benefit rural populations only but also enhances production to have surplus food to be sold for better livelihoods through income generation, improved diet and nutrition. The high yields obtained from irrigated land, coupled with the benefits as listed are therefore indications that irrigation can be a vehicle for long-term development. Mutema Irrigation Scheme in Manicaland Province of Zimbabwe established in 1932 is testimony to this success story. Irrigation schemes act as catalysts for better livelihoods through poverty alleviation. The success of the schemes provide socio-economic benefits to both the community and the country at large. Agricultural lands therefore provide the primary means of livelihoods. They are also revenue sources for developing other sectors of the economy including mining, industry, transportation, health and education. Soneye (2014) argues that, of the 70% land utilised by agriculture in sub-Saharan Africa, it contributes 50% of the gross national product, and is the source of livelihood for over 60% of the developing countries' entire population.

However, maize farmers participating in irrigation schemes in Mashonaland Central Province continue to fail to produce enough for their own consumption as most of the irrigation schemes are not performing as expected. The farmers receive donor support and training by Agritex officials and other developmental agencies to be productive, yet this seems not to produce the desired results. As a result, the farmers suffer from a crisis of unsustainable agricultural production, malnutrition and persistent rural poverty.

Food poverty experienced is attributed to depressed production due to droughts. The poor support to farmers and inequality of land distribution are also contributory factors to food deficits and food insecurity. As a result, the country is now a net food importer as indicated by the importation of 482 metric tonnes in four months from South Africa in 2014. Recently, the country imported 42 000 tonnes of maize through the Food Deficit Programme (*The Herald*, 2016, February 22). One wonders if the grain would suffice as about 1 900 people in Mukumbura Ward 4 only need food aid. Two main features of agriculture at independence (1980) were the duality of agriculture and the high degree of government intervention that intended to stimulate production. The focus on stimulating production by smallholders was seen as a means towards

371

achieving self-sufficiency and food security in rural households (Mutambara *et al.* 2014, Mupaso *et al.* 2014). Small-scale irrigation plays a larger role in rural development to reduce some inequalities (Averbeke and Mohamed, 2012). This is achievable through imparting of new knowledge to the newly resettled farmers and by trying to convince them to change their mind sets. This is where the 3 domains of learning (cognitive, psychomotor and affective) are applied as they aid in the communication process for training to be fruitful.

Throughout Africa, there are hardly any cases of successful and sustainable farmer managed smallholder irrigation schemes. This is in contrast with the view that these schemes offer great potential to improved crop production, secure income and create employment. For example, about 0.1 million hectares in South Africa are under smallholder irrigation with a total of 31 000 plot holders thereby representing about 15% of the total smallholder population. It was further observed that 50% to 75% of these plot holders lived below the poverty line (Averbeke and Mohamed, 2012). A study carried out at Dzindi Irrigation Scheme in Limpopo Province revealed that the poverty rate was 62% among the plot holders.

Studies undertaken by AGRITEX (1999, 2010) and FAO (1999, 2010) indicates that formal smallholder irrigation schemes have performed poorly and are not sustainable. Moreover, these evaluative studies mainly focused on the socio-economic impact of smallholder irrigation schemes in Mashonaland Central (Negomo in Chiweshe), Mashonaland East (Chitora in Mutoko and Wenimbi in Marondera) and Mashonaland West (Ngezi Mamina in Kadoma) and Manicaland (Mutema) Provinces. Studies also undertaken globally and regionally did not study the application of the domains in the training area of the farmers in SIS. Focus was centred on sustainability and revitalisation of the irrigation schemes though most of them recommended training of the farmers in the projects. Despite all the support from various governments, the irrigation schemes are still operating below expectation, not adding to the breadbasket of the national economies, and enhancing food security in families.

Training Needs

A "need is the gap between current and desired (or required) results, or (stated another way) the gap in results between `what is' and `what should be'" (Kaufman, 1994:14). Farmer trainings quality is improved using systematic training needs analysis as this addresses the real problem at heart. The development of irrigation schemes was seen as a famine relief strategy. It was also a move for smallholder farmers to be able to be self-sufficient by managing their own schemes rather than waiting for the government (Rukuni, 1986, AGRITEX, 2010, MoAMID, 2014). The government's emphasis was to reduce dependency on rain-fed agriculture where it was possible. Training was of fundamental value to farmers then as it is now as times change. Agricultural training has also become more necessary after the fast track land reform programme (FTLRP) initiated by the government around 2000s. The Commercial Farmers Union (CFU) also confirms that new landowners had little or no expertise at all (Mwando, 2013) as reflected by maize production drop from 2 million metric tonnes of maize in 2000 to 400,000 metric tonnes in 2010. Since then communal area production has remained depressed. To ensure sustainability of projects for better livelihoods, new training methods ought to be explored. New technologies provide new occasions and causes new capabilities hence people should always increase their knowledge level (Valsamidis et al. 2011, Settle, 2014). Agricultural producers should remain competitive since the field is greatly affected by global market changes.

Manpower development and training is an important aspect of irrigated agriculture. Those farmers who are trained serve as guides to other famers in surrounding communities through sharing knowledge and ideas even during the absence of extension officers. Through proper training and adoption of new systems, the most vulnerable would be able to move from dependency to self-sufficiency and out of the tragic cycle of extreme poverty. New technologies and innovations have emerged in agriculture. Hruska and Corriols (2012) report that the proper use of pesticides by farmers protects the whole nation from risks associated with pesticides use in crops to the consumers. Farmers need further training for them to appreciate and be able to adapt and adopt the new approaches available to get better yields through irrigation systems than dryland farming (Settle, 2014). Training is very dynamic. Its elements cannot be left for long without the possibility of their becoming stagnant or outdated. It is only through systematic assessment of the training needs that will help the quality of farmer trainings to improve. As a result, farmers in irrigation schemes are able to indulge in farming as a business than for peasant farming.

The lack of efficient and effective support to agriculture need to be addressed as this restricts the dissemination of productive farm technologies and commercial skills. The element of agricultural education and training needs reconsideration hence it is the focus of this discussion. The government of Zimbabwe is targeting the training of all farmers to be realised through upgrading of modern teaching and training technologies that address agricultural knowledge and skill challenges or gaps in the farmers. However, the government needs to assess the how, where and when of the training and skills acquisition methods.

Settle (2014), Dossah et al. (2003) and Binala (2016) in their various studies attributed poor performance in smallholder irrigation schemes in SSA to inadequate training. Nkabule and Dhlamini (2013) similarly concluded that low yields at Maplotini Irrigation Scheme in Swaziland were due to limited knowledge. Fanadzo *et al.* (2010) and McCarty (2015) attributed the poor performance of small-scale irrigation schemes in South Africa and Ethiopia respectively to the same factors. In essence, policy-makers afford little or no attention to smallholder farmers in terms of skills and knowledge acquisition.

Settle (2014) observes that farmers need further training for them to appreciate and be able to adapt and adopt the new technologies and innovations available to get better yields through irrigation systems than dryland farming. Training is of fundamental value to farmers as times change. New technologies provide new occasions and causes new capabilities hence people should always increase their knowledge level (Valsamidis *et al.* 2011). Agricultural producers should remain competitive since the field is greatly affected by global market changes.

Mupaso *et al.* (2014), in a study of smallholder irrigation schemes in Chirumanzu in Masvingo Province, recommended that agricultural training be provided to farmers involved in the schemes in order to enhance their productivity. The purpose of agricultural training is not for practical use only but also to encourage adoption by farmers of new practices and technologies to increase production.

Agricultural Extension in Zimbabwe

Agricultural extension can be viewed as a form of communication between agricultural research and farmers, whereby research findings are passed on to farmers. The value of agricultural research is largely lost if research findings are not communicated to farmers in a way that will enable them to improve their farming practices. This chapter thus focuses on the human competence to grasp what is taught and delivered during training sessions. The high level of illiteracy among small-scale farmers contributes to the general low adoption levels of agricultural production technology. Extension education is provided by extension workers who are meant to convey meaningful messages to farmers in a functional rather than formal way. Consideration of the domains of learning is therefore of paramount importance.

Zwane (2012) indicates that the concept of extension is dynamic that a single definition would not suffice. Agricultural extension has three dimensions which, first, considers extension in the face of agricultural performance. The aim is to increase production and income levels in farmer households. Extension is also equated to rural community development. This is the second dimension which aims at advancing rural folk in terms of livelihoods and agricultural development. Finally, it is a form of non-formal education as it provides non-formal agricultural related education to different audiences in the farming communities.

The conception of extension was meant to offer services to the rural agricultural sector for the improvement of farmer livelihoods (Hanyani-Mlambo, 2002). Davis (2009) argues that the service include imparting technological knowledge, management skills, rural development goals as well as non-formal education. Food security's concern long ago in Africa mainly focussed on increasing production, training of farmers as well as improving crop yields. Currently, extension has evolved to go beyond "technology transfer to facilitation, beyond training to learning." (Davis, 2009:48). Farmers are assisted to form groups that deal with issues of marketing and forming partnerships with other service providers and agencies. Agricultural extension can therefore be viewed as a system that facilitate solving of problems, information and skills improvement for people engaged in agricultural production to enhance their living standards. In addition, the skills levels of extension officers require further assessment for optimum output in the schemes.

Alvord introduced agricultural extension in Zimbabwe in 1927 (Alvord, 1933, Hanyani-Mlambo, 2000). Agricultural colleges were later established. Chibero and Gwebi agricultural colleges led in the provision of basic education for extension services through offering a 2-year diploma in agriculture. Later, other agricultural institutes like Mlezu, Esigodini, Rio-Tinto were established, and these also focused on preparing extension workers who had direct contact with farmers. In pre-independence era, quality training was only afforded to white commercial farmers whilst general vocational type of training was offered to the general populace.

Other organisations involved in extension assistance include non-governmental organisation (NGOs) such as Plan International, Oxfam, FAO and Danida, to mention but a few that were involved in Mashonaland Central. Other organisations were farmer organisations like Commercial Farmers' Union and Zimbabwe Farmers' Union.

Since independence, the mandate of the government has been to adjust existing structures to suit present demands. Current agricultural extension focuses on new varieties, technologies and promotion of commercialisation. Government of Zimbabwe currently pays attention to extension-researcher-farmer linkages though there is lack of incentives for extension agents. Hanyani-Mlambo (2013) lamented that there should be good coordination between parties for successful agricultural extension. This helps in avoiding duplication of projects including those that will have failed.

Ozowa (1997) posits that Nigeria classified its farms into small, medium and large scale. The small-scale farmer is the major producer of food consumed in the country with 98% capacity. It has been observed that, on average, smallholder farmers face constraints related to poor extension support, linkages and markets by their governments. This results in dire food insecurity in households and poverty. Oxfam (2015) reported that Zambia, Malawi and Mozambique had a quarter or half of its population under nourished. This is caused by lack of agronomic advice for them to be productive on their farms.

Agricultural Extension Officer

Agricultural extension officers link agricultural research institutions and the farmers as clients. Extension officers ought to have vast technical knowledge and communication skills attained through training to lead successful food security programmes in communities. Extension workers ought to be equipped with strategies to persuade communities to conserve resources they have in their communities. Extension officers are responsible for useful information dissemination to farmers. Communities are able to adopt new practices if they are part of the research and seeing results. It requires the expertise of the extension worker to impart valuable agricultural knowledge to farmers after considering the level of the mind, which encompasses the three learning domains.

Normally, agricultural extension organisations face many challenges that include shortage of well-trained manpower leading to high ratios of farmer to extension agent. Effectiveness of extension efforts is thereby affected. Movement from scheme to scheme is also problematic as no transport is available for use by extension officers. They are provided with motor bikes, which sometimes are not repaired if broken down. Resultantly, the nature of contacts with farmers becomes haphazard. One of the challenges also faced by extension organisations is lack of routine knowledge base of extension officers update. Agriculture is taking another turn and extension staff need to be better informed for them to be able to impart the new information to farmers for improved production. This is why there ought to be training and retraining of personnel involved in smallholder irrigation schemes.

Literature on smallholder irrigation schemes has revealed that, regionally and nationally, small-scale farmers are the main producers of food consumed in most countries. The farmers have tried to achieve some level of efficiency though they face some challenges due to lack of support from their governments (Ozowa, 1997). The observation indicates that small-scale farmers are capable of transforming traditional agriculture if they are afforded with the relevant and adequate information and feasible technology.

In a sector like agriculture, it is difficult for one to claim to know the farmers' needs because of the complex problems faced by farmers on a daily basis. Their needs worldwide rests on trying to solve problems such as soil fertility, weed and pest control, as well as marketing strategies. These problems form the groupings of needs by farmers that should form the basis of all farmer training. This will be in an effort to resolve the problems at hand. Farmers, as adults, do not need knowledge or education for banking, they want information for immediate use as espoused by Knowles (1980). The adoption rate of new seed variety and use of new technology is a key indicator that information dissemination through agricultural extension and training is a very influential factor which needs more attention than what is afforded now.

Analysis of Agricultural Extension Interventions

In the whole of the Southern African Development Community (SADC), Zimbabwe was once recognised as the country with the best extension services. The role of extension is that of transmitting suitable techniques to farmers. Various methods were used for agricultural training. Main extension methods that were used in pre-independence era were:

a) Master Farmer Scheme (MFS)
Alvord introduced the method in the 1920s. The commonly used method could be applied on its own or combined with other schemes. This was a two-year programme where literacy was not required as farmers could be trained theoretically or practically. For one to acquire land in the small-scale farmland, the MFS certificate was a pre-requisite. Records indicate that 40 000 farmers were trained by 1980 when the country attained its independence. However, the programme had the disadvantage of reaching few communal farmers (Naman, 1991). Agents were selected to attend Master Farmer functions so that they could bring change in the communities represented.

b) Training and Visit (TandV) System
This form of agricultural extension was introduced in 1982 by Daniel Benor of the World Bank, the institution that later funded this model of agricultural extension. Extension workers trained leaders who were appointed per group. The leaders would in-turn share the knowledge with other members of the group. Extension personnel would then visit the groups monitoring progress on the imparted knowledge.

c) Farmer Extension Promotion Scheme
Chazovachii (2012) reiterates that thorough and intensive training was offered by this scheme. The government was involved in the scheme by paying

377

promotion agents for services offered. The same principles applied as those under TandV system where the extension officers would then monitor progress among farmers.

d) Group Extension

Farmers were mobilised into groups by extension workers. These groups would be formed according to cropping, villages, or cooperatives who may be buying inputs collectively. The method has the advantage of a wider coverage hence reaches many communal farmers which is important considering the current extension worker to farmer ratios.

Techniques such as role-plays and drama were and are still used as a form of illustrating agricultural concepts or experiences. Field days, agricultural shows and special visits to study various extension programmes were also organised in communal areas. Farmers would share experiences and information during these events. Another technique for dissemination information in the group extension approach is through the radio. This had greater impact in colonial era as farmer groups would gather to listen to programmes and later discuss. During this period `Kunzwa/ukuzwa/listen' was published by Agritex and then distributed to groups free of charge.

Several extension approaches have been developed over the years to work and fit farmer needs. According to Bell *et al.* (2015), these were developed in relation to the `ASK ME' extension framework. The framework refers to *Audience, Solutions, Key* message, *Message* form and delivery and *Evaluation.* This entails that there should be understanding and engagement of the audience, problem solving, identification of key messages and proper delivery of the messages and evaluation in order to improve the whole process of information dissemination. Apart from the four (4) methods used in Zimbabwe in the colonial and post-colonial era, there are others that are being widely used worldwide. These include:

a) *The Commodity-based approach* which mainly focuses on a single crop production or form of farming. This approach aims on extension and research, marketing as well as production increase of particular crops. The method has the disadvantage of not focusing on other farming aspects. Organisational interests control the planning of all activities.

b) *The cost-sharing approach*: The approach works as a cooperative where farmers pull resources together thereby sharing commodity costs. This has the advantage that those with limited means are able to meet all needs.

c) *Farmer field schools approach* is a participatory research method. It makes use of group-based learning technique. It mainly addresses the issue of Integrated Pest Management (IPM). The disadvantage of this approach is that of high costs and time which in turn might affect the sustainability of the whole approach.

d) *Farmer participatory approach* entails farmers being active participants in the planning and carrying out of the different research-extension activities. Farmers plan and implement their own programmes. The method, however, requires farmers who are active and skilled participants to contribute to the activities.

Methodology

The studied schemes were chosen on the basis of proximity to the city centre and also basing on how urban or rural the scheme is. The distances range from 90 km to 250km from the city centre of Harare (MoAMID, 2014). Research was undertaken using historical profiles to gather information concerning training received to date with the farmers. This was obtained from irrigation schemes chairpersons. Systematic desk research was done for online research using the internet and Google Scholar. The guiding terms were poverty, training needs, agricultural extension, food security and domains of learning for each of the schemes. Primary data from agricultural extension officers and experts in agricultural extension services were sought. Secondary data from Agritex and government published reports, press releases and statistical publications were also sourced for the development of this chapter from the Ministry of Agriculture, Mechanisation and Irrigation Development. Peer reviewed and edited articles were also consulted before cross referencing of the data was executed.

Results and Discussion

The study focussed on irrigated maize by farmers in three Mashonaland Central smallholder irrigation schemes. Maize was chosen because it is Zimbabwe's staple food with shortages faced both in urban and rural areas. There is declining productivity due to drought, availability and access to adequate food. There is a potential to increase food supply to meet the demand from irrigated agriculture than from rain-fed agriculture. Sustainability and revitalisation of irrigation systems therefore play an important role in ensuring food security in households through training of the relevant personnel. In assessing the food insecurity situation, Scoones (2013) posits that Zimbabwe

379

has moved from being the breadbasket producing enough food for the population and even exporting to a basket case, where it is almost permanently relying on imports. Maize imports have become more regular since 2000. A study by Nhundu and Mushunje (2010) revealed that farmers performed below average and the major irrigation crops were below the ideal threshold. The same study showed that 65% of the farmers in the irrigation schemes did not have relevant training.

The following table shows the scheme sizes, number of beneficiaries by gender, training offered and cropping pattern of the 16 schemes in Mashonaland Central as provided by the Ministry of Agriculture, Mechanisation and Irrigation Development.

Table 19.1: Irrigation Schemes in Mashonaland Central

	Project Name/Scheme	Land Size (Ha)	District	Number Of Beneficiaries	Year	Trainings Offered	Dist. From Harare	Cropping	M (%)	F (%)
1	Tsakare A	20	Mt. Darwin	40	1998	OandM	200	see list below	80	20
2	Dotito	30	Mt. Darwin	60	2006	OandM	210		78	22
3	Mutondwe	10	Mt. Darwin	20		OandM	190		85	15
4	Mudotwe	64	Shamva	32		OandM	70		85	15
5	Chimhanda	67	Rushinga	134	1992	OandM	250		75	25
6	Principe A	30	Shamva	60	1993	OandM	120		90	10
7	Principe B	30	Shamva	60	1993	OandM	120		88	12
8	Mazivandagara	10	Shamva	20	2000	OandM	140		85	15
9	Kanhukamwe	394	Mazowe	296	1996	OandM	90		80	20
10	Banana	20	Shamva	40	2011	OandM + TFT	125		80	20
11	Eben	20	Shamva	40	2011	OandM + TFT	125		75	25
12	Pfunyanguwo	5	Mt. Darwin	10	2005	OandM	300		85	15
13	Gutsa	12	Muzarabani	30	2014	OandM	350		85	15
14	Chipa	86	Mt. Darwin	41	2005	OandM	160		10	10
15	Tsunda	40	Bindura	113	1990	OandM	90		10	10
16	Chibuli	50	Mt Darwin	33		OandM	220		91	9

CROPPING IS GENERALLY-

Grain Maize			t/ha	6
Groundnuts			t/ha	1.8
Tomatoes			t/ha	27
Onion			t/ha	22.5
Cabbage			Heads	27,000
Dry beans			t/ha	1.8
Green Maize			cobs/ha	39,600

Key: *OandM-Operation and Maintenance, TFT-Training for Transformation
Source: MoAMID, 2014

The results indicated that the general training offered to farmers were Operation and Maintenance and Training for Transformation in all the 16 schemes in Mashonaland Central. The schemes studied were Chimhanda that covers 67 ha with 134 beneficiaries. The composition is made up of 75% male and 25% female beneficiaries. Farmers have been trained in operation and maintenance of the irrigation schemes. Kanhukamwe is 394 ha with 296 plot holders. Operation and maintenance training was offered to plot holders who are 80% male and 20% female. Eben is under 20 ha with 40 beneficiaries. The composition is 75% male and 25% female. In this scheme Operation and Maintenance and Training for Transformation was offered to farmers. Maize harvested was approximately 6 tonnes per hectare in the schemes studied as indicated in Table 19.1. Other crops also grown as indicated included groundnuts, tomatoes, onion, cabbage and sugar beans.

Organisations such as Cooperative for Assistance and Relief Everywhere (CARE) offer training in market research and post-harvest management. The organisation is also involved in the research of suitable varieties for the area. SNV is known for training farmers in vegetable processing using solar driers. Emprendedores and Tecnologia (Entrepreneurs and Technology) (EMPRETEC) and Crops Research Institute for the Semi-Arid Tropics (ICRISAT) are some of the NGOs that are running training courses for irrigated maize farmers in Mashonaland Central in conjunction with Agritex. Deutsche Gesellschaft fur Internationale Zusammenarbeit (GIZ) provides drip kits for irrigation to the farmers in the three schemes. In full (SAMP) is involved in community seed production training (Tundu, 2017, November 27). Such training is mainly done through lecture and demonstration methods. The trainers mainly use Shona and English in their training sessions. The best approach amongst the agricultural extension interventions should be chosen for teaching and learning sessions to yield results. Agricultural extension officers are better placed to inform communities they serve on what best method to use amongst the interventions that may produce better results agriculturally.

Most adults are not comfortable to learn together with their children and wives, therefore, training sessions should be age and gender sensitive (Knowles, 1980). On another note, people who learn in groups are able to share experiences thereby learning from each other like in the Group Extension Approach and the Farmer Field School (FFS). In addition, methods that promote competition amongst farmers, such as the Master Farmer Scheme (MFS) that uses practical or theory lessons, could be adopted. These cater for the different mental capacities of the farmers involved. Where farmers have literacy challenges, training can be conducted using practicals. The certificates issued after attending the MFS act as motivators to farmers to aim to produce more and get the certificate also. Self-actualisation is realised as members become recognised in the community as being lead farmers. In turn food security is realised in farmer households and Zimbabwe at large.

Through the Farmer Participatory Approach, members of the smallholder irrigation schemes are involved in planning and carrying out the research-extension activities. This way members become active participants and are able to convey the gaps in the agricultural knowledge they need filled. Farmers plan and implement programmes according to their needs. As a result, they participate knowing that they are owners of the programmes and not mere recipients of donor-initiated activities (Knowles, 1980).

After all these training programmes are offered to farmers in the irrigation schemes in Mashonaland Central in Zimbabwe. The question is: Are these training programmes addressing the mental capacities of these farmers? Although the teachings may be in vernacular people have different levels of understanding hence the 3 domains of learning cognitive, affective and psychomotor should be addressed to have meaningful messages.

Conclusion and Recommendations

The chapter sought to make a positive contribution to the body of knowledge on the failures of irrigation schemes in Zimbabwe as well as mapping a way forward to get maximum output from irrigated maize. If agriculture in Zimbabwe is going to have a strong and sustainable future, then investment must be done on the most important resource that is the people active in the farming sector. Farmer education is vital in the agricultural sector to ensure sustainable production for better livelihoods through food security for households. It has become more urgent to train farmers after the fast track land reform programme (FTLRP) initiated by the government in 2000. Commercial Farmers Union (CFU) also confirms that new owners had little or no expertise at all (Mwando, 2013) as reflected by maize production drop from 2 million tonnes of maize in 2000 to 400 000 in 2010. Since the FTLRP, communal area production has remained depressed.

Agricultural extension emphasises on the development of human capital through capacity enhancement to make better decisions. Through proper training farmers can manage to learn and communicate effectively with extension officers their problems. Sustainability of projects is therefore achieved if farmers are empowered through appropriate training to fight against poverty by increasing their agricultural production. Extension workers need to be well trained to deal with human behaviour, norms and values. Extension officers need to know their community traditions well, for example, not talking to women in the absence of men. In some areas, women are not household heads and therefore it is taboo to address women on issues concerning their families. Decisions are mostly made by men and it will be fruitless for new techniques to be passed on to women as these might not be implemented.

Extension officers who share knowledge with farmers ought to take cognisance of the three levels of the mind of their agriculture clients. This way change in farming practices can be facilitated to enhance food security in households and Zimbabwe at large. Extension officers, if well trained, can play a pivotal role for farmer empowerment by assisting them in accessing capital in the form of savings or credits. The job is made easier if they are able to organise farmers into associations and commodity groups as discussed in the extension approaches section. Other forms of cooperatives are also born out of such local organisation development. The same method was successful in Taiwan and South Korea where farmer associations played a major role in the promotion of institutional technology (Zwane, 2012). In Zimbabwe, associations like the CFU and ZFU can help in the adoption of new technologies by farmers through their teachings and research linkages by other local non-governmental organisations as well as the government.

Extension services in Zimbabwe are not provided by one source. This calls for proper linkages with other stakeholders. Diverse farmer training needs are best met if different stakeholders like farmer organisations, government, non-governmental organisations and other researchers coordinate to avoid duplication of projects some of which may have failed. Scarce resources are also not depleted as they target where the need is. Proper working relations between extension officers under Agritex and researchers should be established in the bid to meet the dynamism in farmer training needs in small scale irrigation schemes.

Extension officers should spearhead in empowering the farming communities through strengthening of the human resource capacity of both the farmer and extension worker. This would in turn enable sustainability of projects as a goal in rural development. To be successful, the goals and objectives of the training initiatives should be formulated after due consideration of the audience to be addressed and their needs. In order to have meaningful results, the teaching and learning sessions should use the right agricultural extension approach that takes care of the mental capacity of recipients.

Stakeholders in the SADC region should develop strategies that transform the agricultural sector to commercially-oriented than subsistence-based. Farmers need training to progress to entrepreneurial farmers rather than producing food for consumption. Policies to do with infrastructure development budgets for irrigation schemes should also be looked into if Zimbabwe is to be back to its breadbasket status. New technology training information need to reach individual farmers whether in small- or large-scale enterprises if these technological advances would be of agricultural value.

References

Agricultural Technical and Extension Services. 1999. FAO repository: Socio-economic impact of smallholder irrigation development in Zimbabwe. Available online: www.fao.org/docrep/X5594E/X5594e03.htm

Agricultural Technical and Extension Services. 2010. Socio-economic impact of smallholder irrigation development in Zimbabwe. Harare: Government Printers.

Alvord, T. 1933. *An assessment of the impact of smallholder irrigation in Manicaland Province*. A technical paper prepared for the Department of Agricultural Development, Rhodesia.

Aryeetey, G. C., Jehu-Appiah, C., Kotoh, A. M., Spaan, E., Arhinful, D. K., Baltussen, R., and Agyepong, I. A. (2013). Community concepts of poverty: an application to premium exemptions in Ghana's National Health Insurance Scheme. *Globalization and health*, 9(1), 1-12.

Scientific-Report- (2015), Dietary Guidelines Advisory Committee Report - Health.gov

The Standard. (2016), January 22. Zimbabwe gets $200 mln Afreximbank loan to import maize: c.bank governor. *The Standard*, Harare.

Mupaso, N., Manzungu, E., Mutambara, J., and Hanyani-Mlambo, B. (2014). The impact of irrigation technology on the financial and economic performance of smallholder irrigation in Zimbabwe. *Irrigation and drainage*, *63*(4), 430-439.

Averbeke, W. Van and Mohamed, S. S. (2012). *Smallholder irrigation schemes in South Africa: Past, present and future.* Tshwane University of Technology, South Africa.

Bell, J. E. Herring, S C., Jantarasami, L., Adrianopoli, C., Benedict, K. Conlon, V. Escobar, J., Hess, J., and Luvall, C. 2015 P*lanning training programmes.* Medellin , USA: McGraw Hill. Inc.

Binala, L. (2016). Irrigation Cooperative as a Strategy of Peri-urban Poverty Reduction: Case Study of Ward 5 in Epworth, Harare. In *Peri-Urban Developments and Processes in Africa with Special Reference to Zimbabwe* (pp. 55-66). Springer, Cham.

Business Dictionary.com Available online: www.businessdictionary.com/

Chazovachii, B. (2012). The impact of small-scale irrigation schemes on rural livelihoods: The case of Panganai Irrigation Scheme, Bikita District, Zimbabwe. *Journal of Sustainable Development in Africa*, 14(4), 217-231.

Davis, K. E. (2008). Extension in sub-Saharan Africa: Overview and assessment of past and current models, and future prospects. *Journal of International Agricultural and Extension Education*, 15(3), 15 28.

Dossah, B.O., Bashir, D. Ndahi, A.K. and Ahmed, S.D. (2003). Training needs for successful development of irrigation schemes. 29th WEDC International Conference: Towards the Millennium Development Goals.

FAO, (1996). Rome declaration on World Food Security. United Nations Food and Agriculture Organization (FAO) World Food Summit, 1996.

Food and Agriculture Organisation, International Fund for Agricultural Development, World Food Program. (2015). "The state of food insecurity in the world 2014: Strengthening the enabling environment for food security and nutrition. Available online: http://www.faor.org/3/a4ef2d16-70a7-460a-a9ac-2a65a533269a/i4646e.pdf.

Food and Agriculture Organisation. (1999). Smallholder irrigation development Project (Vol. 1). Design and Layout: Fontline Electronic Publishing, Harare, Zimbabwe

Food and Agriculture Organisation. (2010). Socio-impact of smallholder irrigation development in Zimbabwe. Design and Layout: Fontline Electronic Publishing, Harare, Zimbabwe.

Government of New Brunswick. (2015). Economic and Social Inclusion Corporation: What is Poverty? Sea Breezes, N/A.

Government of Zimbabwe, (2014). The 2014 Mid-year Fiscal Policy Review Statement: Towards an Empowered society and a Growing Economy. Presented to the Parliament of Zimbabwe.

Hanyani-Mlambo, B. T, (2013). Strengthening the pluralistic agricultural extension system: A Zimbabwean case study. Available online: www.fao.org/docrep/005/AC913E/ac913e00.htm

Hruska, A. J., and Coriols, M. (2012). The impact of training in integrated pest management among Nicaraguan maize farmers: Increased net returns and reduced health risk. *International Journal Occupational Environmental Health*, 8(2), 191-200.

Jongwe, A. (2014). Synergies between urban agriculture and urban household food security in Gweru City, Zimbabwe. *Journal of Development and Agricultural Economics*, 6(2), 59-66.

Keita, N., Okidegbe, N., Cooke, S. and Marchant, T. (2009). WYE City Group on statistics on rural development and agricultural household income. 2nd Meeting, Italy, Rome 11-12 June 2009, FAO Headquarters.

Knowles, M. (1980). *The modern practice of adult education.* New York: Macmillan USA: Ghostwriting, Promoting press.

Ministry of Agriculture Mechanisation and Development (MoAMID). (2014). Acts Assigned To The Minister Of Agriculture, Mechanisation And Irrigation Development, Government of Zimbabwe: Harare.

Mutambara, S., Mutambara, J., and Darkoh, M. B. K. (2014). Towards sustainable stakeholder engagement in smallholder irrigation schemes in Zimbabwe. *African Journal of Agricultural Research. Vol.* 9(50), 3587-3599.

Mutambara, S., and Munodawafa, A. (2014). Production challenges and sustainability of smallholder irrigation schemes in Zimbabwe. *Journal of Biology, Agriculture and Healthcare*, 4(15), 87-96.

Mwando, M. (2013). Zimbabwe eyes irrigation law to boost farm sector. Available online: http://www.trust.org/item/?map=zimbabwe-eyes-irrigation-law-to-boost-farm-sector. Retrieved 20/7/2015.

Mwendera, E. and Chilonda: (2013). Conceptual framework for revitalisation of small-scale irrigation schemes in southern Africa. *Irrig. And Drain, 62,* 208-220. Doi, 10.1002/ird.1723

Nhundu, K., Gwata, C. and Mushunje, A. (2010). Impacts of Zimbabwe European Union micro-project programme (Zim/Eu MPP) in funding smallholder irrigation projects on food security and income levels: A case study of Mopane Irrigation Scheme in Zvishavane, Midlands province, Zimbabwe. *African Journal of Agricultural Research, 5*(14), 1759-1771.

Oxfam (2015). *Beyond good intentions: Agricultural policy in the SADC region.* Oxford, England, Development Bookshop Press.

Oxford Dictionary. (1971). Available online: http://www.oxforddictionaries.com/definition/english/food-insecurity. Accessed 25 January 2016.

Ozowa, V. N. (1997). Information needs of small-scale farmers in Africa: The Nigerian example. *Consultative Group on International Agricultural Research, 4*(3), 1-25..

Randall, V.R. 2011 Learning domains or Bloom's taxonomy: Big dog's bowl of biscuits Available online: http://www.nwlink.com/donclark. Accessed 25 March, 2015.

Rukuni, M. and Eicher, C.K. (Eds.). (1994). *Zimbabwe's agricultural revolution.* Harare: University of Zimbabwe Publications.

Rukuni, M. (1986). *The evolution of irrigation policy in Zimbabwe: 1900-1986. Research on irrigation in Africa.* Paper presented at the Forum on Irrigation Systems Research and Applications. Cornell University, USA.

Scoones, I. (2013). Irrigating Zimbabwe: Time for some new thinking. Harare, Zimbabwe: Zimbabwe Book Publishers Association.

Settle, W. 2014). *Adapting to climate change.* Toronto: Food and Agricultural Organisation.

Tundu. 20(17, November 27. personal communication.

US Environmental Protection Agency. (2016). 000D75001 Health Effects of Increasing Sulfur Oxides Emissions Draft. Available online: https://nepis.epa.gov/EPA/html/pubs/pubtitle.html Accessed 22 November,

Valsamidis, S., Kazanidis, I., Petasakis, I. and Karakos, A. (2011). A framework for e-learning in agricultural education. In M. Salampasis and A. Matopoulos (Eds.), *Proceedings of the international Conference on Information and Communication Technologies for Sustainable Agri-production and Environment* (HAAICTA 2011), Skiathos.

Vincent, V. and Thomas, R. G. (1961). *An agricultural survey of southern Rhodesia. Part 1 agro-ecological survey.* Harare: Government Printers.

WFP, (2014). Zimbabwe – Monthly food security monitoring. Rome: World Food Programme.

World Bank. 2015. Poverty. Available online: http://www.worldbank.org/en/topic/poverty. Accessed 25 January 2016.

Zhangazha, W. 2014. Rural poverty on the rise in Zim. *The Independent.* September12, Harare.

Zimbabwe Atlas. 2015. Government of Zimbabwe.

Zimbabwe Statistical Agency (ZIMSTATS) Census. 2014. Government of Zimbabwe.

Zimbabwe Statistical Agency (ZIMSTATS). 2015. Government of Zimbabwe.

Zimbabwe Vulnerability Assessment Committee. 2014. Rural Livelihoods Assessment, Report. Food and Nutrition council, Harare, Zimbabwe.

Zwane, E.M. 2012. Does extension have a role to play in rural development? *South African Journal of Agricultural Extension, 6(40),*16-24.

Chapter 20

Reflections on the Performance of the Agenda for Sustainable Socio-Economic Transformation of Zimbabwe.

Tawanda Zinyama

Summary

The chapter assesses the performance of the Zimbabwe Agenda for Sustainable Socio-economic Transformation (ZIMASSET) from 2013 to mid-2017. Within five years, the economic resuscitation blueprint aimed at creating 2.2 million jobs, achieving a gross domestic product growth rate of 7%, improving food security and nutrition, expanding access to social services, reducing poverty and developing physical infrastructure in the country. The chapter argues that, although the implementation of ZIMASSET was still in progress at the time of writing this article, most of its targets were clearly not met. With less than 18-months before the programme come to an end, the major socio-economic challenges the programme sought to address are actually deepening. Several factors explain this scenario: negative economic growth, challenged investment climate, over 80% unemployment, massive company closures, unprecedented factionalism within the ruling party and increased liquidity challenges.

Introduction

The chapter examines the performance of ZIMASSET focussing on related issues and questions. First, it examines the theoretical perspectives. Secondly, it examines the strategic direction and the four clusters of the ZIMASSET. Thirdly, it examines the performance of ZIMASSET from 2013 to 2017. Zimbabwe Agenda for Sustainable Socio-economic Transformation (ZIMASSET), the national economic development plan, was formulated in 2013. It is a brainchild of the ruling party, Zimbabwe African National Union Patriotic Front (ZANU-PF) that culminated from the party manifesto and President Mugabe's inaugural speech delivered on 22 August 2013. It targets at igniting and sustaining accelerated economic growth and wealth creation. The national economic blueprint is also viewed as the pathway to national economic emancipation and total independence.

The development of ZIMASSET came against a background of unfavourable operational socio-economic landscape. Some of the economic and social challenges that led to the adoption of ZIMASSET include severe and persistent liquidity crunch, low industrial capacity utilisation accentuated by countrywide company closures, deterioration in the foreign direct investment and rising formal unemployment, crumbling infrastructure especially of key economic enablers such as energy, transport and communication that eroded viability and competitiveness of local producers in key economic sectors, poor service delivery from parastatals, local authorities and government institutions, severe capacity underutilisation particularly of key resources like productive age, and low value addition (Confederation of Zimbabwe Industries, 2012).

The then prevailing socio-economic scenario was causing suffering to the country and thus exposing the untenable position of the government. A strategic intervention that could assist in turning around of the economy was therefore a necessity. It was against this background that the ZIMASSET concept was conceived. This chapter examines the performance of the ZIMASSET between 2013 and mid-2017. The chapter has four sections, namely conceptualising ZIMASSET, methodological perspectives, presentation and discussion of findings and the conclusions.

This chapter sets out to answer the following research questions whose resolution will go a long way to illustrate the performance of ZIMASSET:
   i)   What accounts for the performance of ZIMASSET?
   ii) What is the interface between ZIMASSET and policy inconsistency?

Methodology

In order to achieve the study objectives, the researcher used as documentary search as a methodology in the collection of data. The study reviewed the work that others have already done on ZIMASSET. The secondary data provided useful information. The study analysed reports on ZIMASSET performance at policy formulation and implementation levels, academic literature, online sources, newspaper articles, international financial institutions (IFIs) reports by organisations such as International Monetary Fund (IMF), World Bank (WB), African Development Bank (ADB), and government publications including Acts of Parliament, National Budget Statements, Mid-term Fiscal Policy Statements, Hansard (Parliamentary Debates) and Monetary Policy Statements. Data from institutional websites were also reviewed. The websites visited include Zimbabwe Revenue Authority (ZIMRA), Treasury (Ministry of Finance and Economic Development (MoFED), Parliament of Zimbabwe, Reserve Bank of Zimbabwe (RBZ), and Zimbabwe National Statistical Agency.

During the field research, purposive sampling was used to select participants from the sampling frame. Interviews were conducted with officials from MoFED, RBZ, Zimbabwe Revenue Authority (ZIMRA), research institutions (Zimbabwe Economic Policy Analysis Research Unit (ZEPARU), Transparency International Zimbabwe (TIZ), Members of Parliament and academics. The researcher also used observations as well as case studies on specific ZIMASSET clusters in order to analyse the issues relevant to the study. The cases in point are the cluster on food security and nutrition (Command Agriculture), social services and poverty eradication and infrastructure and utilities.

Theoretical Perspectives

Within the purview of this study, issues that frequently recur are ZIMASSET, performance, strategic direction and policy discord. To address these issues, the political economy theory is found heuristic as an analytical tool in understanding the social reality and changes extant in Zimbabwe.

This section defines and discusses the characteristics of the ZIMASSET. The words that make up ZIMASSET are also defined. The term agenda refers to a set menu of priorities and action points towards regaining the socio-economic status. In this study, the term agenda in ZIMASSET influences or determines a programme of action. Sustainable refers to the ability to be sustained, supported, upheld, or confirmed. Sustainability is defined as:

A requirement of our generation to manage the resource base such that the average quality of life that we ensure ourselves can potentially be share by all future generations...Development is sustainable if it involves a non-decreasing average quality of life (Asheim, 1994:18).

Thus, this study takes a bi-dimensional approach to sustainability as encapsulated in the ZIMASSET programme. The two dimensions are economic and social sustainability. Sustainability is the ability to continue a defined behaviour indefinitely. Economic sustainability is the ability to support a defined level of economic production indefinitely. Social sustainability is the ability of a social system, such as a government, to function at a defined level of social wellbeing indefinitely. The socio-economic sustainability in Zimbabwe is characterised by limited capacity utilisation and general social ills. High unemployment levels, high death rates, company closures, religious and cultural corruption.

The term transformation refers to radical decision, that is, 'no business as usual' approach. This concept simply means revitalise, identify, enhance and grow. ZIMASSET was envisaged as a five-year economic blueprint. It was a result-based national development framework, crafted to achieve sustainable development and social equity anchored on indigenisation, empowerment and employment creation which largely propelled by the judicious exploitation of the country's abundant human and natural resources. ZIMASSET targeted all Zimbabweans both as individuals and organisations from diversified backgrounds that include public and private sectors. Each one was assumed to have a critical role to play as a leader, follower, employer or employee. The overall thrust was to stimulate economic activities and improve production and productivity. ZIMASSET was envisaged to end hunger and poverty in Zimbabwe and create wealth. The thrust of the strategy further rejected the notion of Zimbabwe as a dumping ground of cheap foreign goods.

The ZIMASSET sought to:

- be a powerful indigenisation tool to eradicate poverty and related social ills,
- provide enabling framework for re-focussing and re-coursing the economy to better channel the energies of Zimbabweans,
- facilitate engagement into capacity building and development discourse for optimisation in the productivity agenda,
- provide strategic link between policy-makers and development players, and
- provide opportunity for progress monitoring and performance management.

A breakdown of the ZIMASSET concept is discussed below. The ZIMASSET was deemed a people-driven and action-oriented national empowerment strategy that provided a framework, challenging the efficacy of the then prevailing strategic and applied systems that include governance, leadership and management approaches, policy and legislation tools, strategic and work plans, expertise, skills base, education and training systems.

Most importantly, ZIMASSET sought to create accelerated economic growth and wealth creation. This was expected to culminate in increased agro-based and multi-sector industries, increased competitiveness of finished products on both local and regional markets, sustaining productivity levels, improved efficient systems, equitable distribution of wealth, high gainful employment opportunity levels, increased disposable income levels, sustainable food security and nutrition, poverty eradication, restored decorous social value systems, and increased happiness index.

ZIMASSET Strategic Direction

Through implementation of the ZIMASSET, the government of Zimbabwe envisioned the growing of a robust economy that is highly competitive in the region and Africa. It also wanted to build an empowered society that owned the means of production. This is aptly captured by the vision of the ZIMASSET: "Towards an Empowered Society and a Growing Economy" (Government of Zimbabwe, 2013: ix). The mission of ZIMASSET is: "To provide an enabling environment for sustainable economic empowerment and social transformation to the people of Zimbabwe" (Government of Zimbabwe, 2013: ix).

The result-based agenda was cluster-based to enable the government to prioritise its programmes and projects for implementation with a view to realising broad results that sought to address the country's socio-economic challenges. The four strategic clusters identified were food security and nutrition, social services and poverty eradication, infrastructure and utilities, and value addition and beneficiation. These clusters are explained below.

Food Security and Nutrition

The thrust of this cluster was to create a self-sufficient and food surplus economy. The ultimate goal was to make sure that Zimbabwe re-emerges as the "breadbasket of southern Africa". To this end, the cluster sought to build a prosperous, diverse and competitive food security and nutrition sector that contributed significantly to national development through the provision of an enabling environment and social transformation. The cluster programmes were said to be aligned to and informed by the Comprehensive African Agricultural Development Programme (CAADP), Draft Comprehensive Agriculture Policy Framework (2012-2032), the Food and Nutrition Security Policy, the Zimbabwe Agriculture Investment Plan (2013-2017), Southern African Development Community (SADC) and Common Market for Eastern and Southern Africa (COMESA) Food and Nutrition Frameworks. In order to realise tangible results on this, the implementation plan and results-oriented matrix were developed highlighting the cluster's key result areas, outcomes, outputs, strategies and the lead institution that spearhead the implementation. The ministries responsible for Agriculture, Environment and Health were leading institutions in this cluster.

Social Services and Poverty Eradication

The thrust of this cluster was supposed to enable the government to improve the living standards of the citizenry for an empowered society and a growing economy. The near collapse of public service delivery, deterioration in public infrastructure, increasing poverty and massive skills flight from public institutions made it critical for the government to implement programmes that enhanced service delivery by all public institutions. In this regard, the government sought to execute robust capacity development initiatives that addressed issues of recapitalisation, engagement and retention of skilled manpower, among other measures. Furthermore, strategies towards empowerment of the vulnerable were implemented in the short to medium term. The cluster also had the following programme areas that were supposed to integrate vertically and horizontally with programmes in other clusters:

- human capital development,
- indigenisation and economic empowerment,
- access to water and sanitation,
- infrastructure,
- access to land and agricultural inputs,
- employment creation,
- gender mainstreaming,
- information and communication technology, and
- resource mobilisation.

The results matrix was developed and the lead institutions in this cluster were Ministries of Empowerment and Indigenisation, Education, Office of the President and Cabinet, Local Government, Public Works and National Housing, Health, Justice and Legal Affairs, Women Affairs and Gender, and Civil Service Commission.

Infrastructure and Utilities

This cluster sought to develop a robust, elaborate and resilient infrastructure in order for the economy to register growth in a manner that is both competitive and effective. This was to be achieved through the rehabilitation of infrastructural assets and the recovery of utility services in Zimbabwe. These services included water and sanitation infrastructure; public amenities; information communication technology, energy and power supply and transport (road, rail, marine and air). The results matrix was developed, and the lead institutions were Ministries of Water Resources and Development; Public

Works and National Housing; ICTs; Energy; Transport; and Office of the President and Cabinet.

The quick wins to be implemented within this cluster were the following: undertaking a national blitz to rehabilitate water supplies, sewerage systems, roads, health facilities and schools in all urban centres, construction and maintenance of trunk and feeder roads through funding from the central government and public-private partnerships (PPPs), speedy construction of schools in rural, urban and newly resettled farming areas in order to decongest existing school infrastructure, stabilising the power situation in the country, and prioritising the implementation of the e-government programme.

Value Addition and Beneficiation

Against the background that Zimbabwe had been losing huge potential economic returns by exporting raw products, the government wanted to provide the necessary support to intensify refining processes of primary goods to fetch more economic value. This strategy was anchored on the private sector playing a key role in the funding and execution of the activities contained therein. The government was expected to provide support in terms of alignment, consistency and cohesion of policies that include the Industrial Development Policy, National Trade Policy, National Tourism Policy, Science, Technology and Innovation Policy, Minerals Development Policy, National Procurement Policy, Indigenisation and Economic Empowerment Policy and Local Authority Licensing and Regulation Policy. The success of the value addition and beneficiation cluster was dependent on the availability of key enablers that include energy, water, transport and ICTs. The lead institutions were Ministries of Energy and Power Development, Industry, Small to Medium Scale Industries, Agriculture, Mining, and Higher Education. Specific programmes to be implemented included the operationalising of the New Zimbabwe Steel project, establishing diamond cutting and polishing centres, full operationalisation of the Chisumbanje Ethanol Project, and establishing agro-processing projects (apiculture, processing and canning of fruits and vegetables, oil extraction, leather projects).

In addition to these four broad clusters, there were two sub-clusters, namely fiscal reform measures and public administration, governance and performance management. The attainment of targets set out in ZIMASSET was underpinned by putting in place robust fiscal reform measures that would enable the treasury to mobilise resources to finance the different priorities identified by the clusters. This would be done through, among other measures, restoring fiscal sustainability and strengthening fiscal management, increasing financial sector stability, tax and non-tax revenue, leveraging land and mineral resources, sovereign wealth fund, public private partnerships, special economic zones, and issuance of bonds both on the local and international markets. The Ministry of Finance and Economic Development was the lead institution.

Another sub-cluster was the public administration, governance and performance management. This sub-cluster was meant to ensure successful implementation of the ZIMASSET. This sub-cluster was supposed to provide an oversight role in coordinating, monitoring and evaluating policies and programmes to ensure coherence with the country's national vision and priorities. It was also expected to deal with ensuring that governance systems were people friendly by providing high quality services to the citizens in an efficient and effective manner. To this end, all public sector agencies in this category were expected to deal with issues of corruption, modernisation of public sector agencies and performance management.

The lead institutions were Ministry of Finance and Economic Development, Office of the President and Cabinet and the Civil Service Commission. The quick wins within this sub-cluster included the following: revamping the operations of State Procurement Board, publishing and implementing client service charters throughout government, introducing performance contracts to senior officials in the civil service, capacitating the anti-corruption agencies to effectively discharge their mandates, intensifying institutionalisation of results-based management (RBM) in the public sector, reorienting public sector employees in order to enhance performance, improving the working conditions of civil servants, and establishing the national productivity centre.

Key Success Factors

The ZIMASSET explicitly defined the key success factors that underpinned its implementation. These were political commitment and leadership from the highest level, strong collaborative partnerships among government agencies, the private sector, citizens and other stakeholders, human capital development programmes to enhance the acquisition of requisite skills, and scientific research and development. Though the ZIMASSET had not yet completed its life cycle at the time of writing this article, the questions that beg answers are: "Is ZIMASSET on course to successfully turnaround the economy of the country by 31 December 2018? Does Zimbabwe have the capacity to correctly articulate the national development vision to spur that growth?

Results and Discussion

Economic Performance Overview

After many dreadful years, the rate of economic growth began to gradually recover from 2009. Hyperinflation was halted following the adoption of a multicurrency system, restarting financial intermediation and imposing fiscal discipline by precluding the option of budget deficit monetisation. As a result of these measures and by further following international recommendations, gross domestic product (GDP) growth was 10.6% in 2012. This was driven by a recovery in domestic demand and strong external demand for mineral exports. However, GDP growth declined to 4.5% in 2013 and 3.1% in 2014. Estimates of GDP per capita vary substantially, though, according to the World Bank, GDP per capita was $820 in June 2014. The rate of inflation decreased from 3.9% in 2012 to 1.6% in 2013. For 2014, the Zimbabwe National Statistics Agency (Zimstat) stated that the inflation rate was - 0.05% due to a lack of capital. This was due to the depreciation of the South African rand, devaluation in international commodity prices, decline in demand for raw materials, de-industrialisation, excessive dependence on natural resources and a declining manufacturing sector.

The manufacturing sector accounted for almost 30% of GDP in 1992, but only 12.6% of GDP in 2014. Unemployment remained very high, though no reliable unemployment statistics existed. According to a 2011 Zimstat survey, 84% of workers are contracted on a self-employed basis by micro, small and medium enterprises. Not all of these workers received payments for their work and only 11% were formally employed. The manufacturing sector had further deteriorated because of a lack of capital to replace failing equipment, unreliable energy and water supply, and political and economic insecurity. This was further exacerbated by the government's unpredictable use of the indigenisation law. Industrial capacity utilisation was almost to 60% in 2011 but had fallen to 40% in 2013 and 36% in 2014. Key factors contributing to the economy's poor performance included political insecurity during an election year, a fragmented regulatory framework for foreign direct investment (FDI) and the extreme fiscal profligacy by the government. Wage expenses accounted for more than two-thirds of government expenditure, with capital and operations accounting for only 6% and 7.5% of total government expenditure, respectively.

At the time of writing, the government had made no appreciable progress on attracting FDI which had declined from $311.3 million in 2013 to $146.6 million until October 2014. For 2015, the economy grew by 3.4% in the agricultural sector, 3.1% in the mining sector, 1.7% in the manufacturing sector, 4.7% in the tourism sector and 0.4% in the ICT sector. In 2013, FDI accounted for only 3% of the GDP, down from 3.5% in 2011. The current account deficit is $3.51 billion or 24% of GDP. It declined to $3.43 billion in 2015. The capital account improved by 11% from $2.76 billion in 2014 to $3.07 billion in 2015 (ZNCC 2014). A major economic constraint is debt distress which totalled $8.40 billion in December 2014. External debt is estimated to be $7.22 billion or 81% of total arrears. The World Bank is Zimbabwe's largest creditor, with domestic debt accounting $1.17 billion. Tax revenue was lower than expected in 2014, totalling $3.04 for the year to October 2014. Nevertheless, as collected tax revenue is equivalent to 28% of the GDP, Zimbabwe is one of the most taxed countries in southern Africa. Gross capital formation declined to 17% in 2013 and the budget balance was -1.7% in 2014.

ZIMASSET Performance

ZIMASSET was announced on 22 August 2013. Its policy goals were unrealistically ambitious. Within five years, the agenda aimed to create 2.2 million jobs, achieve a GDP growth rate of 7%, increase the profitability of the mining sector, improve food security and nutrition, expand access to social services, reduce poverty and develop physical infrastructure. However, while most areas were targeting deficiencies, the proposals were too imprecise to facilitate effective implementation. One academic with the University of Zimbabwe, remarked that the programme borrows from the failed programmes of the past and does not acknowledge reality. Since 2008, international aid had been channelled through a multi-donor fund. In 2013 and 2014, this international aid was not given directly to ministries, but to local civil society organisations. The multi-donor fund had been replaced by the Zimbabwe Reconstruction Fund (Zimref, 2014 to 2019). Zimref targeted private sector development, capacity building and policy dialogue. It was aligned to ZIMASSET. According to the World Bank report, *Doing Business 2016*, the business environment improved with the country moving up 16 places to 155 out of 189 countries. Zimbabwe has experienced reverse urbanisation in recent years as an economic slowdown hampered opportunities in cities. GDP growth declined from 3.8% in 2014 to an estimated 1.5% in 2015 but slightly increased to 1.6% in 2016. This improvement was due to an expansion in the tourism, construction and financial sectors. The poor performance of government revenue against the background of high recurrent expenditures continues to constrain the fiscal space.

The country remained in debt distress, exacerbated by the lack of a diversified export base and declining terms of trade that make it difficult for the country to adjust to changing world demand for tradable goods. These structural weaknesses have constrained the country's ability to generate high and sustainable growth that is necessary to mitigate the debt distress. Moreover, the external position remained under severe pressure in the medium term because of poor export and import performance on the back of an appreciating US dollar. The Public Debt Management Act passed into law in September 2015, was expected to strengthen the legal and institutional framework for debt management. The fiscal space remained constrained due to underperformance of domestic revenues, increase in public expenditures, depressed exports, limited FDI and other capital inflows into the country. This undermined development expenditure and social services provision in both urban and rural areas and exacerbating the incidence of poverty. Financing for urban development, both housing and transport, was negatively affected. The economic policy framework within which ZIMASSET was being implemented in Zimbabwe hardly met the requisite conditions ideal for effective implementation of the national programme. To begin with, the political leadership in Zimbabwe is not morally obliged to create the so-called enabling framework because, except for the few technocrats, the political leadership does not identify with the values that underpinned the ZIMASSET. This, coupled with general inconsistency in overall economic policy formulation and implementation, created a framework that could hardly sustain effective implementation of ZIMASSET.

Food Security and Nutrition Cluster

The 2017 National Budget prioritises agriculture with a total allocation of US$291.6 million proposed, covering key activities related to the following: strategic grain reserve - US$112.5 million, input schemes - US$102 million, supportive personnel/employment costs - US$47.3 million, operations - US$8 million, irrigation development - US$6.1 million, extension services - US$3.385 million, and veterinary services - US$2.68 million, among others. The above allocation together with other agriculture related expenditures incurred during 2016 amounted to US$148.8 million and translated into total agricultural support towards the 2016/17 season of US$440.4 million. The level of support was in line with the 2003 Maputo Declaration by African Heads and Governments on committing at least 10% of national budgetary resources to the sector.

Special Maize Production Programme

Prioritisation of maize production had been scaled up following two successive droughts which drained the fiscus through grain importation to provide for the national grain requirement shortfall. Consequently, starting with the 2016/2017 agricultural season, the government took a deliberate stance to increase grain production to levels sufficient to meet national requirements. This was being implemented through the Special Maize Production Programme. The programme progressed well, with 33 931 farmers contracted having received 76% of their maize seed supply, 38% of compound D, 3% of lime and 20% of fuel as at 6 December 2016. With regards to tillage, as of 6 December 2016, 135260 ha had been tilled, with 33932 ha planted. In terms of financing, a total of US$160 million was mobilised for the programme, with US$85.5 million going towards irrigable land and US$75 million for dry land. In 2017, US$87.5 million was provided for both irrigable and dry land activities. In order to sustain the implementation of this programme on a revolving basis, beneficiaries under this programme were monitored to produce in line with their contract obligations (GoZ, 2016:56-57).

Command Agriculture

This is the Special Maize Production and Import Substitution Programme. This is a policy intervention by government, informed by the imperative to substitute grain imports through increased agricultural production and productivity thereby revitalising various agro-processing value chains and helping the country to re-industrialise (Mnangagwa, 2017:10). The objectives of the Command Agriculture Programme were to:

a)   ensure food security and maize supply self-sufficiency:

b)   produce maize locally and reduce grain imports: and

c)   produce at least two million metric tonnes of maize grain on 400 000 hectares out of which at least 200 000 hectares would be on irrigated land (Mnangagwa, 2017:10).

This programme was funded through the public private partnerships (PPPs) where financiers directly pay suppliers for inputs that were drawn by farmers, with farmers accessing inputs and making loan repayments through grain deliveries to Grain Marketing Board depots on a cost-recovery basis.

Social Services and Poverty Eradication

Level of Socio-economic Development

The problem of Zimbabwe is not so much the structural exclusion of specific demographic groups along gender or ethnic lines, but widespread economic exclusion within the whole population. This exclusion is due to economic mismanagement and a political elite that pursues its own self-interest. According to the World Food Programme (WFP), 72% of the population lived on less than $1.25 a day in 2013 and 2014. In rural areas, the proportion of the poor increased from 63% in 2013 to 76% in 2014 (Zimbabwe Vulnerability

Assessment Report 2014). Nevertheless, the proportion of the rural population needing food assistance has declined due to a very good cereals harvest in 2016/2017 agricultural season. In the 2014 Human Development Index, Zimbabwe gained four places in the overall ranking, but still had a low human development score (0.492).

The inheritance of a once well-functioning schooling system still supports literacy rates above 80% (World Bank). The dropout rate of pupils, especially of girls is higher than that of boys, as many parents can no longer afford school fees or materials. That women have struggled more than men as part of the country's slow economic recovery is reflected in the country's Gini Index which fell to 0.583 (2011). Nevertheless, the life expectancy of women (34 years in 2006) did rise considerably to 60 years (WHO, 2012). This is due to better nutrition and easier access to antiretroviral drugs for those infected with HIV. Budget allocations to the health sector declined during the ZIMASSET era. As an illustration of this, health received 7.1% of total votes in 2014 and 6.6% in 2015. This is against the Abuja declaration where at least 15% of the budget should go towards the health sector. Furthermore, primary and secondary education received 18.5% of total votes in 2014 and 19.4% in 2015. This is also against the Dakar Declaration where at least 20% of the national budget should be allocated towards education. Nevertheless, the country continues to struggle with the outbreak of diseases as water supplies are erratic and the health sector lacks sufficient medicine and trained personnel due to inadequate funding.

Employment and Unemployment
It is striking to note that the problem of youth unemployment in Zimbabwe has reached alarming proportions. Factors that work against the youths included few vacancies in formal employment, inappropriate training, inadequate skills and lack of experience. It has often been suggested that Zimbabwe's education system is inappropriate as it imbues the youth with high aspirations for white collar jobs. Several suggestions have been made to deal with the problem of youth unemployment in Zimbabwe. The suggestions include, among others, the creation of self-employment, promotion of the informal sector and small and medium scale enterprises (SMEs). So far, no tangible results have come out of the various initiatives. The major problems include lack of coordination at national level, inadequate funding for youth projects and the harsh economic environment. Another stark reality in Zimbabwe is that unemployment is unacceptably high among the educated. Two factors explain such a scenario: the higher qualifications attained by the youths following the 1980s' massive education expansion versus the current adverse economic environment.

The reliability of Zimbabwe's unemployment figures is questionable. Press reports give very high unemployment rates estimates for Zimbabwe. These are often disputed by government officials. The Zimbabwe Congress of Trade Unions (ZCTU) and government do not agree on Zimbabwe's unemployment figures. For example, according to ZIMSTATs, Zimbabwe's effective rate of unemployment is as low as 11.3% claiming land reform had created numerous job opportunities and many other people are employed in the informal sector. ZCTU dismissed the claim that unemployment rate in Zimbabwe was as low as 11.3%. According to ZCTU Zimbabwe's unemployment rate in 2014 was well over 80% having been exacerbated by huge job losses in the economy. Confederation Zimbabwe Industries (CZI) documents report of massive retrenchments and company closures.

One explanation to the variation in unemployment rates is said to emanate from the fact that ZCTU's estimates do not consider the new opportunities in the agricultural sector and excludes informal sector employment. However, ZCTU is not alone in estimating that Zimbabwe's unemployment rate is well over 80%. Independent economists, politicians and industry associations also put Zimbabwe's unemployment rate in 2015 at well over 85%. It is true that the majority of those retrenched have taken refuge in the informal sector where remuneration is often poor and working conditions deplorable. In most cases, such people do not consider themselves employed, ZIMSTATs does so. Computing unemployment rates assuming even a vendor in the informal sector is not unemployed may give wrong conclusions in terms of policy formulation. Specifically, the definition employed by ZIMSTATs makes it difficult to find an unemployed person given the prevailing harsh economic environment and increasing poverty in Zimbabwe. Since the implementation of ZIMASSET formal employment has continued to decline as informal activities increased in the economy.

Corruption

One key socio-economic visibly clear in the ZIMASSET is the problem of corruption. This has increased during the ZIMASSET era. There is obstruction of justice and interference in the duties of agencies tasked with detecting, investigating and prosecuting illicit behaviour. The Zimbabwe Anti-Corruption Commission (ZACC) faced this fate when it asked the Minister of Higher and Tertiary Education, Science and Technology Development to appear before it to respond to allegations of fraud, corruption and embezzlement of public funds. The Minister was accused of taking public and government funds earmarked for manpower development to bank roll First Lady's "Meet the People" rallies, the "One Million Men March" in solidarity with President

Mugabe organised by the ZANU-PF youth league and, the procurement and distribution of bicycles to chiefs in his Tsholotsho North constituency. The Minister refused to appear before Zimbabwe Anti-Corruption Commission citing that it was being used by Vice-President, Emmerson Mnangagwa, to settle tribal and factional scores. However, the issue is that the Minister used government resources to finance his political party business against the laws of the country.

Abuse of office has been and is endemic in Zimbabwe, while the major culprits have, in most cases, escaped prosecution. This impunity has fuelled corruption across all sectors of society, including health care, education and sports. The abuse of office has become so rampant that, in some cases, it is accepted as part of the culture and is often institutionalised. According to Partnership Africa Canada (PAC), some $2 billion of revenues from the diamond sector has been lost in the last three years. Public officials who have abused their office, like former Minister of Mines Obert Mpofu, are rarely prosecuted. However, in most cases, the prosecutions are politically rather than publicly motivated.

Public Policy Discord

This was very explicit in the civil servants' 13th month cheque for both 2015 and 2016. The Minister of Finance and Economic Development (MoFED) announced that the government was suspending payments of annual bonuses for two successive years in order to create fiscal space with the ultimate aim of stimulating full economic recovery. The Minister of MoFED categorically stated that:

> To achieve this (full economic recovery), the government has decided to suspend bonus payments to civil servants in 2015 and 2016 and the situation will be reviewed in 2017 in the event that we're able to build enough capacity (Minister of Finance and Economic Development, 13 April 2015).
>
> It's a paradox that industry has been struggling to pay salaries and let alone bonuses, while the government continued to pay. Our industry needs breathing space and heavily taxing the productive sector isn't sustainable. We can't kill the goose that's laying the golden egg" (Minister of Finance and Economic Development, 13 April 2015).

However, during the Independence Day celebrations (18 April 2015), President Mugabe reversed the suspension of the payment of annual bonuses arguing that it was not debated at cabinet level and was not government policy. The monthly wage bill in Zimbabwe as at 30 April 2015 was USD260 million.

This constituted 96 percent of monthly revenue collected by Zimbabwe Revenue Authority (ZIMRA). Implied is that the recurrent expenditure is crowding out the capital expenditure. This characterisation of conflicting policy pronouncements and policy discord was observed by the International Monetary Fund (IMF) country representative:

> The situation is quite challenging, and the conditions have been deteriorating over the past two months. There has been policy inconsistency which might not have been conducive in the terms of traction and momentum that was gained after the Staff-Monitored Programmes (Christian, 2016).

This chapter observes that such a policy environment diminishes confidence in the government. Furthermore, policy incoherencies were visible in reasons proffered for introducing the export incentive in the form of bond notes. The Finance Minister and the Reserve Bank of Zimbabwe (RBZ) governor revealed contradictions over the bond notes. Addressing the 2017 pre-budget seminar in Bulawayo, the Minister of Finance announced that counterfeit bond notes were in the market, way before public campaigns on the security features had been rolled out. The RBZ governor defended the bond notes project by dismissing claims by the Minister of Finance. One of the Vice-Presidents added his support on the bond notes by saying:

> The US dollar is a reserve currency. It is a precious currency to most countries in the world. It's for international transactions. It is not meant for buying snot apple, watermelon, Mopani worms and wild loquat fruit (Mnangagwa, 2016).

The Minister of Finance has become the ram of government failures despite his pragmatic reform-minded policy pronouncements. The Finance Minister has been dressed down for doing his job in the best way he knows. After the Finance Minister announced that civil servants must forgo the 13th cheque for two years to create fiscal space, the President played to the gallery during Independence Day celebrations, throwing the Finance Minister under the bus, after asserting that government workers would receive their salaries despite the dire economic situation. The question one would ask is: Did the Finance Minister make an unsanctioned statement that the government was suspending bonus payment for civil servants? This is improbable and unbelievable. Faced with the heat in the cabinet, the Finance Minister hastily retreated by apologising for his 'procedural mistake' but took the opportunity to paint a gloomy picture of the economic situation. Official figures show that salaries now gobble up 96% of the national budget (GoZ, 2016).

Presenting the 2016 Mid-Year Fiscal Policy Review in September, the Finance Minister announced government's intentions to cut its bloated civil service wage bill through retrenchments. However, the Public Service, Labour and Social Welfare Minister came out guns blazing, saying there would be no layoffs. This revealed that the mixed messages characterised discord and a lack of cogent ideas in government to move Zimbabwe forward. One academic key-informant informed this study that:

> *Contradictory messages also betray the fact that there are no clear economic policies and, hence, potential investors will sit back waiting for clarity as they cannot throw their money in a policy jungle. Already people have lost confidence in this regime and these contradictions vindicate the fact that we have a clueless lot at the helm. We have an economy on autopilot, and we are as good as a people without a government.*

Few months into the year 2016, the Finance Minister and Indigenisation Minister publicly clashed over the implementation of the Indigenisation and Economic Empowerment Act with the Minister of Indigenisation pushing for foreign-owned banks to relinquish at least 51% shareholding to Zimbabwean locals as stipulated by the law and threatening to withdraw their licences if they failed to comply with the law by 30 March 2016. Simultaneously, the Finance Minister argued that banks had submitted satisfactory plans. This forced the President, as the Head of Government, to issue a statement through the Information Minister to clarify the indigenisation policy after the conflicting positions. The statement reads as follows:

> *Conflicting positions in the interpretation of the indigenisation and economic empowerment policy have arisen of late. This has caused confusion among Zimbabweans, the business community, current and potential investors, thereby undermining market confidence. This situation has also led to increase in the cost of doing business, thus further weakening the country's economic competitiveness* (Mushowe, 2016).

However, despite the fact that the President and his government were aware of the dire implications of policy dissonance on the economy, they continued contradicting each other. The Zimbabwe Economic Society (ZES) official aptly observed this during interviews:

> *The new Minister of Youth Development, Indigenisation and Economic Empowerment seems to have taken a hard-line approach that is at odds with pronouncements by the Minister of Finance and Economic Development Patrick Chinamasa during the national budget presentation and also pronouncements from the newly appointed Vice-President Emmerson Mnangagwa.*

405

The Finance Ministry advocated for indigenisation to be handled by line ministries and the Ministry of Youth Development, Indigenisation and Economic Empowerment was supposed to coordinate the policy at cabinet level. However, the key-informants informed this study that the involvement of line ministries had no benefits except putting an extra layer of bureaucracy. This is what the key-informant said:

> *It's just an extra layer of bureaucracy and possible corruption. What this country needs is investment and not such policies. Foreigners are saying we are not giving away anything for nothing, so they are investing elsewhere, even Zimbabweans are doing the same now.*

Therefore, one may be prompted to conclude that there is no policy consistency in Zimbabwe. For instance, the President made an announcement at Heroes Acre that Zimbabwe does not need help from the West (United States of America, Britain, European Union among others) yet at the same time the Finance Minister was in London begging for funds and aid.

The mixed messages show that government does not bother to speak in the same language and, therefore, in the process delaying economic revival and progress. Zimbabwe remains below in the World Bank Ease of Doing Business Report. For example, it fares terribly in the World Bank's Ease of Doing Business survey that puts the country at 171 out of the 189 ranked countries, from 172 in 2014 (Ministry of Finance, 2016). It also ranked 180 out of 189 in terms of the ease of starting a business (*ibid.*). These contradictions in government reflect a lack of cohesion on various issues that include indigenisation, foreign direct investment and the re-engagement of the international community, particularly the West. Policy inconsistencies affect good planning and have an impact on profitability. Furthermore, it increases perceived country risk and impacts negatively on all sectors of the economy. Implied is that the government should be consistent in its policies to allow policy certainty and socio-economic development.

Education

Government spending on education is low. The problem lies not only with allocations but with the disbursement of funds. In 2013, the education sector did not receive the full amount of its allocated budget, and about 90% of the amount was spent on salaries and only 7% on operations. Substantial improvements in the sector are due to donor assistance via the Education Trust Fund, which is administered by United Nations Children and Education Fund (UNICEF). The Fund stood at $160 million in 2013, but the Minister for Primary and Secondary Education hesitated to use the fund. In the past, ZANU-

PF had denounced the money to be illegal. In early 2015, there was not enough money to support the enrolment of about one million children at primary level. This was because the government had broken the constitutional guarantee of free primary education and international donors had not budgeted for this additional cost.

Resource Efficiency

Zimbabwe's budget has been extremely poor in past years. Employment costs have accounted 76% of the total government budget in 2014. This increased to 81% out of a total government budget of $4.1 billion for 2015. In 2014, government expenditure on operations and capital was 7.5% and 6% of the total budget, respectively. The Staff-Monitored Programme (SMP) of the IMF recommended an audit of the civil service sector. In response, the Minister of Finance publicly confirmed the need for streamlining the sector. However, the bloated public administration statistics indicate that the patronage system of President Mugabe's regime was still alive and well. There were an estimated 75,000 ghost workers on the payroll of public agencies, particularly parastatals and the Ministry of Youth. These ghost workers presented a major obstacle to the implementation of any kind of reform programme. It is striking that, though Zimbabwean diamonds are now legally traded on the world market, increased revenues within the diamond sector have not significantly increased state revenues. There were still rumours that senior ZANU-PF officials were involved in the ongoing looting of minerals. In 2013, the chairperson of the parliamentary portfolio committee for mines and energy, Chininga, exposed corruption within the mining sector. He died in a car accident in June 2013. Although the new Mines Minister dissolved the boards of the Zimbabwe Mining Development Corporation (ZMDC) at the end of 2013, the sector remained as opaque as ever and at the centre of the factional struggle within ZANU-PF.

International Cooperation

The European Union (EU) lifted its trade sanctions on Zimbabwe on 30 October 2014 following pressure from southern EU member states. It has also overturned Article 96 of the Cotonou Partnership Agreement between the EU, and African, Caribbean and Pacific countries. From 2002, this Article had blocked the direct provision of development aid to the Zimbabwean government. However, travel sanctions against President Mugabe and his wife, Grace Mugabe, remained in effect. Their foreign held assets also remained frozen. This followed Grace Mugabe's active participation in the eviction of farmers due to personal interests in the land.

The lifting of sanctions by the EU meant that Zimbabwe would also qualify for the European Development Fund. The EU ambassador to Zimbabwe, Philippe von Damme announced that the EU would like to start providing direct financial aid to Zimbabwe. The money would be channelled through local and international NGOs to support good governance, health care services and agricultural development.

Following elections on 31 July 2013 and the subsequent fall of the Government of National Unity (GNU), the factional struggle within ZANU-PF ruling party intensified. The handling of these internecine conflicts by senior officials further damaged the party's credibility. In December 2014, ZANU-PF party's congress demonstrated that a new force within the party had emerged, namely President Mugabe's wife. Grace Mugabe appeared to wield increasing influence over President Mugabe and within the party structures. Although it still enjoyed some credibility within regional organisations, such as Southern African Development Community (SADC) and African Union (AU), Zimbabwe was still improving its links and trust among international institutions like the EU and IMF.

In August 2014, President Robert Mugabe was elected chairman of the SADC under the requirement to rotate the organisation's chairs. This was notable given the lengthy SADC mediation process, South African intervention and President Mugabe's defiance of the SADC Principles and Guidelines Governing Democratic Elections during the 2013 flawed elections. In January 2014, President Mugabe became the deputy chair of the AU. From January 2015 to January 2016, President Mugabe became chair of the AU. Zimbabwe had also been elected into the AU's highest organ, the five-member Bureau of the Assembly of Heads of State and Government. Zimbabwe acted as first deputy chair of the bureau after other countries refused to accept the position due to, among other things, upcoming or recent elections. From 2013, the Minister of Finance and Economic Development, Patrick Chinamasa, opened up a dialogue with the international community. This U-turn was likely driven by the very limited government budget and huge debt overhang. Chinamasa had since agreed to most of the IMF's reform recommendations, despite resistance from many senior ZANU-PF officials.

The Structural Management Approach

The structural approach to solving national problems is problematic as more institutions are created, further draining resources for national development to the wage bill of the bureaucratic nature of these structures. One key informant urges the government of Zimbabwe to make sure that the "national budget allocates more than 50% of the total budget to capital expenditure and at least 25% of the GDP." Zimbabwe's wage bill currently tops the region at 75% of the government's total expenditure, leaving 25% of total budget resources for both operations and capital projects (Zimbabwe Coalition on Debt and Development (ZIMCODD), 2016:30). In the 2014 national budget of US$4.2 billion, 73% of the resources were channelled to finance the wage bill leaving just 11 percent for capital investments and 16 percent for non-wage recurrent expenditure.

In addition to this, the 2015 national budget statement allocated about 81% of resources to the wage bill. This is attributed to the structural approach to problem solving. The structural management approach entails creating various institutions and departments to solve problems. This approach leads to increase in government expenditures as there is duplication of roles. Many structures are created thereby militating against effectiveness and efficiency. Resources are channelled to finance bureaucratic structures, and some are wasted as there is duplication of projects among various government ministries and departments. For example, projects in the Ministries of Youth and Gender are similar. Devotion of a greater chunk of national resources to recurrent expenditures to sustain structures has negated social and economic development evidenced by cuts in social sector expenditure which has led to poor health sector, poor education system and a lack of essential social services. There is needed to strike a balance between consumption and capital investment without impacting negatively on social and economic development.

Factional Politics

The reluctance by President Mugabe to tackle issues around his succession has led to factional infighting within ZANU-PF. The increase in factional politics within the ZANU-PF is likely to ignite violence in the country. Policy coordination in an environment of limited fiscal space becomes more critical to ensure maximum returns from limited resources. In this regard, it becomes imperative for government to coordinate implementation of key projects and consequently minimise wastage of financial and human resources. Policy coordination was affected by factionalism entrenched in ZANU-PF. The two quotations attest to this observation.

Factionalism has become a watchword for ZANU-PF, defeating organisational and unity of purpose, much worse raising fears that the party may as well experience a dangerous schism or gradual weakening...Let us not hear any divisive voice from you... the G40s or .... Lacoste (President Mugabe quoted in *The Herald*, 2016, February12 and 20).

Factionalism is "characterised by leadership aspirations that are steeped towards 'will to power' more than will to transform people's lives (Crisis in Zimbabwe Coalition, 2014)

The factional infighting within ZANU-PF resulted in marginalisation of moderates with links to former Vice-President Mujuru. This facilitated the radicalisation of ZANU-PF as being reform minded was now akin to opposing the hardliners. Factional fights within the ruling party had a negative effect on the efficient operation of government.

ZIMRA Revenue Performance

The Ministry of Finance and Economic Development (MOFED) in the 2016 Mid-Term Fiscal Policy Review revised the economic growth for the year 2016 from 2.7% down to 1.2%. The International Monetary Fund (IMF) was more optimistic projecting a decline of 0.3% in 2016. The major factors behind the decline in 2016 were declining commodity prices, reduction in production capacity across the board (in agriculture, mining, tourism, construction and the service sectors, among others). However, according to the results of the Confederation of Zimbabwe's (CZI) *2016 Manufacturing Sector Survey*, the manufacturing industry's capacity utilisation increased significantly from 34.3% in 2015 to 47.4%. The survey attributed the increase in production levels to Statutory Instrument (SI) 64 of 2016 for companies whose products were protected by the Statutory Instrument.

The Reserve Bank of Zimbabwe (RBZ) intervened in November 2016 and introduced the 5% bond note export incentive aimed at stimulating domestic production for export and to ease the cash shortage. The monetary authorities were also encouraging the use of plastic money and ZIMRA was fully supportive of this because it enhanced tax compliance. The impact of the bond notes was yet to be felt mostly because they were then a very small percentage of the money supply but also because they were introduced towards the end of the year. However, the bank queues disappeared. Maybe people were finally catching up on plastic money. Year-on-year inflation rate during 2016 moved from the negative rate of 2.2% in January 2016 to negative rate of 1.10% as at the end of November 2016 (ZIMSTAT, 2017).

Depressed Economic Growth Affects ZIMASSET

Government failed to meet ZIMASSET short-term targets due to depressed domestic demand and subdued international prices for major exports. The current job losses being experienced in the country were as a result of decline in economic growth.

The decline in economic growth in 2014 can generally be attributed to poor investment performance, low business confidence, liquidity constraints, infrastructure and energy deficits, limited fiscal space, depressed domestic demand and subdued international prices for major exports.

These challenges are responsible for the job loses currently obtaining in the country (Khaya Moyo, 2016).

ZIMASSET targeted economic growth averaging 7.3 percent during the plan period (October 2013-December 2018), with the economy expected to grow by 3.4 percent in 2013 and 6.2 percent in 2014 and continued on an upward growth trajectory to 9.9 percent in 2018. It had already missed these targets. However, the country only managed growth rates of 3.4 percent and 3.1 percent in 2013 and 2014 respectively.

The situation was being further compounded by a public debt that stood at $7.94 billion translating to 56% of the gross domestic product, a figure considered too high by international standards. The manufacturing sector had been on the decline with capacity utilisation decreasing from 57.2% in 2011 to 36% in 2014. This was mainly due to poor agricultural performance, competition from cheap imports, power shortages, dilapidated infrastructure, high cost of capital and lack of access to international finance due to sanctions.

Alignment of National Budgets and ZIMASSET

ZIMASSET Achievements

Notable achievements of ZIMASSET included in areas such as infrastructure projects in energy generation and transmission, transport sector, water and sanitation, ICT, education and health facilities, financial sector stabilisation, re-engagement with the international financial community, improved doing business environment, improved cost of doing business, support for distressed industries, support for agriculture, and advances on the value addition and beneficiation strategy (GoZ, 2015:11).

Industry Performance

According to the 2016 CZI manufacturing sector survey, industrial capacity utilisation increased from 35% to around 75%. Statutory Instrument 64 of 2016 was introduced to curtail importation of products that could be manufactured domestically. Government statistics show that the import bill declined by US$1, 1 billion.

Internet Coverage

Improved access to the internet enhanced access to information, though tariffs for data were still more expensive than in neighbouring countries. Zimbabwe has a relatively high rate of internet penetration for an African country, with nearly 19% of the population having access to the internet. As a

411

result, public access to social media and other online news sources has been steadily undermining the monopoly position of state media. Political posts on Facebook, in particular, attract significant public attention.

Conclusion

Major economic indicators indicate that the crisis is in fact deepening. Several factors including negative economic growth, low levels of investment, lack of skills and inappropriate technologies explain this negative conclusion. What is encouraging, however, is that the government continues to show concern over the state of the economy. The Central Bank captures it well that the economy needs production and is hungry for exports hence the need to do things differently. There is a general acknowledgement; both in monetary policy statements and budget statements that fiscal prudence is sacrosanct in creating an enabling environment that Zimbabwe needs to achieve sustained socio-economic transformation. One of the critical things that challenged the implementation of the ZIMASSET programme is the dearth of policy consistence, without which it is an uphill task to restore stakeholder confidence in the economy and economic policy. The monetary policy statement, budget statements and policy pronouncements, therefore, should be couched around confidence and trust building, which are pre-requisites economic tenets if the country is to address production.

Government ought to mobilise adequate funding in order to pay farmers for their produce on time. This would ensure agricultural productivity and enhanced food security. Paying farmers on time is also a good incentive to enable them to prepare for the winter cropping programme and to increase disposable income. In addition, government ought to complete the implementation of policy measures to address structural reforms that relate to the ease and cost of doing business, fiscal consolidation, state owned enterprises and incentives to expand output and productivity. Addressing the structural reforms would therefore enhance business confidence and attract investment, both domestic and foreign.

The investment climate in the country remains challenged. The impediments to investment include limited resources, high cost of capital, dilapidated infrastructure, obsolete technologies and power and water shortages. The lack of investment in the economy has led to a liquidity crunch, which has affected local businesses. The rate of GDP growth fell from 6% in 2013 to 3.1% in 2014 with the closure of many companies. Furthermore, the unemployment rate is estimated to be 80%. The government needs to negotiate a new debt relief programme. The government must also overhaul public expenditure on the salaries bill which accounts for $4.1 billion or 80% of the government budget. The high cost of public sector wages is largely attributable to huge salaries for management and board members. The government has demonstrated a commitment to the IMF's Staff Monitoring Programme. However, many of the programme's targets have not been met and face substantial resistance from within the government. The slow rate of the programme's implementation has mainly been due to vested interests within the government and ZANU-PF, which fear losing political and economic power.

References

African Economic Outlook (AEO). (2016). Global economic performance. Tunis: AEO.

Asheim, G.B. 1994. *Sustainability.* Washington D.C: World Bank.

African Development Bank Group. (2018). Zimbabwe Economic Outlook: Available online: https://www.afdb.org/en/countries/southern-africa/zimbabwe/zimbabwe-economic-outlook/

Confederation of Zimbabwe Industries (CZI). (2013). Manufacturing sector survey report 2013. Harare: CZI.

Confederation of Zimbabwe Industries (CZI). (2014). Manufacturing sector survey report 2014. Harare: CZI.

Confederation of Zimbabwe Industries (CZI). (2015). Manufacturing sector survey report 2015. Harare: CZI.

Mnangagwa, E. (2017). Command agriculture in Zimbabwe: Myths, lessons and future. Gweru: Midlands State University lecture: 10 May, 2017.

Government of Zimbabwe. (2013). Zimbabwe agenda for sustainable socio-economic transformation (ZIMASSET): Towards an empowered society and a growing economy. October 2013 – December 2018. Harare: Printflow Printers.

Government of Zimbabwe, (2016). The 2016 national budget statement: Building a conducive environment that attracts foreign direct investment. Harare: Ministry of Finance and Economic Development.

Government of Zimbabwe. (2016). The 2017 national budget statement: Pushing production frontiers across all sectors of the economy. Harare: Ministry of Finance and Economic Development.

Zimbabwe African National Union Patriotic Front (ZANU-PF). (2012). The People's Manifesto 2013: Taking Back the Economy – Indigenise, Empower, Develop and Create Employment. Harare: Gmbh, Emporis. ZANU PF Headquarters.

Zimbabwe Coalition on Debt and Development (ZIMCODD). (2016). Zimbabwe's Tax System: Opportunities and Threats for Enhancing Development in Zimbabwe. Harare: ZIMCODD.

Zimbabwe Revenue Authority (ZIMRA). (2016). Revenue performance report for the year ended 31 December 2016. Harare: ZIMRA.

ZIMSTATS. (2013). Poverty, income, consumption and expenditure survey: 2011/2012. Harare: Zimbabwe National Statistics Agency.

ZIMSTATS. (2015). Poverty, income, consumption and expenditure survey: 2014/2015. Harare: Zimbabwe National Statistics Agency.

Chapter 21

A Meta-Analysis of Evaluation of Interventions in Conflict Situations

Shastry Njeru

Summary

The need for a systematic evaluation of the results of programmes is a requirement in both non-conflict and conflict country contexts. The need is even more heightened in violently fragmented societies where the context, knowledge production and research utilisation are difficult to manage or measure. Research on divided societies increases the practical knowledge base for development stakeholders to formulate policy interventions anchored in methodological rigor, timeliness, relevance and usability. For example, the war in Syria has proved to be devastating, attracting different forms of interventions whose impact needs to be measured. In Zimbabwe, the atrocities of Gukurahundi in Matabeleland and Midlands in the 1980s were also monstrous. Ongoing violent conflicts present difficulties for evaluation. In some cases, evaluation results have worsened tensions because their implications or conclusions are perceived to be threatening the interests of one or more of the belligerent groups in the conflict. Paradoxically, evaluation is known as a science of determining objectively and systematically what works and why. Evaluators want to learn from the information gained, and influence change in societies. This is why emphasis on empiricism and rigor in evaluation of policy interventions is important. In evaluation, political conjectures are therefore discouraged in the choice of policy options. Evidence-based policy-making is considered inviolable and this is emphasised in the sustainable development goals. This chapter sought a rethink of the evaluation practice in the light of violent conflicts, reworking it to ensure that appropriate tools and methods are deployed to gather data for effective decision-making by the stakeholders.

Introduction

Violent conflicts account for high human, economic, political and social costs. These costs have "led to increasing shares of development and humanitarian assistance being spent in settings of violent conflict and state fragility" (OECD, 2012: 7). Yet, when the scale of these efforts is considered, it is observed that they do not translate to results. Evaluations have pointed to challenges in "substantial weaknesses in programme design, effectiveness, and sustainable management" (*ibid.* p.7). These challenges have been identified to be affecting project effectiveness, including the clarity of donor support, role of actors purporting to be transforming the conflict drivers, and how the communities affected by those conflicts want them addressed. But there have always been evaluation gaps in the settings of violent conflict. To safeguard against these project weaknesses, a call for institutionalisation of project evaluation has been made and strongly embraced in many countries (Ospina, 2011). Institutionalisation of evaluation is a deliberate effort of setting up national public performance measurement and evaluation systems with traction in the leadership (Angela and Ajam, 2010: 16). It is along the similar principles that the sustainable development goals (SDGs) have called for "follow-up and review processes that examine progress toward achieving" (IEED, 2016: 1) these goals. As a result, all countries are setting up one form of an evaluation system or another.

The SDGs and the UN Agenda 2030 have been adopted and calls are now shifting attention towards the implementation, monitoring and evaluation of these goals in the next few years after implementation, reviews will be made. Evaluation is a major component in the achievement of the SDGs. Evaluation is defined in this chapter as a "systematic measurement for understanding the change in outcomes, outputs or long-term impact *caused* by a policy, programme or intervention. Impact helps to understand why, what and how these changes occurred and any unintended consequences of programmes. Evaluations can inform lessons for other situations" (Puri *et al.* 2015: 7). A lot of public money is being directed towards public projects. There is a realisation by the policy-makers that resources are fungible and there is need to account for them to the citizens. Evaluation is thus becoming a critical requirement at every stage of a programme at the international, regional, and particularly at the national level (IIED, 2016). Such evaluation must go beyond just a measurement, to consider whether progress achieved was equitable, relevant and sustainable (*ibid.* p.1). Yet in the design of the SDGs, there is over assumption that the world would remain the same, and for the next years up to 2030 the tools for measuring the outcomes would not change. There is also a belief that developing would be universal, hence the "leaving no one behind" (OECD, 2016) United Nations mantra. This mantra may be simplistic and sounding like the usual pronouncements by the populist politicians. While this helps to rally everyone towards the United Nations' aspiration of the universal development, an uncritical embrace of this mantra may affect negatively the building of solid evidence from the project intervention claims, particularly in violent conflict situations.

This world has never been at absolute peace since the Treaty Westphalia ending the European wars on religion in 1648. It may not be at peace by 2030 still, adding to the stock of complexity that would affect the evaluation of the SDG interventions in conflict areas. This would affect the universal "no one is left behind" (OECD, 2016: 1) in the global development vision. In practice, conflict areas naturally present complexities, first, by attracting a lot of interventions and interests from a diverse of actors whose individual or institutional orientations, interests in a conflict and methods of addressing challenges are diverse and plentiful. Secondly, conflict areas present additional methodological and ethical challenges for any researcher. These include security challenges, context uncertainty and fast changing situations and these may challenge even the most experienced evaluators or researchers and their results to their core. These fast-changing contexts make it difficult to plan with certainty and precision as expected of the "log-framed" interventions that are the majority of programmes in conflict settings.

Interventions in conflict situations still demand for evaluative thinking (ET). ET is "questioning, reflecting, learning, and modifying ... conducted all the time. It is a constant state-of-mind within an organization's culture and all its systems" (Bennett and Jessani, 2011: 24). In addition, it is "about getting people in organizations to look at themselves more critically through disciplined processes of systematic inquiry ... about helping people ask these questions and then go out and seek answers" (Preskill and Boyle, 2008: 148). ET is characterized by "a willingness to do reality testing, to ask the question: How do we know what we think we know? ... It's an analytical way of thinking that infuses everything that goes on" (Patton, 2005: 10). The UN Agenda 2030 is underlined by this need to review interventions to ensure that all targets adopted in each country are met. This culture must be guided by the consideration of methodological and ethical factors, which affect the way evaluations are commissioned, conduct evaluations, disseminate results and utilise evaluation results.

Conflicts have a tendency of increasing the number of actors and project interventions responding to the needs of the context. These actors come with their values and methods of accessing evidence sometimes at variance with the local tastes and traditions. To be effective in this context, obviously different from those of evaluators (if evaluation teams are not local), evaluations need to be built on sound facets of methodology, ethics and politics (Bush and Duggan, 2013) surrounding an intervention and its evaluation. Unfortunately, the current models of evaluations available have not been responsive to the conflict situations. They have been developed and wired to meet the requirements of peaceful environments characterised by certainty and predictability. To this end, the so called "gold standards" (IEE, 2007) of evaluations or those methods seen as objective (Jones, 2009) in evaluations have been suggested (Sidbald, 1998). The rest of methods which are not part of the gold standard league are downgraded to tools for merely collecting "opinion" (CDG, 2006). Majority of these tools have been developed in the North and have been marketed to the evaluators in the South as the gold standard to be used in the profession, if evaluation results are to be credible. However, conflict environments have a way of resisting these standards because, by their very nature, "conflicts are inherently unstable…unpredictable… (disruptive) and less controllable than non-conflict environments" (Bush and Duggan 2013: 6).

To this end, each conflict zone has its own particularities and can never be *sui generis*. However, while each conflict has its unique factors affecting it, there are few characteristics that can be shared across conflicts, for example, "fluidity, uncertainty, volatility, risk and insecurity" (Bush and Duggan 2013: 7). Interestingly, a conflict on its own is just like an epidemic, it affects the entire spectrum of the environment, leaving a wider impact on how stakeholders affected by it should relate and interact among themselves. By definition, conflict zones must therefore mean broader things beyond the usual militarised zones and culture. They include non-militarised conflict issues such as gender-based violence, class and ethnicity, political violence, structural violence and state organized violence, torture and intimidation (Sceper-Hughes and Bourgois, 2004, in Bush and Duggan, 2013). These challenges confront people in a conflict zone daily and differently, broadening conflicts, problems and those affected. This makes it hard to determine with scientific certainty an impact of an intervention, or to temporalize time between intervention and impact.

In view of conflicts dynamics, do challenges discourage evaluation or research in a conflict zone? Kenneth Bush and Colleen Duggan point to the positivity of evaluation and research in conflict zones. They see evaluation as a social good. Evaluation is thus valued as contributing to increased opportunities for collaboration within and between divided groups particularly where spaces for dialogues have been created (Bush and Duggan 2015: 9). As a result, evaluation cannot be ignored because of the existence of a conflict or militarised situations. Given this central role of evaluation in human progress, and the dangers that evaluators can face in violent situations, how then can the conflict zones be effectively evaluated? What methods, personalities, skills or standards are appropriate for their work in conflict situations? This chapter uses a meta-analysis of the conflict situations to argue for the importance of evaluation of interventions in conflict zones. It argues that it requires more than evaluation craft competency and literacy, it requires evaluators to think and work politically.

Evaluation in conflict zones requires professionals to understand the diversities of a society in conflict. Evaluators (as people whose job involves judging the quality, importance, amount, or value of something) are expected to understand that, in conflict zones, they will be dealing with complexities. This research uses past and on-going conflicts across the world including the conflict in Syria, in the context of the SDGs, to understand these challenges and how evaluation professionals should approach such situations during the course of their work. In the Zimbabwean context, it reviews the long-term effects of *Gukurahundi* (vernacular for "clean out the chaff") atrocities on the long-term moral development and community psyche, and how this affects the relationship between an evaluator and a community member still strained and threatened from speaking about their experiences many years after the actual combat violence. In January 1983, the government of Robert Mugabe launched a massive security clampdown in Matabeleland and parts of Midlands, led by Fifth Brigade, a division of the Zimbabwean National Army (Cameron, 2017). Terrible human rights violations, including murders, mass physical torture and the burnings of property. Members of the Fifth Brigade told locals that they had been ordered to 'wipe out the people [Ndebele] in the area' and to 'kill anything that was human' (*ibid.* p.1). This Korean trained unit was named 'Gukurahundi Fifth Brigade', a ChiShona term that loosely translates to the early rain that washes away the chaff before the spring rains. While the term *gukurahundi* does not only refer to the Fifth Brigade, it also refers to the period of political and ethnic violence perpetrated by the army in Zimbabwe between 1983 and 1985. This period resulted in huge losses for the Ndebele people of Matabeleland and parts of the Midlands estimated to be between 20000-22000 (Coltart, 2016) deaths.

Conceptual Framework

On 25 September 2015, the United Nations General Assembly formally adopted the 2030 Agenda for Sustainable Development. As a successor programme to the Millennium Development Goals, the 2030 Agenda is designed to pave a pathway for eradicating poverty and achieving sustainable development. The Agenda seeks to ensure that no one is left behind by aiming to reach the furthest behind first (ID, 2016). The ambition set by the 2030 Agenda is to eradicate extreme poverty from the globe. However, the empirical evidence suggests that, if current trends continue, extreme poverty will increasingly be concentrated in countries affected by fragility and conflict (*Ibid.*

419

p. 2). These countries face context-specific challenges, including weak institutions and insufficient resources to tackle competing demands (*Ibid.* p.2). Unfortunately, the 2030 Agenda does not prescribe how countries should work towards meeting the SDGs. It is equally silent on how to approach these conflict societies during the implementation of SDGs. Instead, it notes that work on implementing the SDGs must consider different national realities, capacities, and levels of development, and that it must respect national policies and priorities (*ibid.* p.4). But most countries affected by conflict and fragility often have the most limited capacities and resources, and the greatest political challenges. Should there be interventions in fragile conflict situations, similar and more challenges will be presented to the commissioners and practitioners of evaluation projects.

Evaluation

Evaluation may be understood generally as applied enquiry designed at collecting evidence that will be useful in the determination of the "state of affairs, value, merit, worth, significance or quality of a programme, product, policy, proposal or a plan" (Welch, 2011). Programme evaluation requires systematic approaches in assessing its design, implementation and effectiveness in dealing with a challenge affecting the populace. Evaluation, as a field of practice, was born after a realization that there were never enough resources to do all things that one wants to do, and that it takes more than money to resolve complex social and human challenges. Thus, it became a way of justifying project expenditure and future allocation of financial resources including identifying flaws in the completed initiatives in order to ensure that in future such projects will not be funded (McDermont *et al.* 2015: 30). As it is a management tool, evaluation is also a learning aid. Evaluation is considered a rational enterprise seeking to examine the effects of policies and programmes on targeted societies (Njeru, 2015). In this process, it applies objective and systematic methods to assess the extent to which goals are met, and to identify factors associated with successful and unsuccessful outcomes (*Ibid.* p.39). To this end, an authentic evaluation must be based on scientific authority, so that it is more objective and less ideological to be useful in decision-making.

Conflict Situations

Hard to reach or conflict areas are not only militarised conflict zones but may be understood to include sites of social violence, gendered violence, class and caste violence, political instability, state sanctioned intimidation, structural violence, organized and unorganized crimes and genocidal violence (Sceper-Hughes and Bourgois, 2004, in Bush and Duggan 2013). Military or active combat zones are even harder to reach for the obvious reasons. This variegated nature of conflict zones implies the need for methods that will allow for broad range of factors (Bush and Duggan, 2013). The Syrian conflict shows the complex interactions that can present any evaluation exercise as an almost impossibility. It is characterized by violence, large-scale displacements, sectarianism, radicalisation, territorial fragmentation, and the collapse of critical infrastructure. The economy is crippled, control of much of the country's natural resources has fallen to extremist groups, and a host of local and international actors are implicated in the conflict on a daily basis. The Syrian conflict is intractable because these factors appear so interconnected working simultaneously to produce a particular outcome (ARK, 2016).

In Zimbabwe, the post *Gukurahundi* situation in Matabeleland region remained intractable and foreboding such that the community members in the areas such as Tsholotsho, Nkayi, Lupane and Maphisa would not freely discuss their *Gukurahundi* experiences with any degree of freedom expected of citizens in peaceful and democratic societies. Their minds are sieged by years of fear and constant intimidation. Being an evaluator in such circumstances requires one to think "boldly and envision grandly" (Patton, 2012: 80). Expected social innovations must no longer follow the simple linear pathways logic but have to navigate turbulent and uncertain conditions (Njeru, 2015) synonymous with the conflict situations. Thus, the human mind's (in this case, the general mind of an evaluation professional) need for "order, meaning, patterns, sense making and control" (Patton, 2011: 81) has to be decommissioned in the face of unexpectedness so that it experiences a "mission drift" from the traditional. In conflict zones, it is no longer "plan your work, work your plan, and evaluate whether what was planned was achieved" (Patton, 2011: 87). However, the evaluator's mindset in conflict zones must be "plans are fallible, they are based on imperfect information that will be proven wrong" (Patton, 2012: 88) as he/she designs an evaluation strategy.

In the light of the foregoing complexity in conflict zones, Bush and Duggan propose some domains which they say interact to affect the evaluation initiatives and their outcomes (Bush and Duggan, 2013) in conflict zones. These require an understanding when an evaluation is to interact with a conflict situation effectively. The primary domain that affects all evaluations is logistical one. It is about what resources are needed, where are they coming from, how to reach the evaluands in terms of road network, vehicle type, landmines, and how safe are evaluators in doing their work, any cases of kidnapping and ransom demands in the conflict. Once started, a useful evaluation has to be completed. But conflicts can easily affect the security and safety of all involved in the evaluation, including capacity of accessing the conflicted territory and talking to stakeholders on the ground, and this may mean constant changing of the evaluation design and conducting of the evaluation process (p.8). The overarching challenge observed about the conflict zones is their propensity to increasing risks and decreasing predictability. This may affect logistics of evaluation as this may increase the costs of doing the business or price of being involved in the process altogether.

Evaluation is perforated by politics as actors compete for power at all levels (Bush and Duggan, 2013). Actors include international actors pushing geopolitical strategic interests, commissioners of evaluations, insurgents, community leaders and the supposed beneficiaries of that evaluation. An evaluator must balance these actors. Where this fails, if the insurgents deem the evaluation exercise as a counter-insurgency, anyone associated with it becomes their target (*Ibid.* p. 10). Evaluation in Syria would require a smart understating of the existence of a complex network of regional warlords, extremist groups, regime forces, foreign militias, and opposition civilian and military factions interacting with neighbouring countries, mainly Turkey, Lebanon, Jordan, and Iraq, with significant repercussions for those countries (ARK, 2016: 12). This is a huge undertaking for an evaluator but can be done if well-thought-of preparations are made in advance. Thus, politics essentially matters particularly in conflict zone because by its very nature, evaluation process deals with issues that are not "neutral, antiseptic and laboratory type" (Weiss, 1993: 95). Political considerations need to be seriously taken into account, sometimes at the very expense of "clinical and correctness of evaluation result" (Njeru, 2015: 43). Ability to manoeuvre the murky waters of politics means the evaluators will be thinking and working politically.

Evaluating interventions in conflict zones should not be business as usual such as the use of linear methods designed for non-conflict zones. It should not be a process of justifying resource use or future allocations, but something going beyond all this, including building relations and mending bridges destroyed by the conflict. Some authors have suggested a systems approach (ARK, 2016), others reflective models. These approaches emphasise the relationships among a system's parts, rather than the parts themselves. They help to understand the dynamic relationships and causalities between different conflict factors, and the interconnectedness between conflict factors and stakeholders. They operate based on an understanding of "feedback" (causal connections) between conflict factors and helps to understand reinforcing and balancing dynamics in conflict systems (*Ibid.* p.11).

Adding to the complexity of conflict zones, there are no baselines to pre-warn the evaluator about the programmes' conceived theory of change and evaluators should be prepared to work without such prior information.

Evaluators would be working in situations where there will be data challenges from day one as this may be destroyed or seized in transit during conflict, where stakeholders are inaccessible, where there can be censorship of information as a way of controlling the people, where there is competition over the control over data sources and even where there are differences in protocol or practices of data collection. This will affect the generalizability of results and their external validity. Besides, evaluators excited to apply randomized control trials (RCT) as their gold standard in evaluation will find conflict zones very difficult to operate. In most of the cases it will be impossible or unethical to try experimental or quasi-experimental designs, pre or post-testing project participants (*ibid.* p.14). This will make it difficult to pre-gauge the impact in the absence of pre-intervention information (*ibid.* p.14).

In conflict zones, the most challenged phenomenon is ethics. This is because in all conflicts, ethics are the first victim of that conflict. Conflicts are characterized by the "absence of rule of law, societal structures, institutional norms, codes of professionalism" (*ibid.* p. 14). Broadly, the evaluator and the evaluands find themselves thrust deep into ethical dilemmas including "safety and well-being during and after evaluation" (*ibid.* p.14). The evaluator is often under pressure from the financier of the evaluation project (creating the political and methodological problems). For instance, the donor may be emphasising their visibility and worldwide credentials for doing good, not knowing that they will be aiding conflict.

The long-term effects of *Gukurahundi*

The short-term impacts of the *gukurahundi* atrocities have been recorded, an estimated 20,000 people murdered and thousands more suffering psychological and physical wounds from their experience at the hands of the Fifth Brigade. However, it is the lasting impacts of the *Gukurahundi* on Matabeleland's society today that has not been documented. The regime in Zimbabwe closed and refused to permit any open discussions of the massacres on the basis that it would be "opening old wounds". It is evident that those wounds are far from healed, and resentment and anguish still reside in Matabeleland today (Rwafa, 2012: 315). The wounds would not heal because of general denial by the government that atrocities of such proportions ever happened which President Mugabe in 1999 described minimally as a "moment of madness". Lack of acknowledgment has meant that, for the victims of the *Gukurahundi,* their wounds will never properly be addressed. By censoring information about the happenings in Matabeleland and preventing the topic from being openly discussed elsewhere in the country, the government inflicted what is described as a "second wound of silence" (Eastmond and Selimovic, 2012: 503).

The government combined this culture of denying of the ever existence of *Gukurahundi* with a culture of impunity. This has made the collective and individual recovery of the people from that experience difficult. Because the government did not resolve the case of *Gukurahundi* atrocities up to now, many people were left in limbo, more so, when the subject on *gukurahundi* was made a taboo, even those brave enough to talk about it were "quickly shut down" (Teuten, 2015). This is best described in Owen Maseko's case, a Bulawayo artist whose paintings of the *gukurahundi* atrocities led to his arrest in 2010 under charges of "insulting or undermining the authority of the President" (Rwafa, 2012: 324) as well as "the publication of false statements prejudicial to the state" (*ibid.* p.324). With such tight noose over the conscience of the people of Matabeleland, researching or evaluating accountability interventions in this region is just as difficult as in any war situation.

Analysis

Evaluation in Conflict Zones

The following factors need to be considered concurrently when commissioning or carrying out evaluation responsibilities in a conflict zone. Ignoring one or all will affect the chances of completing that evaluation or the utilisation of its results.

The person(s)

Conflict zones evaluation expects a conflict ready or an accomplished evaluator for conflict situations. The qualities of being such an evaluator may be "innate or may be learned or nurtured" (Duggan and Bush, 2015). But the emphasis should be placed on cultural humility for the evaluator, one who is self-conscious and reflective, with skills-set that go beyond the usual social science to have sector specific expertise and experience, strong moral compass, political sensitivities, conflict analysis skills, anthropological and political sensibilities, cultural competences and technical knowledge of the structures in the military zones. Such person is able to work in hard to reach areas or conflict zones and come out with results that are credible, legitimate and utilisable. Working in areas deeply affected by *Gukurahundi* atrocities testifies this difficulty and how hard it may be for someone who is Shona to penetrate these politically closed societies when their names or the language they speak resemble that of the unremorseful perpetrator. The Fifth Brigade, a section of the defence forces that time, was predominantly Shona speaking when it was deployed to Matabeleland to "crush" (Coltart, 2015) the armed dissidents in the region. It is alleged that members of this unit forced people to sing and speak in Shona and failure to do so had grave consequences. A good researcher or evaluator must therefore be a good crisis leader as one of his or her key skill sets.

Ethics

Evaluation in conflict zones requires evaluators to adjust in many ways, including moral and ethical adjustments to address arising concerns in the methods, designs, and sources of funding and how data is reported (Jayawickrama, 2013). The evaluator requires reconsidering critically issues around their entry/contracting, design of his/her evaluation, data collection, analysis and interpretation, communication of results and the utilisation results (Morris, 2007, cited in Jayawickrama, 2013: 26). The evaluator or a researcher doing work in conflict zones should remain guided by research "principles of autonomy, beneficence and justice" through preventing harm and promoting fairness (Jayawickrama, 2013: 27). The issues of fidelity become central where the evaluator is expected to maintain their fidelity and acting in good faith by ensuring that they are loyal, honest and keeping their promises (Newman and Brown, 1996). The evaluators, in this case, do not escape the ethical, Do No Harm, as they ensure their work does not cause harm on others who come into contact with it or expose them to risks.

In approaching evaluation in context which is not of his/her own, an evaluator is advised not to discount the non-Western ways of knowing by infantilizing other ways of knowing. An evaluator should not approach the evaluation context with a "blueprint" or imposing externally generated principles on the local participants as this may cause harm through subordinating local needs and realities (Jayawickram, 2013). In the same vein, evaluators must not impose their own ethics for these may be "unrealistic or undesirable" (*ibid*. p.28). An evaluator, particularly from the North, should not make the mistake of overlooking the Southern ethics as this has the tendency of reinforcing inequality.

Evaluators should by any means try to apply local lens and avoiding placing themselves in position of privilege compared to their evaluands. In fact, Jayawickram suggests that a good evaluator is one who is not "extractive" but one who empowers the voice of participants by sincerely acknowledging their agency and knowledge as insiders (*ibid*. p. 31). In Zimbabwe, the intellectuals from Matabeleland have always complained about the people from Harare (symbols of oppression) designing interventions that patronise the victims of *Gukurahundi*. This has been a cause for tensions between organisations domiciled in Harare and those working on the ground in Matabeleland. Jayawickram cautions such problematic evaluators or researchers and he calls

425

them "myopic" researchers, "who selectively seek, and instrumentally use information that suit the perceived notions, while ignoring realities on the ground and the needs of the communities within which they are working" to acknowledge that they are not assessing "rocks and soil" but individuals who have experienced a conflict" (*ibid.* p. 32).

Since situations are unique and differ all the time, evaluators are required to have a strong understanding of their own values and be prepared to respect the values of others. This calls for developing evaluation humility stemming from cultural humility as personal values can influence one's response to numerous features of the project (Morris, 2007: 200) and the diversity of conflict environments.

Methods used during evaluation in conflict zones

In a complex setting, there is no singular gold standard or blueprint for evaluation. A mixture of quantitative and qualitative methods is suggested due to the complexity and heterogeneity of the contexts (McDermott, 2015: 64). The complex situations refer to "places where society's challenges are more pronounced and the capacity to manage those challenges is diminished" (Ganson, 2013: 11). This complexity involves many issues including "socio-political, including ethnic or religious competition, inter-regional, regional or national tensions, real or perceived discrimination, unresolved grievances, or pronounced disagreement" (*Ibid.* p.12). In such conditions the evaluators are required to reinforce the utility of qualitative and quantitative methods (OECD, 2012). However, there are factors an evaluator requires to take into account as well when approaching a project for evaluation in a conflict setting, which include its level of complexity and operational constraints in the accessing of data (Church and Rogers, 2006). Before picking on a method for evaluation, it is suggested that evaluators carry out "conflict analysis" (i.e., analysing specific issues that may trigger or sustain a conflict) not "context analysis" as is the practice in many evaluators (OECD, 2007: 8-11). This requires an evaluator to have additional skills for analysing violent conflict. While context analysis "seeks a broad understanding of the entire political, economic and social scene, conflict analysis is more narrowly focused on the specific elements that may trigger or sustain the conflict" (OECD, 2007: 24). Conflict analysis includes a "range of political, economic, social, historical and other factors, but focusing on the ones that currently directly influence the shape and dynamics of a conflict. The point is that, not everything in a context is equally relevant to a conflict" (OECD, 2007: 24.). Most evaluators have very little exposure to the tools used on political conflict analysis and they often miss this important aspect of formulating an evaluation design.

In addition, there is also no need to be tied down by pressure to determine intervention impacts of a project. If this becomes the case, the evaluators' singular objective becomes of ascertaining such impacts. In those cases, evaluators end up measuring effects that are too remote or raise expectations of impact too high, even when there is still little agreement on what impact actually means. Impacts relate to higher levels, longer-term effects rather than near-term outcomes. This makes it difficult to attribute impacts to specific interventions, due to the messiness of a conflict zone. Thus, an evaluator working on projects in a conflict zone must be discouraged from any preoccupation with the remoteness of a project's impacts. However, it is important to note the advantage of being focused if one is directed by impacts. This will help the evaluation process in a conflict zone from being diverted by assessing too many effects of interventions on the conflict, whether they were intended or not. Evaluations should take account of individual programme impacts, including cumulative, multi-programme impacts at the strategic or policy level. These are primary and secondary, direct and indirect, positive and negative, intended and unintended (DAC, 2007) effects.

The other factor to look out for and address is the issue of programme/project indicators for an intervention during conflicts. This is not necessarily a resistance to accountability, but the tools used for developing indicators and the indicators themselves do not provide an accurate picture of the changes on the ground and are rarely accompanied by qualitative assessments of the operations under evaluation or their context (OECD, 2007). The straitjacketing resulting from being led by indicators can cause programmers to focus on small objectives and to undertake activities that are limited and therefore unlikely to have significant impacts on conflict prevention or peacebuilding interventions (*Ibid.*). Therefore, a fixation with pre-set indicators has a problem of not responding to changing circumstances, a fact of a conflict situation. Thus, specifying indicators in the design phase of a project for use in monitoring and evaluating a project in a conflict setting in fact limits the evaluation exercise's ability to respond flexibly and effectively to the dynamics of the conflict.

After a consideration of these issues, an evaluator may choose from an array of methods depending on the complexity of the conflict situation, the resources available, the capacity and what needs to be evaluated. Some of the traditional tools include the theory-based ones driven by the theories of change. These seek to understand the space between actual inputs and expected outputs: to understand the "black box problem" (Stame, 2004) and demonstrate 'what works better, for whom, in what circumstances, and why' (Pawson and Tilley, 1997). Despite the contextual complexities stated already, this practice, based

427

on linear models has been dominant. The "logical frameworkers" have adhered to the positivist approach and believe that programmes evaluation must follow a particular logic, of linear, cause and effect trajectory (McDermott *et al.* 2015). Akin to logical frameworks are randomized control trials and other experimental and quasi-experimental designs. The assumption in these approaches is that programme relationships are easy to visualize at planning stage and can be tracked using indicators (Neufeldt, 2007). Those who believe that a conflict cannot be predictable have criticized this approach, asserting that every situation is always unique, lessons are not transferable from one setting to another, and therefore planning can limit, thus, flexibility is the only asset.

In such context of conflicts where everyone mistrusts each other, there are some approaches that can be used, particularly when one is "confronted by budget, time and data constraints, including pressure from government agencies, rebels, politicians, funding and regulatory agencies and stakeholders" (McDermott *et al.* 2015: 65). These include Real World Evaluation where the evaluator draws from a range of mixed methods to address common evaluation problems in real world. Real World Evaluation has the advantage of tackling baseline data constraints by using 'secondary data sources, recall, key informants, focus groups, construct mapping and participatory group techniques' (Bamberger *et al.* 2006: 4). In all the cases of evaluation, key to the success of evaluation is for evaluators to be attentive to addressing methodological bias and unreliable data, including disinformation used as a tactic by combatants or by community members in conflicts to survive. So what wins is when the evaluators apply their humanness to pick the nuances from the communities. This can enable them to relate with stakeholders and make them cooperate better than the technical rigour-ness of the research instrument. Thus, in violent situations absolute science can perform dismally.

Violent situations have a need for fast paced decision-making during implementation of a humanitarian action and real time evaluation approach can be used. This approach helps in bringing strategic focus at a critical stage of the response. For instance, the decision to help the victims of war from the shelled cities of Syria who have decided to leave their homes for neighbouring countries required less bureaucratic process by humanitarian agencies. However, where the relationship between cause and effect is unknown or can only be known in retrospect (Patton, 2010), developmental evaluation is an approach that speaks directly to such complex environments. This evaluation is informed by systems thinking. In Matabeleland region of Zimbabwe, a review of the impact of *Gukurahundi* precisely relied on retrospective thinking which benefited from analysis of non-linear dynamics, as well as allowing innovations and adaptive management (*Ibid.*) of information sources. In combat situations such as Syria,

428

the approach is useful. It believes in the view that "planned interventions must adapt and respond as conditions change suddenly", thus, "planning, execution, and evaluation occur simultaneously" (Patton, 2012: 12). Developmental evaluation is focused on adaptive learning, not accountability.

Outcome mapping and outcome harvesting are some of the approaches emerging from the contribution of analysis thinking. These approaches take the learning and user perspectives and are guided by participative and leaning iterations. They seek to identify strategic actors' contribution to social change outcomes and evaluators want to find out the change in behaviours, actions and relationships of those individuals, groups and organizations influenced by the interventions. In conflict situations, evaluators need to know if an intervention contributed to resolving or preventing a conflict rather than claiming to be sole contributor to ending all violence. This tool for evaluation can be useful only in Matabeleland now where the effects of the direct violence are easy to "harvest", but in an on-going conflict, evaluators have to wait longer until a time when it is able to "harvest outcomes".

In some extreme conditions, some highly developed technical tools have been used to collect data. Geospatial imagery and analysis, integrated with primary data collection in rural areas, has been used as a tool in program management in conflict-affected areas, particularly in Afghanistan. This was used in the assessment of program outputs and outcomes. This method is suitable where setting one's foot on a wider ground to investigate investments can be challenging, and even risky. The imagery analysis allows programme activities and outputs to be mapped on a raster map. This will support the examination of the geographic distribution of investments.

Use of historical high-resolution imagery supports a more detailed examination of program outputs and outcomes, even though this may not be used to explain the changes in human behaviour (Mansfield, 2015). Thus, Geographic Information System (GIS) alone cannot measure some of the more intractable development issues such as shifts in political participation, attitudes to the state, and conflict resolution (*Ibid.* p.25). However still, it is possible to examine whether "program inputs are used at all and, if they are, whether they are sustained for the duration of a program and beyond" (*Ibid.* p.25). For example, an evaluator is able to identify from the images inputs such as greenhouses, poly tunnels, and saplings that will be clearly visible and can be mapped over time and location (*ibid.*). The Zimbabwe Human Rights NGO Forum used the similar technique to document more than 518 single and mass graves of victims of Gukurahundi in about 22 wards in Tsholotsho only (Forum, 2016).

While geospatial is not a panacea for the problems in current performance measurement systems in conflict zones, it makes valuable contributions to the portfolio of monitoring and evaluation strategies for conflict zones. It is important to note that Geographic Information Systems (GIS) is particularly effective at examining physical changes on the ground and therefore it becomes an effective tool for examining the state of infrastructure at a given point in time, such as roads, irrigation works, schools, and health centres. It can also be used to assess some of the social and economic changes that can be attributed to program activities, such as expansion of irrigated land, expansion of residential areas, increased yields, movement into high-value horticulture, and market development (Mansfield, 2015). It is effective in assessing and measuring such change across time and space, particularly when these changes are left out during large-scale surveys focusing on attitudinal change.

Politics

Politics matters in evaluation (Njeru, 2015). The contextual fact that conflict zones are embedded in political dynamics of the particular environment cannot be denied. This makes evaluation a fundamental political activity (Duggan and Bush, 2015: 302). But evaluation does not possess political intent, even though it will have political consequences. On the ground, the evaluators are subject to numerous political pressures stemming from "diverse, intersecting, conflicts, power imbalances, competing interests as well as their own value systems" (*Ibid.* p.302). For the Matabeleland conflict, the Zimbabwean ruling elite want to maintain a narrative that the Unity Accord of December 22, 1987 between ZANU-PF and PF ZAPU brought to rest the issue. It should never be raised, thus making it a taboo. The affected communities want to find a solution but are morbidly fearful to the extent of being sceptical to anyone from "outside" who brings the subject into public discussion. In Syria, entry into the theatre of conflict requires evaluators' ability to identify, engage, placate and secure the confidence of more than 1600-armed militia, the (Islamic State in Iraq and Syria) ISIS and government actors in order to conduct work. This is a costly impossibility. Therefore, evaluators need to be prepared for the political implications and challenges throughout the evaluation process.

In conflict zones, there are more cleavages than connectors. For instance, the conflicts in South Sudan or Syria have become intractable. As an example, Syria is "plagued by violence, large-scale displacement, sectarianism, radicalisation, territorial fragmentation, and the collapse of critical infrastructure" (ARK, 2016: 8). There are more than 1600 fighting groups in addition to the government and ISIS. All these actors and processes result in the contestation for power, and the way they contest that power affect the entire fabric of human security. Besides, the actors make evaluation a costly exercise in terms of protection fees, rents, fines and ransoms that are demanded at various price levels and points by different armed groups met in the course of evaluation.

An evaluator is required to understand centrality of politics at all levels of project interventions. Key to all this is the understanding of the context in which developmental changes take place, alongside an understanding of the purpose and use of monitoring and evaluation (Roche and Kelly, 2012: 8) that follows. Simply put, the developmental changes supported by the evaluation being undertaken happen in four dimensions: "Simple, complicated, complex and chaotic" (Snowden and Boone, 2007). Thus, programmes seeking to change society meet these four dimensions of change throughout their life span, not in simple linear fashion, but in complex, uncontrollable, unpredictable and fast paced ways. This is clearly exemplified by the armed conflicts, but Syria is epitomic due to numerous actors on the ground and the diversity of their needs. These needs, always at cross-purposes to each other, affect whatever programme is implemented in a conflict situation. Thus, the recognition of the political nature of evaluative processes should also be a foundational skill for all evaluation practitioners. They ought to be aware that, by choosing a particular method or area to evaluate in a country or region, they are more likely to privilege the voice and interests of particular groups and they may end up focusing on only one part of the developmental outcomes (Roche and Kelly, 2012: 36). This way, they may inadvertently wade into the conflict mire and risk becoming the target or destroying the project's future.

An evaluator needs to understand that policies his/her evaluation seeks to influence are nurtured through a political process. "They (are) proposed, defined, enacted and funded through political processes and in implementation they remain subject to the pressure that arise out of the play of politics" (Weiss, 1993: 94). Besides, evaluation feeds into decision-making when reports enter the political arena and therefore ought to compete with the other factors that carry weight in the political process (Njeru, 2015: 42). In addition, the programme itself that is being evaluated is not in any way neutral for it happened in environments laden with values that are direct progenies of the rough political process (*Ibid.* p.43). This includes the partisan attack on the evaluation itself, efforts at hostile takeover of the results by those with power or premature embraces of the process. Thus, evaluation requires thinking and working politically. In this case, an effective evaluator is one able to recognise that domestic political factors are much more important in determining developmental impact than the amounts of resources used or the technical quality of intervention models. As a result, successful implementation of evaluation intervention will take place when designs are aligned with a domestic support base that is influential enough to generate legitimacy of the evaluation exercise and overcome the resistance of those benefiting from the status quo. In addition, progressive change on the ground usually involves local political processes of contestation and bargaining among interest groups, and an evaluator can stand to gain more by understanding and responding to these dynamics appropriately.

Conclusion

Conflict zones evaluation cannot be approached with one shoe fits all methodology or approach. Such situations require evaluation expects who are "conflict ready" as well. The challenges in the areas affected by the *Gukurahundi* atrocities in Zimbabwe and what is being experienced in Syria help to conclude that research and evaluation in conflict zones require a transformation in the field of evaluation. The traditional approaches are no longer adequate. A new cadre of evaluation experts with broad range of qualities are the only one that can thrive in the violent conflict field. Such qualities should not deter upcoming evaluators since the qualities of being such an evaluator may be "innate or may be learned or nurtured" (Duggan and Bush, 2015). In addition, the evaluators deployed in conflict zones need to be broad in their competences. But the emphasis should be placed on having cultural humility. An effective evaluator should not only be able to think and work politically, but be self-conscious and reflective, with skills-set that go beyond the usual social science to include sector specific expertise and experience, strong moral compass, political sensitivities, conflict analysis skills, anthropological and political sensibilities, cultural competences and technical knowledge of the structures in the military zones. Such person is able to work in hard to reach areas or conflict zones and come out with results that are legitimate and utilisable. The people with such skill base may be few, but for SDGs, and to ensure that even in conflict zone no one is left behind, there is a need to continuously develop and nurture such skills among members of the evaluation community.

References

ARK. (2016). *The Syrian conflict: A systems conflict analysis,* ARK Group DMCC. Bamberger, M., Rugh, J., and Marbry, L. (2006). *Real world evaluation: Working under budget, time, data and political constraints.* Thousand Oaks, CA: SAGE Publications.

Bennett, G., and Jessani, N. (Eds.). (2011). *The knowledge translation toolkit: Bridging the know-do gap: A Resource for researchers.* New Delhi, India: Sage.

Bush, K. and Duggan, C. (2013). Evaluation in conflict zones: Methodological and ethical challenges. *Journal of Peacebuilding and Development*, 8(2), pp5-25

Bush, K. and Duggan, C. (Ed.). (2015). *Evaluation in the extreme: Research, impact and politics in violently divided societies.* Sage, New Delhi: Sage.

Cameron, H. (2017). The Matabeleland Massacres: Britain's wilful blindness. *The International History Review, 40*(1), 1-19.

CGD. (2006). When will we ever learn? Improving lives through impact evaluation. Report of the Evaluation Gap Working Group. Washington, DC: CGD

Coltart, D. (2015). *The struggle continues: 50 years of tyranny in Zimbabwe.* Auckland Park: Jacana.

Duggan, C. and Bush, K. (2-15). Lessons for researchers and evaluators working in the extreme. In C. Duggan and K. Bush (Ed.), *Evaluation in the extreme: Research, impact and politics in violently divided societies.* New Delhi: Sage.

Engela, R., and Ajam, T. (2010). *Implementing a government-wide monitoring and evaluation system in South Africa.* World Bank, Washington, DC.

European Evaluation Society (EES). (2007). '*EES statement: The importance of a methodologically diverse approach to impact evaluation – specifically with respect to development aid and development interventions.* Nijnerk: EES Secretariat.

Ganson, B. (Ed.). (2013). *Management in complex environments: Questions for leaders.* Stockholm: International Council of Swedish Industry

ID. (2016). Realisation of the SDGs in countries affected by conflict and fragility: The role of the New Deal. *International Dialogue on Peacebuilding and State-building.* Available online: https://www.pbsbdialogue.org/media/ filer_public/72/7b/727b3ec5-d96d-4acf-bcad- 987ee5cb2094/realisation_of_the _sdgs_- _the_role_of_the_new_deal_3.pdf.

IIED. (2016). Evaluation: A crucial ingredient for SDG success. Briefing Paper, Issued in April 2016. Available online: www.pubs.iied.org/17357IIED

Jones, H. (2009). *The 'gold standard' is not a silver bullet for evaluation.* London, England: Overseas Development Institute.

McDermont: , Yousuf, Z., Strecker, J. and Mendez, E. (2015). Fundamental issues in evaluation and research in violently divided societies. In C. Duggan and K. Bush (Ed.), *Evaluation in the extreme: Research, impact and politics in violently divided societies.* New Delhi: Sage.

Neufeldt, R. C. (2011). "Frameworkers" and "Circlers"–Exploring Assumptions in Impact Assessment. *Berghof Handbook for Conflict Transformation I and II.*

Njeru, S. (2015). Developmental programme evaluation in Africa: Politics matters. *Journal of Public Policy in Africa,* 3 (1), 1-18.

OECD. (2007). Encouraging effective evaluation of conflict prevention and peacebuilding activities: Towards DAC guidance. Available online: https://www.oecd.org/dac/evaluation/ dcdndep/39660852.pdf.

OECD. (2012). *DAC guidelines and references series: Evaluating peacebuilding activities in settings of conflict and fragility-Improving learning for results.* Paris: OECD Publishing.

Ospina, S.M. and Grau, N.C. (2011). *Performance measurement and evaluation systems: Institutionalizing accountability for governmental results in Latin America.* Paper to be presented at the Public Management Research Association Conference, June 2011

Oxford Brookes University. (2017). *School of Architecture,* Oxford Brookes University..

Patton, M. (2012). Developmental evaluation for equity focused evaluation. In M. Segone (Ed.), *Evaluation for equitable development.* Available online: www.mymande.org.

Patton, M. (2012). *Essentials of utilisation-focused evaluation.* Thousand Oaks, CA: Sage.

Patton, M. Q. (2010). *Developmental evaluation: Applying complexity concepts to enhance innovations and use.* NY: New York: Guildford Press.

Patton, M.Q. (2005). *In conversation: Michael Quinn Patton.* Interview with Lisa Waldick, from the International Development Research Center. Available online: http://www.idrc.ca/en/ev-30442-201-1-DO_TOPIC.html

Pawson, R. and N. Tilley, N. (1997). *Realistic evaluation.* London: Sage.

Preskill, H., & Boyle, S. (2008). Insights into evaluation capacity building: Motivations, strategies, outcomes, and lessons learned. *The Canadian Journal of Program Evaluation, 23*(3), 147-174.

Puri, J., Aladysheva, A., Iversen, V., Ghorpade, Y. and Brück T (2015). What methods may be used in impact evaluations of humanitarian assistance? Forschungsinstitut zur Zukunft der Arbeit Institute for the Study of Labor, *Discussion Paper* No. 8755 January 2015.

Roche, C. and Kelly, L. (2012). The evaluation of politics and the politics of evaluation: Development leadership programme (DLP). *Background Paper, No.* 11, August 2012.

Rwafa, U. (2007). Representations of Matabeleland and Midlands disturbances through the documentary film *Gukurahundi*: A moment of madness. *African Identities,* 10.(3), (2012): 313-327.

Sibbald, B., & Roland, M. (1998). Understanding controlled trials. Why are randomised controlled trials important?. *BMJ: British Medical Journal*, 316(7126), 201.

Stame, N. (2004). Theory-based evaluation and types of complexity. *Evaluation*, 10(1), 58–76.

Teuten, B. (2015). "A recipe for another war of revenge": The lasting impacts of the *Gukurahundi* on Matabeleland, Zimbabwe. (Unpublished master's degree dissertation). Bulawayo: National University of Science and Technology.

Weiss, C. H. (1993). Where politics and evaluation research meet. *Evaluation practice*, 14(1), 93-106.

Welch, G.W. (2011). A premier on evaluation: Children, youth, families, schools. *Research Methodologies Series*. School of Public Health and Health Services, George Washington.

Chapter 22

Approaches to Sustainable Curriculum Change and Innovation in Zimbabwe

Tendayi Marovah, More Panganayi
and Francis Machingura

Summary

Sustainable curriculum change and innovation involve complex processes undertaken through wide stakeholder involvement guided by qualified and experienced personnel. Nevertheless, the processes are not always perfect, and this results in negative effects on the envisaged curriculum. Most studies on the curriculum focus on evaluating its aims, content and operationalisation though with limited emphasis on sustainable processes in curriculum change or innovation. Drawing on interview data and document analysis from a qualitative case study at two teachers' colleges in Harare, this chapter uses a human development framework focusing on three values. The study used empowerment, equity and participation to argue that processes in the 'new' or revised Zimbabwe Curriculum Framework for Primary and Secondary Education 2015-2022 innovation did not fully uphold sustainable processes and practices in curriculum change and innovation. The chapter addresses part of the broad research question: To what extent did curriculum change and innovation processes and practices in the 'new' Zimbabwe Curriculum Framework for Primary and Secondary Education 2015-2022 contribute towards sustainable curriculum processes and practices? Addressing this question, the chapter uses lecturers' voices from two Harare teacher' colleges to explain and suggest sustainable curriculum change and innovation in an African context. It concludes that lack of sector wide key stakeholder participation, the use of questionable manpower development strategies, an unequal distribution of power and resources among participants and the limited sustainable support structures negatively affect curriculum innovation practices. The study recommends a human development framework with emphasis on three values, namely participation, empowerment and equity as a tool to foster sustainable curriculum processes and practices.

437

Introduction

The chapter provides a platform for engagement with Zimbabwe's educational challenges contemplating a system in which curriculum changes and innovations can flourish. In engaging with these challenges, the chapter focuses on the extent to which curriculum change and innovation processes and practices in the new Zimbabwe Curriculum Framework for Primary and Secondary Education 2015-2022 can be regarded as sustainable. As argued by Marovah and Walker (2016), understanding sustainable educational policy practices within the context of complex contexts that involve historical, religious, cultural, structural, political, environmental, and ethical dimensions adds value to debates on curriculum change and innovation. This understanding acknowledges the multidimensional nature of sustainability issues rather than just focusing on the built environment. It is therefore necessary to interrogate the notion of sustainable curriculum change and innovation by looking at what it entails and how it can be practised as an endeavour to meet sustainable development goals (SDGs). Sustainable processes and practices should be multidimensional and meet the needs of future generations without compromising those of the present (United Nations, 1987, Stallman, 2010, Marovah and Walker, 2016). The curricula must address and meet the needs and concerns of the indigenous people. Although there is literature on teaching and learning for sustainable development across the globe since the launching of the Decade for Education for Sustainable Development (DfESD) and even before (Fien, 2001, 2002, Thomas, 2004, Hayles and Holdsworth, 2006, 2008, Ryan, 2011, Dambudzo, 2015), the chapter notes a limited focus on policy practices and processes linked to sustainability. Dambudzo (2015:11) notes that "education for sustainable development aims at changing the approach to education by integrating practices in all forms of learning." Thus, this chapter calls for a discussion of policy processes and practice in relation to curriculum change and innovation.

The revised Zimbabwe Curriculum Framework for Primary and Secondary Education 2015-2022 is a framework that was introduced by the Ministry of Primary and Secondary Education (MoPSE) following recommendations by the Commission of Inquiry into Education and Training (CIET) in 1999 (Dokora, 2015, Mugabe, 2015). The CIET recommendations have been widely applauded across Zimbabwe and southern Africa yet their implementation have not been fully realised. A number of factors, such as wide involvement of stakeholders, resource mobilisation and reskilling of teachers seem not to have been properly considered in implementing the revised curriculum. As a result, albeit an acknowledgement of the effort made by MoPSE in the curriculum change and innovation process, curriculum development stakeholders raised concerns with the envisaged curriculum. To show that the Zimbabwe Curriculum Framework for Primary and Secondary Education 2015-2022 reform or change process was often characterised by challenges, Mashaya and Tafirenyika (2017) notes that six weeks into the term in which the curriculum had to be introduced, classroom teachers, teachers' unions and school heads were still confused on how this would work in the Zimbabwean context. Mashaya and Tafirenyika (2017) argue that this is a strong indicator of some systemic problems associated with the curriculum innovation.

The chapter draws on empirical data from a study, collected between February and May 2016. From the perspective of teacher educators and one Curriculum Development Unit official, this qualitative and interpretive study aimed at generating an in-depth understanding of curriculum change practices and processes in the operationalisation of the new Zimbabwe Curriculum Framework for Primary and Secondary Education 2015-2022 in two case studies. Since the study sought an in-depth understanding of perceptions of and attitudes towards specified practices, surveys were deemed less effective in generating the type of data that would answer the broad research question. Thus, a case study was preferred despite criticisms levelled against it in terms of lack of generalizability, because it is more context-specific, and therefore important to understanding a phenomenon in its specific situation (Gall, Gall and Borg 2003). On the basis of evidence drawn from one mid-level official from 12 lecturers from two teachers' colleges who are actively involved in the training of teachers and interact with practising teachers at various levels, the chapter argues that the 'new' curriculum changes and innovation do not fully meet sustainable curriculum change ethos. As observed by Bennie and Newstead (1999:150), the 'new' curriculum therefore poses a range of challenges to teachers concerning the underlying assumptions and goals, subject demarcations, content, teaching approach and methods of assessment.

The chapter is divided into five sections which start with a literature review on the conceptualisation of sustainable curriculum change and innovation followed by a brief discussion of three underlying human development values as applied to education. The values are equity, participation and empowerment. The human development framework and its values provide a helpful lens for interpreting the various complexities and contradictions that emerge from the data. The third section provides an overview of the used methodology. Thereafter, the chapter presents findings based on empirical data that demonstrate how curriculum change and innovation processes in the operationalisation of the 'new' Zimbabwe Curriculum Framework for Primary and Secondary Education 2015-2022 either supports or lacks sustainable development values perceived as contributing towards human development. The last section provides possible solutions which may enrich curriculum processes and practices upholding human development values. The solutions potentially open up new avenues for interventions that seek to advance sustainable curriculum change and innovation.

A Review of Sustainable Curriculum Change and Innovation

In trying to understand better the link between sustainability and curriculum change and innovation, this section first explains what curriculum change and innovation is. It then turns to explaining sustainability as it relates to curriculum change and innovation before linking sustainability to the human development framework which is the theoretical base of the chapter. A review of literature would suggest that proposing a definition for 'sustainable curriculum change and innovation' is contestable. To start with, curriculum change and innovation have a number of contested definitions which this chapter will not pursue. For example, Nicholls (1983) and Rea-Dickins and Germaine (1994) define innovation as a fundamental change in ideas, or practices perceived as new which is planned and deliberated. Bennie and Newstead (1999) note that innovation or change in ideas and or practices may involve the introduction of an element or a configuration which was not or had not been there before. Hoyle (1972) suggests that in most cases change is often planned. These definitions do not try to separate change and innovation. For practical reasons, this chapter uses the two terms as inseparable processes and practices. One cannot claim change where there is no innovation or claim innovation where there is no change. Curriculum change or innovation may be either a wholesome change or just a revision making the curriculum different in some way, to give it a new position or direction (Nemat 2015). A curriculum change or innovation may mean alteration to its philosophy by way of its aims and objectives, reviewing the content included, revising its methods and re-thinking its evaluation procedures. Curriculum change and innovation may also be classified using a number of dimensions as suggested by Hoyle (1972) in Table 22,.1.

Table 22,.1: Hoyle's classification of Curriculum change

Dimension	Range
Rate	Rapid or slow
Scale	Large or small
Degree	Fundamental or superficial
Continuity	Revolutionary or evolutionary
Direction	Linear or cyclical

Source: Hoyle (1972)

440

Apart from the above classifications, curriculum change or innovation may be informed by theories of curriculum change such as the diffusion theory or the trans-theoretical model of behaviour change. The diffusion theory assumes that changing curriculum is a systematic, planned sequence in which experts identify a problem, find a solution and then diffuse the innovation to a target context. The trans-theoretical model pays limited or no respect for the interest of other stakeholders where the change or innovation might be used. According to Kelly (2004), stakeholders such as teachers are recipients of the innovation because the initiative is taken by the researchers, the developers and those responsible for ensuring its implementation at policy level. In the Zimbabwean context, the initiative was made possible by a presidential commission of inquiry into education and training (CIET 1999). MoPSE then sought to operationalise the recommendations by suggesting a curriculum framework in line with the CIET recommendations which was then handed down to teachers for implementation (MoPSE, 2017). The main concern is getting the new curriculum framework "right" and then marketing it before it is operationalised (Stenhouse, 1975). This theory and its approach, as will be demonstrated later in the chapter, does not relate to sustainable curriculum change and innovation.

Approaches to curriculum change and innovation may also take different forms such as the three approaches suggested by Nemat (2015): addition, deletion and the reorganisation. The addition approach, in which new elements are added to the existing curriculum, is quite common. The deletion approach, where some elements are deleted, to modify the curriculum is practised either independently or as a simultaneous exercise with the addition approach. At times, a re-organisation approach is adopted. In this approach, nothing is added or deleted but only reconstruction of the existing curriculum is done. The Zimbabwe Curriculum Framework for Primary and Secondary Education 2015-2022 innovation under discussion seems to be inclined more to addition and reorganisation. Thus, in such a complex terrain, this chapter focuses on sustainable curriculum change or innovation processes and practices regardless of how they are defined or what theories inform them. The chapter argues that whichever context, curriculum change and innovation is experienced, it is the manifestation of the distribution of power and resources in society. As observed by Cheng-Man Lau (2001:29), "power is not a fixed entity, but a strong network formed by heterogeneous components". To this end, sustainable curriculum change and innovation ought to pay attention to both the ever-changing strong networks and its heterogeneous components. Having briefly explained curriculum change and innovation, the focus shifts to a deeper understanding of sustainability.

There is a broad agreement within the circles of ESD on the complexity of the concept sustainability (Ryan, 2011). This has led to the adoption of a multidimensional definition seeking to balance and integrate environmental, religious, social, economic and political elements for long term benefits for the greater part of citizens (Newman *et al.*, 2004). This is summarised by the United Nations (1987) definition as projected by the Brundtland Commission Report that sustainability as development meets the needs of the present without compromising the ability of future generations to meet their own needs (UN 1987). However, as observed by Walker and Marovah (2016), if used in a narrow context, sustainability or sustainable development runs the risk of being taken as a 'catch' word currently associated with SDGs. For example, if sustainability is limited to the built environment and economic ends, it loses its real meaning and that has repercussions for curriculum change and innovation. For this reason, it is significant to consider sustainability as applicable in multiple contexts by simultaneously acknowledging its multi-faceted nature (Ministry for the Environment of New Zealand, 2009, Stallman, 2010, Marovah, 2013, Marovah and Walker, 2016).

As observed by Huckle (2008:68), "the politics of sustainability is about the relations that humans are in with other human and non-human agents, how we understand these relations, and what we can do to ensure that they are more sustainable". When applied to curriculum change and innovation, sustainability thus entails focusing on practices and processes that meet the needs of the present without compromising that of the future. The focus should not be limited to aims and content of the curriculum, but how different stakeholders interact in processes of bringing about change and innovation. According to the Ministry for the Environment of New Zealand (2009) and Marovah (2013), sustainability considers public participation, empowerment and equity as key drivers to achieving the well-being of current and future societies. The addition of public participation, empowerment and equity gives emphasis on the significance of ethical and moral processes and practices which promote relational justice through deliberations. Human development framework appraises the role of three human development values such as participation, empowerment and equity. The three human development values are important in advancing curriculum change, innovation processes and practices linked to sustainability.

Human development values and sustainability

The adoption of a human development framework for a more nuanced understanding of curriculum change and innovation practices and processes is motivated by several considerations. First, the framework is informed by the basic development idea of advancing the richness of human life rather than the economy in which human beings live which is only part of it (Sen, 1999). As such curriculum change and innovation practices and processes informed by economic considerations, such as the desire to cut costs at the expense of wide stakeholder participation, are not only unethical but also immoral. Secondly, as argued by Haq, "the basic purpose of development is to enlarge people's choices ... these choices can be infinite and can change over time" (UNDP, 1990:10). Since people's choices are not the same and depend on what they value, it is important to widen stakeholder participation in curriculum change and innovation processes. A critical analysis of the lecturers and principals' perspectives in this chapter is undertaken using three values: empowerment, participation and equity contributing towards human development (Boni and Gasper, 2012, Boni and Arias, 2013).

Using the above three values as a measure, curriculum change, innovation processes and practices undertaken in the introduction and operationalisation of the new Zimbabwe Curriculum Framework for Primary and Secondary Education 2015-2022 do not fully reflect the promotion of democratic principles and sustainability. The vision of enlarging citizens' choices and freedoms to pursue what they value to be or to do is in line with meeting the needs of the present without compromising the ability of future generations to meet their own needs. The third reason for adopting the human development framework is drawn from the multidimensionality of the framework and the interconnected nature of its values: empowerment, participation, and equity. The values place people at the centre of development and, as such, curriculum change and innovation practices should endeavour to achieve that. Therefore, people should not be seen as the means of development), or as skilled manpower, but as the wealth of the nation as well as individuals of moral worth. Curriculum change and innovation processes and practices determine the value accorded to people, either as passive consumers of the curriculum or as its owners and active generators. The multidimensional approach to sustainable curriculum processes and practices is the best foot forward as it calls for parity of participation (Fraser, 1996, 2008, 2009). Parity of participation requires arrangements that permit all stakeholders to participate as peers in social life by dismantling institutionalised obstacles that prevent some members from contributing at par with others (Fraser, 2009).

Alkire (2010) and Ibrahim (2014) explain that empowerment, as envisaged in human development, entails ensuring that people are capacitated to make choices and to transform those choices into desired actions and outcomes. Otherwise it is pointless to involve incapacitated people to make choices and

443

act as decision-makers in cases where transformation of the curriculum is required. To this end, Priestley (2010: 31) argues that:

> Empowered and engaged [Lecturers and Principals] people or participants will respond to change creatively from a wide range of repertoires. Disempowered and/or uninformed individuals will respond narrowly, often to avoid risk.

Closely connected to the process of enhancing the capacity of individuals or groups to make choices in order to transform those choices into desired actions and outcomes, is participation. Participation is a process through which all curriculum stakeholders are involved and have influence on decisions related to curriculum changes and innovations. Whilst participation gives space to stakeholders to be actively and meaningfully involved in curriculum change and innovation processes and practices, it is worthless to have representation which is voiceless or powerless (Fraser, 2009). The participation of stakeholders including youth/students should ensure that changes, innovations and opportunities created do not jeopardise the choices and opportunities of future generations. The effectiveness of participation in fostering sustainable curriculum development, change and innovation is dependent on the existence of a reciprocal relationship between democratic politics and democratic education. As observed by Walker (2010), education operates within the realm of the society which implies that curriculum changes and innovation might influence society as much as society in turn shapes curriculum analysis, change, innovation and implementation. Accordingly, a democratic system of education is indispensable for furthering sustainable curriculum analysis, change, innovation and implementation. Although this assumption is normative, it is necessary as a standard move towards which curriculum analysis, change, innovation and implementation practices and processes should work.

In the same way, to decide by consensus where there is no equitable distribution of power among stakeholders concerned is a subtle way of perpetuating injustice and is thus unsustainable. Equity guarantees equality, peace, fairness and social justice so that whatever curriculum change and innovation processes and practices are undertaken they uphold these guarantees across different dimensions such as gender, age, political and religious affiliations and many others. According to Marovah and Walker (2016), equity extends the notion of interconnectedness of humanity by enabling the accommodation of marginalised and oppressed minority groups within society. In addition, equity is a way of managing society in a sustainable way since the ability or capacity of envisaged changes and innovations to be maintained or to sustain themselves is based on equitable distribution of power and resources.

Equity should adequately capture institutional and structural arrangements which may enhance or inhibit the realisation of sustainable curriculum change and innovation. Contrary to the common view by change theorists that change invites resistance, this chapter argues that sustainable curriculum change processes and practices facilitate positive change (Priestley, 2010). In this case, human development values add value to curriculum analysis, change and innovation processes and practices by emphasising on empowerment, participation and equity. A framework which is silent on these values defeats the course of sustainable curriculum change and innovation.

Methodology

Influenced by a human development framework, this section outlines the rationale and decisions taken regarding the choice of a qualitative research design for this study, the sampling techniques and the sample, data collection, organisation and analysis. In this qualitative study, the processes and procedures were iterative, complex and ever-changing throughout. At each level of this empirical research, the planning, collection of data in situ and its analysis, the spirit of questioning and consciousness of the context in which the curriculum change and innovation was envisaged is evident.

The questions in this research points to the necessity of understanding the lived experiences of lecturers in their context, and their perspectives on processes and practices used in operationalising the new Zimbabwe Curriculum Framework for Primary and Secondary Education 2015-2022. In this case, qualitative methods would be more appropriate for focusing on understanding and interpreting reality (Gall, Gall and Borg, 2003). The phenomenon under study is not straight forwardly perceivable because it is constructed by various perspectives and opinions in multiple ways. Thus, reality about the Zimbabwe Curriculum Framework for Primary and Secondary Education 2015-2022 innovation and change processes is not simply 'out there'. It is different for each participant although there might be some convergences.

Two government primary teachers training colleges, Morgan and Seke Teachers' College, were purposively chosen for this study. They were considered as information rich sites. The sample consisted of seven lecturers from each college (N=7). Participants' names are anonymised in line with ethical promises made during and before interviews. Table 22,.2 and 22,.3 below provides important details of the participants. Two methods were envisaged as necessary in data collection: (1) document analysis, which examined syllabi and reports written by policy stakeholders, (2) in-depth, semi-structured interviews involving each of the participants identified sought to generate essential data needed in qualitative research. The quality of data generated using these methods influenced the interpretation and understanding of lecturers' experiences with regard to sustainable curriculum change and innovation.

Table 22.2: College A: Morgan Teachers' College

	Position of responsibility	Name	Experience in Teacher education	Area of Specialisation
1	Principal	Chihambakwe	+15 years	Practicals
2	HOD1	Nyamasvisva	-10 years	Early Childhood Development
3	HOD2	Liberty	+10years	Theory of Education
4	LIC1	Brian	+10 years	Science and Mathematics
5	LIC 2 *	Moyo	+10 years	Teaching Practice
6	L1	Kunashe	-10 years	ChiShona
7	L2	Monicah	+10 years	Health and Life skills

Table 22.3: College B: Seke Teachers' College

	Position of responsibility	Name	Experience in Teacher education	Area of Specialisation
1	Principal	Nyaude	+15 years	Sciences
2	HOD1	Mukanya	-10 years	Early Childhood Development
3	HOD2	Lorraine	+10years	Practicals
4	HOD3	Matilda	+10 years	Languages and Humanities
5	LIC 1	Sam	+10 years	Teaching Practice
6	L1	Dread	-10 years	Languages
7	L2	Mike	+10 years	Home Economics

From the two tables above, participants from both institutions were recruited from different departments and had vast experience in teacher education. The idea was to get rich information from a cross section of each institution in terms of coverage of areas of specialisation, positions of responsibility as well as gender. One of the lecturers at Morgan Teachers' college, Moyo, is also a leading member of the College Lecturers' Association (COLAZ) in Zimbabwe. Although his views are interpreted as personal, they also help to understand divergent views of teacher educators of different affiliate groups.

A thematic analysis approach, which is a method of identifying, organising, analysing and reporting patterns/themes within data, was adopted for this study (Braun and Clarke, 2006). The process is both inductive and deductive, since some of the codes were predetermined by the theoretical framework, research questions and interview questions. In as much as the process of data analysis and interpretation involved distinct processes, transcription, organisation, coding, analysis and interpretation, the process was not linear or systematic, but complex, iterative and reflexive. For example, the interpretation and analysis were started during interviews as suggestions of themes and possible codes started to emerge. During the transcription of data, engagement with the data also provided a sense of the key issues emerging. This enabled reflexive action during and after the interviews. In the same way, during document review and evaluation or during observations, there were a number of concrete themes and sub-themes that started to emerge. However, the notes written during the early stages of the data generation process were used to draw up a data analysis and interpretation plan. The codes were influenced by several sources such as research questions, interview questions, literature review, theoretical framework, personal experiences and the data itself. The data-sets include interviews of lecturers and a midlevel official from the Curriculum Development Unit as well as notes from document analysis. The qualitative data was analysed and organised using NVivo software. Whilst the NVivo software was useful in organising and managing the data easily, it is not much useful in generating codes or identifying themes from the data. The coding as well as identification of themes still has to be done manually. In the next section, the article reflects on the conditions of possibility for advancing sustainable curriculum change and innovation practices and processes contributing to human development using three human development values to guide the argument.

Results and Discussion

Findings are presented in three broad subsections where voices of participants as well as document analysis are foregrounded and juxtaposed because of the contesting nature of the views. As already stated, the findings are laid against three human development values: participation, empowerment and equity. From the evidence of the document analysis and in-depth interviews, the Curriculum Development Unit officer seems to toe the line of his ministry maintaining that stakeholders' involvement was maximum and effectively utilised as both a practice and process of curriculum change and innovation. The Curriculum Development Unit officer's position on participation was contradicted or dismissed by the other participants. For example, participants from teachers' colleges (lecturers and principals) view the curriculum change and innovation as flawed because of lack of wide key stakeholder participation, use of questionable manpower development strategies to in-service

447

implementers, inequitable distribution of power and resources among initiative participants and limited sustainable support structures. In view of these findings, we concur with Thaba-Nkadimene's (2016) contention that in order for curriculum reforms to succeed, stakeholders at various levels should work harmoniously to cultivate appropriate curriculum change and innovation processes and practices.

Participation of teacher educators

In a $1^{1/}_2$-hour interview, the Curriculum Development Unit member, Tendayi, was asked to share his experiences of the curriculum change and innovation process. His experiences emerged as rich and humbling because of the magnitude of success realised. He admitted however that, "*Despite the sterling effort, the Zimbabwean curriculum change and innovation is far from being perfect*". The process therefore may not be described as perfect. He took note of the limited resources with which they were operating as the major drawback: "We certainly could have done more, resources permitting, but this does not mean that the quality of our work was compromised".

According to Tendayi, every step required in curriculum change and innovation was adhered to. Tendayi notes that, "*We carried out a thorough research before identifying a team of experts from various stakeholders who helped design data collection instruments which were then piloted to a representative sample*". From the above, the main concern is getting the product "right" and then marketing it as ascertained by Stenhouse (1975) and Kelly (2004) described the diffusion theory. What is worth noting is the level of participation of other stakeholders. It appears this linear model assumes that there is a clearly defined audience, a specified passive consumer willing to accept the innovation if it is delivered by experts on the right channel, in the correct manner, and at the right time (Havelock, 1971). It is not surprising that, without shading more light on the level of participation of stakeholders, MoPSE (2015: p.ii) claims that "opportunities for participation were availed through consultations meetings at every school ..." The focus on schools is surprising as this seem to suggest non-involvement of teachers' colleges and universities. In universities, a number of lecturers showed ignorance of the new or revised curriculum. A number of them claimed to have not been involved at all. This official position, though not explicitly stated, is supported by teacher educators whose voices are captured below as they explain their level of participation in the curriculum change and innovation process.

There is consensus among teacher educator participants that the level of teacher educator participation in the curriculum change and innovation exercise was flawed. Both principals of participating colleges, Chihambakwe and Nyaude indicated that they were surprised to hear that the Ministry of Higher and

Tertiary Education, Science and Technology was involved in the curriculum change and innovation process. Principal Nyaude of Seke Teachers' College said: "*Even principals were never involved yet we are the ones responsible for the training of teachers who will then implement the reforms in the new curriculum.*" In Chihambakwe's words "*Our ministry was involved at head office level*". Tendayi affirmed the fact that, in some ministries, only managers were involved: "*Our task was to invite the ministry through the relevant managerial offices, it was not for our ministry or department to detect who should participate in the processes*".

Engaging head office only without the implementers of the curriculum change entails that the level of participation of stakeholders was far from commendable. From Dambudzo's (2015: 13) perspective, "...the entire community should be involved ... Such an approach would bring about change at personal, professional, team and community levels through participation". Given that sustainable curriculum change and innovation processes must involve widespread consultation of all stakeholders, the Zimbabwean new curriculum change and innovation experiences which involved limited head office staff from the teacher educators' ministry rendered the exercise non-sustainable. It will not be surprising for educators not to claim ownership of the new curriculum. Lorraine, the head of department for Practicals at Seke Teachers' College could not hold back her disappointment with the practices in the change process:

> There was zero participation by all of us, I have not heard anyone attending any meeting or workshop relating to the processes of the innovation. We only knew about the changes from the newspapers and debates on radio and television.

Ordinary lecturers also raised the same concerns about their non-involvement in the change processes. Dread observed that every lecturer is an important stakeholder who was supposed to be represented at very early stages of the conceptualisation of the reforms, changes or innovation. For example, he complained that, "... *it is not fair for those on the top to just impose programmes on us to implement*". As one of the key stakeholders, teacher educators were supposed to be fully involved in curriculum change and innovation processes. The idea of participating is one of the human development values regarded as important for people-centred projects (Boni and Arias, 2012). The top-down approach to curriculum change and innovation, as already stated that, failed to enlist support from relevant actors. This led to resistance and lack of buy-in by those who are supposed to implement or benefit from the innovation. The degree of empowerment which also helps shape the depth of stakeholder participation is considered below.

Degree of empowerment by teacher educators

In this sub-section, teacher educators describe the curriculum change process as disempowering and power-coercive. Both principals expressed concern about how this affected their level of participation: According to Nyaude:

> *When you were not involved from initial processes, you are totally disempowered, there are a number of issues I don't agree with, but who do you tell when the innovation is already being operationalised. When that happens, as a key stakeholder in the implementation process you will have to let go otherwise you will be accused of sabotaging the new curriculum.*

The political overtones in Nyaude's voice as testified by the term "sabotage" means the principal's fears are not necessarily based on fear of committing an act of misconduct but the need to be politically correct. This could be part of the explanation why the comprehensive framework, which is widely distributed and referred to, has three introductions, one by the President, the Minister of MoPSE and then the Permanent Secretary of the MoPSE. The emphasis on wide stakeholder involvement by MoPSE is quite notable albeit limited information on the degree of empowerment to articulate issues at stake. Empowerment enables participants to make choices and to transform those choices into desired actions and outcomes (Alkire, 2010, Ibrahim, 2014). Educators were not properly anchored or grounded on the new Zimbabwe Curriculum Framework for Primary and Secondary Education 2015-2022. This seems to have been lacking as MoPSE was more concerned about just having representatives from across the nation, whilst paying limited attention to the quality of participation. This could be the reason why even lecturers felt incapable of handling "new" curriculum issues. As observed by Kunashe:

> *The lecturers are not empowered, we are experiencing difficulties in making decisions on how to move forward with the suggested changes. We needed time to analyse and discuss the changes and how best to introduce them to students who are at different levels of their course, some are already halfway through, others are preparing to go for teaching practice, and some are just starting the programme.*

For someone who was not fully following the new changes as observed above, fitting the curriculum changes and innovation could be a complex process. This is particularly true as one would need to clearly understand what changes affect which area. This lack of contribution is exposed by Monicah's complaint that:

What can I contribute when I have not been involved in conceptualising the new changes? Why were those changes made? Where do we come in as lecturers or educators? I am also keen to learn what the new changes entail" should not be understood as an attitude problem but a genuine concern depicting lack of empowerment to participate at par with those who had an opportunity to be involved from early stages.

Tendayi argued that lecturers just, as any trained teachers, were already skilled with basic skills to interpret "any syllabus from all over the world" making it irrelevant to complain about lack of empowerment. As already observed, this indicates a lack of commitment by MoPSE to participation parity (Fraser, 1996; 2008; 2009). Lecturers did not deny the fact that they already have skills but had reservations about the process:

It is true that lecturers already have skills to analyse and interpret any syllabus in the world, but why should they not be involved in influencing the type of curriculum they will implement. Not all of them should be involved but at least they should be represented.

In this analysis, this chapter does not consider the above request as far-fetched, but rather as a basic ingredient to achieve sustainable curriculum change and innovation. The third sub-section below considers views on equitable distribution of resources and power as projected by participants.

Equitable distribution of power and resources

In as much as Boni and Arias (2013) suggest that, because of individual differences, people need an equitable distribution of opportunities apart from resources (and power) in order for the opportunities availed to them to be transformed into worthwhile doings and beings. However, all participants in this study save Tendayi said the curriculum and innovation processes did not provide for equitable distribution of power. According to Dread, a lecturer at Seke Teachers' College,

Everything was just superimposed, there was no platform for us to ask questions, our principal was not ready to respond to our questions either as he told us to figure out what was required by the new syllabi or possibly as a way of conceding his ignorance on the new curriculum.

A head of department at Morgan Teachers' College, Nyamasvisva affirmed the lack of equitable distribution of power at his station as well. In his words:

I was just told to report to the station to take up extra duties to in-service teachers who had trained as teachers for the general classes to be reskilled for Early Childhood Development teaching

using the new curriculum. The material came a day before the commencement of the training programme, so we had to do with what was available.

From a social justice perspective, Fraser (2009) explains how power can be affirmative or transformative, where the transformative form will be more useful for the advancement of sustainable practices contributing to more just societies. Transformative power challenges the hierarchies of power that inhibit effective participation of citizens in curriculum practices and processes. On the other hand, the affirmative form tends to perpetuate the status quo through its tendency to recognise marginalised stakeholders, but without opening up space for their participation as equals. In this study, the affirmative form seems to be at play in curriculum analysis, change and innovation. Although not referring to practices in teacher education, Dread shared his views in the words:

> *The process of change can best be described as dictatorial and full of threats, we are only lucky that we don't deal with those from Ministry Of Primary and Secondary Education, we hear that headmasters and teachers do not voice their concerns, they just accept what is dictated by authorities.*

The threats alluded to by Dread are both indicators that curriculum change and innovation in the Zimbabwean new curriculum are not in sync with sustainability where stakeholders are expected to express their views without fear of punishment.

Towards Sustainable Curriculum Change and Innovation

Having highlighted challenges that have been encountered on the revised Zimbabwe Curriculum Framework for Primary and Secondary Education 2015-2022, a number of solutions are suggested to address the problems. The proposals are drawn from experiences of the Curriculum Development Unit official, teachers' colleges principals as well as lecturing staff. In order to enhance sustainable processes and practices in curriculum change and innovation, a human development framework foregrounding three values may be useful. The values are empowerment, equity and participation. The feasibility of this proposal depends on opening up democratic space by adopting a bottom-up approach to curriculum change and innovation. When policy stakeholders, principals and lecturers are provided freedoms by removing any forms of barriers, they nonetheless become allies in the processes and practices of curriculum change and innovation, rather than being merely passive recipients of a curriculum thrust upon them from above. Deliberations, in which genuine participatory methods are applied, could be useful in enabling equitable distribution of voice and power among stakeholders such as

452

Curriculum Development Unit members, principals, lecturers and students, to widen the level of participation. The inclusion of students enables continuity which, in human development terms, fosters sustainability. Consultative meetings may also take the form of conferences which, if properly undertaken, provide an opportunity for interaction with a wider circle of academics in the area of curriculum change and innovation. In addition, conferences empower stakeholders with knowledge of international debates on curriculum.

Conclusion

The chapter draws on empirical data from a study collected at two teachers' colleges to analyse and understand how curriculum change practices and processes respond to three human development values. It begins with a literature review on the conceptualisation of sustainable curriculum change and innovation to provide an understanding of how these relate in theory and practice. It then applies three underlying human development values to education. A qualitative research design was then deemed appropriate for a study that sought an in-depth understanding of perceptions of processes and practices in curriculum change and innovation. A case study was preferred and effective to understand a phenomenon in its specific situation despite criticisms levelled against it in terms of lack of generalizability. It is more context-specific and therefore important for an understanding of curriculum innovation and change. It argues for the human development framework and its values as a helpful approach for interpreting the various complexities and contradictions that emerge from the data. The chapter presents findings based on empirical data that demonstrate how curriculum change and innovation processes in the operationalisation of the 'new' Zimbabwe Curriculum Framework for Primary and Secondary Education 2015-2022 either supports or lacks sustainable development values perceived as contributing towards human development. The last section provides possible solutions enriching curriculum processes and practices upholding human development values. The solutions potentially open up new avenues for interventions that seek to advance sustainable curriculum change and innovation.

References

Alkire, S. (2010). Human development: Definitions, critiques, and related concepts. *Human Development Research Paper*, 2010/01, UNDP.

Bennie, K. and Newstead, K. (1999). Obstacles to implementing a new curriculum. In M.J. Smit and A.S. Jordaan (Eds.), *Proceedings of the National Subject Didactics Symposium* (pp.150-157). Stellenbosch: University of Stellenbosch.

Boni, A. and Arias, B. (2013). People first: Rethinking educational policies in times of crisis using the capability approach. *Learning for Democracy*, 3(1), 797-815.

Boni, A. and Gasper, D. (2012). Rethinking the quality of universities: How can the human development thinking contribute? *Journal of Human Development and Capabilities*, 13(3), 451-470.

Braun, V. and Clarke, V. (2006). Using thematic analysis in psychology. *Qualitative Research in Psychology*, 3(2), 77-101.

Dambudzo, I.I. (2015). Curriculum issues: Teaching and learning for sustainable development in developing countries: Zimbabwe case study, *Journal of Education and Learning*, 4(1), 11-24.

Dokora, L. (2015). Foreword in Ministry of Primary and Secondary Education, Curriculum Framework for Primary and Secondary Education 2015-2022.

Fien, J. (2001). Educating for a sustainable future. In Campbell, W.J. (Ed.), *Creating our common future, Educating for unity in diversity* (Ch. 8). Paris: Berghahn Books, WEF and UNESCO Publishing.

Fien, J. (2002). Advancing sustainability in higher education: Issues and opportunities for research. *Higher Education Policy*, 1(5), 143-152.

Fraser, N. (1996). *Social justice in the age of identity politics: Redistribution, recognition and participation.* Paper presented at the Tanner Lecturers on Human Values, Stanford University, California. April 30–May 2, 1996.

Fraser, N. (2008). Reframing justice in a globalising world. In K. Olson (Ed.), *Adding insult to injury: Nancy Fraser debates her critics.* London: Verso.

Fraser, N. (2009). *Scales of justice: Reimagining political space in a globalising world.* New York: Columbia University Press.

Gall, M.D., Gall, J.P. and Borg, W.R. (2003). *Educational research: An introduction* (7th edn.). Boston: Pearson Education.

Havelock, R.G. (1971). *Planning for innovation through dissemination and utilisation of knowledge.* Michigan: University of Michigan Institute for Social Research.

Hayles, C.S. and Holdsworth, S.E. (2006) *Curriculum change for sustainability.* Proceedings of the Built Environment Education Annual Conference (BEECON), The Bonnington Hotel, Bloomsbury, London, 12-13 September 2006.

Hayles, C.S. and Holdsworth, S.E. (2008). Curriculum change for sustainability. *Journal for Education in the Built Environment*, 3(1), 25-48

Hoyle, E. (1972). Sociology of education. *British Journal of Educational Technology*, *3*(2), 159–161.

Huckle, J. (2008). An analysis of new labour's policy on education for sustainable development (ESD) with particular reference to socially critical approaches. *Environmental Education Research*, 14(1), 65–75.

Ibrahim, S. (2014). The capability approach: From theory to practice – rationale, review and reflections. In S. Ibrahim and M. Tiwari (Eds.), *The capability approach: From theory to practice* (pp. 1-28). London: Palgrave Macmillan.

Kelly, A.V. (2004). *The curriculum: Theory and practice* (5th edn.). London: Sage.

Marovah, T. and Walker, M. (2016). Learning for sustainable futures: a human development approach to citizenship education. *Journal of Education*, 65, 54-76.

Marovah, T. (2013). Citizenship education and human capabilities: Lynchpin for sustainable learning environment and social justice. *The Journal for Transdisciplinary Research in Southern Africa* (Special edn), 9(3), 593–607.

Mashaya, B. and Tafirenyika. M. (2017). New curriculum unworkable. *Daily News*, 15 February, 2017.

Ministry for the Environment. (2009). *Rethinking our built environments: Towards a sustainable future.* Available online:
http://www.mfe.govt.nz/publications/susdev/rethinking-our-built-environment/

Ministry of Primary and Secondary Education. (2015). *Curriculum review process: Narrative report.* Harare: The Higher Education Academy.

Mugabe, R. (2015). *Preamble in Ministry of Primary and Secondary Education, Curriculum Framework for Primary and Secondary Education 2015-2022.* Harare: The Higher Education Academy.

Nemat, M.H. (2015). How to approach curriculum revision? *Adv Health Prof Educ.*, 1(1), 41-43.

Newman: , Wiseman, N., Pepper, C. and Kelly, K. (2004). *Training for sustainability: The vocational education and training sector.* Murdoch University: Green Skills Inc, the Centre for Learning, Change and Development, and the Institute for Sustainability and Technology Policy (ISTP).

Nicholls, A. (1983). *Managing educational Innovations.* London: Allen and Unwin.

Priestley, M. (2010). Curriculum for excellence: Transformational change or business as usual? *Scottish Educational Review*, 42(1), 23-36.

Rea-Dickins: and Germaine, K. (1994). *Evaluation.* Oxford: Oxford University Press.

Ryan, A. (2011). Education for sustainable development and holistic curriculum change. Harare: The Higher Education Academy.

Sen, A. (1999). *Development as freedom.* New York: Oxford University Press.

Stallmann, M. (2010). *Sustainable learning environments: The issues and potential policy responses* (Unpublished master's dissertation). Lincoln University

Stenhouse, L. (1975). *An introduction to curriculum research and development.* London: Heinemann Educational Books Ltd.

Thaba-Nkadimene, K.L. (2016). Improving the management of curriculum implementation in South African public schools through school leadership programme: A pragmatic approach. In M.M. Dichaba and M.A.O. Sotayo (Eds.), *South Africa international conference on education 19- 21 September 2016 proceedings: Towards Excellence in Educational Practices.* Manhattan Hotel Pretoria, South Africa, (pp. 188-198).

Thomas, I. (2004). Sustainability in tertiary curricula: What is stopping it happening? *International Journal of Sustainability in Higher Education*, 5(1), 33-47.

United Nations Development Programme. (1990). Human Development Report. Available online: http://www.undp.org/content/undp/en/home.html (accessed23/03/2012).

United Nations. (1987). *Brundtland Report of the World Commission on Environment and Development.* New York: United Nations.

Walker, M. (2010). Pedagogy for rich human beingness in global times. In E. Unterhalter and V. Carpentier (Eds.), *Global inequalities and higher education: Whose interests are we serving* (pp. 219-240)? Hampshire: Palgrave McMillian.

Chapter 23

People Living with HIV and AIDS's Perceived Experiential Attitudes towards Traditional Medicines in Zimbabwe

Tinashe Muromo and Diane Elkonin

Summary

HIV and AIDS bring profound social, economic and public health consequences making it one of the most serious health and development challenges in the world today. It has become common to use traditional medicine concomitantly with allopathic or conventional medicine. This study examined the effect of perceived experiential attitude on motivation to use traditional and alternative medicines (TAM) by people living with HIV and AIDS (PLWHA) in Zimbabwe. The study focused on attitude as a determinant of behavioural intention as depicted in the integrated behaviour model (IBM). Experiential attitudes result from affective evaluation of behavioural outcomes in terms of good or bad. Qualitative data from 20 PLWHA in Zimbabwe who had treatment from traditional healers was analysed using NVivo. In-depth interviews assessed experiential attitudes towards TMA-use. Participants were selected through snowball procedure. Informed consent procedures were followed. Respondents made mostly positive evaluations of the outcomes from their use of traditional medicines. Sustained use of traditional medicine which spanned their childhood was highlighted as one reason for the positive evaluation. Respondents did not only report positive and negative evaluation of outcomes, but also evaluations hanging in the balance, that were ambivalent and appeared to cause a lot of tension. Therefore, the experiential attitude was found to be trichotomous rather than dichotomous as predicted by IBM. It can be concluded that, perceived experiential attitudes are key determinants of PLWHA to use traditional medicines. Policy-makers and health practitioners are recommended to formalize this treatment and healthcare option. Study limitations include non-probability sampling, sample size. Future studies should consider methodological pluralism.

Introduction

Human immunodeficiency virus infection and acquired immunodeficiency syndrome (HIV and AIDS) is a disease of the human immune system caused by infection from the human immunodeficiency virus (HIV) (Kent & Sepkowitz, 2001). This chapter gives an overview of the conceptualisation of traditional and alternative medicine (TAM) including the global use of TAM followed by the Zimbabwean use of TAM for the treatment of HIV and AIDS. The chapter proceeds to present the statement of the problem, leading to the overall study aim and the objectives then the methodology, research findings and finally the conclusions and recommendations. Traditional medicine, referred to in the present research as traditional and alternative medicine (TAM), refers to traditional health practices, approaches, knowledge and beliefs incorporating plant, animal and mineral-based medicines, spiritual therapies, manual techniques and exercises, applied singularly or in combination to treat, diagnose and prevent illness or maintain wellbeing (WHO, 2003; 2013). Complementary and alternative medicine (CAM) is defined as forms of treatment that are used in addition to (complementary) or instead of (alternative) standard treatments. The majority of TAM practices focus on the therapeutic use of herbs and plants while CAM refers to the additional or supplementary forms of treatment. Further, the term conventional/allopathic medicine (CM) (or health care) is used to mean clinical care and prevention in the biomedical scientific tradition. This research study examined the effects of the experiential attitude on the health-seeking behaviours (personal actions to promote optimal wellness, recovery and rehabilitation) of people living with aids (PLWA) in Zimbabwe to choose the traditional health care option as opposed to, or together with, or even before the conventional one.

Use of traditional medicines is prevalent in all parts of the world, among all societies and cultures, under diverse terminologies such as herbal medicine, ayurvedic medicine, unani medicine, acupuncture, traditional Chinese medicine, South African *muti* and *Yoruba ifa*. As an indicator of the pervasive nature of traditional therapies in some societies, in China herbal preparations are estimated to account for 30% - 50% of the total medicinal consumption (WHO, 2003; 2013). Among all traditional medical approaches in that country, the most common modalities were herbal remedies (85.9%) followed by acupuncture (11.0%; Chen et al. 2007). In India, traditional healers use over 2,500 plant species, of which about 100 can be considered sources of medicine (Pei, 2001). While each country has its own TAM practices, it is likely that China and India are not unique in their reliance on alternative approaches to health care.

Frequent use of TAM is not limited to developing countries. In fact, most of the quantitative research assessing the prevalence of TAM has been conducted in the United States (US) and Europe, where interest in CAM increased substantially in the 1990s (Ahmad, 2004; Barnes, McFann, Nahin & Powell-Griner, 2004). CAM use is reported by 40% - 80% of individuals in the United States, Canada, Australia and Europe, with dramatic increases in recent decades in both reported use and expenditure (Boon, 2002; MacLennan, Taylor & Wilson, 1996; Reilly, 2001). There is particularly frequent use by patients suffering from a wide variety of chronic conditions, especially when conventional therapy has had limited efficacy or is not readily available (Muromo & Elkonin, 2016).

Research in developing countries regarding TAM is less well-established, though in one international project conducted by the World Health Organisation (WHO, 2003) approximations showed that alternative therapies were used by about 80% of persons, with usage up to 90% or higher in some rural areas. These TAM use estimates may be especially frequent in Africa (Bukenya-Ziraba, Hoft & Kamatenesi-Mugisha, 2000; Bukenya-Ziraba &Kamatenesi-Mugisha, 2002). As in the US and Europe, limited research in Africa shows that alternative therapies appear to be especially utilised in the management of chronic conditions.

In contrast to the apparently frequent use of TAM for non-infectious chronic conditions, few studies document frequent use of TAM to treat infectious diseases. However, in Swaziland, Mozambique, South Africa and Liberia traditional healers have roles in the treatment of Sexually Transmitted Infections (STIs) (Green, 1994; Friend-du Preez, Formundam, Peltzer and Ramilagan, 2008). Taxonomies of sexually transmitted infections (STIs) and traditional treatment exist among some populations in these countries. STIs are widely believed to respond better to traditional than to conventional management (Green, 1994).

While documentation of the specific herbal remedies that individuals use for various conditions is common, there is little reported on the perceptions, attitudes, beliefs, motivations and other behavioural and cultural determinants that affect the use of TAM. One study found that users of traditional medicines perceived TAM to have greater or equal efficacy compared to conventional medicines (Clement et al., 2007), while another study reported conflicting findings that among cancer patients almost 70% were disappointed with the effects of TAM (Anarado & Ezeome, 2007). Cultural or environmental factors may also play a role in individuals accessing the traditional medical systems in their countries. For example, Drummond, Gelfand, Mavi and Ndemera (1985) in Zimbabwe and Green (1994) in four African countries document more favourable ratios of traditional healers to patients than ratios of conventional health workers to patients. These observations support the central role played by traditional healers and traditional treatment modalities in primary health care in much of Africa. These researchers also conclude that, because traditional healers are perceived to target the spiritual aspects of disease, they may serve an important function in communities' and individual's perceptions about the root origins and causes of many, if not all, illnesses (Carter, 2008; Chinsembu, 2009; Drummond et al., 1985; Green, 1994; Generali, Grauer, King & Russett, 2009).

Since the late 1980s, Zimbabwe's National AIDS Council (NAC) has sought to educate traditional healers regarding HIV and AIDS (Simmons, 2000). Very little research in Zimbabwe, however, has examined how individuals use the traditional and conventional health care sectors in the context of HIV and AIDS. The NAC/Zimbabwe National Traditional Healers' Association (ZINATHA) recommendations focus on using traditional care systems to provide support (rather than treatment) to those affected by HIV and AIDS, to work on developing traditional methods aimed at reducing HIV/AIDS transmission, to increasing awareness of HIV/AIDS for prevention and care of people with AIDS, and creating a supportive environment for those living with the disease (Jijide, 1994). In spite of the fact that ZINATHA and NAC have developed a comprehensive plan for HIV/AIDS management employing both traditional and conventional health care (NAC, 2006), more work is needed on research documenting how this has played out in communities across Zimbabwe . Recent data regarding traditional or conventional medical care for HIV or AIDS–related symptoms from Zimbabwe are scant. Small studies (N ~ 50-250), suggest that a large proportion of Zimbabweans continue to use traditional medical practices, and that some HIV-infected persons use herbal medicines both before and whilst taking conventional antiretroviral therapy (ART) (Benet, Guglielmo, Maponga, Monera &Wolfe, 2008; Sebit et al. 2000; Dolezal et al. 2008). These studies, however, have largely used convenience samples or were conducted in conventional health care settings.

In Zimbabwe, HIV may be treated by practitioners who come from different traditions such as biomedicine, traditional medicine and faith healing. The relatively late introduction of antiretroviral therapy (ART) into Zimbabwe has meant that it came into a context where traditional treatment and healthcare systems were pre-existing and well-established (Broom & O'Brien, 2014). Chitura and Manyanhaire's (2013) study in Manicaland Province in Zimbabwe also reported acknowledgement of the need to have both ARVs and local traditional herbs for HIV and AIDS treatment, pointing out that traditional medicines are at the heart of most communities in Zimbabwe since for most people in rural settings it is the first place they go to if sickness befalls a family. Chitura and Manyanhaire (2013). further discovered that the use of complementary and alternative medicine is popular among people living with HIV and AIDS in Zimbabwe.

The earlier cited recent study by Broom and O'Brien that is similar to this study was carried out in Harare, Zimbabwe to explore the experiences of people living with and affected by HIV. It aimed specifically at documenting, interrogating and reflecting on the patient's perceptions and experiences of biomedicine in relation to traditional medicine and spiritual healing. The study revealed that traditional medicine and spiritual beliefs continue to significantly shape the way in which HIV is perceived, and the health-seeking behaviour of those infected (Broom & O'Brien, 2014). In view of these revelations, they proposed that, even if witchcraft, spiritual healing and superstition based on religion may appear to be niche issues within a broader economic sphere of care, they still control and influence peoples' lived experiences of HIV. Broom and O'Brien contend that in this sense, TAM must "be central to any contemporary understanding of the problem of how to make life-saving therapies efficiently available on a mass scale in a way that is not just tied to drugs but holistically to economic empowerment, food security, nutrition and overall wellbeing" (Broom and O'Brien, 2014: 102). The study advocates for engagement with traditional and spiritual healing, recognising that this is part of culture, individuality and community identity which add meaning to people's lives, and should that these should not simply be regarded as barriers to compliance. This conclusion resonates well with Makadzange and Pearson's earlier observation that "health is grounded in the cultural, spiritual and religious context of Zimbabwean men's lives, … men interpreted sexual-health concerns as due to either natural (disease, psychological stress) or supernatural (displeased ancestral and religious spirits, witchcraft) causes" (Makadzange & Pearson, 2008: 361). Makadzange and Pearson also observed that these perceptions shape the patient's choice of treatment and health service provider.

Dolezal et al. (2008). also had findings that are similar to the preceding when they compared HIV/AIDS-specific quality of life change in Zimbabwean patients at Western medicine versus traditional African medicine care sites. Dolezal et al. maintain that traditional healing is an important component of African culture and society and is the primary system of health care for more than 80% of rural Africans, with the majority of Africans with HIV turning to traditional healing through the course of their illness. In addition to the cultural dimension, as previously shown, Nyika (2007) points out that poor Africans

461

living with HIV/AIDS (including Zimbabweans) rely on traditional and alternative medicine mainly because it is relatively cheaper and more accessible to the poor populations unable to afford allopathic medicines. This is very applicable to Zimbabweans whose country's economy has been performing very poorly over the past 10 years (Barclays Bank of Zimbabwe Limited, 2017)

The scenario presented in the preceding analysis reveals that Zimbabwe is highly vulnerable to threats posed by HIV and AIDS. The most effective response is to put in place programmes to reduce the number of new infections. Recent research has demonstrated treatment as prevention to be very effective (CDC, 2013; ECDC, 2012; NAT, 2011; WHO, 2012). This approach involves targeting the infected person with treatment so that, through reducing their infectiousness, they are less able to transmit the virus (ECDC, 2012). As put by CDC 2013), providing treatment to people living with HIV infection in order to improve their health must always be the first priority. The use of ART to prevent onward HIV transmission has moved to the forefront of public health programmes of HIV prevention because of the heightened tolerance of the medications, cost effectiveness, and the limitations of other approaches (Mayer & Venkatesh, 2011). Treatment reduces the index person's viral load to levels that reduce infectiousness, hence lowering the rate of transmission. This lessens transmission rates, thereby lessening disease burden from a public health point of view as well as reducing morbidity and mortality.

As already mentioned, PLWHA also use traditional medicines. Studies on the use of traditional medicines are therefore very important as they help to inform public health policy, practice and education. It seems, although not documented, this treatment and care option also reduces the index person's viral load to levels that reduce HIV onward transmission. The idea of treatment as prevention is therefore central and a consensus of all, but the decision that has to be made by an infected person is whether to look for traditional treatment, conventional treatment or both. Marachera et al. (2012). reveal that the success rate of antiretroviral therapy (ART) in rural communities of Zimbabwe is low with few children covered on therapy whilst those on ART have a poor health situation worsened by the poor conditions in the remote rural communities. The present study focused on investigating experiential attitude perceptions leading to the choice of treatment with the traditional alternative medicines (TAM) as (a)/n alternative/complement to the conventional or allopathic option. Specifically, the present research focused on the perceived experiential attitude as a behavioural determinant of individuals' choices regarding the use of traditional and conventional health care in Zimbabwe, for the treatment and prevention of HIV/AIDS.

This research provided the first and most comprehensive description, in a country with a high HIV prevalence, of the perceived health-seeking behavioural motivations based on one's experiential attitude that lead individuals to choose traditional versus conventional therapies and health care. It also ascertained when and why these therapies are used along with other perceptions associated with their choices. Beyond this immediate aim, the outcomes of this study provide a basis and resources for building a comprehensive program of research on the choice between traditional and conventional health care for HIV/AIDS in Zimbabwe. As adequately documented in both the results section and the recommendations, there is need for closer communication between those in traditional and modern medicine.

The study adopted a western-developed explanation of health seeking behaviour, "the reasoned action approach" and applied it in a local setting in dealing with the complex issue of AIDS in different socio-economic environment where not much relevant literature is available on the perceived cognitive behavioural determinants of PLWA's motivation to use TAM. Henderson (2011) points out that those studies of a more anthropogenic nature have emphasised the emergence of localised explanatory frameworks for HIV and AIDS at odds with common universal claims. Fishbein (2000) stresses that each of the constructs in the reasoned action approach can be found in any culture or population. He submits that "the theoretical variables contained in the model (the integrated behaviour model) ... have been tested in over 50 countries in both the developed and developing world" (Fishbein, 2000: 275), including Zimbabwe (See Karsprzyk & Montano in Ajzen, Albarracin & Hornik, 2007; Glanz, Rimer & Viswanath, 2008).

Theoretical Framework

This study applied the reasoned action approach as its theoretical framework to identify and understand the specific experiential attitude-based factors that best explain PLWA's motivation to uptake traditional and alternative medicines. Earlier research focused on global determinants of behaviour and was questioned by Fishbein (1967a), Fishbein and Ajzen (1972, 1975) who suggested that attention should be directed to the behaviour of interest and identify its determinants. The challenge related to this approach was its assumption that each behaviour was a result of a unique set of determinants. The reasoned action approach provided a response to this challenge through the theory of planned behaviour.

463

The theory of reasoned action (later modified to be the theory of planned behaviour) was developed to better explain relationships among attitudes, intentions and behaviours (Fishbein, (1967). Intention is perceived as the immediate antecedent of behaviour (Ajzen & Albarracin, 2007). Fishbein distinguished between attitude toward an object and attitude toward a behaviour with respect to that object. Most attitude theorists consider attitude toward an object (e.g., attitude toward HIV) in trying to predict a behaviour (e.g., using TAM). Fishbein demonstrated that attitude toward the behaviour (attitude toward using TAM) is a much better predictor of that behaviour (using TAM) than attitude toward the object (HIV) at which the behaviour is directed (Fishbein & Ajzen, 1975). The present study was accordingly informed and focused on examining the experiential attitude towards the behaviour (using TAM).

Many theorists have described attitude as composed of affective and cognitive dimensions (Conner et al., 2013; French et al., 2005; Triandis, 1980). Experiential attitude, or affect, is the individual's emotional response to the idea of performing a recommended behaviour (using TAM). Individuals with a strong negative emotional response to the behaviour are unlikely to perform it, while those with a strong positive emotional reaction are more likely to engage in it. This study's primary goal was to identify the key beliefs underlying the experiential attitude-based behavioural determinants that best explain PLWA's motivation to use traditional and alternative medicine.

Methodology

This chapter employed a qualitative research design. The study was exploratory, descriptive and interpretative. It explored and described people living with HIV and AIDS who have used traditional and alternative medicine's perceptions and meanings, specifically resulting from their experiential attitudes within the context of the reasoned action approach (Ajzen & Fishbein, 2000), and moved beyond this to complete the data analysis with more explicit interpretations of the attitude-based themes identified in the data. The data analysis was informed by the interpretive phenomenological analysis (IPA) approach (Smith & Osborn, 2003); (Smith, Flowers, & Larkin, 2009); (Willig, 2013). Analysis was done with the aid of NVivo (V.10), a Computer Aided Qualitative Data Analysis Software.

The participants consisted of 8 males and 12 females living with HIV who had treatment from a traditional healer for HIV related illnesses. Data saturated after the 16th interview. Participants were recruited from the City of Harare and the Chiredzi Rural District in Zimbabwe. Four of the 8 males and 6 of the 12 females were from the rural setting while the other 4 males and 6 females were from an urban environment. An urban and a rural setting were chosen in order to cater for their environmental differences. The two selected geographical areas also differ in ethnicity (Shona and Shangani). The sample size was informed by IPA which makes use of small, purposive and carefully selected samples including case studies (Smith, Flowers, & Larkin, 2009). The snowball (or chain, chain-referral, referral) sampling technique was used. This procedure is appropriate when members of special population are difficult to locate (Babbie, 2002); (Newman, 2011).

All the participants were:

(i)   Male or female aged 16 years and above
(ii)   Living with HIV and AIDS
(iii)   People who had treatment for HIV related illnesses from a traditional healer
(iv)   Living in Harare City or in Chiredzi Rural District, Zimbabwe

As already highlighted, the data were analysed using interpretative phenomenological analysis with the aid of NVivo (V.10), a computer aided qualitative data analysis software This analysis focused on how the participants got motivated or formed the intention to use TAM as a result of their experiential attitudes

Results and Discussion

The names (as shown in some diagrams and dialogue boxes) and any other names used in this chapter in reference to PLWHA are pseudonyms; they were used for illustrative purposes only. Any resemblance to actual persons is unintentional. Illustrations with anecdotes during discussions of results should not be perceived as repetitions but rather, various possible interpretations of the same or similar pieces of qualitative data.

Experiential perceived attitude-based TAM-use

Experiential attitude was contextualised as an affective evaluation of perceived TAM use outcomes in terms of good or bad. The respondents showed more perceived positive evaluations of the outcomes. Most of the participants revealed sustained and repeated use of TAM which spanned their childhood. Although there were mixed feelings about the partners' use of TAM, most of the participants also reported positive feelings about the partner's use of TAM. Similarly, the thread of suspicion sprawled to the affect associated with children's use of TAM. However, most of them reported quite permissible and positive experiential attitudes about their children's use of TAM. Data revealed that the experience of participants yielded not only positive and negative evaluation of outcomes as predicted by the reasoned action approach. There were numerous other reported evaluations that were hanging on the balance. There were other outcome evaluations that seemed to be ambivalent and appeared to cause a lot of tension. Therefore, the comprehension of experiential attitude was found to be trichotomous rather than dichotomous (See Figure 43.1 below). This is also illustrated in the cloud in Figure 43.2.

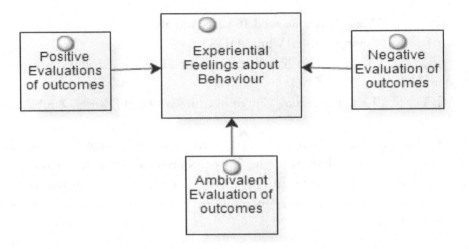

Figure 43.1: Experiential Attitude Model

While the positive and negative evaluations were easy and almost self-asserting, the ambivalent evaluations were difficult and appeared riddled with conflicts.

Figure 43.2: Clouds for Experiential attitude

As shown in the clouds above (Figure 43.2), participants reported positive evaluations in the sense how good, healthy and they like using TAM. Negative evaluations were mostly seen in how they reported the use of ARVs rather than TAM. Ambivalence was also significantly registered as it portrayed elements of various conflicts regarding TAM and its relation and/or comparison to contemporary medicine (CM). Mixing was the indicator of ambivalence. They reported using both healthcare options.

Positive evaluation of outcomes

For the positive evaluations, as shown in Figure 43.3 below, there was positive affect associated with perception of satisfaction with the outcome. These were reinforced and evident in observed emotional attachment to herbalists, subjective resourcefulness and pleasant affect associated with reluctant acceptance from Health Care Workers (HCWs).

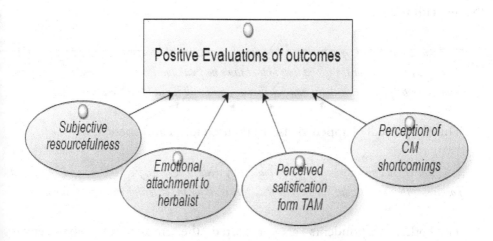

Figure 43.3: Positive Evaluations of Outcomes

Perceived satisfaction from TAM

There appeared to be a general sense of satisfaction as shown below;

I feel better, it is better ... After using traditional medicines, I gain appetite and develop a strong craving for food. I even wake up strong and do my ordinary chores without problems. The health of those on TAM is better than those of people who take pills only. They had a permanent cure. Our conventional medicines just treat the pain, but do not kill the virus.

This satisfaction was reportedly experienced in varying ways. Perception of remarkable improvements was a major one in which *negatisation effect* (purportedly tested negative after taking TAM), *normalisation effect* (reported normal health life after taking TAM) and *contimoxazole affect* (no longer taking ARVs but only cortrimoxazole as a result of TAM-use) were the common affective expressions. Participants reported that these perceived effects motivated them to continue to use of TAM. This is consistent with the reasoned action's prediction that positive evaluations of outcomes positively affect the behavioural intention thereby increasing the probability of the behaviour (TAM-use).

Negatisation effect

Negatisation effect was contextualised as perceived affective experiences characterised by the feeling that TAM literally aided in eliminating the virus from the body to a point where one tests HIV negative. Standing out were some respondents who purportedly eventually tested negative at a mission hospital (Name withheld);

> *I was given TAM by a traditional healer...I returned to the hospital…. And I tested HIV positive… I returned for the second time to that same hospital and I was found negative. I returned again to the hospital for the third and fourth time and I still tested HIV negative*

This purportedly happened also to their children and friends.

> *For my son and a friend in Botswana…they went to be tested for HIV… and were found positive… they used traditional medicines… they went for HIV testing and were found negative.*

The other respondents also reported the mear-negative-experiences (iIncreased CD4 count) as well. Batsiranai narrated her encounter with the doctor who was shocked with her results and almost said, '*could it be that you are negative?*' after the modern medical doctor noticed that the improvement was beyond his/her experience with conventional medicines. Similarly, Charity who, because of the rate she reported her CD4 count to be increasing was convinced that if she continued to use TAM, her results would eventually test negative. Zvamaronga also felt that continued use of TAM can lead to the elimination of the virus. Tinomboedza felt the same.

There appeared to be a strong feeling that TAM would eliminate the virus in the body. While other's experiences were not medically confirmed, cases that were purportedly medically confirmed were extremely exceptional and raised more questions that might be beyond the scope of this chapter. Not only was it raising more health seeking behavioural questions but also pharmacological ones. It seems that the aspiration and reported perceived acquisition of a negative status plays a key factor in the decision to use TAM. These reported experiences and perceptions can also influence others to use TAM. Pharmacological research on such drugs is essential to get a scientific position on the pharmacological actions of such drugs. Results from such studies will inform modern medicine's position on TAM-use.

Normalisation effect

Related to the negatisation effect was the normalisation effect which was contextualised as the affective expressions associated with the feeling of appearing and to have normal health and indistinguishable from healthy individuals. This perception appears a very strong motive towards TAM-use because of the reported effect which greatly deals with issues related to stigma. People would be motivated to take TAM if the perceived effects are such that they do not appear ill after TAM-use and avoid problems associated with stigma, which include but are not limited to segregation and discrimination.

Some respondents pointed out that if a person is on pills alone he will be distinguishable, he said, 'If a person is on pills only, you would notice that s/he is taking pills and is also HIV positive. The one, who takes TAM, would not be noticed. Similarly, others felt that TAM made them more normal. Batsiranai clearly stated that her state had deteriorated but TAM stabilised her and she could now do manual work like other women;

> I am now realising that I have recovered. I can go wherever I want to go. I also carry my tswanda (basket) like other women do. I can also spend the day jogging along the road (Sign of fitness). I can do all the family errands. I am now cooking and eating any food of my choice, without being unnecessarily selective like a sick person. This because I am now strong... the doctor said to me '...Even if you want to carry a child (being pregnant); you are now able to, you can carry the pregnancy' ...initially I was told that I was not allowed to have a child. You see? So, it means that TAM helps...I was like a stick (very thin), when I had a walk, people would think that I would be blown away by the wind. Some would ask, 'is that person going to live up to tomorrow ... will she ever survive?' But I have seen that I have recovered to my normal health ...

Not only was Batsiranai reporting to work like other normal women but she was also now able to reproduce like other normal women. This assertion was also substantiated by Convenor who revealed that her reproductive success was comparable to those who are considered to be healthy. Kushingirira also reported that she felt that she was just functioning normally. She can now cook using nabhodho (big pots) metaphorically to signify normalcy. The metaphor was used to emphasise the satisfaction with TAM. Batsiranai also metaphorically referred to '(*a place I was seated all days) my usual undisturbed normal state*', appearing to imply the normalisation effect of TAM. To her, it now seemed as if she never got sick. She also felt that her current frequency and type of infections were highly comparable to those in good health. It can be seen that Batsiranai has a strong intention to continue using TAM, a finding that is consistent with Fishbein (2000)'s observation that attitude is a strong determinant of behavioural intention. This experiential attitude seems to be deriving from perceived feeling of satisfaction from using TAM. Batsiranai used the stick as a metaphor to exaggerate the state of her deterioration in order to emphasise her satisfaction with the normalisation effect of TAM. Zvamaronga also used the sugarcane to emphasise the same satisfaction;

I keep taking TAM because it is helping me because my new condition is significantly different from my previous sickly state. I was thin and wasted. My hand was like sugarcane (body as thin as sugarcane), but I see that TAM is helping me.

Use of TAM appeared associated with the crossing-back effect in which they felt normal again. There were euphoric reactions to this crossing back as they felt closing the stigma gap and becoming more like healthy others. The reported feeling of being comparably the same as healthy others, especially in appearance and activities they engage in, seemed important in making experiential attitude-based decision to continue using TAM.

Cotrimoxazole affect

Cotrimoxazole affect was subsumed as the affective expressions associated with the feeling of major improvements that would suffice for one to be recommended removal on more rigorous medical treatment and maintained on cotrimoxazole. In a way, cotrimoxazole was used as a measure of wellness from the most deteriorated state of HIV. It was seen as "a safe zone". Generally, it was evaluated as good to be maintained on cotrimoxazoles. Therefore, cotrimoxazole affect was conceptualised as the delightful affective expressions associated with the return to and maintenance on cotrimoxazole. There was a feeling attached to cotrimoxazole especially if one remained on them or if one was reversed to them.

My doctor said, 'right. If you are using TAM, we are now weaning you from pills because the way you have improved means that the TAM you are using is helpful. They removed me from the stronger ARV pills I was taking and gave me cotrimoxazole. I "run" (go) to Chaka (the traditional healer) to take TAM. Recently when I visited the hospital for a review, my CD4 count was very high that is when the doctor said I could now even safely get pregnant…

Expressed positive feelings of taking TAM leading to being '*dropped*' and '*weaned*' from ARVs reinforcing her to her '*run*' and keep on '*running*' to Chaka (the traditional healer) for more TAM are an indication of positive evaluations of TAM-use outcomes.

Clearly, it seems cotrimoxazole affect was a pleasurable affect that was used to measure the sense of security as it helped to estimate HIV deterioration or improvement. Therefore, feeling cotrimoxazoled was comparable to feeling safe. Such an experiential attitude seemed to have been yielding not only repeated use of TAM but also more positive living and proved attractive to most of the participants. Such perceptions appear not to only sustain the use of TAM by PLWHA, but to also direct health-seeking behaviours of others including but not limited to family members and friends towards motivation to use TAM for other diseases and ailments.

Perceived efficiency and permanency of TAM

Positive affect associated with perception of TAM efficiency and permanency both in relation to the elimination of virus and the treatment of opportunistic infections was reported.

So, when she (traditional healer) was giving me TAM I noticed my condition improving. I realised that TAM was effective in fighting the virus because ever since I started to take the TAM, I never got bed ridden

There were perceptions that unlike conventional medicines, TAM does not temporarily treat, it treats forever;

These conventional medicines…heal but temporarily. They only relieve the pain but not treat. However, our traditional medicines treat permanently. Sometimes I would not have the money to go back to see the modern doctor who also has to be paid consultation fees. However, when I get TAM, I know that will be long lasting…

It appears that in addition to perceptions of TAM treatment being relatively cheaper than contemporary conventional medicine (CM), its effects are perceived to be relatively longer lasing or permanent as compared to CM. The issue of reported affordability can be another major motive towards TAM use in Zimbabwe, especially considering the current hard economic times being experienced in Zimbabwe resulting from the general macroeconomic decline.

471

Perception of absence of side effects in TAM

There were also some positive feelings associated with the perception of lack of side effects and no overdose, and allergies in TAM, hence unlike ARVs, you do not necessarily have to keep it beyond the reach of children;

> *It is also rare for a person to be allergic to TAM, and I have never heard of a person who says I have had side effects after taking TAM... I can take AVRs, and can easily take an overdose of the pills. However, even if I pour the whole pocket of TAM, it will never harm me. There is never an overdose of TAM..... It is a type of medicine that could be left in the open. It would not affect or harm a child, even if it were to be taken raw. It would even improve the health of the child. There is nowhere it can affect the child's health because it is not poisonous. There is some TAM I left within my daughter's reach, like I said before; I have done it a number of times. I returned to find that she had taken all of my TAM and drank and finished it all. It did not harm her.*

This was perceived as good compared to the modern medication which has age restrictions, strict dosages and usually written "keep out of reach of children" and have adverse overdose effects. This revelation also implies a perceived positive evaluation of TAM-use that has a direct influence on the behavioural intention to continue to use TAM instead of ARVs.

Perception of superiority of TAM over CM

TAM was also believed to be superior to some conventional medicines (CM) which also included ARVs. An intriguing finding was reported by some of the participants who reported that their relatives died refusing to use TAM, religiously sticking to ARVs;

> *TAM is working better than ARVs for me... And there is no one who knows that I am HIV infected to date, because I never got sick since I started taking TAM. My (relative who was on ARVs) is the one who used to have big problems, but I never had any problem. They said, 'I am drinking pills (ARVs).'... They died taking those pills like that...So I think that the herbs are far much better...*

Some respondents strongly registered regret; they strongly felt that, had it not been that their relatives refused TAM, they would have been alive. For them, TAM is superior to ARVs and has more healing properties than CM which they perceive as only a *'health booster'*.

Perception of life in TAM and CM shortcomings

As a summed point, there was a perception of overall well-being and sustainability of health in TAM. Coded raw in-vivo, this theme was subsumed to capture the positive affective assertions in relation to well-being, life-longevity and good health associated with TAM-use. As a result, this theme can help to concisely capture the affective assertions and the strength of their emotional rooting to the positive evaluations reflecting positive experiential attitude towards use of TAM. This supports Cooke and French (2008)'s findings in their meta-analysis of 33 studies when they documented that attitude has a largest relationship with intention, followed by subjective norms and perceived behavioural control.

There is nothing I can say about TAM because all of them are helpful; most people say that going to the hospital is a waste of time. You would see a person getting well with these traditional medicines.

The positive evaluation of TAM was also implied in the negative evaluation of CM. This was even more when TAM was perceived to help alleviate the perceived shortcomings of CM. Allergies (side effects) of ARVs, assumption of sick role in CM, monotony in the use of CM, 'unnecessary formalities' in CM, failure of CM in other ailments, were the most cited shortcomings among which allergies (side effects) were the most popular. Figure 43.4 is a cloud on the perception of CM shortcomings.

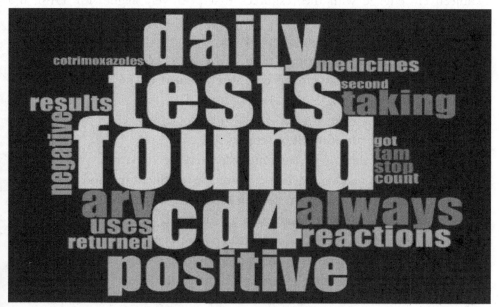

Figure 43.4: Cloud on the perception of CM shortcomings

In this case, it can be inferred that the use of TAM appears to be an escape behaviour that was conditioned by the aversion from CM. The aversion caused negative evaluation because it caused a negative affective outcome (unhappiness). TAM appears to have offered an escape window. Notwithstanding the (in)sufficiency of scrutiny, the presence of the window seemed to be directing these escape behaviours towards TAM which was perceived to be vicariously succeeding, at least in the perception of its efficacy and efficiency. This apparent social learning process might vicariously reinforce the initiation and sustainable continued use of TAM from parents to children, including non-family members who might have had the opportunity to observe and share the positive evaluations and perceptions of TAM use.

Emotional attachment to herbalist and subjective resourcefulness

The positive evaluation of outcome appeared to have an affective association with the source of the treatment. Below is an extract that showed perceived compulsive possessive affection for her herbalist;

> ...*you would see that this person is my spirit medium that protected me and surely that woman I do not want to part with her... (I will not give her away)*

The positive evaluation of outcome was also seen in how the respondents subjectively engage with the resources that positively align with TAM and passively ignore the other resources that might be counter to TAM. With the intention of reducing cognitive dissonance, they selectively engage with only those sources that are consonant with TAM. This subjective resourcefulness was seen in how some participants completely denied any negative or problems associated with TAM.

Ambivalent evaluation of outcomes

Ambivalent evaluation of outcomes captured the affective expressions that posed a conflict in making a decision about the treatment method. This theme emerged as complementary, if not an addition to the traditionally existing dichotomous evaluation of outcomes as predicted by the reasoned action approach. It offered a trichotomous thread of conflicts that the decision-maker goes through. The perception of ambiguity (in)compatibility and multiplicity of the outcomes seemed to draw the decision-maker into a deep seat of conflicts as s/he is torn between and among motivations and goals of varying priorities. Although, it seemed that these ambivalent evaluations would eventually lead to either positive or negative evaluation, it also seemed that some ambivalent evaluations remained as the ultimate answer to not only the use of TAM but also ambivalent use of both TAM and CM. This finding is a conflicting or rather additional revelation to the reasoned action approach that predicts either negative or positive affective evaluations of performing behaviour. The resulting experiential attitude is neither outrightly negative nor positive. As a response to an ailment without cure, assumption of an ambivalent position seemed satisfactory. The present study's findings fit well within constructs of ambivalence as proposed by Lewin in Sanderson (2004) as outlined in Figure 43.5 below;

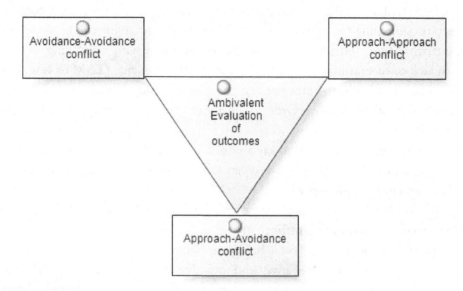

Figure 43.5: Ambivalent Evaluation of outcomes

Approach-approach conflict

Approach-approach conflict is an experience of wanting to do two things that are incompatible (Lewin, 1935 in (Sanderson, 2004). For this study, approach-approach conflict was abstracted as the affective evaluations that were hanging on the balance of the preference for both TAM and CM. As shown in Figure 43.5, the lack of absolute cure, probabilistic conditions of cure in TAM, perceived complementarity of TAM and CM had created mixed affective evaluations, out of which remaining at the balance seemed to be the answer.

Lack of absolute cure made the patients to develop split loyalties as they would not be sure of what would help them. As said by Zvisinei, *they ended up doing the 'Do nots'* because they would not be sure of a better option. This clearly shows how they were forced to develop split loyalties as they were trying to find the solutions and ended up being attracted simultaneously to two or more equally appealing methods. As a result, they ended up doing a lot of trial and error treatments. Absence of treatment of the disease made people susceptible to non-discrimination. The probabilistic condition of healing also appeared to lead to split loyalties;

I told her problem and she said, 'no, wait for me to see if my TAM can boost you on the problem you have.'...she said, 'these are my TAM, if it fails on you, you go back to the hospital.

They would not like to leave it given that there would be some chance that they will improve. The endeavour to counterbalance the perceived deficiencies in both TAM and CM would make the patient prone to split loyalties, wanting to use both CM and TAM. Incompatibility raised by Dread could lead a person to keep on searching for more treatments. The decision-making can be assumed to be marred with tension. Generally, discontentment with everything would lead to lack of discrimination. Lack of certainty of either side (TAM or CM) led to acquisition of both, to eliminate the chances of losing in the event that the answer lies in either of them. Grey spoke about counterbalancing the methods (TAM and CM).

It would seem paradoxical to say a conflict would be solved by staying in it Therefore, ambivalence was, in a way, an answer to the drive towards the use of TAM also in conjunction with CM.

Approach-avoidance conflict

Approach-avoidance conflict is being trapped in making a decision on doing one thing that has both negative and positive outcomes (Lewin, 1935 in (Sanderson, 2004). For this study, approach-avoidance was abstracted as the affective evaluations that were associated with both positive and negative evaluations of using TAM. There were evaluations that seemed to show a conflict in which the decision-maker would be trapped in making a decision of using TAM that has both positive and negative aspects. As shown in Figure 43.6, TAM was understood as characterised by an unfavourable garbage-in-garbage-out (GIGO) concept since both black magic and healing are perceived as coming from the same sources. The perception of divergence of TAM from contemporary, the so-called the 'in-vogue-things', also made TAM less desirable, at least when perceived as using it by the public, yet showing favourable healing outcomes. There was also a fear for self-deception in which some of the participants were sceptical about the veracity of the healing (though perceived) from TAM.

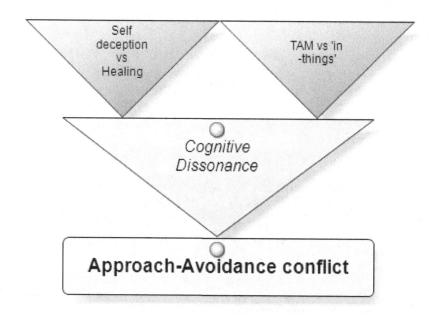

Figure 43.6: Approach-Avoidance conflict

Such tensions about the use of TAM was understood as causing cognitive dissonance since the decision-maker would be holding two conflicting and or opposing cognitions about his or her beliefs and use of TAM.

Self-deception versus healing

There was also some level of confusion as to whether TAM would be healing or not. There was fear of self-deception in which the decision-maker was not sure about the ultimate outcome of TAM-use. This was also seen in the fear for the duplication of treatment together with perceived effectiveness of TAM. Fear of overdose was also revealed although there was never a known case or tangible side effects related to TAM. Most respondents indicated that this was applicable to others. It seems there is denial to establish consonance to their cognitions of TAM.

The tension was mostly seen when the person perceived some improvements in their health they ascribed to TAM. They would start to ponder over whether it was a genuine or fake treatment; independent or duplication of ARVs/CM; right quantity or overdose. Such tensions left the decision-maker in a quagmire of approach-avoidance conflict.

The use of self in TAM trials is also understood as indicative of approach-avoidance conflict, especially when such trials were attempted at self-level and refused and/or condemned on significant vulnerable others such as children to whom possible adverse effects would be accountable to parents.

477

Figure 43.7: Fear of Duplicating Treatment

Traditional and alternative medicine versus 'in-things'

TAM was perceived to heal but at the same time associated with antiquity, backwardness and lack of civilisation. Whilst the patients could be perceived to like the benefits from TAM, that health care choice did not go along with the so called contemporary 'in-things' but perceived as an outdated practice. As indicated by Tatenda, some end up *'running away'* from TAM due to the fear of the label, *'insane'*. The insanity she was referring to was the deviation from the norm, marked dissimilarity from the majority who are following the contemporary 'in-things'. Tatenda preferred to use 'running away' as a descriptor of the non-preference of TAM to indicate how such deviation is sanctioned by the social world through attitude formation. Maybe the question was, are they running away or just imbued in clandestine use of TAM, to save their faces? Some participants confirmed that they engage in clandestine use, *'The reason why they hide is that it is being said to belong to the past, so these days there is what is being called the 'in-thing''*. Therefore, the use of TAM would mean perpetual tension of the approach-avoidance conflict as they continue to like the healing outcome and fear being labelled 'insane.

Avoidance-avoidance conflict

Avoidance-avoidance conflict occurs when a person is being torn between two undesirable choices (Lewin, 1935 in Sanderson 2004). For this study, avoidance-avoidance was abstracted as the affective evaluations that were associated with dislike and dissatisfaction of both TAM and CM. Whilst the CM

478

was largely viewed as having side effects and monotony, TAM also had its own problems that caused the respondents to be tangled in an avoidance-avoidance conflict in which either side was associated with unpleasant affects. Although the respondents had already resolved this conflict (as seen in ambivalent use of TAM and CM), the tension in which both were not preferred were high. Most participants indicated that would not like others to know about their use of both ARVs and TAM. It can be conjectured that due to this avoidance-avoidance conflict, the patients are in desperate search for the treatment that will treat them once and for all and quick fixes

Negative evaluation of outcomes

Negative evaluation of outcome was abstracted to capture the negative affective expressions about TAM. These mostly distracted the user from continuing to use TAM. They can be understood as dissatisfactions with TAM. For some, they felt that TAM would stunt modernisation. TAM was said to help only minor illnesses or as initial assistance before accessing CM. Some respondents also revealed perceptions that ARVs are superior and TAM only acts as auxiliary and cannot substitute ARVs. Incompatibility with ARVs was also found as a negative aspect that brought negative affective evaluations of TAM. This incompatibility was believed to wash away the ARVs from the blood.

Conclusion, Policy Options, Recommendations and Practical Implications

Overall, the respondents showed more perceived positive evaluations of the outcomes of TAM-use. Most of the participants revealed sustained and repeated use of traditional medicine which spanned their childhood. Although there were some negative affective evaluations, the TAM users tried to find ways to overcome these so that they can continue to use it and/or mix with the ARVs or CM. For example, the technique of the 30-minute separation between the ARV and TAM as well as the addition of sweeteners are all some of the methods devised to continue using TAM. Generally, there was great enthusiasm and pro-TAM experiential attitude that promoted continued use of TAM based on perceived positive evaluations of the outcomes. The present research can be summarised as confirming widespread accessibility to and a high frequency of use of traditional medicine in primary health care settings and among HIV-positive individuals in urban and rural areas in Zimbabwe. These findings imply a high potential for traditional health care to interact, and perhaps to overtly interfere, with conventional health care, either in inhibiting access or competing directly with conventional care, perhaps especially in patients without ready access to ART or those not meeting standard criteria for ART. The results serve to inform policy-makers to engage both traditional and conventional medical systems in order to develop a sustainable treatment regime for HIV and AIDS. Based on these findings, it is recommended to the government of Zimbabwe to introduce and/or strengthen policies that aim to mainstream, regularise, formalise, upgrade and quality control the use of traditional medicine and create measures to ensure that traditional and modern medicine can work more effectively and sustainably together. Future related research should conduct similar qualitative studies using strong behavioural theory to determine perceived psychosocial determinants of motivation to use traditional medicines for other illnesses as a formative elicitation phase leading to rolling out of larger national surveys to assess how widely the qualitative themes are shared nationally.

References

Ajzen, I., & Fishbein, M. (2000). Attitudes and the attitude-behavior relation: Reasoned and automatic processes. In W. Stroebe, & M. Hewstone, *European Review of Social Psychology* (pp. 1-33). John Wiley & Sons.

Babbie, E. (2002). *Social research* (2nd ed.). United States of America: Wadsworth Group.

CDC. (2013). *Sexually Transmitted Disease Surveillance 2013*. CDC.

Chitura, M., & Manyanhaire, I. O. (2013). Preferences for complementary and alternative HIV and AIDS treatment among rural residents in Zimbabwe. *E3 Journal of Environmental Research and Management, 4*(6), 0275-0292.

Cooke, R., & French, D. P. (2008). How well do the theory of reasoned action and theory of planned behaviour predict intentions and attendance at screening programmes? A meta-analysis. *Psychology and health, 23*(7), 745-765.

ECDC. (2012). *European Centre for Disease Prevention and Control. Evaluating HIV treatment as prevention in the European context*. Stockholm: ECDC.

Fishbein, M. (1967). Attitude and the prediction of behavior. In M. Fishbein, *Readings in attitude theory and Measurement* (pp. 477–492). New York: Wiley.

Fishbein, M. (2000). The role of theory in HIV prevention. *AIDS Care, 12*, 273–278.

Gelfand, M., Mavi, S., Drummond, R., & Ndemera, B. (1985). *The Traditional Medical Practitioner in Zimbabwe: His Principles of Practice and Pharmacopoeia*. Gweru, Zimbabwe: Mambo Press.

Green, E. (1994). *AIDS and STDs in Africa: Bridging the gap between traditional healing and modern medicine*. Scotsville, Pietermaritzburg, South Africa: Westview Press, Inc., Boulder, Colorado / University of Natal Press.

Henderson, P. (2011). *A kinship of bones: AIDS, intimacy and care in rural KwaZulu-Natal. South Africa:* . KwaZulu-Natal. South Africa: University of KwaZulu-Natal Press.

Jijide, J. (1994). Community-based AIDS Prevention and Care in Africa. In A. Leonard, *Building on Local Initiatives, Case Studies from Five African Countries* (pp. 2-8). New York: Population Council.

Kent, A., & Sepkowitz, M. D. (2001). The New England Journal of Medicine. *The New England Journal of Medicine, 344*, 1764-1772.

Macherera, M., Moyo, L., Ncube, M., & Gumbi, A. (2012). Social, Cultural, and Environmental Challenges Faced by Children on Antiretroviral Therapy in Zimbabwe: a Mixed-Method Study. *International Journal of MCH and AIDS, 1*, 83-91.

Mayer, H., & Venkatesh, K. (2011). Promoting Public Health Research, Policy, Practice and Education. *American Journal of Public Health, 101*(2), 199-200.

NAC. (2006). *National HIV/AIDS Behavior Change Strategy and Priorities*. Harare: National AIDS Council. Ministry of Health and Child Welfare (MOHCW), Health Information and Surveillance Unit, Department of Disease Prevention and Control, AIDS & TB Programme.

Newman, W. (2011). *Social research methods; Qualitative and quantitative approaches*. Boston: Allyn and Bacon.

Pei, S. (2001). Ethno botanical approaches of traditional medicine studies: Some experiences from Asia. *Pharmaceutical Biology, 39*, 74-79.

Sanderson, C. (2004). *Health Psychology*. John Wiley & Sons. Inc.

Smith, J., & Osborn, M. (2003). Interpretive Phenomenological Analysis. In J. Smith, *Qualitative psychology: A practical guide to research methods*. London: Sage Publications.

Smith, J., Flowers, P., & Larkin, M. (2009). *Interpretative Phenomenological Analysis: Theory, Method and Research*. London: SAGE Publications Ltd.

Taylor, T., Dolezal, C., Tross, S., & Holmes, W. (2008). Comparison of HIV/AIDS-specific quality of life change in Zimbabwean patients at western medicine versus traditional African medicine care sites. *Acquired Immune Deficiency Syndrome, 15 49*(5), 552-556.

WHO. (2003; 2013). *Fact sheets*. Retrieved January 6, 2018, from WHO: http://www.who.int/mediacentre/factsheets/fs134/en/print.html

Willig, C. (2013). *Introducing Qualitative Research in Psychology* (3rd ed.). Open Univesity Press.

481

Institutions: Development Catalyst and the Fourth Leg Fundamental to Zimbabwean Sustainability

Abraham Rajab Matamanda and Innocent Chirisa

Summary

This broad overview of this chapter is on institutions and sustainability in the Zimbabwean context. It explores the role of institutions and how they contribute and act as a fourth leg fundamental to sustainability and as a Zimbabwean development catalyst. The chapter begins by acknowledging the diversity and complexities of institutions. Therefore, focus is placed on understanding what institutions are, their nomenclature, the purpose for their establishment and how they contribute to sustainability. In this quandary of attempting to establish what exactly institutions do the chapter is informed by practical lessons from Zimbabwe are then used to examine how selected institutions contribute to the development agenda for the country. It is evident that there are various types of institutions in Zimbabwe which include socio-economic, political and environmental all focusing on specific areas of sustainability and advancing human well-being. The establishment, regulation and operation of some institutions, especially the formal ones is guided by certain statutes and pieces of legislation which assists in keeping the institutions on track as well as enabling the public to hold accountable those responsible in managing certain institutions. However, there are instances when institutions are rendered ineffective due to a number of anomalies which include political interference, corruption, lack of funding and capacity to implement strategic decisions. The chapter thus ends with providing the future direction of Zimbabwean sustainability from an institutional perspective.

Introduction

Institutions are an intrinsic part of socio-economic development because they emerge as constraining entities and enablers of action. Interestingly, institutions do not passively give in to individuals' actions as they are based on a set of rules which help to define what actions and activities can be sanctioned or incentivised (Hodgson, 2006). Therefore, the role of institutions as development catalyst cannot be underestimated. This is especially true in the

Global South where institutions play a pivotal role in facilitating development. Zimbabwe is no exception as institutions contribute to the socio-economic development of the nation. Ironically, it seems institutions in Zimbabwe do not always serve their intended functions due to numerous reasons which call for their scrutiny. It goes without saying that institutions are mandated to advance human well-being, promote development and preserve human rights. Hence, there is a nexus between institutions and sustainability (Knight, 1992). In trying to achieve this sustainability, different institutions are thus established so as to regulate, customise and manage human behaviour with the view to advance sustainability. Considering that sustainability includes social, political, and economic dimensions, institutions may also be categorised into these groups so as to narrow down their focus.

On the whole, it is interesting to note that the list of the types of institutions is not exhaustive as they can be categorised as formal or informal, social, political or economic, based on their function, for example, educational, health, transport management and environmental management. However, there are many factors which seem to compromise the legitimacy of institutions, especially when individuals dominate and override the rules guiding the institutions. When such instances prevail, the function of the institutions will be reduced to shreds thereby impacting on sustainability which aims at advancing human well-being. This chapter thus explores the way institutions act as the fourth leg fundamental to sustainability as a Zimbabwean development catalyst. In making the examination a success, the chapter is structured as follows: first, it defines the term institution, secondly, it considers the types of institutions where general discussion is proffered on the different types of institutions which exist, thirdly, the impacts of institutions on development are analysed, fourthly, the chapter examines the Zimbabwean developmental institutions which is followed by the future direction of Zimbabwean sustainability.

Defining Institution

The term "institution" is broad and has been defined differently by various scholars. Steinmo (2001) provides a narrow definition when he simply defines an institution as rules. Knight (1992: 2) adds on the vagueness of the definition by Steinmo (2001) and goes on to define an institution as a set of *rules* that *structure social interactions* in particular ways. From the second definition, Jack Knight indicates the function of the rules which is meant to influence the structure of social interactions in distinct ways. Scott (1995: 33) takes a broader perspective and defines institutions as regulative, normative and cognitive structures and activities that provide stability and meaning for social behaviour.

From this definition by Scott, it emerges that institutions are much more than rules, but also include the activities which are grouped into three, i.e., regulative, normative and cognitive. It also emerges that these institutions seek to provide stability and meaning for social behaviour which may refer to sustainability. This is so because stability is akin to sustainability which is achieved when there is equilibrium between the three pillars (social, economic and environment). It would thus be justified to argue that the rationale of institutions is to promote sustainability. This may also explain why institutions are sometimes categorised as political, economic and social. In cementing the significance of institutions in promoting sustainability, Hodgson (2006:2) argues that institutions are critical structures in the social realm because they make up the stuff of social life. It may seem that institutions only focus on social aspects of human life, but this is not the case considering that institutions are nested in all facets of human life.

Types of Institutions

There are different types of institutions. First, institutions are categorised as either formal or informal (Ostrom, 1992). Formal institutions are those institutions which are regulative in nature and highly coercive. Helmke and Levitsky (2004) argue that formal institutions are openly codified, since they are established and communicated through officially recognised channels such as through acts of parliament, constitution and various other policies. The emphasis of formal institutions is on laws, regulations and rules which establish the rules of the game. On the other hand, informal institutions are defined as socially shared rules which are often not documented, created, communicated and enforced outside officially recognised channels (Liu, Cheng and Cheung, 2017). Informal institutions may therefore refer to norms, cultures and ethics which help in defining the human behaviour and activities. Liu *et al.* (2017:3) present that both formal and informal institutions exist at different levels as shown in Table 24.1.

Secondly, following on the formal and informal distinction of institutions, Palthe (2014) indicates that institutions may be categorised as regulative, normative or cultural. Regulative institutions are more inclined towards the formal ones and are established based on legal systems say the constitution or acts of parliament. As put across by Ostrom (1992:19-20):

> Enforcement may be undertaken by those directly involved, by agents they hire, by external enforces, or by a combination of these. Rules are useless unless the people they affect know of their existences, expect others to monitor behaviour with respect to these rules, and anticipate sanctions for non-conformance. In other

words, working rules must be common knowledge and must be monitored and enforced.

Table 24.1: Different levels of formal and informal institutions

	Formal Institutions	Informal Institutions
International level	International rules and structures that impact on global development for example International Monetary Fund (IMF), SADC, UNHABITAT, Sustainable Development Goals, New Urban Agenda	Political affinities which influence levels of cooperation together with historical links between countries for example China and Zimbabwe.
National level	Institutions which regulate development at the national level for example: Ministry of Local Government, Environmental Management Agency (EMA), National Constitution, Property rights	Position and attitudes towards women, Patron-client relationships
Local level	Local authorities, Municipal bylaws,	Use of the environment for example method of farming

Source: Adopted from Liu *et al.* (2017: 3)

Examples of regulative institutions include local authorities in Zimbabwe which are governed by the Urban Council's Act chapter 29: 15 as well as the Constitution of Zimbabwe. The activities of the regulative institutions are premised on the behavioural reasoning which is based on the rules and policies which determine what has to be done in line with the prescriptions of the legislative system (Palthe, 2014). Likewise, the evolution of regulative institutions is very slow considering that the change of the systems is subject to legal obligations, hence in most instances regulative institutions are described as being archaic and rigid and fail to adapt to contemporary dilemmas, a situation which compromises sustainability. Normative institutions are described as informal institutions which are mainly established through contact with the immediate environment; hence the legislation system is controlled by moral and ethical systems. Central rudiments of normative institutions are thus through work roles, habits and norms which are uncodified system (Palthe, 2014). Behaviour system is based on the notion of ought to. Hence, in this way normative institutions may be influential in spearheading sustainability considering that it is society which determines what works best for them which

486

they end up normalising. Cognitive institutions are based on cultural systems and are governed by beliefs and values. They evolve through personal desire and social identity, yet change values are internalised.

Third category includes political, economic, and social institutions. Political institutions refer to organisations which create, enforce and apply laws (Boddy-Evans, 2017). These organisations include political parties, trade unions and the legal courts (judicial system). Moreover, considering the definition of institutions proffered by Steinmo (2001) which defines institutions as rules, political institutions in this context may also refer to the recognised structures of rules and principles within which the political parties, trade unions and courts operate together with the responsible government and accountability (Boddy-Evans, 2017). Social institutions refer to a system of behavioural and relationship patterns that are densely interwoven and enduring and function across an entire society (Verwiebe, n.d). In his definition of social institution, Richard Langlois focuses on the regulative aspect of institutions as postulated by Scott (1995), thus social institutions refer to a regularity in social behaviour that is agreed to by all members of society, specifies behaviour in specific recurrent situations and is either self-policed or policed by some external authority (Langlois, 1986: 11). According to Wiggins and Davis (2006: 2) economic institutions are those institutions which perform economic functions which include establishment and protection of property rights, facilitation of transactions and permitting economic co-operation and organisation. At the global level economic institutions include IMF, SADC and ECOWAS while at the national scale Central Africa Buildings Society (CABS), RBZ and Infrastructure Development Bank of Zimbabwe (IDBZ) are examples of such.

Characterising Institutions

A broad understanding of institutions may be facilitated through disentangling the seemingly complex concept of institutions. This understanding may be made possible through providing a detailed discussion on the characteristics of institutions. Thus, institutions may best be explained through contextualising them within the confines of the following characteristics, which help to explain their existence.

Created to serve a particular purpose:
By their nature, institutions are created to serve a particular purpose. This explains why there are different types of institutions including political, social or economic. Such focus also helps to distinguish between institutions' mandate and ultimately avoiding replication of duties between institutions. Considering

that sustainability is multifaceted and focuses on three pillars (social, economic and environment) the same applies also for institutions where each pillar may be governed by a particular institution. For example, the United Nations has different institutions such as Food and Agricultural Organisation (FAO) and World Health Organisation (WHO) which also serve distinct purposes aimed at achieving sustainable development as espoused in the sustainable development goals (SDGs).

Constrain and enable behaviour:

By their nature institutions are founded on the existence of rules and it is common knowledge that rules are somehow responsible for constraining and enabling particular human behaviour. The most critical aspect of institutions is that they are capable of empowering as well as disempowering citizens in different ways. Olson (1997) succinctly explains that institutions are constitutive rules and practices which prescribe appropriate behaviour for certain group(s) in society.

Institutions must be adaptive:

Adaptive is a characteristic that allows institutions to face emerging challenges which may derail the institutions if they lack this critical aspect. Considering the emerging challenges such as climate change, urban informality, water scarcity, proliferation of slums in towns and cities and urban violence which overwhelm society, there is a need for the responsible institutions to adapt and address these challenges with a view to maintain a status quo and sustainability (Crane, 2013).

Institutions evolve and change:

Nothing is constant in this world, everything is forever evolving from one form to the other. The same applies for institutions which are dynamic and constantly evolving so as to conform to the changing societal values, preferences as well as world views (Lewis and Steinmo, 2012). In relation to sustainable development, prior to September 2015, the global development agenda was regulated by the millennium development goals (MDGs), yet post this period, the SDGs have now come to the fore. Hence institutions the world over have been compelled to evolve and conform to the new goals and development agenda espoused by the SDGs. This is a clear indication of how institutions evolve to suit the status quo.

Impact of Institutions on Development

In a broad sense, development refers to any change which occurs with any particular system. However, for it to be hailed and touted, development has to be good, favourable and positive. Development is thus best defined as good or positive change (Chambers, 2013, Bellu, 2011: 2). Interestingly, there are various aspects and dimensions to development considering the fact that the good change may occur in the realm of agriculture, infrastructure, economy and education sector. Ajakaiye and Ncube (2010) demonstrate how infrastructure development contributes to societal progress through promoting human development and citizens' access to better services and goods. It is therefore critical to specify the development in any particular context considering that, although the change may be good, society is not always homogenous, hence, what would be good to one individual or group will not have the same ranking to another group. Sustainable development then becomes the benchmark of good change since it seeks to balance between social, economic and environmental pillars. The result is development which promotes equity, fairness and transparency in society. To achieve this sustainable development, there is need for deliberated action which will be carried out by agents or some authority pre-ordered to achieve improvement to favourable circumstance in both (Bellu, 2011: 2). It is in this context that institutions come into the development matrix and contribute in the formulation and management of rules and laws which will be instrumental in achieving development such that all the three pillars are addressed. The following are some of the impacts of institutions on development.

Conflicts suppress sustainability because they compromise on at least one of the three pillars of sustainable development. Institutions, usually political ones, help in mediating conflicts among different stakeholders (Boddy-Evans, 2017) so that a favourable environment for peace and mutual co-existence prevails within which development projects can be undertaken with much potential for success.

Institutions assist in decision-making considering that they are also based on collective action which may be representative at times. Hence, institutions such as civic organisations, government (at all levels) and political parties have always been instrumental in informing decisions through crafting and implementing policies which they feel will help to promote sustainable development. For example, the sustainable development goals promulgated by the United Nations in 2016 were made on behalf of the world by a few world leaders, yet they have been embraced by most nations across the globe.

489

Institutions also help to address inequalities. Society is usually characterised by various inequalities which are largely based on allocation of resources, hence institutions are created so as to redress these inequalities through stabilising them to sustainable thresholds. As a result, human well-being tends to be improved through encouraging the provision of basic physical sustenance of all in society.

The economy of a country provides basic physical sustenance of society by meeting shelter, clothing, and other necessary supply and services. If the economy of a country is to be sustained, there is a need for economic institutions which will help in promoting economic growth as well as human well-being. In this way, economic institutions help in creating employment opportunities, investment opportunities and industrial growth. Examples of economic institutions include agriculture and marketing systems as well as co-operatives. Agricultural institutions help in guiding, regulating and managing agricultural activities in a country so as to increase agricultural output and subsequently provide food, employment and raw materials for manufacturing industries. At the international level, FAO is an example of agricultural institution which has been instrumental in securing food supply across the globe, especially in the Global South.

Zimbabwean Developmental Institutions

Like most countries around the globe, Zimbabwe has committed itself to Agenda 2030 which relates to the SDGs. Therefore, sustainable development emerges as a fundamental constitutional imperative and an overall strategic objective for the nation. In various sections of the Constitution of Zimbabwe, provisions are made for citizens' rights which are categorised into different groups that include political, civil, economic, social and cultural. There are various sections in the Constitution of Zimbabwe which give an oversight of the various institutions which help to achieve the SDGs. The institutions mentioned in the constitution all play different roles in promoting sustainable development and these include Zimbabwe Human Rights Commission, Zimbabwe Gender Commission and Zimbabwe Media Commission (Government of Zimbabwe, 2013a).

Social Development and Institutions: Experiences and Realities from Zimbabwe

Section 238 of the Zimbabwe Constitution focuses on the establishment of Zimbabwe Electoral Commission (ZEC). ZEC is a political and regulative institution mandated to prepare for, conduct and supervise elections in the country. Moreover, ZEC also ensures that the elections and referendums are conducted efficiently, freely, fairly, transparently and in accordance with the law (Government of Zimbabwe, 2013a: 92). Development is fostered through participation and elections are a means through which citizens get to participate in decision-making processes, especially when selecting leaders. Hence, ZEC plays a critical role to ensure peace and stability in the country through facilitating presidential elections. So far ZEC seems to have played its mandate well since 1980. However, there have been instances where the credibility of ZEC has been questioned with regards to administration of elections. For example, the main opposition party alleged that the 2008 and 2013 presidential elections were rigged, a situation which contradicts sustainability considering that the institution is supposed to act in a fair, just and transparent manner during elections in the country (Nyarota, 2018). In trying to overcome such cases of rigging, ZEC embarked on biometric registration in for the 2018 Presidential elections.

In section 242 of the Zimbabwe Constitution provides for the Zimbabwe Human Rights Commission (ZHRC). The main function of the ZHRC is to promote human rights, right to education, health and decent accommodation as stated in section 242 of the constitution. However, in as much as ZHRC advocates for the promotion of human rights of the country's citizens, there are various instances in the country's history where human rights have been trampled upon. Examples include the 2005 Operation Murambatsvina where 'informal' structures were demolished in the cities and towns around the country. Subsequently, close to 700 000 people lost their homes and livelihoods, a situation which greatly compromised social and economic pillar of sustainable development (Tibaijuka, 2005). Moreover, the failure of the government to timeous address the cholera outbreak in 2008 is another example of human rights which were compromised as the epidemic resulted in the death of at least 4 000 people across the country.

There are several social institutions which help to advance development and sustainability in Zimbabwe, and these include USAID, UNICEF, WHO and World Vision. Most of these social institutions are categorised as humanitarian organisations which focus on issues such as education, health and local economic development. UNICEF has been actively contributing to promoting education in the country as evident from the donation of textbooks and other materials which UNICEF donated to primary and secondary schools across the country. Moreover, UNICEF has always actively engaged in provision of water and sanitation facilities following the cholera outbreak in 2008. USAID and World Vision are mainly focused on providing aid during droughts as well as capacitating small scale farmers across the country with inputs and skills to engage in sustainable agriculture. WHO contributes in the provision of medical facilities and personnel especially in marginalised areas or when epidemics and disasters occur, for example, Tokwe-Mukosi floods where medical assistance was required. However, although these social institutions immensely contribute to sustainable development in the country, there are instances when the development agenda of such institutions has diverted from the local and national priorities, a situation which thus does little in advancing sustainability in the country.

Social institutions are regulative when it comes to promoting public health. In Zimbabwe, local authorities are mandated by the Public Health Act Chapter 15:09 to promote public health. Part IX of the PHA also sets the rules regarding human settlements where focus is on sanitation and housing. In section 83, local authorities are mandated to maintain cleanliness and prevent nuisances in human settlements while section 84 encourages local authorities to prevent or remedy danger to health arising from unsuitable dwellings. In this way, local authorities facilitate public health in towns and cities a situation which helps in maintaining a clean environment as well as preserving a clean environment which promotes human well-being. However, local authorities in Zimbabwe are bedevilled by a plethora of challenges which makes it very difficult for them to achieve their mandates.

Another key group of social institutions contributing to sustainable development in Zimbabwe are orphanages and old people's homes which focus on social issues and development. The rationale of most of these institutions is to promote social well-being of the most vulnerable members of society who include orphans, disabled, aged, women as well as albinos. Examples of these institutions are formal and informal institutions which are largely normative and cognitive as they are established to address specific human needs. Establishment of institutions such as Jairos Jiri Association, Chinyaradzo Old People's Home, Matthew Rusike Children's Home and Tose Respite Children's Home. Jairos Jiri and Danhiko are mainly focused on the disabled members of society who are trained and capacitated so that they get to development life skills which will enable them to sustain themselves rather than solely depend on other people.

Institutions and Economic Development in Zimbabwe

The economy is one pillar of sustainable development. The applies for the country's economy in which the Reserve Bank of Zimbabwe plays a significant role in fostering sustainable development in the country. The Constitution of Zimbabwe provides that the RBZ will be responsible for the following:

- Section 317(1) (a) to regulate the monetary system,

- Section 317(1) (b) to protect the currency of Zimbabwe in the interest of balanced and sustainable economic growth, and
- Section 317(1) (c) to formulate and implement monetary policy.

The provisions of the Constitution clearly indicate the role of RBZ to contribute in promoting economic development. In recent years, RBZ has been put to test considering the economic meltdown which the country has experienced. The institution has had to come up with measures aimed at crafting viable monetary policies which are meant to facilitate the stability of the economy. This has been followed by the introduction of bond notes following shortages in cash around the country. The introduction of bearer cheques in 2005 was meant to ease cash shortages in the country but the move resulted in hyperinflation which greatly affected the economy, thus, in this instance the efforts by RBZ to address cash crisis were futile. However, a successful story is the introduction of the multi-currency in 2009 which resulted in the country adopting the US dollar as a local currency alongside the South African Rand, Botswana Pula and Japanese Yen. Recently, following the cash crisis being experienced in the country, RBZ introduced bond notes and promoted the use of plastic money which has somehow addressed the cash crisis as citizens could alternatively make use of plastic money. However, the efforts undertaken by RBZ show that the institution is somehow adaptive as it usually comes up with strategies that address particular problems confronting the country, though they are not always the best.

Infrastructure is considered to be an intrinsic component of sustainable development and there are various institutions which contribute in infrastructure development (Africa Development Bank Group [ADBG], 2011). In the context of Zimbabwe, it is evident that economic institutions and social institutions have been instrumental in promoting infrastructure development. Over the past years, building societies played a critical role in facilitating housing development in the country. Evidence is abound of projects which have been undertaken by institutions such as CABS, NBS, FBC and CBZ. In addition to building societies, some insurance and pension companies have immensely contributed in infrastructure provision as evident from the developments by NASS which include Eastgate, High Glen Shopping Centre and Westgate Shopping Centre. All these developments add onto the infrastructure in the cities and towns of the country thereby enabling the provision of goods and services to the citizens. During the past years, the Infrastructural Development Bank of Zimbabwe (IDBZ) has been making great strides in infrastructure development in various parts of the country. Examples include housing projects in various towns across the country, road infrastructure development and water treatment plants (ADBG, 2011).

Economic development in Zimbabwe is also facilitated by the Office of the President and Cabinet (OPC) through policies and reforms which focus on various issues such as agricultural development, SME sector growth as well as property rights. The land reform programme which was undertaken in the early 2000 was a remarkable reform and considered as one of the most successful reforms by the OPC. However, the land reform programme has had mixed reactions from various sectors as some proponents argue that its intended benefits were not realised. This is so because, although the land reform programme resulted in some indigenous people being allocated land under various schemes, the displacement of the white farmers left many farm workers without employment and housing as they were not allocated land. Other proponents argue that the land reform programme resulted in massive land degradation as the farmers went on to abuse the environment through deforestation, illegal gold mining, overgrazing and stream bank cultivation, practices which were not done by the white farmers (Marongwe, 2003). Overall, the land reform programme is described as chaotic and failing to achieve the desired results of equitably distributing the land to those who desperately needed as it. Evidently, the elite ended up getting large farms, a situation which somehow perpetuated the inequality which existed when the white farmers owned much of the land.

Recently, the OPC introduced the command agriculture which was a special programme on maize production for import substitution. Specifically, the programme aims at ensuring that the country produces enough grain to feed itself. To facilitate the success of the programme, some farmers were identified and allocated inputs, irrigation and mechanised equipment to boost agricultural output and subsequently retain the status of the country as the breadbasket of Southern Africa. In addition to command agriculture, the economic blueprint, Zimbabwe Agenda for Sustainable Socio-Economic Transformation (ZIMASSET) was crafted to empower society and growing the economy of the country. ZIMASSET is another programme which was initiated by the OPC with the aim of fostering sustainable development through a focus on different clusters which include infrastructure and utilities, food security and nutrition, Social services and poverty eradication, value addition and beneficiation, fiscal reform measures, public administration, governance and performance management (Government of Zimbabwe, 2013b)

Institutions and Environmental Development in Zimbabwe

The environment is an intrinsic component of development in Zimbabwe as it contributes in the provision of goods and services which help to support livelihoods provide food, raw materials as well as sustain ecological balance and integrity. In this regard, there are several institutions in Zimbabwe which focus on the environment with a view to promote environmental sustainability as espoused in the SDGs and various other national environmental plans. The Environmental Management Agency (EMA) is one such institution with the mandate to protect the environment. The Ministry of Environment, Water and Climate (MEWC) also assists in environmental conservation in the country through development and implementation of policies and strategies which restrict unsustainable practices.

Local authorities also place a significant role in environmental protection in the country. The role of local authorities in environmental conservation is stipulated in the RTCP Act, Urban Councils Act and Environmental Management Act, which all encourage local authorities to promote environmental conservation and protection in areas of their jurisdiction. Local authorities such as City of Harare engage in environmental conservation through reserving pen spaces in their development plans as well as the city Master Plan. Although measures are put in place to inform land use development through development control, there are instances when the legitimacy of City of Harare as well as other local authorities have been disregarded. In this way, decisions made by local authorities or guiding their mandates have been rubbished mostly by politicians. A case to note is the continued degradation of environmentally sensitive site through housing development, a move which is not supported by City of Harare, yet the Minister of Housing may give a directive for development to be done in such sites (Muchadenyika, 2015).

The Future of Zimbabwean Sustainability

From the foregoing discussion, it emerged that there are various institutions which seek to promote sustainable development in Zimbabwe. These include social, political and economic institutions. Although there are successful stories which have been written, there remain some shortcomings with regards the institutions in achieving sustainability in Zimbabwe. This is so because there is a myriad of challenges which stifle the effective operation of the institutions. Subsequently, the future of Zimbabwean sustainability is compromised because of these challenges. Political interference in the operations of some institutions, particularly local authorities, greatly compromises their integrity and service delivery which, eventually, result in failure to achieve sustainability in the country. The political interference is also evident in the operation of ZEC, the electoral board, a situation which compromises effective citizen participation and ultimately democracy. There is also the issue of limited fiscal space and financial resources a situation which makes it difficult to achieve some of the set goals such as the command agriculture programme which required a lot of financial resources. Another challenge is in funding infrastructure development, a situation which results in housing deficit as well as poor infrastructure and services being delivered which then compromise sustainability. Achieving sustainability in Zimbabwe is also made difficult by the rapidly increasing urban population coupled with increasing informality which result in housing shortages and environmental degradation as people seek livelihoods and shelter in environmentally sensitive sites. Moreover, the rapid urbanisation is not concomitant with industrialisation, a situation which exacerbates unemployment rates thus reducing the standard of living among most urbanites. Sustainability inn Zimbabwe is also compromised by the existence of gaps in policy implementation and coherence which means that achieving sustainability becomes very difficult in such instances.

Conclusion

The chapter has proffered a discussion on the utility of institutions in championing sustainable development in Zimbabwe. It addressed the issue of institutions through providing for their definition, types and characteristics. Through defining and characterising institutions as well as highlighting on the impacts of institutions on development, the chapter set the tone for an examination of the development and institutional dimensions in Zimbabwe, with a view on sustainability. It emerges that there are various institutions in Zimbabwe which play different roles in promoting sustainable development. However, there are numerous of shortcomings which have been identified and these include lack of funds, political interference and policy inconsistency. In trying to improve the viability of the institutions in the country with a view to promote sustainability, the chapter recommends the following:

• Good governance with regards the management and operation of the institutions in the country, particularly the public institutions which are more vulnerable to political interference.

• There is also a need for dialogue and follow-up action with regards to financing of development projects, such as the command agriculture, which usually end up benefiting a few elites at the expense of the majority of the citizens.

- Another critical consideration is the issue of capacity building aimed at enhancing the scope of the civil society so that they contribute significantly to national agenda rather than engage in activities which do not align with national development goals and objectives.

References

Ajakaiye, O., & Ncube, M. (2010). Infrastructure and economic development in Africa: An overview. *Journal of African economies*, 19(suppl_1), i3-i12.

Boddy-Evans, A. (2017). *The complete story behind powerful political institutions.* ThoughtCo.: New York.

Chambers, R. (2013). *Ideas for development.* London: Earthscan.

Crane, T.A. (2013). *The role of local institutions in adaptive processes to climate variability: The cases of Southern Ethiopia and Southern Mali.* Boston Oxfam America.

Government of Zimbabwe. (2013a). *Constitution of Zimbabwe Amendment (No 20).* Government of Zimbabwe: Harare.

Government of Zimbabwe. (2013b). *Zimbabwe agenda for sustainable socio-economic transformation (Zimasset).* Government of Zimbabwe: Harare.

Helmke, G., and Levitsky, S. (2004). Informal institutions and comparative politics: A research agenda. *Perspectives on politics*, 2(4), 725-740.

Hodgson, G. M. (2006). What are institutions? *Journal of Economic Issues*, XI(1), 1-25.

Knight, J. (1992). *Institutions and social conflict.* Cambridge: Cambridge University Press.

Langlois, R.N. (1986). The new institutional economics: An introductory essay. In R.N. Langlois (Eds.), *Economics as a Process: Essays in the New Institutional Economics.* Cambridge: Cambridge University Press.

Lewis, O. and Steinmo, S. (2012). How institutions evolve: Evolutionary theory and institutional change. *Polity*, 44(3), 314-339

Liu, S., Cheng, I. and Cheung, L. (2017). The role of formal and informal institutions in small tourism business development in rural areas of South China. *Sustainability*, 9(7), 1-14.

Marongwe, N. (2003). *The fast track resettlement and urban development nexus: The case for Harare.* Paper Presented at the Symposium on Delivering Land and securing Rural Livelihoods: Post-Independence Land Reform and Resettlement in Zimbabwe, Mont Clair, Nyanga, 26-28 March 2003.

Muchadenyika, D. (2015). Land for housing: A political resource – Reflections from Zimbabwe's urban areas. *Journal of Southern African Studies*. 41(6): 1219-1238.

Nyarota, G. (2018). *The graceless fall of Robert Mugabe: The end of a dictator's reign.* Cape Town: Penguin Books

Olsen, J. P. (1997). Institutional design in democratic contexts. *Journal of Political Philosophy, 5*(3), 203-229.

Ostrom, E. (1992). Institutions as rules in use. In *Crafting institutions for self-governing irrigation systems* (pp. 19-39). San Francisco: ICC Press.

Palthe, J. (2014). Regulative, normative and cognitive elements of organizations: Implications for managing change. *Management and Organizational Studies, 1*(2), 59-66.

Scott, W.R. (1995). *Institutions and organisations.* Thousand Oaks, CA. SAGE.

Steinmo, S. (2001). Institutionalism. In N. Palsy (Ed.), *International encyclopaedia of the social and behavioral sciences.* New York: Elsevier Science.

Tibaujuka, A. K. (2005). *Report of the fact-finding mission to Zimbabwe to assess the scope and impact of Operation Murambatsvina by the UN Special Envoy to Zimbabwe,* Nairobi: UNHABITAT.

Verwiebe, R. (n.d.). *Social institutions.* Department of Sociology University of Vienna Rooseveltplatz 2 1090 Vienna AustriaWiggins, S. and Davis, J. (2006). Economic institutions. *IPPG Briefing, 3.* Manchester: IPPG.

Printed in the United States
By Bookmasters